Washington's Partisan War,
1775–1783

Mark V. Kwasny

★ ★

Washington's Partisan War, 1775–1783

★ ★

The Kent State University Press

Kent, Ohio, & London, England

© 1996 by The Kent State University Press, Kent, Ohio 44242

Library of Congress Catalog Card Number 96-14559

ISBN 0-87338-546-2

Manufactured in the United States of America

03 02 01 00 99 98 97 96   5 4 3 2 1

Library of Congress Cataloging-in-Publication Data

Kwasny, Mark V. (Mark Vincent), 1959–

  Washington's partisan war, 1775–1783 / Mark V. Kwasny.

    p. cm.

  Includes bibliographical references and index.

  ISBN 0–87338–546–2 (cloth : alk. paper) ∞

    1. New York (N.Y.)—History—Revolution, 1775–1783—Campaigns.
2. Middle Atlantic States—History—Revolution, 1775–1783—
Campaigns. 3. New York (State)—Militia—History—Revolution,
1775–1783. 4. Washington, George, 1732–1799—Military leadership.
I. Title.

E230.5.N4K9 1996

973.3'447—dc20   96–14559

British Library Cataloging-in-Publication data are available.

★ ★ ★

Contents

★ ★ ★

Maps

★ ★ ★

Acknowledgments

MANY PEOPLE helped me greatly during the course of writing this book and deserve my thanks and gratitude. The staffs at several locations made the job of finding and using sources much easier. In particular, I want to thank the staff members of the New Jersey State Library, Trenton, New Jersey; the New-York Historical Society and New York Public Library in New York City; the New York State Library, Albany, New York; and the Connecticut State Library and Connecticut Historical Society, Hartford, Connecticut. In addition, the library staff at The Ohio State University, and especially the people who run the interlibrary loan office, were very helpful.

Everyone at the Kent State University Press has been helpful and supportive of my efforts. I would like to thank in particular Dr. John T. Hubbell, director, Julia Morton, senior editor, Linda Cuckovich, assistant editor, and Beth Wilson, the copyeditor, for all of their advice. Their efforts helped me produce a better book.

For financial support, I owe the Center of Military History, United States Army, a huge debt for the Dissertation Year Fellowship that enabled me to travel and type full time as I wrote the original draft. In addition, the Graduate School and College of Humanities of The Ohio State University provided fellowships that let me concentrate on my personal work.

Ron McLean of the Graphics Services at The Ohio State University provided me with a set of maps that nicely complement the text. His detailed work, his ability to concentrate while I sat looking over his shoulders, and his willingness to put up with my constant little corrections all contributed to the making of a great set of maps.

While writing the original draft, I received advice and criticism from Dr. Harry Coles (who sadly passed away before this book reached completion) and Dr. Paul Bowers, who read each chapter and provided a valuable critique of my work. Dr. Alan Aimone and Dr. Ira Gruber discussed with me the original ideas and supported my request for the army's fellowship. Dr. Clyde Ferguson read my manuscript for The Kent State University Press and provided extensive analysis and criticism, including over thirty handwritten pages of notes, advice, and corrections. His painstaking review helped immensely during the revision of the manuscript. Dr. Allan R. Millett, my adviser and mentor throughout my graduate studies, provided invaluable assistance from the first step. I owe much to his support, recommendations, and criticisms throughout the long process of producing this book.

Finally and most importantly, I must thank my family for putting up with me and my book over the past several years. To "Napoleon," who kept me company during the countless hours typing and reading, I appreciated your company and wish you were still by my side. My children, Katherine and Michael, could not understand why I spent so many hours in front of a computer, but they accepted my work as necessary. Most of all, I dedicate this book to my wife, Barbara, who put up with my need to travel and spend many hours on the book, helped edit the early drafts, listened to my endless stories about the Revolutionary War, and kept encouraging me when it all seemed to be too much work. Thank you for your constant support and understanding of my history obsession.

★ ★ ★

Introduction

THE SMOKE from the opening clashes of the war at Lexington, Concord, and Bunker Hill had barely settled when the newly appointed colonial commander in chief, George Washington, arrived outside British-held Boston. Within a matter of days, he expressed his opinion of the New England militiamen who filled the colonial army to the Continental Congress: "All the General Officers agree that no Dependence can be put on the Militia for a Continuance in Camp, or Regularity and Discipline during the short Time they may stay." Almost eight years later, as the war slowly ground to a halt, Washington expressed a far different opinion: "The Militia of this Country must be considered as the Palladium of our security, and the first effectual resort in case of hostility . . . ."[1] These two viewpoints summarize the dual nature of the militia in the American Revolutionary War, and of Washington's employment of the militia throughout that war. They are not contradictory but complementary statements. Washington never changed his opinion as stated in the first quote, but he came to recognize the truth as expressed in the second quote.

During the eight and one-half years of warfare, the colonial, and later state, militia forces filled a critical need in the military policy and strategy of the rebellious Americans. Though their activities in the South and in upstate New York have been recognized, even in the middle colonies of Connecticut, New York, and New Jersey, militiamen performed vital duties and participated in all levels of the fighting.[2]

The war in the middle colonies was a partisan war. The campaigns of the regular forces of Britain and America are well known, but these armies did not operate through an empty countryside. Surrounding them were swarms of small detachments consisting of militia and regular soldiers maneuvering around the massed formations and creating a swirl of activity through which the armies moved and fought. That the American Revolutionary War in the South was as much a partisan war as it was a clash of regular field armies is well recognized, but it was just as true in Connecticut, New York, and New Jersey.[3]

The Whig militia forces that existed at the commencement of the war were at the heart of this partisan activity in the North. These militia units were what today would be called the reserves, to which the colonists turned when an immediate crisis arose. From the beginning the political and military leaders of the rebellion saw a clear distinction between militiamen and Continental soldiers, who served in the regular army under the control of Washington and the other Continental generals. Militiamen remained under the authority of their state governments and served with the army only on a temporary basis.

Both in their capacity as a local military force and as a support for the regular army, the Whig militiamen of the Revolutionary War participated in, and helped create in North America, what was then called the *petit guerre*. Such warfare was not unknown in the eighteenth century, as a 1760 pamphlet demonstrated: ". . . the *petit guerre* may not improperly be deemed a kind of miniature Portrait of the great Art of War. The same Deceptions, *Manoeuvres*, and Stratagems, are frequently used by the Commander of a Party, and by the General of an Army . . . ." This pamphlet concluded that the partisan corps

> consists of a Body of light Troops, from One hundred to Two thousand Men, separated from the Grand Army to secure its March, to protect the Camp, to reconnoitre the Country or the Enemy; to surprize their Posts, or their Convoys; to form Ambuscades; and, in short, to put to Practice every Stratagem that may harass or disturb them.[4]

A partisan from the American war, Johann Ewald of the Hessian *jägers*, used no less an authority than the Maréchal de Saxe to define irregular warfare as war waged by small parties to patrol, raid, gather information, reconnoiter, forage, and protect the main army from surprise. Ewald perhaps best summarized this type of warfare: "Little war was continuous war."[5]

The American war was exactly that. Militia forces were engaged in a constant battle with the Tories, who remained loyal to the British government, and with British and German detachments. Whether along the coasts or on the roads between the camps of the main armies, these partisan activities raged throughout the war, and the militia units from the colonies around New York City participated in this warfare at all levels. They defended their colonies and states on their own, they filled the long-term militia units created to defend the more endangered areas, and they coordinated with the regular army to fill its ranks or to harass the movements of the British army. In addition, the militia had the primary responsibility of controlling the Tories. In this capacity, Whig militiamen protected the slowly emerging state governments and limited how much the Tories could help the British with information, supplies, and manpower.

The British reaction to this partisan war is difficult to ascertain. British histories tend to ignore the Whig militia and lump all colonial forces together.[6] During the war itself, however, generals and lower-grade officers recognized more clearly the type of war that they faced, and reacted to the partisan aspects. The British commanders in chief, Sir William Howe and Sir Henry Clinton, tended to blame the Whig militia for much of their troubles, but they also needed a scapegoat, and the armed population of the rebellious colonies was a good one. That the partisan qualities of the war had an impact on the British in the middle region is clear, but how large an impact is difficult to determine.

The very nature of this type of warfare also makes it difficult to be specific concerning the numbers of combatants involved in many of the clashes or to narrate every skirmish that the militia fought. Enough information is available, however, to make clear the nature of this partisan war. The interminable list of engagements demonstrates that Ewald was right: this was "a continuous war."

From the outset of the war, control of the militia was split between the provincial and national leaderships. The governments of Connecticut, New York, and New Jersey maintained their sovereignty over their military forces, but had to share them with the Continental and later the Confederation Congresses, and especially with Washington and the Continental generalship. The successful coordination of local and national requirements, and the use of the militia to fulfill both sets of needs, was a key component of the ultimate American victory.

Washington's role in this irregular warfare is perhaps the most misunderstood aspect of his generalship. The traditional rendition of his contempt for militiamen and his obsession with creating a European-style army overlooks his partisan side.[7] His initial view of the militiamen was complex. He disliked their unreliability, yet he understood some of their partisan qualities. He then learned from experience their strengths and weaknesses as regular soldiers and as partisans, and his willingness to employ them as partisans increased over the years. In particular, his skill at coordinating the militia and regulars for a wide range of duties, and his ability to exploit the militia's strengths when it acted alone or in conjunction with the army, were two of the main reasons for American success in the war in the middle states. For a better understanding of Washington's generalship, it is necessary to recognize the many facets of Washington's use of the militia in the war fought around the British stronghold of New York City. Washington was a skillful general who could make the best use of whatever materials he had available.

The region consisting of Connecticut, New York, and New Jersey was the primary theater of operations for the main armies of both sides in this war, as well as the scene of this brutal partisan war. It is the key theater, where the British tried to win the war in the first years and, except for two major campaigns, where the largest armies of both sides remained from 1776 to the end. For this reason, the area around New York City is an excellent place to show the partisan war in the North. In addition, the state governments that emerged in Connecticut, New York, and New Jersey were relatively stable, which means that their militia policy was not subject to radical political shifts. The command structures in the states, and the personalities involved, did not change much over eight years.

Howard H. Peckham, in *The Toll of Independence*, has provided invaluable statistics that demonstrate the extent of the partisan war that occurred in the middle colonies and states around the field armies.[8] Based on a compilation of his statistics for the whole war, the militia participated on its own in 191 engagements in Connecticut, New York, and New Jersey, compared with 194 clashes in North Carolina, South Carolina, and Georgia, the theater of operations for Nathanael Greene's well-chronicled Southern campaign. The statistics for the number of engagements in which militia and Continentals participated together show that in these three Northern provinces there was a high degree of coordination between the two types of military formations. In Connecticut, New York, and New Jersey the militia and Continentals combined in 485 engagements; they did so in North Carolina, South Carolina, and Georgia 260 times.

These numbers clearly suggest that the militia in Connecticut, New York, and New Jersey was extremely active throughout the war. Despite the traditional view, the militia's duties and the operations of the main armies were not two separate wars but one combined and chaotic conflict fought on many levels. The lack of interest in the participation and activities of the militia in the warfare around the city of New York, therefore, ignores the vicious, small-scale partisan war that occurred in the area. For a deeper understanding of the war around New York City, the militia must be put back into the history of the fighting in the region. The ability of the leaders of the rebellious colonies, and later of the United States, to coordinate the different military formations and to meet the requirements of the local, state, and national leaderships proved decisive in their ultimate victory over the British in the American Revolutionary War.

Washington's Partisan War,
1775–1783

★ CHAPTER ONE ★

Initial Plans and Preparations
for the Use of the Militia,
1775–1776

THE FIRST CLASH at Lexington, Massachusetts, in April 1775 ignited a war that pitted the colonial militia against the might of the British Empire. The American colonies contained no standing military forces of their own at that time. The colonists relied instead on their internal militia organizations for immediate security needs, and on the British army and navy for meeting larger and longer-term threats. Thus, when the fighting started in Massachusetts, the American rebels immediately turned to their colonial militia forces for their defense, and "the best troops in the royal army, were seen, to the surprise and joy of every lover of his country, flying before the raw, inexperienced peasantry."[1]

The proper use of these citizen soldiers was a complex issue that challenged the rebels, or Whigs, throughout the war. The Whigs could use their militia forces as the basis for a united field army, or avoid a national army altogether and use the militia as independent armies within each colony. On the other hand, the rebel leaders could create a national army of full-time soldiers and rely on the militia organizations as local security forces within the individual colonies. While deciding these issues, the Whigs also had to improvise a workable system for controlling the militia. Company and regimental officers, colonial governments, and the emerging national Congress and Continental officer corps all had claims on the militia,

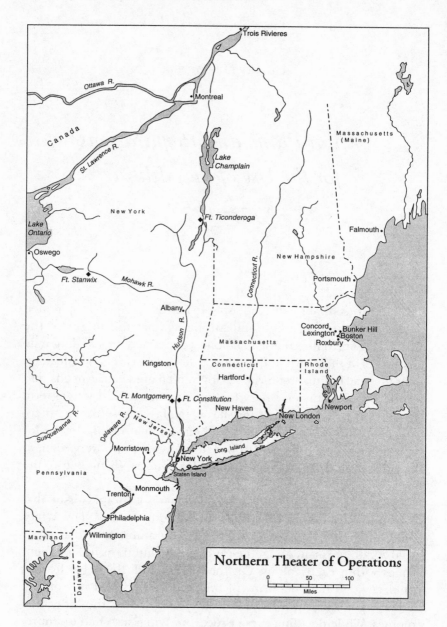

Northern Theater of Operations

and the American rebels had to forge a working relationship among these different levels of authority. By the spring of 1776, the American leaders had established the basic principles concerning the control and proper functions of their militia forces. Though these principles received many challenges during the long war, at least the rebel leaders had established a basis of understanding and agreement from which to work.

The British were not overly concerned about these rebel preparations to employ the militia. Except for General Thomas Gage, who warned that the battle near Bunker Hill showed the Americans could be effective soldiers, and perhaps except for Lord Jeffrey Amherst, commander in chief in England, British military and political leaders held the colonists in contempt. British army officers who had served in North America prior to the outbreak of war dismissed American military abilities and argued that the colonists would make the worst possible soldiers.[2]

Much of this negative attitude toward colonial military prowess came from the experiences of the French and Indian War. British military leaders from that earlier war saw the colonists as cowardly, sickly, selfish deserters. A British surgeon in Boston in 1775 had several other criticisms: Americans were "a drunken, canting, lying, praying, hypocritical rabble without order, subjection, discipline, or cleanliness," and their army would "fall to pieces of itself." The consensus was that the militia could not stand up to British regulars. William Howe, who later succeeded Gage in command of the British army in North America, believed a British soldier was worth two American soldiers. The song "Yankee Doodle," sung later by Americans in praise of the country people who made up the militia, was at first popular with the British soldiers, who sang it in derision of the American militia.[3]

Despite this contempt, some British leaders seemed to understand the nature of the war they faced in 1775. Henry Clinton, who would become the third British army commander in North America, and William Howe both saw the wider dimension of the war that made this contest different from the typical European wars of territorial conquest. As Clinton said in 1776, the British had to persuade the American people to return to their former allegiance by winning their hearts and minds, to use a modern phrase. Sir James Murray, a Scottish officer, recognized a key problem for the British when he described the colonists in 1775 as "3,000,000 exasperated to the last degree and enflamed to the highest pitch of enthusiasm; we have too many instances of what that enthusiasm has been capable of producing not to be very doubtful of the event." This enthusiasm, combined with a country one thousand miles long, worried Murray, notwithstanding the general contempt for colonial soldiers.[4]

The British who criticized the militia, however, misunderstood the colonial soldiers and what they had become by the 1770s. Though the praise the militia received in 1774–75 from rebel leaders was as exaggerated as the British contempt, the militia organizations of the colonial era had evolved during the previous wars. By the time the fighting started in 1775, the colonists could turn to what was, in effect, a semiprofessional military institution and not just a loosely controlled rabble of local militiamen. Even as George Washington tried to turn this semiprofessional force into a professional army, the colonial governments had available these local militia units to serve within and outside of the individual colonies. In effect, each colony had its own provincial army that could help defend it and its neighboring colonies, as well as control the people residing within those colonies.[5]

Whether these rebel militia forces would be effective or not, obviously, was a matter of great concern to the Whigs, but the colonial leaders had little choice. They had to turn to the militia in the spring of 1775. The colonial governments, however, which officially controlled these militia forces in April 1775, were not all safely in the hands of the Whigs. The colonies of Connecticut, New York, and New Jersey, in particular, provided three contrasting examples of the stability and political leanings of the colonial governments in 1775, and therefore of the ability of the Whigs to employ the militia.

Connecticut's colonial government proved to be the most stable and easily converted to the Whig side, due mainly to the fact that its colonial governor, Jonathan Trumbull, Sr., supported the Whig cause against the British government. Trumbull's patriot leanings and the firm Whig control of the General Assembly made it unnecessary to form new legislative and executive branches. In fact, Connecticut was the only colony of the thirteen able to shift from peace to war without restructuring its political system, government, governor, or committees.[6]

As the only colonial governor who joined the rebellion, Trumbull deserved much credit for the calm political transition in Connecticut. This sixty-four-year-old governor had opposed the earlier actions of Parliament and possibly had been involved in the early activities of the Sons of Liberty against British authority. After his election as governor by the Assembly in 1769, he had worked to avert an armed clash with the British, but when news of the fighting at Lexington and Concord arrived at his home in Lebanon, Connecticut, he immediately began to take measures to support the armed colonists against the British military. The first Connecticut militia troops ordered to Boston received their supplies from Trumbull's personal stock of goods. Throughout the war, his home and store were his war office, from which he issued his executive orders and met his Council of Safety. In recognition of his unique status, the British king, members of Parliament, and current British periodicals all denounced Trumbull as the "Rebel Governor of Connecticut." Tories had a special hatred for Trumbull, and after receiving death threats and warnings of a possible kidnapping, he had to accept a guard detail around his Lebanon house.[7]

The actions of this "Rebel Governor" and the legislature enabled Connecticut's government to begin immediately to prepare for war. In fact, the General Assembly had ordered improved efforts at organizing and training the militia forces in December 1774. On April 26, 1775, just six days after Trumbull received word of the fighting in Lexington, a special session of the General Assembly met and the members passed an act providing for one-fourth of the militia, about six thousand troops, to be equipped and readied for the immediate defense of the colony. The legislators appointed David Wooster as the colony's major general of militia and Israel Putnam as brigadier general. Putnam, a stout, burly man with a head of bushy white hair, was a favorite among the militia.[8]

At the same time, the relationship between the legislative and executive branches concerning the control of the militia clarified quickly in Connecticut. In May, the Assembly created a Council of Safety to aid the governor when the Assembly was not in session. Trumbull was to meet with the council whenever necessary. Altogether, the council met 913 days during the war, and Trumbull attended every session. The Assembly also declared it would command the militia being mustered; when it was not in session, the governor and the council would command the troops.[9]

The Connecticut Assembly also recognized the need for some freedom of action at a more local level. The legislators directed that the militia officers be prepared to muster and lead their men on their own initiative in case of a sudden British attack. When the British raided the coast later in the summer, the militia responded as desired, spontaneously, without waiting for orders from the colonial government.[10] The Whig-run government of Connecticut provided well for the immediate, short-term defense of the colony.

New Jersey's government did not make as smooth a transition as that of Connecticut. William Franklin, son of Benjamin Franklin, had received his appointment as governor from the king in an effort to gain favor with his father. As a Tory who fully supported the royal authority in the colonies, William tried to circumvent the rebel activities but steadily lost influence to the Whigs. In February 1776, militiamen commanded by Colonel William Winds briefly held Franklin under armed guard, but he was soon released. Franklin assumed that the Whigs wanted him to flee so that they could proceed to create a new government unhindered, as already had been done in New Hampshire, but he refused to leave. Later, hearing that British commissioners were on their way to Staten Island, Franklin called the General Assembly to meet in June 1776. The Whigs then made their move, and a detachment of militia commanded by Colonel Nathaniel Heard arrested Franklin. The Whig-controlled Provincial Congress sent Franklin to prison in Connecticut, where he remained a prisoner until 1778. After his release, Franklin resided in New York until the end of the war.[11]

Despite Franklin's efforts to maintain his authority, the Whigs slowly took power and organized the Provincial Congress in the summer of 1775. Particularly conspicuous in this movement were William Alexander, a future general of the Continental Army, and William Livingston, the future governor of New Jersey. Alexander, better known as Lord Stirling, was a good-looking, hard-drinking fifty-year-old Whig leader who helped energize the Whigs throughout 1775 and early 1776. The Provincial Congress began to usurp the powers of government, including command of the militia, and the Committees of Correspondence and Observation ran the local county governments. Finally, after the old General Assembly met for the last time in November 1775, the Whigs had a firmer control of New Jersey's political machinery.[12]

While this power struggle occurred at the upper level of New Jersey's government, initial preparations for war began at all levels. New Jersey inhabitants held town and county meetings, where they decided to muster and ready their militia for any emergency. Quickly, local militia units stopped communication between New Jersey Tories and British officials outside the colony. The new Provincial Congress began to exert its control over the militia in June 1775. The Congress adopted regulations and instructed four thousand of the enrolled militia to hold themselves as Minute Men in constant readiness to take the field in New Jersey or a neighboring province. These Minute Men were to stand ready for four months and then be relieved by other militiamen. In addition, two brigadier generals were appointed. One of them, Philemon Dickinson, was a conspicuous leader of the New Jersey militia throughout much of the war. The Congress also drafted a plan to regulate the militia, issued a call for the people of New Jersey to arm themselves and prepare to defend their liberty, and urged that command of the militia be entrusted only to known patriots who supported the Whig cause.[13]

In addition, the New Jersey Congress recognized the need for local initiative, and ordered the militia and Minute Men to assemble at their respective captains' homes in case of a sudden alarm or invasion. The officers nearest to the source of the alarm would immediately lead their men to oppose the enemy while they sent warnings to their superior regimental officers. The regimental officers would inform their general officers and then march all or part of their regiments to support the local officers.[14]

The Whigs of New York had the most difficulty gaining control of their colony. In January and February 1775, the New York Assembly had rejected the authority of the First Continental Congress and had refused to appoint delegates to the Second Continental Congress. These actions had shocked many American patriots. Despite this political hesitancy, the news about Lexington and Concord increased the influence of the Whigs. In New York City, the Sons of Liberty already controlled the streets, and when news of the fighting in Massachusetts arrived, they unloaded ships destined to carry food to the British in Boston. The Whig patriots then announced the port was closed, seized 550 arms from the royal magazine in the city, and distributed the guns to volunteers, who began to drill and march through the city. These armed citizens then placed control of the city government into the hands of the Committee of 100. The Loyalists, as the Tories were also called, remained quiet in the face of this armed threat. By May 1 the immediate danger of violence had calmed, and the Whigs were firmly in control of the city. In early June, the Committee of 100 ordered the one hundred British soldiers in the city to leave.[15]

At the same time, the Whigs were gaining power throughout the entire colony. The rebel Committees of Correspondence helped establish a new Provincial Congress, which began to exert its authority over New York as it recommended that the people arm themselves. Meanwhile, Alexander McDougall, a key Whig leader and a member of the Provincial Congress, took command in New York City. A tall, handsome, hot-tempered Scotsman, whom George Washington called a "brave soldier and disinterested patriot," McDougall spent the month of May organizing seven companies of militia in case more British soldiers came to New York.[16]

This promising beginning for the Whigs received its first check after May 26, when a British warship, HMS *Asia*, entered New York harbor and its captain trained its guns on the city. Matters became more complicated for the Whigs when the royal governor, William Tryon, arrived June 25, 1775, the same day that the newly appointed rebel commander in chief, George Washington, rode through New York City. Tryon wisely waited on board his ship until Washington's welcoming ceremonies had finished. A former governor of North Carolina with a harsh reputation, Tryon had received the appointment as governor of New York in 1771, and in June 1775 was returning from England, where he had recommended reconciliation with the colonists. Upon his arrival in New York, however, he immediately began to rally the Tories, and with the *Asia* in the harbor lending force to Tryon's actions, the Whigs had to move more cautiously. Tryon also moved carefully because he did not have the military force on hand to stop the Whigs, who were raising five thousand troops for their defense, and he believed that the Provincial Congress had for the moment wrested away most of his political power. Tryon decided against issuing a call for the old colonial Assembly to meet because he felt it was better to sit quietly than to take action and be rebuffed. In addition, he lived in fear of the actions of the mob in the city, unaware that Washington had left orders with Philip Schuyler, the Continental general in New York, to leave Tryon alone unless he tried to take forceful action. This uneasy truce lasted through the summer.[17]

Despite this forced truce, the Whigs increased their power by regulating and organizing the militia forces of New York. The New York Provincial Congress adopted a Militia Bill in August 1775 that ordered every fourth man of the militia to act as a Minute Man. This Congress, the county Committees of Safety, and the specific district leaders would decide if local military watches were necessary. George Clinton, future governor of New York, was appointed brigadier general of Ulster and Orange counties. The congressmen also authorized the militia to act on its own, if necessary, to defend New York from British attack. The Militia Bill directed that upon insurrection, invasion, or any other alarm, the militia companies closest to the enemy or insurgents were to oppose the enemy on their own; the officers on the spot were to inform their regimental commanders, who would support the local defenders with part or all of their regiments. The Congress recognized that some counties in New York could get help faster from adjacent counties or from neighboring colonies than by contacting the Provincial Congress first; thus the committees of these counties received authority to call on such aid when necessary. Therefore, both in law and in practice, New York's leaders, as well as those of Connecticut and New Jersey, recognized the dual nature of the command of the militia within the colonies. The committees and Congresses took control, but the militia could also be an autonomous military force.[18]

Even as the colonial governments began to organize and command the local militia forces, the emerging national authorities began to exert some control over the militia. The Continental Congress, George Washington, and the other Continental generals all played a part in the employment of the militia. With the emergence of this national leadership, however, two difficult issues arose: the need to decide between the competing demands placed on the militia

by the national and colonial authorities, and the relationship between those two levels of control.

The Continental Congress and General Washington showed their
preferences concerning these difficult issues early in the initial year
of the war. Though Congress's active role in controlling the militia
later declined, at first it took an active part, especially in establishing
the relationship between the national and colonial authorities over
the provincial soldiers. The main question concerned the extent of
Washington's powers over the colonial militia, and whether Washington, as commander in chief, commanded the colonial forces or
the colonial governments retained control. His commission from
the Continental Congress appointing him commander in chief officially put him in command of all forces raised or to be raised by the
United Colonies. Whether this definition of his authority covered
the individual colonies' militia was unclear.[19]

The Congress itself was ambivalent concerning Washington's powers over the colonial militia. The members basically accepted
the ultimate power of the local leaders over their own militia units,
though at first congressional orders suggested Washington had control over the militia. A congressional committee in the fall of 1775
empowered Washington to call on the militia as necessary to fill
the army, and as the army began to dissolve in November, Congress
passed a resolution authorizing Washington to call on the militia
and Minute Men of New England. But when questions arose concerning the extent of these powers, the Congress hesitated to give
Washington full authority over the militia soldiers. Instead, it decided that Washington had to receive the permission of the executives of the colonies involved. The president of the Congress, John
Hancock, personally wrote to the New England governments to explain this resolution and to urge them to send all the aid that Washington requested.[20]

The Continental Congress's ambivalence left Washington the responsibility of establishing a working relationship with the colonial
governments. Washington himself understood from the beginning
one of the basic aspects of this war: he had to maintain good relations between the army and the people, and of course the governments of the people. Due to this realization, he avoided any challenge to the existing or emerging political powers. He strove to work

with the colonial governments and protect them as much as possible, in order to convince the colonists that the army was in the field to obey and defend the colonies.[21]

He created the necessary relationship in several ways. He made a clear distinction between Continental and militia soldiers. If a unit was considered militia, if it was put into the field and maintained by a particular colonial government, Washington considered himself unauthorized to issue that unit orders without permission from the involved colonial government. In addition, Washington worked through the individual governments when he needed to raise more militia or keep part of the militia in the field longer than expected. As the old army dissolved and a new one was organized during the winter of 1775–76, Washington asked the Massachusetts and New Hampshire governments to send men, and was pleased with the fast response. In fact, the Massachusetts legislature offered to raise more than requested if he believed it necessary. As Washington needed every man he could get, he asked Massachusetts, as well as Connecticut and New Hampshire, to send even more men.[22]

Another way Washington tried to maintain good relations with the colonial governments was through his understanding of their needs. Farmers who spent too much time in the ranks of the militia could not grow food, and the colonial governments depended on their farmers to supply the food needs of the colonies and the national army. It is not surprising that the seasonal needs of planting and harvesting were often cited as reasons for dismissing or not calling in the militia. In July 1775, for example, Washington called for an extra one thousand militia, then decided that the latest intelligence on the enemy, other expected reinforcements, the numerous calls already made on the militia, and the inconvenience of calling "Militia in the midst of Harvest" were good reasons to cancel the call.[23]

He also realized the need to maintain control of the Loyalists in the colonies and agreed with the measures taken by the colonial governments. In fact, he often suggested strong actions against the Tories, as in this advice to Governor Trumbull:

Would it not be prudence to seize on those Tories who have been, are, and that are known to be, active against us? Why should persons who are preying upon the vitals of their Country be suffered to stalk at large, whilst we know they will do us every mischief in their power? These Sir are points I beg to submit to your serious consideration.

He approved of Connecticut's laws to restrain and punish people who acted against the colonies, and urged the other governments to follow its example. He informed the colonial leaders that the militia of each colony had the responsibility for controlling the populace.[24]

Unfortunately for the rebels, the need to balance local demands and national requirements often caused strains between the colonial and national leaderships. Though the Continental Congress at first helped to set guidelines, ultimately Washington had the responsibility of establishing the necessary balance between the colonial and national duties of the militia. The issue of local defense, and whether detachments of Continental soldiers would scatter throughout the colonies and support the militia at every threatened point, proved to be a particular source of friction between the colonial governments and the national leaders. Washington and the members of the Continental Congress, however, set their policy early in the war, and together presented a unified front to the pressures from the individual colonies.

The requests by individual colonies for detachments of the Continental Army began as early as July 1775, when the Massachusetts General Court requested a detachment from the army to protect the inhabitants of its coast from British raids. Washington conferred with his general officers and the members of the Continental Congress present in camp, and then responded. His answer is very important because it established the precedent for his response to all subsequent requests. He answered that it was not consistent with his duty

to detach any Part of the Army now here on any Particular Provincial Service. It has been debated in Congress and Settled that the Militia or other Internal Strength of each Province is to be applied for Defence against those Small and Particular Depredations which were to be expected, & to which they were Supposed to be competent.

He went on to explain his larger view of the war:

> It is the Misfortune of our Situation which exposes us to these Ravages, against which in my Judgment no such Temporary Relief would possibly secure us—The great Advantage the Enemy has of transporting Troops by being Masters of the Sea will enable them to harass us by Diversions of this kind; & Should we be tempted to pursue them upon every Alarm, The Army must either be so weaken'd as to Expose it to Destruction or a great Part of the Coast be Still left unprotected . . . .

He finished with a personal lament:

> It would give me great Pleasure to have it in my Power to extend Protection & Safety to every Individual, but the Wisdom of the General Court will anticipate me in the Necessity of Conducting our Operations on a General and impartial Scale, so as to exclude any first Cause of Complaint & Jealousy.[25]

Washington's answer showed a careful analysis of the nature of the war that the British were capable of conducting and of the proper role of the militia in local defense. He wanted to keep the army concentrated and avoid separating it into little pieces reacting to every thrust by the British. The Congress supported this position, and thus the national political and military leadership agreed on one aspect of the relationship between the army and the militia: the army would concentrate on national defense while the colonial militia remained available for more local needs.

This decision meant that Washington expected the militia to defend the colonies against British raiders and plundering parties. After a successful British raid on the coast of Rhode Island, he commented to Nicholas Cooke, Rhode Island's governor:

> I had flattered myself with the Hope, that the Vigilance of the Inhabitants on the Islands & Coasts, would have disappointed the Enemy in their late Expedition after live stock. I hope nothing will be omitted by the several Committees, & other Officers to guard against any future attempts . . . .

Washington worried that such successes would encourage the British to launch more raids. When General Wooster, who was stationed on Long Island in the fall of 1775, asked for protection for the island's inhabitants, Washington responded that the danger of these raids was less than the danger of fragmenting the army. "Upon this Principle I have invariably rejected every Application made me here, to keep any Detachments on the coast for these purposes."[26]

In August and September 1775, this policy caused friction between Washington and the government of Connecticut. In early August, Governor Trumbull wrote to Washington that he was holding along the Connecticut coast two Continental companies which were bound for the army at Boston. Trumbull then ordered another company of new recruits raised for the Continental Army to remain on the coast. At first, Washington accepted this interference because British ships were in Long Island Sound. In September, however, Washington informed Trumbull that unless the British fleet was then attacking, the Continental recruits along the coast should be sent to the army. A week later, Washington reinforced his request by quoting a resolution of the Continental Congress that ruled against the use of Continental soldiers for the defense of a particular colony. When the Connecticut government ignored these requests, Washington sent a "peremptory requisition" for those men. The Council of Safety finally obeyed Washington's orders, but Trumbull complained to Washington that Connecticut would now have to raise more militia to protect its coast. Trumbull added that the people of Connecticut would continue to defend the rights and liberty of the colonies, "and of our own in particular."[27]

Though Washington realized he could not please everyone, he was concerned that this policy might threaten the good relations between any colonial government and his command. He therefore assured Trumbull that he intended no disrespect toward Connecticut's ruling bodies by his "peremptory" order, and repeated that he understood the defensive needs along the coast. He reaffirmed his desire to protect everyone, but warned that to scatter the army would make his operations dependent on the actions of a few British ships. Naval raids along the coast, he argued, were not a major threat to the colonies. Fortunately for the future relations between Washington and the government of Connecticut, this episode was the only case of real friction between Washington and Trumbull. Despite other disagreements concerning Washington's policies, the two men maintained a cordial correspondence throughout the war.[28]

Washington did bend his rule momentarily after the British burned Falmouth, Massachusetts, to the ground on October 18, 1775. The British had initiated a policy of laying waste the coast of New England, and struck first at Falmouth. In response to pleas for help from the stricken town and its neighbors, Washington at first answered that though he abhorred "the Savage Barbarity of the Enemy," he could send no detachment to the area. He finally relented and ordered a battalion of riflemen to the north. In November, Washington warned that should more help be required,

it is incumbent on the People of the Country to exert themselves for their and the Public's defence, the Continental Congress are so much of that opinion, that they have recommended it to each of the Colonies to provide for their particular internal safety.[29]

Thus, the Congress and Washington had formulated the basic principle for the defense of the individual colonies by early 1776. Though Washington had experienced an example of the kind of resistance such a policy would face, he was determined to adhere to the principle of a concentrated army and a locally based militia for defense.

Another issue concerning the use of the militia caused more friction, this time between Washington and the Continental Congress. The members of the Congress decided early in the war that the militia was to be used as a source of reinforcement for the Continental Army. Many Whig leaders, in fact, preferred the idea of relying on the militia as the primary military organization. According to this opinion, if the militia forces were led by loyal officers, militia soldiers alone could overthrow the British. Pursuant to this policy, the Congress continually urged the colonial governments and Washington to fill the army with militia. In the fall of 1775, a congressional committee urged Washington to attack Boston, and suggested that he request Minute Men and other militia forces, if necessary, from the neighboring colonies. Though Washington followed the recommendation of a Council of War and did not attack, the Congress had shown its belief that the militia was a source of ready reinforcements for the regular army.[30]

Washington did not agree with this policy. His experiences in the French and Indian War left him with a poor opinion of militiamen as regular soldiers. In command of an enlarged regiment of Virginia militia in the 1750s, he became so discouraged by the poor showing of the local soldiers that he often thought of quitting. Too few were willing to serve, he believed, and too many were willing to desert. Washington sensed even then that an attack on the enemy stronghold of Fort Duquesne would offer more security for the frontier than relying for defense on the inadequate militia force available. In addition, the provincial troops lacked the necessary subordination to make good soldiers. Washington wrote during this earlier war, "discipline is the soul of the Army," but training for militia soldiers was haphazard at best.[31]

This traditional view of Washington's attitude and his contempt for the militia has, however, received too much emphasis. As Washington's noted biographer Douglas S. Freeman concluded in his discussion of Washington's French and Indian War experiences, "Whatever the future might hold, then, Washington would have no faith in the militia." Even while developing this healthy distrust of the soldierly qualities of the militia, Washington recognized the usefulness of such men. In his own description of his first battle by the side of Major General Edward Braddock along the Monongahela River in 1755, Washington stated that he not only offered to lead the Virginia militia against the foes hidden in the woods, but he praised the willingness shown by the provincial troops to advance into the trees to engage the elusive enemy.[32]

Building on this view of his earlier experiences with the militia, Washington presented a more complex attitude toward the use of the militia in the Revolutionary War than the traditional description allows. He indeed wanted to create a regular army in which discipline and control would improve his soldiers' ability to fight the British, but he did not disdain to use the militia in some function, even in conjunction with the army. Later in the war, he willingly used it in a variety of roles outside of the army. He preferred the idea of using the militia in emergencies, where the local availability and possibly large but temporary numbers could be of value for the short term. From the beginning, the use of militia units as long-term reinforcements to the Continental Army never appealed to Washington. Unfortunately, the army was rarely strong enough on its own, which often forced him to rely on the militia to strengthen it in emergencies and over the long haul.

Indeed, Washington had to call on the militia from the very beginning, because the colonies had no regular military force and the Continental Congress hesitated to commit fully to a professional army. His unhappiness at having militia soldiers fill his army has been described by historians and military analysts for two centuries, yet rather than refuse on principle, Washington gave in to the reality of the situation. While recruiting the original army in July, he asked Massachusetts for a temporary militia reinforcement. The crisis in the winter, as the original army dissolved and a new one formed, forced Washington once again to turn to the militia to reinforce the army. Still, as Continental enlistments filled slowly, he complained to the Continental Congress:

> . . . I fear I shall be under the necessity of Calling in the Militia and minute men of the Country to my assistance[.] I Say I fear it, because, by what I can Learn from the Officers in the Army belonging to this Colony, it will be next to an impossibility to keep them under any degree of Discipline, & that it will be very difficult to prevail on them to remain a moment Longer than they Chuse themselves, it is a mortifying reflection to be reduced to this Dilema . . . .[33]

Despite his fears that the ill-disciplined militia would "destroy the little subordination I have been labouring to establish, and run me into evil . . . ," Washington called for three thousand militia from Massachusetts and two thousand from New Hampshire. His unpleasant experiences as commander of the Virginia militia regiment in the previous war can be seen in his grumbling that the militia troops were "not to be depended upon for more than a few days, as they soon get tired, grow impatient, ungovernable, and of course leave the Service—what will be the consequence then, If the greatest part of the Army is to be composed of such men?" These provincial troops were engaged to serve only through mid-January, when, "according to custom, they will depart, let the necessity of their stay be never so urgent."[34]

The duality of Washington's approach to the militia, however, began to emerge from the first. Misgivings notwithstanding, Washington planned to use the militia while it was with him, thus reflecting his attitude that it could be useful on a short-term basis. In a Council of General Officers on January 16, 1776, Washington and his subordinates agreed on a plan to attack Boston even as he tried to raise a new army. Washington requested thirteen regiments of militia from Massachusetts and its neighbors "to take advantage of circumstances," but this determination waned in February as the militia came in slowly. Finally, another council advised against an attack because less than half of the militia had arrived. Though he temporarily set aside the project, Washington still favored an attack at that time, despite the negative advice and the lack of militia.[35]

Another opportunity to use the militia as a temporary boost to army strength arose in February and March 1776. Washington planned to lure the British out of their Boston defenses by taking possession of Dorchester Heights and threatening the harbor with his reinforced artillery. He requested that the militia of the towns nearest to Dorchester and Roxbury be ready to join the army upon a given signal, to help repel the expected British attack on the heights. The militia turned out quickly during the crisis days of March, and after the event, Washington expressed his pleasure with the provincial troops. He soon discharged these temporary reinforcements because stormy weather had prevented the impending British counterattack.[36]

Despite Washington's strong reservations concerning the use of militia troops to fill the army, he was willing to risk battle with them if an opportunity arose. This dual attitude toward the militia was the hallmark of his policy for the provincial troops. He would rather not rely on them as full-time reinforcements, but would not disdain to use what was necessary and available.

Washington preferred to use the militia in capacities separate from the army, where it was more effective. Circumstances, however, did not yet give him a chance to employ the militia in a variety of roles; the siege of Boston provided few opportunities to engage in the kind of war he would later wage to great effect around New York City. At Boston, the British remained relatively quiet in their lines, so the employment of small detachments and harassing parties of militia soldiers was difficult. Washington, however, showed his determination, even around Boston, to engage in a kind of war where the characteristics of the militia would be valuable. He tried to cut all communication between the British and the countryside, and prevent the British "from penetrating into the Country with Fire & Sword, & to harass them if they do . . . ." Should the British march out of Boston, he planned to do "everything in my power to distress them."[37]

Thus, Washington began to formulate his views on the place of the militia in his operations and the larger war. In fact, the colonial militia forces increasingly took center stage due to a lack of a regular army, and due to the Whig reliance on the provincial troops for control of the people as well as for local defense. The British held these colonial soldiers in contempt, but the political and military leaders of the rebel Whigs depended on them from the first. As the Whigs gained power over the colonial governments, control of the militia organizations remained firmly in their hands. How well the militia would shoulder the burdens relegated to it remained to be seen.

★ CHAPTER TWO ★

Early Defense of the Middle Colonies, 1775–1776

EVEN AS the rebel colonists went through the process of organizing the governments and formulating their policy, the militia soldiers shouldered their guns and took the field in defense of the colonies. The war clearly would not wait for the colonial leaders to hammer out the finer points concerning the employment of the provincial troops. Amid the chaos of hurried militia calls, Tory dangers, and threats of invasion, the national and colonial leaders had to implement their policy and coordinate the competing calls on the militia.

In the first year the internal threat posed by the Loyalists proved to be less than the Whigs of the middle colonies expected, though the fear remained strong. Controlling the people, however, proved to be a role the militia handled well, partly because the militia had been used for social control before the revolt occurred. In the months following the opening battles of Lexington and Concord, the local rebellious militia forces helped ensure the continued dominance of the Whigs within the colonies and helped guarantee that the Loyalists could not initiate a countermovement among the people. The colonial Whig governments of New Jersey, New York, and Connecticut in particular passed laws to restrain and punish those people unfriendly to the cause, and to stop anyone who sent intelligence or supplies to the enemy, or who spoke out against the Whig governments or the United Colonies. Anyone raising or joining a unit to serve with the British army or navy would be imprisoned, and insurrections against these Whig governments or their militia forces were suppressed. Unfortunately for the Tories, the British did not realize how scattered the Loyalists were, and how well the local Whig militia forces could enforce these new laws by intimidating the Tories through the use of local and county committees. These committees forced Tories to take oaths of allegiance to the rebellion, and even imprisoned or exiled such unwanted people.[1]

The external threat posed by British naval power proved to be a more immediate concern as the colonies faced the danger of possible invasions and raids beginning in the summer of 1775. The Whigs in Connecticut, New York, and New Jersey feared British raids along their extensive and exposed coasts. Connecticut's coast on Long Island Sound, New York's Staten, Manhattan, and Long Islands, and New Jersey's coast across from Manhattan and Staten Islands were all open to an enemy who controlled the water. The Whigs in Connecticut and New York, in particular, spent an anxious year fending off raids and awaiting the expected large-scale British invasion. New Jersey's coast remained relatively safe the first year, but the New Jersey government still exerted itself to help defend New York. Thus, even as the rebels solidified and maintained their power in these three colonies, they turned their attention to the seacoasts of New York and Connecticut.

At first Connecticut's Whig leaders had an easier task defending themselves than did the Whigs in New York and New Jersey, due mainly to the calm transition of power in the opening weeks of the war and to the fact that Connecticut did not face as extreme an internal threat as New York or New Jersey. The few who spoke out against the Whig takeover in Connecticut were quickly silenced, and the only real threat to rebel control there occurred in its southwestern parts. Several militia officers in New Haven and Fairfield opposed taking up arms, but the Whigs immediately ousted them. When most of the militiamen in Fairfield spoke out against the rebels, the Connecticut Assembly sent in two hundred Whig militia who surprised and dispersed the suspect soldiers without resistance.[2]

This internal security enabled the Connecticut government to focus on the threat to its coast, which was fortunate for the Connecticut's Whigs because they found that they had to rely mostly on themselves for local defense. New York's and New Jersey's defenses were closely linked due to their proximity to the Hudson River and Staten Island, and Connecticut militia often marched to New York's support, but rarely did neighboring militia forces come to Connecticut's aid. Governor Trumbull and the Connecticut General Assembly recognized this situation and immediately began to prepare their defenses. They were fortunate that the internal threat was not more serious, because this relative safety freed the Connecticut militia forces to concentrate on colonial defense.

Connecticut's Assembly ordered several militia units along the coast by the end of May 1775: one regiment at New London, one regiment split between Greenwich and Stamford, and another regiment stationed from Guilford to Stamford. These militia soldiers took their places along the coast just in time, for the raids in the Sound began in late July. On July 26, British ships appeared off New London, and reinforcements of militia were ordered there. On August 6, ships plundered Fisher's Island, where "a Large Number of Men were Soon Collected under arms . . . ." The governor and the Council of Safety met in early August when the council announced it expected more attacks on the coast. It urged Trumbull to order one-fourth of the men from five different regiments to be ready and equipped, and to hold themselves as Minute Men. These Minute Men would turn out immediately in an emergency, but stay only for a few days.[3]

The British ships in the Sound hovered off the coast, keeping the port towns in constant alarm, and the calls from these coastal towns for more men multiplied. Lyme's committee feared for the livestock near the coast, and asked if one or two companies could be spared from the defenses of New London. Trumbull answered that the men could not be spared. Instead, he urged the town to set up its own coastal watch, as other towns had done. When British ships fired on the town of Stonington, the colonel there called in the area's men. By the time the firing ended on August 30, almost eight hundred armed men were at Stonington harbor. Trumbull reissued orders for the coastal regiments to hold one-fourth of their men ready for duty as Minute Men, and then ordered new detachments of militia to New London, Stonington, New Haven, and Lyme.[4]

The Connecticut Assembly remained very concerned with coastal defense through the fall and winter of 1775 and 1776. The General

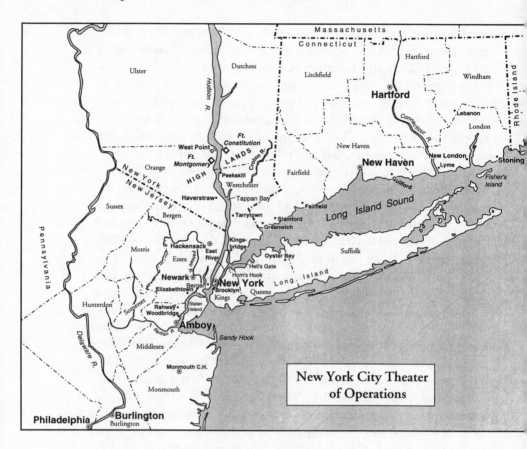

New York City Theater
of Operations

Assembly, and during its recess the governor and the council, passed
acts and resolutions for raising companies for the port towns, and
ordered the construction of defensive works in places such as New
London and New Haven. In December, Trumbull informed the Assembly of the need for more Minute Men for defense, and for the
further fortification of the principal ports. The Assembly responded
with acts to continue the companies stationed on the coast, and to
raise another body of Minute Men to be held ready for instant service. These Minute Men now consisted of one-fourth of the entire
militia of Connecticut, and were placed under the direction of the
governor. They were to serve until January 1, 1777, at the latest. In
addition, the Assembly gave Trumbull and the council the power to
reinforce or disband such units along the coast as they believed best.

The legislature thus put control of the militia that was actually in the field into the hands of the executive, and even gave the executive some power to call out the militia.[5]

The system of depending on Minute Men for each emergency ultimately proved awkward. Calling out men each time a few ships approached a harbor used up provisions and emptied the countryside of farmers. By April 1776, Trumbull understood this, and he began using his executive power to bypass orders from the council and to order additional companies to stand guard along the coast. New London, Fairfield, and New Haven, in particular, received reinforcements.[6]

While Connecticut waged its somewhat isolated war to control the Tories and defend its coasts against British raids, the rebels in the middle colonies prepared for the war to hit the New York shores. Unfortunately for the Whigs, they had to control a potentially dangerous internal Tory threat in New York. New York, however, benefited from its close proximity to New Jersey and Connecticut because its neighbors' militia could march to the aid of New York when necessary. New York quickly became the focal point of the defensive measures of the Whigs in the middle colonies throughout the first year.

Fear of a British invasion of New York developed soon after hostilities began in Massachusetts, and rumors spread of a British naval force sailing to New York City. Since New York's political situation was divided and the Whigs were not fully in control, the Whig-controlled committees wrote to the Continental Congress for advice even as the committeemen started sending women and children from the city and mustering trusted militiamen. Tories kept spiking the cannons, so the Whigs moved some of the guns out of the city. In May, when HMS *Asia* arrived, Whig preparations slowed. The British hoped this naval presence could control the important crossings and passes along the Hudson River, and later support any British troops who might be sent to New York City.[7]

The New Yorkers' request for advice opened the door for the Continental Congress, which began to take action for the defense of New York. First it requested Connecticut's government to send forces to New York City. This move reflected the suspicions caused by New York's divided political situation and the hesitancy of the New York General Assembly to accept the authority of the Continental Congress.

Connecticut's legislature, showing more willingness to send troops to New York than to Boston, ordered two thousand militia to muster on its western frontier under the command of Major General David Wooster. Upon a request from the New York Provincial Congress, these troops held their position in Connecticut for the moment. The Continental Congress urged New York's Congress to arm and train its own militia and collect a number of soldiers in the city, and the New York legislators initially followed this advice.[8]

When the members of the Continental Congress learned that the New York Provincial Congress hesitated to allow Connecticut soldiers to enter its territory, and Connecticut's government hesitated to send its troops into New York without permission, they decided to take more direct action. Their urgency was heightened by the belief that three thousand British troops were on the way to New York, and by their knowledge that the New York Congress had not actually raised its own militia. New York was thus defenseless. The Continental Congress resolved that the Connecticut militia should occupy certain posts in New York, but it did not actually have the authority to send orders to the colonial governments. The national legislators therefore urged the New York Provincial Congress to request Connecticut's men, and recommended that the Connecticut government send the men upon New York's request. Wooster received special instructions from the Continental Congress to be ready to move on a moment's notice. The national and New York governments both singled out the Highlands, a mountainous region along the banks of the Hudson River near Peekskill and the future site of West Point, as a site deserving special care, and men were ordered to secure this vital region. New York's legislators then realized the danger of a British invasion and requested Connecticut's men. Wooster received orders from the Connecticut government to enter New York with his militia force and camp within five miles of New York City.[9]

As Wooster prepared to move, he needed to know if the New York Provincial Congress or the Continental Congress had any authority over his men while they were in New York. He asked for permission to act directly on requests or orders from the New York Congress rather than waiting for orders from Connecticut. The need for freedom of action by the field officer was apparent. The governor's Council of Safety of Connecticut ordered Wooster to obey commands from both the Continental Congress and the New York Congress until he received different instructions.[10] All three levels of control—local, colonial, and national—had to cooperate.

When intelligence arrived that no British troops were actually on their way to New York, the New York Congress asked Wooster to halt where he was. The Continental Congress again intervened and asked Governor Trumbull to order Wooster's force to New York City despite the vacillation of the New Yorkers. The Continental Congress feared the British troop transports might still sail to New York. Trumbull ignored the New York request in favor of the advice of the Continental Congress, and Wooster continued his advance with about fifteen hundred men. By July 1 they arrived on the Hudson River, within two miles of New York City. New York's delegates to the Continental Congress apparently were ashamed of the actions of their provincial leaders, because in late July they wrote to New York's Committee of Safety, expressing the hope that in the future New York would be able to depend upon its own exertions for defense.[11]

After this awkward beginning, Wooster's men remained the focal point of a controversy over control. New York's Congress ordered Wooster to send four companies of the Connecticut militia to Long Island in order to protect the livestock there, and it ordered the Long Island militia to support Wooster's men. On August 9, Wooster arrived with 450 men at Oyster Pond, where the local militia joined him. His soldiers skirmished a few days later with a British party trying to plunder the livestock on nearby Fisher's Island. At this point, Wooster asked Trumbull to release him from the order to obey the New York Congress, as its loyalties were still under suspicion. The Suffolk County Committee of Long Island then asked him to remain on the island because its own militia had been ordered away by the Continental commander of the region, Major General Philip Schuyler. The members of New York's Congress seconded the request. Neither the New York Congress nor the Suffolk County Committee would interfere with Schuyler's orders because Schuyler was a Continental general. For the moment, Wooster stayed.[12]

Next, New York's legislators asked Wooster to send one of his militia companies to defend the Highlands, but he refused. He had instructions from Washington to keep his troops concentrated unless ordered otherwise by Washington or the Continental Congress.

Schuyler suggested the Continental Congress clarify the situation, because Wooster did have orders to concentrate his troops for the defense of New York City. Both Wooster and the New York Congress turned to the Continental Congress for a decision. Instead, Washington intervened. First, he agreed that a colonial congress could not interfere with the orders of a Continental officer, and thus New York's congressmen were right not to countermand Schuyler's orders. Washington then recommended that Wooster keep his troops on Long Island as long as Wooster believed best, but to remember the importance of the lines of communication that crossed the Hudson River at the Highlands. In other words, Washington hesitated to countermand Schuyler's orders or to ignore the request of the New York Congress, and thus he released Wooster from the order to keep his troops concentrated. When Wooster received Washington's letter, he returned to New York City, which seemed the best place from which to defend all the vital sites.[13]

This small crisis in command helped demonstrate the confusion concerning the different levels of authority over the militia. A colonial government ordered its own militia forces into the field, and had some influence over who could command them. The Continental Congress and Washington had a higher authority over Continental officers and soldiers, but they could not overrule a colony's orders for its own militia. A third party, New York's government in this case, had limited powers over the militia of another colony, and none over Continental forces or officers. The militia officer in the field had to weigh the different orders and make sense out of them. Wooster wisely appealed to the Continental Congress and Washington for clarification, but in a more pressing emergency the field officer might not have the luxury to await such a decision.

Later in August, the British ships in the harbor and the rebels in the city nearly came to blows. Isaac Sears, a New York radical, had already threatened to seize the hated Tory governor, William Tryon, despite Washington's orders to leave Tryon alone. On August 23, a rebel party probably led by Sears broke into Tryon's home, but the governor was not there. During the early hours of August 24, the Whig militia took more forceful action, seizing the royal cannons from the battery at the southern tip of Manhattan. After an exchange of musket fire between the rebels on shore and British marines in a boat from HMS *Asia*, British naval Captain George Vandeput ordered a broadside of his ship's guns fired into the city. Though the cannon fire did little damage to the city and did not hurt anyone, Vandeput wrote later the same day that the "people are leaving town in great numbers . . . ." Women and children in particular fled, fearful that open hostilities had begun.[14]

After this hostile exchange, however, tempers cooled. The day after the firing, Tryon met with the members of the Provincial Congress and the New York City Committee as well as his own councilors. The uneasy truce that had lasted throughout the summer was reestablished at this meeting. Tryon convinced the Whig leaders to agree not to seize any more British cannons and supplies in the city, and to continue to send provisions to the British ships in the harbor. This suspension of hostilities lasted throughout the fall months, as each side decided the other was too strong to be challenged, but it also led to further suspicions among the rebels concerning New York's loyalties to the Whig cause.[15]

Despite the truce, New York City still sat on a powder keg. Vice Admiral Samuel Graves in Boston warned Vandeput not to allow the exchange of fire to interrupt the flow of supplies to the British ships in the harbor. Were the mayor of New York to let that flow of supplies stop, Vandeput had instructions to level the house of "that traitor Sears." If the rebels attacked the ships, Vandeput had permission to defend himself and to destroy the American ships around him, as well as the rebels' houses in the city. Though Vandeput believed the mayor was under the control of the "rioters" in the city, he took no further hostile actions.[16]

There may have been a truce between the rebels and warships, but not between the Whigs and Tories. Queens County, Long Island, was a major concern for the Whigs because they believed it had a large Tory population. In September, the New York Committee of Safety ordered Alexander McDougall to send two militia companies into Queens County to disarm the Loyalists. The Tories prepared to resist, and McDougall canceled the expedition when he realized how strong the Loyalist forces were. Whig suspicions of New York's stance only worsened. In October, the Provincial Congress learned of a plan by Tories near Peekskill, in the Highlands, to assemble and support any actions by the British. The Congress ordered in a militia force that seized the Tories before they could do any damage. The truce with the navy notwithstanding, the rebels continued to maintain their power on the land, and Tryon despaired of regaining control. Finally, fearing for his own safety in the city, Tryon took refuge on board a British ship in the harbor on October 19.[17]

Ironically, even as the British lost control of the people and territory of New York, they planned on shifting the war to that colony. In early August, the British government in England requested General Thomas Gage's opinion about seizing New York City immediately and making the Hudson River the seat of war for the next year. Gage agreed that New York would be a good choice because the army could link with the numerous Loyalists and cut the rebel communications over the river. He added, however, that he could not split his force to take the city at that moment. Meanwhile, Tryon added his voice to the discussion, arguing that a force of five thousand to six thousand regular soldiers in New York could stop the rebels and bring the people back to their proper allegiance. Such a British force in New York, he believed, would make the rebels split their forces and could spread an awe of British might throughout the colony. Like his colleagues in the military, Tryon believed that the mere sight of British soldiers would lead the wayward colonists to return to a peaceful obedience to the British government. The British command finally made its decision in September and ordered Major General William Howe, who replaced Gage as commander in North America, to plan to shift to New York, before winter if necessary.[18]

After the events of August–October, however, and despite British plans, New York City remained relatively quiet for the rest of the year. The Whigs spent this time preparing the defenses of the city for the invasion they correctly expected but did not realize had already been planned. One location of primary concern continued to be the Highlands. The Continental Congress ordered Wooster's militiamen still in New York to shift to the Highlands, and it urged the members of the New York Provincial Congress to plan with New Jersey's and Connecticut's governments on the best methods to reinforce the Highlands in case of an invasion. At the same time, Washington wanted the views of the Continental Congress concerning the Continental Army and the defense of New York. Should he send part of his army to New York immediately, or should he depend on the militia of New York for local defense? A committee of the Congress brought Washington the response: Washington's army was too weak to be split, and should therefore be kept around the main British army in Boston. Consistent with the previously declared principle of concentration, both the Congress and Washington expected the militia to defend New York against any sudden invasions.[19]

Governor Tryon, meanwhile, spent the final two months of the year urging the British to move to New York sooner rather than later. Believing rebel spirits had abated, he only awaited the arrival of a few thousand British soldiers to reestablish royal control of the province. He suggested to the British government in England that the friends of Britain were numerous still, but that rebel abuses were growing. Tories had to endure tarring and feathering, plundering, imprisonment, and threats to their lives. Despite these difficulties, Tryon promised up to three thousand provincial troops would join the British force upon its arrival. Howe, though, decided in late November that the year was too far advanced to shift bases before winter, and that his army was too weak to send detachments from Boston. When Tryon learned of General Howe's decision concerning New York, he must have been bitterly disappointed.[20]

Isaac Sears was one rebel who excelled at abusing Tories. On November 23, he entered New York City with about eighty mounted volunteers from Connecticut, where he had gone in disgust at the truce in New York City between the Whigs and the British on their ships. He and his volunteers seized Loyalist James Rivington's printing press and left town without opposition. On his return trip to Connecticut, he disarmed some Tories in Westchester County. The New York Provincial Congress sent an official protest to Governor Trumbull for allowing such actions to proceed from Connecticut, but the raid still spread fear among the Loyalist population of New York. The Tories in Queens County expected a similar raid, and therefore banded together and publicly declared their intention to defend themselves. Altogether, about fifteen hundred men armed themselves.[21]

Unaware of Howe's decision but painfully aware of the growing tension within New York due to events such as Sears's raid, the Whigs stepped up efforts to provide for the defense of New York in November and December 1775. The Continental Congress once again took direct action. It recommended to the New York legislature that one man be put in command of the forts in the Highlands and of the militia of Dutchess and Ulster counties. The New York Committee of Safety, which acted for the Provincial Congress during its recess, appointed George Clinton commander. The thirty-six-year-old Clinton, who had a long and important career during the war, was a trusted supporter of the Whig cause but had had no experience in the militia since the French and Indian War. Nevertheless, he was chosen over more experienced candidates, such as his brother James, possibly due to his support of the first Continental Congress and his membership in the Provincial Congress and the second Continental Congress.[22]

The Continental Congress also turned to New Jersey for more help for New York. The congressmen worked, in particular, through Lord Stirling and William Maxwell. Stirling commanded New Jersey's eastern militia until he became a Continental colonel in November, and Maxwell commanded the province's western militia forces. Stirling's appointment to the Continental Army put him in overall command of all of New Jersey's soldiers, militia and Continental alike. Therefore, in late November, the Continental Congress ordered Stirling to collect the troops in New Jersey and station them as close to New York as possible. A week and a half later, it ordered Stirling to send the men into the Highlands and New York City.[23]

In January 1776, the Continental Congress sent orders for New Jersey and Connecticut militia to enter Queens County in order to disarm the Loyalists and apprehend their leaders. Upon further reflection, the Congress canceled Connecticut's part in the operation. New Yorkers disliked Connecticut interference more than New Jersey intervention, and therefore Lord Stirling received orders to reinforce the New Jersey militia with three companies of his Continental soldiers. Colonel Nathaniel Heard led twelve hundred soldiers onto Long Island and seized about one thousand guns without opposition. On their way home, Heard's soldiers took three suspected Tories from Staten Island, another stronghold of Loyalists. When the New York Congress protested this final action, the three men were released.[24]

Fears for the safety of New York heightened in January when a British fleet prepared to sail from Boston. Washington believed its intended destination was New York, but his warnings went unheeded by the New York Provincial Congress, which feared provoking an attack by the ships already in the harbor. Washington urged the Continental Congress to take further action and to order New Jersey troops back onto Long Island to prevent a landing. At this point, Major General Charles Lee requested permission to go to New York from Boston. A tall, thin, almost emaciated man with a large nose that the soldiers ridiculed, Lee was a man of talent and experience. He wanted a chance to implement his harsh views on how the war should be fought and how the Tories could be suppressed by confiscating their property and perhaps forcing them to flee. He also believed that New York should be either strongly defended or destroyed, and since neither the New York nor the Continental Congress had done enough for New York's defense, he urged Washington to send him to do the job. He was confident he could raise a strong force of Connecticut volunteers to go with him, and he knew Stirling's Continental regiment was available at Elizabethtown, New Jersey.[25]

Few on either side of the war questioned the importance of New York City. Washington in particular had no doubts concerning the need to hold the city, but he feared he might overstep his authority by sending Lee to command in New York. He therefore asked the advice of Continental congressman John Adams, who was visiting the army at that time. Adams, who called New York the "Nexus of the Northern and Southern Colonies," agreed with Lee's plan for defending New York City and eliminating the Tory threat. Washington then sent Lee instructions to collect a volunteer force, proceed to New York City, prepare its defenses, secure the Highlands, and disarm all unfriendly people, apprehending them if necessary. He gave Lee the authority to use the troops in New Jersey as necessary, and he asked Governor Trumbull to help Lee raise Connecticut volunteers. In addition, Washington informed Stirling of Lee's power, and he wrote to the New York Provincial Congress regarding Lee's instructions. In support of Lee's operations, Trumbull and the Council of Safety ordered two militia regiments of 750 men each to assemble, and three hundred other volunteers collected in western Connecticut.[26]

As the colonial patriots prepared to defend New York, British forces were also in motion. The British were not, however, contemplating an occupation of New York at this time. Lieutenant General Henry Clinton sailed from Boston on his way to South Carolina, with orders to stop at the major ports along the route to consult with the royal governors, collect intelligence, and gather supplies. Governor Tryon had written to General Howe that the fleet could get supplies from New York, and therefore Clinton planned to stop in particular at New York City.[27]

The rebels did not know that the British had no plans to occupy New York City, and thus even as the British fleet finished its preparations to leave Boston, Lee traveled through Connecticut in late January, inviting the militia to assemble and march for New York immediately. The New York Provincial Congress and Committee of Safety, however, had not yet received word from Lee or Washington concerning Lee's purpose, and therefore they preferred to maintain the uneasy truce between the inhabitants and the British on their ships. Lee's impending arrival with the Connecticut militia threatened both this truce and New York's sovereignty, and New York's congressmen wanted the Connecticut troops to stay in Connecticut until they had a chance to discuss the situation with Lee. When Lee learned of the wishes of the New York legislators, he immediately informed the Continental Congress that he would continue to New York despite the fears of the New Yorkers, because they did not know the danger that faced them. He would compromise and take only part of the twelve hundred troops he had collected so far. Lee then informed New York's Congress of this decision, assuring its members that his object was to prevent a British lodgement and not to start hostilities. About this same time in late January, the Provincial Congress received Washington's letter explaining Lee's instructions, and it then ordered that Lee and his troops be admitted to New York City. Realizing that the situation in New York was tense and confused, the members of the Continental Congress ordered a committee to New York to try to get all the parties to cooperate for the defense of the city and its environs.[28]

The British fleet with Henry Clinton and almost five hundred British soldiers left Boston at the end of January, and Washington sent urgent warnings to hurry preparations in New York, and to disarm the Tories and seize their leaders. Temporarily immobilized in Connecticut by an attack of gout, Lee sent Colonel David Waterbury and part of the Connecticut force in advance. He believed that the Connecticut militia and Stirling's Continental troops could hold New York until he himself arrived with the rest of the Connecticut force.[29]

The committee of the Continental Congress arrived in New York City on January 30, and Waterbury's advance force began to arrive outside New York City at the beginning of February. The New York Committee of Safety urged Waterbury to remain outside the city until Lee recognized the authority of the Provincial Congress over the Connecticut soldiers, but Waterbury refused to accept any authority above Lee's. The committee from the Continental Congress resolved the standoff by rejecting both parties' viewpoints and instead putting Waterbury under the command of the committee of the Continental Congress. The Committee of Safety and Waterbury both accepted this arrangement.[30]

Then the British fleet carrying General Clinton and his troops arrived in New York harbor on February 4 and Clinton met with Tryon. Nothing further was contemplated at that moment, however, much to the disappointment of Tryon, who continued to urge action by the British army and navy to help the greatly abused Loyalists. Clinton's force remained in the harbor for the moment.[31]

Lee, too, arrived on February 4, and within a week he had about eighteen hundred soldiers in the city. He was glad, however, that the committee of the Congress was there, because he was still unsure of his authority in New York. New York's leaders were unhappy about Lee's arrival, and he was somewhat surprised that the New York legislators and Committee of Safety had accepted his presence. Notwithstanding the sullen reception, Lee began to prepare the defenses of the city, Long Island, and the passes in the Highlands, in case the British still in the harbor made any hostile moves. He asked Governor Trumbull to send the rest of the militia raised for New York, and he asked the Continental Congress to order to New York City a force of Philadelphia Associators, that city's militia. The New York Provincial Congress stirred itself and ordered four battalions of militia to be raised for the defense of New York City.[32]

The city, "Now a City at Waar [sic]," was in a state of panic at the arrival of the British and rebel forces. Lord Stirling arrived with one thousand soldiers the same week as Lee, while the New York militia began to collect on Long Island. Lee put all the soldiers to work preparing entrenchments. Meanwhile, New York's neighbors continued to send help. Governor Trumbull and the Council of Safety ordered to New York the militia that had not accompanied Lee, and the Continental Congress convinced the Pennsylvania government to send a battalion of 720 Philadelphia militiamen, and persuaded the New Jersey legislators to send a battalion of 720 Minute Men. In addition, New York's Congress asked for, and received, an additional seven hundred New Jersey militiamen, led by Colonel Heard, to occupy Staten Island in order to remove the livestock and defend the island against any raids. The county deputies on Staten Island were unhappy about Heard's impending arrival, but the New York congressmen assured the islanders that the New Jersey soldiers had orders only to protect the island and people from a British invasion. Heard crossed to the island with his men and awaited further orders from the New York Provincial Congress, while the island's inhabitants threatened to kill any of his troops who tried to disarm them.[33]

Inside New York City, Lee took a harsh approach to dealing with the Tories. One of his first actions upon his arrival was to announce that one hundred Tories would be executed if the British ships fired on the city. He then proceeded to harass the Tories by publishing a list of suspected Loyalists and ordering them to be disarmed. Without obtaining permission from the Provincial Congress, he sent a militia force onto Long Island to disarm the Tories. He ordered, then canceled, a simliar expedition to Staten Island. He also had Isaac Sears administer an oath to the Tories and identify those who refused to take such an oath. The New York Provincial Congress protested Lee's actions. Its members informed Lee that trying and punishing New York citizens was within the power of the Congress and not of the military. Lee answered characteristically that in an emergency, there was no time for niceties and proper forms, and though he might be criticized for being rash, his motives were good.[34]

The results were also good for the defense. Alexander McDougall had thought the divided loyalties within New York would make it impossible for any substantial work to be done on the defenses. Under Lee's direction, however, the necessary work was being accomplished. McDougall himself deserved some of the credit. He worked hard to lessen tension between Lee and the civilian leaders of New York, and managed to convince Lee to work with the Provincial Congress and soften his demands on that body. Through a combination of brusque directness and diplomatic maneuvering, the military and civilian leaders in New York were taking important steps for the defense of the city.[35]

This feverish activity by the defenders was not matched by an equally aggressive British plan. Since Henry Clinton had no orders to occupy the city, he contented himself with surveying the rebels in town and watching them, on February 11, seize unopposed the royal supplies and cannon left on southern Manhattan. The next day, Clinton and the fleet sailed from New York. Tryon lamented that the rebels were allowed to plunder royal property unmolested but realized the only possible response would have been to use the fleet to destroy the city. After these events, Tryon had even less influence in New York. He dissolved the New York Assembly and called for elections in an attempt to fill the new Assembly with more loyal subjects, but his candidates were decisively defeated. He eventually dismissed this Assembly, too. Tryon then accepted the advisability of moving the remaining British warships from the East River to the Hudson River. New York City was no longer literally under the guns of the British.[36]

As the British forces withdrew, Lee had time to ponder the future defenses of the New York City area, and he was not encouraged. His true feelings about the Minute Men and temporary militia soldiers who had poured into the city finally emerged. They were good for nothing, he complained, and had he known their true quality, he would have prevented them from coming in the first place. He wanted militiamen who would serve longer terms. Despite the fact that the British force had left, he wanted more reinforcements. He urged the New Jersey government to ignore the advice of the Continental Congress to halt its troops and instead send another militia battalion. He also suggested that several thousand Continental soldiers should ultimately take over the defense of New York. Meanwhile, his own forces were shrinking rapidly. As of February 22, he had only the remaining five hundred men of Stirling's Continental regiment and the two Connecticut militia regiments, both of which were to leave in less than three weeks. Though New York's Congress had ordered the raising of four battalions, Lee knew they would not be ready for months.[37]

At the same time, the Continental Congress sent orders for Lee to ride south and take command of the Southern Department in anticipation of Henry Clinton's invasion. Philip Schuyler assumed command of the Middle Department of New York, New Jersey, Pennsylvania, Delaware, and Maryland. Brigadier General William Thompson and Lord Stirling, who was promoted to brigadier general on March 1, were Schuyler's subordinates in the department and would command in southern New York while Schuyler stayed in the north.[38]

As Lee prepared to leave at the end of February, the defense of New York relied heavily on the militia of the area, Lee's scorn notwithstanding. Altogether he had about seventeen hundred organized soldiers, mostly militiamen from Connecticut, a few New York militia, and the remnants of Stirling's Continentals. These soldiers were scattered around the area—erecting defensive works in the city itself, on Long Island, and at Horn's Hook, which commanded the pass at Hell's Gate. The Connecticut militia units were to leave March 12, but upon Lee's urging, the Continental Congress intervened and convinced them to stay until March 25, when reinforcements from New Jersey and Pennsylvania were expected. Overall, Lee was angry with how little had been done for the defense of New York and assumed little more would be done once he left. As a parting shot at the Tories, Lee ordered many to be taken into custody, and even suggested that their children be held as hostages for their good behavior.[39]

The events around New York City from the summer of 1775 through February 1776 demonstrated where the militia fit into the early war effort by the colonists against the British. In the absence of a sufficient garrison of Continentals, militia forces were the primary source of manpower for this port town. Washington clearly understood this important function of the militia in the defense of New York. While supporting the efforts to secure New York against the Tories, he urged the governments of the neighboring colonies to send more men.

On the other hand, the difficulties of a policy that relied on a local militia plagued the commanders in the area. Local leaders such as Wooster and Waterbury had to work with vacillating political leaders. Lee had to deal not only with the hesitant New York government but also with the Continental Congress. His anger at the erratic

Minute Men and short-term militia suggests a problem inherent in a system of defense built on such soldiers.

The potential crises around New York City in 1775 and early 1776 thus showed that when an emergency arose, the colonial leaders and the Continental authorities immediately turned to the militia, just as the colonists had turned to the militia when the first shots rang out in April 1775. The initial policies of Washington and the Continental Congress, and the early efforts by the Whigs of Connecticut, New York, and New Jersey to secure control of the people and the colonial governments, had been successful. The threats to this area, however, and to New York City in particular, had just begun. Throughout the rest of 1776, first the colonists and then the British concentrated their forces around New York City and fought for this vital "nexus." The American defenders faced challenges to their policies, but during the coming struggles, the presence of the militia proved to be a vital support to the American cause.

CHAPTER THREE

The Armies Arrive at New York, March–August 1776

Soon after Charles Lee left for South Carolina, his successors in command at New York were wrestling with problems similar to those he had had to face. These problems grew more complicated between March and August 1776, as the rebel leaders in the middle colonies had to adjust their defensive plans in response to the arrival of both the Continental Army and a powerful British military force. The task of coordinating militia and regular forces to face this new scale of warfare posed a challenge to the principles that Washington, the Continental Congress, and the colonial governments had established during the previous months.

Lee left for the South at the beginning of March, and General Philip Schuyler officially took command of the New York City area. Schuyler, however, remained in Albany, and Lord Stirling became the commander on the spot. Somewhat overwhelmed by his temporary command, Stirling nevertheless tried to maintain the defenses and secure militia reinforcements. Alexander McDougall's presence continued to ease the problems of the local Continental Army commander by stimulating the New Yorkers to greater efforts and easing tension between the civilian government and the military command.[1]

Stirling's job became even more complicated after General Washington sent his troops and artillery onto Dorchester Heights in March 1776 and the British decided to evacuate Boston. Washington expected the British to sail directly to New York City, and accordingly he began to send detachments of the army to that city. If the British arrived in New York before the Continental Army could march across New England, Stirling and the local militia would have to hold. Fortunately for Stirling, the number of militia had continued to increase since Lee's departure. To help strengthen the defenses further, Washington urged Stirling to ask the New Jersey government to send one thousand militia, and Washington himself wrote to Governor Trumbull to request two thousand militia for New York. Washington hoped that these forces, combined with the militia from the New York countryside, could hold the place until the army arrived. For the long-term defense of New York, the Continental Congress ordered that eight thousand Continental soldiers be raised, but this would take a long time. In the meantime, the Continental Congress empowered Stirling, or his successors, to call on the militia of New York, New Jersey, and Connecticut as necessary. To support this resolution and Washington's earlier appeal, the Congress asked Trumbull to prepare Connecticut's militia to respond to requests for men from the commander in New York.[2]

Having settled earlier on the policy of depending on militia to defend everywhere except where the army was concentrated, Washington, Stirling, and the Continental Congress had no choice now but to depend again on the militia. Unfortunately, Stirling had only a few Continentals left in the city and about four thousand militiamen in the area, and many of the militia soldiers from Connecticut wanted to go home and plant their crops. To strengthen his force temporarily, Stirling detained some soldiers who were on their way to Canada. In order to secure reinforcements, he exercised the powers granted by the Continental Congress and followed Washington's advice. He sent requests for more militia from Connecticut, New York, and New Jersey. Altogether, he expected to receive perhaps two thousand extra soldiers.[3]

New York's neighbors responded to the several pleas for help. Trumbull and the Council of Safety decided they could send men immediately, without waiting for the legislature to act, because by law Connecticut militia could respond to an emergency in a neighboring colony—and the threat to New York constituted such an emergency. Trumbull ordered two thousand militiamen to be raised and sent to New York. The New Jersey militia at first did not respond as quickly. Several companies in New Jersey hesitated because a New Jersey law forbade its militia to leave the colony without legislative action. Many militiamen also believed that the Continentals in New Jersey should go instead. Stirling argued that orders of the Continental Congress superseded New Jersey law, and that he and the Congress were also preparing the defenses of New Jersey. His appeal achieved some success, and of the one thousand militia Stirling had requested from New Jersey, about two hundred had arrived by March 20. As these militia troops began to arrive, Stirling put them to work preparing more defenses. New York then provided two hundred Continental soldiers, the first contingent of the New York Continental regiments being raised. Meanwhile, on Long Island, Brigadier General Nathaniel Woodhull of the New York militia received permission to react to any sudden invasion without waiting for orders from the Committee of Safety or the Continental commander in New York.[4]

On March 20, Brigadier General William Thompson arrived and by seniority of rank took command of the defense of New York City and the area around it. Upon his release from command in New York, Lord Stirling returned to New Jersey to help forward its defenses and to call out more militia to build roads and fortifications. Thompson joined the Continental Congress and Washington in urging the New Jersey government to support Stirling and hasten the defensive preparations. They also recommended that the New Jersey militia of Bergen, Essex, and Middlesex counties go onto and fortify Staten Island while the colony's interior militia should be sent to New York. New Jersey's Committee of Safety ordered the raising of three militia battalions, totaling two thousand men, to be sent immediately to New York.[5]

Without the support of the thousands of militia troops that the neighboring colonies ordered out, Stirling and then Thompson would have commanded only a few Continental soldiers around New York City. More help was on the way, however, because after the British fleet and army left Boston harbor on March 27, Washington hurried additional Continental units toward New York. He also ordered Major General Israel Putnam to take command in New York. Soon confidence grew in New York as Continental and militia soldiers arrived from the east and west. In fact, by early April, Putnam commanded about seven thousand soldiers. The streets were filled with barricades, and on every headland and commanding spot of ground around the city stood fortifications either completed or under construction. In addition, the uncertain truce that had reigned in the city for months between the British on their ships and the forces in the city, had finally ended with Putnam's declaration on April 7 that hostilities had commenced. By mid-April, with the city safe for the moment and with much of the Continental Army already in New York and the rest on its way, the Continental Congress requested Putnam to release as many of the Connecticut and New York militia as possible, and all of the New Jersey militia.[6]

The militiamen had served their temporary duty of local defense according to the defensive policy of Washington and the Continental Congress, and now the Continental Army took over the defenses. The American defenders had taken advantage of the availability of the militia at any threatened point, a benefit that General Schuyler understood. Commanding in Albany and trying to maintain the colonial toehold in Canada, he asked the Continental Congress to order more Continental soldiers to Canada rather than to southern New York. He argued that the militia provided an immediate reinforcement for New York City whenever necessary, whereas in Canada this option did not exist. The Congress ordered Washington to send four Continental battalions to Canada.[7]

Meanwhile, as Washington hurried the last of the Continental Army from Boston to New York, a request arrived for a detachment of Continentals for local defense. Governor Nicholas Cooke of Rhode Island feared the British might try to invade his colony, and he therefore asked for the Continental units marching nearby to divert into Rhode Island. Washington, consistent with the principle set forth earlier, refused to halt any Continental units in Rhode Island for local defense. Though Rhode Island was exposed to a naval attack, Washington believed the defense of New York was too critical and in need of all the army. He did allow the last division of troops leaving the Boston area to march through Rhode Island as a precaution, but he remained inflexible concerning the basic policy.[8]

Preparations for the defense of New York and the neighboring colonies of New Jersey and Connecticut advanced as the different parts of the army arrived. Facing the possibility of an invasion by the powerful British navy and army, the defenders realized that New Jersey's coast was important for the defense of southern New York. Since most of the Continental Army was available to defend New York, much of the New Jersey militia originally ordered to New York now could remain in New Jersey. Therefore General Philemon Dickinson, who had replaced Stirling as commander of New Jersey's eastern militia, ordered the militia to begin erecting defensive works at such key spots along the coast as Newark, Elizabethtown, Rahway, Woodbridge, and Amboy. One battalion of New Jersey militia remained on Staten Island because that island's defense was considered critical to the defense of New Jersey. The New Jersey Committee of Safety then resolved that one-fourth of the militia would serve as Minute Men ready to assemble at a moment's notice.[9]

In addition to New Jersey's shoreline, the defense of New York's Highlands remained a topic of concern. The two main forts in the area, Montgomery and Constitution, were too important to be held even partially by militia. The colonial defenders feared that the many Tories known to live in and near the Highlands might attack the forts in conjunction with the expected British invasion of New York. Therefore the fort garrisons, which already consisted primarily of Continental soldiers, received more regular soldiers to replace the remaining Minute Men.[10]

Connecticut, more isolated from the New York–New Jersey coast and therefore from the Continental Army concentrating around New York City, still depended more on the exertions of its own militia. Trumbull and the Council of Safety ordered the militia units near the coast to be ready to move instantly upon an invasion. To ensure a more efficient large-scale mobilization when necessary, the Assembly passed several acts to regulate the use and mustering of the militia, ordered cavalry units to organize, and increased the monetary fine for disobeying a summons to active service in the militia. In addition, all men in Connecticut were urged to arm themselves and, if not already enrolled in the militia, to form themselves into companies. The Assembly also ordered two new regiments to be raised, to serve for a maximum of one year. One of these regiments would defend the principal coastal towns, especially New London and New Haven, while the other would remain ready to march to any threatened area within Connecticut or a neighboring colony. Another act provided for almost one-third of the militia of Connecticut to be detached from regular duty in order to serve as Minute Men holding themselves in constant readiness. These Minute Men would serve three-month tours of duty. At the same time, the Connecticut government and its militia made efforts to discover and apprehend leaders of conspiracies against the Whig leadership in the colony. Militia officers usually did such work and afterward reported their efforts to the General Assembly.[11]

The advantages that the Whigs in Connecticut had due to the calm transition of power continued to show. The executive and legislative branches worked well together, preparing specific detachments for service and improving their command and control over the militia. The Whig leaders in New York and New Jersey, relying on their ad hoc committees and provincial legislatures, moved more slowly, especially in the area of improved militia regulations.

While the colonial governments took advantage of the spring months to organize and prepare for the expected arrival of the British armament, Washington used the time to establish himself in New York and improve relations with the local governments. After complying with a request from the Continental Congress in May to dismiss most of the militia currently serving in New York, he contacted the colonial governments and formulated plans for how the militia would be recalled. He especially wanted to know how long it would take the New York Congress to collect up to twenty-five hundred militia in a crisis, and he suggested it make the necessary arrangements in advance. He recommended to the governments of New York and New Jersey that they coordinate their plans for responding to an emergency. For his part, he promised to establish lookouts to give as much warning as possible of the approach of the British fleet. The New York congressmen agreed to do everything they could to prepare their militia forces for a speedy response to an invasion. They established a committee with powers to order out the militia and appointed places of rendezvous for the troops. In addition, they resolved to raise two more militia battalions to serve the colony for three months.[12]

Washington also urged the New Jersey and Connecticut governments to prepare their militia to come to New York's aid. For New

Jersey he suggested new regulations to improve the efficiency of its militia forces, and he asked both colonies' governments to allot a certain number of militia to march on the first notice of the enemy's approach. As he explained to Governor Trumbull, if such preparations were initiated only after the enemy arrived, and requests for militia reinforcements had to go through all the necessary forms and channels, the needed relief would come too late.[13]

At the same time, Washington hoped to cooperate with the local legislatures, but he was not averse to forcing his will upon them when necessary. Soon after his arrival in New York, an issue of contention arose between him and the New York government concerning the continued communication between the city and the British ships in the harbor. He could excuse such behavior earlier due to the weakness of the city's defenses, but with the army on hand and with hostilities having officially commenced, such an excuse was no longer valid and the illicit correspondence had to stop. The next day, April 18, the Committee of Safety ordered all communication to cease, and Washington quickly issued a proclamation in support of this action.[14]

Understanding the need to maintain control of the people as well as to defend territory, Washington supported the suppression of the Loyalists. He promised to do all he could "to root out or secure such abominable pests of Society," and to send forces onto Long Island to frustrate an expected rising by the Tories. In late May, as he prepared to go to Philadelphia to confer with the Continental Congress, he instructed his temporary replacement, General Putnam, to give all military support possible to New York's efforts to seize leading Tories in the city and its environs, especially on Long Island. The population of that island remained suspect in the eyes of the colonial defenders due to past events, despite the fact that few islanders had actually spoken in favor of the British government. That the inhabitants had not openly renounced their former allegiance was enough.[15]

As the feared British attack on New York had failed to materialize, the defenders had enjoyed the luxury of a relatively calm spring to fit the Continental Army into the defensive arrangements. This calm ended when the British fleet arrived at Sandy Hook on June 29, and the British army began to occupy Staten Island in early July. General

William Howe conferred with Governor Tryon, and they quickly saw the results of the rebel efforts around New York. The rebel army, according to Howe's observations, was strongly placed on Long Island and in New York City. Howe agreed with Tryon that many Loyalist Americans in Connecticut, New York, and New Jersey only awaited an opportunity to join with the British army. The British leaders on the spot did not fully appreciate the efforts by the Whig politicians and militia to isolate and eliminate the Tories.[16]

As British forces amassed around Staten Island throughout the summer months, colonial preparations took on more urgency. Even as the colonial leaders declared their independence and the colonies became states within the United States of America, the state governments of Connecticut, New York, and New Jersey continued their efforts to improve their militia forces and to cooperate with Washington and the American army around New York City. Faced by the now very real threat to New York City, the defenders tried to remain consistent to their policies and guidelines for the use of the militia even as the conditions for their use in New York changed dramatically.

As the colonial governments made the transition to state governments, the different stages of organization in the governments of New Jersey, New York, and Connecticut remained noticeable. Connecticut's government was still the most organized and under the firmest Whig control. Its militia muster laws, which empowered the colonels of the militia regiments to call out their men upon invasion by land or sea, were adequate to cover sudden emergencies, though they could not provide for the massive need that the large British buildup in New York would demand. Governor Trumbull, however, could supplement these laws with orders for the colonels to muster their men upon his or Washington's request. Trumbull and the Connecticut government decided that for the moment, new militia regulations were unnecessary.[17]

New Jersey and New York began the summer with their provisional governments and committees. New Jersey, however, changed that in the summer of 1776. After the royal governor, William Franklin, was sent to prison in Connecticut, New Jersey's Whig leaders adopted a constitution on July 2, 1776, that ended all allegiance to the British Crown. On July 18 the provincial government changed its name to the Convention of the State of New Jersey. The constitution provided for a General Assembly, a governor, and a council. The governor would be "Captain-General and Commander in Chief of all the Militia, and other military force" of New Jersey. The people of New Jersey would elect their first governor in the fall. For the summer, the Convention continued to run the state. The Whigs of New York moved even more slowly. No firm political coalition formed during the summer of 1776, and increased dangers from British attack and Loyalist uprisings prevented the emergence of a new government throughout the year. Though the New York Convention tried to form such a government, the New York Whigs did not adopt a new constitution until 1777.[18]

Even as the Whigs organized new state governments, they had to maintain their control of the people and the political machinery. The arrival and buildup of the British army and fleet off Staten Island through the summer of 1776, however, encouraged the Tories and therefore increased the internal threat to Whig dominance. The governments of all three middle states continued to work strenuously to isolate and eliminate the Loyalist danger within their borders.

In June, the New York Convention authorized Washington to secure dangerous persons in New York. To help deal with the Tories, the Convention created a secret committee that functioned until the end of the war. When the committee received word of dangerous activities or people, the members would call on militia or even Continental detachments to help. Whig fears possibly magnified the number of Tories in New York, but the rebels saw a grave danger to Whig control in the British sympathizers, who could cause insurrections and influence people to turn against the new state government. This assumed Tory influence scared many inhabitants and led some people to go over to the British army. Therefore, the Convention declared that anyone who was loyal to the British was guilty of treason, and it charged the county committees to apprehend all suspected persons. Militia officers performed such duty. The committees and officers also tried to stop the Tories from sending any help to the enemy. George Clinton fully supported these anti-Tory activities. One of his driving principles was to eliminate pro-British sentiment in New York, and as a brigadier general of the militia, he issued orders for Tories to be tried, jailed, or even exiled.[19]

Matters became more serious in August, after the British forces had assumed alarming proportions. The Convention ordered the local committee of Kings County, Long Island, to investigate a report that the inhabitants of that county did not plan to oppose the enemy. The Convention resolved that if this report were true, the Kings County committee "be empowered to Disarm and Secure the Disaffected Inhabitants, to remove or Destroy the Stock of Grain, and if they shall Judge it necessary, to lay the whole Country Waste. . . ." After a detachment of the Continental Army took post on Long Island, the committee received authority to apply to the Continental commander, Major General Nathanael Greene, or any other Continental officer on the island for aid in executing these orders. As the number of openly defiant Tories was usually inflated, the committees rarely took such extreme measures.[20]

New Jersey faced a similar threat from the British presence, and consequently from the Loyalists. The Provincial Convention ordered the committees of New Jersey to disarm all who did not subscribe to the Whig cause or who refused to obey the laws of New Jersey, and instructed its militia officers to seize suspected Tories and post guards to prevent anyone from going to the enemy. Monmouth County was a particularly troublesome region, and the Convention more than once had to order militia from Burlington County into Monmouth County to help the local militia apprehend Tory insurgents. In July, Convention members ordered four hundred militia soldiers into the county to disperse a suspected Loyalist stronghold, but the roughly one hundred Tories dispersed quickly. The Convention, however, excused Monmouth militiamen from duty outside the county except to fill the quota of militia that the Continental Congress requested that summer. Somerset County also had to send militia detachments into Hunterdon County to help Hunterdon's militia control the Loyalists.[21]

The dangers that the Whigs of New York and New Jersey faced elicited the aid from the national authorities as well. The Continental Congress sent requests to the state governments to "suppress Insurrections, and to promote good Order and Obedience to Laws in the United Colonies . . . ," and resolved that anyone who worked or fought against the states would be guilty of treason. As New Jersey struggled to maintain order in Monmouth County with its own militia, the Congress ordered the Pennsylvania legislature to send a part of its militia destined for the army to Monmouth County instead, to help the local inhabitants.[22]

Washington had a strong interest in the suppression of the Loyalists and the isolation of the British army and fleet from those British sympathizers, and he even used Continentals to support some of these activities. In particular, he supported the efforts to remove suspected Tories from Long Island. He also wanted all suspected people removed from New York City, and when New York's government hesitated, he acted on his own. His efforts to clear the city of dangerous people earned him the thanks of the New York Convention delegates, who appreciated his initiative at a time when the continuing political divisions of New York prevented action. In addition, Washington asked the governments of New York and New Jersey to take stronger measures to control their own Tories, and he supported their efforts as often as possible, allowing some New Jersey militiamen from counties that had a severe Loyalist problem to return home. Washington especially urged Livingston and New Jersey's legislature, as well as General Clinton and the New York county committees, to prevent all communication between the Tories and the British. This would prevent the enemy from getting needed supplies and information.[23]

Connecticut's relative isolation from the British buildup outside New York City spared it from the worst fears of Tory dangers during the summer of 1776. Loyalists, however, still posed a potential threat. Governor Trumbull confided to Washington that though his firm belief in the cause steeled him against any British actions, still the internal threat worried him. In an effort to restrict the movements of people possibly hostile to the United States, the Connecticut Assembly directed that a person had to have a certified pass to travel within the state. Civil authorities, as well as militia generals and officers, would inspect these passes, and the larger towns received encouragement to establish watches to apprehend those who traveled at night. In this way, the Connecticut government attempted to limit the ability of the Tories to concert any actions against its state.[24]

Connecticut's distance from the British concentration also meant its coasts were somewhat safer from immediate danger. Its political leaders, however, still acted decisively in support of New York, as they had in 1775, ordering one-fourth of Connecticut's militia to muster and hold itself ready to march. In July, the governor and the Council of Safety ordered three regiments of the Connecticut horse militia to New York, to serve until the militia of the surrounding states could collect. In August, with the harvest over, the governor and the council ordered fourteen regiments to be raised to join Washington in New York, despite the concern of those along the Connecticut coast that the shore defenses had been stripped. The Assembly appointed Brigadier General Oliver Wolcott to command this detachment, while Brigadier General James Wadsworth commanded the Connecticut militia already in New York. Governor Trumbull also called for individual volunteers to enlist and go to New York, and he asked the town leaders to incorporate all householders not already in the militia and send them to New York.[25]

New York had to defend not only its coast and islands but also the shores of the Hudson River, and especially the Highlands. Unfortunately for New York, its government's efforts to mobilize the militia and get the men back into the field did not go as smoothly as the mobilization in Connecticut. Whig leaders of New York City promised three thousand of their city militia to support the army, and the New York Convention promised Washington it would provide all the help it could. Promises notwithstanding, the militia forces of New York assembled slowly. The Convention also tried to raise militia reinforcements for the Highlands while it called on the northern counties to send men to the aid of the army in New York City. In addition, the legislators ordered all the militia of Orange, Dutchess, and Ulster counties to be ready to turn out on a moment's notice. The Convention warned Washington, however, that despite these efforts to mobilize the state's forces, the numbers would not be great due to several factors: the number of Loyalists in New York, the exposed state of Long Island, the British forces already on Staten Island, a lack of arms, and the need to reinforce the Northern army.[26]

Complicating matters for the New York leaders were British efforts to disrupt and threaten rebel movements. Within days of their arrival in early July, the British ships *Phoenix* and *Rose* sailed up the Hudson as far as Tappan Bay, near Tarrytown and Haverstraw, about forty miles above New York City. The local militia regiment in Orange County guarded along the shore and turned back one landing attempt on July 12. Orange County's committee wrote to the nearest Continental officer for help, and the New York Convention ordered militia reinforcements into the area from the neighboring counties. George Clinton, who commanded the militia near the Highlands, ordered men from his posts to help the Orange County militia, and he believed a stronger force could be collected within a few hours from the neighboring towns if necessary. In fact, Clinton confidently ordered the local militia officers to prevent any landings unless they could let a small party land and then destroy it. He urged the officers to occupy the passes in the rough hills along the river, and he warned them to remove all livestock from the area. In response to his orders, sentries took positions along the shores, and when British soldiers landed, militiamen concentrated quickly to limit their depredations. The superior mobility of the British along the river, however, usually meant that any landing party could escape before a formidable militia force could concentrate. Still, by July 18, about six hundred militiamen had collected at Peekskill, and some two hundred guarded the western shore.[27]

In order to relieve pressure along the Hudson shores, the American defenders launched two fire ships on August 16, in an effort to destroy the pair of British ships. Despite the dangers of being burned or blown to bits, several Connecticut militiamen on one of the burning craft stayed aboard long enough to toss grappling hooks onto a British ship. They escaped with only one missing, but the experiment failed and the British ships were not destroyed. The British naval commander, however, was so alarmed that he ordered the *Phoenix* and *Rose* downriver, running past the guns of the American forts and rejoining the British fleet on August 18. After the ships fled, George Clinton ordered the excess militia along the river to join him at Kingsbridge, where he took command in mid-August. Clinton reported that the forces along the river at that time were dwindling, with a few Continentals remaining along the western shore, three hundred militia on the eastern shore, and only two hundred militia near Peekskill.[28]

Some New York leaders were not encouraged by the prospect of relying on the militia for so much of the defensive force. Robert Livingston, a member of the New York Convention, pleaded with Washington to send regular troops rather than depend on the militia to defend at Kingsbridge, where the main line of communication crossed a bridge and connected the mainland with Manhattan Island. Alexander McDougall urged the recruitment of longer-term militia or regular soldiers: "Regiments engaged without time, are more to be depended on for the defence of the Country, than those embodied for a short period."[29] Though Washington sympathized with such sentiments, there was little he could do.

Unlike Connecticut's government, New York's had no executive, and therefore New York's legislature relied more on its militia officers to run its militia on a daily basis. George Clinton, in particular, emerged as one of New York's leading militia generals. He had just spent three months in the Continental Congress, where he had voted for the Declaration of Independence and had met Washington. While in Philadelphia together, Washington and Clinton had conferred about New York as the next arena of the war, and in the process had begun their lifelong friendship. After returning to New York, Clinton took command of a militia brigade that was partially responsible for the defense of Forts Constitution and Montgomery in the Highlands. He had the authority to order the local militia to assemble or go home, and even New England militia units stationed in the Highlands turned to him when they wanted to leave in July. He and a Council of War decided to dismiss all but three hundred of the New Englanders, as he believed three hundred enough to defend the eastern shore of the Hudson River. When those British ships and land forces threatened the river valley in mid-July, Clinton took charge by ordering out further militia detachments and removing supplies from harm's way. Local militia officers wrote to him for reinforcements, and he kept in communication with Washington in New York City, especially concerning the strength of the Highland defenses.[30]

At the same time, Clinton watched out for the good of his soldiers and the local inhabitants. To protect the inhabitants of the area, he ordered his militia officers to put in jail any man who abused the local people. During the harvest season, he persuaded the Committee of Safety to grant a few days' leave to some militiamen so they could return to their farms to tend their crops, and he dismissed some of his own troops due to "the Busy Season of the year & the Great Injury the Country must sustain by detaining Industrious Farm-

ers from Home any longer than absolute Necessity requires . . . ."
Typical of the requests to allow militiamen to remain at home was
that of Hezekiah Howell. Both his son and grandson were in the
Orange County Troop of Light Horse. After Clinton called the troop
into the field in August, Howell asked Clinton to allow his son or
grandson to return to his farm. He worried that without help, he
could not sow his winter grain or collect his hay. The local Committee of Safety got involved and asked Clinton to release the young
men. Fortunately for the farmers of the area, Clinton and the committeemen often allowed such absences. Bad weather that summer,
however, just as often delayed the haying and, therefore, the return
of some of these men.[31]

In early August, Washington suggested to the New York Convention that Clinton take command of all militiamen mustered for the
defense of the Highlands along the Hudson River. The Convention
members agreed, and appointed him to command all militia raised
in Ulster, Orange, Dutchess, and Westchester counties. In addition,
the Convention authorized him to call on those counties to hurry
their men to Kingsbridge and to call out their troops of horse to
position as he believed best. This authority over the counties extended until the end of December 1776. Clinton immediately began
to order out the necessary militia for the defense of the Highlands
and Kingsbridge, and he personally took command of the
Kingsbridge area in August. The Convention left it to Clinton to
keep Washington informed of the situation at Kingsbridge.[32]

The New York Convention ordered Clinton to take command
at Kingsbridge because the members were concerned about this
critical communication link between Manhattan and the mainland.
The Convention therefore increased Clinton's authority and empowered him to call on whatever militia forces were necessary to defend
that vital spot. Ultimately, the delegates in the Convention hoped
to create an "army" of New York and Connecticut militia amounting
to six thousand men to guard the Kingsbridge crossing. By mid-
August, however, Clinton had only about seven hundred men under
his command.[33]

The British army and fleet at Staten Island also directly threatened Long Island, its inhabitants, and its large number of cattle,
sheep, and other livestock. The New York Convention resisted removing

these animals because that would ruin the inhabitants and, in addition, because it believed the local militia could protect the people and their livestock. An estimated eight hundred militia had already collected on the island, and the Convention members believed that such a force should be enough to stop small raids. The Convention had Washington's assurance that he would send help should a large British force invade. Later in August, when Major General Greene's Continental force took post at the west end of the island, the Convention sent orders to the militia of Kings and Queens counties to join his force, and in response to the British landing in force on the western end of the island in late August, the Convention ordered Brigadier General Nathaniel Woodhull to post his militia as near the enemy as possible, to prevent further excursions eastward. If the British advanced toward him, Woodhull was to destroy all supplies and animals, to keep them from the British.[34]

Meanwhile, throughout this tense summer, New York's militia did not passively sit and wait for the hammer blow. Militiamen tried to isolate the enemy from the countryside and stop Loyalists from sending supplies and intelligence to the British or from joining the enemy. Clinton posted guards along the river to capture Tories and remove the boats to prevent further communication. In addition, Clinton used militia parties to bring in New Yorkers who refused to muster.[35]

British soldiers on Staten Island threatened not only parts of New York but also the coast of New Jersey that lay adjacent to the island. The Convention of the State of New Jersey tried to meet this British concentration by expanding its mobilization. The Convention members ordered out thirty-three hundred militia upon a request by the Continental Congress, and they promised Washington they would do everything possible to complete the brigade of New Jersey militia already on its way to New York. In August, the Convention called out half of all its militia, without exception, to serve for one month, and then to be replaced by the other half.[36]

Command of these militia forces remained in the hands of the officers in the field. Brigadier General William Livingston, who in June took command of the militia of the eastern half of the state, became prominent in the urgent preparations to defend against the British army assembling on Staten Island. In general, Livingston decided when militia units had to be called out or dismissed, and if units had to be repositioned. He wrote to Washington and other Continental generals for permission to reposition militiamen who had been attached to the army, and New Jersey militia officers in New York turned to him to intercede for them with Washington. Washington worked through Livingston to position units, as did Brigadier General Hugh Mercer of the Continental Army, who was in New Jersey to help prepare its defenses. Finally, Livingston used New Jersey militiamen to round up other militia soldiers who refused to serve when called. Detachments intercepted both New Jersey and Pennsylvania deserters and resisters.[37]

Livingston's attention focused in particular on defending the coast adjoining Staten Island. He called in militia forces from the counties nearest the coast and combined them with several militia units that Washington had released from the army to garrison the coast. Several hundred militiamen erected breastworks on Elizabethtown Point while more than four hundred men took positions in Amboy. Livingston placed one battalion in Newark, another at Hackensack Ferry in Bergen County, and several companies at Woodbridge. Harvest season hampered efforts to get men out, but many still assembled with spirit. In their effort to prevent any landings or small raids along the coast, these militiamen skirmished frequently with British soldiers on the opposite shore. On July 21 a British force tried to land on Bergen Point, but the musket fire of the coastal guards killed three and turned them back without loss to the defenders. By August 22, fifteen hundred militia were in and around Elizabethtown, where Livingston had his headquarters, and a large force of New Jersey militia was with Mercer at Amboy and Woodbridge. Although Livingston feared that a strong attack from Staten Island could overpower his defenders, their presence at least provided some semblance of defense.[38]

The Continental Congress took a direct and active role in helping these states face the British armament. Maintaining its confidence in the militia soldiers' ability to act as a reserve for the Continental Army or even to fight as a front-line force, the Continental Congress on June 3, 1776, voted to assemble in New Jersey what it called a "Flying Army" of ten thousand militiamen from Pennsylvania, Maryland, and Delaware. In addition, the Congress ordered 13,800 militia to reinforce the Continental Army in New York. This second requisition included fifty-five hundred men from Connecticut, three thousand from New York, and thirty-three hundred from New Jersey. John Hancock, president of the Congress, explained that the crisis demanded more men faster than could possibly be raised and trained for the regular army, and therefore the Congress had resolved to call out the militia. The congressmen believed that the "Militia of the United Colonies are a Body of Troops that may be depended upon. To their Virtue, their delegates in Congress now make a solemn Appeal." They specifically referred to the growing collection of militiamen in New Jersey as "Our army of Militia." John Adams explained that the congressmen did not necessarily believe that militiamen were equal to regulars in combat, and he even admitted that relying on the militia could lose America an occasional battle, but such a dependence would leave the United States in "less danger of Corruption and Violence from a standing Army, and our Militia will acquire Courage, Experience, Discipline and Hardiness in actual service." As President Hancock concluded, however, calling the militia was "the only effectual step that can possibly be taken at this juncture . . . ."[39] Perhaps high, lofty ideals were not as important at this point as simple expediency.

The state governments responded to the calls for militia, as well as to new pleas from Washington. As related, New York's legislature tried to call out its men to join Washington and guard its coasts and islands, while the governments of New Jersey and Connecticut passed resolutions to fill their new militia quotas. When Washington requested permission to call two thousand men of the Flying Army to New York City, the Continental Congress agreed, and asked for New Jersey militia to replace them. New Jersey's government complied with the new request. The Congress then asked the Pennsylvania government to increase its quota to fill the militia army.[40]

The Congress also understood the nature of warfare well enough to realize that it could not make all necessary plans in advance. The best way to handle the changing needs of the coming campaign was for the states to empower Washington to call on their militia when necessary. Hancock sent letters asking the governments of Connecticut, New York, and New Jersey, in particular, to authorize Washington to call on their militia in an emergency. In this way, he explained, the civil powers would be supporting the military power, and the whole strength of the governments could be drawn to the crisis point. Washington thanked the Congress for the support and expressed confidence that if the governments gave him such powers, many advantages would accrue. The governments of Connecticut, New York, and New Jersey all complied quickly with the Congress's request. In addition, the members of Congress empowered Washington to employ the troops in the Northern army, the Flying Army in New Jersey, and the Continental Army in New York City however he believed best. When the Congress directed Brigadier General Hugh Mercer, Washington's selection for commander of the Flying Army, to send militia to the coast of New Jersey, President Hancock carefully added that Mercer should follow the Congress's instructions only if they did not interfere with Washington's orders.[41]

Unhappy as usual with the forced reliance on militia forces to fill the armies, Washington still recognized the need for them. The calls for help had begun to arrive from all quarters as soon as General William Howe and the first corps of the British army arrived on Staten Island. The Highlands needed men, the Continental force on Long Island had to be strengthened, and pleas for assistance from New Jersey's coast, Long Island, and the shores along the Hudson River all had to be answered. Washington was pleased to hear that the states were exerting themselves to muster and send their militia.[42]

Requesting militia reinforcements, and actually getting them into the field were two different matters, however. Washington requested to the state governments to send their militia as quickly as possible. Worried that they would arrive too late, he urged Connecticut and New Jersey in particular to hasten their men in small detachments, if necessary. By the end of June, with only twelve hundred militia on hand, he lamented to President Hancock, "I have wrote; I have done every thing in my power to call them in, but they have not come, tho' I am told that they are generally willing."[43]

July and August were the harvest months, and this further slowed the assembling of the militia. In late July there were only three thousand militia in the Flying Army instead of the ten thousand called by the Continental Congress, and as of the first week in August, only half of the militia called to New York from New Jersey, New York, and Connecticut had assembled. Washington hoped that after the harvest ended, the men would muster and he would have an army of about fifteen thousand soldiers, but "as Harvest and a thousand other excuses are urged for the Reasons of delay," the militia's arrival was uncertain at best. In fact, in Hunterdon County, New Jersey, militia-men brought clubs and beat their colonel and captain for trying to take them from their fields. Throughout the summer and coming fall, many desertions from the militia ranks were due to the need to take care of the crops. By mid-August, however, the situation began to improve as the states assembled their forces, and Washington even grew confident that the army could defeat the British.[44]

Despite these shortages and delays, Washington did not often exert his full powers but instead tried to work through the state govern-ments and their appointed generals, as he had before the arrival of the British forces. The command arrangements erected earlier re-mained in place. For Connecticut, this meant working through Gov-ernor Trumbull for an increase in militia or to arrange for several militia regiments to be available at his call. When New York's legisla-ture presented its idea to create a six-thousand-man force at Kings-bridge, Washington asked Trumbull if Connecticut could help.[45]

The proper channels of command and communication in New Jersey and New York were still confused, and Washington worked through the state legislatures, the different committees, and the vari-ous militia generals. In June, since New Jersey did not yet have a governor in place, its legislature had authorized Washington to call on the New Jersey militia generals if he needed men, and he communicated in particular with General Livingston concerning the assembling, dismissing, and positioning of the militia. Washington occasionally used General Hugh Mercer to coordinate with Living-ston, while Livingston kept Washington informed of the numbers and positions of the militia units. Washington's only dealings with the New Jersey legislature were general in nature, as when he urged a larger call for militia reinforcements or suggested improved militia regulations.[46]

As the New York Whigs had not set up a new government yet, Washington still had the perplexing job of working through the New York Convention, its committees, and George Clinton. For example, Washington cooperated with the legislature and the committee it sent to him for the removal of livestock from the islands, and with another committee created to handle the Hudson River defenses. The legislators in return promised to work with Washington and ask his advice on matters concerning the militia. In particular, however, Washington worked directly through Clinton, especially for the river defenses. He left Clinton in charge of moving, mustering, and dismissing the militia along the river, and Clinton kept Washington informed of his situation. Ultimately, in August, Washington and the Convention agreed on the appointment of Clinton as commander of all New York militia called out on both sides of the river.[47]

Despite Washington's strenuous efforts not to bypass civilian authority, the pressing exigencies of the growing crisis around New York City forced him occasionally to make use of the powers granted him by the Continental Congress and the state governments. He had the authority, if necessary, to call directly on the militia of the neighboring states, and he used this power sparingly to requisition both New Jersey and Connecticut militia units during the summer buildup. Often directly through the subordinate militia officers, though occasionally through one of the state-appointed militia generals such as Livingston in New Jersey, Washington called the state troops to his army. In an effort to cooperate with this use of discretionary power, Governor Trumbull informed Washington in early July that seven militia regiments in western Connecticut had orders to obey any direct requests from Washington. Washington called on them in August.[48]

In the presence of the growing British military juggernaut, Washington faced a different operational situation than he had outside Boston. At New York, the British were amassing an overwhelming force that could strike out to capture the islands and defeat Washington's army. The siege of Boston, however, had given Washington the chance to formulate the basic roles for the militia, and despite the altered circumstances, he maintained his policy of employing the militia in a variety of functions. Thus, faced with the disagreeable task of relying on the militia, Washington exhibited the true mark of leadership by accepting reality and using the available resources.

He linked militia with Continental units for the defense of key places such as the Highlands, the New Jersey coast across from Staten

Island, and Long Island. In addition, he understood that militia-men could fight British regulars best from behind defensive works, and therefore urged their officers to have the men practice firing from behind parapets. His plan was to have the better-trained and better-disciplined soldiers contest the approach of the enemy in the field. As would occur at the battle of Long Island and often there-after, this careful division of battlefield duty did not survive the real-ity of combat.[49]

Washington's preference was to employ the militia separately from the regular army, particularly for local defense. Having denied re-quests for detachments of Continental soldiers to guard coasts and ports throughout the first one and a half years, Washington now felt obliged to return militia units from the army to New Jersey to allow them to defend the coast against the growing British force on Staten Island. In Washington's opinion, the local "Militia, Independent of other Troops, being more than competent to all purposes of defen-sive War," could adequately guard the coasts and thus allow him to continue concentrating the army. This viewpoint held true even for Mercer's Flying Army in New Jersey. Washington planned to keep Mercer's army concentrated as well, and to rely on local, temporary militia units to respond to threats along the shore. Though he still received requests for Continentals, and occasionally acquiesced, as when he allowed a Continental regiment to help guard the eastern end of Long Island, he usually expected the militiamen not already in the field to turn out for defense. When militiamen did their job, such as preventing the landing attempt from the British ships up the Hudson in July, he praised their "Vigilance and Activity." Wash-ington's confidence in the local troops seemed well placed, as the number of militia in the field, independent of the Continental and Flying Armies, increased during August. Clinton had fourteen hun-dred along the Hudson, and Livingston had one thousand at Elizabethtown.[50]

Washington, however, was still disappointed with the number of militia who joined the two American armies in New York and New Jersey, but "as harvest will soon be over and that Plea, at an end," he hoped that the number would increase soon. Once the militia was assembled, he planned to start a campaign of harassment and raids. He had had little opportunity around Boston to employ the militia forces in this aggressive manner, but at New York the possibilities were more open. Washington also liked the idea of a militia force around Kingsbridge. Then, if the enemy invaded north of the American positions on Manhattan and Long Islands, there would be "an Army to hang on their Rear, [which] would distress them exceedingly." In late August, just prior to the battle of Long Island, the British sent men across to Long Island, and Washington asked Governor Trumbull to send one thousand militia onto eastern Long Island to harass the enemy's rear and flanks, and annoy their parties collecting cattle. Constant skirmishing between the British soldiers and the Continentals and militia occurred along the enemy's lines on the island.[51]

Washington's aggressive nature, in fact, did not allow him to plan a purely passive defense. When the British landed on Staten Island and the New Jersey militia began to assemble, Mercer urged an attack on their quarters. Washington agreed, and at a Council of War in mid-July, he proposed using "a Partisan party, with a view to alarm the Enemy and encourage our own troops," who, Washington believed, wanted something positive to be done against the British. Soon after, he and Mercer agreed on the need to raid and surprise the British camps wherever possible. Mercer assembled about thirteen hundred men and prepared to cross to Staten Island on the night of July 18, but high winds and bad weather forced a cancellation of the enterprise. By late July, Mercer estimated the enemy force at ten thousand, far too many to attack with a small militia force. Washington, however, had Mercer continue to examine the possibilities, though no attack occurred before the British crossed to Long Island in late August and precipitated the first large-scale battle of the war.[52]

Washington, thus, had specific views on how to work with the states and their militia. He had formulated these plans through the first year, and did not change his basic ideas throughout the spring or summer, even as both the American and the British forces concentrated around New York City. The British arrival gave him the opportunity to expand his thoughts on how to employ the militia. Washington's own appreciation of the importance of the militia to his plans is evident in his impatience at the British delays before opening the action. He was worried that William Howe was procrastinating so the militia would grow tired and leave. Washington knew that if the militia did leave, he would be in serious trouble. In late August, he watched his army grow to about twenty-three thousand men, over half of them militiamen, as militia poured into New York City and its environs. Washington needed every soldier to fight the British.[53]

Finally the calls of Washington and the Congress had succeeded. As the struggle for New York City was about to open in late August, Washington had reason to be thankful for the presence of the militia. Though this gratitude at first was based primarily on the realization that he needed the militia simply to be able to stay in the field and fight, the active campaigns ahead would enable Washington to demonstrate a flair for making a virtue out of necessity. He would come to view the militia not only as a necessary evil but also as a reliable fighting force in its own element.

★ CHAPTER FOUR ★

New York Lost and New Jersey Saved, August 1776–January 1777

THE ACTIVE campaign for the main armies opened August 27, 1776, when General Howe's army attacked Washington's lines on Long Island. For the next five months, the contending armies maneuvered and fought through New York and much of New Jersey, culminating in the American attacks on Trenton and Princeton in December and January. During those months, the political and military leaders of the United States turned to the militia to fulfill the functions and duties established in the months of preparation. The ensuing crises of the loss of New York City, the British invasion of New Jersey, and Washington's winter counterattacks forced the rebel leaders to modify their policies for the use of the state militia. Throughout this difficult campaign, however, the militia played a significant role in maintaining the American army in the field and ultimately in help-ing it to recover much of the ground lost early in the campaign.

The American concentration of forces reached a peak in the last days of August. At this time, Washington's plans for this growing army revolved around a strategy known as a war of posts. By using fortified positions to guard key locations, Washington hoped to weaken the enemy army as it took each successive post. The first link in his chain of defended sites was the western end of Long Island, where he placed about thirty-five hundred men under the command of Major General Nathanael Greene. As of mid-August, about half of Greene's command consisted of the militia of Brigadier General Nathaniel Heard's brigade of New Jersey militia, parts of two Long Island militia regiments, and some Connecticut levies. Washington and Greene had mixed emotions about this combined force of regulars and militia. They were both disappointed that the Continental Congress had not provided for an army of regular troops, yet they were confident that this mixed force could defeat the British if the Americans fought from behind breastworks.[1]

On August 22, with their own army finally concentrated, the British began crossing from Staten Island to Long Island, where the first troops landed unopposed. By August 26, they had about twenty thousand troops available to fight on Long Island. Washington still feared a British descent on Manhattan itself, so he reinforced Long Island with only eighteen hundred men, including Colonel Gold S. Silliman's Connecticut militia regiment. On August 24, Washington sent four more regiments to the island, raising the total there to about seven thousand defenders. Unfortunately for the Americans, the command situation on the island became confused during these final days. Greene became ill and Major General John Sullivan took command on August 20. Sullivan, a thirty-six-year-old New Hampshire general, was a short, tough-looking man who had a reputation for bravery almost to the point of recklessness. Possibly because of this foolhardy reputation, Washington replaced Sullivan with Major General Israel Putnam on August 23.[2]

While both sides funneled troops onto Long Island, the skirmishing began between the advance units of the two armies. Washington's plan to keep the militia separated from the army, even when operating within the vicinity of the main British army, began to take form on Long Island as the officers on the spot employed militia units as partisan forces to engage the enemy and harass British movements. Later a hallmark of Washington's militia strategy, this policy received its first large-scale test on Long Island. As the British advanced toward Flatbush, which lay near a wooded area, the Americans "made their first appearance," according to Sir James Murray, a Scottish officer in the British army. Colonel Silliman's Connecticut militia had taken post at Flatbush about half a mile in front of the American positions along the Heights of Guana. The militia soldiers and British advance troops began exchanging shots, and throughout a three-day halt by the British after they secured Flatbush, the Americans "kept up a constant kind of dirty firing," according to Murray. The British had about thirty casualties during this running skirmish. One advantage that Murray saw the Americans use was the terrain around Flatbush, which "was entirely after their own heart covered with woods and hedges . . . ."[3]

Meanwhile, to the east of the British army stood Brigadier General Nathaniel Woodhull with almost one hundred Long Island militia. Following orders from the New York Convention, he set up a chain of guards across the island within six miles of the British camp, and within two miles of the British mounted troops. Woodhull tried to prevent Tories from communicating with the British while he ordered his own mounted force to herd all of the local cattle to the eastern end of the island.[4]

Adhering to his principles, Washington urged Putnam to place the rest of the militia and least experienced troops within the trenches around Brooklyn, and to depend on the better soldiers to defend the heights that ran along the front of the Brooklyn position. Putnam, however, did not follow Washington's advice. He stationed a mixed force of three thousand regulars and militiamen along four miles of these heights on the coast road, at Flatbush Pass, and at Bedford Pass. These Continentals and militia from Pennsylvania, New Jersey, New York, and Connecticut were supposed to stop the British from getting to Brooklyn. No force held Jamaica Pass on the American left.[5]

Unfortunately for Putnam and the American defenders, the British took advantage of the opening at Jamaica Pass. General William Howe employed his twenty thousand soldiers to execute a flank maneuver that was more successful than even he anticipated. Using five thousand men to attack along the coast road, and another five thousand to create a diversion near Flatbush and Bedford passes, Howe and ten thousand British soldiers spent the night of August 26–27 marching around the defenders' left flank. Early in the morning of August 27, Lieutenant General Henry Clinton, who had recently rejoined the army from his unsuccessful Southern expedition, led the van of the British army through Jamaica Pass and into the rear of the American forces holding Bedford and Flatbush passes.[6]

The surprised and partially surrounded American soldiers put up a stubborn if short-lived resistance. Between the opening of the battle

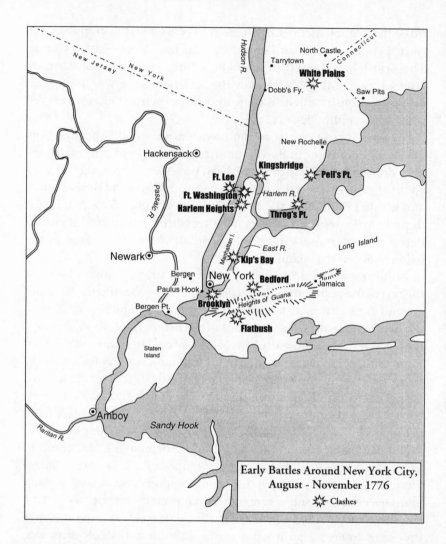

Early Battles Around New York City,
August - November 1776
Clashes

around 8:30 A.M. and the final rout of the last of the defenders at
2 P.M., there was a wild melee. Murray even admitted that the Americans "gave us several very heavy fires." Slowly but relentlessly, the
British marched behind each American position, routing and capturing many American soldiers and officers. General Sullivan, who
commanded the left of the line along the heights, surrendered after
a dramatic resistance, described thus by an American eyewitness:
"the last I heard of him, he was in a corn Field close by our Lines

with a Pistol in each Hand, and the Enemy had formed a Line each side of him, and he was going directly between them." Sullivan later returned to the Continental Army in September, after being exchanged.[7]

Lord Stirling, commanding along the coast road, held out the longest. He kept the British diversionary force at bay until almost noon, and then found the main British force behind his position. His mixed force of Continentals and militia tried to fight its way through the British to the American lines at Brooklyn, but after as many as six assaults, Stirling and the troops by his side found themselves completely surrounded, and finally surrendered. Others slipped through the British grasp. Michael Graham, a Pennsylvania militiaman, still recalled the chaos and horror of the moment over half a century later. With enemy troops firing from all directions, his unit became divided. He joined another group of men passing by, and they all fired a volley at the nearest enemy, then retreated again. Graham finally entered a marsh behind Stirling's original lines, and under the cover of an American artillery barrage from the Brooklyn lines, he slipped safely into the American camp.[8]

The British had routed the entire American line along the heights. Total rebel casualties were 1,097 men, whereas the British lost just under 400. Howe considered, but quickly rejected, the idea of an immediate assault on the Brooklyn lines. Though confident that his army could capture the second rebel position that same day, he saw no reason to lose British soldiers when the enemy lines could be taken by a regular siege. He reasoned that defeating the rest of the rebel force on Long Island would not have defeated the entire rebel army. Howe also had another concern: "[T]he most essential duty I had to observe was, not wantonly to commit his majesty's troops, where the object was inadequate. I knew well that any considerable loss sustained by the army could not speedily, nor easily, be repaired."[9]

Howe's opinion was consistent with his earlier statement that two American lives were not worth one British life. This concern, however, proved to be one of Washington's greatest weapons. Whether conscious of Howe's attitude or not, Washington's partisan use of the militia and parts of the Continental Army, as well as his willingness to stand and fight, played against Howe's desire to conserve his troops. Washington's effective blending of partisan and regular operations, initiated on Long Island, would inflict a growing number of casualties on the British.

The day after the battle, as the British opened their siege lines, Washington accompanied a reinforcement to the island that brought the American force up to ninety-five hundred men. The Continentals and militia manned the trenches on August 28–29 as skirmishing continued. Meanwhile, Washington, Governor Trumbull, and members of the New York Convention supported continued efforts to defend eastern Long Island. The Convention members asked Washington and Governor Trumbull to send men to the eastern end of the island to contest the British advance in that direction, and though Washington could not spare men from his army defending Brooklyn and Manhattan, he urged Trumbull to send one thousand Connecticut militiamen. He hoped this force would create a diversion on the flanks and rear of the British lines around Brooklyn, while the New York legislators hoped the militia could protect the local inhabitants and livestock. Their hopes were weakened when Brigadier General Woodhull's small force of island militia tried to make a stand August 28 at Jamaica, about eleven miles east of Brooklyn. The British captured them and killed Woodhull.[10]

Even as he urged resistance on eastern Long Island, Washington decided to abandon Brooklyn. During the night of August 29–30, Continental and militia volunteers manned the army's boats, and under the supervision of Alexander McDougall as well as of Washington, the American army evacuated Long Island in silence. The British found the Brooklyn lines deserted on the morning of August 30. Remaining on Long Island at that point were a detachment of two hundred Continentals, commanded by Lieutenant Colonel Henry Livingston, and a few local militia, all to the east of the British force in Brooklyn.[11]

Now on his own, Colonel Livingston tried to maintain his position on Long Island. Livingston and several Long Island inhabitants quickly wrote to Trumbull for help because most of the island militia had either retreated with the main army or had surrendered to the British. In an effort to rally the rest of the islanders, Livingston and his small detachment began an advance toward the enemy army to harass its foraging parties. Few of the local inhabitants, however, joined Livingston. At the same time, Trumbull started preparations for almost fifteen hundred Connecticut militia to cross Long Island Sound and join Livingston. Washington continued to urge Livingston to "pursue every step which shall appear to you necessary and Judicious, for annoying and harassing the Enemy, and to prevent their foraging," but to get off the island when it became too dangerous. As British parties advanced toward him, Livingston tried again to rally the remaining people to him, but many of the islanders were frightened, and preferred to submit. Livingston disarmed several Tories and retreated with his men to the mainland in the first week of September.[12]

Livingston and Trumbull, however, did not give up all hopes of contesting the British occupation of Long Island. Livingston crossed to the island with a small force in the second week of September for another attempt to save or destroy the livestock; they failed, and returned to Connecticut. As Trumbull prepared a new militia detachment to join him, Livingston returned to the island a few days later to prevent more people from swearing allegiance to Britain. He then combined his Continental detachment with 280 Connecticut militia to go a third time to the island, to help evacuate Whig families and their livestock. Another detachment of Connecticut militia crossed the Sound by itself, penetrated about thirteen miles inland, and brought off several families and numerous cattle and sheep. All of these forays occurred by mid-September. By that time, Washington had decided diversions on the island were of little further use, though he supported continued efforts to help friendly citizens escape the British. Livingston and several units of Connecticut militia remained along the Sound, ready to cross over and harass the British and Loyalists or help the Whigs. General George Clinton of the New York militia tried to raid Long Island from New Rochelle, New York, but bad weather prevented him.[13]

On Manhattan, Washington had his hands full dealing with the militia still attached to the Continental Army. After the retreat from Long Island, the militia began to leave without notice or permission. Washington ordered Major General William Heath, who had taken command at Kingsbridge, to stop any militiamen fleeing the army. This "impulse for going home" and the militia's lack of discipline provided ample reasons for Washington to vent anew his frustration concerning the forced reliance on the militia to fill the army. He wrote to Congress, "No dependence could be [placed] in a Militia or other Troops than those enlisted and embodied for a longer period than our regulations heretofore have prescribed." He laid out his argument, one to be repeated throughout the war, that only "a permanent standing Army" could properly defend America. The "Check" on Long Island, rather than inspiring the militiamen to greater efforts, had only made them anxious to leave the army. Even as Washington began to utilize the militia in a variety of partisan roles, he consistently condemned the need to attach militia units to the regular army.[14]

Disgust notwithstanding, Washington still had little choice. The decision of the Continental Congress to use the militia as a reserve for the field army could not be overcome at this point. The congressmen, however, began to reconsider their confidence in the state troops. They sent out orders to the Continental battalions left behind in Rhode Island and Massachusetts to concentrate in New York, as a "greater reliance is to be placed in them than a Militia . . . ." The Congress also passed a resolution, on September 16, to raise a new army of eighty-eight Continental battalions.[15]

Washington tried to make the best of the situation and use the militia units where he thought they could serve most effectively. His first concern as his army concentrated on Manhattan Island was to prepare for an attack at any point. He ordered all the militia over which he had authority to join the army, and requested more militia from the adjoining states. He positioned the militia regiments already with his army and the Flying Army in New Jersey to defend the exposed coasts, and he ordered General Hugh Mercer, commander of the Flying Army, to send him about one thousand men and to position a party on the Jersey shore opposite Fort Washington on Manhattan Island. Washington then asked the New York government to send reinforcements to Kingsbridge and the Highland forts. He urged Governor Trumbull to hurry the mustering of the Connecticut militiamen and to position them along the Sound, so they could join the army when the British tried to cross to the mainland. The government leaders of both states promised to send as many militia soldiers as they could. Washington even convinced the Massachusetts legislature to send about four thousand of its militia. The Continental Congress supported his efforts with a call to all the states north of Virginia to send "all the aid in [their] power to the Army at New [York]."[16]

As he concentrated the militia with his army, Washington encouraged the militia on the British flanks to take a more active role. He asked Mercer to study the possibility of a diversionary attack on Staten Island and, as shown, he at first urged Trumbull and Henry Livingston to continue the raids and harassment on Long Island. He even favored such partisan activities in the face of the enemy army while it sat on Long Island, informing Heath and George Clinton that he "should much approve of small harassing parties, stealing, as it were, over in the night, as they might keep the enemy alarmed, and more than probably bring off a prisoner, from whom some valuable intelligence may be obtained."[17]

While Washington prepared the defense of New York City and the mainland, the New Jersey Whigs installed their newly elected governor, William Livingston, at the beginning of September. Elected on August 27, the tall, slender militia general came from a prominent New York family that had gained some social prestige in New Jersey. Governor Livingston proved to be a staunch supporter of the revolt, and earned the hatred of the British with his sarcastic writings aimed at the British government. More important for the war effort, Livingston quickly became a good friend of Washington's, despite some friction during the coming crisis in New Jersey. Upon taking office, Livingston immediately suggested that the legislature work on improved regulations for the militia. This struggle between governor and legislature over laws to regulate the militia would last the entire war. One suggestion Livingston considered was the adoption of six-month tours for the militia, rather than the monthly rotation then employed.[18]

As its new government took shape, New Jersey's defense depended on Mercer and his Flying Army of militia. Most of the New Jersey militia in the field were in this army, which was stationed along the coast across from Staten Island, and on Bergen Point and Paulus Hook. Mercer, however, agreed with Washington's idea concerning a diversionary attack on Staten Island, and even as he prepared to defend the coast, he continued to study the possibility of an attack.[19]

While the New Jersey Whigs reorganized their government, the New York Convention quickly ordered the militia officers of Orange, Ulster, Dutchess, and Westchester counties to prepare their men to repel the expected invasion of mainland New York. The legislators, however, exhibited little confidence in the ability of the militia to prevent an invasion, as they informed Washington: "we cannot by any Means advise your Excellency to trust for its prevention to any Militia, which we can at this time call out." The Convention members nevertheless ordered six hundred militia to reinforce the Highland forts when they learned that Washington could not detach men from the army to defend the Highlands. In addition, part of George Clinton's militia brigade guarded along the Harlem River, and one regiment reinforced the Kingsbridge area.[20]

Governor Trumbull and the Council of State also responded to Washington's urging. They immediately sent two regiments of militia horse to join Washington in Westchester. In addition, they ordered the militia units along the coast to be prepared to march toward New York to join the army, to create a diversion on Long Island, or to cover the country as necessary. Trumbull wanted to be ready to take advantage of any opportunity and to respond to the next request that Washington sent. That request came, and by the end of the first week of September, Trumbull ordered the militia to join Washington.[21]

The British victory on Long Island, and the threatened invasion of Manhattan and the mainland, increased the danger posed by the Loyalists. In New York, the Whigs were especially worried that the Tories would rise up in support of the enemy. Therefore, the Committee of Safety ordered parties of militia into the field to bolster efforts to prevent Loyalists from going over to the enemy. George Clinton attempted to remove from two Long Island regiments any disloyal militiamen who were trying to return to Long Island and possibly join the enemy, and he asked the Convention to order out other militia to help round up Tories and deserters. Trumbull aided these efforts by ordering a detachment of Connecticut horse militia to help in "scouring the Country, and preventing or supressing [sic] any risings of our eternal Enemies."[22]

These efforts by the governments of Connecticut, New York, and New Jersey to muster and employ their militia became increasingly difficult. The defeat on Long Island and the overwhelming strength of the British force convinced many Whigs that they could not win this war quickly, a realization that discouraged the militia and slowed the response to the many appeals for the men to take the field. In addition, the Loyalist threat, especially in New York and New Jersey, and the need to use the militia for local defense inhibited the reinforcement of Washington's army. The New York Convention, in fact, feared to call out a greater proportion of militia from the four counties nearest to New York City due to the large number of Tories and slaves in the area, and because of the exposed situation of the counties along the Sound and the Hudson River. The Convention therefore could not comply when Washington requested further reinforcement for Kingsbridge, though the members ordered the militiamen still at home to be ready if absolutely necessary. Washington understood the situation in New York and accepted the Convention's decision. Trumbull, meanwhile, ordered to New York only the militia regiments that were not needed to guard the coast, and even then companies at certain ports received permission to remain at home on guard.[23]

The long-awaited attack on Manhattan Island occurred September 15. By then, in an effort to defend all possible landing sites on the island, Washington had split his army into three parts: Putnam kept his division at the southern end, General Heath commanded a force nearer the northern end, and in the center, along the East River, stood General Greene's division, which consisted primarily of militia. A Connecticut militia brigade in Greene's division was entrenched along the shore of Kip's Bay, the spot where the British decided to direct their attack. The militiamen did not hold the spot long. A bombardment of almost eighty guns from nearby British warships leveled the militia's breastworks, and the Connecticut state troops broke ranks and ran. Despite Washington's personal intervention, the retreat turned into a rout as the fleeing Connecticut militia ran into another militia brigade and a brigade of Continentals, both of which joined in the general panic. The British troops landed unopposed and began to march west to cut off Putnam's division. Over three hundred Americans became British prisoners during the landing operation.[24]

The retreat did not end until the American army reached Harlem Heights. Putnam's division barely escaped from the southern end of the island, and his rear unit, Colonel Silliman's Connecticut militia regiment, found itself cut off by the advancing British units. Silliman, however, kept his men in the woods and they slipped past. The British pursuit caught up with Silliman's rear guard, and he formed about three hundred of his militiamen on a hill and repulsed a British charge. The British backed off, and Silliman led his men to safety on Harlem Heights.[25]

The rout of the militia at Kip's Bay simply reinforced Washington's opinion of the worthlessness of militia soldiers in combat against the British army. The day after this most recent defeat, he vented his disgust to President Hancock: "this disgraceful and dastardly conduct" gave him "great surprize and mortification . . . ." He began to despair of winning the war with such troops. General Hugh Mercer in New Jersey echoed this opinion after a party of Pennsylvania and New Jersey militia fled from Paulus Hook in the face of a naval bombardment on September 15.[26]

New York City had been lost, but Washington was not ready to surrender all of Manhattan Island. He placed about ten thousand men along Harlem Heights, keeping another six thousand troops near Kingsbridge to guard his escape route to the mainland. On September 16, the British advanced toward Washington's lines, and Washington struck back in frustration. Several Continental units spearheaded the counterattack, but when the British began to retreat, Washington sent forward Continental and militia regiments. By noon, about eighteen hundred American soldiers were engaged, with Generals Putnam, Greene, and George Clinton in the field directing the pursuit. One of the militia units that advanced was the Connecticut militia regiment that had first panicked at Kip's Bay. When the running battle ended, the British had lost as many as two hundred men, whereas fewer than one hundred Americans had fallen.[27]

This battle of Harlem Heights allowed Washington to display an important characteristic. The day after he had watched in disgust as the militia bolted, he sent the same men forward to fight British regulars. Washington would not give up on the militia. Rather than refuse to use them, he found ways to work them into his operations and battles.

In the days after the clash at Harlem Heights, the Continentals and militia fortified their positions while militia reinforcements arrived from New Jersey, New York, Connecticut, Massachusetts, and New Hampshire. Militia and Continentals also took position along the Hudson River to defend the fortifications there, and militia units began to construct defensive works along the east side of the Harlem River. Washington sent General Greene to take command in New Jersey, and Mercer became Greene's second in command. The Flying Army in New Jersey consisted at this time of five thousand militiamen maximum, a far cry from the fifteen-thousand-man army that the Continental Congress had called for earlier in the summer.[28]

The main British and American armies remained relatively inactive in their lines on the heights for almost four weeks while General Howe concentrated his forces and prepared the naval component for another amphibious landing. During this lull, Washington and Governor Trumbull hoped to renew offensive action on Long Island to prevent the British from enlisting the local inhabitants into their army, and to help remove any Whigs and their livestock. Washington sent George Clinton to Connecticut to organize such a raid. At the same time, he ordered Major General Benjamin Lincoln with his Massachusetts militia to coordinate with Lieutenant Colonel Henry Livingston's Continentals, who were still in the area, and the local Connecticut militia for an expedition to Long Island. Governor Trumbull even secured support from Rhode Island. The raiding party numbered about twelve hundred by mid-October, but bad weather kept delaying its departure, and later in October, Washington canceled the plan because he needed the men in New York.[29]

On October 12, the impasse on Manhattan ended as British troops landed at Throg's Point, which was in effect an island at the end of a peninsula jutting into the Sound due east of Washington's position at Harlem Heights. Washington had posted a small detachment of Continental riflemen at this point, and these men, supported by Continental reinforcements, stopped the British advance at the narrow pass leading from the landing site to the mainland. Thus, Howe found his amphibious flanking movement thwarted. Washington, however, did not wait for Howe's next move. On October 16, urged by General Charles Lee, who had recently returned from his command in the South, Washington ordered a retreat off Manhattan Island.[30]

The British executed another amphibious assault at Pell's Point on October 18. Despite stiff but brief resistance, they succeeded this time because Pell's Point was a wider peninsula connected directly to the mainland. The two armies marched northward on parallel courses over the next few days until Washington's army reached White Plains on October 21. Washington left behind a detachment of six hundred men at Kingsbridge and a mix of fourteen hundred Continentals and militia at Fort Washington on Manhattan.[31]

As the British approached White Plains, their leading troops skirmished with detachments of Continentals and militia. On October 28, the British army attacked Washington's advance position, which Washington had ordered forward to harass British deployments. This American force consisted mostly of Connecticut militia, who volleyed several times with the British troops and even drove them back before the British opened fire with their artillery and forced an American retreat to Chatterton's Hill, on the American right. The British army advanced against the hill and ran into Brigadier General Alexander McDougall's command of sixteen hundred men, also mostly militia. The defenders fired a heavy artillery barrage and repulsed the initial British assault, but the British charged again with a reinforced corps. First the militia and then the few Continentals of McDougall's force retreated off the hill. The defenders inflicted about three hundred casualties on Howe's army and had about two hundred losses of their own.[32]

While the two armies faced each other outside White Plains after this engagement, the British units remaining on Manhattan captured Kingsbridge on October 29. On November 1, Washington suddenly pulled his army back to North Castle. Deciding that Washington now preferred to avoid a general action, Howe halted the pursuit. Thus, as November began, the British army remained split near White Plains and on Manhattan. Washington had his main force at North Castle, while General Greene commanded the garrisons of Fort Washington on Manhattan and Fort Lee just across the Hudson River. Brigadier General Samuel Parsons commanded a brigade at the Saw Pits along the Sound, near the border between Connecticut and New York. Washington continued to guard against a British advance in any direction.[33]

While the main British and American armies maneuvered and fought in late September and October, Washington and the members of the Continental Congress continued their efforts to secure more troops. They sent new pleas for help to all of the governments of the New England states, and Connecticut in particular responded to the requests. Since the thirteen Connecticut militia regiments that had already joined the army had dwindled to about seven hundred men by late September, Washington decided to discharge them and ask for new units as quickly as possible. Governor Trumbull and the council ordered nine militia regiments, about three thousand infantry and three hundred cavalry, to join Washington's army in Westchester County. In addition, the Connecticut Assembly put Major General David Wooster and his militia command under Washington's command. Wooster's force of about 400 infantry and 150 cavalry had been guarding the Connecticut–New York border near the Sound since the British landing at Pell's Point in mid-October. Wooster had orders to assist the Continental Army and annoy the enemy in any way possible. Washington thanked Trumbull for these spirited efforts to support the army.[34]

Washington's dual, though consistent, attitude toward the militia continued to show itself. Even as he gathered it and used it to fight, he hammered away on his by now well-known theme that the militia was an unreliable source of manpower for the army. In late September, Washington's disgust at the general behavior of the militia, despite his employment of it on Harlem Heights, burst forth in a letter to the Congress: "To place any dependance upon Militia, is, assuredly, resting upon a broken staff." Militiamen came and went at will, their lack of discipline spread to others, and Washington was not sure "whether the Militia have been most serviceable or hurtful upon the whole; I should subscribe to the latter." The militia also tended to lose equipment in battle faster than Continental soldiers, especially when facing a British attack. This willingness to throw away guns and any other encumbrance when fleeing battle worsened Washington's already strained logistical support. The worst offenders in all of these offenses were those men called out for temporary aid, but militia soldiers mustered for several months' service also were questionable. Washington feared he would again have to rely almost exclusively on the militia when the present army's enlistments expired at year's end and a new one had to be recruited. Other generals, including Nathanael Greene and George Clinton, agreed with this estimate of the militia.[35]

If he wanted a change in the system, Washington knew he had to overcome both popular opinion and the congressmen's prejudice in favor of the militia. As he explained to his brother:

Matters in this Quarter, have by no means worn that favourable aspect you have been taught to believe from the publications in the Gazettes. The pompous Acct. of the Marches, and Counter Marches of the Militia, tho' true so far as relates to the Expense, is false with respect to the Service . . . .[36]

Much to Washington's surprise, the members of Congress in general came around to his views during September and October. When the militia failed to respond to the crisis after the retreat from Long Island, the Congress on September 16 ordered the raising of eighty-eight battalions of regular soldiers. As Congressman Francis Lightfoot Lee explained, the members of the Congress decided to raise a regular army so "that we shall not have recourse to the militia, but upon extraordinary occasions." These Continental soldiers would be enlisted for the duration of the war. Hancock informed the states that a strong Continental Army would be formed because the "heavy and enormous expense consequent upon calling forth the Militia, the delay attending their motions, and the difficulty of keeping them in Camp, render it extremely improper to place our whole dependence on them."[37] This overly ambitious goal of a large regular army would never be met.

In spite of his disgust, Washington understood that militiamen were often the only men available for some duties. He needed information on the British plans for New Jersey and the South, and asked Mercer to use his militia to obtain it. Washington also began to use militia detachments for forward defense. Militia units would take position in advance of the army and hold as long as possible if attacked, while Washington prepared his response to the British move. As described earlier, Washington used such a tactic at White Plains, where the first British attack hit a militia force in front of the main position; only after defeating it did the British attack Washington's main line. In addition, Washington and even the Continental Congress continued to use the militia to isolate the enemy from their Loyalist friends, and in general to control the Tories throughout the area. Washington detached a party of Massachusetts militia from his position at Harlem Heights to help the New York Convention prevent a feared Tory uprising after three British ships sailed up the Hudson River in early October. When New York's Committee of Safety warned him that it did not trust its own militia, Washington sent a New Hampshire regiment to act under the Committee's orders. The Continental Congress asked Governor Livingston to send two New Jersey militia companies to stop the communication from the New Jersey coast between Loyalists and the British fleet.[38]

Even as the national leadership urgently called for the militia, the state forces remained the first line of defense for the state governments. The militia of Connecticut continued to defend the coast from British invasion and Loyalist raids from Long Island. New York's government tried to muster New York's strength both to support Washington and to defend itself. While four hundred militiamen of Ulster and Orange counties marched to Peekskill, Orange County officials mustered militia to guard the western shores of the Hudson River. Though Clinton's brigade remained attached to the army, he used parts of it to protect and remove supplies from the area.[39]

New York militiamen also had to contain the growing internal threat. When the British advanced onto the mainland, daily warnings of Tory uprisings alarmed New York's leaders. In response, the legislators created the Committee for Detecting Conspiracies "to call out such detachments of the militia or troops in the different counties, as they may, from time to time deem necessary for suppressing insurrections." In addition, the committee took command of the militia rangers of Ulster and Orange counties. The Convention then asked the militiamen and Continentals already stationed in the area to help capture local inhabitants who had enlisted in the British army. Suspects were simply removed from the area. When the British army entered eastern New York and neared the Connecticut border, the Connecticut General Assembly sent its own committee to apprehend dangerous persons. This Connecticut committee applied to General Wooster for help from his militia defending the area.[40]

In New Jersey, the Flying Army was the main line of defense. The time of service for part of the New Jersey contingent of the Flying Army, however, ended in mid-October. Governor Livingston, who had little actual power to call out the militia unless the enemy invaded the state, asked the Assembly to replace the departing soldiers. He again urged the Assembly to improve the militia regulations, but the legislators did not act. Meanwhile, Mercer, who had continued to study the possibility of a diversionary raid against Staten Island, finally launched his raid on October 15. Attacking with a mixed force of about six hundred regulars and militia, the raiding party engaged a group of Tories, British, and Germans. He lost two men killed and three or four wounded, but captured about twenty prisoners.[41]

Mostly ignoring these rebel efforts to rouse the people, General Howe shifted his army on November 3 from White Plains to Dobb's Ferry on the Hudson River, and within ten days the British had withdrawn to Kingsbridge. While the British pulled back, Washington sent small parties, from his camp at North Castle, back toward White Plains to harass pro-British inhabitants and impede British movements. Washington and his generals then decided to split the army in New York, sending part into New Jersey to join the Flying Army and protect against a British advance toward Philadelphia. Accordingly, Washington detached three thousand men to reinforce General William Heath's command in the Highlands, and appointed Major General Charles Lee to command the portion of the army remaining in New York. Lee was to guard as much of New York as possible, and to command General Wooster's detachment of Connecticut militia in western Connecticut. Washington left Lee orders to follow the British into New Jersey should they invade in strength. The militia would then be responsible for guarding New York and Connecticut. After Washington departed with the rest of the army for New Jersey, Lee sent troops to reoccupy White Plains, and by mid-November his men were entrenching there and north of the Croton River.[42]

Meanwhile, as Washington prepared to lead his reduced army across the Hudson into New Jersey, he asked Governor Livingston to replace the New Jersey militia already with the army and to have the rest of his state's militia ready to support Washington's move. Washington wrote to General Greene, who still commanded Forts Lee and Washington, on either side of the Hudson River, to order Mercer and his Flying Army northward in support of Greene's position. Leaving Lee and Heath behind, Washington's army then marched toward King's Ferry at the end of the first week in November, and soon afterward began crossing into New Jersey.[43]

Even before Washington crossed into New Jersey, Governor Livingston warned the general that the New Jersey militia might not respond to the governor's calls. He promised Washington that he would do all he could to get the militia into the field, "but whether they will obey the order God only knows . . . ." Livingston began issuing the necessary orders to the militia officers but feared that the weak militia regulations of the state, which had no provisions to force people to serve, would undermine efforts to muster the state forces. The government could only levy fines against those men who refused to take the field. The governments of Connecticut and New York had similar regulations and faced similar difficulties throughout the war. The New Jersey legislature was reviewing the regulations, but as of November, it had made no revisions.[44]

As the Americans split their army and the New Jersey government prepared for the war to shift to its state, Howe made a sudden move against Fort Washington, the rebel stronghold on Manhattan Island that Washington had kept garrisoned. Despite the fact that British ships had already sailed past this fort and Fort Lee, Washington still hoped that the defenses would obstruct British use of the river. Greene was the immediate commander of the area, but Washington personally inspected the fort as late as November 16, the day the British attacked. The garrison, which numbered just under three thousand men, consisted mostly of militiamen from the Flying Army. Washington hesitated, and ultimately made no decision concerning the abandonment of the fort. Perhaps he clung to the idea that the militia could fight effectively from behind defensive works, and therefore might be able to hold in the face of the British army. If that was his reasoning, it proved incorrect. Howe sent eight thousand troops against the fort, and by 3 P.M. on November 16, the garrison had surrendered. The British captured over twenty-eight hundred men, and lost over four hundred in the fight. Greene blamed the loss on the militiamen, who, he claimed, panicked unnecessarily.[45]

Ironically, the ultimate blame for this defeat perhaps rested on Washington's confidence in the militia, a confidence shaken at Long Island and New York but renewed at Harlem Heights and White Plains. Washington was still measuring the true worth of the militiamen, on whom so much depended. Events in November once again caused him to despair of finding any useful employment of the militia attached directly to the main army.

After the fall of Fort Washington, which was renamed Fort Knyphausen, after Lieutenant General Wilhelm von Knyphausen, the commander of the German troops under Howe's command, the

British began the invasion of New Jersey. Howe first planned to capture Fort Lee, on the Jersey side, to open the entire Hudson and to gain a road into New Jersey. On November 18, British troops commanded by Major General Lord Cornwallis crossed the river about seven miles north of Fort Lee. General Greene ordered the evacuation of the fort on November 20, but the withdrawal became confused and rushed, much to his disgust. Militia soldiers from the Flying Army composed most of the garrison, and Greene blamed their lack of discipline for causing the flight and the loss of about one hundred men whom the British captured.[46]

Washington initially planned to resist this British invasion of New Jersey by using the Continentals brought from New York and the militia of the Flying Army, but the troops of the Flying Army were due to go home soon. When they left, Washington would have only a few small Continental regiments and the few New Jersey militia whom Governor Livingston had been able to collect. He decided around November 20, as Greene abandoned Fort Lee, to call General Lee to join the army in New Jersey. Washington then began a retreat to New Brunswick in order to join the remainder of the Flying Army and the few Continentals stationed in New Jersey. He urged Livingston to keep assembling the militia. By November 22, Washington's fleeing army was at Acquackanonk on the Passaic River.[47]

As Washington retreated and the British followed, the Continental Army and its supporting militia dwindled in size. The Continental force had shrunk to about three thousand men by November 21, while the Flying Army consisted of four hundred to five hundred militiamen. Great efforts were then initiated to affect a concentration of all possible militia and Continental soldiers in New Jersey. Livingston continued to order out all of the New Jersey militia, and he authorized Brigadier General Philemon Dickinson to assemble them. Washington asked President Hancock for an order of the Continental Congress to the New Jersey and Pennsylvania Continentals in the Northern army to join him in New Jersey, and the Congress passed the necessary legislation. In addition, the Continental Congress, on Washington's pleading, called on the Pennsylvania government to raise the militia of Philadelphia and the counties near the Delaware River. It also asked for five hundred volunteers from Delaware and as many volunteers as possible from Maryland.[48]

Despite these urgent appeals for reinforcements, Washington at first received few men as he retreated southward through New Jersey. The immediate source of help, the New Jersey militia, failed to respond to the crisis. Governor Livingston's orders to the northern counties of New Jersey produced few results. New Jersey's legislature ordered the raising of four battalions of long-term militia, but they would not be immediately available, and the New Jersey government gave Washington little encouragement to expect many to muster. Besides, the militiamen north of New Brunswick could not get to the army even if they wanted to, because the British occupied the northeastern portion of the state. A committee from the Continental Congress informed Livingston that the Continental Congress would pay for the extra soldiers called out in this emergency, but even this offer gained little. An essay in the *Pennsylvania Journal* tried to spur the Pennsylvania and New Jersey militia to action with a warning that the cause depended on the militia of those two states, and if the militiamen failed now, they deserved to be slaves. Nothing succeeded in raising the New Jersey militia. Militia soldiers went home when their time of service ended, and other men refused to serve. The problem increasingly was a combination of fear of British military might, which led many New Jersey inhabitants to accept the king's forgiveness and protection being offered by the advancing British army, and the still inefficient New Jersey laws. On November 30, the time of enlistment for the New Jersey and Maryland brigades of militia in the Flying Army ended, and Pennsylvania's enlistments were up on January 1. The New Jersey and Maryland men refused to stay longer. The strength of the Continental Army and the Flying Army continued to shrink.[49]

Still, as Washington led his disintegrating army through New Jersey, he did not forget the other duties of the militia and Continentals. He sent scouts and detachments to harass the enemy's movements and gather intelligence. When he received information of a possible uprising of Tories in Monmouth County, he detached a New Jersey militia regiment from his already weakened army to prevent the insurrection. He authorized the commander of the local militia regiment to attack any armed group, and to call to his aid any local New Jersey militiamen he thought necessary.[50]

Washington, the army, and the state of New Jersey all needed help, and on December 1, New York's Committee of Safety began

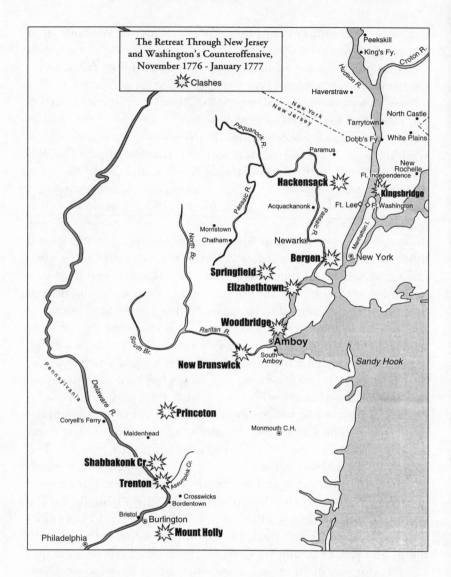

The Retreat Through New Jersey
and Washington's Counteroffensive,
November 1776 - January 1777
Clashes

preparations that would lead to an eventual counteroffensive in northeast New Jersey. The committeemen asked Governor Trumbull to help create a force of six thousand militiamen from their two states to join the Continental brigades of Major General Lee and of Major General Horatio Gates, who was marching south from the Northern army, according to the orders of the Continental Congress.

The committee suggested this combined force could end the panic in New Jersey and threaten the flank of the British army marching southward through New Jersey. Otherwise, the British would march easily through New Jersey, which the New York committee believed had strong Loyalist sympathies. At that time, about nine hundred New York militiamen were in the field, and more militia from the nearby counties had orders to join Lee and Gates.[51]

For the moment, however, Washington could only continue the retreat. His efforts to procure reinforcements from the adjacent states failed. The plan set in motion by the New York Committee of Safety, had he known of it, would not have altered the situation. Washington had only four thousand men, including one thousand New Jersey militia, and new men were coming in slowly. A large reinforcement was expected from Pennsylvania, but not for a couple of weeks. Washington therefore decided on December 1 to retreat through New Jersey, cross to the western side of the Delaware River, and there await the reinforcements. On December 3 he reached Trenton. He could not understand why Lee had not joined him, but he still hoped that when the expected reinforcements of Continentals and militia arrived, he could rally the New Jersey militia. Even in this emergency, Washington refused to call Heath from his position in the Highlands because he believed the Highland passes were too important to risk.[52]

General Lee's failure to join Washington in time to defend New Jersey was due to Lee's views on the campaign. When Washington crossed into New Jersey, Lee became commander of the forces in New York. In that capacity, he faced a problem similar to what Washington faced: how to keep his militia soldiers with him in the field. Lee tried, unsuccessfully, to convince the militia to stay longer; and though the New York Committee of Safety ordered its militiamen to serve until the end of the year, no matter when their times of service ended, only a few men stayed. Lee also asked the governments of Massachusetts and Connecticut for help. Washington's order of November 21 for Lee to join his army in New Jersey thus placed Lee in a dilemma. Lee decided to send two thousand of Heath's four thousand men from the Highlands and to keep his own corps of Continentals and militia in New York. Washington vetoed this proposal and again ordered Lee's division into New Jersey. Lee and the members of the New York Convention were unhappy with Washington's insistent demand for Lee's troops. Lee personally believed he was performing a better service in New York by protecting the forage in the area and pinning down a large British force near Kingsbridge. When the British in New York withdrew their advance parties in late November, Lee finally agreed to enter New Jersey. No militia reinforcements, however, had arrived to replace his troops and protect the New York countryside.[53]

As Lee prepared to leave in late November, the forces remaining in New York prepared their defenses. General Heath tried to maintain some control over the local Tories and to obstruct the river passage through the Highlands. He sent a small brigade of New York militia to Haverstraw to protect against an invasion there and to control the Tories in that area. Washington, meanwhile, approved Lee's requests for more Connecticut militia but doubted the Connecticut government could provide any. He still did not approve of Lee's constant delays, but Lee promised to move at the beginning of December with four thousand men. Since Lee was taking most of the Continentals from New York, the New York Convention ordered all possible militia forces in the field to join George Clinton in the Highlands, and all militiamen of Ulster and Orange counties not already in the field to be ready to muster and repel invasion attempts on the west side of the Hudson.[54]

Connecticut's leaders also prepared for an attack. As of mid-November, Wooster's militia brigade, which had only five hundred of the two thousand men ordered to join it, guarded the port towns near the New York border. Lee asked Wooster to extend his forces to defend the Saw Pits as well, because Lee could spare no men. Meanwhile, a small British raid at Stamford was met and repulsed by about fifty local militia troops, and the British secured only two or three cattle. In response to Lee's call for more men in late November, the Connecticut Assembly ordered four militia battalions to march for New York to serve until March 1777. Trumbull then asked the Continental Congress to station two Continental battalions along Connecticut's coast to bolster the defenses against further raids. The Congress agreed.[55]

Despite the frantic efforts to strengthen the forces in New York, the defenders had no more success than Washington had in New Jersey. Heath sent George Clinton and five hundred of his militiamen from Peekskill to reinforce the Highland forts on December 1, but most of the other New York militia went home despite the pleading of the New York Convention. When Lee finally crossed to the west side of the Hudson River on December 2–3, he left in New York only Heath's command in the Highlands and Brigadier General Joseph Spencer and a small force of Continentals and militia, about three thousand total, guarding the New York border near the southwestern corner of Connecticut. Spencer had orders from Lee, however, that if a large body of militia did not reinforce him soon, Spencer should retreat to the northeast and join a body of Massachusetts militia who were supposed to arrive soon.[56]

At this point in early December, Washington lamented the course of the campaign so far. The army was scattered, and New York and New Jersey remained vulnerable to further British attack. Washington especially hated leaving so much of New Jersey undefended because he had hoped to stop the British near Hackensack in northern New Jersey, or at least at New Brunswick. Without militia support, however, he had been forced to retreat. He had initially left about twelve hundred Continentals at Princeton with the hope that he would return soon, but had ultimately withdrawn the entire army across the Delaware. He regretted having to depend on the militia for his main support, and again begged the Continental Congress for a strong regular army. He argued that the repeated calls on the militia probably had weakened its response. He also understood that the presence of the British in New Jersey endangered families and homes, and kept many militiamen at home. In addition, the British offered a pardon to all rebels who laid down their arms, and the growing number of Tories joining the British in New Jersey helped persuade and intimidate the Whig militia from taking the field.[57]

The important influence of the militia on the main operations of the regular armies became clear during this retreat. Even Washington suggested that with the proper support from the militia of New Jersey, he could have stopped the British. He still hoped that a strong turnout in December could reverse the situation. He regretted the dependence on the militia, yet acknowledged that with it, he could operate. Washington's ambivalence toward the militia remained.

As Washington retreated to the Delaware River and Lee fretted over the defense of New York, the British advanced across New Jersey.

At first, General Howe planned only to occupy eastern New Jersey, where he would station a large force to collect forage and supplies. He expected Washington to retire behind the Raritan or even the Delaware River. Cornwallis therefore pursued this objective after capturing Fort Lee on November 20. Eight days later he took possession of Newark and continued to follow Washington toward New Brunswick. Throughout this march the British army met little opposition.[58]

When Cornwallis approached New Brunswick, part of the American army remained on the south side of the Raritan River. The armies exchanged a brief cannonade, after which the American force fled. Cornwallis then halted, in accordance with Howe's plan to end the campaign and put his army into winter quarters along the Jersey coast in New Brunswick, Elizabethtown, and Newark. Howe reconsidered, however, and decided to continue the pursuit of the retreating Americans. The advantages to be gained by reaching the Delaware River, and possibly crossing and capturing Philadelphia, were great; and even just occupying positions along the river would keep open the option of a winter strike at the rebel capital. In addition, many Loyalists assured Howe that Washington's army was disintegrating, and if pursued further, the rebels would disperse. Howe therefore joined Cornwallis at New Brunswick and led the advance.[59]

The British army crossed the Raritan River on December 6 and reached the banks of the Delaware River two days later. Washington's army, however, had finished crossing the Delaware the previous day. Finding that the rebels had taken or destroyed all of the boats along the river, Howe halted the pursuit and established a chain of posts across New Jersey from Trenton and Bordentown on the Delaware to New Brunswick. The advance positions near the river were deliberately kept strong in case an opportunity to cross arose later, and other posts were set up near Burlington to protect Monmouth County, which contained strong Loyalist sentiment. Howe realized this string of garrisons across the state was too long, but he wanted to maintain control over as much territory as possible. The number of inhabitants responding to his November 30 proclamation offering amnesty to the rebels further encouraged Howe, who later defended his actions to Parliament by claiming three hundred to four hundred people per day came to his army seeking a pardon.[60]

In addition, Howe believed the garrisons would be "in perfect security," relying as he was on "the almost general submission of the country to the southward of this chain . . . ." He left a total of six brigades of soldiers in New Jersey under the command of Major General Sir James Grant, who maintained his headquarters at New Brunswick. At the far end of his line Howe placed Colonel Carl von Donop with about three thousand German troops in Trenton and Bordentown, only five miles apart. Another detachment of British troops garrisoned Princeton, twelve miles from Trenton. Colonel von Donop wanted to concentrate the German troops in Trenton, but Howe ordered him to hold Bordentown and even Burlington to provide full protection for Monmouth County. Howe clearly meant to help the people of New Jersey return to their allegiance to the royal government. After his return to England in 1778, Howe defended his actions by stressing that protection of the people was his main objective. He was convinced the rebels had submitted.[61]

Washington dreaded the consequences of this British occupation and worked frantically to gather a force with which to strike back into New Jersey. He clearly understood as well as Howe why the British were able to occupy so much territory: "they have not found the least Opposition from the People of Jersey . . . ." Much to Washington's consternation, many people in New Jersey were submitting and seeking protection under Howe's offer of pardon. Once the American army was huddled behind the Delaware River, the New Jersey militia continued to ignore Washington's pleas to join him, and the Pennsylvania militia did not react much better. As usual, he complained to President Hancock of the militiamen's "lethargy" and "backwardness," and concluded "that no reliance except such as may arise from necessity, should ever be had in them again . . . ." By mid-December, Washington had collected about fifteen hun-dred militia from Philadelphia, but little from the rest of the state. In fact, Washington began to lump the militiamen of New Jersey and Pennsylvania together for their lack of spirit in the crisis. General Greene saw only a slight distinction between the Pennsylvania and New Jersey militia. He believed the Jersey men acted out of fear, but that the Pennsylvanians stayed home due to disaffection to the cause. General Heath described the New York militia in equally disparaging terms: "It is vain to trust to a militia . . . ." He complained that too many militiamen who joined him went home a few days later.[62]

The failure of the militia to join Washington or resist the British advance thus led not only to Washington's flight but also to Howe's confidence. As of early December 1776, neither Howe nor Washington understood the difficulties that could be involved in occupying large areas of hostile territory. Washington could only see how the militia's weakness had lost most of New Jersey, while Howe believed the Americans would no longer resist British advances. The weakness of the American military position without the militia was clear: when the local militia forces did not resist, Washington's small Continental Army could not resist the British or prevent the occupation of the countryside.

Washington did not despair, however, as he kept calling on the governments and people of New Jersey and Pennsylvania for help. He wrote to the Pennsylvania Council of Safety and to individual militia colonels in that state, and he wrote to General Lee somewhere in New Jersey and to the militia generals of New Jersey. Pennsylvania's council authorized Washington to call on the militia of two counties along the Delaware River, which he did. He also applied to Massachusetts for four thousand militia and wrote to the Continental commander in Rhode Island to send him what militia he could find in New England. Meanwhile, Connecticut's leaders continued preparations to send four battalions of militia to New York, and the Continental Congress again wrote to the Maryland government for support. Despite these efforts, Washington wrote on December 21 that few militia had arrived, perhaps two thousand Philadelphia militia. After that date, additional Pennsylvania and Philadelphia militiamen finally began to arrive. Washington ordered them to guard the ferry crossings on the river and to raid into New Jersey in order to attack British supply convoys.[63]

Lee's division finally arrived around December 20. Though long overdue, his men were welcome. They were so late because Lee had entertained hopes of saving the campaign on his own. Washington's reputation as of December 1776 was not high, whereas Lee believed his was. Acting on this belief, Lee was reluctant to do what Washington ordered. He ultimately did enter New Jersey on December 4 with about four thousand troops, but rather than race to find Washington, Lee thought he saw strategic possibilities from his position on the flank and rear of the British army that was advancing south. From northeast New Jersey, Lee believed he could "annoy, distract, and consequently weaken [the British] in a desultory war . . . ." He tried to collect the militia of northern New Jersey but had little success. His presence did force Cornwallis to detach a guard to cover his northern flank, and British troops occupied Hackensack, Elizabethtown, and Amboy, but the British did not halt their pursuit of Washington. Finally, Lee learned that Washington had abandoned New Jersey altogether and that the British had occupied towns from New Brunswick to Trenton. Uncertain of his next step, he waited at Morristown between December 8 and 11, then decided to attempt to join Washington across the Delaware. Unfortunately for Lee, the British captured him on December 13 and his second in command, General John Sullivan, led the remaining troops south and joined Washington within a week, with about two thousand men.[64]

General Horatio Gates was bringing another Continental reinforcement from the Northern army. Leading four regiments, about six hundred men, Gates followed a route northwest of Lee's division. He crossed the Delaware River on December 15 and joined Washington a few days later. Washington had hoped fifteen hundred New York militia would join Gates en route, but the militiamen had refused to leave their state. By December 22, after the addition of Sullivan's and Gates's corps, Washington's little army still numbered only about three thousand Continental soldiers.[65]

While hiding behind the Delaware River with this weak force of Continentals and the few militiamen available, Washington contemplated what to do next. He knew he could not abandon New Jersey indefinitely, or the rest of the people might return fully to their allegiance to the Crown. He therefore encouraged blows against the British posts throughout the state while his army grew in strength. Thus, immediately after retreating across the Delaware River, Washington began urging new efforts in New Jersey. His army at that moment was too weak to act, but rather than wait until the desired reinforcements arrived, he wrote to other officers to spark the desired resistance.

As early as December 7, as his army first crossed the Delaware, Washington ordered Heath with his Continental troops to cross from

New York into New Jersey to protect and rally the people, and ultimately to join the main army. Lee supposedly was doing the same
thing in northeast New Jersey at that time. The New York Convention, knowing only of Lee's move into New Jersey, supported Lee
with a call to all the militia of Ulster and Orange counties to muster
under George Clinton's command and cooperate with Lee or Gates,
who was expected to be in the area by then. The Convention ordered
Clinton to try to rally the militia of northeast New Jersey, suppress
the Tories of that area, and cooperate with whatever Continentals
he found in an attack on the enemy's rear. When the Convention
heard Washington had also ordered Heath out of New York, the
members amended their orders. Clinton could take the New York
militia no farther from the Hudson than Haverstraw, in order to be
near the Highlands if needed. The Convention also begged Washington to leave Heath in the Highlands and instead allow the New
York militia to help northeast New Jersey.[66]

Heath, however, followed orders and crossed the Hudson in mid-
December with about five hundred Continentals. New York militiamen from the west side of the river began to assemble, and George
Clinton hurried across the river to join them. Heath then sent reconnaissance parties toward Hackensack, captured about fifty Loyalists, and tried unsuccessfully to attack a Tory regiment at
Hackensack Bridge. Washington wrote to Heath on December 16
that the British had stopped their advance southward, and Heath
therefore should return to the Highlands. On his way back, Heath
should again attack the British posts around Hackensack if possible.[67]

Clinton, who by then had twelve hundred New York militiamen,
joined Heath at Hackensack on December 16. Clinton ignored the
Convention's latest orders to stop at Haverstraw because he knew
the militia did not like to be called out and then told to stop and sit.
Heath and Clinton discovered that the enemy had fled Hackensack,
but that a large body of British troops was moving across the Hudson
River from the previously captured Fort Washington, and other enemy parties were marching up from the south. Clinton and Heath
retired to Paramus to cover the country and avoid this reportedly
strong enemy force. As he retreated, Clinton detached militia units
to guard several of the towns in nearby parts of New York and New
Jersey, and to apprehend Tories. Washington, hearing of Heath's

and Clinton's latest moves, reversed his orders and encouraged Heath to continue his efforts in New Jersey as long as possible, to prevent the British from extending their control over too much territory. He still firmly believed that the defection of many in New Jersey was due in part to the absence of an army in their midst to face the British. Heath's combined force of Continentals and New York militia was better than nothing, and might encourage the people of northeast New Jersey. Heath apparently agreed, though he had not received Washington's latest advice. On December 19, Heath ordered a raid by Clinton and Brigadier General Samuel Parsons with about five hundred men, half Continentals and the rest from Clinton's militia. Parsons and Clinton launched a surprise attack on a Tory regiment near Bergen Woods and captured twenty-three Tories while losing only one man killed.[68]

The New York Convention then informed Clinton that it approved of his deviation from its orders to stop at Haverstraw and left all future moves up to him. Clinton's scouting parties continued to hunt down Tories and skirmish with the enemy with some success. Heath finally received Washington's December 16 order to return to the Highlands, and was in Peekskill a week later. Clinton, who had about two thousand militia at this time, extended his posts to cover the ground left unprotected by Heath's withdrawal. Though worried that the British brigade near Newark and the three hundred enemy troops at Hackensack might cut off his advance regiments, Clinton maintained his forward positions to protect those who had recently returned to the American side and to harass the enemy, especially the growing number of Tories in the area. Despite the presence of British troops, however, he did not want to keep more militia soldiers in the field than necessary. He believed half of his force could be sent home because his original goals had been accomplished, and one thousand men were enough to defend the passes and inhabitants on the west side of the Hudson River. The Convention asked him to keep all of the men in the field a few days longer, in case the British suddenly attacked the passes, and then to dismiss half of the men if he believed it safe.[69]

While Heath and Clinton were harassing the enemy in northeast New Jersey and New York, the New Jersey militia began to reemerge elsewhere and resist the British. Local militiamen, commanded by

Colonel Jacob Ford, Jr., began to harass the enemy posts around Woodbridge. On December 11, Ford led a raid into that area and secured several hundred head of livestock. Ford's militiamen also captured Tory leaders and shot a British forage master. The next day, with his brigade scattered and British reinforcements on their way from Elizabethtown, Ford decided to reconcentrate his militia at Chatham and await help from Lee, who was in nearby Morristown. A few days later, however, Sullivan led Lee's division to the south, removing that possible source of support. Then another detachment from the Northern army, consisting of about 350 Continentals, neared Morristown. These men were not part of Gates's corps, which was marching through New Jersey farther to the west. As this Continental force approached, Brigadier General Alexander McDougall, who had been forced to leave Washington's army and remain in New Jersey due to poor health, received a plea from the local militia leaders and the citizens of Morristown to stop these Continentals and use them in New Jersey. The leaders of Morristown warned McDougall that if no Continentals supported their efforts, the militia would disband. Heath also believed that these new troops should be kept with the militia. McDougall agreed, and ordered the Continental soldiers to cooperate with Ford, who now had almost one thousand militia operating against the enemy at Springfield. Even with the support of this Continental detachment, Ford's force decreased to seven hundred men in a few days.[70]

Washington approved of McDougall's decision, and on December 21 sent Brigadier General William Maxwell of the Continental Army to take command of the combined force, with orders "to harass and annoy the enemy in their Quarters and cut off their Convoys." If the main body of the enemy left New Brunswick and moved south toward Trenton, Maxwell should attack their rear or at least annoy their march. Maxwell was to rally the local militia to his force and to prevent people from joining the enemy. McDougall was pleased with Washington's decision but still feared New Jersey was in trouble. Ford's numbers fell to about two hundred men by December 22, and McDougall and Ford retreated to Morristown to avoid being trapped by the vastly superior enemy forces in New Brunswick, Elizabethtown, and Newark. Calls went out for the militia to rally to this force. Despite their shrinking number of troops, McDougall and

Ford hoped to stay in the area until Washington could create a diversion in their favor.[71]

The New Jersey militia thus were returning to the fight. British detachments faced increasing resistance in the middle weeks of December as militia parties hovered around the British positions in New Jersey. A major cause for this resurgence of the local militiamen was outrage at the behavior of the occupying army. British and German troops committed so many depredations against the people of New Jersey that Washington later condemned the "infamous mercenary ravagers, whether British or Hessians." The British and German actions, ironically, were in part an angry reaction to the growing number of skirmishes between both armies' patrols and scouts. Thus, depredations and raids created more of both.[72]

These localized threats had weakened British control in the area, but Washington knew more had to be done, and he knew he had to use his army before it went home. He had about twenty-five hundred regulars with him in the days before Christmas, but he realized that by the end of the year, only fifteen hundred Continentals would remain. In addition, militia reinforcements continued to arrive, and detachments of Pennsylvania militia still raided into New Jersey, causing several skirmishes near Trenton between American patrols and the German troops stationed along the river.[73]

Besides the desire to use the army before it melted away, Washington understood the need to make a more dramatic strike in support of the people of New Jersey. Despite the growing resistance, the British occupiers were still gaining ground with many of the inhabitants. As late as December 22, British Commissioners for Restoring Peace in America concluded that many active rebels in New Jersey were taking the oath of allegiance to the Crown. The commissioners believed that much of New Jersey had submitted, and some in Pennsylvania also were taking the oath. Howe decided on December 20 that the submission of the people and the general desire for peace that had met the army called for a change in plans for 1777. An early capture of Philadelphia should, he believed, end the rebellion. Even in New York, the people were joining the British. The former royal governor of New York, William Tryon, had already recruited about eighteen hundred Loyalists to fight, and he believed all of the inhabitants of Long Island were ready for peace. Thus, the British plan was still working. Howe had created a feeling of superiority and strength with the British army by avoiding defeat, showing the weakness of the Continental Army, and slowly convincing the people to reconcile.[74]

Washington therefore had to make a move with the remnant of his army scattered roughly thirty miles along the south side of the Delaware. The twenty-five hundred Continentals held from Coryell's Ferry to a point across from Bordentown, New Jersey, and the Pennsylvania militia guarded from there to Bristol. Militia Colonel John Cadwalader commanded the Pennsylvania militiamen, most of whom were Philadelphia "Associators." He had perhaps one thousand of them, in addition to a regiment of Maryland and Pennsylvania Germans. Washington also could count on Brigadier General Philemon Dickinson and small detachments of New Jersey militia under his command. The New Jersey militia spent the ten days preceding Christmas searching the river valley for all the boats in the area. Washington clearly had not only defense on his mind but also possibly the need for boats to recross the river into New Jersey.[75]

As Washington neared a decision to reenter New Jersey, the skirmishing along the river bank increased. General Dickinson sent New Jersey militia patrols from behind the Delaware to scout into New Jersey for information on the enemy's positions, while farther south Pennsylvania militia detachments continued to enter New Jersey. Donop's German troops found themselves constantly engaging in brief clashes with these militia units. Dickinson at one point shelled his own home near Trenton when he found a German detachment occupying it. Yet despite the growing resistance along the river, the German commander in Trenton, Colonel Johann Rall, remained unconcerned. He did ask for reinforcements from General Grant to clear out these raiding parties, but Grant urged Rall not to worry. Grant, who was contemptuous of the rebels, believed he could maintain peace and order in New Jersey with a handful of troops.[76]

These skirmishes led Colonel von Donop to a critical decision just days before Washington crossed the Delaware. In the second week of December, Major General Israel Putnam, who commanded in Philadelphia, sent Colonel Samuel Griffith and five hundred to six hundred militiamen, mostly from New Jersey, on a raid toward Mount Holly, eighteen miles south of Trenton. Donop ordered two hundred men to find this raiding force, but the German troops re-treated in the face of Griffith's superior numbers. On December 22, Donop ordered another reconnaissance toward Mount Holly. Finally, he personally led a detachment of one British regiment and one Hessian battalion, two thousand men, from Bordentown toward Mount Holly and skirmished with the rebel militia on December 23. Griffith retreated after the brief clash. Donop's response to the militia's advance, however, had removed the reserve force from Bordentown and further dispersed the British army in New Jersey. Rall in Trenton now had no supporting forces nearby. As Captain Johann Ewald of the Hessian jägers wrote, Donop was "Led by the nose to Mount Holly . . . ." Though not part of a preconceived plan, Griffith's advance materially aided Washington's decision to attack Trenton.[77]

Washington thus made his well-known attack on Trenton at an opportune moment. The militia, especially of New Jersey, had struck at the British occupation, and now Washington brought the army back into the fight. The man who just two weeks earlier had com-plained that "no reliance" could be placed on the militia now used its operations to advantage. With British forces watching Heath, Clinton, Ford, McDougall, and Griffith, Washington employed the army and militia directly under his command to hit the isolated post of Trenton. These diversions, such as Griffith's, were not part of a preplanned strategy, but were part of Washington's overall policy for using the militia. In addition, Washington was an opportunist, al-ways a good trait in a general.

Washington's plan in late December envisioned a three-column assault across the Delaware River against the Hessian post at Tren-ton. Rall held that town with fourteen hundred troops; most of the supporting troops were either with Colonel von Donop at Mount Holly or at Princeton, twelve miles away. Washington and the re-mainder of the Continental Army, about twenty-four hundred regu-lars, crossed the Delaware River north of Trenton during the night of December 25–26 and marched against Trenton. In support of his move, Brigadier General James Ewing commanded a detachment of militia ordered to cross the river just to the south of Trenton and get behind the Hessian force in town. Farther down the Delaware, Colonel Cadwalader and about eighteen hundred Pennsylvania and Delaware

militiamen near Bristol had orders to cross into New Jersey and create a diversion to draw British attention away from Trenton. Ewing's
command, however, did not cross the river that night, and Cadwalader's men crossed but then returned to the Pennsylvania side. Washington made this move unsupported by the militia attached to the
army.[78]

Washington tried to encourage his men before this dangerous
operation by ordering a reading of the inspiring prose of Thomas
Paine, whose pamphlet *The Crisis* had been published in Philadelphia on December 23. Militiamen and Continentals responded to
the emotional plea to continue the fight and remain with the army
even past the end of their terms of enlistment. The Continentals
rose above the hardships of the night by crossing the river, though
no amount of inspirational rhetoric sufficed to get and keep the
militia across the river that night.[79]

On the road from the river crossing to Trenton, men in General
Sullivan's column found and routed a company of Hessian infantry
from the home of General Dickinson, who was still on duty across
the river in Pennsylvania. General Greene, meanwhile, marched his
column along a road to the north of Sullivan's route. Together, the
two columns hit Trenton a little before eight in the morning on
December 26, and the Continentals charged down the streets, yell-
ing Thomas Paine's inspirational line, "This is the time to try men's
souls." The battle was over in less than two hours. For the loss of four
killed and eight wounded, Washington's force killed Rall and about
twenty other Hessian soldiers, and captured over nine hundred enemy soldiers. Despite this stunning success, Washington quickly retreated his small army back to Pennsylvania that same day. Since no
other column had crossed to support him, he decided not to risk
too much.[80]

The supporting forces, however, soon began to move. General
Putnam, still in Philadelphia, sent seven hundred more militia on
December 26 to join the men who had operated near Mount Holly
with Colonel Griffith. This combined force totaled more than
fifteen hundred men. Washington asked Putnam to remain in New
Jersey and try to assemble the local militia. The next day, before
he learned that Washington had returned to Pennsylvania,
Cadwalader crossed fifteen hundred militiamen into New Jersey sev-

eral miles south of Trenton. Even after learning of Washington's retreat, he decided to stay in New Jersey and advance to Burlington
because he heard the enemy was retreating toward South Amboy.
Washington suggested to Cadwalader and Putnam that they delay
further operations until he recrossed the river and joined them with
the Continentals. He ordered the rest of the militia units that had
remained in Pennsylvania during the attack on Trenton to cross to
New Jersey. Washington planned to concentrate every man he could
in New Jersey.[81]

Cadwalader's information was correct. The British response to the
Trenton attack was an immediate retreat. Despite General Grant's
ridicule, Donop ordered the scattered garrisons to withdraw toward
South Amboy. This retreat not only encouraged Cadwalader's advance but also helped convince General Ewing to cross his militia
into New Jersey. By December 28, the British were concentrating
their separated detachments at Princeton.[82]

In order to distract the British further and create a diversion in
his favor, Washington urged a continuation of the attacks in northern New Jersey. His goal clearly was to drive the British out of New
Jersey completely, or at least limit their holdings to the coast. He
wrote to McDougall to use the combined force under his and
Maxwell's command to encourage the militia and harass the enemy
whether the British advanced or retreated. If nothing else, McDougall
and Maxwell should keep their force together and await the arrival
of Washington's army. Maxwell and McDougall called the militia of
the area to assemble January 1, and convinced their Continental
soldiers to stay two weeks longer. They then extended their outposts
and patrols toward the enemy and daily brought in British, German,
and Tory prisoners. McDougall informed Washington that the enemy soldiers did not venture far from their positions in the towns
along the coast. Unfortunately for Maxwell's and McDougall's plans,
the New Jersey government did not take an active role in these proceedings, and thus no one was coordinating the statewide effort to
muster the militia. The Continental generals and militia officers instead took control.[83]

Meanwhile, the concentration of American soldiers at Trenton
kept growing. To aid Washington's efforts, the Continental Congress
vested Washington with authority to take any steps necessary to handle

the current crisis. He could request any militia he needed from any state, requisition from the inhabitants whatever he needed if the local people refused to sell, and imprison anyone who was disloyal to the cause or who refused to accept Continental money in payment for what Washington had to take. He also had permission to do whatever was necessary to convince the soldiers with the army to stay in the field past the end of their enlistment, but Washington only tried to encourage, not force, the men to stay past the end of December. President John Hancock sent pleas to the governors, including Livingston and Trumbull, to cooperate fully with Washington's demands. The New Jersey government, however, had basically ceased to function by December 1776. Washington therefore issued his own address to the people of New Jersey for the militia to muster, and he sent militia colonels throughout the state to gather those militia who responded.[84]

Washington recrossed his Continentals into New Jersey, and by December 31 he had about twenty-two hundred men, mostly regulars, in Trenton, though the numbers continued to decrease rapidly. His personal appeal to the Continental soldiers to stay with him succeeded in convincing only about fourteen hundred men to remain. Washington forbade these troops to plunder the Tories and ordered them to have mercy on women and children. He hoped to avoid angering the inhabitants as the British army had. While Washington assembled and addressed his army at Trenton, Colonel Cadwalader massed a force of about thirty-five hundred men between Bordentown and Crosswicks. These men were mostly Pennsylvania militiamen, plus Philemon Dickinson's small New Jersey militia corps and a few New England Continentals. Cadwalader led this mixed command into Trenton on January 2. Including this recent augmentation, Washington had an army of about five thousand troops.[85]

While the American forces assembled at Trenton, the British concentrated at Princeton. Hearing of the growing rebel army at Trenton, General Grant advanced his main force from New Brunswick to Princeton, where General Cornwallis joined him and took command of the reinforced army of approximately eight thousand men. The British moved quickly to defeat the resurgent rebels because they understood how the American victory at Trenton would encourage the local militiamen to take up arms again. As George Inman of the

17th Regiment wrote, the rebels were "daily receiving from their late success large reinforcements." The leaders of both sides now realized how fragile was the British hold on New Jersey.[86]

On January 2, Cornwallis advanced south toward Trenton with roughly fifty-five hundred soldiers. Left behind were Lieutenant Colonel Charles Mawhood's brigade of about twelve hundred men at Princeton and Brigadier General Alexander Leslie's brigade of the same number at Maidenhead, about halfway between Princeton and Trenton. To slow the British march, Washington posted an advance force of about six hundred troops, mostly Continentals with a small party of New Jersey militia, just south of Maidenhead. Brigadier General Roche de Fermoy officially commanded, but he returned to Trenton and Colonel Edward Hand of the Pennsylvania riflemen took command. Cornwallis's force pushed Hand's men back, but twice Hand stubbornly slowed the British progress. At Shabbakonk Creek, Hand's corps made a stand for three hours with few or no casualties. Again in the northern outskirts of Trenton, Hand's men stopped the British for an hour. After a brisk clash in which about fifteen Americans were killed or wounded and about thirty British and Hessian troops were killed or wounded, Hand finally ordered his men across Assunpink Creek southeast of Trenton, where Washington's main army stood. The New Jersey militiamen were the last to cross the bridge.[87]

Washington learned of the British advance as Hand's detachment retired. From the American army's position behind Assunpink Creek, Washington watched the British and German troops occupy Trenton on January 2. Rather than stand and fight Cornwallis the next day, Washington used the night of January 2 to maneuver his Continentals and militiamen around the British left flank and along a back road to Princeton.[88]

Early in the morning of January 3, Washington's army of about five thousand soldiers ran into Lieutenant Colonel Mawhood, who was in the process of leading the 17th and 55th regiments out of Princeton to join Cornwallis. Mawhood's third regiment, the 40th, remained in Princeton. As his men neared Princeton, Washington detached Brigadier General Hugh Mercer with about 350 veterans of previous battles to take and guard a bridge on the main road south of town. Mawhood saw Mercer's movement and immediately led the 276 men of the 17th Regiment, which he had nearby, to attack. With this detachment, Mawhood routed Mercer's force and mortally wounded Mercer. About one hundred yards behind Mercer were Cadwalader's inexperienced militia, who fled in the face of the British cannons and charging infantry. Mawhood had scattered almost fifteen hundred men with his small band of soldiers.[89]

Hearing the firing, Washington raced back from Sullivan's column, which had marched ahead toward Princeton. Rhode Island and Virginia Continentals and Hand's Pennsylvania riflemen followed a short distance behind Washington to reinforce Mercer's battle. Not waiting for the support, Washington rallied the fleeing militia, who quickly re-formed, and personally led Cadwalader's men back toward the British. The opposing lines stood and fired volleys at each other until Sullivan's Continentals arrived, joined the militia, and forced the British to retire. Mawhood led the remainder of his troops off the field, across the bridge south of Princeton, and down the road to General Leslie's brigade at Maidenhead.[90]

While the brief but fierce battle raged just south of Princeton, Sullivan's weakened column of possibly six hundred men halted in front of part of the British 55th Regiment, situated on a hill in front of Princeton. When the men of the 55th heard of Mawhood's retreat, they withdrew into Princeton and joined the 40th Regiment. After only slight resistance, the British troops retreated to New Brunswick. Sullivan's men occupied Princeton without the loss of a man.[91]

The whole battle lasted only about forty-five minutes. South of town, the fighting cost Washington forty-four casualties. British losses were somewhere between Howe's admission of seventeen killed and two hundred wounded or missing, and Washington's claim of two hundred or more killed or wounded, and over three hundred captured. Whatever the actual numbers, Washington's army had taken Princeton behind Cornwallis's army and scattered Mawhood's brigade. In the words of an American parody of the day that mocked the British regulars, "some underpaid Doodles they cut us to crumbs."[92]

Cornwallis realized what Washington had done when he heard the cannon fire from the direction of Princeton and then received information from Leslie. He immediately set his army in motion up the road to Princeton, reincorporating Leslie's brigade as he passed through Maidenhead. The Americans, however, were several hours ahead of Cornwallis's troops, who were slowed by an American rearguard left at the bridge south of Trenton. In his anxiety to get to New Brunswick before Washington could attack it, Cornwallis hurried his men and left behind a number of broken-down wagons with two hundred soldiers to guard them. The next day, about twenty New Jersey militia cavalrymen surprised this British guard, who fled. The horsemen took the wagons to Washington.[93]

After his victory at Princeton, Washington considered attacking New Brunswick that same day, as Cornwallis feared, but due to the fatigue of his men, Washington instead led them toward the mountains near Morristown. Cornwallis continued the pursuit for a while, but then swung east and marched his troops into New Brunswick. The British concentrated their forces there and in Elizabethtown to await the enemy's next move.[94] Thus ended Washington's counteroffensive to rally the people of New Jersey and shatter the British stranglehold on the countryside.

The larger campaign, however, had not ended. The pair of victories in New Jersey encouraged the militia, and Washington heard that New Jersey militiamen were flocking to the army and taking the field on their own throughout the state. He admitted that the Pennsylvania militia, who had been with his army during the previous critical weeks, could do little more, but he wrote on January 5: "I must do them justice however to add, that they have undergone more fatigue and hardship than I expected Militia . . . would have done at this Inclement Season." In order to keep up the pressure in New Jersey, Washington ordered Putnam to move the force he had been assembling in Bordentown to Crosswicks, to watch the enemy in that area. He decided to shelter his army at Morristown rather than conduct further active operations, especially as the number of Pennsylvania militia decreased daily.[95]

Meanwhile, skirmishes between New Jersey militia, with the support of detachments of Continentals, and British and German troops increased. For a couple of weeks after Princeton, militia and Continental units of varying sizes engaged British and German forces in several clashes. On January 5, New Jersey militiamen attacked a British foraging party and inflicted four casualties. On January 6, Brigadier General Maxwell led about fifty New Jersey militia against a party of British and German troops near Elizabethtown, inflicting about ten casualties and taking forty prisoners. When a British captain of the Grenadiers traveling alone was killed on his way to join his company, General Howe described and defined both the death of this officer and his opinion of the partisans forming a ring around his army: "some lurking villains who murdered him in a most barbarous manner, which is a mode of war the enemy seem from several late instances to have adopted with a degree of barbarity that savages could not exceed." In the face of this growing resistance by the militia of New Jersey, the British patrolled the roads leading to New Brunswick daily, and even withdrew their garrison from Elizabethtown to concentrate all of their men in New Brunswick. General Maxwell, with a mixed force of Continentals and militia, fell on the rear guard of the enemy retreating from Elizabethtown and captured seventy men. By mid-January, the British forces were stationary at New Brunswick.[96]

As this partisan war spread through New Jersey, even Washington admitted that he had little control over most of the action. When General Cornwallis asked for safe passage through the state for the British wagons taking supplies and money to the Hessian prisoners, Washington replied that he would prevent any part of his army from interfering, "But cannot answer for the Militia who are resorting to Arms in most parts of this State, and exceedingly exasperated at the Treatment they have met with, from both Hessian and British Troops."[97]

While Washington and the militia attacked in central New Jersey, George Clinton continued to harass the British and Tory units on the west side of the Hudson in northeast New Jersey. Clinton urged the local militia of Orange County, New York, and northeast New Jersey to assemble, and pleaded with the men of his brigade to stay in the field past their time. Many left for home, however, and Clinton did not blame them. He tried to explain to General Heath, who was back in New York, that no matter how loyal the militiamen were, they would not remain in the field long if kept inactive. In addition, he was discouraged because the enemy had returned to Hackensack, despite his efforts to protect the place. As of the beginning of the new year, the enemy had in the area about six hundred regulars and Tories, who had plundered Hackensack and Paramus. Clinton was too weak to stop them, though he kept out large patrols every night to protect the country as much as possible. The New York Convention tried to help on January 1 by authorizing him to call out a further one thousand militia from Dutchess, Ulster, Orange, and Westchester counties.[98]

By January 4, the members of the New York Convention changed their minds. Now believing there was little more Clinton could do, they gave him permission to dismiss all but five hundred of his militia when he believed it best. Before he dismissed them, Clinton wanted to attack Hackensack one more time, but on January 5 the enemy retreated again in haste. He sent a party to collect any supplies and secure any Tories who were left behind, then released all but five hundred of his militia. He stationed the rest to guard the countryside.[99]

Washington initiated one final move against the British. He ordered Heath to advance from Peekskill toward New York City, to threaten the British stronghold and possibly force them to weaken their army in New Jersey. This was not a new idea. In December he had asked the governments of Connecticut and Massachusetts to direct their militia to Peekskill, to cooperate with Heath. In response, the Massachusetts legislature ordered six thousand militiamen to New York, and four battalions set out from Connecticut. The New York Convention, meanwhile, started preparations on its own for an expedition into Westchester County to protect the inhabitants and attack the British in New York, and called out the militia to support the division in the Peekskill area. When Heath left northeast New Jersey in late December to return to Peekskill, he informed Washington that he would cooperate with Major General Benjamin Lincoln, the Massachusetts militia commander. Heath's Connecticut militia brigade, however, had gone home. Washington urged him, if possible, to attack the enemy anyway.[100]

The Massachusetts militia started to arrive on January 4, and the New York militia began to rendezvous at North Castle. Washington's victory at Trenton, in particular, had inspired the people of New York and even New England. Washington again urged Heath and Lincoln to advance toward New York. If the enemy withdrew any men from New Jersey, Washington would try to take advantage of the weakness. After sending about two thousand of the Massachusetts militia to join Washington, Heath prepared to advance down the Hudson River. On January 8 he began to move slowly, and within ten days he had assembled all his forces, about three thousand militia, near the enemy's lines. He began to besiege Fort Independence, near Kingsbridge, on the same day, hoping a successful attack would encourage the militia to stay longer despite the bad weather.[101]

Howe did not respond to this threat, thus upsetting Washington's plans. Word of the arrival of the rebel militia on January 18 and the Americans' demand of surrender by the Hessians and British rangers defending the fort reached Howe quickly, but he was not worried. He knew the inclement weather would force an early halt to the operation, just as Heath feared. Howe considered trying to cut off the rebels but decided such a maneuver was impossible. Instead, he began to plan his campaign for the next summer.[102] Washington's grand plan to threaten both New York and New Jersey simultaneously had failed.

Before retreating, Heath's militia skirmished with the mostly German garrison of Fort Independence for several days, while American parties carried off quantities of forage from the area. On January 28, Heath and his generals decided they could not take the fort or the city because the enemy was too strong and the militia was not capable of an assault on the fortifications. In addition, they believed they could protect the inhabitants, control the Tories, and forage from a safer position farther back. Therefore, on January 29, Heath retreated from in front of the British lines and sent detachments of militia to Tarrytown, New Rochelle, and White Plains. When news of the withdrawal spread, the members of New York's Convention were not happy with Heath. Washington, too, was disappointed, especially since two days earlier he had sent a plea to Heath not to give up the operation, if at all possible. Washington believed that little had been accomplished, and that he could have used the militia force to better advantage in New Jersey.[103]

Despite Heath's failure to achieve any substantial results, the idea had been good, and once again the militia had responded to the crisis. In fact, throughout the weeks from mid-December until late January, more than twelve thousand militiamen from Delaware, Pennsylvania, New Jersey, New York, Connecticut, and Massachusetts, in particular, had responded to the crisis. About one thousand New Jersey militia had originally joined Ford and McDougall around Morristown, another two thousand New Yorkers had been with George Clinton and Heath in northeast New Jersey, two thousand Massachusetts militia had crossed the Hudson to join Washington in early January, three thousand more New England militia had formed Heath's advancing force against Fort Independence, and a mass of over thirty-five hundred Delaware, Pennsylvania, and New Jersey militia had joined Washington right after Trenton. In addition, a number of small militia units had sprung up and operated on their own along the British lines, and had skirmished with British and German detachments. Other militia forces garrisoned the forts in the Highlands, New York's Committee for Detecting Conspiracies had militia detachments hunting Tories, and Connecticut had militia guards in its coastal towns and along the New York–Connecticut border.[104]

Supporting this popular uprising, perhaps 3500 to 4000 Continentals remained in the field. Washington had had about 2400 Continentals on the Delaware River, McDougall about 350 around Morristown, and Heath about 800 in northeast New Jersey. Thus, in the midst of winter, perhaps 12,000 militia soldiers took up arms and fought alongside the remnant of the Continental Army to retrieve the situation in New Jersey, even while other militia defended parts of New York and Connecticut.

The militia clearly had a decided impact on American fortunes in 1776–77. The numbers that participated in the counteroffensive help explain how the Americans were able to force the British to evacuate much of their New Jersey conquest. Washington and his small band of Continentals were critical to the success of the operations, but so was the militia. Washington did not recover so much ground with three thousand Continentals huddled along the Delaware River; he did so with that army, the supporting militia of Delaware, Pennsylvania, and New Jersey, the militia forces in northern New Jersey, and those in New York on both sides of the Hudson River. With possibly sixteen thousand soldiers operating against the British on an arc from the Delaware River to Westchester County, the British retreat into a few fortified posts along the coast becomes more understandable.

The American reaction to this sudden reversal of fortunes between November and January was divided. The initial disaster in New Jersey brought forth more denunciations of the reliance on militia from both Washington and the Continental Congress, as its Executive Committee demonstrated in the following lament: "Pray Heaven that American States may never more be obliged to call Militia to the field. It is the most ruinous, destructive, expensive way of supporting a war that human invention can devise." Yet the militia of the states from Pennsylvania to New England, in particular, helped retrieve the situation, and Washington and Congress also recognized this. Washington had great praise for the Pennsylvania militia, and Congressman Richard H. Lee wrote: "America, without an army, is formidable in its militia. For sudden exertions, the Militia certainly do well, but they cannot bear the continued discipline of camps and campaigns." Governor Trumbull wrote in the midst of the retreat through New Jersey, "The Militia are certainly a respectable body of Men, but without constant imploy [*sic*], they will grow impatient . . . ."[105] The praise of the militia was now tempered by a recognition of the very real limitations of the state militia forces.

The British leaders, too, seemed to gain increased respect for the rebel militia forces, at least initially after the battles of Trenton and Princeton. William Howe and Henry Clinton, who were considered to be among the best of the British generals, saw their carefully executed strategy shattered by Washington and the militia. Howe's hopes of ending the rebellion by convincing the rebels that fighting was futile disappeared after this campaign. Instead, he explained to the home government on January 20 that the defeats in New Jersey were a greater setback than at first feared, and that the rebels had been greatly encouraged. Showing a clear understanding of how battles inspired or discouraged the local militiamen, Howe admitted that only defeating the enemy army would end the uprising.[106]

Equally aware of the dangers of these defeats was Lord George Germain, Secretary of State for the American Department, who was responsible for diplomacy as well as naval and military affairs for the West Indies and North America. In other words, he was responsible for running and winning the war against the rebel colonists. He wrote to General Howe that the victories in New Jersey would encourage the rebels to fight more, and therefore the army had to be on guard not to be surprised. In an interesting admission, he warned Howe that though the Americans were contemptible soldiers, they should not be taken too lightly: "For, as the same effects are often produced by dissimilar causes, that very pusillanimity which prevents them from facing you in the open field may occasionally operate like courage itself and instigate them to seek opportunities of attacking by surprise." If the colonists continued to resist, he advised, Howe might have to make them suffer seriously enough to convince them to return to their proper allegiance. Howe and Germain were beginning to think along the same lines: only a major defeat of the rebel forces would succeed.[107]

Others' opinions were mixed. Captain Ewald of the Hessian jäger forces also recognized the vast change wrought in New Jersey. Washington had been on the run and the war almost over, then four weeks later the British and German troops were on the defensive. "This great misfortune," he decided, would "surely cost the utter loss of the thirteen splendid provinces of the Crown of England . . . ." Lord Cornwallis, however, wrote to Germain that the damage done by Washington was mostly repaired in a few days. Loyalist newspapers even described Princeton as a British victory.[108]

One man definitely learned from this operation. George Washington's reputation improved dramatically after this campaign because Washington was not above learning and improving. His basic views on the proper use of the militia, as set forth during the first year of preparations, proved correct but partially irrelevant. His reluctance to use militia units to reinforce the Continental Army, and his desire to use militiamen exclusively for local defense, control of Tories, and harassing and raiding enemy detachments, sounded nice on paper, but without a large regular army, such niceties were impossible to execute. He did employ the militia for such separate duties, but he also used militiamen to strengthen the army, and again proved willing and even anxious to take offensive actions with the militia. Rather than relegate the militia to an unimportant secondary role, as his oft-stated opinions might have led him to do, Washington integrated the militia into his operations and put it to use.

The main lesson that this campaign taught Washington was painfully clear: unless the Continental Army was enlarged dramatically, it could not stop the British on its own. Neither could the militia prevent the British from moving almost at will and even occupying large areas. When the army and militia worked together, however, the British were ejected from most of the state and confined to the coast. Therefore, Washington realized that only in combination could the regular army and state irregulars effectively stop the British. This need to coordinate partisan activities, local militiamen, and his Continentals was the key, and would become the hallmark of Washington's strategy. He would not resort simply to a hit-and-run strategy, nor would he stand toe to toe with the British army. He clearly had abandoned the strategy of a war of posts, too. He would instead use a mix of regular operations and partisan warfare, hitting the British from many directions while keeping the main army ready to move in once the British were distracted or weakened. This partisan warfare had emerged somewhat on its own in New Jersey, with great success. His subordinates, most notably Nathanael Greene, would also learn this lesson from Washington's campaigns and use the same approach with great success in other theaters. Thus, the campaign in New Jersey provided a valuable education to Washington and Greene.

Altogether, Washington emerged from this first major campaign as a solid leader of a revolutionary war. He recognized the limitations of the citizen soldiers with whom he had to deal, and tried to use them where their strengths could be maximized. He managed to stay on good terms with the state governments despite his continued refusal to detach portions of the army for local defense. He also understood the need to encourage the people with the army, and to keep fighting. Perhaps most important of all, he understood the need to prevent the British from establishing undisputed control over large areas of territory. Washington had already proven himself to be a competent commander in chief and leader of a rebellion.

This campaign thus tested the decisions and plans of 1775–76, and overall the Americans' preparations withstood the test. Though setbacks occurred, the Americans followed the basic principles of their plans reasonably well, which helped them overcome the disasters and recover their fortunes. Most important, the militia showed its worth. Not only did militiamen perform their local duties for the states, but they kept the army in the field in New York, allowed the army to return to the field in late December, and helped keep the British contained in well-defended posts. In a very real way, their presence determined the fortunes of the campaign. When the militia failed, so did the Americans, and when it supported the war effort, the Americans were victorious.

CHAPTER FIVE

Partisan War Erupts,
January–May 1777

WINTER DID not mean the cessation of activity. Washington and Sir William Howe, knighted for his victories around New York City in August and September, both settled their armies into winter quarters in January 1777, but the fighting did not stop. In fact, the partisan war that had erupted in the final weeks of 1776 continued almost uninterrupted throughout the winter. The war had taken on a different character around New York, and the leaders of both sides had to adapt. Washington in particular had to learn to engage in such a war with a small regular army and the larger but unpredictable state militia forces.

After the battle of Princeton, Washington's strategy for the winter of 1777 was clear: he "would not suffer a man to stir beyond their Lines, nor suffer them to have the least Intercourse with the Country." He thus initiated a war of small detachments in New Jersey against enemy parties that emerged from their lines. To execute this harassment, he coordinated militia and Continental forces to attack exposed British posts and foraging parties, raid enemy supplies, and cut all communication between the enemy and the country. He urged Generals William Heath and Samuel Parsons to launch raids from Connecticut against enemy positions on Long Island, while he ordered out a series of small parties of Continentals and militia to sweep the area near the British lines. He hoped to collect all of the livestock and wagons, prevent the British from stockpiling supplies for the coming months, and thus delay the opening of the campaign in the spring. The parties collected most of the useful animals. Washington then established advance parties to watch for enemy movement. He summarized the goal of all of these steps to General Heath: "This would Oblige them to forage, with such large covering parties, that it would in a manner harass their Troops to death." Washington added that "by keeping four or five hundred Men far advanced, we not only oblige them to forage with parties of 1500 and 2000 to cover, but every now and then, give them a smart Brush."[1]

The Americans were successful in several of these engagements, but just as important to Washington, win or lose the British were taking casualties. The rejuvenated New Jersey militia forces, in particular, played an effective role in this partisan war on their own, as well as in conjunction with the Continental detachments that Washington sent forward. In late January, General Philemon Dickinson and four hundred militia soldiers plunged through an icy stream, attacked and defeated an equal number of enemy foragers near Somerset Courthouse, and captured nine prisoners, forty wagons, and about one hundred horses. On February 1, a foraging party of two thousand soldiers emerged from the enemy's lines near New Brunswick, and ran into a rebel foraging party of five hundred Continental light infantry under the command of Colonel Charles Scott and a party of two hundred militia. In the ensuing clash, the British ultimately retired after taking about one hundred casualties, while the Americans captured the British wagons and hay with the loss of twenty-four wounded and killed, at most. A few days later, a British foraging party ran into almost four hundred rebels and exchanged a few volleys before the American party retreated.[2]

The militia and Continentals became rather sophisticated in their methods of surprising enemy foragers. Parties would learn where the British tended to search for supplies, then arrive the night before an anticipated British raid. The rebels would hide through the night and surprise the foragers the next morning. Another ploy the Americans used involved disguising a few soldiers as local farmers, who then drove a herd of cattle near the British lines. Supporting infantry and cavalry units would hide nearby to ambush the British should they try to capture the herd. The first few times the Ameri-

cans tried this trick, the British ignored the bait, but as meat supplies dwindled in New York City, British and German troops finally
overcame their caution, came out to capture the herd, and fell into
the ambush.[3]

This fighting escalated throughout the winter. General Cornwallis
led a foraging party of 1,750 British and German troops on February
8. Near Quibbletown, they ran into American riflemen, who stubbornly resisted until British artillery forced them to retire. Both sides
continued to skirmish throughout the day until Cornwallis's party
returned to the British lines. In mid-February, a British party of about
sixteen hundred soldiers, commanded by Colonel Charles Mawhood,
tried to surround a rebel party within ten miles of Amboy. The British split their forces and engaged the rebels in a patch of woods.
The Scottish officer Sir James Murray described it thus: "The fire
was prodigiously heavy at one time but p[er] favour of some pretty
large trees, which by a good deal of practise we have learnt to make
a proper use of, my Company suffered very little." The rebels retreated with little loss, then as the British returned toward Amboy,
the Americans tried to surround them. The firing continued on all
sides during the entire march back to the British lines. On February
18, a party of 250 New Jersey militia joined fifty Pennsylvania militia
to attack a Tory regiment about three and a half miles south of New
Brunswick. They surprised the Tories, captured about sixty of them,
killed four, and wounded one. The New Jersey militia lost one man
killed.[4]

Pennsylvania militiamen increasingly joined the New Jersey militia and the Continentals in this growing melee in New Jersey. Major
General Israel Putnam sent a party of five hundred Pennsylvania
militia into Monmouth County to secure a pile of provisions collected there by local Tories, and the advance guards skirmished with
the Tories. Putnam also sent Pennsylvania riflemen to the coast near
New Brunswick to snipe at passing boats, which they did with some
effect, and he kept out patrols within sight of the enemy's sentries.
Brigadier General William Maxwell issued standing orders to the
militiamen under his command to assemble each morning on the
road to Woodbridge. On February 18, he took a party of 120 militia
and was marching down that road toward the British lines when he
spotted about 500 enemy on the same road. He concealed his force

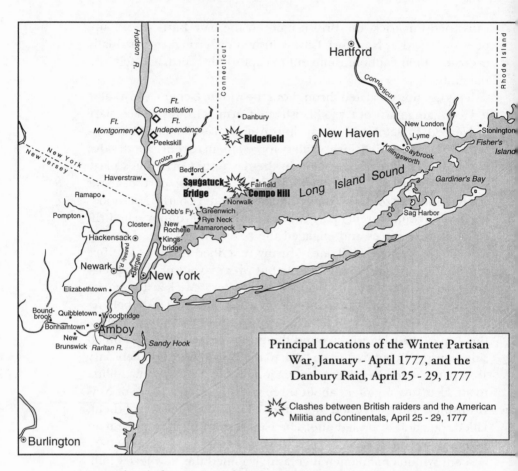

Principal Locations of the Winter Partisan
War, January - April 1777, and the
Danbury Raid, April 25 - 29, 1777

Clashes between British raiders and the American
Militia and Continentals, April 25 - 29, 1777

to await reinforcements, but the opposing force marched off toward
Amboy. An enemy foraging party of about twenty-five hundred men
came out in late February; Maxwell concentrated the nearby American troops, attacked the British, inflicted nine casualties, and forced
them to retire to Amboy. Maxwell lost five men. Meanwhile,
Dickinson established a continuous line of sentry posts along the
enemy's front. In late February, soldiers from Lord Stirling's division forced in enemy foragers who had emerged from the British
lines near the coast.[5]

Into the spring this constant skirmishing raged. The British
needed supplies, and so continued to send out foraging parties of
several hundred men or more. On April 12, General Cornwallis led

a large party of British and German troops to surprise five hundred rebels commanded by Generals Benjamin Lincoln and Anthony Wayne near Boundbrook. Cornwallis's force struck suddenly that night, and as Captain Johann Ewald of the Hessian troops described the impact on the Americans: "The guard was partly cut down and partly captured, the three cannon seized, and the two generals fled without their breeches." For the loss of seven men wounded, Cornwallis captured about forty rebels. After Cornwallis's detachment left, however, Lincoln's troops resumed their former position. Ewald admitted that the surprise scared the rebels for a few days only, after which the harassment resumed. On May 10, Major General Adam Stephen launched his division of fifteen hundred Continentals and militia against three British regiments near Bonhamtown. In the ensuing skirmish the Americans inflicted possibly seventy casualties on the British while suffering only half as many losses.[6]

While this skirmishing spread, Washington ordered out patrols of combined forces to gather information. In particular, he employed General Philemon Dickinson's New Jersey militia along the British lines to detect any movement by the enemy and to send that information back to Major General Nathanael Greene, who was nearby with his Continental division. In this way Washington used the militia as scouts as well as part of a forward defense to shield the main army, which was still in camp near Morristown.[7]

Overall, Washington was pleased with the results of this winter war. He watched with pleasure as the size of enemy foraging parties in New Jersey increased, and in mid-April, he admitted that even though his forces had consisted mostly of militiamen throughout the winter, they and the few remaining Continentals had harassed the enemy exceedingly well. Washington conducted what he believed was a successful partisan war with the combined forces of the Continentals and militia.[8]

While the partisan war raged unabated in New Jersey, New York became the arena of a similar war. The Hudson River was a natural corridor for the British to utilize when they wanted to run raids into rebel territory. The Highlands region, in particular, remained an area of particular concern for the American rebels. Brigadier General Alexander McDougall took command in the Highlands in February 1777, when General William Heath left for Massachusetts. He quickly learned that the river valley would be a scene of partisan activities similar to what he had witnessed in New Jersey in late 1776. McDougall's main duties were to prevent the British from landing along the river and collecting supplies, and to protect the supply magazine created at Peekskill. Total defenders for the Highlands in early February were six hundred Massachusetts militia, a New Hampshire regiment, and four small Continental regiments that contained only six hundred men. Worse yet, many of the militiamen would leave on March 1. George Clinton's brother James remained with McDougall and used his own considerable influence over the local people to persuade about one hundred of the New York militia to stay after March 1.[9]

Still, the number of defenders kept declining after March 1, and McDougall feared a sudden attack by boat against the post at Peekskill. After sending two of his weak Continental regiments to strengthen the garrisons of Forts Constitution and Montgomery on the Hudson, he had only two small Continental regiments to defend Peekskill. George Clinton, who retained command of the militia along the rivers, called out the local militiamen to join McDougall, but few responded and Clinton preferred not to force them out with the busy spring farming season approaching. Only about one hundred militia soldiers defended along the west side of the river.[10]

In mid-March, General Sir William Howe decided to take advantage of the rebel weakness along the river and ordered a raid to destroy the magazine at Peekskill, which was only about forty miles upriver from New York City. He sent about five hundred soldiers, and they landed on March 23 near Peekskill. With only 220 men from two Continental regiments in town that day, McDougall retreated after destroying as large a portion of the supplies as possible. The British burned the rest. McDougall wanted to fight but feared that if the British destroyed his small detachment, the forts north of him would be exposed. As long as his small Continental force was in the field, he reasoned, he could contest an advance on the forts and be a rallying point for the militia. He had learned from the New Jersey campaign and instead protected his men, and ordered the militia to reinforce Fort Constitution. The other two Continental regiments already sent up the river garrisoned Fort Montgomery. On March 24, McDougall sent out parties to skirmish with the British advance guard. The American soldiers hit the British from two sides, inflicting fifteen casualties while taking only seven, and the British retreated to the main body of troops. Washington approved of McDougall's conduct.[11]

While McDougall retreated and skirmished, George Clinton tried unsuccessfully to assemble the militia to defend Forts Montgomery and Constitution. He ordered three militia regiments to reinforce the forts, and parts of two other regiments to reinforce the guards along the western shore of the river. He personally went to Fort Montgomery on March 24. He also urged the local militia officers along the western shore to attack the enemy's rear if the enemy made a move toward the forts. The militiamen along the western shore, however, responded slowly. They preferred to stay home and protect their own property. Fortunately for George Clinton and the rebel defenders, the British raiding party instead returned to New York on March 25 after destroying Peekskill.[12]

Another exposed part of New York was Westchester County, which became known as the "Neutral Ground." The southern part of this county became the battleground for Whig and Tory militia, thieves who had no loyalty to either side, and soldiers from both armies. By May 1777, no one was safe in Westchester. Not only was the county situated between the lines of the two armies, but it also produced many Loyalist units, including a Tory cavalry unit that William Tryon raised and James DeLancey commanded. These "Cowboys," as the Tories were known, collected supplies and deserters from the British ranks and clashed often with local Whig forces.[13]

The objectives of the American defenders in Westchester County were to collect forage, prevent the British from gathering supplies, and skirmish with the enemy troops. General William Heath was in command of the defense of New York along the river and in Westchester until he left for Massachusetts in February. After his retreat from Fort Independence near Kingsbridge in late January, he established a line of posts from Dobb's Ferry on the Hudson to Mamaroneck on Long Island Sound. In addition, he tried to coordinate his patrols with General Wooster's Connecticut militiamen who were in New York near the Connecticut border. He even considered a surprise attack on Fort Independence in early February, but agreed with the Massachusetts militia commander, Benjamin Lincoln, that such a maneuver was too risky. Instead, he relied on the militia of New York and Connecticut to guard Westchester and harass enemy foragers and scouts.[14]

His trust proved well placed, as about nine hundred New York militia remained along the lines in late February despite the cold weather. Wooster, who had taken a position at New Rochelle after his participation in Heath's move against Fort Independence, had 882 Connecticut and 87 New York militiamen on February 17. The British, on the other hand, had 1400 men at Kingsbridge and Fort Independence. Wooster, who tried to prevent foraging by the British and Tories in the area, retreated on February 24 to Rye Neck. From Rye Neck he continued to send patrols to stop the enemy's foraging until his men's enlistments ended March 15. By that date, most of the Connecticut and New York militia had gone home, and only 160 New York militiamen maintained a post in the beleaguered county. Enemy foragers regularly gathered provisions from the area. William Duer of the New York Convention requested, but did not expect, more help from Wooster, who had no men left, and from General McDougall, the new Continental commander in New York. Duer meanwhile organized the local Westchester militia into ranger companies under the command of officers who knew the ground. Washington and the other Convention members urged Duer to remove or even destroy the forage and livestock. Washington also urged Wooster to return to New Rochelle when he had more men.[15]

McDougall sent a few of his Continentals to Westchester before the March 23 raid on Peekskill, and the Convention ordered more militia into the area, but these efforts proved insufficient. As of April, the organized force defending the county consisted of 140 men, despite the fact that the county militia totaled about 1400. The Tories and British foragers thus had an almost free hand, and they collected horses and other livestock daily. George Clinton ordered one-fourth of Westchester's militia to assemble in April, but as of April 21, no one had responded to this latest call. McDougall hoped the Convention would take further steps.[16]

The partisan activities that erupted in New Jersey and spread to New York also flared in Connecticut, especially along the Sound. Brigadier General Samuel H. Parsons, stationed in Lyme, was in charge of recruiting for the Continental Army in that area. While stationed along the Sound, he decided to use the new volunteers, as well as Colonel Henry Livingston's Continental regiment still in Connecticut, to raid Long Island and seize Tories and British supplies. He suggested a larger raid of eight hundred to one thousand men to capture the enemy's guards, an idea that Washington liked and that the Connecticut government said it would support and enlarge with about three thousand militia. Washington, however, called off the planned expedition in late March because the enemy was too strongly positioned on the island. As late as May 23, however, Colonel Return Jonathan Meigs led a party of volunteers and Continentals across the Sound and raided Sag Harbor. Striking Lieutenant Colonel Stephen DeLancey's Tory battalion, which was foraging on the eastern end of Long Island, Meigs and his men killed six and captured ninety men, and burned the Tories' boats and forage. Meigs returned to Connecticut without the loss of a man after traveling over ninety miles in twenty-five hours.[17]

As the winter gave way to early spring, a new threat began to appear off the coast of Connecticut. British naval forces, which had been present in the Sound at times during 1775 and 1776, became more aggressive. Small militia detachments already garrisoned many of the port towns along the coast, but when British ships hovered off Fairfield throughout March, the local militia commander, Brigadier General Gold S. Silliman, called in several hundred militia to guard the town. Fairfield's leaders warned Governor Jonathan Trumbull that without more aid, the town might have to be evacuated. Trumbull's only advice was for them to complete their Continental quota, in the hope that he could then get permission to station more Continental soldiers on the coast. Meanwhile, other ships threatened New London. When rumors spread in early April that the British were going to raid Danbury to destroy the supply magazine there, the state government ordered General Silliman to assemble his militia brigade to defend the area.[18]

Speculation grew throughout April that Danbury would be the target of a large British raid. Washington even suggested that Parsons concentrate the new Continental recruits in Danbury while they awaited their time to move to Peekskill. This concern was well founded because, unbeknownst to the Americans, General Howe had received advice from Secretary of State George Germain that the king wanted diversions on the New England coast to slow Continental recruiting, to stop rebel privateers, and to pin down troops in these provinces. At the same time, rebel fears of another raid up the Hudson River increased, and then seemed confirmed, when several British transports and ships anchored off Dobb's Ferry around April 25.[19]

Speculation ended on Friday, April 25, when former Governor William Tryon and eighteen hundred British troops with six cannon landed without opposition at Compo Hill, about eight miles west of Fairfield and four miles east of Norwalk. The British marched seven miles inland that night, still without opposition. Saturday morning, April 26, they met little resistance during their twenty-two-mile march to Danbury. Colonel Jedediah Huntington, the Continental commander in Danbury, had only fifty Continental soldiers with him when the British arrived, and therefore he retreated to some hills north of town. Tryon's men entered the town, but when he learned that the militia was assembling, Tryon ordered the supplies and some houses burned. Huntington's numbers, meanwhile, increased to about two hundred Continentals and a few militiamen, but this force was still too small to bother the enemy party in town.[20]

So far, the British had met no opposition, but the rebels were preparing to fight. General Wooster, who was in the area, hurriedly assembled a small party of local militia, a few Continentals, and some convalescent soldiers. General Silliman began collecting a similar force. Meanwhile, Brigadier General Benedict Arnold had been in New Haven, brooding over his lack of promotions and considering a resignation. When he heard of the raid on Danbury, he quickly raced northward and joined Silliman and Wooster. The three men, with a force of about one hundred Continentals and possibly six hundred Connecticut militia, arrived at Bethel, four miles from Danbury, at 2 A.M. on April 27. Heavy rains and the fatigue of a thirty-mile march that day prevented an immediate attack on the British still in Danbury. Later that morning, Sunday, April 27, the Americans divided their command. Arnold with Silliman's detachment of about four hundred men blocked one road from Danbury to the coast, and Wooster with two hundred troops took a position on the other road to the coast. Tryon, however, left Danbury on April 27, along the road to Ridgefield, and bypassed the two roads the rebels were guarding. Arnold and Wooster began to follow Tryon's troops, who moved slowly because they took along a herd of captured sheep and cattle.[21]

Arnold's men, moving faster than the encumbered enemy column, slipped ahead of the British and reached Ridgefield first. Another one hundred local militiamen joined Arnold during the day, and with these five hundred men, he quickly threw up entrenchments across the road. Meanwhile, Wooster's militia troops followed the British closely and opened a running fight that lasted to within a few miles of Ridgefield. Tryon's raiding party then ran into Arnold's barricade in the afternoon of April 27. During the confused fighting around Ridgefield, Wooster's men were closing in on the British rear when Wooster received a mortal wound and his militia fled. Tryon, however, still had to deal with Arnold. British and American lines exchanged volleys in a heated firefight that lasted about an hour. At one point, Arnold's horse was shot out from under him within a few yards of the British troops, but he slipped free of the fallen horse, shot an advancing enemy soldier with his pistol, and escaped. Ultimately, Tryon forced his way through the rebel line and Arnold's men retreated. The British camped in Ridgefield overnight.[22]

Despite the setback, the local militiamen continued to rally to Arnold as he retreated toward Norwalk. Meanwhile, Governor Trumbull, who had no other Continentals in the state to order to the area, ordered all the militia west of the Connecticut River to join Arnold, even though this left the coast "naked, and greatly exposed . . . ." Before being wounded, Wooster had sent orders to the militia of the immediate area to assemble at the Saugatuck Bridge over the river between Fairfield and Norwalk. Hopes that General McDougall would march to the area from Peekskill went unrealized as he spent April 27 frozen in place by the British ships moving up the Hudson River.[23]

The British resumed their march to the coast on Monday, April 28. Throughout the morning, the raiding party met small detachments of militiamen disputing every good defensive spot along the road, while other locals fired at the British from houses and behind walls. In addition, militia parties and Huntington's Continentals from Danbury hovered near the rear of the British column. Meanwhile,

Arnold collected the militia still arriving and prepared to make another stand in front of Saugatuck Bridge, while Silliman tried to rally the militia that had been scattered by the defeat the day before. At 11 A.M., the British ran into Arnold's force, which now numbered about seven hundred, making its stand in front of the bridge. The Americans fired a few rounds from a cannon, but a Tory guide led Tryon's men to a ford north of Arnold's position and the British slipped across the river. Local militiamen kept pouring in, and Huntington's Continentals and the militia that had been following the British also joined Arnold's force, which reached somewhere between twenty-five hundred and four thousand men during the day. Arnold led his growing detachment across the river in pursuit of the British. An enemy rear guard retreated upon the American approach, and the main body of British troops formed on Compo Hill, near the landing place and under cover of the guns from the British ships. Arnold engaged Tryon's men in a brisk skirmish, while the British began to embark their plunder and their troops. Arnold frantically tried to persuade the militiamen to attack up the hill, but most of them retreated when fired on by the British cannons. A British bayonet charge finally scattered the Americans, and the last enemy troops embarked and sailed east at sunset.[24]

McDougall, meanwhile, decided on Monday, April 28, that the British ships in the river were not launching a raid. He therefore marched with twelve hundred men toward Bedford, hoping to intercept the British if they moved toward the Hudson River from Ridgefield. On Tuesday, McDougall's detachment reached Bedford, where he learned that the enemy had returned to the coast on the Sound. Since he could not catch the raiders at that point, he decided not to risk Peekskill further and instead returned there. Washington approved of his conduct.[25]

Losses during the Danbury raid were not ascertained, but the Americans estimated theirs at about thirty killed and seventy wounded. They claimed to have buried thirty British dead, and to have captured forty to fifty. Washington personally believed the British loss was much greater, possibly 60 killed and 120 wounded. Both Arnold and Wooster, who died of his wound, received much praise for their efforts with the militia, and the Continental Congress promoted Arnold to major general. The Connecticut militia did not receive as much praise. Arnold criticized the militiamen's retreats at Ridgefield and during the attack on Compo Hill, and Massachusetts Congressman John Adams was unimpressed by the militia's resistance:

> We have a fine Piece of News this Morning of the March of 2000 of the Enemy, and destroying a fine Magazine there— and the stupid sordid cowardly torified Country People let them pass without Opposition.
>
> All New England is petrified, with Astonishment, Horror, and Despair, I believe in my Conscience. They behave worse than any Part of the Continent. Even in N. Jersey 2000 Men could not have marched so far.

Washington at least believed that the British had been punished enough to make them hesitate before trying such a raid into the interior again. The British, of course, estimated their losses differently, and Howe did not even mention in his official report how many were lost in the raid.[26]

The raid on Danbury, however, brought into question Washington's steadfast belief that the militia were adequate to the defensive needs of the states. The response of the Connecticut militia units demonstrated both the strengths and the weaknesses inherent in such a system. Within two days the British landed, marched over twenty miles inland without opposition, and burned the supplies in Danbury. Then the militia forces began to converge on the area and contest the British return to their ships, but the British still withdrew without serious loss. On the other hand, that possibly four thousand militiamen assembled within four days demonstrated what a local militia could do if given enough time. Even Howe admitted that Tryon received "intelligence that the whole force of the country was collecting," and therefore had to burn the supplies rather than take them with him.[27] Thus, Washington's reliance on the local militia to defend the coasts proved insufficient, though the presence of the militia and a few Continentals at least prevented anything worse from happening.

On the other hand, Washington's acceptance, and even encouragement, of a partisan war using those same militia proved effective through the winter and spring. As the Whig civilian observer Mercy Otis Warren observed, perhaps "these smaller depredations and inconsiderable skirmishes, served only to keep the spirits in play, and preserve the mind from the lethargic state, which inaction or want of object creates." Still, the war became a brutal, deadly affair. The constant raids and skirmishes, and the need for the British commanders to send out ever larger foraging parties, played against Howe's desire to avoid casualties. In fact, Hessian Captain Johann Ewald praised the New Jersey militia by admitting in February that "Since the army would have been gradually destroyed through this foraging, from here on the forage was procured from New York." Scottish officer James Murray described the British and German frustration with the constant sniping and ambushes:

> We have a pretty amusement known by the name of foraging or fighting for our daily bread. As the rascals are skulking about the whole country, it is impossible to move with any degree of safety without a pretty large escort, and even then you are exposed to a dirty kind of *tiraillerie*, which is more noisy indeed than dangerous . . . .

Murray added that this skirmishing was still "a little troublesome," and that he could not travel along the coast road unless accompanied by a detachment of troops. No one was safe outside of the British lines.[28]

The British and Germans noted an even worse effect. Instead of spending the winter resting in quarters, the soldiers were on duty most of the time. German journals noted how the soldiers along the lines went to bed fully dressed because the rebels attacked so often and kept the outposts constantly alert. The adjutant general of the Hessian forces, Major Baurmeister, admitted that the rebels had "been harassing our quarters from all sides in spite of their continual losses. While our loss has been negligible, the troops have been much fatigued." George Inman, a member of the British garrison in Amboy through the winter, described life in Amboy as "irksome and unpleasant Quarters, being out almost every day, wch harrass'd the Garrison much." This fatigue also turned to anger as the tired British and German soldiers grew bitter toward the rebels.[29]

The British high command worried about the lasting effects of this winter war. Sir William Howe grew pessimistic as the casualties increased, and he began to urge more Tories to enlist in the Tory units attached to the army. He even had to bring men and supplies from Rhode Island to New York because the rebel war against the foragers was so effective. Secretary of State Germain was equally depressed by the news that Howe sent throughout the winter. In April, on the eve of the next campaigning season, Germain expressed concern for the troops because not only had they been unable to rest from the previous summer and fall operations, but they would not be able to recover from the winter's exertions before the summer arrived.[30]

The rebel leadership, however, knew that despite the effects of this partisan war, they had to plan for the summer campaign, when the British would initiate large-scale operations once again. Washington and the state political leaders did not believe partisan activities alone would stop future British efforts, and therefore the political and military leadership at the state and national levels made preparations for a renewal of the regular war as well.

The Connecticut government had efficiently supported the war effort during the 1776 campaign, and therefore faced few legislative problems. The major concern in Connecticut throughout the winter was how to enlist the required Continentals. The Danbury raid, however, created consternation in Connecticut over the safety of its coast, and an enemy raid from New York into southwestern Connecticut in early May increased this concern. The governor and the Council of Safety ordered more militia guards into the port towns and decided that two battalions of 728 volunteers each be raised to serve until the end of the year, to guard the coast and southwestern frontier. "His Excellency," as the Connecticut legislature decided to title the governor, empowered the militia generals and other officers to assemble their militia units to resist any invasion without waiting for orders from superior officers or the government. A sense of impending doom hung over the state as Governor Trumbull told the Assembly that Connecticut was surrounded by threats.[31]

Reacting to this feeling of danger, Trumbull reminded the Continental Congress that it had given him permission the previous December to keep two Continental regiments in the state. He wanted the Continentals to help guard the coast and relieve the militia from the constant guard duty, and he wanted a detachment of four hundred Continentals to guard Greenwich. Trumbull feared, correctly, that the British raids were part of an attempt to create a panic in Connecticut, interfere with efforts to raise soldiers for the regular army, and prevent the Connecticut government from sending its own men into neighboring states. General Parsons meanwhile ordered the Continental troops already raised in Connecticut to New Haven and Danbury, where they could guard western Connecticut and still be close to Peekskill if needed.[32]

New York's Whig leaders faced a more difficult task in preparing for the summer campaign. Since the Whigs had not yet organized a new government, and therefore had no executive, the New York Convention continued to rely on its militia generals in the field. George Clinton, in particular, remained the primary commander of militia in the New York City area, retaining his command of the militia of Westchester, Dutchess, Ulster, and Orange counties. In addition, he was in charge of the effort to obstruct the Hudson River in the Highlands. In late March, the Convention empowered him to call out any or all of the militia of those four counties to defend against invasion and to reinforce the Highlands and the posts west of the Hudson. At the same time, the Continental Congress appointed him a brigadier general in the army and officially gave him command of the Highland defenses. Clinton believed too much was asked of him and the few militiamen in the field, and half seriously contemplated resigning his command and serving as a private in the militia. He did try to resign as a major general of the militia in May, but the Convention depended on him and refused to accept his resignation.[33]

When Clinton did not receive the full cooperation from the county authorities, he let the Convention know it. The leaders of one town even had the nerve to ask the Convention if they should obey his orders. In addition, by late April, only one-fourth of the men he had called had actually assembled. The problem, Clinton informed the Convention, was that the local militia officers did not exert themselves to muster their men. He urged the Convention to devise a better way to enforce calls to raise the militia, because the threat of court martial for delinquent officers was not sufficient. The Convention members made no immediate response to these problems.[34]

The British raid against Peekskill in March did galvanize the militia for a brief time, and militia reinforcements began to converge on the Highlands immediately after the raid. George Clinton used the authority granted him by the Convention to order out one-third of the militia of Ulster and Orange counties, which would number twelve hundred men if all responded. In addition, he ordered eight hundred militia from Dutchess County to the Highland forts. As usual, however, a much smaller total of militia ultimately assembled. By the third week of April, not one man of the eight hundred ordered from Dutchess County had arrived. On the west side, a greater proportion of militia turned out in Ulster and Orange counties, though some companies did not send a man.[35] Despite his new authority from the state Convention and Continental Congress, Clinton could not mobilize the militia with any degree of certainty.

Orange County defenders needed to guard against not only raids along the river but also the enemy posts in northeast New Jersey and on the west bank of the Hudson south of the Highlands. As early as February, George Clinton ordered out five hundred militia of Ulster and Orange counties to secure the post at Sydman's Bridge on the west side of the Hudson River near the New Jersey border, and to garrison the more forward posts of Hackensack and Closter in New Jersey. Clinton appointed Colonel Levi Pawling to command this force. These militiamen were to protect the friendly inhabitants, suppress the growing number of local Tories, and annoy the enemy posts as much as possible. Washington then ordered Clinton to extend his coverage of New Jersey, and in late February, despite the fact that only about 350 men had assembled, Clinton ordered Pawling to extend his posts west to the Passaic River. When accomplished, these extended lines formed a chain of posts from the Hudson River across northeast New Jersey. Such a line helped prevent British sympathizers in Passaic from sending provisions to the enemy. Upon Clinton's request, the Convention attached a detachment of rangers to Pawling's regiment.[36]

Clinton then warned the Convention that Pawling's men were enlisted only until April 1, when the approaches to Orange County would be left undefended. During the British raid on Peekskill, Pawling's small force retreated to Ramapo to prevent the enemy from landing behind it. On March 31, Clinton ordered 500 militia to replace Pawling's men, but the militiamen were reluctant to leave their homes undefended, and by April 18, only 365 had arrived at Ramapo.[37]

While guarding against attack by the British army, the Whigs also strove to protect themselves from internal threats posed by the Loyalists. Colonel Pawling used his militia to arrest men working for the enemy, and the Committee for Detecting Conspiracies commanded a company of rangers to thwart real and suspected dangers. When several armed men on their way to the enemy were captured, Clinton urged that a severe example be made of them. He believed that many militiamen who stayed home when called did so due to fear of these armed Tories roaming the countryside. After Clinton received a report of British recruiters enlisting New Yorkers to join the British, he quickly sent a militia detachment to apprehend them, with orders to kill anyone who tried to escape. In early April, parts of two Orange County militia companies marching to Sydman's Bridge stopped and helped capture a large group of Tories. Clinton, busy scouring the country around Fort Montgomery for Tories, approved of the militia officers' initiative. On April 21, the state Convention issued to each county committee a recommendation to exert itself to apprehend all dangerous persons.[38]

The hunt for Tories continued into May. Brigadier General Alexander McDougall sent men disguised as Tories to search for enemy recruiters in the Highlands, and George Clinton had militia parties out hunting down a force, estimated at over 150 Tories, armed and marching to New York City. Several were ultimately captured. As Clinton feared, the Loyalist threat was strong enough on the west side of the river that some Whig militiamen were afraid to muster for fear of Tory spies among them. The state Convention authorized the county committees of Orange and Ulster to detect and stop Tory insurrections and to call on the local militia when necessary. As Tories continued their raids from New Jersey into New York, New York Whig militia parties went into northeast New Jersey to hunt down Tory bands.[39]

As the campaigning season neared in late April, efforts to muster more men heightened. To encourage the militia, George Clinton decided that he or his brother James should be personally stationed in the Highlands on the west side of the Hudson. He also ordered out an additional five hundred militia from Orange County to guard the passes in the western Highlands. He sent orders to the militia officers of Orange and Ulster counties to prepare to march on a moment's notice. The Convention ordered the creation of two longer-term militia regiments to serve in the Highlands, and George Clinton hoped these units would make further calls on the local militia unnecessary. Westchester County also needed help because the few militiamen in the field could not maintain a line across the entire county in front of the enemy. Tories therefore plundered nightly and forced the American militia to stay on watch every night.[40]

Despite these efforts by New York's leaders, when General Putnam arrived at Peekskill to take command of the Highlands in late May, the number of soldiers in the area was small. Putnam estimated his force at 2000 men, mostly militia, with an additional 200 men garrisoning Fort Constitution and Fort Independence near Peekskill (not to be confused with the British-held Fort Independence near Kingsbridge), and 740 in Fort Montgomery. This was not a strong force, especially since most of the men were local militiamen.[41]

The Whigs in New Jersey faced a political crisis as well as a military threat. New Jersey's government had to resume functioning after the disaster of the previous campaign, and Governor William Livingston was determined to correct the problems that had led to the government's collapse. On January 24, Livingston informed the New Jersey Assembly that the British had taken advantage of the defects in the New Jersey militia laws, and now those defects had to be removed. Agreeing with this criticism, Washington argued that if the laws remained untouched, New Jersey's government would be of little use in the coming campaign. Both men urged the state legislature to stop relying on monetary fines to convince men to serve. Washington bluntly wrote: "We want Men, and not Money." The Assembly began consideration of new militia laws, but one month later, in early March, Livingston's confidence in the Assembly's ability to correct the problem was not strong:

Our Assembly, after having spent as much time framing a Militia Bill, as Alexander would have required to subdue Persia, will at last make such a ridiculous Business of it, as not to oblige

a single man to turn out who can only bring him[self] to con-
sume three gallons of Spirits in Toddy per Annum less than he
does at present.[42]

True to his prediction, the bill under consideration still allowed a
man to avoid serving in the field simply by paying a fine. Livingston
considered this unacceptable, and wrote to the Assembly that it had
to pass a bill that would enable him to call out the strength of the
state. That meant making a man serve, provide a substitute to serve
for him, or face "Consequences [that] will [be] dreadful beyond
Expression." With the current bill under consideration, Livingston
feared that he would be unable to comply with the calls of Washington or the Continental Congress on New Jersey. Washington could
not believe the Assembly passed such an ineffective law, especially as
the enemy would probably move soon, and then the "Assembly may,
perhaps, wish that their Militia were in the Field." Livingston urged
the Assembly to create a council empowered, in an emergency, to
call out the militia in whatever numbers were necessary to act under
its orders.[43]

On March 15, the Assembly finally passed two bills. One authorized the governor, in case of invasion, to call out part or all of the
militia with the advice of the Assembly or, in its recess, of a council
that was to be established. The militia thus called could be used to
help the army or a neighboring state. Militia officers also were to
assemble their men upon an emergency, without awaiting orders.
Anyone who refused to serve had to pay a maximum fine of thirty
pounds. The second act created a Council of Safety to support the
governor in calling out and issuing orders to the militia. The Assembly thus continued the practice of allowing militiamen to avoid service
by paying a fine, and Washington and Livingston both saw problems
with this provision. In addition, the acts maintained the limitation
of service for New Jersey militia to one month at a time. The Assembly did, however, help the situation by creating the council, which
would enable the executive branch to function even in the absence
of the legislature.[44]

While Livingston and the Assembly debated militia laws, the governor and the generals in the field tried different methods to get
the militia into service. As early as January 14, Livingston instructed

Brigadier General Philemon Dickinson to compel delinquent militiamen to join the army. In February, Dickinson sent a small battalion to its home county of Sussex to muster the rest of the local militia brigade, and Brigadier General William Maxwell tried the same technique in Morris County. When Major General Israel Putnam ordered militia soldiers called out in February to serve or pay their fine, Livingston informed him that he approved of Continental officers compelling the militia to serve but preferred that Putnam not accept fines. He explained to Putnam that since the laws were so weak, Livingston instead based his February call for more militia not on the laws but on the constitutional principle that during an invasion a commander in chief must have the power to call out the militia. Therefore, fines would not be accepted. Instead, he wanted Continental officers to force the militia to serve. Putnam accepted monetary fines anyway, because he believed that if he forced militiamen to serve, he would simply have to keep them under guard.[45]

Though active in framing militia laws, the New Jersey government did not control the militia while it was in the field. Livingston wrote to Washington that he was pleased to hear of the activities of the New Jersey militia and that the militia turned out in great numbers, but he seemed to take little actual control of assembling or commanding the militia. As in New York, militia generals like Dickinson and Nathaniel Heard had more power over collecting the militia than did the government. Livingston urged Dickinson to use discretion when forcing militiamen into the field and to apply to Continental officers for help if necessary.[46]

In early April, to be ready for the opening of the campaigning season, Livingston ordered Colonel David Forman to call out half of the militia of Burlington and Monmouth counties, General Heard to call out half of the militia of Somerset, Hunterdon, and Sussex counties, and Brigadier General William Winds to call out one-third of the militia of Bergen, Essex, and Morris counties.[47] Whether the militia would respond under the new laws remained to be seen.

In May, Governor Livingston responded to a request from Washington and issued orders for one thousand militiamen to join General Heard at Pompton. The few New York militiamen in northeast New Jersey could not defend the area. Livingston, however, seriously doubted the New Jersey militia would assemble. Heard, meanwhile, with the four hundred-odd men he had, tried to protect the area against Tory raids such as the one on May 13. On that day about three hundred Tory recruits left Bergen and tried to surprise a party of seventy Whig militia at Paramus. The American commander heard of the threat and withdrew, and in the morning fog the Tories fired at each other. The enemy retreated with ten dead and several wounded, while the Whig militia had one killed and two captured. Heard pursued the Tories with his four hundred men but failed to catch them. He then left about two hundred men to guard Paramus. Meanwhile, David Forman, recently promoted to brigadier general, commanded three hundred militiamen guarding a stretch of one hundred miles of coastline including Sandy Hook. The Tory element in Monmouth County, where Forman was based, remained strong, and Forman had difficulty guarding the coast while watching for internal problems caused by the Loyalists.[48]

As warm weather returned, the New Jersey government would turn its attention to this internal Tory threat but through the winter, the main concern was the partisan war against the British posts and the Tory units that were joining the British army. The need to control the people and prevent British sympathizers from gaining influence was not forgotten, however, as Livingston made clear in January: "As to the Tories, that have been active against us, we shall make rough work with them, as soon as the state is reduced to a little more tranquility." Through the winter and early spring, the New Jersey government and militia had enough to do to help Washington keep the British enclosed within their lines and make them pay with casualties each time they came out to forage. Livingston believed the people of New Jersey had helped do that.[49]

Washington, too, spent the winter and spring planning for the coming campaign. Even as he helped direct the growing partisan war, he looked toward the summer and where the militia would fit into the army's next operations. He did not mislead himself or ignore the implications of the previous year's events. Before the winter was over, he began sending appeals to the state governments from Virginia to New England for militia reinforcements. He also urged those governments to complete their Continental units, but until that was done, he had to have militia to prevent losing all the advantages he had gained in December and January. As of February 20,

Washington estimated the forces under his immediate control at four thousand, mostly militia, because most of the Continentals' enlistments had ended. As usual, he did not have definite numbers because the militia came and went with such rapidity.[50]

Washington had vague hopes of replacing the militia with newly recruited Continentals in March, but was disappointed (though not surprised). The time of service of much of his militia ended in March, however, and so he again wrote to the governments to send militia if their Continentals were not ready. One fact he did learn in 1776 was that Connecticut was a source of great strength, and he wrote once more to Governor Trumbull for men. He asked Trumbull for two thousand men to go to Peekskill, and added a dejected lament to his request: "I flattered myself, that I should never again be under the necessity of trespassing upon the public Spirit of your State, by calling upon her for another supply of Militia . . . ." As of mid-March, his army had 981 Continentals, and about 2000 militia who were engaged until the end of March. In a letter to Robert Morris, the depressed general concluded that if he were not reinforced with something soon, "the Game is at an end."[51]

The previous months of disasters and successes had taught Washington to use combined forces of militia and Continentals to good advantage, as well as to employ the militia on its own. He now used militia parties for "waylaying" roads and guarding local points such as ferry crossings. He asked George Clinton to station New York militia near Passaic Falls, New Jersey, to stop the inhabitants from sending provisions to the enemy, and requested a party of New Jersey militia to remove supplies kept within reach of the enemy. As he concentrated his growing army in April, Washington ordered militia units to guard the interior parts of the country to protect the inhabitants against possible attacks by Loyalists. In addition, he used militia detachments to collect deserters.[52]

Washington also had learned to understand militia soldiers. They could not be used for some things, such as a serious attack on the British army. They could, however, harass and annoy small parties, as he had them doing throughout the winter and spring. Militiamen could not be driven, but had to be led by their officers and slowly disciplined to army life. Praise was also important, and many of his letters were to militia units thanking them and praising their exploits. In particular, when a unit executed an especially brilliant exploit, he applauded its skill.[53] Thus, Washington was acquiring skill in handling the unpredictable militia forces on which he found himself dependent.

The growing realization of his need for the state forces reinforced Washington's desire to maintain good relations with the state governments. During the crisis of the early winter, the Continental Congress had authorized him to call on the states whenever he needed militia, and he did so, but he was always careful to go through proper channels. When he wanted Connecticut to furnish men, he asked Governor Trumbull, promising that the men would not have to go past Peekskill. Requests for New Jersey militia had to follow a more complicated route, as Washington had learned in 1776. As the government still did not have an efficient system for mustering militia, Washington worked in particular through Generals Dickinson and Maxwell while advising Governor Livingston of the steps he took. Maxwell was a Continental general but also a native of New Jersey with some influence. For New York, he contacted Alexander Mc-Dougall, the Continental commander in the Highlands until General Putnam took command in May 1777. McDougall then sent Washington's requests to the state Convention. Washington was especially impressed with George Clinton, who often anticipated his desires.[54]

Washington did not want to compromise on his principles against dividing the army for local defense. He protested efforts by the Rhode Island government to raise Continental battalions for its own defense, and informed Generals Parsons and Silliman in Connecticut that he could not allow Continentals to be stationed in small parties along the coast, nor could he spare any men from the army. Other such requests also met with refusals. On the other hand, the new Continental recruits remained in Connecticut throughout the winter and spring, and helped resist the Danbury raid, while Washington allowed one Continental regiment to be stationed in Westchester County until the New York Convention exerted itself and called out its militia.[55]

Washington thus showed that he could learn from experience while remaining true to his principles. As he grudgingly accepted the role of the militia in the operations of the regular army, he readily adopted the strategy of a partisan war as well. Though firmly rejecting efforts to scatter Continental detachments for local defense, he slowly and quietly acceded to necessity on occasion. With the approach of the campaigning season for the main armies, he was maturing as a commanding general.

Washington and the Continental Congress spent late April and May anticipating the British strategy and trying to be ready for whatever stroke Sir William Howe contemplated. The Congress continued to give Washington a free hand as the legislators confined themselves militarily to supporting his calls for men and urging the state governments to cooperate. In April and early May, the Congress requested 4500 militia from the governments of Delaware and Pennsylvania, and asked the New Jersey government to send Washington as many militia as the commander in chief needed. President John Hancock expressed the hope that these militia reinforcements would be enough to enable Washington to succeed in the coming campaign. Vestiges of the old confidence in the militia to form part of the field army still remained.[56]

With the support of the Congress and his growing understanding of the nature of the war being fought, Washington made preparations to shift from the partisan war of the winter and spring to a more active campaign for the main army. As of May 20, he estimated his army at about eighty-two hundred Continentals. He accordingly sent out requests for large numbers of militia, and the Continental Congress repeated its earlier pleas. He said that by May he had hoped not to have to resort to calling militia, but the enlistment of Continentals had gone too slowly. Disappointed he may have been, but again he was not particularly surprised.[57]

Washington, however, did not know if the states could even supply him with the requisite militia, let alone the requested Continentals. New Jersey had failed in 1776, New York had trouble fielding any kind of force, and Connecticut was preoccupied with its coastal defenses. If the states did not furnish their militia, Washington would have a serious problem in the next campaign. Added to that was the growing realization that militia units alone could not handle the local defensive needs. Thus, as the 1777 campaign opened, Washington, the Congress, and the state leaders had serious doubts concerning how well the militia forces of the middle states could meet the growing demands that the military and political leadership had placed on them.

CHAPTER SIX

The Militia Takes Over the Defenses, May–December 1777

WASHINGTON WAS caught on the horns of a dilemma. Would General Sir William Howe make the Hudson River the objective of the coming campaign, or would the British attack Philadelphia? As the British army prepared to open its campaign for the summer of 1777, Washington found himself trying to guard against all possibilities. He thus had Continentals and militiamen scattered from the New Jersey coast to Long Island Sound in Connecticut. With his regular army under strength, and the state militia forces still unpredictable, the commander in chief faced a perplexing summer.

Unsure of Howe's ultimate objective for the 1777 campaign, Washington forged a flexible strategy that would enable him to rush to the defense of the Highlands or Philadelphia. In order to accomplish this plan, he relied heavily on the militia to flesh out his Continental troops in New York and New Jersey. First he positioned his forces to hold the Highlands against a sudden assault and to attack the British in New Jersey if an opportunity arose. He then sent a committee of generals to view the Highland defenses, and held meetings with his generals on the advisability of attacking the different British posts in New Jersey and New York. He also planned to position a force in White Plains to watch the enemy in that area and to protect Connecticut. Another part of his strategy was a continuation of the partisan war. Washington suggested to Putnam at Peekskill and to Parsons in Connecticut that they attack nearby enemy posts, using Continentals or militia, but to execute such raids only if they were confident of success. As late as June 8, just five days before the British advanced into New Jersey, American soldiers raided onto Staten Island and skirmished with a Hessian outpost.[1]

Putting this flexible strategy into effect, as well as adhering to his principle of concentration, Washington began to consolidate the Continental Army in May. While he pulled in the Continental units stationed along the Jersey coast, Washington watched with pleasure as militia detachments replaced the Continentals and formed a line across the state in front of the army. General Dickinson had temporarily resigned due to family needs, and therefore General Nathaniel Heard commanded the New Jersey militia guarding from Elizabethtown to Hackensack. By early June, three hundred New Jersey militiamen defended Newark, two hundred guarded Elizabethtown, two hundred defended Rahway, and a small party held Pompton. Washington urged Heard to keep out scouting parties to warn of any enemy moves, so that Heard would "have an Opportunity of calling in the Country to your assistance . . . ." Washington placed militia troops in positions behind the army to guard supplies and erect defensive works for safe havens in case the army had to retreat.[2]

Washington was unsure how to help the militia prepare fully for the coming campaign, which would be different from the partisan war fought through the winter. As he explained, however, to Major General John Sullivan, he believed that if the militiamen "will only agree to fall upon the flanks of the Enemy upon their march, in small parties, without any regular order, they may harass and impede them very much." Since the British army remained within its lines into early June, Washington continued to send small parties of Continentals and militia on raids against the enemy's posts and on scouting missions. According to Washington's plan, when the British did advance, his generals were to detach parties to harass the British army's movements and secure passes to dispute its advance. These actions would give the rest of the Continental Army time to move up and would allow the militia time to attack the enemy's flanks.[3]

The warm weather brought an increase in the number of requests for Continental detachments. Washington, however, was busy concentrating his army and therefore did not change his official stance. He even became more stringent in enforcing his policy. He wrote to Parsons and Trumbull in Connecticut that he could no longer allow Continentals to remain in Connecticut because he needed them for the vital defenses in the Highlands. Trying to prevent complaints or arguments, Washington explained that the state leaders had known from the beginning that the British would harass the coasts, and he could not defend every mile of shore. In addition, he knew of no detachment of Continentals in any state where the enemy did not have an established post. Washington feared, correctly, that the enemy was raiding Connecticut, in particular, in a deliberate effort to divide the Americans and divert attention from the main goals. He would not be misled, however, and therefore remained determined to concentrate the army. He promised to defend Connecticut as well as possible if the condition of the army allowed him to do so. Washington then had to deny similar requests from Massachusetts and even from parts of New Jersey. His answer was that he could not defend every individual in the United States.[4]

As May ended and June began, Washington and his generals noted with interest British preparations for some move in New Jersey. General Sullivan, who commanded a division of about sixteen hundred men at Princeton, found himself on the main route between the British in New Brunswick and Philadelphia. He therefore stayed in constant communication with Major General Benedict Arnold, who commanded in Philadelphia, concerning the British buildup at New Brunswick and the deployment of the Whig militia in the area. In his instructions to Brigadier General Prudhomme de Borre, one of his brigade commanders, Sullivan showed that he had learned from Washington's strategy for dealing with a British advance. Sullivan warned de Borre to avoid a general fight, in which he would be defeated by superior numbers. Instead, de Borre should harass the enemy, dispute each step, and keep up roadblocks. By delaying any advance, de Borre would allow time for the rest of the army to concentrate and for the militia to attack the flanks of the enemy force.[5]

Washington's preparations to meet their offensive did not go unnoticed by the British. By mid-May, Sir William Howe's scouts had noted that the Continentals to their front were withdrawing. Despite Sir James Murray's expressed bravado that "It will soon be over no doubt," the commanding general was not as confident. In late 1776, Howe had thought that the submission of the people of New Jersey presaged the end of the rebellion, and the occupation of Philadelphia would complete the job. The defeats at Trenton and Princeton had not materially altered his plans, which had been based on the hope of receiving at least fifteen thousand reinforcements. He had planned to march across New Jersey and at the same time to launch an offensive from Rhode Island toward Boston. By early April, however, Howe was reconsidering his plans. By then he knew that he would receive few reinforcements, and he admitted to Secretary of State George Germain that a march across New Jersey would be long and difficult. Therefore, he now favored moving against Philadelphia by sea while abandoning New Jersey. His frustration was clear as he admitted to Germain that he did not believe he could end the war that year. Though he had little fear that the rebel congress could raise the fifty thousand men it had called for, still the rebels "will have a numerous militia in the field, in addition to their standing force, with a tolerable train of artillery."[6]

Since Howe believed his actions were so limited due to the lack of men, he promised little help for the British army that would operate out of Canada in 1777. He committed himself only to using the provincial corps under the command of William Tryon, whom Howe had promoted to the temporary rank of major general of the Loyalist units. Howe carefully explained to General Sir Guy Carleton, who commanded in Canada, that any force operating against Ticonderoga, in upstate New York, would have to do so without much help from New York City. At best, the corps left on the lower Hudson River might be able to open a line of communications past the Highlands and the rebel forts.[7]

After the resignation of his command in 1778 and his subsequent return to England, Howe wrote a defense of his actions during his command in North America. Though clearly written with an eye to defend his measures, his later statements reflected his attitude in the spring of 1777. In his justification he explained how he faced the fifty thousand men whom the Continental Congress had called, "exclusive of the large bodies of militia, who were to be collected on the shortest notice. I mentioned at the same time the spirit infused into the people by their leaders from the strongest assurances of procuring the assistance of foreign powers . . . ." In his letter to Germain of April 2, 1777, he discounted the possibility of the rebels raising fifty thousand troops, but his consideration of the militia was present.[8] Clearly, the resistance by the militia soldiers of New Jersey had influenced his thinking to some degree as early as the spring of 1777.

His explanation as to why he abandoned plans for an offensive in New England also showed how his thoughts, at least after the fact, reflected his experiences with the militia. He dismissed assertions that the British army could have been better employed in New England by saying that the New England colonies not only were the most heavily populated provinces, "but their militia, when brought to action, the most persevering of any in all North America; and it is not to be doubted that General Washington, with his main army, would have followed me into a country where the strength of the Continent, encouraged by his presence, would have been most speedily collected." He agreed, in early June 1777, to launch raids against Massachusetts, but only if such raids did not interfere with the main campaign.[9]

Howe thus recognized, both after the fact and during his tenure as commander, that the presence of the militia had to be considered. He also recognized the relationship between the regular rebel army and the willingness of the local militia to fight. Whether he was truly concerned with the militia or simply looking for excuses, he considered the rebel militia a good enough cause to blame for his failures.

Consistent with his views stated originally in a letter of January 20, 1777, Howe repeated in his later narrative that a move against Philadelphia would force Washington to fight. "And as my opinion has always been, that the defeat of the rebel regular army is the surest road to peace, I invariabley [*sic*] pursued the most probable means to forcing its Commander to action . . . ." His actions in the spring of 1777 showed that Howe was indeed thinking along such lines. He wanted to maneuver Washington and the rebel army into a fight, defeat it, discourage the rebels and especially the militia, and force the submission of the people, as had begun to happen in New Jersey in the fall of 1776. Therefore, on April 2, 1777, he wrote to Germain that he planned no offensive into New Jersey unless an opportunity presented itself.[10]

Such an opportunity, he believed, presented itself in June 1777, and Howe thus began to concentrate the British army in New Brunswick throughout the first half of the month. In response, Washington and a council of generals decided to draw all but one thousand Continentals from Peekskill to reinforce the army in New Jersey. Washington was convinced that Howe was about to move against Philadelphia. He ordered General Sullivan at Princeton to avoid a full engagement if the enemy moved toward him, and instead to fall back while leaving out parties to harass the enemy's moves. Sullivan's letter to General de Borre, written two days before Washington sent these orders to Sullivan, showed how similarly these two men thought. Washington also sent a Continental regiment and two independent companies to Morristown to join the militiamen who were protecting supplies, and he ordered Colonel Daniel Morgan and his corps of light infantry to the front lines to scout and to attack the British flanks during any maneuvers. Despite Washington's efforts to fit the militia into the army's operations, he continued to complain to the Continental Congress that a dependence on the militia impeded his ability to resist a British advance. Major General Nathanael Greene, on the other hand, wrote with confidence that the militia would slow any British march toward Philadelphia.[11]

New Jersey's government made a last minute effort to support Washington's army. The Assembly passed a law that authorized the governor, with the consent of the new Council of Safety, to station any number of guards anywhere in the state. Governor William Livingston subsequently ordered out the militia of the southwest counties. Washington instructed Sullivan to use as he believed best any militiamen who responded to Livingston's call. In addition, Philemon Dickinson returned to New Jersey and the legislature elected him a major general of the New Jersey militia.[12]

Despite the impending British advance in New Jersey, the American leaders still worried about New York's defenses. George Clinton commanded Fort Montgomery, with about 400 Continentals and 500 militia, and Fort Constitution, with about 130 Continentals and 120 militia. About 70 militia guarded Fort Independence, near Peekskill. Clinton ordered out part of the Westchester County militia, and though the county committee had trouble filling that order, it did order three companies of rangers to be raised. Major General

Israel Putnam ordered four hundred Continentals from Peekskill to White Plains to harass the enemy, protect supplies, and surprise the enemy post at Morrisania. After Washington sent his call for all but one thousand of the Continentals from Peekskill, Putnam ordered the Continentals to join Washington. Washington also urged Brigadier General James Clinton to keep as large a body of militia as possible assembled on the west side of the Hudson, to coordinate with Nathaniel Heard in New Jersey to protect that area. George Clinton ordered one hundred newly recruited Continentals to join his brother at Sydman's Bridge to reinforce the weak force on the west side.[13]

General Howe personally arrived at New Brunswick on June 12, and during the night of June 13–14 the British army advanced from New Brunswick in the hope of luring Washington off the mountain between Quibbletown and Middlebrook where he had taken position, and into a pitched battle. Leaving two thousand men to guard New Brunswick and a corps of German troops in Amboy, Howe's army advanced in two columns, the first on the road toward Somerset Courthouse and the second on the road toward Princeton. General Cornwallis, commanding the first corps, stopped on June 14 near Somerset Courthouse, while the second corps swung in behind Cornwallis's troops on the road to Somerset. At this point Howe stopped the advance in the hope that Washington would descend the mountain and move toward the Delaware River to protect Philadelphia. Throughout the day, rebel and British parties clashed, including one skirmish at the rear of Cornwallis's corps that left almost forty Americans dead and wounded. The British lost about fifteen men.[14]

Washington reacted to the British advance cautiously. He sent his baggage wagons from the front so that the army would be free to harass the enemy's rear or flanks, and to attack if an opportunity arose. He ordered Sullivan to move closer to him, to prevent the enemy from marching between Sullivan's division and the main body of the army. He also instructed Sullivan to keep out small parties of militia and Continentals to scout further British moves and skirmish with the enemy. That the Americans executed such scouting and skirmishing duties efficiently, the Hessian partisan Johann Ewald later attested to: "The Americans are very skillful in placing such small ambushes for their own safety in front of their outposts, which has cost many an Englishman or German his life or his freedom."[15]

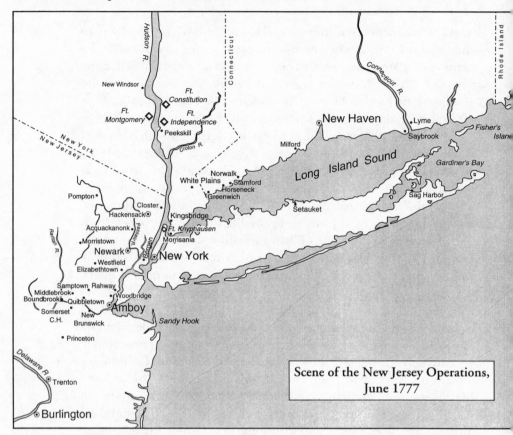

Scene of the New Jersey Operations,
June 1777

Once the British halted, Washington spent the rest of June 14 ordering all the militia possible to collect and join the army. He kept out light troops to skirmish, but did not venture an attack on the main British army. Sullivan received orders to take post to threaten the British right and rear if they advanced, and to attack and confine their advance posts. Sullivan at this time had about twenty-one hundred Continentals, a growing number of New Jersey militia, and about five hundred Pennsylvania militia.[16]

From June 14 to June 18, the British remained stationary between New Brunswick and Somerset; rivers guarding both flanks protected the army from attack. Washington kept the main part of his army in position near Middlebrook, and Sullivan, nearby at Sourland Hills. As Ewald succinctly put it: "General Washington, who neither moved nor let himself be lured out of his strong position by this demonstration, sent out several detachments daily which observed and harassed our army, whereby constant skirmishing ensued." As he waited, Washington collected all the Continental and militia troops he could. "In the mean time," he explained to Arnold, "I intend by light bodies of Militia, countenanced by a few Continental Troops, to harass them and weaken their numbers by continual skirmishes." Rebel troops even attacked the German force at Amboy on June 16.[17]

Much to Washington's satisfaction, New Jersey militiamen turned out with spirit to support Washington, and he wrote to General Philip Schuyler that they "seem determined, in conjunction with the Continental Troops, to harass and oppose the Enemy upon their march thro' the Country." Dickinson informed Washington that five thousand to six thousand militia were on the road to join the fight. With everything going well for the moment, Washington played a waiting game, as he explained to Major General Benedict Arnold:

It is an happy circumstance, that such an animation prevails among the people. I would wish to let it operate and draw as many as possible together, which will be a great discouragement to the Enemy, by showing that the popular Spirit is at such a height, and at the same time, will inspire the people themselves with confidence in their own Strength, by discovering to every individual the zeal and Spirit of his neighbours.

Once the militia had turned out and made its impression on the enemy and the people of New Jersey, Washington planned to dismiss all but two thousand of the militiamen, unless the enemy moved again. These two thousand men he would keep for a month to reinforce the army and allow him to rest the Continentals. On June 17 he wrote to Arnold not to send any more Pennsylvania militia for the present. Still on the way were two thousand Continentals, most of whom had already crossed the Hudson River from Peekskill on their way to join Washington.[18]

Finally concluding that Washington was not going to venture forth to engage in combat, Howe contemplated and ruled out as imprudent an attack on the rebel defenses. He therefore decided to begin the real campaign, a sea movement against Philadelphia, and accordingly ordered the British army to return to New Brunswick. On June 18, the British began their retreat toward New Brunswick and arrived there the following day. Sullivan's division followed this retrograde movement, finding houses and barns burned. Militia, light horsemen, and Continental riflemen harassed the British rear as they marched, but the rivers on the British army's flanks protected it from direct attack.[19]

Washington and the American defenders were jubilant over this apparent victory, and they gave the New Jersey militia much of the credit for stopping the British advance. Washington was particularly impressed, concluding that if Howe had planned to move to the Delaware, he had found greater opposition in New Jersey than expected. After castigating the militia for the previous two years, Washington's following praise of it must have been a surprise to the Continental Congress: "For I must observe, and with peculiar Satisfaction I do it, that on the first notice of the enemy's movements, the Militia assembled in the most Spirited manner, firmly determined to give them every annoyance in their power and to afford us every possible aid." He believed Howe retreated when, as he described it to President Hancock, Howe heard people were "flying to Arms in every Quarter, to oppose him." Brigadier General Henry Knox agreed, writing that Howe "found himself almost blockaded in an open flat country" and that New Jersey militiamen showed no sign of the "lethargic spirit that possessed them last winter." Knox concluded that no country can be permanently conquered "where the inhabitants are unanimous in opposition." Brigadier General Samuel Parsons believed that every man capable of carrying a gun had taken to the field to resist the British. The Massachusetts historian of the war, Mercy Otis Warren, perhaps best captured the attitude of the people of New Jersey when she concluded that they were "disgusted and alienated by the barbarity of his [Howe's] troops," and that most of the people were armed, enraged, and ready to fight. Washington, in fact, was so impressed that in November 1777, when he needed reinforcements during the Pennsylvania campaign, he reminded the New Jersey militia how its exertions had stopped the British in June. He also praised the exertions and ready support of the Pennsylvania militia.[20]

Even the British recognized the part that the New Jersey militia played in the operation. After the war, Johann Ewald used the actions of the New Jersey militia as an example of skillful partisan war:

What can you not achieve with such small bands who have learned to fight dispersed, who know how to use every molehill for their defense, and who retreat as quickly when attacked as they advance again, and who will always find space to hide. Never have I seen these maneuvres [sic] performed better than by the American militia, and especially that of the Province of Jersey. If you were forced to retreat against these people you could certainly count on constantly having them around you.

General Howe did not give the militia all the credit for ruining his effort to catch Washington, but he indirectly admitted that the presence of the militia helped induce him not to attack Washington at Middlebrook. In his postwar narrative, Howe defended his decision to avoid battle partly on his inability to keep open his line of communication with his base at New Brunswick. He would have had to detach too many soldiers of his eleven-thousand-man army to guard his communications if he had tried to march further into the interior to find and fight the rebel army. After such a battle, he either would have had to return to his base through rough country, or advance on Philadelphia. He believed, however, that he could not have maintained a supply line overland through New Jersey. The militiamen helped make Howe even more cautious.[21]

Howe's army, however, remained in New Jersey, and skirmishing between the British and American scouts and patrols continued day and night along the lines between the two armies. Washington's main army advanced, and his light troops occupied Boundbrook, Quibbletown, and Samptown. On June 22, the British army evacuated New Brunswick and marched to Amboy. British and rebel parties clashed throughout the day, and several times the small skirmishes escalated into larger affairs. Rebels harassed Cornwallis's rear elements from nearby woods until Cornwallis sent a detachment that dispersed the Americans with several casualties on both sides. The Queen's Rangers, a Loyalist cavalry unit originally raised by Colonel Robert Rogers in 1776, were protecting the right flank of the retreating

British army when they became too separated from the main body of troops. A large party of rebels suddenly attacked the Rangers, killing and wounding about half of the Tory unit. Brigadier General Alexander Leslie led the 71st Highland Regiment and the Hessian jägers, elite light infantry, to secure a hill in front of the British column. Leslie's force ran into about six hundred rebels and fought a fierce little engagement before capturing a few American cannons and the heights. Finally the British army camped at Amboy in the evening of June 22.[22]

During the British withdrawal, Washington detached units of Continentals and militia not only to harass the British march but also to watch the rivers for enemy supplies on the move and to guard the coast against any new enemy advances until the army could concentrate. He meanwhile moved the rest of the Continental Army toward Amboy, seeking an opportunity to attack before the enemy crossed to Staten Island. On June 23, with Howe's force concentrated in Amboy, Washington dismissed the New Jersey militia troops who had assembled during the initial alarm. He praised their bravery while skirmishing with the enemy and assured them that "while the same spirit remains, no danger is to be apprehended from their [British] future attempts." He also decided that the enemy's lines were too strong to warrant an attack.[23]

With the British again confined within their lines, Washington began to reestablish the old posts around the state, including ordering Heard to return to Pompton with five hundred militia. For the next couple of days, the Americans remained uncertain as to Howe's next move. Reports circulated that British troops were crossing to Staten Island, yet General Heard reported that Howe still had a large camp south of Amboy on the road to New Brunswick. While both armies eyed each other around Amboy, skirmishing continued along the lines. The rebels frequently advanced against the enemy outposts, and on June 25, Howe sent out a large detachment to attack and scatter these parties.[24]

Howe was about to begin crossing the army to Staten Island when, on June 25, he learned from prisoners that the rebel army had left its mountain position and had advanced to Quibbletown, and that Stirling's corps of three thousand men had taken post to the left of the enemy army. Another party of seven hundred rebels had moved to the left of Stirling. Assuming that the Americans were planning to attack Amboy as the British army crossed to Staten Island, Howe decided to strike suddenly and try to precipitate a battle. At 2 A.M. on June 26, the British army advanced in two columns toward Quibbletown in the hope of hitting Washington's left flank.[25]

Howe's right column, under Cornwallis's command, ran into the rebel party of seven hundred men on the Americans' far left flank, and the firing alerted Washington to the maneuver. Washington's use of forward units to intercept and warn of enemy moves worked. From 3 A.M. to noon, the running battle raged. Washington, believing correctly that Howe's objective was either to force an engagement or to isolate and trap Stirling's division, quickly pulled his army back to the heights near Middlebrook that he had occupied during the previous British advance. At the same time, he detached parties of light infantry and militia to attack the flanks of the British army. Cornwallis's column continued to advance and attacked Stirling's corps, which was well placed in some woods. After a stiff fight, Stirling's troops retreated. The rebels lost up to 500 men, and the British force had possibly 130 casualties. Cornwallis followed the fleeing rebels to Westfield, where the extreme heat of the day forced a halt to the pursuit. The other column, under Howe's personal command, joined Cornwallis at Westfield, and the army camped there during the night of June 26.[26]

The British retreated to Rahway on June 27 and entered Amboy the next day, burning and pillaging as they marched. During the nights of June 28 and 29, the main part of Howe's army returned to Staten Island, and Cornwallis with the rear guard finished the withdrawal on June 30. Throughout this crossing, the rebels made no appearance. Washington stationed two brigades near Woodbridge to watch their moves but did not attack. After the British army reconcentrated on Staten Island, Washington decided to release most of the New Jersey militia to let the people collect their harvests. He also ordered General Heard to keep at most 150 of the 500 militiamen at Pompton.[27]

Meanwhile, on June 19, when Howe first withdrew his army to New Brunswick, Washington worried that Howe might make a sudden move up the Hudson River. Even though the enemy army remained in New Jersey, Washington ordered the two thousand Continentals on their way from New York to return to Peekskill. He instructed General Putnam to use militiamen to replace any Continentals on guard duty at supply magazines, to station Continentals at the most critical places, and to use the best militia for posts of secondary importance. He urged George Clinton to ask Putnam for reinforcements to strengthen Fort Montgomery if necessary. At this time, Clinton had 420 Continentals and 480 militia at that fort, with another 250 men nearby at New Windsor. Fort Constitution contained 265 Continentals and 109 militia, and 215 militia defended Fort Independence.[28]

Preferring to keep the Continental soldiers concentrated near the Highland forts, Washington forbade Putnam to send a Continental brigade to White Plains. Though Putnam obeyed, he believed a regular brigade was necessary at White Plains to gather information on British ship movements and to restrain the enemy's scouts and rangers from plundering the area. Putnam also believed some people might return to an allegiance to the United States if protected, and he even suggested that James Clinton should send men down the west side of the river for the same purpose. Washington finally accepted Putnam's recommendation, but warned Putnam to return the brigade to Peekskill immediately if the enemy moved upriver. At the same time, Washington urged George Clinton to call out a strong force of New York militia to reinforce Peekskill and the nearby posts until the army could move closer. He asked Putnam to help call in the militiamen, and promised not to keep them long. Washington hoped to know Howe's plans soon. To make matters more difficult at this uncertain moment, he had to detach one brigade from Peekskill to the north because of the growing enemy threat to Ticonderoga.[29]

When the British withdrew onto Staten Island, Clinton responded quickly and ordered four Dutchess County militia regiments to Peekskill, four regiments from Ulster and Dutchess counties to Fort Montgomery, and one regiment from Orange County to reinforce his brother at Sydman's Bridge. Before calling out more of the militia from Ulster and Dutchess counties, Clinton and the Council of Safety waited to see if the men from the northern parts of those counties would have to march north instead, to help against General John Burgoyne's advance from Canada. Clinton also asked

Putnam for a reinforcement for Fort Montgomery, because Clinton believed an attack on the fort would be sudden and would be over before help could arrive. Putnam wrote to the militia colonels for help, too, and he wrote to Governor Jonathan Trumbull to forward all the Continentals in Connecticut. In addition, Putnam asked Trumbull to send one or two militia regiments to White Plains or Horseneck to protect Connecticut from raids by Tories, in case the enemy moved upriver. Meanwhile, his brigade at White Plains skirmished with an enemy force of three hundred to four hundred men, and Putnam ordered another regiment down to support the brigade.[30]

Still uncertain as to Howe's intentions, Washington began to move his army toward the Hudson River at the beginning of July. He left a couple of infantry regiments and some mounted troops to guard the New Jersey shore against small raids, and urged Sullivan, whose division was nearest to New York, to try to capture Tory recruits near Bergen. As the British army began to embark from Staten Island in early July, Washington's moves became hesitant and the army stopped. On July 11, he again began to edge his men toward the Highlands, ordering Sullivan's division to cross the Hudson and join Putnam. The Continental Congress, meanwhile, ordered the governments of New York and the New England states to reinforce Washington with all the militia he needed. By July 21, both Sullivan's and Stirling's Continental divisions had joined Putnam near Peekskill, while the rest of the army continued to move closer to the river on the west side. As he neared New York City, Washington began to contemplate possible attacks on the enemy's advance posts around that city. His headquarters was within twenty miles of the Hudson River when he received information of the British fleet standing out to sea and setting sail to the southeast. He immediately halted the army until he could gather further information.[31]

As the Continental Army withdrew from New Jersey, the government and militia of that state stepped in to replace it and to control the Tories, thus relieving Washington of the concern for that state's defenses. In early July, Governor Livingston and the Council of Safety ordered out four hundred militia to apprehend Tories in Bergen County, and similar efforts suppressed most disaffection in Sussex County. The militia detachment in Bergen County captured several Tories who were on the council's list. To ease the burden of defense in New Jersey, Washington dismissed all of the New Jersey militia attached to the army except one hundred men who were guarding supplies. Militia units already on guard near the coast and in Monmouth County remained on duty to resist enemy raiding parties and to help Washington gather information on the whereabouts of the British fleet. Washington then warned Livingston that he would soon remove the two Continental regiments left near Newark, and Livingston ordered Dickinson to position fourteen hundred militia along the coast from Acquackanonk to Amboy, to defend and even to raid Staten Island if an opportunity arose.[32]

In New York, the defense of the Highlands against the expected attack devolved onto Washington and the Continental Army. Washington warned Putnam to obstruct all roads in the Highlands that he did not absolutely need. As aggressively minded as his commander, Putnam suggested an attack against the enemy force at Kingsbridge, which he estimated at eighteen hundred men. The garrisons in the Highland forts themselves continued to fluctuate. On July 18, 448 Continentals and 435 militia defended Fort Montgomery; 117 Continentals and 115 militia were posted in Fort Constitution; and only 143 militia garrisoned Fort Independence.[33]

The New York Whigs also took an important political step toward greater efficiency at this time. In July, they adopted a new constitution that created an executive in the body of a governor and provided for a two-house legislative body. The governor had a three-year term, instead of the one-year appointments in New Jersey, and he would be the commander in chief of the New York militia. The people of New York voted for their governor, whereas in the other states the legislative bodies elected the governors. George Clinton won this first gubernatorial election almost unanimously, due mostly to the soldiers' votes. Washington was pleased with the result. Clinton's experience as a soldier, a role he would continue to fulfill, would aid him as the wartime governor of New York. His influence over the militia and his blunt, energetic style also helped get things done.[34]

Elected in July and due to take office on August 1, George Clinton delayed leaving his command at Fort Montgomery while an attack was expected. He also refused to leave his post without Washington's permission. On August 1, Clinton officially became governor, and though Washington hated to lose his services as an officer, he believed Clinton would prove to be a valuable asset as governor. Clinton therefore left the fort and became governor, but declared in his first week that due to the present emergency, he would prorogue the legislature until later in the month.[35] Clinton had to juggle the roles of governor, militia commander, brigadier general in the army, and commander of the Highland forts.

While Washington and the governments and militia of New York and New Jersey responded to the maneuvers of the British army throughout June and July, the defense of Connecticut remained independent from the Hudson River operations, though Washington continued to call on Connecticut militia to help defend New York. In mid-June, Washington ordered all the Continentals in Connecticut to join the army. He denied the Connecticut government's right to keep two Continental battalions for its own defense. The Connecticut Assembly accepted Washington's decision and ordered the raising of two state militia battalions for the defense of the coast and the southwestern frontier. Governor Trumbull regretted the need to pull more men from their farms, but he preferred that inconvenience rather than endanger the common good. Parts of the militia companies stationed along the coast were drafted to help form these regiments. The first of these regiments, commanded by Colonel Roger Enos, sent three companies to New Haven, two companies to Greenwich, and one each to Stamford, Milford, and Fairfield, while smaller parties were ordered to other port towns. One company was later shifted from New Haven to Norwalk. The second regiment, commanded by Colonel John Ely, covered the coast from Lyme and Saybrook to the east. In this way, the two regiments helped defend the entire coast and frontier from the New York border to the eastern end of the state. In addition, the Assembly made available to Washington one-third of the militia from the coastal units and one-fourth of the interior militia. Washington could call on these units in an emergency, and the men would serve for three months. The Assembly asked Washington not to call them from the state unless absolutely necessary. Trumbull assured President John Hancock that the people of Connecticut would exert themselves "as far as can possibly consist with their own internal security and the cultivation of their lands."[36]

While the rebels prepared for the worst in New York and along the Sound, Sir William Howe turned his attention farther south. As his army embarked during the opening days of July, he spelled out his ideas. Having decided to avoid a difficult march through New Jersey, yet still eyeing Philadelphia as a worthy objective, Howe planned to sail with the fleet and army up the Delaware River and capture the rebel capital. Should Washington bring his army into Pennsylvania, Howe instead would sail up the Chesapeake Bay. He watched with satisfaction as Washington edged ever closer to the Hudson River, because that would mean an easier campaign in Pennsylvania. Should Washington threaten New York City, Howe could send reinforcements to that city, and if Washington moved north against Burgoyne, Burgoyne would be in no danger and the rebel chief would be between British forces to the north and in New York City. If Washington moved to Pennsylvania, that would leave Burgoyne free to operate as desired.[37]

Throughout these plans, the influence of the militia again showed indirectly. Instead of marching through New Jersey and thus staying close to New York, Howe felt the necessity of sailing around the New Jersey militia. He seemed to feel no fear for New York City at the hands of either Washington's army or the militia. In his own way, Howe demonstrated an accurate assessment of the rebel militia forces. They were a problem when moving though the open field or trying to occupy large tracts of territory, but they could not threaten fortified positions or maneuver rapidly between the states.

Behind, in command of the British garrison left in New York City and its environs, remained Lieutenant General Henry Clinton with some latitude to act as opportunity afforded. Henry Clinton's primary objective, however, was the defense of New York City. Howe took about fourteen thousand men with him to face Washington's army and "almost any number he pleased of militia." Though written after his return to England, this phrase suggested what Howe wanted to emphasize as a key impediment to his efforts to subdue the rebellion. He believed that he left an estimated eighty-five hundred soldiers and a small body of Tory militia with Clinton, though Clinton claimed that he had only seventy-two hundred troops.[38]

As the British fleet sailed southward, Washington began to shift his divisions toward the Delaware River. Sullivan's and Stirling's divisions were recalled from the east side of the Hudson River, and Washington began to move his headquarters south. When the fleet was sighted along the southern part of the New Jersey coast, Washington called for two more Continental brigades from Peekskill. By the end of July, he estimated that the entire Continental Army would soon be in Philadelphia. Washington then halted the army to await further sightings, keeping Sullivan's division at Morristown so that it could return to Peekskill if necessary. On August 1, he heard that the British fleet had last been seen steering east. Fearing that Howe might double back and make a sudden move up the Hudson River, Washington sent orders for the army to swing north once again. He ordered Sullivan to return to Peekskill. Then to avoid too many countermarches, Washington halted the army until he could gather more definite information.[39]

As Washington and the army maneuvered through New Jersey in anticipation of the fleet's destination, the militia had to take over the defenses of the Hudson River valley just as the New Jersey militia had replaced the army in June. On July 25, Fort Montgomery contained 419 militia and 444 Continentals, while Fort Constitution had 121 militia and 119 Continentals. A party of 130 militia garrisoned Fort Independence. The militia at Fort Montgomery was due to leave at the end of July, and Governor Clinton asked Putnam for a reinforcement from Peekskill. Washington warned Putnam and Clinton that he probably would have to withdraw most of the Continentals from Putnam's command, and he urged them to call on one thousand to fifteen hundred more militia from New York and Connecticut. Clinton and Putnam agreed that one thousand militia would be enough, five hundred from each state, and they sent a request to Governor Trumbull. Because it was the busy farming season, they expected difficulty in getting the men to assemble, but Clinton issued the necessary orders in New York and asked the legislature to help. Washington gave Putnam permission to call on Sullivan's division near Morristown if the British appeared on the river.[40]

Despite these preparations, Putnam's force was not impressive. As of July 31, after the Continentals originally called by Washington had left and many of the militia had gone home, Putnam had 2347 Continentals on the east side of the Hudson. He needed five hundred at White Plains and five hundred at the forts, leaving about thirteen hundred for Peekskill and the passes. He estimated the enemy to have five thousand to six thousand at Kingsbridge and

Fort Knyphausen. On July 31, Washington made a further demand for men, which left only two thousand Continentals with Putnam. Washington suggested that Putnam fill the garrisons with additional Connecticut and New York militia.[41]

After Washington heard on August 1 that the British fleet had shifted to an easterly course, preparations intensified along the Hudson. Not only did Washington countermand his orders and send the two Continental brigades and Sullivan's division back toward Peekskill, but he urged George Clinton to call out every militiaman possible and to stay at Fort Montgomery personally, if consistent with his new office. Clinton had already ordered out 810 militia for long-term service at Fort Montgomery, but now he sent orders for four more militia regiments to go to Fort Montgomery, another to go to Sydman's Bridge, and three others to assemble at Peekskill. This call, however, interrupted efforts to raise the 810 long-term militia for Fort Montgomery. Putnam wrote to Trumbull to send all possible aid from Connecticut. By the beginning of the second week of August, Putnam reported to Washington that the New York and Connecticut militia were coming in fast, with the New York militia regiments ordered to Peekskill and Fort Montgomery already at their posts. Clinton warned, however, that in the harvest season it would be difficult to keep them with their units.[42]

As Washington hesitated in New Jersey through the middle weeks of August, all he could do to help New York was to urge the collecting of militia. He also expressed his pleasure to Putnam that Governor Clinton resumed his command at Fort Montgomery: "there cannot be a properer man upon every account." New York militiamen kept assembling, but when the British fleet did not arrive immediately, Putnam released many of them to gather the harvest and to return immediately after it was collected. Washington, unaware of Putnam's decision, advised Clinton to judge how long the militia should stay in the field. He reminded Clinton that the militia "is a Resource which must be sparingly employed" and he "would have them detained no longer than is absolutely necessary." Clinton, meanwhile, ordered three hundred militia down to White Plains for two months, to protect the inhabitants.[43]

During this flurry of activity, the Connecticut government removed any fears that it might withhold its men for its own defense. Governor Trumbull ordered the closest parts of Colonel Enos's regiment to Peekskill on July 30, and he told Putnam to apply to Brigadier General Gold S. Silliman, still commanding on Connecticut's southwestern frontier, if he needed more men. In addition, Trumbull had other militia regiments ready to move if necessary. Silliman sent three regiments to Peekskill without official orders from his government, and on August 5, Brigadier General Oliver Wolcott of the Connecticut militia responded to calls from Washington and Putnam by ordering parts of three militia regiments to go to Peekskill without awaiting Trumbull's authorization. The governor and the Council of Safety approved of Silliman's and Wolcott's actions, and they ordered seven hundred more militia to be drafted and sent to Peekskill. Of these, four hundred were to ride horses to the New York border in order to speed their arrival. Brigadier General Andrew Ward took command of this detachment. Altogether, Connecticut started about three thousand militia toward New York by the end of the first week in August.[44]

Despite the Connecticut government's exertions, the initial detachment of Connecticut militia did not provide as much help as planned. Of the three thousand men ordered to New York, only four hundred actually marched into New York by mid-August, and some of them stopped at New Bedford because they refused to leave southwestern Connecticut undefended. The Connecticut militiamen in New York then grew tired of waiting, and with no enemy fleet in sight, Putnam could not convince them to stay, especially as they had been engaged for no specific time. Washington was surprised at this exodus of Connecticut militia troops, and urged Putnam to inform the Connecticut government of the situation and to ask for militia engaged to serve a minimum of three months. Putnam asked Trumbull for at least two thousand men for three months. General Ward's detachment, increased to one thousand men, finally arrived in late August and joined a Continental detachment at White Plains to distress the enemy and protect the inhabitants. Trumbull promised to discuss with the Assembly the need for two thousand more men for three months and the need to relieve those men already in New York. He did remind Putnam of Connecticut's long coast, Rhode Island's calls for help, and the men sent to the north, but despite these other demands placed on Connecticut's militia, it continued to supply men for Putnam. The Connecticut Assembly decided to send the two thousand men requested by Putnam and Washington.[45]

On August 21, Washington learned that the British fleet had been spotted off the Virginia Capes in mid-August. He set the army in motion once again to march to the defense of Philadelphia. As the army finally left New Jersey, the Continental Congress had Washington send a request to Governor Livingston for one thousand New Jersey militia to go to New York and replace an equal number of New York militia in the Highlands. These New Yorkers would then go to fight Burgoyne in northern New York. Livingston ordered Brigadier General William Winds to collect and send the desired one thousand militiamen, who were to serve until November 1. Livingston informed Washington, however, that he expected only three hundred of the men actually to go.[46]

The uncertainty of Howe's movements and the marches and countermarches of the Continental Army did not diminish Washington's partisan streak. While his army waited in New Jersey through the middle of August, he ordered a brief reconnaissance of Staten Island, and Monmouth County militia sent him the desired intelligence. Washington then suggested to Sullivan the possibility of a descent onto Staten Island if the defenders were weak. Sullivan took the initiative, and on August 21 he launched a large raid against the British and German units on Staten Island. Crossing at two different points with about two thousand troops, including a detachment of New Jersey militia, he hoped to surprise and surround the scattered enemy posts, then concentrate and attack the larger British garrison in Richmond, across the water from Amboy. Sullivan achieved an initial surprise on the morning of August 22, hitting and routing the four hundred men of Brigadier General John Skinner's Loyalist rangers. Then Sullivan lost control of the expedition as his men began to straggle and plunder. Meanwhile, the alarm sounded on the island, and a German battalion and the British 52nd Regiment attacked Sullivan's troops and drove the rebels back toward their boats. Sullivan began the difficult maneuver of crossing to the New Jersey mainland while being pressed by the enemy, safely removing all but his rear guard of one hundred men before the British and Germans attacked again. Sullivan ordered the boats to return to Staten Island to pick up these last men, but the frightened boatmen refused to row to the shore in the face of the hostile fire. About forty of the rear guard surrendered, and the rest swam to safety.[47]

Altogether, Sullivan's men marched fifty-one miles in twenty-two hours. Losses for both sides were uncertain, though Sullivan claimed to have lost a maximum of 25 killed and wounded, with about 140 men captured by the British. The British reported killing up to 250 rebels and capturing over 300 men. On the other side, Sullivan declared the capture of 140 enemy soldiers, whereas the British admitted to 80 men missing, with only about 12 killed and wounded. Much to Sullivan's disgust, a court of inquiry was later held because of the lost rear guard, but Sullivan defended his decisions and the court ruled that he was to be commended for his actions.[48]

Without a preconceived plan, the same day that Sullivan attacked Staten Island, two other offensive movements commenced. Brigadier General Samuel Parsons had been ordered by General Putnam to return to the Connecticut coast with some Continentals and to coordinate with local militia in order to raid Long Island. On August 22, Parsons crossed the Sound with about seven hundred Continentals and militia, and landed at Setauket on Long Island. He immediately demanded the surrender of 150 Tories defending a stockade near the town. After five hours of musket and artillery fire, the Loyalists held firm and the rebels retreated to Connecticut. Both sides took a few casualties. Meanwhile, in a third American move, Putnam sent about six hundred troops toward Kingsbridge, where General William Tryon commanded. Tryon advanced to meet the rebels, who withdrew rather than engage his force. Neither side took casualties in this feint against the British redoubts at Kingsbridge.[49]

Despite the lack of results from these moves, the Americans were able to keep the pressure on Henry Clinton in New York City throughout the rest of August. Parsons with his Continentals and militia remained along the Sound in southwest Connecticut, while Sullivan with his Continentals and the New Jersey militia continued to threaten another raid onto Staten Island until withdrawn into Pennsylvania to rejoin the main army. Putnam, however, dismissed the short-term militia with him at the end of August when the British fleet was sighted in Chesapeake Bay. Only 600 New York militiamen, all that had been mustered so far of the 810 militia assembling for long-term service, remained with Putnam.[50]

For the moment, the danger of a sudden British assault up the Hudson River had subsided. Despite the frustrations of depending on the militia, once again it had responded to the crisis, and militia-men from Connecticut, New York, and New Jersey had supported Putnam's small Continental force. The Connecticut government had ordered three thousand men, New Jersey's called for one thousand, and New York's government ordered out eight regiments, for a total ordered out in these three states of possibly six thousand soldiers. Far fewer showed up, but had the British attacked, the numbers may have been greater.

Most of the Continental Army was well beyond supporting dis-tance by late August, and therefore the continued defense of these three states rested in a large measure on the militia. For Connecti-cut, Parsons' Continentals who remained near Horseneck bolstered the defense of the New York–Connecticut border. The front line of defense there, however, depended on General Silliman. He stationed part of his militia brigade and detachments of the local militia in the towns along the border.[51]

For New Jersey, the removal of the army left its defense almost entirely up to the state militia. Guards occupied stations along the coasts of Monmouth, Essex, and Middlesex counties, but the British still sent small raiding parties across to New Jersey. The governor and the Council of Safety sent militia parties to hunt down enemy recruiting agents who were trying to augment the Tory units in the British army, and the government had to replace the two New Jersey Continental regiments that Washington had recently called to the army after leaving them behind as long as possible. An added diffi-culty were the many inhabitants of Bergen County who had Loyalist sympathies and therefore refused to serve at all. Thus, Livingston and the council felt the state too hard pressed to comply with a re-quest for five hundred militia to reinforce Horatio Gates in north-ern New York. They did order out the one thousand militiamen for the Highlands when the Continental Congress requested the men.[52]

War weariness was settling into New Jersey by the fall of 1777, and the New Jersey militia was exhausted after its exertions since Decem-ber 1776. Livingston therefore had little hope of collecting enough militia to supply an adequate defense against a larger attack. He again urged the Assembly to pass a stronger militia law that would compel militiamen to serve rather than just pay a fine for delinquency, and the militia officers of several regiments sent petitions for a more effective militia law, but all the Assemblymen passed was a resolution to take such an act under consideration. Despite Livingston's order for fourteen hundred militia to guard the coast across from Staten Island, as of September 7, only four hundred had collected. With Bergen County mostly disaffected, and the western New Jersey counties sending their men to Washington in Pennsylvania, Livingston feared that the eastern half of the state would be ruined. He therefore asked the Continental Congress to shift fifteen hundred Continentals from Peekskill to New Jersey in the hope that the militia would rally to this contingent of regulars. The Congress agreed, and ordered Putnam to prepare to send the fifteen hundred men. Washington then ordered Putnam to send the detachment.[53]

After Sir William Howe left New York City, Lieutenant General Henry Clinton had the unenviable task of defending the city and helping, if possible, Burgoyne in upstate New York and Howe in Pennsylvania. Rejecting William Tryon's view that the only way left to subdue the rebels was through a brutal war to terrorize the Americans into submission, Clinton preferred trying to regain the rebels' allegiance. In order to use the limited resources to maximum effect, he employed New York Loyalists with family ties to colonists living in New Jersey and in the Hudson River valley, men such as Brigadier General Cortland Skinner, to collect information on the rebels. In this manner Clinton relied less on patrols and outposts, which had to fight with militia parties, to gather intelligence. The rebel Committees of Safety and other such groups, however, were able to limit these new British methods to a degree. Still, during Henry Clinton's tenure as commander in New York, and then as commander in chief, the British effectively anticipated many American movements and plans.[54]

As Henry Clinton tried to discern the rebel plans, he decided he had to take action to support Howe's and Burgoyne's operations. Though Clinton could not know it, Burgoyne was already complaining to Secretary of State Germain that no one was assisting him. Henry Clinton did not believe an opportunity to attack up the Hudson had arisen as of mid-September, with Parsons threatening Long Island, Putnam guarding the Hudson, and two brigades still in

New Jersey threatening Staten Island. Clinton, however, believed New York City itself was safe. Therefore, hearing of Burgoyne's advance and Howe's landing and march into Pennsylvania, Clinton launched a raid into New Jersey. He seemed to have a vague hope that such a move would help the other two British armies, possibly by pinning down troops and preventing further reinforcements from going to the north or south. In addition, he was executing a diversion for a future raid up the Hudson River.[55]

In the evening of September 11, Clinton led about one thousand British, German, and Loyalist troops into New Jersey. They landed at Elizabethtown Point and met no initial opposition. Another detachment of one thousand to fifteen hundred men crossed into New Jersey near Fort Lee. The American defenders were caught by surprise and gave no immediate resistance. Colonel William Malcom, commander of a Continental detachment at Ramapo, sent a party toward the enemy while he tried to collect the militia of the area and warn New York Governor George Clinton. Governor Livingston informed General Dickinson, who commanded the New Jersey militia opposed to the British force, that no further men were available because Livingston had to send a large force to reinforce Washington. When Washington heard of the British attack in New Jersey, he ordered Putnam to send one thousand more Continentals into New Jersey, in addition to the fifteen hundred already ordered. Brigadier General Alexander McDougall, whose brigade was part of this new contingent, had orders to join Dickinson and oppose the enemy in New Jersey, and then to march to Washington in Pennsylvania if the enemy returned to Staten Island.[56]

Throughout September 12–13, local militia skirmished with Henry Clinton's men as they marched to Newark and collected cattle, horses, and sheep. On September 14, Clinton sent the German troops to Bergen with the livestock while he led a contingent of the corps toward Hackensack to join the men who had entered New Jersey near Fort Lee. Meanwhile, Dickinson and Malcom continued to call out the nearby New Jersey militia, and Putnam obeyed Washington's orders, sending McDougall and twelve hundred Continentals to pursue the enemy. Dickinson, overestimating the enemy at four thousand men in New Jersey and fearing that they planned to march through the state, asked for help from the western militia while

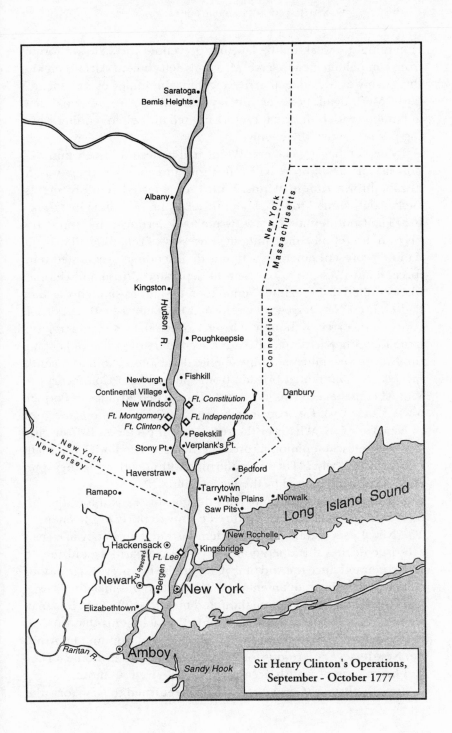

Saratoga
Bemis Heights

Albany

Kingston

Hudson R.

Poughkeepsie

Newburgh
Continental Village
New Windsor
Ft. Montgomery
Ft. Clinton

Fishkill

Ft. Constitution

Ft. Independence

Peekskill
Stony Pt.
Verplank's Pt.

New York
New Jersey

Haverstraw

Ramapo

Bedford

Tarrytown
White Plains
Saw Pits

New York
Massachusetts

Connecticut

Danbury

Norwalk

Long Island Sound

New Rochelle

Hackensack
Ft. Lee
Kingsbridge

Passaic R.

Newark

Bergen

New York

Elizabethtown

Raritan R.
Amboy

Sandy Hook

Sir Henry Clinton's Operations,
September - October 1777

lamenting the weak militia law that prevented the state authorities from compelling men to serve. Malcom's detachment skirmished with the enemy as McDougall arrived within nine miles of the enemy's party. McDougall, however, initially had only 731 Continentals and 200 militia with him, and therefore limited himself to sending scouting parties toward the enemy.[57]

By September 17, General Winds had collected fifteen hundred militia, and Dickinson had one thousand men on their way to Elizabethtown to join Winds. With the expected reinforcements, Dickinson planned to have about three thousand militia in a day or two. The Continental Congress wrote to Governor Livingston to use his own discretion concerning the necessity of retaining all his militia in the present emergency rather than sending a requested reinforcement to Washington. Then the separated British and German forces united at Bergen on September 16, and as suddenly as they had entered New Jersey, they returned to Staten Island. Dickinson concluded correctly, though in reverse order, that the raid was just a large foraging party after all, with a secondary objective of keeping the New Jersey militia at home. General Parsons, who had recently moved his Continental brigade from southwestern Connecticut to White Plains, believed his move and a threatened advance by Putnam toward New York City convinced General Henry Clinton to return to New York City. Whatever the reason for the sudden British withdrawal, American opinion favored the view recorded by Connecticut soldier John Wyllys: "They are returning without effecting their purpose, after being pelted by the Jersey militia."[58]

Losses were light on both sides during this expedition, though both sides claimed to have captured twenty to thirty of the enemy.[59] The New Jersey militia, however, demonstrated an important characteristic during this operation. Despite war weariness and the effort expended since the end of 1776 to repulse two previous invasions of New Jersey, the militiamen responded well to this imagined large-scale invasion. Close to three thousand men took the field in a matter of days to join the small Continental detachments that hurried into the state. Even without the presence of the Continental Army, the New Jersey state troops fought in defense of their homes. They had had a taste of British occupation and desired no more.

After the British, Germans, and Tories returned to New York, the

New Jersey militia returned home, and the New Jersey defenses remained weak throughout the rest of September. At most one thousand militiamen were with Dickinson at Elizabethtown, and he planned to take them to Washington. Since this move would leave New Jersey defenseless, Washington suggested to Dickinson that he leave some of the militia on the coast to ease the fears of the people. The march of 130 Tories through New Jersey on their way to Staten Island increased these fears. The local militia, however, captured about seventy of these Loyalists. The state government tried to improve its ability to defend the state and control the Tories by voting to continue the Council of Safety for another year in order to assist Livingston with the militia, and the legislature passed another revision of the militia laws. This new law empowered the governor to call up to half of all the militia should the enemy invade, and any militiaman who refused to serve or provide a substitute would pay an increased fine. Dickinson meanwhile decided not to accompany the militia units that went to Washington. By October 3, he had only 100 militia at Acquackanonk, 230 at Newark, 160 at Woodbridge, and 200 stationed in Monmouth County.[60]

Next door in New York, the government and militia officers tried to man the defenses as more and more Continentals went to New Jersey, Pennsylvania, and upstate New York. Governor George Clinton called out militia detachments to increase the force in Westchester County and to bolster the garrisons of the Highland forts, and like Governor Livingston, he urged the Assembly to strengthen the militia laws that had been devised at the beginning of the war. The Assembly agreed, and created a committee to work on the revisions. Meanwhile, Putnam's Continental force continued to decline. McDougall and the Continentals sent to New Jersey never returned, continuing instead to Pennsylvania, which left Putnam only seven hundred Continentals at Peekskill and Parsons's brigade at White Plains. Washington understood how much his calls for reinforcements weakened Putnam's force, but he believed Putnam could hold the Highlands with the remaining Continentals and the local militia.[61]

When Putnam informed Governor Clinton of his weakness, Clinton ordered six militia regiments to Peekskill, two other regiments with about nine hundred men to Fort Montgomery, and three regiments with another nine hundred men to the west side of the Hudson River. These units were all that he could call forth because the rest of the state's militia had to help in the north. Putnam asked Governor Trumbull to send three thousand Connecticut militia to Peekskill, to serve until the end of the year. General Oliver Wolcott again did not wait for official orders but immediately ordered half of his brigade to Putnam. To Wolcott's disappointment, only four hundred men responded to his call to go to New York. Putnam, meanwhile, received orders from Washington to send to Pennsylvania more Continental soldiers from his command, including Parsons's brigade from White Plains.[62]

As Parsons withdrew from Westchester County, he asked General Silliman to cover the county with his militia. Putnam asked Clinton for even more New York militiamen, but Clinton repeated that the eleven regiments already ordered out were all he could get, unless the Assembly passed better laws and thus enabled him to require more service from the militia. These demands for more New York and Connecticut militia did not succeed, and Putnam reported on September 29 that he had only two hundred to three hundred men from each state. Just one thousand Continentals remained, including Parsons's brigade, which stayed in New York after all. By this time, rumors of British reinforcements and a possible attack up the river were circulating, and Governor Clinton sent new urgent orders to the militia colonels to get their men collected. To make matters worse for Clinton, the Westchester County committee informed him that it expected an attack soon and had therefore ordered out its militia, which would make it difficult to muster men from Westchester for the defense of the Highlands. News from Connecticut was a little better. Trumbull wrote that Colonel Enos's regiment was on its way to Peekskill, and six hundred more militia had been ordered to join Putnam as soon as possible. Enos's regiment plus the six hundred men, however, did not add up to three thousand reinforcements.[63]

In early October, Putnam's fears of a sudden attack increased as he estimated the enemy's force in New York at nine thousand men. The New York militia still would not assemble, and Connecticut's militia was still supposedly on its way. Trumbull and the Council of Safety ordered detachments from four brigades to hurry to Peekskill to help with the situation. Washington, however, seemed to underestimate the threat to the Highlands. He informed Putnam that the Continentals left with Putnam, combined with the militia, should be enough to defend Peekskill and the Highlands. On the other hand, with upstate New York and Philadelphia both threatened, Washington also had little choice but to rely on a few Continentals and the militia to defend the Hudson River valley.[64]

As of early October, with most of the Continentals from the Highlands on their way to Pennsylvania or northern New York, and the militia responding slowly to the calls for men, Lieutenant General Henry Clinton chose his time well to attack the Highlands. The British general had been in correspondence with General John Burgoyne, who was having difficulties in upstate New York. Burgoyne had warned Clinton in late September that he could not hold out much longer unless he received some help from New York City. Clinton seemed to have hoped that the foray into New Jersey would help, but when it failed to achieve that goal, Clinton contemplated another operation up the Hudson River. With the arrival of seventeen hundred reinforcements on September 24, Clinton began to eye the Highland forts. He wrote to Howe of his idea to make a quick strike at Forts Clinton and Montgomery, and possibly open a line of communication to Albany. Though he was pessimistic about how much could be done with two thousand to three thousand soldiers, which is all he believed he could spare from the New York defenses, Clinton launched his raid up the Hudson in the first week of October.[65]

In order to confuse the rebels, Henry Clinton opened his operation with a series of diversions, including a raid into Westchester County. A British force marched through Westchester to the Saw Pits in the first days of October. While the British foragers collected livestock, the Connecticut militia responded to the threat and chased the raiders back to New Rochelle. A few days later about six hundred Tories under General Tryon, who was still the royal governor of New York, landed at Tarrytown and marched toward the Connecticut border. A Connecticut militia unit composed of light cavalry entered New York, followed Tryon, and then chased Tryon and another raiding party away from Connecticut. A ranger company skirmished with other British raiders operating in Westchester, while another Connecticut militia regiment chased off a party of 137 enemy light horsemen. On October 9 Colonel John Mead led 400

Connecticut militiamen to the Saw Pits to discourage further raids, and General Silliman ordered a regiment to take position in White Plains.[66]

Meanwhile on October 3, Henry Clinton's main operation commenced when about eleven hundred troops embarked from New York City and landed near Tarrytown the next day. A second division of the same number marched overland from Kingsbridge and joined the first division at Tarrytown. A third division of about eight hundred troops embarked on October 4, and all three divisions, roughly three thousand soldiers, combined at Verplank's Point on October 5. The few rebel troops there withdrew without firing a shot. British galleys sailed on to Peekskill to cut the rebel line of communication across the river at that place.[67]

This attack was not a total surprise to the Americans. They had heard reports of an impending attack for days, and when several small ships came up river and landed troops at Tarrytown on October 4, Putnam ordered out parties to harass and slow their march, and asked Governor Clinton to order the militia to assemble. Governor Clinton wrote to his brother to sound the alarm guns and call in the Orange County militia. The governor was disappointed that so few militia collected initially, and by the time the British concentrated their troops at Verplank's Point on October 5, few militia were in the field. Some of the militiamen on the west side of the river moved farther inland rather than risk having to fight the British. Putnam promised Governor Clinton that he would send reinforcements from Peekskill if the British made a move against Fort Montgomery. The New York Assembly, meanwhile, adjourned and left the fighting up to the governor.[68]

On October 6, all but four hundred of the British force embarked from Verplank's Point and crossed to the west side of the river, where twenty-one hundred men landed at Stony Point. About five hundred men remained on the boats. General Henry Clinton divided these twenty-one hundred men into two columns. He personally led twelve hundred men toward Fort Clinton, while Major General John Vaughan led five hundred regulars and four hundred Loyalists inland to pass behind Thunder Mountain and attack the rear of Fort Montgomery, which was situated a few miles north of Fort Clinton. Major General Tryon commanded the British rear guard and reserve.[69]

As the British column advanced toward Fort Montgomery, it brushed aside a rebel advance guard of thirty men about two and a half miles from the fort. The other British column reached Fort Clinton and waited until Vaughan's column was ready to strike Montgomery. Governor George Clinton, in command at Fort Montgomery with fewer than five hundred men, most of whom were New York militia, ordered out more detachments to oppose the British advance west of Thunder Mountain on the route to the rear of the fort, but the British division was too large to be slowed by small parties of about one hundred men. Meanwhile, about one hundred men, under the command of the governor's brother James, were the only defenders of Fort Clinton. The British attack on Montgomery opened about 5 P.M. on October 6, and General Henry Clinton launched a bayonet attack on Fort Clinton as soon as he heard the firing from Fort Montgomery. The British galleys on the river opened fire on Montgomery to support the British land attack.[70]

The battles for the two forts raged until after sundown. Fort Clinton finally fell without the British firing a shot, after a bitter but short defense. The rebel commander, James Clinton, was bayoneted in the thigh and barely escaped in the dark. Fort Montgomery's garrison held out a little longer. General Vaughan demanded its surrender, but Governor Clinton sent a subordinate officer to inform the British commander that the Americans would not surrender. However, they would accept a British surrender and promised to treat the British well. In response, Vaughan launched a bayonet attack and a wild melee ensued. The British finally captured the fort around 8 P.M., but many of the defenders escaped. Governor George Clinton escaped down the side of the hill and crossed the Hudson in a boat at night. Altogether, the British lost about 200 men while taking the two forts, but they captured 100 or more rebels, and wounded or killed another 150 men.[71]

The next day, October 7, British commander Henry Clinton sent a summons to the garrison of Fort Constitution, just upriver from the recently captured forts, to surrender. When the American defenders fired on the British flag, he ordered General Tryon to embark his men and take the fort by force. Tryon arrived on October 8 and found that the rebel garrison had fled after burning the fort. The British destroyed the chain and boom that the rebels had

stretched across the river, and thus opened it for the British amphibious force to continue further to the north.[72]

Between October 5, when Henry Clinton landed at Verplank's
Point, and the loss of the third fort on October 8, General
Putnam sent no Continental reinforcements to the governor, despite
his promise. The British fooled him on October 6 by leaving four
hundred men on the east side of the river at Verplank's Point while
they crossed to the west side and attacked the forts. Meanwhile, British boats threatened a landing at nearby Fort Independence and
Peekskill on the east side. Putnam had only about twelve hundred
Continentals and three hundred militia, and he decided he could
not chance sending men to the west side to help Governor Clinton
or his brother. When Putnam heard the firing from the forts on
October 6, he belatedly detached five hundred men to help the two
garrisons, but the forts fell before the reinforcements could get across
the river. On October 7, Governor Clinton conferred with Putnam,
and they decided to retreat northward. George Clinton would rally
his "broken but brave forces," as he described them to the legislature, on the west side, while Putnam would defend on the east bank.
Putnam said he would send a Continental regiment to join the
governor's force.[73]

Putnam, however, had acted quickly to call for help. As soon as he
realized that the British were advancing up the river, he sent out
calls for men to the governments of New Jersey and Connecticut. As
early as October 4, when the British first moved upriver, he wrote to
the militia colonels of the Connecticut regiments stationed near the
New York border to forward their men to Peekskill. General Parsons, whose brigade remained in New York, then raced to Connecticut to speed the march of the militiamen, hoping to get at least two
thousand men to rendezvous soon near Poughkeepsie. By October
11, General James Wadsworth of the Connecticut militia informed
Governor Trumbull that Parsons had one regiment of his brigade
plus one thousand other Connecticut militiamen near Peekskill, and
more Connecticut militia were arriving.[74]

When Washington heard of the British attacks, he realized that
he might have weakened the Highlands too much, and quickly asked
Governor Livingston to send all possible New Jersey militia to help
Putnam. Livingston asked his Council of Safety, and it resolved to

send up to one thousand men to New York. Livingston feared that the usual difficulties of mustering militia would render the aid useless, but he hoped that at least Dickinson could immediately send some of his one thousand men that were guarding the coast at Elizabethtown. Despite the presence of one German and five Tory regiments on Staten Island, Dickinson dispatched Brigadier General Winds with three hundred troops on the road to New Windsor. The rest of the militia ordered out by the council would join Winds when ready. Winds wrote ahead to George Clinton for orders, and ultimately joined James Clinton and a small force of New Yorkers near New Windsor on October 19. By October 23, Winds had about six hundred men, and more were still coming to join him.[75]

It was well for the defenders of New York that their neighbors made such efforts, because the British did not immediately return to New York City. After landing troops at the abandoned Fort Constitution on October 8, Henry Clinton sent General Tryon farther upriver. Tryon destroyed the Continental Village and returned the next day to Fort Montgomery, where General Clinton remained with the main body of his force. The British also maintained the detachment at Verplank's Point as a threat to the rebels on the east side of the river. Fortunately for the Americans, the reinforcements kept arriving. By October 9, Putnam had about twelve hundred Continentals and fourteen hundred militia on the east side of the Hudson, while Governor Clinton had two hundred Continentals, some of whom had escaped from the forts, and three hundred New York militia on the west side. The governor and Putnam conferred again, and decided to hold Fishkill and New Windsor as long as possible. If the British pushed upriver, they would fall back toward Kingston. They assumed Albany and the relief of General John Burgoyne were the objectives. Governor Clinton wrote to General Horatio Gates in northern New York for help, and after Gates's success at the battle of Bemis Heights on October 7, he was able to send several hundred militiamen to Albany.[76]

George Clinton, meanwhile, was having trouble getting the militiamen on the western side to assemble in as great a number as he wished because they wanted to stay home and protect their own families. They came to camp in the morning but returned home at night. Putnam had a similar problem getting militia out on his side of the river. The Continental regiment that Clinton expected Putnam to send him did not materialize. Putnam instead ordered a militia unit to cross from the east side of the river to the west. Governor Clinton not only believed that the militiamen would not cross the river, he even urged an officer of the regiment to tell the men to stay on the east side with their families. Meanwhile, the Council of Safety was trying to get all males sixteen and over to rendezvous at their alarm posts in case the enemy advanced farther.[77]

The real hope of the New Yorkers lay, however, with Governor Clinton. The unsuccessful but stubborn defense of Fort Montgomery had increased his reputation as a man of talent and strength, and as far away as Massachusetts, his resistance was praised. John Wyllys, a Connecticut soldier fighting alongside George Clinton and the New York militia, managed to weave together his New England prejudices against New Yorkers with an accurate portrayal of Clinton's influence over the people who were rallying to him in the present crisis:

> We are at present on the West Side of the River, under the Command of Governor Clinton—Never had a man a more absolute Ascendancy over people, than he has over the Inhabitants of this part of the Country—They are now gathered round their *Chief*—a stout hardy race—armed with good, long Musquets— in high Spirits—exulting in their behaviour at Fort Montgomery & wishing for another opportunity—In short they do not appear like Dutchmen; but have the manners of N. England; from whence I believe they sprang—Their Governor deservedly has their Esteem—few men are his Superior.[78]

Governor Clinton was at New Windsor on October 12. He kept strong parties forward of his position to watch the British moves and enable him to remain between the British and Kingston. He asked the Council of Safety to send the available militia from the north to him so that he could concentrate his force. Putnam's command, meanwhile, continued to grow at Fishkill to about six thousand men, of which five thousand were militia. This number included about fourteen hundred Connecticut militia commanded by General Silliman and another two thousand Connecticut militia led by General Andrew Ward. Putnam felt confident enough of his numbers to detach

Parsons with two thousand men to return to Peekskill and hold that town, and even to reconnoiter Kingsbridge in case an opportunity to strike at the British base presented itself. At the same time, Putnam retired northward with the rest of his troops to parallel the British movement up the Hudson. General Gates approved of Putnam's decision to move north, and promised on October 15 to send help to Putnam once Burgoyne surrendered, which Gates expected any day.[79]

Putnam retreated to the north to counter the British commander's final move of this operation. General Henry Clinton decided to make one last effort to help Burgoyne, and therefore sent General Vaughan with two thousand provincial troops and supplies for five thousand troops up the Hudson. Vaughan's detachment sailed northward on October 15, plundering and destroying rebel houses and vessels along the river until they reached Kingston the next day. There they ran into a rebel force with fourteen cannons positioned behind a breastwork. Vaughan needed to move farther upriver to get information on Burgoyne, so he landed troops to dislodge the rebels and prevent their interrupting his communications with Henry Clinton or harassing his return down river. Governor Clinton raced ahead of his men, who were marching northward from New Windsor, in order to be with the men at Kingston before the British attacked, but even his presence could not offset the numerical imbalance. Unfortunately for George Clinton and the rebel defenders, despite a heroic forty-mile forced march in twenty-four hours, the troops from New Windsor were still about four miles from Kingston when Vaughan launched his attack. The few defenders resisted briefly, then continued to fight from within the houses and behind some small defensive works in town. The British captured the rebel cannons, and when they came under fire from the Americans in town, Vaughan ordered his troops to destroy the town. Both sides had only a few casualties.[80]

On October 17 and 18, Vaughan and the British troops and ships slowly moved a few miles farther north, burning buildings near the river, while Governor Clinton followed along the west bank to protect the supplies removed from Kingston. Putnam moved up the east side, leaving detachments in Fishkill and Poughkeepsie. James Clinton, with some New York militia and the New Jersey militia commanded by Winds, advanced on New Windsor. Vaughan stopped about forty-five miles south of Albany and sent two messengers to discover Burgoyne's situation. When he learned of Burgoyne's surrender to Gates on October 17, he decided he could furnish Burgoyne no further help. Becoming wary of the growing number of rebels on both banks of the Hudson, which he estimated, somewhat accurately, at five thousand men with Putnam on the east side and about fifteen hundred men with George Clinton on the west side, Vaughan decided to return downriver to the base in New York City.[81]

While the British remained north of Kingston, George Clinton kept near them with about one thousand men. He believed that Henry Clinton had originally planned to advance to Albany but Burgoyne's surrender had forced a change in plans. When he learned of the fate of Burgoyne's army, Governor Clinton quickly wrote to Gates for reinforcements. If he could have four thousand additional men, two thousand on each side of the river, he could attack the British. James Clinton, meanwhile, collected and stationed the militia he had from New Jersey and from Orange County along the Hudson River near Newburgh. Unfortunately for these plans to attack the British during their withdrawal, the Clinton brothers were not in communication with Putnam, who was still on the east side of the river.[82]

Ignoring the hostile moves of the rebels, Vaughan's command sailed down the river between October 23 and 25, passing New Windsor on the twenty-fourth and reaching Fort Montgomery the next day. Vaughan returned to New York City on October 26 without further incident. Henry Clinton, meanwhile, had hoped to retain the Highland forts, but General Howe sent orders for him to send substantial reinforcements to Philadelphia and to destroy the Highland forts. Howe believed that Clinton could not maintain a line of communication with the forts during the winter, and therefore they were not worth trying to hold. Clinton had the forts dismantled and withdrew to New York City.[83]

The Americans followed the British along both sides of the river, reoccupying Fishkill and New Windsor in strength. Reinforcements, meanwhile, were on their way from Gates's army. In all, Gates sent fifty-seven hundred Continentals, which increased Putnam's force to about nine thousand men at the end of October, including some newly arrived militia. This total did not include the New York or Connecticut militiamen who had served during the crisis days because Putnam dismissed them when he heard the northern reinforcements were close at hand. At the same time in early November, the Clinton brothers were still on the west side with their party of New York militia, which George Clinton tried to reinforce with a call for five hundred more militiamen from Orange and Ulster counties. General Winds and his New Jersey militia returned home.[84]

As Putnam advanced down the river with his reinforced corps, he contemplated his next step. General Gates, who was on his way to join Putnam, advised Putnam to reoccupy the posts along the Hudson immediately and then send a large force into New Jersey to prevent the British from marching overland to help Howe in Pennsylvania. Putnam consequently held a council of war with his officers, including George and James Clinton, and they decided that four thousand men should go to Haverstraw, one thousand should remain in the Highlands to repair the forts, and the rest should march toward Kingsbridge to divert the enemy's attention and be ready to take the offensive if an opportunity arose. Washington at first agreed with these plans and even urged Putnam to march men down both sides of the river, not only to retake the Highland forts but also to grab New York while it was weak.[85]

Washington then changed his mind and decided not to leave the newly arrived Continentals in New York. Soon after he heard that the British had returned to New York, he ordered Putnam to send the majority of the northern brigades to the Continental Army in Pennsylvania so that he could concentrate all available forces against Howe's army in Philadelphia. Putnam sent these troops, which left him only Parsons's Continental brigade and three New York Continental regiments, altogether about eighteen hundred men. To replace the men, Washington again tried to take advantage of the availability of local militia units by urging Putnam to call in additional militiamen as reinforcements. Washington hoped that with the remaining Continentals and the supporting militia, Putnam could retake and hold the Highland posts. The commander in chief justified withdrawing the Continentals from New York because the British had recently shifted men from New York to Philadelphia. Though he understood that the people in New York would feel alarmed and deserted by this withdrawal, Washington believed they would ultimately realize the logic of it.[86]

Washington's decision to call the Continentals from New York meant that Putnam's plans had to change. Putnam, however, still wanted to send a force to White Plains to harass and threaten the British lines, and he still hoped to attack New York. He therefore asked the Connecticut government for two thousand to three thousand more militia and promised that an attack would be made. Washington approved of a more limited plan. Putnam should no longer try to attack New York, but Washington suggested that he could threaten an attack on Long Island, and Washington asked General Dickinson to threaten Staten Island. He advised Dickinson and Putnam to collect boats and men, and make it look as if they planned to attack New York City. Washington even sent a spy into Howe's camp to spread the word that a large force of New Jersey militia were going to attack Staten Island while New York militiamen attacked New York City. Clearly he believed that the threat of a militia attack carried some weight with the British. The Continental Congress, which agreed with the plan to reoccupy the posts in the Highlands, appointed Gates to take command of the forces there and authorized him to apply to the state governments of New England, as well as to those of New York and New Jersey, for militia reinforcements.[87]

General Dickinson had initially suggested to Washington the idea of a coordinated move against Staten Island and New York. Throughout the fighting along the Hudson River in October, he commanded opposite Staten Island a force of militia that on October 24 numbered only seven hundred men. Washington's repeated calls for reinforcements in Pennsylvania and southern New Jersey had stripped much of New Jersey's strength. Dickinson had planned to send most of the men currently with him to Washington, but the militiamen refused to leave the eastern shore defenseless and the Council of Safety forbade Dickinson to leave. Therefore, in early November, Dickinson and Washington decided that if the militia would not leave the coast, it might as well make itself useful by attacking Staten Island. Nevertheless, Dickinson ordered 160 more men from his detachment to Washington despite the objections. He believed that he could increase his militia force to twelve hundred men for a raid, but he promised Washington that he would attack Staten whether he raised more troops or not. According to his intelligence reports, the enemy had only one thousand to twelve hundred men on the island. The New

Jersey Assembly supported Dickinson's idea for an attack on Staten Island by ordering General Winds to call out his militia again.[88]

In the end, Putnam and Dickinson both executed versions of this aggressive plan. First, Putnam decided to move with the majority of his force toward White Plains, where the fighting had continued to rage since the British diversionary forces had raided toward Connecticut in early October. Putnam and Parsons had received reports of this raid, but during General Henry Clinton's operation up the Hudson River, they could do nothing about it. On October 29, after Clinton's amphibious force had returned to New York City, Parsons sent 150 Connecticut state troops and a detachment from his Continental brigade in the Highlands to White Plains. The rest of Parsons's brigade followed, arriving on October 31. Parsons's men captured about thirty of the horse thieves, as Parsons called them, as well as six Tories and six of the enemy's mounted raiders. A Connecticut militia regiment then joined Parsons at White Plains. The presence of Parsons's troops and the capture of several of the raiders helped ease the situation for the Whigs in the area because many of the Tories who lived nearby disbanded their units and fled to Long Island. The rest of Putnam's small army, meanwhile, moved toward Kingsbridge in an effort to pin down the British in their defenses and protect their own foragers.[89]

Putnam planned to pursue Washington's and Dickinson's idea about simultaneous threats, if not attacks, against New York City and Staten Island. Still disappointed that his Continental force had been so weakened, Putnam asked Governor Trumbull to send the three thousand militia to help him attack Fort Independence near Kingsbridge, and possibly even New York City itself. He was not confident, however, that the Connecticut government could furnish many men. Trumbull regretted having to call out more militia but believed the situation demanded action, so he ordered six hundred militiamen to join Putnam for two months. Few new men trickled into Putnam's camp, and as of November 11, Putnam had with him only two thousand men, mostly militia, and some of them were to leave at the end of November. Despite Putnam's pessimism, Dickinson, who was collecting militia in New Jersey, noticed that Putnam's advance toward New York City had caused alarm within the British lines.[90]

On November 27, the simultaneous moves against New York City and Staten Island took place. A detachment of Putnam's Continentals made a feint against Fort Independence and skirmished with the enemy garrison; both sides lost about three killed. To support Dickinson's anticipated move onto Staten Island, Putnam sent Parsons with his and another Continental brigade toward Kingsbridge to draw British attention from Dickinson's efforts. Dickinson, who had collected fourteen hundred militiamen, two hundred more than the maximum force he expected to assemble, led his troops onto Staten Island that same day. He tried to slip his men behind the Tories and Germans stationed on the west side of the island, but the enemy heard of his approach and escaped the trap. Dickinson's force then skirmished with the enemy throughout the day, capturing two and killing five or six while losing three captured and ten wounded. After eight hours on the island, Dickinson returned his force to the New Jersey shore without molestation. Favoring his effort on the island was a heavy tide that day, which prevented the British from sending reinforcements from Manhattan or Long Islands.[91]

Dickinson and Governor Livingston were unimpressed with Putnam's feint against New York, and Washington also expressed his disappointment with the results of the coordinated maneuver. The British and Germans were unmoved as well, as evident by their lack of comment on the rebel advances. Putnam, however, claimed to have achieved a signal success in lower Westchester County by breaking up the Tory units of light cavalry, as well as the groups of thieves and bandits who plagued both sides in the neutral ground between the two armies. That at least three thousand militiamen had assembled for these movements was also a success for that time of year.[92]

After receiving news of these movements, Washington ordered Putnam to concentrate all of his time and resources on defending and rebuilding the Highland forts, and to call in his detachments from Westchester County. He worried that the British might repeat their move up the river in the spring and wanted the defenses better prepared. Washington also asked Gates, whom the Continental Congress had put in overall command of the forces along the Hudson River, to concentrate on the river works and to call on the New England states for more militia to help build the fortifications. Gates instead went to Philadelphia, and Putnam remained in command. Washington then asked Governor George Clinton to support Putnam's efforts, take personal charge of the works along the river, and call out any necessary militia. Putnam complied with Washington's orders, called off his operations in Westchester County, and ordered his forces back to Peekskill. He then warned Trumbull that this withdrawal would uncover that part of the country, which also contained the road to the Connecticut border, and he complained that only fifteen of the six hundred Connecticut militiamen ordered to him had arrived. At the same time, he asked Governor Clinton for New York militia to take over the protection of Westchester County.[93]

Despite the limited results of the operations, for the second straight year the militia had supported winter diversions against New York City and its environs. The militia had again proved inadequate for immediate defensive needs but had shown its willingness to respond after the initial British advance, and thus limit British movements and help force them to return to their starting point. The sequence of events during the Hudson River raid resembled that of the Danbury raid in April.

After Putnam and Dickinson ended their offensive operations against the British, the local militiamen returned to their duties of defending the Highlands and coasts, raiding enemy posts, and hunting Tories. Governor Clinton, who had been working on the river fortifications and obstructions ever since the British had retreated in mid-October, complained that Putnam had been too busy in Westchester County to help him. Most of the New York, Connecticut, and New Hampshire militia with Clinton departed on December 15, and Clinton was left with one small, tired Continental regiment. He hoped Putnam's imminent return from White Plains would free more men to work on the fortifications and to man the defenses. Meanwhile, in Orange County, on the west side of the Hudson, the Continentals withdrew, but the local rangers maintained an active campaign against the Tories by sending small parties past the enemy's lines and burning Loyalists' houses. Tories occasionally crossed from Staten and Manhattan islands and took off inhabitants before the local Whig militia could organize. They released the captives on parole or held them to exchange for Tories captured by the Whigs.[94]

When Trumbull received Putnam's warning about the withdrawal of the troops from Westchester County, he ordered out additional militia to defend the area but left the actual number to be assembled up to General Silliman, who still commanded the militia in the southwestern part of Connecticut. Trumbull also promised Putnam that he would address the Assembly concerning the failure of the Connecticut militia to turn out and reinforce Putnam in November. Apparently most of those men called to serve paid a fine instead of going to New York. Connecticut's militia laws punished delinquent militiamen with only a monetary fine, similar to the law in New Jersey, but this was the first major incident of that provision interfering with the use of the Connecticut militia. Trumbull said that the matter was out of his power, but he would discuss it with the Assembly.[95]

General Parsons returned to Connecticut in December and at Norwalk took command of a small detachment of Continentals and some Connecticut militia. From there, he decided to resume the raids on Long Island. On the evening of December 9, he launched an expedition with some of the Continentals and militiamen to destroy the enemy ships being used to collect wood on Long Island, to remove or destroy all supplies that they found, and to attack a regiment stationed on the island. Part of his party did not cross the Sound due to rough weather; one ship ran aground and fifty-five men were captured by the British. Parsons landed on Long Island with about three hundred men, and on December 10 they destroyed one ship and exchanged shots with the crews of several other ships just off the coast. On December 10, more men joined Parsons from New London, and this reinforcement helped him slip his command past the enemy ships and return to the mainland. He brought twenty prisoners with him, his only losses being the men captured while crossing to Long Island. When Washington heard of this raid, he cautioned against further such efforts, urging that the commanders in New York and Connecticut instead concentrate on the defensive works along the Hudson River.[96]

In New Jersey, the few militiamen left in the field to defend the eastern shore maintained their positions. As of early December, Governor Livingston ordered five hundred militiamen to guard at Elizabethtown, one hundred at Newark, and sixty at Woodbridge.

Dickinson took advantage of the lull in the season to go home and attend to personal business, but he promised to return in an emergency. Meanwhile, the New Jersey militia continued the bitter war against the Tories, especially in Monmouth County. In constant skirmishes, Whig and Tory militiamen fought as the Whigs tried to isolate the Loyalists from the British lines and to protect pro-Whig inhabitants from the ravages of Tory raids. This civil war was brutal and showed no signs of abating after two and a half years. Governor Livingston best summarized the Whig view of the New Jersey Tories: "A Tory is an incorrigible Animal: And nothing but the Extinction of Life, will extinguish his Malevolence against Liberty."[97]

As these local clashes continued, the campaign of 1777 around the British lines in New York ground to a halt. It had been a busy year, beginning with the winter partisan war and ending with that small-scale war still raging. The main regular armies of both sides had drifted out of the theater, but the maneuvers and fighting between the regular units and militia remaining in the area had been hectic and confused.

The events around New York, however, had demonstrated the growing importance of the Whig militia in the defense of the United States. Even the British were beginning to recognize the nature of the war that they had on their hands. Sir William Howe informed Secretary of State George Germain on November 30 that "in the apparent temper of the Americans a considerable addition to the present force will be requisite for effecting any essential change in their disposition and the reestablishment of the King's authority . . . ." Nicholas Cresswell, an English journalist who traveled in America during part of the war, showed a combination of contempt and admiration for the rebels when he expressed shock that "General Howe, a man brought up to War from his youth," could "be puzzled and plagued for two years together, with a Virginia Tobacco planter." After Howe's retreat from New Jersey in June of 1777, Cresswell had written:

> Washington is certainly a most surprising man, one of Nature's geniuses, a Heaven-born General, if there is any of that sort. That a Negro-driver should, with a ragged Banditti of undisciplined people, the scum and refuse of all nations on earth, so long keep a British General at bay, nay, even, oblige him, with

as fine an army of Veteran Soldiers as ever England had on the American Continent, to retreat, is astonishing.

Sir James Murray, who had a comment on everything occurring around him, perhaps best described the British attitude toward the partisan war spreading around them: "It is a barbarous business and in a barbarous country."[98]

The Whig militia deserved much of the credit for making this war "a barbarous business." With the bitter civil war between Whig and Tory parties and the deliberate partisan activities that Washington employed and encouraged, the fighting often degenerated to a level where the discipline and large-scale fighting ability of the British army could be overcome by the rebels. That the state governments kept calling forth their militia strength and that the militiamen kept answering the calls, at least in emergencies, showed that the American rebels would fight long and hard for their independence. Just as important, the different state governments and militia forces continued to work together. The Connecticut government and militia did not renounce the larger war to concentrate on their own defenses. In New York, the Whigs organized a new government to enable them to use their militia more effectively, and they elected George Clinton as governor, a wise choice at least militarily. The New Jersey militia showed that its failure in 1776 was a fluke and that the state troops of New Jersey would fight tenaciously to avoid further British occupation.

The Continental Congress followed the role it had adopted in late 1776 by letting Washington handle the field operations. The congressmen limited themselves to supporting him with letters to the state governments. When Washington left the New York–New Jersey area, they did assume a slightly more active role. The Congress had developed confidence in Washington's handling of the theater but, with him gone, felt compelled to step in and help direct activities.

Washington's ability to coordinate Continentals and militia in the field against the British army showed itself in June 1777. When he moved the army to Pennsylvania to meet Howe's army, he relied on the militia, with the support of a few Continentals, to hold the Highlands. He expected the militia to handle the needs of local defense against British raids, and though he may not have believed the militia really were up to the challenge, necessity forced him to rely on it anyway. The presence of the militia at any threatened point was one of the advantages that the Whigs enjoyed, an advantage that allowed Washington to concentrate his Continentals wherever the British army went. Washington explained this aspect of his strategy to Jedediah Huntington of Connecticut:

> Great Dependence is placed upon the spirited Exertions of the Militia of the Country as the Continental Army cannot be every Place where the Enemy are easily and quickly transported by Water. If the Militia of every State were as deservedly reputable for military Order and Prowess as the Jersey, they would be as formidable to the Enemy as the continental Troops, because our Marches are eluded by their Navigation, whilst the Militia of the Country are in every Place ready to defend their own pleasant Habitations.[99]

Thus the availability of the militia enabled Washington to shift the army to Pennsylvania and send reinforcements to northern New York without surrendering the Highlands outright.

What was becoming clear, however, was that militiamen could not defend against attacks by sizable British forces without sizable Continental support. They failed in Connecticut against two thousand soldiers, they failed against two thousand in New Jersey in September, and they failed against three thousand in New York in October. In all three cases, the militia did rally after the initial losses, and its presence helped to limit British gains and to hurry the British out of the area. Thus it was only partially successful on the defense.

Another pattern becoming clear concerned the willingness of the militia to serve. The season of the year and the presence of the Continental Army did not seem to have a material effect on whether the militia responded when called, though the presence of at least a few Continentals did inspire the militia to fight longer. The deciding factor, however, seemed to be the level of immediate danger. To the credit of the militiamen, the more critical the crisis, the more quickly the militia responded and the greater the number who mustered. Generals and politicians had trouble getting militia units filled and then keeping militia soldiers in the field just to guard against possible attack. When an attack occurred, however, the militia responded without being called. A man like Washington, who liked order, discipline, and preparedness, had trouble accepting this pattern because he never knew in advance what numbers to expect, and therefore he could not plan ahead.

Thus, the proper place of the militia in this war had clarified. Militiamen were effective when fighting a partisan war against enemy parties of a few dozen to a few hundred, and they were effective against Tories. In addition, they could operate as partisans on their own and in conjunction with Continental detachments. Their availability anywhere in response to an emergency was a great benefit, but planning ahead with the militia was difficult. Militia units did not fight well on a larger scale, and they therefore proved to be ineffective as part of the army in stand-up battles against large British forces. They were partisans and therefore could serve best in that capacity.

Washington clearly understood all of these attributes of the militia. He also never gave up urging the creation of a large, regular army that would eliminate any dependence on the militia. As he was unlikely to get such an army, he set aside his wishes and instead made use of what he had. He employed the militia where he believed it was best suited, and he grudgingly admitted the good, and at times even essential, service that the militia did provide. He also had to face the fact that the militia on its own could not stop enemy raids, but this weakness could be rectified only by spreading Continental units around to support the militia for local defense. So far, he had resisted taking this step.

CHAPTER SEVEN

The Militia
in a Changing War, 1778

THE WAR changed dramatically in the year 1778. The alliance between the governments of the United States and France, signed in February 1778, had far-reaching consequences for the contest between Great Britain and the United States. The immediate effect was the British decision to concentrate their forces in New York City, in anticipation of shifting their major effort in North America to the Southern states. This development had a direct impact on the fighting in the middle states in 1778 as the two main armies prepared to return to the New York City area and the partisan warfare raged unabated around New York City.

Until news of the French alliance arrived in May 1778, the main British and American armies remained in Pennsylvania. As the Continental Army shivered in the cold and trained at Valley Forge, the defense of the country around New York City remained in the hands of the state governments, local Continental generals, and state militia forces. Though Washington and the Continental Congress tried to support the local efforts, they were far away and had no immediate control. The officers and government officials in the area, therefore, had to provide for the defense of the coasts and Highlands, and with few Continental soldiers available, the militia had the primary responsibility for manning the defenses, launching raids, skirmishing with enemy parties, and isolating the British from the countryside.

The Highlands remained the focus of attention for the defenders in the middle states, especially since the old forts had been destroyed in October 1777 and new works had yet to be erected. In January 1778, the Continental commander in New York, Major General Israel Putnam, held a council of war at which the officers chose West Point, opposite old Fort Constitution, as the site for the new defensive works. Constant delays, however, postponed the beginning of construction, and a frustrated Governor George Clinton ordered seven hundred New York militiamen to muster in February to help with the works and defend the area. He asked the governments of Connecticut and Massachusetts for twenty-three hundred more men. Clinton hoped that when these three thousand militia soldiers assembled, they could coordinate with the few Continentals stationed in the Highlands and finish the works. Despite these efforts, however, the new works had not even been started as of March 10.[1]

Understanding that it would take some time for the militia of New York, Connecticut, and Massachusetts to gather, Governor Clinton also asked for the help of two Continental regiments then stationed in northern New York. Washington obliged, and ordered three small Continental regiments to the Highlands. Even before these reinforcements arrived, Brigadier General Samuel Parsons, in command at West Point, initiated construction with the few men he had. To protect the Highlands while Parsons's troops worked and the militia regiments of New England and New York assembled, Clinton urged the New York Assembly to remove all Tories from the vicinity of the new forts. He then ordered out six temporary companies of militia to guard the approaches to the Highland defenses. The governor promised Parsons that he would take personal command of the militia if the enemy advanced.[2]

Alexander McDougall, promoted to major general the previous October, arrived in March 1778 and temporarily replaced Putnam as commander in the Highlands. In order to protect the newly initiated works, McDougall concentrated five small Continental regiments, eight hundred men total, at West Point on the west side of the river, and positioned four equally small regiments on the east side of the river. As these regiments were so weak, he requested further militia forces to gather at West Point and Fishkill. Governor Clinton agreed with McDougall's dispositions and ordered the necessary militia to muster for temporary duty while the longer-term militia regiments formed. A confident McDougall informed Washington on April 13 that the partially completed fort at West Point was strong enough to resist a sudden attack, though he planned to erect more works on the nearby heights. A month later, however, the works were still only half completed because many of the militia ordered to help with the construction refused to stay in camp for more than a few weeks. As of June, the defenses at West Point were still incomplete, and Clinton continued to order out further temporary militia detachments to supplement the work parties.[3]

The area south of the Highlands also lay open to British raids, and Governor Clinton directed part of the long-term militia unit ordered out in February to defend Westchester County and prevent any communication between the Loyalists and the British army. The partisan fighting that had raged since 1776 continued in that county, though the British sent fewer parties from their lines in the winter. Still, a Continental regiment remained at White Plains to support the militia against the British troops and Tories who did raid. As winter gave way to spring, British excursions became more frequent, and the local militia met and fought the British and Tory parties whenever they left the British lines. Lieutenant Colonel Morris Graham in particular used his New York militia regiment to good effect, despite the fluctuation in numbers from over five hundred men in the field in mid-March to about two hundred in May. He stationed his regiment near Fort Independence, which was a part of the British defenses near Manhattan Island, to watch for any British moves and to engage raiding parties as they issued forth from the British stronghold.[4]

On the west side of the Hudson River, local militiamen worried that the forage stored in the area would attract the attention of the British. Therefore, to protect these supplies, the Orange County militia regiment assembled and remained in the field until Washington finally ordered Parsons to remove the forage. Throughout April and May, the local militia regiment still had to guard the shore whenever British ships appeared. Orange County officials asked the state government for more help, but Governor Clinton denied the request on the basis of a policy similar to the one that Washington followed: since many areas needed protection, the local militia had to provide the necessary defense for its own region.[5]

In Connecticut, the Assembly ordered companies of twenty to twenty-five militiamen to be stationed in the principal port towns along Long Island Sound, and to serve for the entire year. In addition, the Assembly ordered the formation of two state brigades of 720 men each to serve until March 1, 1779. The men in these brigades would be liable for duty wherever necessary. Particular ports, such as New Haven, occasionally received companies from one of the organizing brigades to reinforce their guard companies. When the guards failed to muster or simply left for home early, as happened at Stamford and Norwalk in April, the regional militia general ordered temporary drafts from his local brigade to supply the necessary guards. At the end of May, the Assembly ordered the raising of two battalions of 728 men each (the number of men in a brigade and a battalion was not always different) to serve for two months in or out of the state as necessary. In early June the Assembly ordered a muster of all Connecticut militia in response to a British embarkation from New York.[6]

Meanwhile, local militiamen and the few Continentals in the state defended the southwestern border near New York. Brigadier General Gold S. Silliman commanded the militia brigade in southwestern Connecticut, though as of February, he had available only 390 of the 700 men ordered to active duty in the area. Silliman admitted, however, that proportionally this was a better response than had occurred with any earlier militia call. These men's enlistments ended March 1, and Silliman feared that the border would then be defenseless. Governor Trumbull persuaded Putnam, who at that time in February still commanded the New York–Connecticut region, to move the Continental regiment in Hartford to the Saw Pits in order to support the militia. When the assembled militia soldiers left on March 1, Silliman acted without waiting for orders and replaced those men who went home with other soldiers from his brigade. The Assembly later approved his actions while expressing the hope that the two long-term militia brigades then assembling would be able to furnish guards for the southwestern regions before Silliman's latest detachment went home. On May 1, however, Silliman once again had to order temporary militia forces into the field because the state brigades had not yet been fully assembled. Trumbull advised Silliman to order out sufficient numbers to serve two more months. Late in

May, the Assembly ordered the men who had already enlisted in the two state brigades to march to the Saw Pits.[7]

New Jersey's militia was also busy during the winter and spring, especially against Tory and British foraging parties. Militiamen guarded along the coast but could not prevent all communication between the Loyalists and the British in New York City. The Council of Safety specifically ordered a company of rangers into Bergen County to support a militia party already there, trying to stop the Loyalists from supplying the British. Meanwhile, the British ran daily raids into New Jersey to collect forage and supplies, and New Jersey militia parties occasionally intercepted them. In early April, the council advised Governor William Livingston to order out more of the Bergen County militia to prevent these British excursions and also to remove all the grain within reach of the enemy. In addition, the New Jersey militia worked for Washington by gathering information, as well as occasionally raiding Staten Island and taking a few prisoners. As these constant duties exhausted the militia near the coast, the New Jersey Assembly wrote to the Continental Congress in April that the militia was fatigued, the state had no Continentals defending it, and therefore the Assembly wanted the Congress to send help soon. For the moment, however, the militia had to serve as best it could.[8]

The state governments of Connecticut, New York, and New Jersey tried to improve the efficiency of their militia forces by clarifying the different levels of control over the militia and considering legislative revisions of the militia laws. In New York, Governor Clinton retained direct control of the state troops, calling out the militia and asking the New England governments for support. He coordinated efforts within New York between the militia and the local Continental commanders, and commanded the movements and placement of the New York militia when in the field. The Assembly functioned mainly in a supporting role for the governor. It helped advise on the selection of West Point as the site of the new fortifications on the Hudson River, and tried to promote Clinton's work in reconstructing the defenses in the Highlands. In addition, the legislature authorized the Continental commanders in the area to call on the militia if necessary. The division of authority in New York's government over assembling the militia seemed to lie between temporary or short-term calls on the militia, which the governor authorized, and calls for longer-term militia units, which the Assembly handled. When he wanted seven hundred militiamen to serve throughout 1778, Clinton asked the Assembly to provide them, and it passed the necessary act on March 31. Clinton urged the legislature to control the Tories of the area, and the Assembly responded by passing an act authorizing the governor to remove dangerous people.[9]

Governor Clinton wanted new militia regulations to enhance his ability to assemble the militia when necessary, and he was angry at the Assembly's hesitation to enact such a bill. The Assembly continued to study the issue, however, and finally passed a new law April 3, 1778. This law authorized Clinton to call out part or all of the state's militia, at his discretion, for the defense of New York or any other state, though soldiers could be ordered out of the state only for a maximum of forty days. Local officers retained the power to assemble their commands in an emergency without waiting for orders. Punishments for delinquent soldiers remained similar: militiamen who refused to muster when called could only be fined. The new law also ordered all men who were exempt from regular duty with the militia to enroll themselves in companies liable for service in case of invasion or insurrection. Thus, the executive had his powers strengthened in relation to calling out the militia, but the problem of how to compel a militia soldier to serve remained. Despite this continued weakness, Clinton still had confidence in the militia, especially since news of the French alliance had encouraged the men.[10]

Connecticut's Assembly maintained more control over its militia by ordering out the coastal guards and raising the two brigades for longer duty. During active campaigns and immediate emergencies, Trumbull and the Council of Safety often stepped in when the Assembly was in recess, but during quieter months, the Assembly could handle the job. Indicative of its confidence in the state militia, the Assembly did not revise its militia laws.

In June, the Connecticut Assemblymen responded to calls for help from New York's government by ordering four regiments of militia to be raised and sent to New York. Putnam, who was at that time in Hartford, believed the militiamen would not leave their own businesses "till the Enemy have made some *vigorous Push*, when perhaps their assistance may be too late." In response to further requests from General Gates, who had taken command in New York by then, the Connecticut Assembly increased the long-term force earmarked for New York to 1000 men in six regiments and, as mentioned, ordered that two state regiments of 728 militiamen each be enlisted to serve for two months in Connecticut. By June 18, on the eve of the summer campaigning season, only 723 of these 1000 men had actually joined the six regiments bound for New York, so the Assembly ordered one of the new two-month regiments to join the force going to New York. Trumbull confidently estimated these steps would provide a reinforcement of 1631 privates.[11]

The activities of the New Jersey Assembly resembled those of the New York Assembly more than those of the Connecticut Assembly. Governor Livingston and the Council of Safety handled the duty of ordering out temporary parties of militia and rangers. Though the Assembly did occasionally pass resolutions for the establishment of long-term militia units during these first months of 1778, it left the role of militia commander to the executive branch. The Assembly, however, worked on improving the militia laws, especially after Governor Livingston urged it to revise the laws and raise regiments that could serve for one year rather than continuing to follow the current system of monthly tours of duty for the militia. The Assembly passed an act on April 14 that authorized the governor, with the consent of the legislature—or in its recess, of the council—to muster and position up to half of the state's militia upon a request from Washington, another Continental general, or a neighboring state's executive. In case of invasion, insurrection, or other alarm, the governor could immediately call on all of the militia. Local militia officers retained the authority to assemble their troops in an emergency without waiting for orders from superiors. Except in the case of an actual invasion or insurrection, however, the militia still could serve for only one month at a time, and any soldier who refused to muster when called only had to pay a fine. Thus, the New Jersey Assembly, just like its neighbors in New York and Connecticut, did not solve the problem of enforcing orders for the militia to assemble, nor did its law help keep the militia in the field for longer periods of time.[12]

Livingston assured Washington that he would call out the militia whenever Washington requested, but he was unsure if the men would assemble even with the new law. Livingston, however, still had enough confidence in the militia to write for the newspapers, under the pseudonym "De Lisle," that "most of the laurels that have been earned since the commencement of the war, have been gathered by the militia." Writing in April, "De Lisle" believed that the British would never be foolish enough to try to cross New Jersey again after the "drubbing" they had received in 1777. Livingston was confident that the militia would rush to oppose any such march, but he hesitated to call the militia out until the British actually committed themselves in New Jersey.[13]

Jealous of their military powers, these governments acknowledged only a limited authority for the local Continental commanders over the militia in the area. General Putnam, who commanded in New York during the first weeks of the year, could ask Trumbull to send Connecticut militia to replace those going home, but he never had the full authority to call on the militia as he wanted. When he left for Connecticut in mid-February, his temporary replacement, General Parsons, also complained of a lack of authority over the militia. He had to ask Governor Clinton to order out New York militia to help with the West Point works. In mid-March, when Washington ordered General McDougall to take command in the Highlands, he asked the Continental Congress to grant McDougall all the powers necessary to do the job. McDougall received some increased authority to request militia from New York and the New England states, but not to order out any militia directly. In late May, General Gates returned and took command with the same authority the Continental Congress had granted him the previous fall: he could call on the militia of New York and the adjacent states, but he still had to work through the state governments.[14]

From Pennsylvania, Washington and the Continental Congress tried to maintain some control over the activities in the area around New York City. Though Washington wanted the new works in the Highlands completed as quickly as possible, he preferred to leave it up to the commanders on the scene to decide how many men were necessary for the work. He asked Governor Clinton to support the local Continental commanders, and he asked the Continental Congress to reinforce the Highlands because, as he wrote on March 24, to "depend too much upon Militia, is in my opinion putting every thing to hazard." He then sent his orders for the three Continental regiments to move from northern New York to the Highlands. After

Gates wrote that horse soldiers were necessary, Washington ordered a cavalry detachment to join Gates on the Hudson River. In addition, he made suggestions on how to use the militia in the area. He suggested a possible raid into New York to capture the British general, Sir Henry Clinton; he ordered Continentals to help the Orange County militia remove forage from near the river; and he wrote to Parsons to concentrate all of his men near the fortifications while sending out only light infantry and cavalry troops toward the enemy. He also left some Continentals in Monmouth County to help protect an important salt works.[15]

The Continental Congress limited itself to appointing commanders in New York in Washington's absence and to urging the state governments to help the Continental generals in New York. In November 1777, it had given Gates command along the Hudson River with power to call on the states for all necessary help. In February 1778 it appointed Governor Clinton commander of the Highland fortifications with the powers originally planned for Gates. In April, when the Congress appointed Gates to command all the troops on the Hudson River and in the Northern Department, it granted him full power to call on the governments of New York and New England for militia, though it cautioned Gates to call on the militia soldiers sparingly, as they were expensive to maintain and such calls interfered with their farming. The Congress asked the New York and Connecticut governments to help Gates in every way possible, and it urged Gates to confer with Governor Clinton and take his advice.[16]

Characteristic of Washington was his desire for some offensive action, even during the winter and spring. Washington, as well as the Continental Congress and Governor Trumbull, urged a possible attack or diversion against the British in New York to help the main army in Pennsylvania, and they believed that the New England militia would willingly turn out for such an enterprise. Washington suggested the possibility to McDougall when he commanded in the Highlands, and he accepted McDougall's decision against such an attack. The Congress urged General Gates, as he took command in New York in April, to consider such an attack, but only if Washington approved of the plan. Washington definitely approved of the idea, but Gates also considered such an attack too risky. Governor Clinton hoped that sometime in late May or early June the Highland defenses would be strong enough to justify sending the main force toward New York City. The militia might be more willing to support an offensive at that point, and perhaps an attempt would then be possible. No attack occurred.[17]

As the spring passed, it became increasingly clear that the British army, commanded by its new leader, Lieutenant General Sir Henry Clinton, was about to evacuate Philadelphia in response to the French alliance. Washington therefore increasingly concentrated his attention on the militia of New Jersey. He asked Governor Livingston for estimates of the number of militia his government and generals could get into the field, and how long it would take to get the men collected. To lessen the response time, Washington urged Livingston to develop a plan for drawing out the state's forces in the shortest time possible. Washington also kept in contact with Major General Philemon Dickinson, who had returned to New Jersey to command its militia. He warned Dickinson of the expected British evacuation of Philadelphia and the probable British march through New Jersey to New York City, and recommended that Dickinson personally prepare to assemble all the militia possible. Two New Jersey Continental regiments were sent to support the New Jersey militia by late May, and Washington promised Dickinson that he would soon send Brigadier General William Maxwell and the other two New Jersey Continental regiments to coordinate their movements with Dickinson's militia. Washington hoped that this combined force could impede and injure the British army if it did move through New Jersey, or at least restrain British detachments and prevent depredations. On May 25, Washington ordered Maxwell and the second pair of New Jersey regiments into New Jersey to link up with the first two Continental regiments, thus forming the New Jersey brigade under Maxwell's command. Maxwell had orders to cooperate with Dickinson, hover around the enemy's flanks, destroy bridges, and block the roads with trees. Maxwell met Dickinson and they began to send a steady stream of information to Washington on British preparations.[18]

As June began, Washington believed that the New Jersey militia and Maxwell's brigade could effectively harass any British march toward New York. Livingston's own confidence in the good spirits of his state's militia raised Washington's hopes. Washington even described to Dickinson how to use the militia to best effect:

I take the liberty of giving it to you as my opinion also, that the way to annoy, distress and really injure the Enemy on their march (after obstructing the Roads as much as possible) with Militia, is to suffer them to act in very light Bodies. . . . as the Enemy's Guards in front flank and Rear must be exposed and may be greatly injured by the concealed and well directed fire of men in Ambush, This kind of annoyance ought to be incessant day and night and would I think be very effectual.

Dickinson meanwhile acted on Washington's recommendations and asked Livingston to assemble the militia, but the governor preferred to wait until the danger actually appeared. As of mid-June, just before the British left Philadelphia, Washington's preparations for New Jersey were as complete as possible. He had eight hundred Continentals with Maxwell in New Jersey, and he had alerted the state's militia. If the British did march through New Jersey, his only decision would be whether to attack the enemy's army with his own army in an all-out effort or only in detachments.[19]

Washington, however, had no guarantee that the British would march through New Jersey. They could embark and sail directly to New York, which would enable them to threaten the Hudson River defenses. Acting on this concern, Washington warned Gates as early as April of a possible push up the river by the British. He urged Gates to keep any Continental recruits who arrived from New England, and suggested that Gates use his powers to call in militia to complete and man the works around West Point. Though he denied a request from Gates for reinforcements from his army, Washington promised that Maxwell's brigade in New Jersey would move immediately to New York if the British embarked. Washington contemplated the necessity of a direct march from Pennsylvania to New York, ignoring the British army even if it withdrew through New Jersey, but he preferred the idea of following any British march through New Jersey in order to harass it and make use of the New Jersey militia.[20]

General Gates, meanwhile, tried unsuccessfully to prepare the defenses in New York for any sudden British move. He followed Washington's advice and sent requests to Governors Clinton and Trumbull for reinforcements of Connecticut and New York militia. The officers of the militia stationed near the British lines in Westchester

County and along the New York–Connecticut border warned Gates that the British were preparing to make some movement that the militia currently in the field could not possibly prevent. On May 30, Governor Clinton ordered out further detachments from several militia regiments in the southern portions of the state, and he planned to take the field personally to help Gates. By the second half of June, however, as the British prepared to evacuate Philadelphia, the turnout of the militia in New York was disappointing. Few had arrived from Connecticut, and Clinton urged the Assembly to do something to help get New York's militia ready.[21]

Caught on the horns of a dilemma, Washington was unsure of his next move. His dilemma was over his immediate options, especially since the French alliance and brewing war between France and Great Britain almost guaranteed that British strategy would change. He felt certain that the British would make one last effort to win the war before the weight of French intervention could be felt, and he wanted to be ready for whatever plan they tried. Washington therefore contemplated his general strategy and how he would use the militia in the operations about to commence. His two basic strategic options were to concentrate immediately against New York or Philadelphia, or to stay near the British army and follow whatever moves it made. To attack either British stronghold would entail using numerous militia, which would be costly and leave the results doubtful. He decided on a wait-and-see approach in order to take advantage of opportunities that might arise. He estimated the number of Continentals who could take the field in his army at eleven thousand, with another fourteen hundred Continentals at Wilmington, Delaware, eight hundred already in New Jersey, and about eighteen hundred more on the Hudson River. Thus Washington planned to keep his army near the British army in Philadelphia, and if the British marched through New Jersey, as he expected, he would follow. If they sailed to New York, he would rush directly to the Hudson River.[22]

In order to augment Washington's army, the Continental Congress empowered him in April to call on the governments of Maryland, Pennsylvania, and New Jersey for a total of five thousand militia. He hesitated, however, to call out such a large number, partly because he believed he could not get so many militia to assemble, and also because he hated to distress the states unless absolutely necessary. He therefore decided to wait as long as possible, and to limit himself, for the moment, to writing the state governors to have their militia ready when called. He planned to use the militia in a harassing role, as he advised Dickinson, since he still believed that undisciplined soldiers fought better in small detachments. He planned to draw in all the Continental detachments and concentrate the army, his usual practice, and to replace those forward detachments with militia. This policy would allow the army to fight at full strength while employing the militia in roles for which it was better suited.[23]

Washington's opponent in Philadelphia was making his own preparations in the spring of 1778. Lieutenant General Sir Henry Clinton arrived in Philadelphia in early May to succeed Sir William Howe as commander of the principal British army in North America. Intellectually, Clinton understood the war in America as well as anyone. He was well read, and he realized the connection between economics, geography, and politics in the war. Unfortunately for the British, Sir Henry Clinton was not as good at putting his considerable knowledge to work. Admittedly, he took command at a difficult period of the war. The signing of the Treaty of Amity and Commerce between the United States and the king of France had led almost immediately to the decision by the British government to attack French holdings in the West Indies. For this operation, Secretary of State George Germain informed Clinton in March, even before he had taken command, that Clinton would have to send five thousand soldiers from the British army in North America to the Caribbean theater, and another three thousand troops to complete the conquest of Florida. With his weakened army, Clinton was to evacuate Philadelphia and concentrate in New York City, and there await the outcome of new negotiations between the rebels and the British government. Should the negotiations prove unsuccessful, Clinton had permission to evacuate New York City if necessary and to split his army between Rhode Island and Canada.[24]

The Carlisle Commission, which handled these negotiations with the rebels, failed when the Continental Congress refused to consider any terms except independence, and Sir Henry Clinton had to implement his previous orders. In early June, Clinton decided that he could not transport the entire British army, dependent Loyalists, horses, and supply trains all at the same time. Even if he had had enough transports to carry everything, Clinton feared being delayed at sea and thereby giving Washington an opportunity to attack New York City with his combined forces. Clinton therefore planned to march his army and supply wagons across New Jersey, and thus protect New York while his army was on the move.[25]

Interestingly, when Clinton wrote to Lord George Germain of his decision on June 5, he informed him that he expected little delay in New Jersey. In his memoirs, however, written after the war, Clinton remembered that when he made his decision to cross New Jersey, he knew he had to face not only Washington's rebel army but also the militia, which Washington could call out "to any magnitude . . . ." These militiamen, Clinton argued in his memoirs, "were little inferior in perseverance and courage to his [Washington's] best soldiers." Though it would be difficult to say that considerations of the rebel militia influenced his decision to cross New Jersey, after the fact Clinton seemed to indicate that the rebel militia was a consideration in his planning.[26]

The campaign opened on June 15 when the British army began crossing from Philadelphia into New Jersey, using Cooper's Ferry over the Delaware River. Clinton and the British rear guard left Philadelphia on June 18, and the last units of the army left Cooper's Ferry the next day. The British army had committed itself to New Jersey, and that state's government and militia responded immediately. On June 16, Governor Livingston and the Council of Safety ordered out half of the militia, exclusive of those men already in the field, and Livingston informed Dickinson that the rest of the militia had orders to turn out on Dickinson's command. The officers were to communicate directly with Dickinson for orders. The Assembly had already sent orders to Brigadier Generals Nathaniel Heard and William Winds to muster their brigades. Dickinson lamented to Washington that he had failed to convince Livingston to order out the entire state militia force at once, but he still had confidence that the New Jersey militia would turn out with spirit. Washington warned Dickinson that he relied on the militia to obstruct the enemy's march and to send intelligence regularly.[27]

The skirmishing began almost immediately. Even as the British army crossed the Delaware River, the Hessian jägers and British grenadiers were in constant contact with rebel parties. The British advance

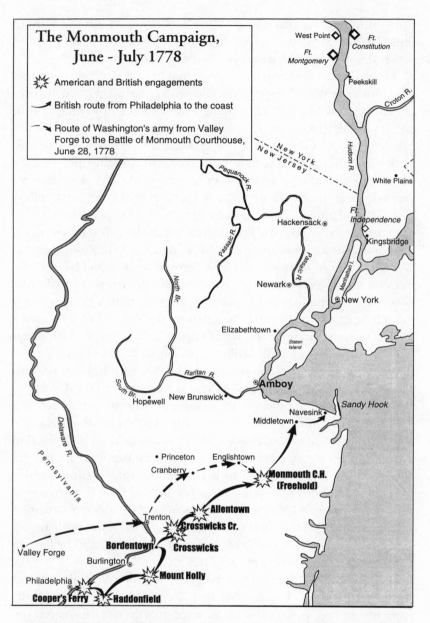

The Monmouth Campaign,
June - July 1778

American and British engagements

British route from Philadelphia to the coast

Route of Washington's army from Valley
Forge to the Battle of Monmouth Courthouse,
June 28, 1778

camped at Haddonfield on June 17, and the next day, Johann Ewald of the jägers noted: "As soon as day broke the militia received us with sharp rifle fire, and a part of the light troops of Washington's army hung on our rear guard. The skirmishing continued without letup." General Wilhelm von Knyphausen's leading column moved slowly due to all of the destroyed bridges along the roads.[28]

The militia and Maxwell's Continental brigade in New Jersey began implementing Washington's ideas for harassing the British. Dickinson and Maxwell coordinated their forces in writing and in person as they both sent out small detachments to fire at the enemy, fall back, and then contest the crossing of creeks and streams. Dickinson's numbers continued to increase during the opening days of the operation, and he sent ever more parties to destroy bridges and take positions to annoy the enemy. Skirmishes and brisk volleys constantly erupted. Dickinson reported to Washington that the obstructions were slowing the British, but that the British at times moved even more slowly than necessary. Washington asked Major General Benedict Arnold to send a party of Pennsylvania militia from Philadelphia to harass the enemy's rear. Meanwhile, from Pennsylvania, Washington sent forward Colonel Daniel Morgan's light infantry detachment of six hundred Continental soldiers, which joined Dickinson's militia near the British army in New Jersey. Livingston expressed pleasure at the militia turnout so far, though he complained that the militia could only "skirmish & run. In Junction with the grand Army we might make them pay dear for their March."[29]

Washington then began to move his army in response to the British march. On June 18, he sent six brigades toward the Delaware River with the rest of the army under orders to follow. He decided to enter New Jersey and act according to circumstances. To stay informed, he asked Dickinson to keep sending information both to him and to Governor Livingston, as he did not have time to correspond directly with Livingston. Dickinson kept up a steady stream of intelligence to Washington's headquarters. The army itself began crossing the Delaware north of Trenton on June 21, and by late on the next day, the entire army was back in New Jersey.[30]

By June 20, the British army had reached Mount Holly, but not without difficulties. Ewald described the march into Mount Holly from his vantage point with the advance guard: "On this march the head of the queue and both flanks were constantly annoyed by the enemy." General Henry Clinton was surprised that the rebels did not offer stiffer resistance at Mount Holly, which he considered a strong position. There was only a brief clash that left five rebels dead and two prisoners. Clinton paused at Mount Holly on June 21 to concentrate his army.[31]

Dickinson took advantage of the British pause to withdraw most of the Continental detachments from near the British army in order to have them ready to join Washington if required. He estimated he had one thousand militiamen with him at Bordentown on June 21, and a large force of militia remained in Elizabethtown, watching the enemy forces on Staten Island. Dickinson reported that small militia parties had skirmished with British flank and rear guards during the British march to Mount Holly. General Arnold, meanwhile, sent a few volunteers and part of one Continental regiment from Philadelphia into New Jersey to join the militia parties harassing the tail of the British army. Washington sent two light infantry companies to join Morgan's corps near the British army, and he urged other Pennsylvania militia units to cross into New Jersey and harass the British rear.[32]

Governor Livingston then began to question Washington's strategy in New Jersey. He could not understand why Washington wanted to impede the British march unless he planned to engage the British army. Livingston preferred the idea of hurrying the British on their way through the state. He found a sympathetic ear in Major General Charles Lee, who had rejoined the Continental Army in May 1778 and had resumed his position as second in command. It was Lee's opinion that the army should avoid a general action, and many of the other generals agreed.[33]

Despite the governor's concerns, the New Jersey militia and supporting Continentals continued to follow Washington's instructions to harass and slow the British. On June 22, when the British left Mount Holly, General Dickinson concentrated his men at the bridge over Crosswicks Creek. Having decided to make a stand at the bridge, he called in his scouting parties, which brought his force up to almost thirteen hundred militia soldiers. Maxwell, his Continental brigade, and about two hundred other militia were nearby in Crosswicks itself to support Dickinson. An advance of 120 militia marched out to meet the British, but fled upon sight of the enemy army. On June 23, with the Queen's Rangers leading, the British army neared Crosswicks. About seven hundred men advanced to rebuild the bridge over the creek, but the musket and cannon fire from

Dickinson's force stopped them. Major John Simcoe, commanding the Rangers, deployed a detachment of light infantry on the left and his dismounted dragoons on the right, and approached the dismantled bridge with the intention of crossing the remaining timbers. Dickinson, fearing a flank maneuver by the British attackers, withdrew his men as night fell. He had lost about ten men. He left six hundred militiamen on each flank of the enemy's route, and small detachments remained near the British army's front to continue obstructing the roads.[34]

On June 24, Clinton's army crossed the bridge over Crosswicks Creek and headed down the road toward Allentown. Morgan followed in the afternoon, and Dickinson attached three hundred militia to Morgan's corps. A party of forty horsemen and a detachment of militia harassed the British rear as it crossed the bridge and continued to follow the British column. A few militia stayed in front. Dickinson meanwhile ordered Maxwell's brigade and more militia to Allentown, to parallel the enemy's left flank, while Dickinson and the remainder of the militia stayed farther back on the British left. Expecting to have upwards of two thousand militiamen in the field within a day, Dickinson informed Washington that he would keep the main body of militia always on the British left unless Washington ordered it to another position.[35]

At the same time, other detachments from the surrounding countryside and from the army were converging in New Jersey. The force sent by Arnold from Philadelphia, 240 regulars and 50 volunteers, crossed Cooper's Ferry on June 23 and followed the enemy's route. North of Trenton, the Pennsylvania militia turned out slowly. About forty crossed into New Jersey on June 23. Washington sent Brigadier General Charles Scott with fifteen hundred Continentals toward Allentown, to fall on the enemy's left flank and rear and to cooperate with any other forces operating in the area. He also ordered Morgan to move around to the enemy's right flank, using local militiamen as guides. As of June 24, Washington had five detachments of the Continental Army in the field that were coordinating with the militia to harass the British march. Morgan was moving toward the enemy's right, Scott was on his way to the rear and left, a detachment of cavalry had been sent to join Scott, the Continentals from Philadelphia were at the enemy's rear, and Maxwell was still on the left. Almost thirty-six hundred Continentals were cooperating with more than twelve hundred militia near the moving British army. Washington asked Dickinson to supply militia guides for all of these detachments.[36]

The British general faced a critical decision at this point in the campaign. Up to June 24, Clinton had generally moved along the route that led directly to the Hudson River and Staten Island, but now he had to make a choice. Having received information that Washington and Lee had crossed the Delaware with the main army and were assembling the militia from the surrounding provinces, and that General Gates was coming from the north with another corps to join Washington on the Raritan River (an erroneous report), Clinton believed that the path northward was increasingly risky. In addition, he assumed that Washington would continue to avoid a general action and instead try to attack the British baggage train, which was twelve miles long and under the protection of Knyphausen's leading column. On top of these concerns, the daily skirmishing continued, the rebels had destroyed most of the bridges, and they had filled the wells, which was a critical problem in the scorching heat of June. Stragglers were leaving the British and German ranks in increasing numbers, and the rebels were capturing these men, including one officer who, according to George Inman of the 17th Regiment, was "a Mr. Nesbit, a Lieut. in our Regt. but he was no great loss to us or an acquisition to them." Clinton therefore ordered the army to alter its course and march toward Sandy Hook through Freehold and Navesink. This route would shorten the march and thus lessen the dangers posed by Washington's army, the enemy parties hovering around the army, the heat, and the straggling.[37]

Dickinson informed Washington on June 23 that he still believed the British were moving more slowly than necessary, possibly to lure Washington into a general engagement. Washington agreed, and as the British army, led by Simcoe's Rangers, marched to Allentown on the next day, Washington held a Council of War to discuss whether he should risk battle. Lee remained strongly opposed to any attack against the British army, preferring to allow the British easy passage through the state. He had little faith in the American army's ability to fight the British successfully. As a result of the strong resistance to a full attack displayed by his officer corps, Washington limited himself to detaching Brigadier General Anthony Wayne, on June 25, with one thousand more Continentals to join the forces hovering around the enemy army. He also ordered the Marquis de Lafayette to take command of all the forces operating near the British, both those detached from the main army and the militia units taking the field on their own. Washington then ordered another Continental brigade to join Lafayette's corps, which grew to a strength of about four thousand men from the army and twelve hundred militia. Lafayette had orders to coordinate with Dickinson to annoy the enemy's left and rear, and to attack with his entire force if an opportunity arose. On June 26, Washington gave in to General Lee's demand that he, as second in command, should lead this large advance corps, and Washington sent Lee with yet another Continental brigade to take command of the entire force. Washington urged Lafayette not to wait for Lee but to strike the enemy whenever possible. He advanced the rest of the main army to Cranberry, about midway between Princeton and Englishtown.[38]

Meanwhile, the British army continued to fight its way eastward. On June 24, Simcoe found the bridge at Allentown still standing but guarded by a party of rebels. The defenders, however, fled after Simcoe's advance fired a couple rounds of artillery. The British detachment then crossed the remaining timbers of the bridge without firing a shot. Another party of rebels approached Simcoe's Rangers, but the militiamen quickly ran when they realized that the Rangers were British soldiers. The British army camped at Allentown that night, and the next day continued toward Freehold and Sandy Hook. The skirmishing lasted throughout the day as the rebel harassing parties appeared in ever greater numbers near the British army.[39]

On June 25, as the British moved down the road toward Freehold and while their rear guard was only six miles beyond Allentown, Dickinson entered Allentown with his militia. Scott's light infantry detachment arrived at Allentown that day, and Morgan's corps continued on its way to the British right flank. Though the skirmishing still occurred daily, Morgan reported that the enemy usually kept in a tight formation that made it difficult to attack isolated parties. The New Jersey militia, however, continued to hover around the British army, looking for any opportunity to inflict damage. Over 200 militiamen were on their way to the right flank to operate with Morgan, and more than 250 others were trying to stay in front of the enemy army to impede its advance. Another 150 militia were supposed to join Scott on the enemy's left, and the rest of the militia divided and took turns operating near the British. All of these detachments sent a steady stream of information to Dickinson and Washington, which helped Washington decide on his next steps.[40]

On June 26, Dickinson stayed close to the enemy rear as the British army marched to Freehold and camped within four miles of Monmouth Courthouse. During the day, fighting between the British advance party, consisting of the Hessian jägers, and the rebel detachments intensified. At one point, Simcoe had to race forward with his Rangers to support the jägers, but the rebels fled. The next day, the British army rested at Freehold, but the American parties surrounding the British maintained the pressure on their outposts. One rebel party attacked the pickets of a German brigade in Knyphausen's corps and forced the Germans to deploy their cannon before they withdrew.[41]

As the British concentrated at Freehold, Dickinson informed Washington that he had about one thousand militia with him near the British army and that he would put himself under Lafayette's command. His numbers were again increasing at this point, and Dickinson believed that the near approach of the main American army would encourage the militia to assemble even more quickly. Meanwhile, Morgan's corps finally gained the right (southern) flank of the enemy and immediately sent out small parties to make contact with the British army and to cooperate with the militia parties in the area to annoy the British as much as the compact formation of the British allowed. Between the British and the coast, other militia forces continued to collect. Small parties cut down trees and bridges, and the detachment ordered to get in front of the British managed to do so on June 26 with two hundred men. Another one hundred Monmouth militiamen were nearby. Farther to the north, Brigadier General William Winds left Elizabethtown on the twenty-sixth with about one thousand militia and began to advance toward Freehold. He had not gone far before he stopped at New Brunswick because he believed the bridges ahead of him were down. The next day, he started out from New Brunswick, but upon hearing that the twenty-five hundred enemy troops on Staten Island had boats and were in motion, he quickly returned to Elizabethtown that same day. Disappointed with this failure to assemble even more men around the British army, Washington sent orders on June 27 for Winds to turn around again and march toward Middletown.[42]

With almost five thousand Continentals and about twenty-five hundred New Jersey militia hovering around the British army camped near Monmouth Courthouse in Freehold, Washington moved closer with the rest of his army. On June 27, he ordered Lafayette's corps to Englishtown, which was within seven miles of Freehold. In Englishtown, Lafayette would be within supporting distance of the main army and would occupy a central location where all the detachments could concentrate. Washington also urged Lafayette to coordinate his movements more closely with Dickinson, so that Dickinson's militia would be able to help if Lafayette engaged the enemy. Lee joined Lafayette the same day and took command of the entire advance corps. Dickinson and his militia, meanwhile, edged closer to the British positions. The main American army then moved to within three miles of Englishtown. Fearing the British would reach Middletown and be safe from attack before he could engage them, Washington ordered Lee to take the reinforced advance corps and attack the British rear on June 28.[43]

As the armies neared a showdown, neither commander had definite plans to engage in full-scale battle. Sir Henry Clinton had limited intelligence on the movements of the American army. Relying on his few cavalry to scout and report enemy positions, he found himself almost blind due to a lack of mounted troops. He barely had enough to guard his flanks and screen the advance. The rebel militiamen and Continental detachments around the British army deserved much of the credit for Clinton's lack of information because they kept the British scouting forces busy protecting the marching army. Thus, the rebel army advanced, almost unnoticed, within a few miles of Clinton's army by the end of June 27. Washington's plans were also unclear. He did not necessarily intend to fight a major engagement with the British army, yet he probably felt some pressure to fight. He could not let the British march across the entire state of New Jersey without a battle.[44]

Whether it was intentional or not, the two main armies finally came to blows on June 28 near Monmouth Courthouse in Freehold,

New Jersey. At 4:15 A.M., Dickinson wrote to Washington that the enemy was preparing to leave. He sent out parties to gain more information while he led two hundred to three hundred militia forward to try to detain the British. He continued to send updated information to army headquarters throughout the morning. When Washington received this initial information, he set the army in motion toward Freehold. The British, meanwhile, formed into two columns, and the first, led by General Knyphausen, left with the baggage train at dawn. As Knyphausen's corps moved off, General Clinton watched the rebel reconnaissance party advance toward the northern flank of the British rear guard. At 7 A.M., Clinton ordered Simcoe's Rangers to disperse the rebel detachment, which Simcoe proceeded to do. Crossing heavily wooded terrain, Simcoe attacked the rebel militia with his cavalry and forty grenadiers. The grenadiers fired one volley, and the militia fled. The Rangers then charged and scattered another militia party advancing past Simcoe's right flank. At this point, Simcoe noticed a larger enemy force advancing toward him, and he withdrew his cavalry and grenadiers. Dickinson's militia scattered, retreated behind the advancing corps, and played no further part in the battle.[45]

The large rebel force that Simcoe saw was Lee's advance corps hurrying forward to join Dickinson. Lee left Englishtown at sunrise and reached Dickinson's position in time to see the skirmish between Simcoe's Rangers and the militia. Lee watched as the militia retreated, re-formed, and advanced again in its attempt to get around Simcoe's northern (right) flank. Dickinson informed Lee that his own left flank was unprotected, and Lee ordered two militia regiments from Dickinson's unengaged militia to move off to the north and guard the engaged militia's left flank. Using a New Jersey militia captain as a guide, Lee then advanced his corps of Continentals to attack what he thought was the enemy rear guard of two thousand troops. The battle of Monmouth had begun.[46]

Knyphausen's column with the baggage was well under way, and the second column, commanded by Lord Cornwallis, had begun its movement when, about 10 A.M., Lee's cannons opened fire on the British rear guard. Aware by this time that Washington's entire army was approaching, and knowing that enemy parties still threatened both flanks of his marching army, Clinton concluded that the only way to protect the baggage train and force the rebel commander to pull in his flanking detachments was to attack the main army advancing toward him. Clinton therefore decided to fight. Hoping that his attack would induce Washington to engage in a general action, Clinton ordered Cornwallis's column to turn around and rejoin the rear guard, which was quickly done. He also ordered the 17th Light Dragoons and an additional British brigade to return from Knyphausen's corps. With a little over half of his army immediately on hand, Clinton launched an attack on Lee's corps. Lee's forward units, which had advanced past Freehold, quickly fell back behind the town. Despite the intense heat, the British guards and grenadiers charged the new rebel position on the heights behind the town. Lee's line, consisting of the Continental brigades sent out under Generals Scott, Lafayette, and himself, withdrew further in the face of this British onslaught.[47]

While the battle raged past Monmouth Courthouse in Freehold, Washington hurried his army forward to join Lee's corps as it grappled with a large portion of Clinton's army. Washington met Lee as his corps retreated from its second line on the heights behind Freehold, and after an exchange of heated words, Washington placed his newly arriving Continentals and Lee's retreating soldiers along a new line near some rough and marshy ground. As the day stretched on, the British advanced, the Americans stopped their charge, and then launched a counterattack of their own, which was promptly repulsed by the British. As night finally fell, both armies disengaged. Washington's army had held its third and final line, and the British occupied the heights behind Freehold where Lee had tried to hold his second line.[48]

As the two regular armies fought, the rebel militia continued to hover around the area but did not actually engage in the battle after Dickinson's militia dispersed early in the morning. Morgan's corps of light infantry and militia maintained its position to the south and west of the British line of march. Washington ordered Morgan to refrain from engaging the British because Morgan was too far from the main American army to receive any support should Clinton turn on him. A party of light troops and militia did attack Knyphausen's column in an attempt to capture or destroy the British baggage train, but Knyphausen skillfully repulsed the assault with little loss.[49]

Both armies were exhausted from the fighting and the heat of the day. The British rested until 10 P.M., and then Clinton ordered his men to follow Knyphausen's route. Washington decided the next day that pursuit was impossible due to the heat, the fatigue of his soldiers, and the head start gained by the British during the night. Clinton planned to attack any pursuing forces, but since there were none, his army continued its movement on June 29 unmolested. Only a few rebel light troops watched the British army's march.[50]

The battle of Monmouth showed the growing capabilities of the Continental Army. Washington held the battlefield the next day, which allowed him to claim that he had forced the enemy from the field. Though Clinton claimed that he had accomplished his object of dispersing a detachment harassing the rear of the British army and forcing Washington to call in his flanking parties, Washington's claim of success rings truer. Washington had called in several, though not all, of the flanking parties. On the other hand, the Hessian jäger Captain Johann Ewald recorded in his diary after the battle: "Today the Americans showed much boldness and resolution on all sides during their attacks." Losses, as usual, varied according to the person reporting them. Ewald estimated that both sides lost about 1100 men, but Clinton admitted to only 147 killed and 234 wounded and missing. Washington, on the other hand, reported that his army buried 249 of the enemy dead. American losses ranged anywhere from about 360 to over 1000 total. The only agreement between the two commanders was that both armies were exhausted by the end of the day and neither could continue the fight.[51]

The day after the battle, as his army retreated toward the coast, Clinton still feared the surrounding American parties. Suspecting that Washington might try to establish a blocking force on the good defensive terrain near Middletown, between the British army and the coast, Clinton ordered Major General James Grant to move ahead and secure the Middletown position, which Grant accomplished on June 29. The rest of the army arrived at Middletown the next day, when Clinton resumed the march to a hilly position at Navesink, where he waited throughout the rest of that day and July 1 to see if Washington would advance. Clinton planned to attack Washington should the rebel army approach Middletown. Unfortunately for Clinton, he had again lost contact with the American army, which had already turned toward the Hudson River by July 1. When the American army did not appear, Clinton moved his army to Sandy Hook on July 5 and immediately began embarking his men. On July 5–7, the British army transferred to New York City.[52]

Where were the pursuing Americans during these final days of the operation? Though the campaign was not over, the New Jersey militia thought it was. Dickinson reported his force greatly reduced the day after the battle, and believed that if he tried to get it to follow the British, considering the heat and the soldiers' desire to go home, he would have perhaps one hundred left on June 30. He hoped the detachment of militia in front of the enemy would stay at least another day, but that party had already decreased to 150 militiamen. Washington urged Dickinson to persuade the militia to stay until the enemy was out of the state, because the surrounding militia helped contain enemy marauding parties and continued to annoy the British flanks. Washington meanwhile ordered Morgan to press the enemy's rear and capture any enemy stragglers. Maxwell had orders to keep his New Jersey Continental brigade near Monmouth to support Morgan if necessary.[53]

Though Dickinson tried to obey Washington's request, he had difficulty retaining even three hundred men on June 30. By late that day, he had half that number, and more were leaving constantly. He understood that it was an important time of the season for farming, but he was disappointed that the militiamen did not stay at least until the state was totally free of British soldiers. He dejectedly reported to Washington that he had no prospect of executing Washington's orders. Brigadier General Winds was still at Elizabethtown on June 30, despite Washington's orders for him to intercept the British army, and he informed Washington that he could still assemble six hundred to eight hundred militia north of Amboy by July 1 if Washington wanted. He promised to gather boats and prepare to cross to the south side of the Raritan River. Closer to the enemy army, Morgan continued to pursue and even engaged its rear guard in a brief skirmish near Middletown on July 1.[54]

Except for Maxwell's Continentals and Morgan's force of militia and Continental light infantry, Washington gave up the pursuit on June 30. He believed that the terrain around Middletown and Sandy Hook was too easily defended and would provide protection for the

British from any attack while they were embarking. He therefore dismissed the rest of the militia who had helped in the pursuit of the British, and on June 30 started the army toward the Hudson River. The parties of light troops, including those commanded by Morgan and Maxwell, remained near the British position on the coast in order to prevent quick excursions by the enemy into the interior. Once the British left the coast, Maxwell took post near Elizabethtown, while Morgan's corps rejoined the main army. Assuming the British commander would next turn his attention to the Hudson River and the new fortifications around West Point, Washington planned to cross the Hudson River and join Gates.[55]

In fact, even before the British had reached the coast and transferred back to New York City, the American commanders had turned their attention to the Hudson River and the Highlands. Washington informed Gates on June 21 that he could send no reinforcements to New York as long as the British remained in New Jersey, but should the enemy evacuate the state, he would hurry to the Hudson. To prepare for any contingency, Gates and Parsons both informed Governor Trumbull that the Connecticut militia who had been ordered to New York still had not arrived at the Highlands or along the New York–Connecticut border. Gates thought he might help Washington during the march through New Jersey by making a feint against New York City. He therefore moved the main body of his Continental troops to White Plains. If nothing else, he hoped he could prevent British reinforcements from being sent to New Jersey. While at White Plains, Gates, who understood George Clinton's influence over the militia of the area, asked the governor to take personal command at West Point. The British, however, did not react to this movement to White Plains. As July began, Gates continued to call on the Connecticut government for a reinforcement of militia, but by the end of the first week of July, the British were stationary on Manhattan, Staten, and Long Islands, and Washington's army was nearing the Hudson. The active campaign came to a halt, at least for the moment.[56]

Once again, the British had marched through a portion of New Jersey as they had in 1776, and as they had threatened to do in 1777. The militia's performance, however, and Washington's use of the militia had both improved since 1776. The main lesson Washington had learned was twofold: that the militia took the field and fought most willingly when an actual crisis occurred, such as the invasion of New Jersey, and that despite this willingness to respond to an emergency, the militia still needed to have the support of the army, or the people would not resist for long. In addition, Washington learned that the militia worked best in smaller detachments rather than concentrated with the army. Working on this knowledge, Washington had sent out numerous Continental detachments in 1777 and again in 1778 to encourage the militia and to take advantage of its partisan capabilities. Bolstered by these Continental contingents, the militia turned out in June 1778 to help Washington pursue and harass the British army.

The results of this march through New Jersey were not lost on Washington or the British. Washington clearly understood the important role the New Jersey militia played in the campaign across New Jersey in 1778. In his General Orders of June 29, he expressed his thanks to Dickinson and the New Jersey militiamen "for the noble Spirit which they have shewn in opposing the Enemy on their march from Philadelphia and for the Aid which they have given by harassing and impeding their Motions so as to allow the Continental Troops time to come up with them." Used in that manner, the militia contributed greatly to the operations of the regular army. Washington estimated the total loss to the British army in New Jersey to be two thousand of their best troops.[57]

Captain Ewald agreed with this estimate of British losses. He compared this retreat, as he called it, to Xenophon and the march of the ten thousand Greeks. With roads and bridges ruined, drained by three weeks of the hottest weather, harassed daily by the rebels, he believed the "whole province was in arms, following us with Washington's army, constantly surrounding us on our marches and besieging our camps." He had a chilling summary of the operation: "Each step cost human blood." These words from Ewald's diary, as well as the daily recollections of Simcoe, represent testimony from two of the leading officers in the advance and rear guards that this march was punctuated by daily clashes between rebel parties and British outposts. On the other hand, the British commander, Sir Henry Clinton, gave little indication at that time that he considered the American resistance to be anything other than a minor inconvenience, and in his postwar account, he concluded that the march met with little interference. This attitude seemed to be the official British view of the campaign in June 1778. This operation, however, was also the last time Clinton tangled with the New Jersey militia, and even in the midst of his march to New York, he had decided against the route through northern New Jersey, where the militia had already shown its ability to stop a British army in its tracks. He instead went through Monmouth County, where loyalist sentiment was stronger. Perhaps his actions spoke louder than his words.[58]

With the arrival of the British army in New York City, Washington faced a new opportunity to attack the British. French intervention, which had already influenced British strategy and led to their withdrawal from Philadelphia, at this point affected Washington's strategy. In early July, as he led his army toward the Hudson River, Washington learned of the approach of a French fleet. The possibility of a French naval force arriving on the North American coast was not a new consideration, and ever since the treaties had been made public in the spring, there had been talk of direct French intervention in the British–American war. In June, Washington had even sketched a general plan for attacking the British in New York City. Now it seemed more than just a possibility. General Winds, who kept Washington up to date on the approach of the fleet, informed him that he could probably collect up to three thousand New Jersey militiamen, especially since the harvest was almost complete. The Continental Congress asked Washington to cooperate with the French and authorized him to call on the militia of New Jersey, New York, and the New England states for as many soldiers as he believed necessary. The Congress urged the state governments to supply whatever reinforcements Washington requested. While the army hurried toward the Hudson River, Washington sent requests to the governments to assemble their militia.[59]

As the army approached the river, Washington ordered detachments of Continentals and militia in New Jersey and New York to take positions near the British fortifications in order to watch for any British movements and to prevent Loyalists from supplying the British with food or information. Maxwell sent a detachment from his Continental brigade to Monmouth County to maintain order and to communicate with the French fleet, which arrived off Sandy

Hook in the second week of July. The fleet commander, Vice-Admiral Comte d'Estaing, immediately opened communication with Washington. As the two leaders sought pilots who could direct the fleet over the sandbar in front of New York harbor, the Continental Army crossed the Hudson River between July 15 and 18, and by July 19 Washington had established his headquarters at White Plains in anticipation of the projected allied attack.[60]

Washington's hopes for a combined land and naval attack against New York ended abruptly when the pilots supplied to d'Estaing and Washington failed to find a channel into New York harbor over the shallow sandbar. By mutual agreement between French and American commanders, the fleet instead sailed for Rhode Island to cooperate with Major General John Sullivan in an assault on the British post at Newport. On July 22, Washington sent two thousand Continentals from his army to reinforce Sullivan and urged Governor Trumbull to send all possible Connecticut militia to Sullivan, even if it meant stripping the coast.[61] The first attempt to coordinate the Continental Army and the militia with a French fleet had failed as quickly as it had started, long before the state governments could supply the requested militia reinforcements. Washington would have to wait for other opportunities.

The British army had done little to interfere with the growing combination of American and French forces against New York. General Henry Clinton casually informed Secretary of State Germain on July 27 that Washington seemed to have planned an attack on New York with the French fleet, but that the fleet had subsequently left for Rhode Island. Responding to Clinton's warning of a projected attack on New York, Lord Germain showed a clear understanding of the connection between the urgency of the crisis and the number of militia that Washington could retain with the army. He correctly predicted that no matter how many militia responded to the calls from Washington and the Continental Congress, once the French left, the rebel army most likely would immediately decrease in numbers.[62]

As events unfolded in the equally unsuccessful attempt to capture the British post in Newport, Rhode Island, Washington turned his attention to reestablishing the defenses of the Highlands and the line of posts around the British throughout New York and New Jersey. As of July 25, there were nine hundred Continentals in the

Highlands, four hundred near Hackensack, eleven hundred in Maxwell's brigade at Elizabethtown, and just over eleven thousand in the main army near White Plains. The militia attached to the army posts decreased rapidly, as Washington found it increasingly difficult to collect any sizable militia force once active operations waned. A small contingent of New York militia provided part of the garrison of West Point, and when these men went home in late August, Washington asked Governor Clinton to replace them. Clinton agreed to order out five hundred militiamen, but the busy time of the season for farmers and the weak punishment for delinquents combined to slow the muster. Still, about three hundred men had assembled by September 16. Around the same time, the militiamen of the two Connecticut state regiments in New York reached the end of their enlistment and headed home.[63]

Washington created a mixed force of Continentals and militia to guard Westchester County. In late July, an American party of two thousand infantry and two hundred cavalry, regulars and militia, foraged throughout Westchester County without opposition from the enemy. In addition, small detachments of militia had standing orders to forage in the area. In August, Washington gave Brigadier General Charles Scott command of a newly created Light Infantry Corps, which included Continental infantry, a New York state regiment of militia, and the Continental dragoons whenever the cavalry were in the county. This corps provided a forward defense between the army and the British. Scott guarded all roads and kept scouting parties out as near to the enemy's lines as possible, to collect information and prevent any surprise moves against the Continental Army. Scott also stationed patrols along Long Island Sound in New York to watch the British fleet and check for reported advances by the British army. The number of militia in Scott's corps dwindled constantly, but militiamen continued to do duty along with the corps throughout September.[64]

The British counterparts to the new Light Infantry Corps were the Hessian jägers and the Queen's Rangers. Simcoe's Rangers, including a rising young officer, Lieutenant Colonel Banastre Tarleton, clashed in several brief fights and attempted ambushes on both sides. Simcoe personally believed these constant patrols and skirmishes were a mistake for the British army. He explained in his journal:

they appeared to him to be particularly dangerous, and totally useless. The inclinations of the Americans, though averse from tactical arrangement, had always been turned to patrolling, in their antiquated dialect, *scouting*: the Indians, their original enemies, and the nature of their country, had familiarized them to this species of warfare, and they were, in general, excellent marksmen.

In consequence of this opinion, Simcoe limited the number of patrols he dispatched to a few strong parties. When Washington withdrew the main American army from White Plains in early September, Simcoe credited the move to the constant check given to the American light troops by the Rangers and jägers.[65]

Maxwell's New Jersey brigade, meanwhile, remained in New Jersey during the fall. Maxwell positioned detachments of Continentals and militia to watch the British fleet and to guard against raids from Staten Island. In mid-September, he reported to Washington that he expected a large descent on New Jersey, and he asked if he should apply to Governor Livingston to prepare the militia to assemble. Washington urged caution and recommended against calling the militia immediately. Instead, he suggested Maxwell only prepare the signals, which were usually large bonfires on local heights, that could be used to call the militia to muster and to cooperate with the Continental brigade if an attack occurred.[66]

Washington increasingly demonstrated this new policy of avoiding unnecessary duty for the militia while the armies remained quiet. He still relied on the militia to respond to any emergency and to cooperate with nearby Continental detachments in fighting raids or invasions, but otherwise he counseled against calling out large bodies of militiamen. In addition, he showed a growing tendency to detach parts of the Continental Army to defend along the coasts and between the two armies' outposts. He stationed Continental detachments in New Jersey, Westchester County, the Highlands, and even in Norwalk, Connecticut. One main reason for the dispersal of the army was to ease logistical concerns. Yet he also wanted detachments near the coasts and the enemy posts to help relieve the state governments and militia forces of some of the burden of daily defense, and to support the militia in its daily activities.[67]

Fortunately for the weary militia, the internal threat from Tories had receded greatly by this point in 1778. In Connecticut, where the Whig government had quickly established control, the threat from British sympathizers had never been strong. In New York and New Jersey, the Whigs had faced a more dangerous situation, especially during the different operations of the British army. By the late summer of 1778, however, the Whigs had established firmer control, though they still had to deal with some recurring problems. Livingston and the Council of Safety ordered militiamen into Monmouth County to protect the inhabitants from Tories and to attempt to stop the flow of supplies from that county to the enemy, but he did not believe his state had the military strength necessary to stop this communication on its own. Elsewhere, militia parties hunted and apprehended Tories considered dangerous to the state. In New York, the activities of Tories and robbers, who professed allegiance to neither party, forced Governor Clinton to employ companies of rangers and other militia detachments along the Hudson River to intercept or disperse these parties.[68]

Just as the armies settled into their quarters, a new problem arose for Washington. In late August, after the aborted attack on Rhode Island, the French fleet sailed to Boston, and Washington suddenly faced the possibility of a resumption of active operations. Fearing that the British might attempt to attack the French with the British fleet and a landing party, Washington contemplated moving his army to the east to help the French. In anticipation of this move, he asked Governor Clinton for more militia to garrison the Highlands should the Continentals be withdrawn, and he recommended that Clinton prepare the state's militia for a general muster in case the British issued forth from New York City. The governor issued a call for five hundred militiamen and assured Washington that he could collect a strong force if the enemy advanced. During the first weeks of September, Washington pulled the main army back from White Plains and sent two Continental divisions to Danbury, Connecticut, one to West Point, and two to Fredericksburgh, where they could defend New York and be ready to move eastward if necessary. Pursuant to his policy of avoiding unnecessary calls on the militia, Washington urged Sullivan in Rhode Island to delay calling the militia but to be prepared in case the British did attack the French in Boston.[69]

While the army pulled back from its forward position, Washington ordered Brigadier General Scott to advance his Light Infantry Corps nearer to the enemy to watch for signs of an advance and to protect American foragers, who had orders to collect all of the forage between the Highlands and New York City. If the British attacked, Scott had to secure all possible supplies and immediately inform Governor Clinton. Sir Henry Clinton, however, had no plans to attack Washington or the French in Boston. Since he had orders to dispatch eight thousand soldiers to the West Indies and Florida and another two thousand men to Canada, General Clinton believed that his army in New York was too weak to undertake any extensive operations. The British commander did advance a large detachment in mid-September; Scott's force withdrew slowly while skirmishing with it, and Clinton attempted nothing further. The British then remained quiet in Westchester County except for a brief excursion by about four hundred soldiers on September 20. Scott eventually pulled back a couple of miles to a more secure position. Washington ordered Putnam, whose division had gone to West Point, to discharge the New York and Connecticut militia still with him because there seemed little danger of an attack by the British army. The Continental Army remained poised to move eastward or westward, spread from Danbury to West Point, with Scott's corps near White Plains, when news arrived in the second half of September that the British fleet, which had been out to sea, had returned to New York, and the possible threat to Boston and the French fleet had ended. Washington halted any further moves toward the east.[70]

Though the participants did not know it at the time, when Washington halted his army's preparations to rush to Boston, he brought to a close not only the active campaigning of the main armies in 1778 but also the active period of campaigns in the North. For the previous three years, the British government had thrown just about everything it could at the rebellious colonists in an attempt to subdue the uprising in the Northern colonies, and Washington, the Continental Army, and the state militia forces had parried almost every blow aimed at the middle states along the Atlantic coast. Washington and the British were back where they had been in the summer of 1776, and at this point, the British had to turn their attention to the growing international war. As a result of this expanding war, the British government halted its efforts to crush the Northern states and instead turned its power against the Southern states. Due to this decision by the British leaders, the war around New York City saw fewer operations by the massed regular armies, though the partisan war between the outposts of the two armies would rage on, unabated.

During the warfare in the Northern states between 1775 and 1778, Washington and the militia of Connecticut, New York, and New Jersey had forged a working relationship that proved successful. While the militiamen served their states as local defenders and internal security forces, they also participated in a partisan war that grew over the years. On their own and in conjunction with Continental detachments, the militia soldiers met the enemy parties sent to raid, forage, and attack American posts, and they responded with raids of their own against British posts on the islands and in Westchester County. In addition, the partisan strategy that Washington used in 1777 and 1778 allowed the state troops to rally to the army in order to harass and impede British advances into the states.

Clearly the militia did not handle all of its duties equally well, but during these three years the American leaders learned how best to use the militia. Its strength lay in its ability to respond to threats anywhere, usually more quickly than the army could get to the scene. Militiamen would collect and fight wherever the British or Tories appeared, and could do so effectively, though for short periods of time and only against smaller British forces. They performed best when directly supported by Continental detachments, as they showed throughout the maneuvers of 1777 and 1778. Their unwillingness to assemble before a crisis occurred, and their resistance to staying in the field any longer than absolutely necessary, irritated Washington and meant that the British often could launch raids against relatively unprotected areas, such as the Danbury raid in April 1777. The militia, however, responded quickly and then fought well while containing these raids and harassing the raiding parties.

The state governments of Connecticut, New York, and New Jersey found it increasingly difficult to assemble their militia forces and maintain them in the field despite the dangers posed by the massive British operations. Even the relatively stable government in Connecticut had difficulties raising militia units by late 1777. Legislative efforts to redress the problem had so far failed. Though the governments at times raised militia units for longer service, the main reliance continued to be on the local militia to assemble in a crisis and to serve in the area until Continentals or other militia could arrive, then to go home whether the crisis was over or not. This system did not change even after repeated events showed that long-term units would provide steadier defense and allow Washington to estimate his strength and capabilities better. The militia continued to be a local, temporary force available on call but undependable in regard to numbers and length of service.

The three governors in the area were to varying degrees supporting the war effort in the theater. Jonathan Trumbull and the Connecticut government remained sources of strength and stability. William Livingston had urged his government to reform the weak militia laws, but so far he had proved to be the weakest of the governors. Washington often worked directly with Dickinson, who proved to be a valuable asset to the New Jersey militia and to Washington, and he deserved much of the credit for making the New Jersey militia an effective military force even when the state government failed to act decisively. George Clinton of New York had shown himself to be the most versatile of the three governors. As governor, he continued to serve as a field commander of the militia along the Hudson River even while he ran the government, working with the legislature to organize and improve the militia. He had emerged as a key figure in the war around New York City, and he got the most out of the state of New York despite the occupation of several counties by the British and the multiple threats to the state from the north, west, and south.

George Washington emerged during these three years as an effective commander in chief of a mixed force of regulars and militia. As the Continental Congress increasingly left the operation of the war to Washington and his generals, Washington developed his own strategy for fighting the British. Resisting from the beginning the effort of the Congress to rely on the militia to fill the regular army, Washington preferred to use the army and the militia for separate duties, a basic policy that remained largely unchanged. Failures by the militia, however, such as at Danbury in 1777, shook his confidence in its ability to provide for local defense, and by the fall of 1778, he began to provide detachments of the army to support the militia in local emergencies.

Over the years, Washington learned how the militia performed best. He supported the militia in the field with Continentals and used the militia in smaller detachments where its lack of discipline and staying power had less impact. He established a system of forward defense in which the advance forces of militia and Continentals gathered information, warned of British moves, and skirmished with and impeded British advances in order to give Washington time to react with the main army. These strategies and tactics allowed the militia to act in the role of partisan, and did not force militiamen to perform duties for which they were not suited. In addition, Washington gradually realized the futility of calling for large militia reinforcements every time he anticipated active operations. The militiamen were important at home as well, especially for the agriculture of the states. In the first couple of years, he called on the militia constantly, but by 1778 he delayed such calls until he was sure of the need.

Thus, Washington merged his initial intuition concerning the militia, gained from personal experiences before the Revolution, with the knowledge gained in the first years of the Revolutionary War to forge an effective strategy to fight the British and maintain the rebellion. He could appease his aggressive nature with raids and harassing tactics while awaiting an opportunity to engage the British army on favorable terms. His was not a war of posts, but more a fluid war of maneuver, skirmish, and occasionally full-scale battle. As long as the British kept coming out of their camps and fighting, he could use the militia and detached regulars to inflict damage while protecting the main army.

Washington therefore had already shown himself to be an effective commander of a disorganized country with no organized military force. Politically, he maintained good relations with the state governments and worked through them when he needed the state militia forces. Though he would have preferred to have a strong standing army, he modified his wishes to the reality of the situation, and by 1778 he showed a clear understanding of the usefulness of partisan warfare around the British. In particular, he coordinated Continental and militia forces well, which was an important aspect of this war. If Washington had been unwilling or unable to use the two different military forces together, the American war effort in the first three years would have been severely weakened. Instead, he used both forces to advantage and thus combined a strategy of partisan warfare with the traditional strategy of maneuvering armies in the field. He must be credited with fashioning this strategy, which, in the able hands of Nathanael Greene, would prove so effective in the South.

In fact, according to a recent historian, the British themselves learned from Washington's strategy. When they turned their attention to the South, Germain urged Henry Clinton to employ the American method of combining the militia with the regular army. Crediting the American leaders with effectively using the militia, Germain advised General Clinton to use small forces of regular troops as rallying points for the Southern Loyalists. When both sides employed such a strategy, as happened in the South in 1780–81, the result was a war of partisan ferocity that equaled or even surpassed the war in the middle states.[71]

As the war entered a new phase in the middle states, with the British army concentrating in New York City and the emphasis of the field operations about to shift to the South, would the experiences and lessons of the first three years remain valid? Washington understood the value of partisan warfare, especially around an active British army, but he now had to make use of those partisan abilities against a less active foe. Faced with these new conditions, and the possibility of further French intervention, Washington and the militia had to meet new challenges as well as the usual difficulties of maintaining the American position around the British stronghold of New York City.

CHAPTER EIGHT

Frustration and Partisan Fighting, 1778–1779

THE RETURN of the main British and American armies to the New York City area brought to a close the Northern phase of the war. The active operations of the concentrated armies, which punctuated the campaigns of 1776–78 and which led to several full-scale battles between the contending armies, ceased after the fall of 1778. During the remaining five years of the war, the British and Americans concentrated on the growing Southern campaigns, while in the middle states, the two protagonists sparred with each other in detachments and raids but the opposing armies did not lock horns. On the other hand, the annual arrival of a French fleet in North America and Washington's desire to cooperate with his ally kept open the possibility of American operations on a grand scale.

The American leadership had developed serious concerns by this point about the availability and efficiency of the militia forces. The militia clearly was incapable of stopping large British raids on its own, and Washington already allowed detachments of Continentals on occasion to support the militia in local defense. In addition, the number of militiamen that the state governments could muster had been declining, despite the occasional efforts to pass new militia laws. Washington therefore had to adapt not only to the changing circumstances of the war but also to the diminishing capabilities of the militia. Ironically, even as the militia grew less reliable, the war in the middle states became more of a partisan war for which the militia's style of fighting was better suited.

As the American leaders faced this uncertain situation, Sir Henry Clinton, the British commander, contemplated his future strategy. He had to send the eight thousand troops to the West Indies, as ordered by the government in England, which would leave in New York and Rhode Island about seventeen thousand men. Of these, he had to leave four thousand in Newport, which left him thirteen thousand men, about half Germans and Tories, to guard the posts on Staten, Manhattan, and Long Islands, as well as to run operations against the rebels. Despite Clinton's hopes of enlisting a great number of Tories, volunteers were fewer than desired, and their emphasis on raids made them difficult to control. Altogether, Clinton was unsure if he could even hold his positions, and definitely ruled out offensive operations until reinforced. Major General William Tryon of the Loyalist Corps still urged a war of desolation and terror against the rebels, but despite Tryon's advice and orders from the British government to seek a decisive battle with Washington's army, Clinton preferred a defensive policy. This decision led to smaller-scale operations and skirmishes but no major battles or campaigns through the rest of 1778 and all of 1779.[1]

Still, Clinton was not adverse to seeking opportunities to hurt the rebels and collect needed supplies. Pursuant to this policy, he launched simultaneous excursions into New Jersey and up the Hudson River in September 1778. Major General Charles Cornwallis with five thousand men crossed the Hudson River on September 22 at Paulus Hook and camped between New Bridge and Fort Lee two days later. Meanwhile, Lieutenant General Wilhelm von Knyphausen went up the east side of the Hudson River with about three thousand troops and camped near Dobb's Ferry. Knyphausen's force was supposed to attract Washington's attention and watch his movements, while Cornwallis's men in New Jersey stripped the countryside of anything usable. Clinton's long-range plan was even more clever: his two columns could combine within twenty-four hours, and by commanding the river crossings as far north as the Highlands, the British blocked Washington's easy access across the river. Clinton estimated that it would now take Washington ten days to assemble his army, and if the rebel chieftain tried to concentrate his army in New

Jersey, he would have to leave the mountains and risk a general battle. Thus, Clinton hoped to gather supplies and possibly lure Washington into a decisive battle on favorable ground.[2]

With his army spread from Danbury, Connecticut, to West Point, New York, Washington suddenly faced what seemed to be a repeat of the July 1777 operation by Sir William Howe, but this time in New York and New Jersey simultaneously. He decided to respond in the same manner as he had in 1777. First, he sent a Continental brigade to the west side of the Hudson to support the militia parties north of the British in New Jersey, and then he ordered Brigadier General William Maxwell to move his Continental brigade from Elizabethtown toward Hackensack to support the New Jersey militia in that area. In addition, he moved Brigadier General James Clinton's Continental brigade to Peekskill to be near West Point in case this move turned into an attack on the new fortifications. He also warned Brigadier General Charles Scott, who commanded the Light Infantry Corps in Westchester County, to watch for any attempt by Knyphausen's corps to march up the river and slip past him.[3]

While Washington shifted his forces to meet the new threat, the militia responded immediately. Brigadier General William Winds took command of about six hundred New Jersey militia who mustered near Cornwallis's column, while an Orange County militia regiment assembled and entered northeast New Jersey to restrain British foragers. To increase the number of militia rushing to the area, Governor William Livingston and the Council of Safety called out all the militia of the six nearest counties to join Maxwell, and New York's Assembly ordered the Orange County officers to collect as many militiamen as necessary.[4]

As soldiers from both sides concentrated in northeast New Jersey and southern New York, the fighting began. Scott's corps slowly fell back while skirmishing with Knyphausen's advance troops. In New Jersey, Cornwallis's patrols clashed with several militia parties that were removing cattle, grain, and forage from the area. Despite the efforts by the local militia to strip New Jersey, Cornwallis's foragers still found much of use. To Sir Henry Clinton's disappointment, however, Washington did not concentrate his army or offer battle, and even the militia mostly kept at a distance, all of which limited the fighting that occurred.[5]

Then, learning that a large body of militia and a regiment of Continental dragoons were near Tappan, General Clinton tried to capture them during the night of September 27. Major General Charles Grey led a detachment from Cornwallis's force in New Jersey, while the 71st Regiment and Lieutenant Colonel Simcoe's Rangers from Knyphausen's column crossed the Hudson River in order to intercept the rebels' retreat. Unfortunately for Simcoe and the 71st, three deserters warned the militia of the impending attack, and Simcoe's boats were three hours late, so the militia escaped. The Continental dragoons, commanded by Colonel George Baylor, did not fare so well. General Grey surprised the regiment, and few escaped. Grey's force then ran into a small militia party, killed several, and captured many others. Altogether, the British lost one man killed, while Baylor's regiment lost at least seventy killed, wounded, and missing, and the militia lost many more.[6]

Despite such disasters, New Jersey's militia continued to muster. By September 28, Winds had one thousand men near Hackensack, and Brigadier General Nathaniel Heard had arrived at Elizabethtown with four more regiments, about one thousand men total, to support Maxwell. Washington hoped the two Continental brigades in New Jersey, as well as the New York and New Jersey militia around the British posts in New Jersey, could keep the enemy from extending its lines. To coordinate the different American detachments, Washington sent Lord Stirling to take command of all the troops in New Jersey. He also ordered two more Continental brigades to West Point.[7]

As of September 29, with the two raiding columns maintaining their positions in Westchester County and northern New Jersey, Washington had his forces positioned around the British, ready to respond to any new threats. The center of the army was near the Highlands, a brigade of 700 men guarded West Point, and Major General Israel Putnam was moving to West Point with 1390 more Continentals. James Clinton's brigade of 820 Continentals was nearby, and another Continental brigade of 740 men was at Fishkill. A division of 1100 Continentals was only twelve miles from Fishkill, and 3030 Continentals were at Fredericksburgh. The left wing of the army was at Danbury with 4560 Continentals. Scott's advance corps of seventeen hundred regulars was at North Castle, and two brigades of fifteen hundred Continentals were in New Jersey. In supportof the Continentals in New Jersey were an estimated three thousand New Jersey militia and a party of one hundred New York militia. Few New York militiamen were operating with Scott's corps. Altogether, thirty-two hundred Continentals and about thirty-one hundred militia were operating near the two British forces of approximately eight thousand men. While keeping the majority of the army disengaged and ready to maneuver, Washington surrounded the British in both states, limiting their advances while thwarting General Clinton's hopes of enticing him into battle.[8]

Typically, as the operation dragged on, the local militiamen began to go home. In order to encourage them to stay, Stirling ordered part of Maxwell's brigade to move closer to Cornwallis's column. Stirling also asked Governor Livingston for more militia, and by October 4, he had with him Generals Heard and Winds with about sixteen hundred militiamen. The state troops, however, continued to melt away, despite Stirling's and Livingston's repeated efforts to muster more men. By October 6, only about four hundred militiamen remained of the sixteen hundred two days earlier. Meanwhile, Cornwallis had received reinforcements, and his sixty-two hundred men continued to forage and patrol near the American positions. Washington warned Stirling not to risk his shrinking force, but instead to back away and limit himself to restraining British patrols.[9]

Sir Henry Clinton finally decided that nothing further could be accomplished in this operation. In addition, the naval convoy taking the eight thousand soldiers from New York to the West Indies was ready to sail, and Clinton therefore ordered the two columns to return to their camps. Knyphausen returned to Kingsbridge on October 10, and Cornwallis left New Jersey three days later. Stirling followed Cornwallis with his Continentals, and once the British had left the state, he posted one Continental brigade at Newark and Maxwell's at Elizabethtown. The remaining Continental dragoons he placed at Westfield. He ordered militia detachments to remain on guard along the coast. In Westchester County, Scott's Light Infantry Corps reestablished itself in the county as Knyphausen withdrew.[10]

After General Clinton withdrew his parties into the defensive positions around New York City and sent the eight thousand men south, the main British and American armies remained in their camps throughout the winter and spring of 1778–79. Detachments, however, ventured forth as the raiding and partisan fighting continued to rage. All along the coasts of Connecticut, New York, and New Jersey, the state militiamen defended against British and Tory raids while launching their own raids against British and Tory posts.

Raids by Connecticut militia maintained a constant pressure on the British occupation of Long Island, where Tories and Germans provided most of the defense. William Tryon arrived at the east end of the island in September with about one thousand additional Loyalists to ensure the good behavior of the inhabitants, who had to take an oath of allegiance to the king or flee to Connecticut. In November, Simcoe's Rangers were ordered to make their winter camp at Oyster Bay, and a detachment of British grenadiers garrisoned Jamaica, thirty miles away. Simcoe did not like his precarious position, threatened as it was by Connecticut militia and a detachment of Continentals in Connecticut.[11]

The threat of raids emanating from Long Island haunted the inhabitants of Connecticut's coast as well. Connecticut's Assembly positioned detachments of twenty to seventy men from the local militia regiments along the coast for defense, and Governor Trumbull and the Council of Safety determined when and where to send reinforcements for these coastal guards. Throughout the spring of 1779, Trumbull often shifted the position and strength of these guards in order to match the maneuvers of the British, German, and Tory forces on Long Island. Finally, in May 1779, the Assembly ordered the formation of two state militia regiments, not liable for Continental duty except in an emergency, to serve until March 1, 1780. They were to help in the defense of the coast and the southwest border near New York.[12]

Showing a continued willingness to use Continental detachments to support these local defensive efforts, as well as a need to spread his army in order to find more forage, Washington placed General Putnam's division of three Continental brigades near Redding, Connecticut, for the winter of 1778–79. He made this decision even before Governor Trumbull requested such an arrangement. Though Washington prohibited Putnam from placing large detachments along the coast, by March 1779, he had given Putnam increased latitude in positioning small detachments at several ports to help guard against minor incursions. Despite these precautions, the enemy continued to send raiding parties across Long Island Sound, especially as spring weather returned in March and April 1779. On March 25, a party of twenty-five Tories crossed to Compo, between Norwalk and Fairfield, and burned several mills filled with grain and flour before returning to Long Island. On April 18, a party of Loyalists crossed to Connecticut and captured Brigadier General Gold S. Silliman.[13]

This direct Continental support ended in April when Washington ordered Putnam to regroup his division at Redding in anticipation of the annual spring concentration of the army for the coming campaign. Enemy raids increased after the Continentals withdrew from the coast, and Trumbull applied unsuccessfully for Washington to keep one or two Continental regiments on the coast. Washington regretted the difficult choice he had to make between concentrating the army and responding to these calls for help. In fact, using almost the same words he had been employing since the war began, he lamented to Major General John Armstrong of Pennsylvania: "To please every body is impossible; were I to undertake it I should probably please no one. If I know myself I have no partialities." He explained to the Continental Congress that he could not send more help from the Continental Army despite the fact that the enemy seemed determined to continue this "predatory war" and the state militia units seemed unable to defend their states.[14]

The situation along the southwestern border of Connecticut was equally dangerous. The Assembly stationed one state militia regiment in the southwestern corner in early October 1778, but the 350 men could not stop the frequent raids into Connecticut by regulars and Tories from New York. In February 1779, several hundred British, German, and Tory soldiers led by Tryon surprised the Americans at Horseneck and took possession of the town. Brigadier General Silliman, who commanded the district until his capture in April, called out his and an adjacent brigade's militia to oppose them, while Putnam rallied the few Continentals and militia who had retreated from Horseneck and combined them with other soldiers stationed at Stamford. He marched this hastily formed detachment toward Horseneck, but the raiding party had already finished plundering the town and had begun its return march to New York. Putnam sent in pursuit a party that captured possibly fifty men. Altogether the invaders lost sixty-three soldiers; Putnam estimated his total casualties at twenty men.[15]

In the spring of 1779, the Assembly ordered reinforcements to Greenwich, but the inhabitants requested even more help as enemy parties continued to plunder by land and water. In June 1779, Colonel John Mead, Silliman's replacement in the southwest part of the state, wrote to Trumbull that his regiment could not hold much longer. Large enemy parties threatened to raid from New York, and soon the border between British-held territory and Connecticut-controlled territory would be pushed back to Stratford, and Greenwich and Stamford would be lost. Trumbull asked Washington for help throughout the winter and spring, but Washington responded that the Light Infantry Corps near Kingsbridge should provide protection for Connecticut as well as New York. Putnam also provided some help through April with detachments from his division at Redding.[16]

Throughout the skirmishing in 1778–79, the Assembly made further efforts to improve the efficiency of its militia laws. It increased the amount a man could be fined for failing to serve when called but did not create sufficient penalties to compel men to serve. In fact, as late as October 1780, Trumbull told the Assembly that the militia still had to be better organized.[17] None of the three state governments went beyond monetary fines for delinquent militiamen.

In New York, the presence of a substantial portion of the regular American army in 1778–79 eased the burden on the militia. In Westchester County, the local militia had the support of the Light Infantry Corps, commanded by General Charles Scott, who had orders to supply and support as many militia detachments as the local militia commander believed necessary in order to protect the farmers. Scott meanwhile spread out his parties to help the militia guard the area, and even the Continental cavalry patrolled between the Hudson and the Connecticut border. A Hessian officer, Major Baurmeister, gave testimonial to the efficiency of these American patrols: "Their patrols are good, cautious, and quickfooted. Enjoying the affection of the residents, they know all our movements."[18]

Despite these efforts, raiders still attacked and plundered the livestock of the county, causing the inhabitants to ask for more help. Even larger detachments from the British army operated along the

Hudson River throughout the late fall of 1778. On November 12, Lieutenant Colonel Simcoe and his Rangers marched to Rye, where they attacked the forces of one of the most feared rebels, a Colonel Thomas. Colonel Thomas tried to defend his house with five men, but Simcoe's men rushed the house and killed Thomas and three others. In a larger operation, Sir Henry Clinton sent Brigadier General William Matthews and about four thousand soldiers up the Hudson on December 2, while Brigadier General Sir William Erskine led a party of about two thousand men overland from Kingsbridge to Tarrytown. A third detachment of fifteen hundred men sailed to Tarrytown to support either of the other two parties. Clinton's objective was the baggage train and rear guard of Washington's army, which supposedly were going to cross the Hudson River at that time. Erskine had to dislodge the militia from Tarrytown after what Captain Johann Ewald called a "stubborn fight," while Matthews landed at Verplank's Point on December 5, two days too late. The delays in getting there had allowed the rebels to remove their baggage and cross their soldiers before the British arrived. The third party landed at Stony Point in search of other supplies and briefly skirmished with local militiamen. The several detachments then returned quickly to New York City.[19]

During that same month, Washington withdrew the Light Infantry Corps from its exposed position to put it into winter quarters. General McDougall, once again in immediate command of the Highlands, asked Governor Clinton to send three hundred militia to cover southern Westchester County until the Continentals were in their winter quarters, at which point he would send patrols into the county and relieve the militia. Clinton issued the necessary orders. Putnam sent two hundred Continentals from his camp in Redding, Connecticut, to Westchester County, and he urged McDougall to send parties to the Hudson River. By the end of December, McDougall had sent 220 men into Westchester with orders to hang any Tory raiders they caught. Throughout the rest of the winter and spring of 1779, McDougall tried to combine these Continental and militia detachments to stop the Tory raiders, but the plundering continued.[20]

The effort to stop the trade of goods and information between Tories outside the city and the British army within the city hit a peak in January 1779. That month, the British army in New York City went through a dangerous crisis, which the rebel patrols helped to heighten. Stockpiles of provisions fell to critically low levels for the British garrison, and some soldiers survived on grits instead of bread. The horses had no oats for days. In addition, the weather was extremely cold. This combination of cold and hunger led soldiers in the garrison and local inhabitants to collect and eat the geese and ducks that had frozen to death in great numbers. When the Americans learned of the British difficulties, they pushed their patrols closer to the British outposts in order to stop the people in the country from sending provisions into the city. Washington was not involved in this event; he was in Philadelphia between December and February, and Major General Stirling had temporary command. The crisis ended when a provision fleet arrived in late January. In the following months, the New York militia tried continuously to stop the Tory trade into the city, but despite the exertions of companies of rangers and other detachments, who were busy hunting Tories who robbed and harassed inhabitants friendly to the American cause, all efforts to prevent some communication between the British garrison and nearby Loyalists failed.[21]

The partisan warfare raged along New Jersey's coast too. Monmouth and Bergen counties, and the coast across from Staten Island, were all open to British and Tory raids, and New Jersey militiamen and Continental units left in the state by Washington worked together to limit these forays. For the protection of Monmouth County, which had been a source of problems since the commencement of the war, Governor Livingston and the state legislature called out detachments of militia to stand guard along the coast. Livingston also asked Washington for help from the Continental Army, and Washington stationed a detachment of Continentals in Monmouth County at the beginning of 1779. This detachment helped stop a raid in January and made it possible for Livingston to dismiss part of the militia guarding the coast. Across from Staten Island, Maxwell's Continental brigade remained at Elizabethtown throughout the fall and winter. Militiamen took positions on the coast and in the principal coastal towns so that the Continentals could stay concentrated in Elizabethtown. In northeast New Jersey, Bergen County rivaled Monmouth County for its difficulties. Livingston requested Continental aid for Bergen in November 1778, and Washington ordered a

Continental brigade to spend the winter at Paramus. In addition, mostly for improved logistics, seven Continental brigades spent the winter in Middlebrook. Militia detachments also were posted along the coast to isolate New York City and Staten Island, and to guard against raids.[22]

William Franklin, former royal governor of New Jersey, warned the British government that the rebel posts along the coast of New Jersey could distress the British garrison if they remained in place. In particular, Maxwell's brigade of about eight hundred Continentals in Elizabethtown became the main target of British planners. On February 25, Sir Henry Clinton sent two British regiments and the light infantry of the British Guards, about twenty-five hundred soldiers, to New Jersey. Landing between Newark and Elizabethtown, their immediate goal was to surprise Maxwell's brigade. Unfortunately for the British, militia guards along the coast learned of the landing and sent warnings to Maxwell, who assembled his brigade and abandoned his forward positions in Elizabethtown and Newark. Maxwell's Continentals and the local militia then offered stiff resistance to the British landing party, which hastily retreated toward its boats. For the loss of at least forty soldiers, the British gained little. The Americans lost about thirty men.[23]

The raids kept coming as General Clinton continued to pursue his policy of raids and small-scale operations. He wanted to collect supplies and hurt the Americans while not risking the entire army or its vital position in New York City. In March, 650 men raided near Middletown and surprised an American regiment at Shrewsbury. During the early morning hours of April 27, about eight hundred British soldiers entered Monmouth County. The nearby Continental detachment retreated quickly while the local militia began to assemble. About 150 militiamen had arrived when, around 3 P.M., the British retreated to their boats. Brief skirmishing ensued until the British party was gone. As the *New-Hampshire Gazette* sarcastically reported, the British usually launched such raids in the night and then fled before the militia could muster. If the militia ever assembled even half the number of the British, the militia would be "sufficient to drub them." After fleeing, according to the newspaper article, the British "then magnify in their lying Gazettes, one of those sheep-stealing nocturnal robberies, into one of the Duke of Marlborough's victories in Flanders." In May, about five hundred British troops marched through New Bridge deeper into Bergen County. The Continental commander in the area sent forward patrols to link with the local militia, which turned out quickly. The raiders withdrew after a short stay.[24]

In April 1779 Washington warned Livingston that he would be removing the Continentals from Monmouth soon, and Livingston ordered out detachments of militia to replace them. In May, Washington told Livingston that he was about to withdraw Maxwell from the coast as well, and again Livingston ordered out militia detachments to take Maxwell's place. Maxwell began to pull out in mid-May even though only seventy militiamen had arrived. Livingston ordered the seventy men to stand guard, and if compelled to retreat before a British raiding party, at least they would be a rallying point for other militia. Only 120 militia had arrived by the end of May, and Livingston ordered part of a new state regiment to guard the exposed coast. Until this reinforcement arrived, monthly militia replacements were to stand guard. Finally, in June, Livingston and the Council of Safety resolved to raise a state regiment of one thousand militiamen to protect the coast from New York to Monmouth until the end of the year. Of these, 300 would defend south of the Raritan River, about 450 would garrison across from Staten Island, and the remaining 250 would guard the coast in Bergen County. Livingston ordered the local militia officers to use detachments from their units as coastal guards until the state regiment was complete.[25]

The New Jersey Assembly also made an effort to improve and strengthen its militia laws but had only limited success. The Assembly tripled the fine for delinquent troops, but Livingston remained unhappy. He argued that money could not defeat the British, that instead laws were necessary to compel the militia to turn out when called or to face harsh punishment. The annual attempt by the lawmakers to increase the penalties, however, was over, and no new law concerning penalties for militiamen would be enacted until 1780.[26]

Governors Trumbull, Clinton, and Livingston all missed what could have been a valuable opportunity in the spring of 1779 to improve the efficiency of the militia in their states. Major General Friedrich von Steuben sent to the three governors copies of his new regulations that established general principles for disciplining and training the soldiers of the United States, including the militia. His ideas were based on the simplified instructions that he had used successfully as inspector general of the Continental Army at Valley Forge during the winter of 1777–78, and that had been published by an act of the Continental Congress in March 1779. He explained to Governor Trumbull: "It is then in our Militias that we must find the real Strength which we are to oppose to that of great Britain . . . ." He hoped these regulations would be "the means of rendering that Militia capable to supply the Want of a well regulated Standing Army, at least as much as lies in our Power." He believed that through the use of the simple training program, militia regiments as well as Continental regiments could learn the necessary principles. Such training would, he argued, lead to advantages when the militia joined with the army or when it fought on its own. Livingston and Clinton both agreed that implementation of the regulations would probably be beneficial, but they did not believe it possible during the war to find the time and inclination among the militia to learn the new principles. All three state governments chose to ignore the offered manuals.[27]

Washington must have been disappointed by this decision because, even as he prepared for the 1779 campaigning season, he urged the state governments to prepare their militia forces and complained to the Congress of the expense and danger of depending on the militia. Perhaps a better trained militia could have made his job easier. Washington, however, could not worry about such details at this point. His thoughts instead turned to the need to have militia forces available to him. Washington and his generals, therefore, spent the spring contacting the governors. General McDougall, still commanding in the Highlands, coordinated with Governor Clinton to have the militia of the area ready to assemble on his orders. Washington asked Governors Livingston and Trumbull for estimates of the number of militia available for the summer, and suggested that they establish the necessary signals to call out the militia when needed. Livingston ordered the creation of the necessary signals, a series of prepared bonfires that in an emergency would be lit to spread the word throughout the region for the militiamen to join their units. Livingston also informed Washington that General Dickinson, supported by Generals Heard and Winds, would again command the

New Jersey militia. Trumbull urged the Connecticut Assembly to do everything possible to support the war effort, and he promised Washington that he would prepare a regiment of militia specifically for duty in New York if needed.[28] Washington and the state governments continued to cooperate fully, and this coordination of effort at the state and national levels remained the strength behind the American military.

Beyond the effort to prepare as many men as possible to take the field, Washington took a wait-and-see approach in 1779. His basic strategy revolved around how many men he could get, whether the British would initiate active operations, and whether the French fleet would arrive. Due to the lack of a large regular army, and to the unpredictability of militia numbers, Washington, as usual, could not plan far in advance.

The British, on the other hand, were busy formulating their objectives for the coming campaign. As early as November 1778, Secretary of State George Germain urged Sir Henry Clinton to continue the raiding policy inaugurated in the fall of 1778. Germain believed that such raids could keep the coastal regions in a state of alarm while destroying rebel ships, supplies, and commerce. Germain understood that the Americans were having great difficulty creating a regular army and had to depend on the militia to continue the war. Therefore, he wanted Clinton to intensify the raiding war in 1779 by using a corps of four thousand men along the New England coast and another four thousand in Chesapeake Bay. These operations, he believed, would keep the militia forces of those regions busy and unable to join Washington. Then Clinton could use the remainder of his field army to maneuver against Washington in order to force the rebel chief to fight a decisive action or to hide in the Highlands. Either way, Germain expected this plan to open new territory to British influence and allow the loyal inhabitants, whom Germain believed to be a majority of the colonists, to reassert their allegiance to the king. Germain's plan showed a clear recognition not only of the political nature of the war but also of the important role of the rebel militia. If the militia were pinned down in local defense, Washington's small regular army could be defeated or at least isolated. Then the people, free of interference from the rebel army and the rebel militia, could rejoin the royal banner.[29]

The Photographs

Governor Jonathan Trumbull. Lithograph by J. H. Bufford, in I. W. Stuart, *Life of Jonathan Trumbull, Sen., Governor of Connecticut* (Hartford, 1859).

"General George Washington before the Battle of Trenton." Painting by John Trumbull (1756–1843). Courtesy of The Metropolitan Museum of Art, Bequest of Grace Wilkes, 1922. (22.45.9)

Sir William Howe, by C. Corbutt. Courtesy of the Anne S. K. Brown Military Collection, Brown University Library, Providence, R.I.

Silhouette of William Livingston, cut by Peale Museum. From the Collection of The New-York Historical Society.

Governor George Clinton (1739–1812), attributed to Charles Wilson Peale. From the Collection of The New-York Historical Society.

Sir Henry Clinton (dated 1787) by Thomas Day (c. 1732–c. 1807). Courtesy of
The R. W. Norton Art Gallery, Shreveport, La.

Clinton's own plans were not so clearly defined. On May 5 he informed Germain that until he received reinforcements, he could form no plan of operations. He promised to send General Matthew and twenty-five hundred men to Chesapeake Bay, but beyond that, he refused to commit himself. Clinton decided, however, to launch a campaign up the Hudson River later in May, but only for the limited object of threatening both sides of the river, which might induce Washington to draw in his troops from the banks of the river. Clinton estimated Washington's army at eight thousand men, "besides a numerous militia who were ready to turn out at a moment's warning," according to the constant refrain in his postwar memoirs.[30]

Clinton chose as his immediate geographic objectives Verplank's Point, on the east side of the river and Stony Point, directly opposite on the west side. These two positions, which the Americans were in the process of fortifying, commanded King's Ferry, the main line of communication across the Hudson River south of the Highlands. By taking these locations, Clinton hoped to force Washington to concentrate his army and fight for control of the communication link between New England and the states west and south of the Hudson. Accordingly, Clinton started up the river on May 28 with one corps while Simcoe's Rangers led a second corps on an overland march that stopped at the Croton River on June 3. Out in front of Simcoe's advance force was Lieutenant Colonel Banastre Tarleton, scouting and skirmishing.[31]

Upon learning of this British movement, General McDougall immediately notified Governor Trumbull that Washington might need the militia from western Connecticut. McDougall asked Governor Clinton to prepare the local militia, and the governor issued warnings to the officers. Washington, meanwhile, began to move the three Continental divisions that had wintered in New Jersey toward the Hudson River. As the British continued up the river toward King's Ferry on May 29–30, Governor Clinton ordered the militia of Orange and Ulster counties to West Point, and that of Dutchess County to join McDougall directly on the east side of the river. Major General John Vaughan and fifteen hundred men landed on May 31 at Taller's Point, about eight miles below Verplank's Point, and General Henry Clinton led the rest of his party against Stony Point. The Americans there set fire to the defensive works and fled, and General

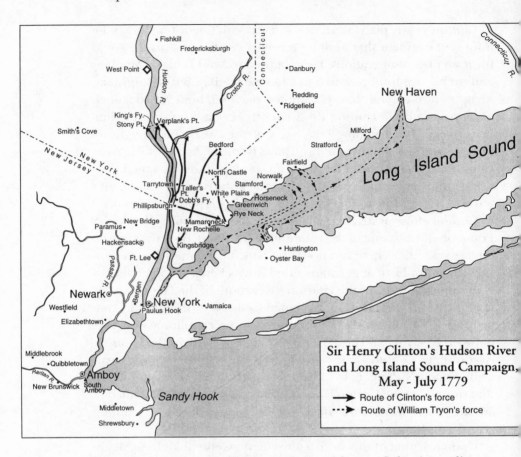

Sir Henry Clinton's Hudson River and Long Island Sound Campaign, May - July 1779

→ Route of Clinton's force

···▶ Route of William Tryon's force

Clinton took possession of Stony Point without a fight. According to Major General James Pattison, who accompanied General Clinton's column, for the first few days "the militia were impertinently trouble-some by coming down in small Bodies, and firing upon our Jager Post, but five or Six of them having been dropt by our Rifle Shot, they thought fit to disappear . . . ." The militia avoided the British post after that incident.[32]

On June 1, the British at Stony Point opened a battery and shelled the American fort across the river on Verplank's Point. After one shell exploded in the fort and killed three of the defenders, the Americans evacuated the fort and ran right into General Vaughan's column, which was advancing from Taller's Point. Forced back into the fort, the garrison of seventy-four men quickly surrendered to

Vaughan's party. Altogether, in the operations on both sides of the river, the British had only one casualty.[33]

As the British captured Stony Point and Verplank's Point, Washington urged McDougall to concentrate his forces around the Highland forts and apply to the governments of New York and Connecticut for even more militia if necessary. He advised Governor Livingston to be prepared to call out New Jersey's militia should the Hudson River attacks prove to be a feint to draw men out of New Jersey. Washington had already ordered the three Continental divisions stationed in New Jersey to march to New York. At that time, McDougall had six Continental brigades on hand in the Highlands. The New York militia meanwhile began to collect, and Governor Clinton arrived at Fishkill to take personal command on the east side of the river.[34]

After the relatively easy capture of the two forts, the British commander halted further operations. Sir Henry Clinton had hoped that Washington would concentrate his army and fight for the forts, but since the rebel chief continued to avoid a battle, Clinton began fortifying the two points. Without reinforcements, he believed a further advance up the river to be too dangerous. Washington meanwhile frustrated Clinton by keeping his divisions well away from the British positions. He stopped the main portion of the army, on its way from New Jersey, at Smith's Cove, about ten miles from Stony Point. McDougall held West Point with about seventeen hundred men, but the rest of his division stayed on the east side of the Hudson about nine miles south of Fishkill. Governor Clinton and the New York militia from the east side of the river remained with McDougall, and six hundred militiamen guarded the roads on the west side that led from Stony Point to West Point. The governor promised to support any militia units that took positions near the British posts and skirmished with them. Farther east, one-fourth of the Connecticut militia units from the counties west of the Connecticut River had orders to march to New York, and in early June the first contingent of these soldiers began to collect at Fredericksburgh, New York.[35]

On June 5, Washington began detaching small Continental parties from the nearby divisions to cooperate directly with the militia forces operating near the British posts along the river. He hoped that the Continentals would encourage the militia in the field to be active. He also warned the Continental generals to be careful not to attack friendly forces by mistake, since small militia parties were out on many of the roads. He wanted to avoid an unfortunate clash between friends.[36]

Despite this initial flurry of activity, no major movements occurred for several days. In fact, part of the British force operating along the river returned to New York. After a week of inaction, the militia began to go home, even though about five thousand British soldiers remained at Verplank's Point and about one thousand more at Stony Point. Washington decided, however, that since part of the British force had just returned downriver and the main portion of the Continental Army was now nearby, the militia could be dismissed. He accordingly told Governor Clinton to dismiss the New York militia. Washington was convinced that the British had taken the two points only to interrupt the most convenient American line of communication over the river, and therefore further operations were unlikely. Governor Clinton was pleased to relieve his militia, especially in this busy season for farmers. Washington also dismissed the Connecticut militia assembling in New York. To be safe, he ordered the Continental dragoons into Westchester County to watch the British army and, while they were there, to help fight British and Tory raiding parties. Washington expressed his disappointment that the New Jersey militia had been unable to create a diversion from its side to help the situation along the Hudson River.[37]

Just in case the British had plans for further operations in New Jersey or New York, Washington urged Governors Livingston and Clinton to be prepared to call the militia again. Should the British advance, his plan was to assemble the militiamen, join them with all the Continentals not garrisoning West Point, and dispute every foot of ground leading to that fort. Sir Henry Clinton, however, had no plans to advance further up the Hudson River. Having decided that without reinforcements he could not move beyond Verplank's Point and Stony Point, he withdrew more soldiers from the new garrisons during the last week of June, and by July 1 he had taken post with the withdrawn troops at centrally located Phillipsburg, where he was within twenty-four hours of the new forts as well as of Staten, Manhattan, and Long Islands. The garrisons remained at the newly captured forts, working to strengthen them.[38]

Not wanting to leave matters as they were, Washington decided on July 1 to attack Verplank's Point and Stony Point. He firmly believed that when the enemy raided and distressed the countryside, he could not sit by idly with the army. Unfortunately for his plans, the British did not remain passive. Just as Washington was planning his counterstroke, the British suddenly moved again.[39]

The latest move was still part of Sir Henry Clinton's overall plan to lure Washington into battle. In late June, Major General William Tryon embarked on a raiding expedition against the Connecticut coast. In order to support Tryon's actions and to be ready to march toward Connecticut if necessary, Clinton positioned his field force at Phillipsburg. Then, if Washington moved to help Connecticut, Clinton hoped to catch Washington's army as it crossed the Hudson River or out in the open after crossing the river. On June 30, Tryon's raid commenced when a small British fleet threatened Fairfield. About two hundred men landed, set fire to several houses and barns, and reembarked before the militia could collect. The militia and naval force then fired several cannon shots at each other, and the fleet sailed off in the night.[40]

The rest of the fleet, with the larger landing force commanded by General Tryon, set sail on July 3, but a lack of wind delayed it so that it did not arrive off New Haven until July 5. On that day, Tryon and about twenty-six hundred soldiers landed in two divisions and marched into town, brushing aside a spirited defense by a party of local militia. One division entered the western part of New Haven, and Tryon led the other column to the east side. As the local militiamen collected, those men on hand took and held the bridge that connected east and west New Haven, thus preventing the two raiding columns from rejoining. The militiamen skirmished with both British detachments throughout July 5 and 6; on the sixth, the western column forced a crossing to the east side to escape the mounting pressure from a growing militia force. With the number of militia soldiers swelling rapidly all around him, Tryon decided to reembark his corps on the evening of the sixth. Behind lay the smoldering ruins of several buildings in New Haven. The British lost about eighty men in the two-day battle, while the militia lost perhaps fifty.[41]

Governor Trumbull quickly ordered three militia brigades to move to the coast, and he asked Washington for help. Anticipating

Trumbull's plea, Washington had already ordered Brigadier General John Glover, whose brigade was en route from Rhode Island to New York, to march to the coast if the British raided Connecticut. Washington also ordered Brigadier General Samuel H. Parsons to Connecticut, to organize and command the militia collecting haphazardly along the coast. These actions were taken none too soon, because on July 8, Tryon's raiders landed near Fairfield and marched to the town under continual but ineffective cannon fire from the small militia force on hand. On the morning of July 9, they burned most of the town because militiamen had fired on them from the houses. Under constant fire, the British returned to their ships and reembarked that morning. By that time, a large number of militia had assembled.[42]

While these coastal raids were occurring, General Henry Clinton moved his mobile corps, which had risen to seven thousand men, from Phillipsburg to Mamaroneck on July 8, in order to support Tryon's efforts and to be ready should Washington move to Connecticut's aid. The next day, Clinton moved to Bryam's Bridge, even closer to the Connecticut border. Norwalk's civilian leaders and General Parsons both asked Washington for help from the army to bolster the militia against this dual threat from the fleet and the land force. Parsons meanwhile ordered the few Continental infantry left in Connecticut to the coast, and the Assembly ordered militia reinforcements to Greenwich and to the coast east of Greenwich. In response to the pleas for assistance, Washington started Major General William Heath toward Connecticut with two Continental brigades. In addition, Trumbull wrote to the Massachusetts Council for help from its militia.[43]

Despite the mounting opposition, Tryon kept attacking. After stopping briefly at Huntington, Long Island, for supplies, he returned to Connecticut, and on July 11 landed his soldiers near Norwalk. Major General Oliver Wolcott had on hand seven hundred militiamen, but instead of immediately attacking the landing party, he decided to wait until Parsons and the few Continentals arrived. On July 12, the British advanced through the town and beyond against little opposition from the local militia. Parsons with 150 Continentals and another party of militia finally joined Wolcott, bringing his numbers up to about eleven hundred, though Tryon estimated he faced at least two thousand men. This reinforced corps stopped the advancing British in their tracks. The fighting then raged back and forth throughout the twelfth. At one point a part of the militia retreated, but the state soldiers rallied quickly and helped push Tryon's men back. Tryon withdrew his corps to Norwalk, burned the town to the ground, and reembarked. Parsons praised the militia and Continentals for a brave and orderly defense of Norwalk, and when Washington heard of the action, he applauded the fighting spirit shown by the militiamen. Even "if the opposition they give is not absolutely effectual, it serves to discourage the enemy and make them sick of such excursions."[44]

While Tryon battled the militia and Parsons's regulars at Norwalk, Heath continued edging nearer to Bedford, New York, but bad weather slowed his progress. He sent orders to Parsons to bring the Continentals from Connecticut to join his division, but Parsons asked Washington to countermand these orders. The regulars were the only soldiers in Connecticut on whom Parsons could rely, and he wanted to retain them to support the militia. While awaiting a reply, Parsons moved his force toward Stamford in anticipation of another amphibious raid. At the same time, the British corps marching overland through New York entered Bedford ahead of Heath and burned it. In Bedford, Sir Henry Clinton's army was only fifteen miles northwest of Stamford, but instead of marching into Connecticut, Clinton returned to Kingsbridge. The American concentration continued unabated: Heath moved around Bedford and arrived at Ridgefield, Connecticut, on July 13; Glover, marching from Rhode Island, halted his brigade at New Haven; and one thousand Massachusetts militiamen prepared to go to the aid of Connecticut. Then, as suddenly as they had started, the coastal raids ended in mid-July. Parsons wrote to Washington that Connecticut still needed help, but since the raids were probably only a diversion to weaken the Highlands, he concluded that the destruction of a few ports was not as important as the defense of West Point. Observing that the British raiders had not tried to march far inland, and avoided any large-scale fighting, Parsons was convinced that the raids posed no real threat.[45]

Tryon had been preparing to continue the raids when, on July 13 at Huntington, he unexpectedly received orders from General Clinton to cancel the expedition and return to New York. Sir Henry Clinton called off the raids against Connecticut because "all the militia of the country were assembling in arms," Clinton recalled in his memoirs, and because Washington had not accepted the bait. The main portion of the rebel army had not come out of its defenses, and therefore the raiding parties were taking too many casualties for such paltry results. Tryon admitted to Clinton afterward that the number of militia opposing his raid was great at New Haven, even greater at Fairfield, and vastly increased at Norwalk. Clinton estimated Tryon's losses at almost 150 men. The Connecticut militia, bolstered by a small detachment of Continentals, had limited the success of Tryon's operation and thus helped ruin Clinton's overall plan.[46]

Washington finally launched his own counterstroke on July 15, when Brigadier General Anthony Wayne stormed Stony Point with his corps of twelve hundred Continental light infantry. For the loss of about 100 men, Wayne inflicted more than 130 casualties and captured over 440 men, almost the entire garrison. Wayne's men then turned the British guns at Stony Point against the British fort on Verplank's Point to support an anticipated attack by General Heath, who was marching his Continental division from the Ridgefield–Bedford area toward Verplank's Point. The British commander in chief, however, reacted quickly, canceling his own plans, embarking the field force on July 19, and racing up the Hudson River toward Stony Point. He sent his cavalry and light infantry back to the Croton River to intimidate the Americans, and he embarked a second corps and ordered it to sail directly to the support of the fort on Verplank's Point. Learning of the British moves, Heath canceled the attack on Verplank's Point and retreated, and Wayne destroyed and evacuated the fort on Stony Point. General Clinton arrived near Stony Point and remained with the main British field army in the hope of luring Washington into a battle, but again Washington avoided contact. Clinton reestablished the garrison on Stony Point and returned with the rest of the army on July 20 to Dobb's Ferry. Three days later, he withdrew his army to the main lines around New York City. Washington decided against further attacks and informed Governor Clinton that unless the British returned upriver, he did not need the New York militia for the moment.[47]

This series of maneuvers that Sir Henry Clinton had initiated in late May ultimately achieved little for the British commander. Wayne's successful attack on Stony Point depressed Clinton, weakened his resolve, and led him to draw his forces into a tight perimeter around New York City. He had taken a chance and allowed William Tryon to test his ideas for laying waste the coast of Connecticut, even though Clinton personally disliked the idea. After the fact, Clinton argued that the destruction went against his orders, and he never gave Tryon an independent command again. Perhaps this bickering merely represented Clinton's growing frustration. On August 21, he lamented to Lord Germain that the season had been wasted. He believed that by then, Washington had probably prepared his defenses, and Clinton despaired of ever luring the rebel chieftain into a general action. The capture of Verplank's Point and Stony Point was supposed to have been the start of offensive operations, but as of August, Clinton had no further plans. The new posts were no longer important, and Clinton assumed he would abandon them soon.[48]

Washington was not privy to Clinton's despair, so he prepared for further British movements. He urged the Continental Congress to energize the state governments and get them to prepare their militia forces in case the British received reinforcements and resumed active operations. His dependence on these militia soldiers was apparent in his warning to the Congress that the army was extremely weak and he had little hope of recruiting men to fill the ranks. "The only succour then that we can expect in case of exigency, must be derived from the Militia."[49]

The Connecticut Assembly agreed with this sentiment and bolstered its defenses. In early August, it ordered four thousand militiamen to guard the entire state coast. Of this force, about twenty-five hundred men were ordered to watch the coast from New Haven to the New York border. Frequent alarms throughout the month kept these guards on edge, so Washington maintained a Continental division of 1050 regulars nearby to ease the fears of the Connecticut government and militia. Major General Robert Howe, commander of the division, which included Glover's brigade and a cavalry detachment, had orders to patrol along the southwest border and to attack nearby British posts if possible. Washington warned Howe, however, not to call the militia detachments from their assigned posts.[50]

The close proximity of the outposts of the two armies continued to take its toll on both sides. Simcoe noted on August 8 that, for the first time since leaving winter quarters, the men of the Queen's Rangers were able to remove their coats at night, with strict orders in case of alarm to form undressed. They left their bayonets fixed to their guns even at night. Connecticut militiamen and Tory raiders fought constant battles along the border between New York and Connecticut. The Connecticut militia sent patrols throughout the countryside to search for Tory parties, and if a patrol met any Tories, it warned the local militia units, which immediately took the field. The Connecticut militia also raided into New York on its own. Major Benjamin Tallmadge led one such raid with one hundred mounted men to New Rochelle, where he fought a thirty-minute battle, killed and captured several of the enemy, then returned to Connecticut.[51]

Washington even used regulars for such raids. On August 19, Major Henry Lee led four hundred Continentals against Paulus Hook in New Jersey. In the ensuing battle they killed about 50 men and captured over 150 of the garrison. Lee lost perhaps a dozen of his own men. On his way back to the army, Lee ran into about thirty Loyalists and lost a few men in the ensuing clash, and then his corps was harassed by a nearby British detachment. Both sides had learned the art of raiding and skirmishing.[52]

Later in August, the British reacted to the continued raids onto Long Island from Connecticut by reinforcing the garrisons on the island. The British light infantry, the 17th Regiment, and the Queen's Rangers went to the assistance of the small posts on Long Island. The Americans, not knowing the reason for this buildup, worried that the British were about to attack Connecticut. That state's Assembly quickly sent orders to the militia generals to have their brigades ready to move on an instant's notice. The Massachusetts government offered to send its militia if the British invaded again, as they had in July. Along the coast, the guard detachments in the port towns were beefed up to fifty men each.[53]

On September 26, 1779, the war around New York City intensified. The Continental Congress resolved that day that Washington was to cooperate with an expected French fleet. When he received this news, Washington broke into a flurry of activity to secure an army to use when the fleet arrived. The very next day, he wrote to the governors of the states stretching from Pennsylvania to the north, including Governors Trumbull, Clinton, and Livingston, that the French fleet was supposedly on its way and he would need a large supply of militiamen should the fleet arrive. Washington therefore asked the governors to prepare their state troops for two or three months' service with the regular army, but to delay actually mustering them until he was more certain that the French would really join with him. Altogether he requested four thousand men from Connecticut, twenty-five hundred from New York, and two thousand from New Jersey. In addition, he wanted two thousand militiamen from Massachusetts and fifteen hundred from Pennsylvania. He promised all the governors that this was the minimum force necessary. Clearly, Washington's plans to collect twelve thousand militiamen and use them in an offensive against New York City were contradictory to his stated opinions on the effectiveness of militia in regular operations, but he had no choice. With the French expected off the coast at any time, he could not hope to enlarge the Continental Army to the requisite number quickly enough to besiege and assault the British defenses.[54]

The governors of New York and its immediate neighbors reacted swiftly. Governor Clinton assured Washington that New York would furnish every man possible. The Assembly strengthened Clinton's powers by passing a law on October 9 that increased the fine for delinquent militiamen by 500 percent and that enhanced the governor's powers to call out the militia for longer periods of time. Still unsatisfied, Clinton urged more, and in March 1780, long after the current crisis had ended, the Assembly belatedly increased the fine again. As of October, however, Clinton had to be content with the limited improvements. Meanwhile, New Jersey's Assembly responded to Washington's plea by passing an act on October 9 to raise four thousand men. Governor Livingston could order the men to assemble at any time, and they would be liable for service until December 20. Livingston openly expressed his surprise that the legislature had acted so promptly. Governor Trumbull and the Council of Safety ordered out four thousand Connecticut militiamen to serve three months with the army, and the Assembly confirmed this action with an official act on October 14. Washington promised Trumbull personally that he would not call the men to him unless the French appeared. In fact, Washington carefully avoided calling any of the militiamen to the army until he was assured of the French arrival. He explained this decision in a letter to the Comte d'Estaing, the admiral in command of the French fleet. He felt strongly that he should not inconvenience the states until he knew with certainty that the French would come, and he also wanted to guarantee that the militia soldiers would remain with the army for several months. If he called them out too soon, they would go home in the midst of the operation.[55]

As October passed and November began, the hopes for joining with d'Estaing decreased. On November 14, Washington wrote to the Continental Congress that he believed it would be best to give up the idea of a joint operation. It was nearing winter, the army was not properly clothed, and he did not trust the militia to turn out and serve for long in the inclement weather. When Washington received news of d'Estaing's earlier attack and repulse at Savannah, Georgia, he immediately wrote to the state governments to release their militia units from the obligation of holding themselves ready. He also dismissed the Massachusetts and New York militia that had already arrived. The French would not be coming this year.[56]

While the Americans prepared for an offensive that never occurred, the British contracted their lines in anticipation of a shift southward of another part of the New York army. On October 21, the British burned and evacuated their works on Verplank's Point, and two days later, the garrison abandoned Stony Point. At the same time, Sir Henry Clinton ordered the evacuation of the post in Newport, Rhode Island. The possibility of French naval intervention in the North worried Clinton, who reasoned that the Rhode Island base could not be held with inferior naval forces and therefore served no further purpose.[57]

The British then made a move into New Jersey that led Washington to believe a large invasion was under way, though it was only a cavalry raid by Simcoe's Rangers. The British, fearing that Washington's preparations to attack New York were real, learned of a collection of boats that the Americans were moving from the Delaware River to New York to assist in the assault. Simcoe requested and received permission from Clinton to cross into New Jersey and destroy the boats. Simcoe also learned that Lee's cavalry had left Monmouth County, where they had been stationed, which left only the militia to stop the Rangers. Simcoe, however, who had a grudging respect for the local soldiers, admitted that "those, tumultuously assembled at the moment of the execution of the enterprise, could, possibly, impede it."[58]

Simcoe led the Rangers from Staten Island into New Jersey on October 26. Pretending to be from Washington's army and searching for Tories, they passed Quibbletown without incident. Then a rebel recognized Simcoe, quickly sent a warning to Governor Livingston, and the chase commenced. The Rangers raced through Boundbrook and found eighteen boats, which they destroyed. Knowing that the country behind them swarmed with rebel militia, Simcoe led his men past Somerset Courthouse to New Brunswick, all the while hearing alarm guns being fired throughout the countryside. When a few shots rang out near the rear of his column, Simcoe told some women in nearby houses to warn the pursuers, estimated at only four or five men, to stop shooting or he would burn every house he passed. Ahead, Simcoe ran into a small party of New Jersey militia behind logs and bushes. Fearing that Lee's Continental cavalry could be nearby, Simcoe tried to discover a safe way past when, in a brief encounter with the militia, he was captured. The Rangers continued on, ran into an ambush and lost three men, and finally reached the heights northeast of New Brunswick. The militiamen were assembling nearby when a detachment of the Rangers charged. The militia fled. The Rangers then crossed the Raritan River to South Amboy and reembarked for Staten Island. Altogether, the Rangers had marched eighty miles and lost four killed and six captured, including Simcoe himself. He returned to active duty on December 31, 1779.[59]

When this raid commenced, Washington heard that the British had invaded New Jersey with five thousand men, and he responded as he had in the fall of 1778. He sent two Continental divisions into northeast New Jersey while he concentrated the rest of the army in the Highlands. A third division was already in New Jersey. In the end, Washington found the British numbers had been greatly exaggerated, and only a small raiding party had landed. The divisions returned to their camps near the Hudson River.[60]

In Connecticut, the greatest danger to the state government's control in the fall and early winter of 1779 remained in the southwest corner of the state. Throughout the summer and fall, Major General Oliver Wolcott had maintained a large detachment of militia in the area, against Washington's advice, in an attempt to maintain some political control. As of early October, however, only 200 militiamen guarded Horseneck, and this number was down to 130 at the end of November. Enemy parties plundered the area daily, and the local militia commander requested at least six hundred to seven hundred men. By the end of the year, most people loyal to the United States had migrated out of the area, which left the region sparsely inhabited by people who were coldly neutral to both sides. In effect, southwest Connecticut did not politically belong to the state of Connecticut any longer.[61]

Concerned lest this political defection continue, Trumbull asked Washington to place Continentals in Connecticut for the winter. Washington replied that he would keep Brigadier General Enoch Poor's New Hampshire brigade of Continentals in Danbury, and a couple of cavalry regiments east of there, and these units would keep patrols along Long Island Sound. As of mid-December, Poor had twelve hundred men at Danbury, and four hundred Light Dragoons were posted near Hartford.[62]

Monmouth County, New Jersey, also received special treatment for its known Loyalist sentiments among many of the inhabitants. In November, Washington sent a Continental detachment and part of the army's dragoons to the county to further limit Tory activity. When the times of service for the few militiamen in the county ended, Livingston requested more Continentals, and Washington agreed to do what he could, though he expressed his disappointment that the militiamen were going home. Livingston ordered 200 more militia into the county immediately to protect against "Freebooting Tories," and ordered 290 militiamen to replace them in March 1780.[63]

Another danger zone in New Jersey was the coast across from Staten Island. In November, the British began amassing troops on Staten Island, and Washington feared that they were about to raid into New Jersey. Accordingly, he ordered three Continental divisions, which had taken position near Quibbletown, to send out light infantry detachments to support the militia. At the same time, Washington had to weaken his army by sending a large portion of it to the South to counter a growing British threat in Georgia and South Carolina. As the size of the British encampment on Staten Island grew, and the British fleet prepared to sail, Washington asked Governor Livingston once again to prepare the New Jersey militia for a sudden call to arms, especially now that the Continental Army had been so weakened. The New Jersey Assembly issued the necessary orders to prepare the signal fires and guns, which would be fired to call in the militia. Washington also urged Governor Clinton to have his militia ready in case the British went back up the Hudson River.[64]

These preparations proved unnecessary. Sir Henry Clinton was not eyeing New Jersey or the Hudson River. Having decided that the campaigning season had been wasted, he turned his attention toward the South. Leaving twelve thousand troops to defend the New York City area from Washington's army and, as he recalled in his postwar memoirs, "as many militia as he [Washington] pleased to embody in the neighboring populous provinces, which were little inferior in practice and courage to the Continentals," Clinton sailed south on December 26 with approximately seven thousand soldiers. Agreeing with Clinton's assessment of the campaign, Hessian Captain Johann Ewald summed up the year's achievements rather bluntly: "This is now the third campaign where we have continually lost in the end what we won with the first rush in the beginning."[65]

Throughout his postwar memoirs, Clinton repeated his litany about a "numerous militia," supposedly available everywhere. Such a practice may have been simply his attempt to find an excuse for his ultimate failure in North America, but it is interesting to note what body he chose to blame for his problems.

On the other hand, Washington was relatively pleased with the 1779 campaign. As he informed the Continental Congress, the "enemy have wasted another Campaign . . . ."[66] With this statement he echoed Sir Henry Clinton's admission. By following his policy of shielding the army with militia and Continental detachments while launching aggressive raids against British posts, Washington checked British operations and limited the success of British raiding parties in New Jersey, New York, and Connecticut.

Thus, by the end of 1779, the militia had maintained its critical role in American military planning and operations, and to a degree continued to exert some influence over British planning and operations. The two main armies did not engage in full-scale maneuvers and battles against each other between the fall of 1778 and the end of 1779, though large portions of each army did take the field more than once. In this kind of war, the American militia took on an even greater importance. As a shield for the main army, as local defense for the states, and as support for a possible joint allied attack on New

York City, militiamen continued to fill a vital role. Their record in the different roles remained spotted, however, and Washington increasingly detached Continental forces to guard along coasts and support militia units in the field. Still, Washington's policy toward the use of the militia remained relatively consistent despite the changing nature of the war in the middle states.

CHAPTER NINE

Lost Opportunities, 1780

As THE WAR in North America entered its sixth year, both sides were searching for a way to end the conflict successfully. Though victory continued to elude the British and Americans, for fleeting moments in 1780 the opposing army commanders had high hopes. From Rhode Island to New Jersey, the two armies threatened to lock horns and finish the fight, even as larger detachments went to the South. Ultimately, the armies would remain distant and the state militia forces once again would help fill the space between them.

While the remnants of the British army that had not gone south shivered in New York City and its environs during the cold winter months of 1780, and the American army remained scattered from Connecticut to New Jersey, the partisan war between the two armies raged through yet another winter. In Connecticut, the Assembly ordered militia companies, ranging in size from fourteen men in Branford to ninety-seven in New Haven, to guard the ports. As the militia guardsmen came and went, often without orders, town officials petitioned for more guards and occasionally the local militia general would order out a reinforcement on his own authority. The Assembly also ordered the creation of two state militia regiments of 440 men each to serve for the entire year, but as of May, it was still trying to complete the regiments. Washington, meanwhile, kept Poor's Continental brigade and the Continental cavalry in Connecticut until spring. Despite these defenses, Tory and British parties raided along the coast throughout the winter and spring, plundering and taking local inhabitants prisoner. Most of the small guard companies could not hope to stop these raids, but they could at least resist the raiders while the local militiamen assembled. The invaders, however, usually escaped before the local militia concentrated.[1]

The militiamen along the southwestern border guarded against similar raids, and launched attacks of their own. On January 18, Captain Daniel Lockwood and 131 Connecticut militia soldiers attacked a Tory camp near Morrisania and captured about 15 Tories. A Loyalist unit pursued Lockwood's party, caught up with it, and in the ensuing battle, Lockwood lost between forty and sixty men. With the southwest portion of the state engulfed in this bitter struggle, Trumbull convinced the Continental dragoons in Connecticut to support the militia near the New York state line. Colonel John Mead, the militia commander in southwest Connecticut following General Gold S. Silliman's capture, had the authority to call on the nearby Continental generals in New York as well as in Connecticut should the enemy attack him. In early March, fearing such an attack, Mead asked for help from General Robert Howe, who had recently replaced General McDougall as the commander in the Highlands due to McDougall's ill health. Mead explained that the local militia was fatigued and the area was consequently defenseless. Before answering, Howe contacted Washington, who responded that he could not send Continentals to guard against every threatened raid. The Assembly ordered a reinforcement of about two hundred militiamen for Greenwich in April and five hundred more in May, but the raiders kept returning and the inhabitants threatened to leave the area. In June, General Silliman, who had finally been released, ordered three hundred more men from his brigade to Horseneck, but most of the men preferred to pay a fine rather than serve. Tory parties subsequently found Horseneck defenseless and took possession. Howe finally ordered the Continental dragoons to the southwest border, and the Tories left. Connecticut militia detachments reestablished their posts in the region and continued to skirmish with the Tory bands.[2]

Across the state border in Westchester County, Tory raiders were also a danger. To help New York, the Continental Congress agreed to pay the state for the raising of eight hundred New York militiamen, and Governor Clinton, who in April won reelection to three more years as governor, ordered part of this eight hundred to guard Westchester. Still the Tories continued to raid, driving off live-stock and forcing the inhabitants to flee. On February 3, roughly 600 British, German, and Tory soldiers attacked a Continental regiment of 250 men stationed only 17 miles north of Kingsbridge. They killed and wounded almost forty Continentals, including several men burned to death in a house, and they took over ninety prisoners back to New York City. Along the west bank of the Hudson River, Clinton ordered out a detachment of Orange County militia to join General Howe's Continental division to prevent further depredations.[3]

Such attacks, however, were not as frequent anywhere in New York this winter because the British garrison feared for its safety while General Clinton and a large portion of the army were in South Carolina. General Wilhelm von Knyphausen, who commanded the army left on the islands around New York City, and Major General James Pattison, who was the commander of the garrison and of New York City itself, instead spent the winter preparing for a possible attack by Washington's army. In fact, it was their turn to call out the militia for defense. Due to the severely cold weather, the rivers froze so completely that cannon were dragged across the Hudson River and cavalry units marched across the ice to Staten Island. This condition only worsened the garrison's fears. Therefore, Pattison decided to call out all Loyalists, seventeen to sixty years of age, in order to man the defenses. With the help of William Tryon, they mustered 2660 Tories in seven days. Thus, with the British garrison concerned about being attacked, most of the soldiers remained inside the defensive works on the surrounding islands.[4]

Though he did not contemplate a winter attack on New York City, Washington considered Staten Island a prime target. He strongly urged raids onto the island, and on January 15, 1780, Major General Lord Stirling led three thousand men, mostly Continentals, across the ice from the mainland to Staten Island. Planning to isolate and capture part of the garrison on the island, Stirling advanced between the main British corps and a detachment consisting of the Irish Volunteers and Simcoe's Rangers, who had been transferred to the island from Long Island. The defenders were too few to take the field against Stirling's three thousand, so they stayed in their defensive works throughout the day. While Stirling's force sat in front of the British positions, New Jersey militiamen crossed to the island and plundered the local inhabitants. Efforts by the garrison commanders to assemble the Tory militia on the island failed, and Simcoe began to despair, fearing he would be captured again. Just as he contemplated trying to escape to the mainland, he learned that Stirling's corps had retreated. Stirling had realized that he had lost the advantage of surprise, and that several of his men were suffering from frostbite caused by the extreme cold. The Rangers pursued and captured seventeen stragglers. Stirling's command returned to New Jersey on January 16 without having engaged the garrison on the island.[5]

The participation of the Continentals in this and many other raids clearly demonstrated the increased availability of the regulars to engage in this partisan war. Most of the raids in which the Continentals participated were during the late fall, winter, or early spring, when Washington was more willing to allow detachments to leave the army. When spring arrived, Washington still concentrated his forces.

To counter such strokes, General Knyphausen used raids and partisan strokes similar to the ones launched by the Americans, and he thus acquired a reputation for trying to help the friends of the British and hurt their enemies. On the night of January 25–26, a Major Lumm of the British 44th Regiment led more than three hundred infantrymen from Staten to Newark, where he surprised the garrison, killing eight and capturing thirty-four without loss to the British party. At the same time, a detachment of about 130 Tories crossed the river to Elizabethtown, where they surprised and captured about 60 men. Simcoe proposed a quick raid into New Jersey to capture Washington, and Knyphausen approved of a limited operation. Simcoe took two hundred dismounted Rangers and early on February 1 entered Woodbridge, which was undefended. From there he moved inland, ran into a rebel patrol, and returned to Woodbridge as the alarm guns boomed and signals flared. At dawn, New Jersey militiamen appeared near Woodbridge and Simcoe retreated to the coast, turning at one point during the withdrawal to assault the pursuing militia. Simcoe's Rangers crossed the ice under fire from the Jersey shore. Both sides lost a few men wounded. Unimpressed by the resistance on this raid, Simcoe summarized his contempt for the New Jersey militia: "the whole of the affair being between single men, the Rangers were infinitely better marksmen than the Jersey militia." On March 22, two detachments of three hundred men each crossed the Hudson River into New Jersey in order to surprise a party of three hundred Continentals. The Continentals retreated from one detachment, then ran into the second column, and each side fired several heavy volleys into each other. As the militia from the surrounding area quickly mustered, the British raiders withdrew through New Bridge. Altogether the British lost about sixty men but brought sixty-five prisoners to New York.[6]

Attacks such as these kept New Jersey in a perpetual state of alarm through the winter and even into the spring. In March, about five hundred British troops entered Hackensack. As they returned toward the coast, only one hundred Continentals and thirty militia followed them. In April, a detachment of four hundred men executed a similar raid into Bergen County. In response, Governor Livingston and the Council of Safety ordered militia detachments to every exposed point along the shore. In addition, mounted militiamen patrolled across from Staten Island, militia troops with the support of Continental dragoons guarded Bergen County's coast, and militiamen on their own watched for raids in Monmouth County. By June, Maxwell's Continental brigade was back at Elizabethtown, having been withdrawn from its advanced and isolated post during the winter to avoid making it the object of even more raids. The New Jersey Assembly by then had ordered the mustering of 624 militiamen: half would guard south of the Raritan River, one-third would defend Bergen County, and only 47 would watch the coast across from Staten Island. The Assembly clearly had great confidence in the presence of Maxwell's brigade to protect that last stretch of coast.[7]

Many of these British raids were against Continental detachments near the coast. Though Knyphausen was willing to launch expeditions into New Jersey, he believed that the American regulars were a worthy target, whereas the scattered militia guards were, at best, a suitable target for Tory raids. That there were so many Continental units near enough to the shore to be attacked showed how far

Washington had relented on his previous refusals to detach parts of the army for local defense.

Undaunted, and perhaps even encouraged, by this partisan conflict, Washington spent the spring months contemplating the possibility of active operations. Following the traditional, if still unsatisfactory, pattern of previous years, during these months he urged the state governments to prepare the signals and their militia for any emergency. When the British concentrated their forces on Staten Island in March, Washington advised General Howe to be ready to call out the militia if the enemy attacked up the Hudson River. If the British invaded New Jersey instead, as Washington expected, Howe should attack their rear from across the Hudson. Since such a maneuver would inevitably weaken the Highlands, Washington expected New York militiamen to strengthen the garrisons of the forts. Governor Clinton promised Howe that his men were ready.[8]

At the beginning of April, Washington estimated his army at 10,400 men, but the units were still scattered from Connecticut to New Jersey. This strength, moreover, would probably not grow, and might even shrink during the year through detaching more men to help the South and through soldiers going home. In fact, twenty-eight hundred Continentals were leaving at the end of May, when their enlistments expired. Washington, "relying on the internal strength of the Country," still hoped to launch an attack as a diversion to help the South at least. He therefore informed the governors of his preparations for calling the militia to the army should an opportunity arise.[9]

While Washington's plans were no more specific than this vague hope, the opposing commander in New York studied his options. General Knyphausen learned that Washington had detached parts of his army to Chesapeake Bay, to Albany, and to Pennsylvania. British intelligence estimated Washington's strength in New Jersey at four thousand men concentrated around Morristown. The rest of the American army was in New York and Connecticut. In addition, reports had come in to headquarters from spies and Tories that the New Jersey militia were tired and would stay home in peace, and that the New England Continental brigades wanted to desert. Knyphausen therefore decided to invade New Jersey in strength, with about six thousand soldiers, in order to harass the rebel army and learn if the reports were true.[10]

Accordingly, Knyphausen led six thousand men, all that could be spared from the New York defenses, from Staten Island to Elizabethtown during the night of June 6. His specific plan was to march inland swiftly, take a position in the Short Hills between Springfield and Chatham on the first day, and then march quickly the next day against Washington at Morristown. Then Washington, encumbered with baggage wagons, would have to risk a general engagement or abandon much of his supplies and artillery.[11]

Unfortunately for Knyphausen, the reports concerning fatigue and dissatisfaction among the American ranks were wrong. A disappointed Knyphausen concluded: "I found the disposition of the inhabitants by no means such as I expected; on the contrary they were everywhere in arms . . . ." General Maxwell was on the alert in Elizabethtown, and he led his eight hundred Continentals in a slow withdrawal to Connecticut Farms, all the while sending out the alarm to the nearby militia. As the militia units assembled rapidly, the British and Germans met constant impediments from broken bridges and the delaying actions of Maxwell's Continentals and the militia, who occupied every defensive position possible. Captain Ewald of the German jägers described it thus: "General Knyphausen had hardly landed and marched off when he ran into enemy parties which made his every step troublesome." At Connecticut Farms, near Springfield, the defenders numbered about twenty-five hundred men as the militia rallied to Maxwell's command. For three hours, Maxwell blocked Knyphausen's advance until the German general concentrated his forces and finally shoved Maxwell's troops out of the way.[12]

As Knyphausen's army advanced and the forward detachments skirmished, Washington ordered his generals to collect the militia and move toward Knyphausen's flanks. At the same time, he led the main American army from Morristown to the Short Hills, behind Springfield. When Knyphausen learned that Washington had beaten him to the Short Hills, he halted his advance rather than fight Washington's army and the militia, especially in light of the fact that the people seemed animated and hostile, contrary to the intelligence reports. Knyphausen also received word from Sir Henry Clinton that the returning British army from South Carolina would be at Sandy Hook in a few days, and Knyphausen decided to withdraw to the coast and await Clinton's arrival. After burning Connecticut Farms,

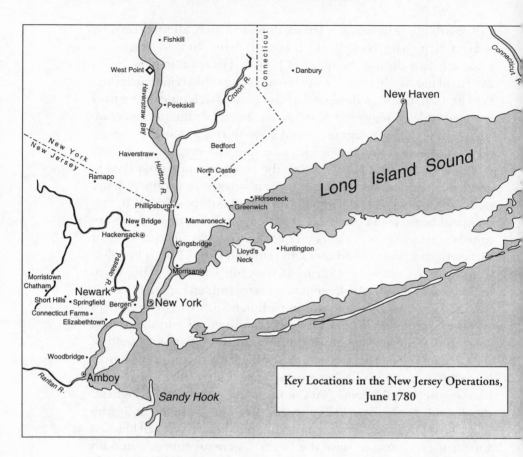

Key Locations in the New Jersey Operations,
June 1780

the army withdrew during the night of June 7 to Elizabethtown. The
Americans followed the retreat and attacked the rear of the British
column but were repulsed.[13]

Washington, unsure of what the object of this maneuver had been,
had strong praise for the militia: "The Militia have turned out with
remarkable spirit and have hitherto done themselves great honor."
That the enemy army remained in Elizabethtown and maintained a
bridge of boats to Staten Island worried Washington, and he therefore determined to mass as many troops as possible while skirmishing with the enemy outposts. He ordered Maxwell back toward
Elizabethtown to provide a forward defense and shield for the main
army, and he sent forward other Continental detachments to work
with the militia to harass the British and Germans. Knowing that

Knyphausen had a large cavalry force, he urged these advance parties to stay in the woods as much as possible. On June 11, General Dickinson returned to New Jersey, and in obedience to orders from Governor Livingston, he ordered out the entire state's militia force. Though Washington was pleased with the spirit shown so far by the New Jersey militia, he feared that General Clinton would return from the South, join the army already in New Jersey, and thus prolong the operation. This possibility worried him mainly because by then he knew the capabilities of the militia as well as anyone. "The militia of the State have run to Arms and behaved with an ardor and spirit of which there are few examples," he explained to a Continental Congress committee, "but perseverance in enduring the rigors of military service is not to be expected from those who are not by profession obliged to it." In a few days, he suspected, most of the militia would go home whether the enemy army had left or not. Once again he urged the Continental Congress to devise a way to increase the regular army.[14]

As the initial invasion force remained quiet day after day in New Jersey, Governor Livingston requested help from the Pennsylvania militia. On June 13, however, Washington asked Dickinson to dismiss about half of the roughly three thousand New Jersey militia who had assembled. If Knyphausen's army advanced again, the rest would have to be recalled. The Continental Congress asked the state governments from Maryland to New England to prepare their militia in case Washington had to call on them. Meanwhile, along the Hudson River, General Robert Howe expressed his fear to Washington that the British might make a sudden move against the Highlands under cover of the feint in New Jersey. Washington agreed with Howe's suspicions and urged him to use militia to reinforce the garrison. Howe therefore asked Governor Clinton for eight hundred militia immediately. Clinton ordered nine hundred men to join Howe. On the other hand, should the British advance again in New Jersey, Washington wanted Howe to create a diversion in New York.[15]

Knyphausen's army, however, did not move for over two weeks. During that time, the outposts of both armies skirmished continually. The Hessian Adjutant General, Major Baurmeister, described this fighting as well as his grudging respect for the rebels: "They make sudden irregular attacks that resemble surprises and are excellent marksmen. We have not yet learned to meet them the same way and not to offer them our front." On June 17, General Sir Henry Clinton arrived by ship in New York. The transports bringing his army from the South were a few days behind him. Clinton was mildly surprised and even disappointed to find Knyphausen already in New Jersey because he had had vague ideas about trying to surprise Washington in camp. Now, Washington was prepared and the entire country was in arms.[16]

When Washington received news of a large British fleet approaching from the South, his fears for the Highlands increased. Leaving at Springfield two Continental brigades and the Continental cavalry, about twenty-five hundred men under the command of Major General Nathanael Greene, he began moving the rest of the army already in New Jersey toward the Hudson River. At the same time, he asked Trumbull to send the available Connecticut state militia regiments to West Point and to order two thousand to three thousand more militia to join Howe. Trumbull and the Council of Safety ordered two thousand militiamen and one of the state regiments to march immediately for West Point, and Trumbull ordered twelve hundred more men to be held ready to go to New York on Howe's orders. Meanwhile, Howe asked Governor Clinton to prepare all available New York militia to join him.[17]

In an attempt to take advantage of Washington's apparent uncertainty, the British commander in chief ordered Knyphausen to pressure the Continental division left in his front, while he would lead a corps up the Hudson River. Clinton could then attack Washington's rear if he turned back to help his division in Springfield. Part of Clinton's Southern army, led by Simcoe's Rangers, joined Knyphausen in New Jersey, while a corps commanded by Major General Alexander Leslie prepared to sail up the Hudson. The two forces advanced on June 23. Knyphausen marched inland while Leslie, accompanied by Clinton, sailed up to Haverstraw Bay.[18]

General Greene informed Washington that the British army was advancing toward Springfield and that he was going to have to retreat because he had few militia at the moment, though others were collecting. Despite the growing threat to New Jersey and New York, the New Jersey militiamen had continued to go home even as Livingston strove to assemble other men to replace them. When Washington learned of the new advance in New Jersey and of Greene's fears, he halted his army's movement toward the Hudson.[19]

While Sir Henry Clinton waited along the Hudson River, on June 23 Knyphausen advanced in two columns toward Connecticut Farms and Springfield. With Simcoe's Rangers in the advance of one column on a flanking march, Knyphausen led the other down the direct road to Greene's position at Springfield. Both columns skirmished with American militia and Continental parties who slowly fell back toward Connecticut Farms. Throughout this second advance, the Americans "fought in a manner that shows honour may be got by destroying them, but a double advantage to the state by bringing them to be good subjects; they were, however, always beat," according to the new royal governor of New York, General James Robertson.[20]

Generals Greene and Stirling immediately called for the New Jersey militia to hurry to them. Washington redirected his army's march from the Hudson back toward Morristown in case Knyphausen's advance was more than a diversion. Meanwhile, at Connecticut Farms, Knyphausen's force struck Maxwell's brigade and a few collected militiamen, and despite the good defensive terrain, superior numbers compelled Maxwell to retreat to Springfield, where he joined Greene's other brigade. When Knyphausen's column reached Springfield, it found Greene's Continentals and militia entrenched and ready for battle. Greene's men repulsed several assaults before the second column led by the Rangers outflanked Greene's position. He then withdrew his corps to the Short Hills behind Springfield, under cover of an attack by Dickinson and a detachment of the New Jersey militia against the flanking column. Knyphausen, with his forces reunited in Springfield, declined to renew the battle.[21]

Instead, Knyphausen had his men set fire to several of the buildings in Springfield and then begin the march back toward Elizabethtown that same day, June 23. Greene immediately pursued, sparking a running battle all the way to Elizabethtown. He sent ahead about 120 Continentals, who joined with the growing number of militia detachments to hover on the retiring column's flanks and rear. Greene followed cautiously with the rest of his Continentals. The retreating army and Greene's advance parties remained in constant contact until Knyphausen's force reentered Elizabethtown.

Knyphausen's rear guard, again the Rangers, suffered the worst during this day of fighting, as Simcoe often had to use his cavalry to dislodge pursuers who came too close. According to Simcoe, Greene's militiamen and light infantry kept up a constant fire from nearby trees throughout the day, and despite the presence of his Rangers, the militia maintained its pressure until Knyphausen's corps had reached the coast. Between midnight and 6 A.M. on June 24, Knyphausen's men crossed to Staten Island. Losses for this day of fighting were estimated to be a few hundred casualties for both sides.[22]

When Washington learned of Knyphausen's sudden withdrawal, he turned his army around once again and hurried back toward the Hudson River, fearing a sudden move up the river by Sir Henry Clinton's force. General Howe asked Trumbull to send additional militia, and Governor Clinton ordered out all of the Dutchess County militia to rendezvous at Fishkill. He then left for Fishkill to take personal command of the militia. Washington and the army arrived at Ramapo on June 27, but by then it was clear that the British did not intend to attack up the Hudson River. Washington wrote to the governments of Massachusetts and Connecticut to recall their militia, and asked Howe to dismiss the New York militia. He also wrote to Governor Clinton to praise New York's efforts in the emergency, and Howe thanked Trumbull for the strong reinforcements that Trumbull had ordered to his support. In New Jersey, General Greene left it up to Dickinson to decide to keep or dismiss the New Jersey militia, though he advised Dickinson that the sooner he dismissed the New Jersey militiamen, the better for the farmers.[23]

General Sir Henry Clinton had decided against further operations because Washington had so far avoided battle and Clinton saw little chance of luring the rebel chief into a general engagement. Therefore, after he had taken his force up the Hudson on June 24, the corps had sailed back downriver, disembarked at Phillipsburg, and begun foraging in the area. Overall, Clinton was pleased with Knyphausen's attack on the remaining Continentals in New Jersey, but concluded that once Washington's army and the militia had collected, there was little more to be gained. Clinton instead concentrated Knyphausen's men with his own at Phillipsburg to await word of the possible arrival of a French fleet. General Robertson agreed with Clinton's favorable impression of the operation in New Jersey. He credited Knyphausen with killing many rebel militiamen, which he hoped would discourage them the next time the British advanced, and the invasion secured some forage that normally Washington's army would have used. When Secretary of State George Germain heard of the maneuvers, he expressed a hope that Clinton's return to New York would dampen rebel morale and convince the militia not to join Washington's army. Thomas Hughes, a British subject traveling through the states at that time, was not as impressed, however, summarizing the expedition rather sarcastically: "A very pretty expedition: six thousand men having penetrated 12 miles into the country—burnt a village and returned."[24]

Washington, on the other hand, was genuinely pleased. Once again he had thwarted a British operation and had inflicted losses without committing his army to risky battle. Throughout both of Knyphausen's advances, the militia acted as an effective partisan force and shield for the army. Washington concluded: "The Militia deserve every thing that can be said on both occasions." A popular verse that circulated through New York City after the return of Knyphausen reflected the growing American contempt for the British army:

> Just not long before,
> Old Knip
> And old Clip
> Went to the Jersey Shore,
> The rebel rogues to beat;
> But at Yankee-farms,
> They took the alarms,
> At little harms,
> And quickly did retreat.
>
> Then, after two days' wonder,
> Marched boldly on to Springfield town;
> And swore they'd knock the rebels down;
> But, as their foes,
> Gave them some blows,
> They, like the wind,

Soon changed their mind,
And, in a crack,
Return-ed back
From not one-thrif their number.[25]

One reason that Sir Henry Clinton had abandoned the operations in New Jersey and had concentrated his army in New York was his knowledge that the Americans were expecting a French fleet along the coast sometime soon. In fact, as early as May, Washington had received news of the impending arrival of a French fleet in North American waters. The commanders in New York City, however, were skeptical. Intelligence from spies and Tories in New Jersey said that the Americans expected a French fleet, but that the Congress had not raised taxes and the state governments had not called out the militia. The British leaders believed that the rebels would take advantage of any increased expectations created by the French fleet to raise men and taxes, and therefore they were not convinced.[26]

Yet even before Knyphausen invaded New Jersey, Washington had initiated efforts to create a large Continental force to join with the French in a possible attack against New York City. He had urged the Continental Congress to convince the state governments to draft men into the army from the militia if necessary, because, as he explained, the "Militia are too precarious a dependance to justify such an attempt, where they form a material part of the plan." Should the Congress actually follow his recommendation and create a larger regular army, he would still need to call for aid from the militia. Based on his May estimate that the British force in New York numbered 15,000–17,500 soldiers, he wanted 35,000–40,000 men for the attempt on New York. The French, he hoped, might bring five thousand troops, but he was unsure. The Continental Army, if completed as desired, would number 22,680. He would therefore need 17,320 militiamen from all of the states north of Virginia. He had thus thought it best to begin the arduous process of assembling them immediately in May, because if the French fleet did arrive, there might be little time left to collect the militia.[27]

On June 2, the Committee of Cooperation, which the Continental Congress had sent to coordinate plans with Washington, issued letters to the governments of the states of Virginia and all those to the north of Virginia, asking for their militia to be readied by July 15. Connecticut's quota was 2250, New York's was 1575, and New Jersey's was set at 945. Altogether, the committee and Washington asked the states to provide 21,780 militiamen, an increase from his May estimates, to cooperate with the army. The committee urged the state leaders to complete their Continental quotas as well. On June 30, Washington postponed the target date for the rendezvous of these massive militia forces to August 25, but he warned that if the French arrived sooner, the militia would have to join him immediately. The British, who began to note Washington's strenuous efforts in June to gather men from the states, started to worry that the impending appearance of a French fleet might encourage the wavering Americans to take the field.[28]

The French did arrive sooner, but went to Newport, Rhode Island, instead of joining Washington near New York City. On July 10, the French fleet appeared off Rhode Island, and Sir Henry Clinton learned of the fleet's position on July 18. Suddenly the tables were turned, and instead of defending against attack, Clinton devised a bold plan to strike the French at Newport. Unfortunately for Clinton, his earmarked force was not fully embarked until July 27, when he had the fleet set sail immediately. Clinton and the fleet waited in Huntington Bay until July 31, but no favorable opportunity presented itself.[29]

As the French quickly entrenched in Newport and called in the militia of the area, Washington decided that he had no time to march his army to Rhode Island to support them. Therefore, the only way to help the Comte de Rochambeau, the French army commander, was to threaten or even attack New York. Since the militia was supposedly assembling in order to join the army anyway, he planned to use those militiamen who had already mustered to support his thrust at the British defenses. Even before the British had embarked on their ships, on July 21 Major General Anthony Wayne led 1600 infantry and 400 cavalry to attack a blockhouse held by 160 Tories in New Jersey across the river from Manhattan. The Tories repulsed the assault, inflicting over sixty casualties on Wayne's force while losing only twenty-one men. Washington, meanwhile, led the Continental divisions from the New Jersey mountains toward the Hudson River, and General Robert Howe stationed a mixed force of Continentals and New York militia at West Point, then moved the rest of his division and some attached New York militia troops forward. Governor Clinton ordered the militia officers of the adjacent counties to ready their men, and Governor Livingston ordered part of the New Jersey militia to rendezvous on August 1 at Morristown and there await Washington's orders. Washington ordered two Connecticut state militia regiments available for his use to join him and asked the commanding officer of the militia then assembling at Danbury to come forward. He also asked Governor Trumbull to prepare two thousand more militiamen in case he needed them. He urged Livingston to send immediately the New Jersey state regiment and the contingent of militia that were ready, and to prepare the rest of New Jersey's militia for action. He wrote directly to General Dickinson that he would be pleased to have Dickinson command the New Jersey militia in New York. Finally, Washington directed the militia units already en route from Massachusetts and New Hampshire to march to West Point. While trying to muster the militia reinforcements, he concentrated the regular divisions near Peekskill by the end of July.[30]

The militia began to arrive slowly in early August. About 250 New Jersey militiamen were already on their way, and Livingston's Council of Safety convinced him to call out 945 others to join Washington. Only 150 New Jersey militia soldiers, however, were at the Hudson River as of August 8, and a mere 448 of the 945 men called had assembled at Morristown by August 10. Then the number of militiamen in New York began to increase. The New England militia began to arrive at West Point after the tenth, which freed most of the New York militia in the Highlands to march forward and join the army in the field. After this, more men kept arriving. As of August 12, about 250 New York militia, over 1500 Massachusetts militia, and more than 650 New Hampshire militia made up the garrison at West Point, and more than 500 other militiamen from Massachusetts and New Hampshire were defending other posts around West Point. A detachment of New York militia guarded Haverstraw. At least twelve hundred Pennsylvania militia were marching toward New York, and Washington counted on the Connecticut militia, which was on its way, and other detachments of New York militia to support the army in its advance. Almost three thousand militiamen were already on hand, and perhaps another two thousand were on their way by mid-August.[31]

While Washington tried to assemble an army and threaten New York, Sir Henry Clinton became doubtful of success against the prepared French positions, and he increasingly worried about the safety of Staten Island and the other advance positions around New York City. Clinton therefore canceled the intended operation against Rhode Island and returned to the city in early August. Washington's army, which had grown to about twelve thousand, had already advanced to the Croton River when the British fleet returned to New York harbor. Washington canceled his own offensive plans and returned with the main army to the west side of the Hudson River.[32]

Throughout the rest of August, Washington urged the further collection of the requested militia because he still hoped to convince the Comte de Rochambeau to cooperate in an attack on New York. On August 17, about thirty-seven hundred militiamen were actually in the field, including eight hundred from New York and five hundred from New Jersey. The Connecticut militia, however, still had not arrived. Again the Committee of Cooperation asked the state governments to furnish their quotas because a second division of French troops was expected, and the American army had to be reinforced.[33]

By late August, Washington was becoming increasingly discouraged at the poor turnout of the militia in the second half of the month. The time of service for the militia of New Jersey had already ended, and the men were heading home. Altogether, less than one-fourth of the militiamen who were called actually had assembled. Washington took this opportunity to inform Congress once again that long-term enlistment for soldiers was necessary. The state governments, he added, would probably agree now because, with an army based on longer terms of service, he could stop making constant calls for the state militia forces. General Greene, whose name would become synonymous with the militia in the South, echoed this opinion. He decided in early September that anyone who knew about the militia would agree that twice the number of militia was necessary to afford the same protection given by half the number of regulars.[34]

It was too late, however, to influence the current campaign. The chances for a joint operation were slim, and when Washington learned that a British fleet had blockaded the second French division in Brest, France, he asked the governors to dismiss the militia already raised. If an opportunity arose later, he would have to recall the militiamen and hope they returned. Refusing to give up totally, in mid-September Washington met the French commanders in Hartford, Connecticut, to discuss a possible offensive. He warned General Greene, who took command in his absence, to watch for the arrival of another French fleet. If one appeared, Greene should immediately call for the militia to reassemble.[35] No new fleet appeared, and for the third time the projected Allied assault on New York City failed to materialize.

The British high command was not as sure that the threat of a joint assault on New York City had passed, though the new royal governor, James Robertson, exuded confidence. He concluded that despite Washington's growing numbers, New York was in no danger. By his calculation, on September 1, seventeen thousand regulars could be concentrated within twenty-four hours, and five thousand inhabitants could be armed. Thus, Washington's moves carried no threat to the British stronghold, with or without the rebel militia. Sir Henry Clinton, however, placed his strength closer to thirteen thousand fit for duty, against Washington's twelve thousand and five thousand French, and possibly three thousand more French soon. Based on these numbers, he decided that he did not have enough men to defend New York City, and most assuredly was too weak to resume offensive operations.[36]

On the other hand, in an attempt to ease the threat against New York City and possibly scatter Washington's forces, Clinton took advantage of an opportunity that he had been maturing through his communication with Benedict Arnold, the disgruntled general in the military forces of the United States. In July 1780, Arnold had returned to field duty and taken command of the fort at West Point as well as of the four thousand men garrisoning it and nearby forts. That was the situation as of September, when Clinton decided to make use of Arnold's unhappiness. Still fearing an attack on New York, Staten Island, and Long Island, he assumed that West Point would be the site of the rebels' main supply magazine. Therefore, with the hope of capturing West Point and perhaps the garrison, and disrupting Washington's entire campaign, Clinton sent Major John Andre to negotiate directly with Arnold. Clinton's plan fell apart when Andre was captured by a party of militiamen who, despite

Andre's offer of a large bribe, took him prisoner. Arnold heard of Andre's capture and fled to some British boats on the Hudson River.[37]

When Washington learned of these events, he worried that the British might try to follow up their surprise with a sudden attack on West Point. At this point he had about ten thousand Continentals and only four hundred militiamen concentrated on the west side of the Hudson, and about eight hundred Connecticut militia at North Castle. Since he had not expected a resumption of active operations, Washington had dismissed the rest of the militia. He quickly concentrated what militia he had near West Point to support the garrison of Continentals and New England militia, and ordered two other Continental divisions to West Point. He wanted the New England militia dismissed when these two divisions arrived. As usual, when West Point was threatened, Washington tried to replace all militia in the garrison with Continentals. The incident passed, however, without an attack on the Highlands.[38]

The scare over West Point marked the end of active operations for both sides in 1780. The experiences of that frustrating summer, however, led Washington to take up his favorite theme with the Congress: the augmentation of the regular army. As the following quotes demonstrate, five years of war had clearly taught Washington the different merits of full-time soldiers and local militiamen. He wrote to Congress:

> Regular Troops alone are equal to the exigencies of modern war, as well for defence as offence, and whenever a substitute is attempted it must prove illusory and ruinous. *No Militia* will ever acquire the habits necessary to resist a regular force. Even those nearest the seat of War are only valuable as light Troops to be scattered in the woods and plague rather than do serious injury to the Enemy.

He wrote to the state governments in the same tone:

> America had been almost amused out of her liberties. We have frequently heard the behavior of the Militia extolled upon one and another occasion by Men who judge only from the surface, by Men who had particular views in misrepresenting, by

visionary Men whose credulity easily swallowed every vague story in support of a favorite Hypothesis. I solemnly declare I never was witness to a single instance that can countenance an opinion of Militia or raw troops being fit for the real business of fighting. I have found them useful as light parties to skirmish the Woods, but incapable of making or sustaining a serious attack.

He continued in the same letter:

I mean not to detract from the merit of the Militia; their zeal and spirit upon a variety of occasions have intitled them to the highest applause; but it is of the greatest importance we should learn to estimate them rightly. We may expect everything from ours that Militia is capable of, but we must not expect from any, service for which Regulars alone are fit.[39]

Coming after the summer failure to increase the number of regular soldiers and the need to call up masses of militia to fill the army for the planned campaign, Washington only repeated what he had been saying for five years. The militia had its place, but that place was not attacking entrenched British and German regulars and besieging New York. Perhaps Washington's greatest strength as commander in chief of the American rebellion was his realistic approach to problems. He understood the reality of the war, that he had to use the militia because he would not get an army strong enough for all its tasks, and he also understood the merits and faults of the militia. He did not, however, cease striving to create the optimal military establishment for the tasks ahead of him. On the other hand, he did not refuse to work under less than perfect conditions. He instead tried to employ the militia in the roles he saw as best for it, including the jobs of partisan and scout. His frustration boiled over when he was forced to make plans that meant using militiamen where they were ill-suited.

As the main armies settled into their quarters, the partisan war again flared in the usual locations along the coasts and between the advance positions of the two armies. Westchester County lay directly between the two armies and bore the brunt of the constant raids by both sides. While the Continental Army operated in the county during September, the local people had a measure of protection. When the army withdrew in late September after the Arnold scare, the terror returned. Relentless Tory raids forced more and more of the inhabitants to flee farther from the British stronghold. As of November, about two hundred Continentals were operating with the local militia, but the Tory raiders still harassed the remaining occupants. When the Continental Army went into winter quarters in December, the locals looked to Governor Clinton for help, requesting at least seventy additional men to guard. Clinton ordered out the seventy men and promised to ask Washington for more Continentals, but he did not expect Washington to increase the detachment that remained in the county near Bedford. Clinton instead urged the local residents to muster their own militia units to defend themselves as much as possible. At the end of the year, however, few men were guarding Westchester County. By then, North Castle had been broken up by raiding parties and Bedford had been burned, and the inhabitants of Westchester felt abandoned. The British used the area to gather supplies almost unhindered and to transport supplies into New York City from Connecticut. General Heath, back in command in the Highlands, ultimately did increase the Continental detachment near Bedford to two thousand men to try and stop the Tories and ease the inhabitants' fears.[40]

In New Jersey, the presence of part of the army did not alleviate the need to call out militiamen to guard the coasts and Monmouth County. In October, the governor and the Council of Safety began a monthly call for militia detachments from less exposed parts of the state to furnish additional guards for Monmouth County. Along the coast facing Staten Island, Livingston and the council called out detachments of militia for short tours as guards throughout the summer and fall. As winter approached, Livingston asked Washington if any Continentals could help defend the coast, and Washington responded that he could spare only a few men to guard the line of communication between Morristown and the Hudson River. He did promise that these detachments would occasionally send patrols toward the coast, but the main body of troops would have to stay far from the coast so as not to encourage the British to make a strike at it. The Assembly then called out an additional 284 militiamen to join those already assembled. As for Bergen County, the story was the same. Washington informed Livingston that he could not place strong Continental detachments in the area when winter began, and the council had to order militia to guard. To handle all of these needs, the Assembly resolved in December that 820 men would be raised for the defense of the state to serve throughout 1781.[41]

Along the Connecticut–New York border, both sides raided each other throughout the summer, fall, and winter. The Connecticut Assembly tried to maintain a sizable force in the area, but the number of militiamen on guard fluctuated greatly. The two Connecticut state militia regiments that joined Washington for the summer operations had returned to Horseneck by October, but Tory attacks continued. In November, the Assemblymen ordered one thousand men to defend the region, but halved this number in December as winter began.[42]

The most threatening partisan activity centered on the Long Island Sound war between Tory and Connecticut militia parties. Both sides plundered each other and took civilians and militiamen captive to be held for ransom, exchange, or parole. The numbers involved on both sides grew ever larger. In late August or early September, about sixty British and Tory raiders crossed the Sound to Horseneck in whaling boats. Upwards of four hundred to five hundred local militiamen rallied, met the invaders, and captured them. Amphibious raids by Connecticut militiamen were so bad that more and more British and German regulars joined the swelling number of defenders on the island. Captain Ewald estimated that the New Englanders kept about one hundred boats along the Sound and often roamed the island with strong detachments. The jäger corps and Simcoe's Rangers went onto the island in the fall, bolstering to about one thousand the number of regulars guarding the north coast.[43]

General Sir Henry Clinton considered the threat to Long Island serious enough in November to urge Vice Admiral Marriot Arbuthnot, commander of the British fleet at New York, to keep his ships in Gardiner's Bay on the east end of the island. Clinton feared that with the French fleet in Rhode Island, if the British fleet left Long Island Sound unguarded, French and New England troops would cross to the east end of Long Island and be joined by the inhabitants living there, "who are in general disaffected. And the consequence of such an event would be most fatal, particularly at a time when my great detachments to the southward have so much reduced the army under my immediate command." He repeated his warnings on December 9, pleading with Arbuthnot to remain in Gardiner's Bay or risk giving the enemy control of the Sound. Such an occurrence, Clinton believed, "would assuredly have a most dangerous effect at any time . . . ." Clinton hoped that Washington's army would diminish considerably at the end of the year, but he feared that Washington could take advantage of an opportunity on Long Island to bolster morale and induce the regulars to stay, and get the militia to join him in greater numbers. In this respect, Clinton clearly understood the fragile nature of American enlistments and militia participation. As winter set in, Clinton became less worried about the island, though he convinced Arbuthnot to maintain his station at least until January.[44]

Brigadier General Gold S. Silliman of the Connecticut militia took an extraordinary step during the fall and early winter. As commander of the militia in southwest Connecticut, he was responsible for protecting the inhabitants near the New York border and along the coast. In order to accomplish that goal, he took the initiative in an attempt to stop the constant raids against civilians of both sides for plunder and prisoners. On September 23, he wrote to Colonel G. G. Ludlow, the British commander at Lloyd's Neck, Long Island, that "this predatory kind of Warr I conceive tends not in the least to bring to a close the great dispute between Britain and America . . . ." He offered to punish any American caught plundering Long Island if Ludlow would restrain his people from raiding Connecticut. Ludlow agreed to try. Silliman then stopped one unauthorized plundering party from leaving Horseneck and ordered another uncommissioned American raiding party arrested. Ludlow, meanwhile, informed Silliman on December 1 that he was "extreamly mortified to find" that a privateer had plundered Connecticut's shore and taken six people. He returned the people on his own initiative and promised to make the ship's captain answer for his conduct.[45] In this hostile partisan conflict, two men at least tried to ease the horror of war for those people caught between the warring sides.

In December, Silliman heard that the new British general, Benedict Arnold, was about to attack the Connecticut coast with a large force. When Trumbull learned of the rumored invasion, he quickly asked Washington for a detachment of Continentals to support the militia. The Duc de Lauzun, a brigadier general in the French army stationed in Rhode Island, offered the services of his corps should Arnold attack Connecticut. The feared raid, however, did not occur.[46]

In fact, the entire year of 1780 resembled that rumored invasion by Arnold. Despite great expectations on Washington's part, he gained little that year. He thought he would have the opportunity to end the war with the help of the French, and then he hoped to take advantage of Sir Henry Clinton's move to Rhode Island, but neither materialized. The British also grasped for, but failed to seize, opportunities in June, when Clinton returned from the South to find Knyphausen and Washington facing each other in New Jersey, and in July–August, when Clinton considered but ultimately aborted the operation against Rhode Island. The Arnold escapade in September, in light of these lost opportunities, seemed more like an act of desperation than a real chance to hurt the American forces.

Throughout these missed opportunities, militia operations resembled those of 1778–79. The state governments tried to improve the efficiency of their militia forces again in 1780, as they had almost every year so far, but did not resolve the basic problem of how to compel men to serve. All three state governments increased the fines for delinquent soldiers, but this monetary policy did little good. The governments could still assemble large numbers of militia for specific and limited operations, or in times of actual emergency, but they could not plan ahead when large forces were needed to take the field for long periods, and they could not maintain large forces for any length of time. More important, however, the three governments continued to cooperate with Washington as fully as possible, and this cooperation between state and national leaders remained one of the key components of American success.

To bolster the flagging number of militia that the state governments could muster, and in recognition of the limitations of the local militia forces, Washington followed the trend of recent years and allowed numerous Continental detachments to cooperate with militia units for local defense. Though he spread his army as much for logistical reasons as for the strategic goals of supporting the militia, while the army units remained scattered through three states, he freed more regulars for duty along the coasts and between the two armies.

Washington ignored his own instincts concerning the militia only when it came to dealing with the French. He seemed to view a joint operation with the French with mixed emotions because of the forces he would have to use. With no other choice, he called for a large number of militia to fill his ranks in the summer of 1780, as he had in 1778–79, yet at every opportunity he complained that any operation dependent on the militia was doomed to fail. Judging by the small proportion of the required militiamen who actually assembled, it is doubtful such large forces of militia could have been collected. In addition, Washington did not exude confidence in the militia's ability to contribute to the operation even if it did join him. Yet each year he tried to collect such a force. His overwhelming desire to capture New York and win the war with one decisive victory seemed to cloud his usually perceptive judgment of the militia's capabilities. Possibly this annual exercise in futility reflected his belief that he had to put up a good front for the allies, and he knew that he could get the requisite number of men from no other immediate source.

On the other hand, Washington's military principles were sound, and his desire to take New York City reflected a keen sense of strategic understanding. A few years after the war, Washington demonstrated this strategic sense when describing an earlier war, the French and Indian War. Back in the 1750s, as he remembered it, after Major General Edward Braddock had lost the battle along the Monongahela River in 1755, enemy raids had devastated the Virginia countryside. According to Washington's post-Revolution recollections, in the 1750s he had urged the Virginia legislature to exert itself to capture Fort Duquesne, the source of the raiding parties. Only through capturing the means of such raids could they have been stopped.[47] Washington seemed to have applied the same principle to the capture of New York. Only by removing the source of the Tory, British, and German raiding parties could the middle states be safe. Washington's view of the art of war was sophisticated and complex, and his nature was strong. He was an aggressive fighter who wanted to take the war to the enemy, and when the opportunity seemed to present itself, as with the arrival of a French fleet, his desire to take the offensive overruled his caution against using the militia in such a role.

Still, no full-scale battles occurred between Washington's army and the British army, but both sides maneuvered for advantage and several times a general engagement seemed imminent. In such operations, Washington could employ the militia as he preferred, as a partisan force hovering around the British. He cannot be credited with deliberately forcing the conflict into this more partisan phase of raids and partial maneuvers because the British allowed that to happen when they shifted the emphasis to the South. Washington, however, took advantage of the new circumstances by protecting his army while hurting the British with mixed forces of militia and Continentals. Whether this damage was inflicted in the open field or along the coasts against raiding parties mattered little to Washington.

What becomes clear during the operations of 1780, as well as 1778–79, is a fact that the British commanders understood but is often missing from modern descriptions of the war around New York City. When a British army, estimated by its commander as thirteen thousand effectives, remained inactive in the face of Washington's army, often estimated by Washington and the British at perhaps four thousand men in New Jersey, as was the case in the spring of 1780, it is hard to understand why the British did not just go forth and destroy Washington's minuscule force. And later, when Clinton returned from the South to New York, he hesitated to engage Washington even when his army outnumbered Washington's seventeen thousand to ten thousand. What is often missing in such descriptions is the fact that between the two armies were thousands of militiamen, some assembled in active units but most scattered in small parties or still at home, and also parties of Continentals distributed throughout the three middle states. Any estimation of the opposing sides must take into account these loosely controlled forces as well. Then the hesitation of Sir Henry Clinton or Wilhelm von Knyphausen in 1780, as well as of Sir William Howe earlier, to operate in the open field against Washington's army becomes more understandable. The importance of the militia in the operations of the regular field armies, as well as in the raging partisan war of raids and depredations, becomes clear.

CHAPTER TEN

The Militia Helps
Seize an Opportunity, 1781

THE LEADERS of the United States had no reason to believe that 1781 would yield results any different from the previous three years. They could hope that this year would be different, that the long awaited joining of the French and Americans would occur, but skepticism was strong and doubts intensified during two mutinies in January. Despite the presence of the French army and fleet in Rhode Island, the Continental Army was still weak and the militia undependable when it came to planning war-winning blows. Few American military or political leaders, therefore, could have predicted the stunning events that would unfold in 1781, and the important role the militia of the middle states would play in the final great victory achieved so many miles from New York.

Before the attainment of that victory, Washington faced one of the war's greatest internal threats to his command. On January 1, 1781, the Pennsylvania Continentals, who were stationed in New Jersey, mutinied. Brigadier General Anthony Wayne, commander of the division, feared that the British might try to take advantage of the crisis, and therefore ordered the New Jersey Continental brigade to Chatham, to get between the mutineers and Staten Island. At the same time, the Council of Safety advised Governor William Livingston to call out part of the New Jersey militia instantly and place Major General Philemon Dickinson in command, which he did.

The militia began assembling near Chatham immediately. The council ordered Livingston to call out even more militia on January 7.[1]

Wayne's fears were well founded. The British high command had been expecting some such event since the previous summer. British leaders had always believed that provincial soldiers were ill-disciplined and too prone to desertion, and this event supported that belief. As early as the summer of 1780, New York's new royal governor, General James Robertson, had believed that the Pennsylvania troops were ready to quit the service. In fact, this belief had been one of the reasons that he had supported General Wilhelm von Knyphausen's decision to invade New Jersey the previous June. Therefore, when the British commander, Sir Henry Clinton, learned of the mutiny on January 3, he was not surprised. He instead quickly tried to take advantage. Though he did not believe that the mutineers were planning to join the British, he nevertheless sent them offers of protection and help.[2]

The tense situation escalated rapidly as the Americans attempted to resolve the crisis before the British could intervene. Dickinson placed detachments of New Jersey militia at Crosswicks, Hopewell, and South Amboy, and near the Pennsylvanians' camp at Trenton. From these positions, the militiamen guarded the roads that led from Staten Island to Trenton. Washington meanwhile prepared to send one thousand Continentals with Major General Arthur St. Clair from New York if the mutineers did not lay down their arms. He expected General St. Clair to coordinate with the militia and to take whatever action was necessary against the mutineers. Washington also informed Governor George Clinton of the mutiny and warned that he might need the help of the New York militia, especially to defend West Point, if further mutinies occurred in New York. The two men met on January 6 at New Windsor, where Clinton assured Washington that he could assemble one thousand militiamen at West Point within four days.[3]

The British were aware of these steps taken to suppress the mutiny and keep the mutineers away from the British, but Sir Henry Clinton was determined to try and reach the Pennsylvanians. He moved four thousand of the elite troops of the army in New York to Staten Island in preparation for an expedition into New Jersey, and he planned a diversion up the Hudson River to keep the northern

New Jersey militia busy and to prevent Washington from sending men from New York. At first, Clinton was confident of success, but he hesitated to invade New Jersey prematurely because he feared such a move would simply reunite the rebel army. Instead, he limited himself to sending messengers to the mutineers with offers of help.[4]

Getting these messages through to the mutineers, however, proved very difficult because the New Jersey militiamen carefully guarded the coast and all the roads inland. The Pennsylvanians themselves informed a committee from the Continental Congress that they had no plans to go over to the British and that they would, in fact, join Wayne and the militia if the British invaded New Jersey. Sir Henry Clinton's analysis of the situation was correct.[5]

On the other hand, the mutineers were angry that the militia seemed to be threatening to attack them, and warned that they would lay waste to the country if the militia acted before the situation had been resolved. The militiamen, however, had no desire to act, at least not until negotiations had been tried. They in fact believed that the Pennsylvanians had legitimate grievances that should be redressed. While the standoff between the army and the mutineers continued, Sir Henry Clinton remained hopeful. His hopes were finally dashed when the Pennsylvania troops spurned his offers and turned the two messengers who had made it through the militia guards over to the Continental Congress. The spies, as the Congress labeled them, were hung. After the Congress discharged over one thousand Pennsylvanians, the rest of the division returned to duty on January 15, and Dickinson dismissed the militia. Two days later, Clinton learned that the mutineers had reached an accommodation, and he returned to New York City.[6]

Within a week the New Jersey Continentals, who were also stationed in New Jersey, followed the Pennsylvanians' example and mutinied. Washington immediately ordered Major General Robert Howe to take command of a detachment of Continentals to quell the latest insurrection and gain the unconditional submission of the mutineers. He urged Howe to gather all the New Jersey militiamen possible by warning them of the danger to civil liberties when armed men dictated terms to the government or army. Washington informed Governor Livingston that he had sent a force to put down the latest mutiny and asked him to prepare the New Jersey militia to help.[7]

Once again a British presence on Staten Island heightened the pressure on Washington to resolve the situation quickly. When Sir Henry Clinton heard of the second mutiny, he ordered General Robertson to Staten Island to be ready to take advantage of any opportunity. The British, however, found no opportunity with this mutiny either. The New Jersey mutineers were in Chatham, making their demands, when they learned that the New Jersey militia was assembling in great numbers in Springfield, with the intention of putting down the mutiny by force if necessary. The mutineers then became alarmed and returned to their barracks, where Howe surrounded them with his Continentals on January 27. Howe knew that he could call on the militia in case the New Jersey Continentals refused to submit, but instead, the New Jersey regulars gave up and the second mutiny ended. The Whig leadership of New Jersey was pleased with the actions of the local militia during both mutinies, and expressed confidence that the militiamen would help quell any such future incidents.[8]

While mutinies wrecked the Continental Army, the state governments were busy with the usual efforts to use and improve their militia forces. The New Jersey Assembly tried once again to improve its militia laws on January 8, when it passed a new act that ultimately only reorganized the counties into new brigades. The system of monthly tours of duty and the monetary penalty for refusing to serve both remained in effect. In late January, the Assembly adjourned until May, authorizing General Dickinson to call out the whole of the state's militia in an emergency but prohibiting him from sending militiamen into neighboring states without the consent of the Assembly or the Council of Safety.[9]

In the nearby states of New York and Connecticut, the local militia spent the winter and spring months fighting the constant raids from Long Island and New York City. In Connecticut, the government maintained guard companies in the ports along the Long Island Sound to protect against these raids, and as usual, the people of these coastal towns asked the Assembly for even more guards, despite the fact that these townsmen also raised their own small guard detachments from the local inhabitants. Particularly dangerous was an organization known as the Associated Loyalists, which the British government officially sanctioned at the end of 1780. The Association, which included many Tories who had previously fled Connecticut and now resided on Long Island, used that island as a safe haven from which to launch raids. During the first weeks of 1781, the Associated Loyalists attacked Norwalk, New Haven, and Branford. Brigadier General Gold S. Silliman, who still commanded the local militia brigade in southwest Connecticut, warned Governor Trumbull that this predatory war showed no signs of letting up, and if the inhabitants did not get more help, they would abandon the area. The Assembly tried to furnish extra guard companies when possible, but the detachments remained small, ranging in number from eighty-six men in New Haven to twenty-one in Killingsworth.[10]

These small guard details could not stop the raiding parties from Long Island. The raiders would plunder or burn a few houses and barns while the outnumbered coast guards retreated, then the local militiamen would assemble, and the raiding party would reembark and escape. In retaliation, Trumbull and the Council of Safety called for volunteers to raid Long Island. Occasionally even Major Benjamin Tallmadge and some of his Continental dragoons would join the militia in these attacks across the Sound. As late as June, while the regular armies massed for the summer operations, Tory and Connecticut militia units crisscrossed the Sound, attacking each other's towns. Clearly, Silliman's efforts the previous year to end the brutal raids had failed.[11]

Along the southwest border of the state, the savage war worsened. Colonel John Mead, commander of the militia detachments posted in the area, reported on January 3, 1781, that he had only thirty-nine men at Stamford, and that the enemy raiders had free run of Horseneck, which they plundered and raided daily. Though he sent patrols to Horseneck each day, he refused to remain there until he had on hand the five hundred men that the government had ordered to him. He warned that Stamford would be lost next because it was in as bad a condition as Greenwich had been a year ago, and Greenwich was now in a no-man's land between the American and British outposts. Silliman urged the militia officers of the area to assemble and send their men to Mead as required, but as of the end of the first week of January, Mead had only one hundred men.[12]

The few remaining inhabitants of Greenwich complained bitterly to Trumbull that the enemy raiders plundered at will, paroled the people, and collected supplies for the British. Even some Whig militiamen plundered indiscriminately between the lines. Mead informed Trumbull of an even more dangerous trend: many people who had been friendly to the rebellion were laying down their arms. In order to relieve the situation somewhat at the end of the first week in January, Mead called out four companies from his own local regiment to serve for eight days. Silliman meanwhile sent orders that all suspicious people were to be apprehended. The governor and the council ordered all brigadier generals of the militia to compel their officers to detach the required men for southwestern Connecticut, but there was no way to enforce this order. At the same time, the governor issued orders for two hundred more men to join the five hundred originally designated to guard the southwest frontier. Silliman issued a fourth order in late January to the officers to send their men. Finally, the situation began to improve during February, and by March 1, Mead had reestablished a post in Greenwich. The enlistments of many of his men, however, ended soon, and Mead feared he once again would be left with no men.[13]

On March 24, Trumbull and the council appointed Brigadier General David Waterbury to command the forces in southwest Connecticut, but the perilous situation did not improve. In fact, on April 16, Waterbury reported that he had with him only one hundred men, though with the help of the local inhabitants he was harassing the Tories as much as possible. The number of militiamen serving with him increased somewhat in May and June, and Waterbury was able to hold Greenwich throughout those months.[14]

Next door in Westchester County, the inhabitants suffered from the same kind of raiders that plagued southwestern Connecticut, while the Westchester militia tried to stop the Tories and even attack their bases. The New Yorkers asked for help from the Continental detachment in the county, commanded by Lieutenant Colonel William Hull, to attack Morrisania, which was the base of the noted Loyalist raider Colonel James DeLancey. Though not confident of success, Washington allowed Major General William Heath, the overall commander of the Continentals in the area, to support the attack with some of his troops. Heath reinforced Hull's Continental detachment, and General Samuel Parsons went forward to take command.[15]

During the evening of January 21, the mixed force of Continentals and militia advanced southward. Parsons asked Colonel Mead to advance from southwest Connecticut to support the attack, but Mead refused to do so. As he neared Morrisania, Parsons detached parties of Continentals and mounted militiamen to guard the roads leading to the area in order to isolate the Tories, and then sent the main body of troops to attack the Tory base. In the ensuing clash at Morrisania, Parsons's men, under the immediate command of Colonel Hull, killed about thirty of DeLancey's corps, captured fifty-four, and burned all of the huts used by the men. In addition, they took a large stock of forage and some cattle and horses. Hull's detachments lost twelve men killed, thirteen wounded, and six missing. The next day, Hull retired with his prisoners and livestock, but the Tories regrouped and pursued. Parsons concentrated his scattered detachments and advanced to support Hull, but then British soldiers arrived to help the Tories, and Parsons finally had to make a stand on a nearby hill. After one of Parsons's parties withdrew toward Eastchester, followed by part of the British force, Parsons's artillery fired on the remaining British and Tories, and they retreated toward New York City. Parsons then withdrew his men as well. The local militia praised the Continentals for their work in the raid, and Parsons hoped that the success would afford some relief for the local inhabitants.[16]

This attack, however, did not end the threat to Westchester County. While the local militia maintained a constant guard, the inhabitants continued to petition the New York government for more militia to reinforce the Continentals already stationed in the county. As Captain Jeremiah Fogg of the Bedford militia explained, presumably with a touch of exaggeration, the men in his command needed relief "to enable them to sleep with their wives at least once a week without fear—Such Separations, should the War continue a Century, might prove fatal in point of propagation." Governor George Clinton was not exaggerating when he wrote to John Jay in praise of the efforts of the local militia of Westchester County:

Its Militia often unsupported & left alone to resist the Enemy, have maintained their Ground beyond the most sanguine Expectation. Every Man, indeed every Boy, has become a Soldier, and I do not believe a superior Spirit of Bravery & Enterprize ever possessed a People, and I have the Pleasure to assure you this Description is equally applicable to the Inhabitants of Orange County South of the Mountains.[17]

Despite these heroic efforts, the raids continued. As late as mid-June, a local militia officer, Major Nathaniel Delivan, complained that the Tory raiders commanded by Colonel DeLancey were continually "bating and barking." The local militia usually could not assemble before the plunderers were on their way home. When the French army marched through Westchester County in July, its officers were shocked by the devastation in the area wrought by this partisan war. They noted that the inhabitants were in communication with the British, that the Whig residents had abandoned their homes, and that many of the homes had been destroyed. The area was stripped, according to Jean-François-Louis, the Comte de Clermont-Crevecoeur, "not surprisingly considering that this region has been a battlefield for three years." Actually, the hapless people of Westchester had been caught between the contending armies for six years, and the scars were deep.[18]

On the west side of the Hudson River, the number of raids increased as the winter ended. In mid-March, about two hundred enemy troops emerged from Paulus Hook and advanced toward the west end of Dobb's Ferry. Heath sent 150 Continentals to support the militia, who quickly assembled, attacked, repulsed, and pursued the raiders. The militia recaptured all of the plunder. Near Poughkeepsie, militia detachments patrolled both sides of the river for plunderers and for Tories who had enlisted with the enemy. Also in March, the New York Assembly passed a new law providing for the creation of a state militia regiment to serve throughout the year. The soldiers of this new regiment would be used to defend the frontiers, including the southern regions near the British army. Governor Clinton began issuing the necessary laws in April for the raising of this regiment.[19]

On May 15, a party of one hundred Loyalists began to construct a blockhouse on the former site of Fort Lee in New Jersey. The local Whig militia, commanded by Colonel Richard Dey, immediately began to assemble around the Tories. Fearing that a blockhouse on that site would enable the British to harass more of the countryside and possibly interfere with future operations, Washington ordered Colonel Alexander Scammell to take his Continental battalion, join the assembled militia in the area, and attack. He warned Scammell not to inform any militia officers ahead of time of the plan, or the information might leak out. By the time Scammell arrived, however, Dey's militia had attacked and forced the Tories to leave the unfinished works. Dey's men were busily destroying the works when Scammell arrived.[20]

At one point, Washington had to reverse the usual pattern of winter requests for detachments of men. Instead of the militia and governors asking for Continentals, Washington issued an urgent appeal in February to the governors to prepare their militia to come to the army. Having sent a large detachment to Virginia earlier in February, he feared that the British might try to take advantage of the weakened state of his army. Therefore, he wanted New Jersey's and New York's militia ready to assemble. Governor Clinton, in Albany at the time, had instructed Washington to contact the militia officers directly if a need arose. Washington therefore wrote to the militia officers of New York to prepare for any emergency. He also wrote to General Dickinson, according to the instructions of the New Jersey Assembly, to have that state's militia prepared. By 1781, the state governments, at least in New York and New Jersey, allowed Washington to bypass the normal chain of command when calling on the militia. He did inform Governor Livingston of his actions, and Dickinson informed Washington that he had issued the necessary orders. The Comte de Rochambeau offered to march most of the French army from Rhode Island to reinforce Washington, but Washington responded that this was unnecessary. He hoped to be able to hold with the help of the new Continental recruits coming in and the large body of militia that could usually be collected in an emergency. The British, however, did not attack.[21]

In Philadelphia, meanwhile, the national legislature finally solidified itself with a formally written government. On March 1, the Articles of Confederation established a new framework for the government of the United States. Under the Articles, the new Confederation Congress asked all of the states to keep a well-regulated militia. The Congress had the power to make the rules for the military, and officially it could direct the operations of the land forces. It also decided on the number of men the army would have and made requisitions to the states for men, but the Articles had no mechanism for enforcing these decisions or requests. In fact, the new government remained uncommitted to the ongoing debate with Washington concerning the need for a regular army. In actuality, the transition from the Continental Congress to the Confederation Congress had little impact on the military and manpower policies of the United States during the war. The Confederation Congress even continued to send advice and directions to Washington. It resolved in April that he should send another detachment to the South, and that he be authorized to call on the state governments of New York and New England for any necessary militia to replace the men. Washington sent the detachment.[22]

On May 21, Washington met the Comte de Rochambeau at Hartford, where they discussed their plans for the summer. The French commander informed Washington that Admiral Comte de Grasse was on his way to the West Indies with a large fleet and a small land force. The American and French commanders agreed that should de Grasse arrive along the North American coast, New York or Virginia was the likely place for combined operations. Washington preferred ending the war with his favorite project, the capture of New York, but for the moment, uncertain of de Grasse's destination, he and the French leaders decided simply to unite the French army from Rhode Island with Washington's army near New York City and try to take advantage of the weakened state of the British army, which also had sent detachments to the South. Washington immediately wrote to the state governments from Pennsylvania to New England that in view of this planned combination and possible attack, all Continental regiments had to be filled and large numbers of militia had to be prepared. As of May 24, Washington reported the army's strength at nine thousand men. He asked for over six thousand more militia, which was far less than he had demanded in past years when trying to coordinate with the French. Washington seemed to have learned that he stood a better chance of getting what he asked for if he made a more conservative request.[23]

Connecticut's Assembly responded quickly to Washington's request. It immediately decided that the two state militia regiments, which it had ordered to be raised in February, would be completed and sent to New York along with other detachments that would total twenty-one hundred men, six hundred more than Connecticut's original quota. New Jersey's Assembly, on the other hand, postponed its consideration of the need to prepare its quota of five hundred men. In New York, General Parsons complained to Governor Clinton that the roughly six hundred militiamen that New York's government was supposed to maintain at West Point were not there. He emphasized that he needed to have the militia to complete the garrison up to the three thousand men required should active operations commence.[24]

In mid-June, Washington asked the state governments to have their militia join the army by July 15. Fearing that he would not be able to assemble as large a force as he had hoped due to a poor militia turnout, he asked Rochambeau to urge the Comte de Grasse to bring a French force with him. Meanwhile, he reduced Pennsylvania's quota of militia because its men were busy supporting the Continental and militia forces in Virginia. To cover for this reduction, he increased New Jersey's quota to 750 men and Connecticut's to 2100.[25]

Washington clearly had little confidence in the militia to assemble on time and in the necessary numbers. Plans based on the use of substantial militia forces were risky, as he had written more than once. Unlike earlier years, when preparing for possible joint operations with the French, Washington approached the 1781 campaign slightly more realistically. Perhaps this time he sensed that there was a real chance the French fleet would arrive and he could accomplish something. Still, he based much of his hopes on a military organization that was undependable for such large operations.

Throughout the rest of June, Washington and the state governments attempted to collect the required men. In Connecticut, Governor Trumbull and the council complied with an urgent request from Washington for an additional eight hundred men to serve for three months, and General Waterbury prepared his command of twenty-one hundred men then assembling in southwest Connecticut. Washington sent a similar plea to Governor Clinton for an extra eight hundred New York militia, and he warned the governor that he might have to ask for even more in an emergency. On July 1, the New York Assembly ordered that the desired soldiers be raised, to serve until December 1. It also authorized Clinton to call out other detachments of militia as might become necessary during the campaign. The militia raised for this operation would be subject to Washington's orders. To help New York, Washington asked for six hundred militiamen from Massachusetts to defend northern New York so that the New York government could concentrate most of its militia in the southern part of the state. Continuing raids in the southern part of Orange County interfered with the muster when in late June the inhabitants of that region asked to be excused from furnishing their quota of militia for the new units being raised. They instead requested permission to raise a guard to protect their own frontiers. Clinton, however, continued to focus on the collection of the necessary men.[26]

New Jersey's Assembly finally acted on June 27 when it authorized Livingston to call out 750 militiamen to serve for three months rather than the usual one month. The men were to assemble at Morristown by July 15, and would be under the command of Colonel Sylvanus Seely. Tory raids, however, threatened to inhibit the muster in New Jersey. Excursions in June forced the inhabitants of Bergen County to petition the New Jersey government for protection from Tory plundering, and farther south, a larger expedition attacked Middletown. On June 21, Brigadier General Cortland Skinner, a Tory, led seven hundred British regulars, three hundred Loyalists, one hundred jägers, and eighteen cavalry from Staten Island. They landed near Middletown and marched into the town, looking for sheep and cattle, but much of the livestock had already been removed. The raiders collected what animals they could find and herded them to Navesink, opposite Sandy Hook. The rapidity of this march prevented the local militia regiment from organizing, though small groups of militiamen harassed and skirmished with the raiding party throughout its march. These militiamen hovered on the flanks of the invading corps and fired from behind trees, fences, and whatever other cover they could find. Though the local defenders could not stop or destroy Skinner's party, they forced Skinner's men to stay concentrated and not send out smaller detachments to plunder a wider area. Altogether Skinner had about five casualties and five men missing, and the local militia lost about the same number of men.[27] Despite the interruption of such raids, perhaps launched deliberately by the British to interfere with the attempted muster of the militia, the governments and militia of the middle states strove to supply Washington with the men he needed to coordinate with the French in the coming campaign.

American efforts to collect an army did not go unnoticed by the British command. In fact, the possibility of a joining of the French and American forces had been preying upon Sir Henry Clinton's mind since the beginning of the year. Understanding the nature of the American military, Clinton warned Secretary of State Germain in January that should the French receive reinforcements this year, the rebels would be encouraged and Washington's army would be greatly increased, no matter how weak it was after the mutinies. Germain, however, hoped that the mutinies would so weaken Washington that Clinton could continue to send detachments to Virginia to reinforce the British corps already operating along the James River there. This reinforced party, commanded by Benedict Arnold, could then coordinate with Lord Cornwallis, who was operating in the Carolinas, to secure the Southern colonies.[28]

Germain also pressured Clinton to attack West Point, an attack Germain believed should have occurred either the previous September or during the winter. In April, Clinton defended his decision not to attack West Point at either earlier time because Washington had at both times twice the force Clinton could use, besides the militia, "which might have been readily collected in the three populous and warlike provinces adjoining . . . ." Arnold later supported Clinton's defense by estimating Washington's army the previous fall at ten thousand men, and even after January 1, probably about six thousand. Arnold elaborated on Washington's reserves: "I ever supposed that upon any emergency he could draw forth a considerable body of militia which would depend on the local situation of his army, perhaps from two or three to five or six thousand in as many weeks." Clinton promised to attack West Point at the first opportunity.[29] Clearly the militia were beginning to influence Sir Henry Clinton's thinking in 1781. Whether he really feared the rebel militia or only used it as a scapegoat, as of 1781 the militia began to loom ever larger in the mind of the British commander in chief.

Clinton's thoughts turned from the offense to the defense in June. As he calculated the growing American army, his fears for New York grew. Estimating the Continental Army at six thousand, and the French at another six thousand, he then added possibly seven thousand New England militia and perhaps another three thousand from New Jersey. Thus, he explained to Germain, Washington probably would have over twenty thousand men as well as "a militia as I have always said warlike, inveterate and numerous." Clinton judged his own numbers at 10,931 effectives, not nearly enough, in his opinion, to handle Washington's force. Still, he hoped to hold out in New York as long as the British fleet remained superior to that of the French.[30]

To be safe, however, Clinton wanted more men for the defense of New York. He therefore began a line of reasoning that would ultimately lead to the disaster at Yorktown. In mid-June, he wrote to Cornwallis, who by then had abandoned the Carolinas and had entered Virginia to join the corps already there. Clinton explained to Cornwallis that he had sent to the South over seventy-seven hundred soldiers and that Major General William Phillips, who had replaced Arnold, commanded about fifty-three hundred men in Virginia. This many men, Clinton believed, should have been more than enough to subdue the Southern provinces by then. Threatened with a siege, Clinton decided it was time to reconcentrate his forces in New York. Accordingly, he ordered Cornwallis to take a defensive position in Virginia and send some of his men to New York. When reinforcements arrived from England, they could begin to plan their next campaign.[31]

Thus, indirectly, Clinton's image of American forces, which was intricately wrapped up with his view of the numerous militia surrounding New York, began to affect his strategic view. The chain of events set off by this decision to call for men from Virginia would have far-reaching consequences for the British and American forces in North America.

While Clinton fretted in New York City, the French army left its camps in Newport on June 11 and crossed Connecticut; by July 1 the vanguard had reached Ridgebury. Washington spread the word that the long-anticipated attack on New York was about to take place. Inside the British defenses, the talk of an attack was seen by some as a ruse to keep Clinton from detaching more men to the South. Clinton, however, clearly believed the threat was real. Washington, meanwhile, ordered all available militia and Continentals to move forward and rendezvous near the British outposts on July 2, his target date for the announced attack against Manhattan Island. He asked Rochambeau to have the French army at Bedford by that date, and requested that Governor Clinton have the New York militia ready to join the army if the attack succeeded. In support of the main advance, he wanted the Duc de Lauzun's corps to join 200 Continental cavalry, 350 militia commanded by Waterbury, and three companies of New York militia soldiers in an attack on Morrisania on the same day.[32]

Rochambeau redirected the French march and sent Lauzun's Legion to Bedford, where the Continental dragoons joined it on July 2. Meanwhile, the Continental Army left Peekskill and were within a few miles of Kingsbridge on the second. Major General Benjamin Lincoln, who commanded the advance force, led forward eight hundred men to attack Fort Independence near Kingsbridge while Waterbury prepared his detachment of Connecticut militia to begin the secondary attack against Morrisania.[33]

At this point, whatever Washington's ultimate plans for the day were, everything became confused. It seems that both armies had moved detachments toward each other on July 2. As Lauzun, the dragoons, and Waterbury neared Morrisania, and Lincoln's corps marched ahead of the main American army, Sir Henry Clinton sent about eighty regular infantry, under the command of Lieutenant Colonel Andreas Emmerich, to ambush Lincoln. Clinton then received intelligence that the main American army was nearby, and he became worried that Emmerich would be surrounded. He therefore ordered out another detachment, 240 men led by Lieutenant Colonel Wurmb, to cover Emmerich's retreat. As Wurmb followed Emmerich, he found the former site of Fort Independence already held by Lincoln's troops, and he immediately attacked and retook the fort. Emmerich, meanwhile, was waiting in ambush near Phillipsburg when he noticed a large number of boats moving down the river and realized something bigger than a raid was occurring. After attacking a small party of American troops, he quickly retreated in the direction of Fort Independence. A detachment of jägers drove back an advance party from Lincoln's corps and Emmerich joined Wurmb safely.[34]

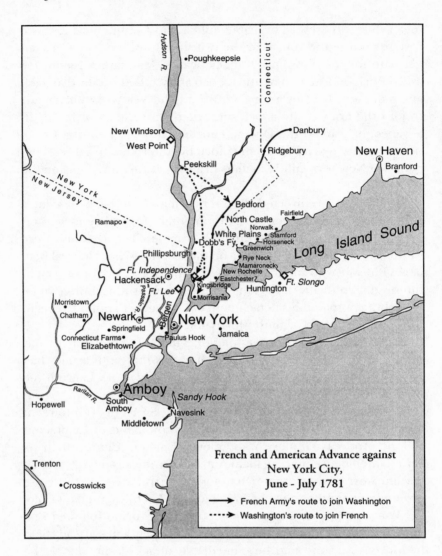

French and American Advance against
New York City,
June - July 1781

——▶ French Army's route to join Washington
----▶ Washington's route to join French

While this small battle raged between Lincoln's men and the parties with Wurmb and Emmerich during the night of July 2 and the
early morning of July 3, Lauzun and Waterbury moved closer to
Morrisania. Waterbury had just begun the attack with the Connecticut and New York militia against DeLancey's base when the sound of
gunfire from the direction of Fort Independence interrupted the
operation. Lauzun decided to march to the sound of the guns, a

move that Washington later approved because the necessary surprise for Waterbury's attack had thus been lost. Waterbury pressed his attack anyway, while Lauzun raced westward. Lincoln learned of Lauzun's approach and tried to pin down Emmerich's and Wurmb's corps to allow Lauzun to attack their flank, but the trap failed, and despite their superiority in cavalry, Lincoln and Lauzun were unable to prevent the escape of Wurmb's and Emmerich's detachments. By noon on July 3, the fighting had died down around Fort Independence. Waterbury finally gave up his effort to destroy Morrisania and retreated later in the evening before British reinforcements could encircle him.[35]

Washington reconnoitered the British defenses during the afternoon of July 3, but decided that nothing further could be accomplished that day. He instead withdrew the main army, which by then had edged near to Kingsbridge. The American army had about fifty casualties and the British forces perhaps a little more than thirty total. The French corps had no losses. Waterbury's action resulted in few, if any, losses on either side. When Washington pulled his units back, the British maintained all of their posts, including the Tory base at Morrisania. Whether Washington had actually planned to attack the defenses at Kingsbridge and initiate a battle for New York City is uncertain. One of the more skeptical British officers, Major Frederick Mackenzie, admitted that the American and French maneuvers suggested that a serious attack, at least on the advance forts, had been contemplated. If nothing else, Washington had used the day of skirmishing as a reconnaissance in force.[36]

Still, Washington had come closer than ever before to realizing his great objective of attacking New York City. Though the preliminary moves had failed, he had at least moved aggressively, which suggested a real intention to attack. Most of the militia had yet to collect, so this advance in early July consisted of Continentals and French soldiers, with a few supporting militia units. These units he sent off on a subsidiary operation while he directed the main body of regulars toward the point of attack near Kingsbridge. Perhaps this separation of militia and regulars was a key to the method Washington planned to employ should a full-scale assault ever be tried. Militia forces would be used to guard the rear areas and launch diversions while the main work would be left to the Continentals and French.

For the moment, however, Washington backed away from the city. On July 3, the French and Americans marched back to North Castle, where they stayed for three days, then advanced to White Plains. During this march the French learned firsthand how badly this region had been devastated by the war. Lauzun's corps and Waterbury's militia remained behind to patrol the roads that led north and east from Kingsbridge. Washington kept the Allied forces together, awaiting further reinforcements of militia and Continentals. While camped on the edge of this stripped area and near the British outposts, American and French parties foraged southward into Westchester County. Several caches of hay and oats, destined for New York City, were found along the coast. Usually detachments of fifteen hundred soldiers and a troop of French hussars accompanied the French foraging parties. In the process, this no-man's land between the two armies continued to be ruined by the war. On July 17, Lauzun's Legion skirmished with Colonel James DeLancey's Loyalist cavalry, and on July 22, a larger than normal corps of French and Americans advanced toward Kingsbridge and occupied the site of Fort Independence. Under cover of this large column, foragers collected the cattle of the area. Another column, including Waterbury's Connecticut militia and Lauzun's Legion, again attacked DeLancey's Tory cavalry near Morrisania. They destroyed the Loyalist base, drove the Tories onto some nearby British ships, and then joined the main body near Kingsbridge. Altogether the concentrated force numbered several thousand. After staying near Kingsbridge through July 23, the French and Americans withdrew at sunset.[37]

The few French forces left in Rhode Island, meanwhile, launched a raid that proved Sir Henry Clinton's fears for Long Island were well founded. The previous fall and winter, Clinton had convinced Admiral Marriot Arbuthnot to guard the eastern end of Long Island Sound due to his fear that the French would attack Long Island, and in mid-July 1781, the French did exactly that. On July 10, about two hundred French soldiers embarked; they landed at Huntington two days later. Once on the island, however, the French raiders did not fare so well. They formed a line of battle outside the local fort, which supposedly had only fifty men as a garrison, but despite this numerical advantage, the French commander, Baron d'Angely, ordered a retreat. The French lost three men killed.[38]

While the Continentals, militia, and French engaged in the partisan war, additional militia forces assembled slowly. Governor Trumbull and the Connecticut Assembly continued to issue orders for the state regiments and the other required militia units to assemble and march to New York, but as of July 20, the militia officers were still trying to muster their men. In New Jersey, Colonel Seely had collected only 100 of the expected 750 militiamen at Morristown. With the season advancing rapidly, Washington held another conference with the French commanders on July 19 in order to discuss future operations. He remained convinced that New York should be the primary objective, but if Admiral de Grasse's fleet was late or the French remained convinced that they could not get their ships across the sandbar into New York harbor, Washington accepted the possibility of moving the combined army to Virginia. In that case, he would garrison West Point adequately and leave some Continentals and militia to cover the country around the British lines, then take the rest of the French and American armies to Virginia to operate against Cornwallis, who was at that time campaigning against the Marquis de Lafayette.[39]

While the Allied army sat at White Plains throughout July, the British army sat in New York City. Sir Henry Clinton continued to urge Cornwallis to send two thousand to three thousand men from Virginia, though Clinton's plans for these additional men were unclear. He wrote to Germain about an expedition to Philadelphia, but he informed Cornwallis that his position in New York was in danger from the Allied forces, which he estimated at almost fourteen thousand. This estimate included a large force of militia that he assumed had already joined Washington. As he explained to Cornwallis, he could only imagine what effect this large army "will have on the numerous and warlike militia of the five neighbouring provinces," but he feared that even more militia would join the rebel army.[40]

Not everyone shared this awe of the "warlike militia." General James Robertson agreed with Clinton's numerical estimate of Washington's forces, but explained that most of the rebels were "raw soldiers." Others in New York tried to understand why Clinton simply sat while the rebel and French armies camped so close for three weeks. Instead of attacking, Clinton sent for reinforcements from Cornwallis. Clinton's image of the American forces supported by the militia, and the presence of the French army, kept him frozen in place.[41]

By July 21, Washington had militia lookouts in southern New Jersey watching for de Grasse's fleet. He warned Waterbury that he planned to move the army soon, and therefore the militia had to guard closely the roads running from New Rochelle to Eastchester. The expected militia reinforcements, however, continued to assemble slowly. Seely reported that despite using every method he could think of, he had only about 180 men at Morristown on July 29. Washington asked him to send forward those he had collected. Livingston's Council of Safety advised the governor to order four companies of militia that were currently guarding the coast at Elizabethtown to join Seely. Major General Alexander McDougall, who had returned to the army after serving briefly in the old Continental Congress, informed Washington that only small parties of Connecticut militia had arrived at West Point. The Connecticut government continued to have problems collecting its men despite Trumbull's efforts to urge the officers to send their quotas.[42]

On August 2, Washington's growing frustration manifested itself in a letter to the Confederation Congress. He had written twice to the governments of the states north of Maryland, he complained, in an effort to collect a strong militia force as soon as possible. As of the second, however, he had only 200 militiamen from the Connecticut state regiments, 176 other militiamen recently detached from local Connecticut militia units, and about 80 men from New York. The two hundred soldiers from the Connecticut state regiments and the eighty New Yorkers had been with the army since he had left winter quarters. He informed the state governments that his army was little stronger on August 2 than it had been when it had started the operation in June. The French, who had joined him several weeks earlier, faced the possibility of sitting out the rest of the year without achieving any substantial results. Over the next few days a few Massachusetts and Connecticut militia trickled in, and the New Jersey government ordered further parts of its state regiments to join Seely, but Washington feared he would have to revert to the defensive and give up hope of ending the war that year. Governor Livingston wrote to Washington that he was embarrassed for the United States, and for New Jersey in particular.[43]

The next two weeks were equally frustrating for Washington. Though still hopeful of executing some form of an offensive, he received little encouragement to expect the needed reinforcements. Trumbull renewed his orders for the militia to muster but could only hope the orders had some effect. Seely arrived at Dobb's Ferry, but as of August 10, had only about 390 men. The French and American armies, however, remained poised near New York City, with the advance corps and Waterbury's militia still near the British outposts in Westchester County. Washington refused to give up on his cherished project.[44]

Washington should not have been surprised by the result so far of the summer campaign. In none of the previous three efforts to prepare for an Allied operation had the militia responded as desired, and the units that he had requested were usually slow to assemble and understrength. Washington perhaps expected too much of the militia this time. He had learned of the militia's limitations and he had understood since the fall of 1776 that he should not try to concentrate large bodies of militia with the army for field operations. It would seem that Washington's overwhelming desire to attack New York and end the struggle with one blow continued to cloud his usually clear perception of the militia's limitations.

As the waiting game dragged on, the British did little to interfere with the American plans. By late July there was little doubt among the British that de Grasse was on his way and that Washington wanted to attack New York. The skeptical staff officer, Major Mackenzie, believed that General Clinton should mass all available troops and attack the rebels in New York, which would at least dampen their spirits and make them concentrate their own forces, which would be difficult for them to do. Showing an understanding of the logistical problems faced by the Americans, he decided that the policy of sending British detachments to many different colonies was a mistake because it allowed the rebels to employ all the locally available militiamen when most of those militia units could not be used elsewhere. If the British concentrated in New York, most of the militia forces would be too far away, and therefore useless to them. Mackenzie also had a very low opinion of the rebel militia, an opinion that seemed to be shared by many of the British generals but not by Clinton himself. Clinton actually planned to advance in mid-August after receiving about twenty-four hundred German reinforcements, but on August 19 Washington suddenly withdrew all of his advance forces to North Castle and Clinton's resolve dissipated. He continued to sit.[45]

Meanwhile in Virginia, Cornwallis had ended his operations and selected the port of Yorktown as his base. He cited Clinton's urgent requests for men as the reason that he halted his army's maneuvers and took a post at Yorktown. He was preparing to send men to New York if still necessary.[46] Thus, Clinton's view of the militia, the presence of the French, Washington's maneuvers, and poor communication between the two principal British army commanders combined to lead Cornwallis to hole up in Yorktown while waiting for Clinton to decide what to do next.

In mid-August, Washington's hopes and the campaign gained new life. Washington received dispatches from Admiral de Grasse that his French fleet was on its way to Chesapeake Bay; as a result, Washington accepted the inevitable change in plans and decided to move the Allied army to Virginia. Perhaps the failure of the militia in the middle states to assemble also helped change his mind. He appointed General Heath to command in New York after the army moved south. Washington decided to leave behind with Heath seventeen Continental regiments, a regiment of Continental cavalry, and a few independent units, altogether about three thousand men, and whatever militia and state regiments remained in service. Heath's primary job would be to defend West Point and the Highlands, and to protect the inhabitants and supplies in the area. Washington recommended to Heath that he stay on the defensive, but not to ignore any opportunities to strike enemy posts or detachments, and to use the cavalry, the New York state militia regiments, Waterbury's militia, and any other light parties available to "carry on the Petit Guerre with them . . . ." Washington also prepared letters to the governments of New Jersey, Connecticut, Massachusetts, and New Hampshire, asking them to send their militia, even though the main army was leaving, because the enemy army in New York still posed a danger to the area.[47]

As in 1777, Washington depended on the militia to help defend the area when the main army left. This time, however, he left a stronger Continental force than he had given General Putnam in 1777. Washington again demonstrated that he had learned from past disasters. Experience had shown that the militiamen might not turn out to help take the offensive, but they usually would turn out to defend their own states. Combined this time with a sufficient force of regulars, they should be able to hold against the British army left in New York.

Washington moved the French and American armies into New Jersey during the third week of August. As the Allied host marched through New Jersey, he ordered the New Jersey Continental brigade, reinforced by an independent Continental regiment, to the heights between Chatham and Springfield on August 19. Seely's militia joined this detachment a few days later. This combined force had orders to scout toward Staten Island and help prevent any surprise attack from that quarter. Heath, meanwhile, ordered a detachment of infantry, all of his cavalry, and a party of New York militia to advance near the British outposts in New York while he marched the rest of his army back to Peekskill. He then urged Waterbury to protect his militia, and Waterbury withdrew his men to Horseneck on August 20. Governor Clinton ordered the New York militia already operating in Westchester to remain there until relieved by other troops.[48]

At the end of August, Washington asked Heath to send the letters he had prepared earlier, asking the governments of neighboring states to continue sending their militia to support Heath's army. Washington wanted five hundred militiamen from New Jersey and fourteen hundred from Connecticut, and he expected twenty-two hundred men from New Hampshire and Massachusetts. Governor Clinton would furnish whatever local militia he could muster. Altogether, Washington expected over four thousand militia to support Heath.[49]

Sir Henry Clinton was unsure of the meaning of Washington's maneuvers. He hoped that this move into New Jersey meant Washington was returning to his defensive position near Morristown, possibly to detach more troops to the South. Therefore, on August 27, Clinton informed Cornwallis that he should keep all of his men for now, and if Washington did not resume an aggressive posture, Clinton would send men to Virginia. When Washington kept moving through New Jersey, Clinton at first wondered if Washington's plan was to attack Staten Island, but he quickly realized that the entire Allied army was moving to the South. Suddenly, Clinton was worried. He estimated Cornwallis's force at six thousand to eight thousand, whereas Washington and the French could probably muster eight thousand Continentals and another seven thousand to eight thousand

French, once Washington's Allied army joined Lafayette's corps and incorporated the reinforcements with de Grasse. In addition, there would be the numerous militia soldiers, if the Americans could arm them. Clinton contemplated a diversion into New Jersey but quickly dismissed the idea when he heard from Cornwallis that de Grasse's fleet was already in Chesapeake Bay. He and his generals in New York agreed that if Washington had any hope of capturing Cornwallis, no diversion would turn him from his goal. Meanwhile, Clinton feared that if he embroiled his army in a fight in New Jersey, it would only delay the possibility of sending help directly to Cornwallis, which was the only method Clinton saw of relieving him.[50]

Complaints against Clinton's inactivity in New York grew throughout September, especially after the British fleet returned from an unsuccessful attempt to break the French blockade in Chesapeake Bay. Some, such as Mackenzie, believed that an immediate move through New Jersey to Philadelphia would be useful, though they perhaps underestimated how much the New Jersey militia could interfere with such a march. Mackenzie himself had admitted on August 29 that once Washington was across the Delaware, there was nothing they could do from New York. Others grumbled that Clinton should never have allowed Washington to cross the Hudson River and move through New Jersey without a fight. Such complaints were immaterial, however, because as long as Clinton kept his sights on a direct relief effort to Virginia, the British army in New York City made no moves into New York or New Jersey.[51]

William Heath, of course, did not know how long the British inaction would continue. Since a major invasion of New Jersey could begin at any time, he had to be ready to move to that state's defense as well as maintain a credible defense of the Hudson River and Highlands. With only about three thousand Continentals left to him, Heath was glad to see the Massachusetts and Connecticut militia arriving daily. He kept his headquarters in Peekskill and sent out patrols toward the British positions. The remaining New York militiamen guarded along the river near the city. Heath issued orders to all of the militia regiments serving with his army to form ranger companies for extra patrols, and he instructed off-duty militiamen to exercise in small squads and companies. He clearly envisioned the proper use of the militia in the same terms as Washington did.[52]

Fearing that the British might raid and plunder Connecticut and New Jersey in an effort to draw his forces away from the Highlands, Heath promised Washington that he would keep his forces as concentrated as possible and support the militia with small detachments that would not endanger the Highlands. When the British raided New London, Connecticut, on September 6 and threatened to attack other Connecticut ports, he received many calls for help. Heath responded sparingly, sending only twenty dragoons and two hundred Connecticut Continentals toward Stamford. He also alerted one other brigade to be ready to move if necessary. The Connecticut Continentals marched as far as Bedford before the fleet in the Sound returned to New York. The regulars immediately returned to Peekskill. In defense of his meager support, Heath explained to Trumbull that he had received pleas for help from New Jersey and northern New York as well, and if he sent men to every threatened spot, his army would dissolve and leave the critical posts along the Hudson River defenseless. He promised to counter any British moves if they did not occur too far from the river.[53] Heath was experiencing firsthand the frustrations that Washington had had to live with since 1775.

The people of New Jersey fully expected a British invasion, especially when British troops concentrated on Staten Island and remained there throughout September. Joseph Reed, president of the executive council of Pennsylvania, promised Governor Livingston that he would send help from the Pennsylvania militia if the British attacked. The Confederation Congress resolved on September 10 that the governments of New Jersey and Pennsylvania should each furnish three thousand militiamen to repel the expected invasion of New Jersey. Heath would not send a large Continental force, but he prepared to send such small detachments of Continentals as might be necessary to help New Jersey. The militia had the primary responsibility of countering any sudden thrusts into New Jersey. This time the Congress did not ask Washington to order the commander in the Highlands to send Continentals to New Jersey, an action that in 1777 had led to the weakening of the Highlands just before Sir Henry Clinton attacked.[54]

Throughout the rest of September and the first half of October, fears persisted that the British were going to invade New Jersey, especially after several thousand British soldiers embarked onto ships in New York harbor. Livingston ordered Colonel Seely to keep his five hundred New Jersey militiamen at Connecticut Farms and to send patrols along the coast to prevent raids and illegal trading with the enemy. Livingston warned Heath that Seely's force could help stop small raids, but if the British invaded in force, Livingston would need help from Heath. In response, Heath sent a detachment to Ramapo, where it could cover the passes into the mountains and be available to help the New Jersey militia. Livingston was satisfied with this move. The New Jersey Assembly, meanwhile, decided that the governor had ample authority to call out the additional three thousand men called for by the Congress. The threat of imminent invasion ended when the British fleet set sail October 19.[55]

Before the fleet set sail, Heath spent September and the first half of October preparing the defenses of the Highlands in case the British moved up the Hudson River instead of into New Jersey or to the south. He asked Trumbull to send the rest of the Connecticut militia to fill its quota, as set by Washington before he had left for Virginia. When Heath sent the Continental detachment to Ramapo to ease the fears in New Jersey, he again reminded Trumbull about the deficient number of Connecticut militia. On October 12, as the British fleet got ready to set sail, Heath asked Trumbull to prepare all of the militia of western Connecticut to be ready to move to the Highlands in case the British attacked up the river. Connecticut's Assembly authorized Trumbull to take whatever measures he believed necessary. Heath also expected the help of the local New York militia should the British attack.[56]

Probably oblivious to these defensive preparations around him, Sir Henry Clinton consulted his generals concerning his proper course of action. In mid-September, after the repulse of the British fleet by the French outside Chesapeake Bay, he decided to wait until a more favorable opportunity arose to get the fleet into the bay. Clinton informed Secretary Germain that he still considered the possibility of a strike against Philadelphia, either overland or by ship, but only if Cornwallis made it clear that he could not hold out any longer. "But I confess to your lordship, notwithstanding, that I do not think any diversion will induce Mr Washington to stir a man from the object before him . . . ." This was high praise from the British commander in chief. Clinton and his amphibious relief force finally sailed on October 19, arrived at the mouth of Chesapeake

Bay on October 24, learned of Cornwallis's surrender five days earlier, and so returned to New York.[57]

As it became clear to the Americans that the British planned to sail southward, thoughts turned from defense to offense. Thomas McKean, president of Congress, asked Washington if Heath should consider striking New York while part of the British army was gone. McKean believed he could get five thousand militia to Heath within two weeks. Washington wrote to Heath suggesting the possibility of an attack, but he refused to order Heath to act. Heath liked the idea and on October 17 asked Governor Trumbull to prepare fifteen hundred militia, and Governor George Clinton, an equal number. He remained secretive, however, and would not explain his exact plans to either governor. Clinton informed Heath that the New York militiamen had been under orders all season to hold themselves ready, and he firmly believed they would turn out again if called. Heath then explained to Clinton his plan to attack New York if the British actually sailed south. Yet he took no action when Sir Henry Clinton finally did leave for Virginia. On October 30, Heath informed Washington that the British in New York had indeed been weakened but were still strongly placed in good defensive works, and that he had little chance to attack them successfully. He carefully explained that the quality of the soldiers he would have to use in the attack discouraged him from making the attempt. Presumably Washington understood this hesitation to attack fortifications with militiamen.[58]

While these events took place in New York and New Jersey, General Waterbury returned to Connecticut in August from cooperating with the French and American armies in New York, and resumed his defense of southwest Connecticut. The Council of Safety at that time ordered Waterbury to collect all of the livestock between the American and British outposts, and to apprehend all suspected people and send them to the governor to be tried. In addition, Waterbury revived the practice of sending out daily scouting parties toward the New York border to watch for raids. Throughout the fall his numbers fluctuated, but he had about 530 men along the border at the end of October.[59]

The raiding war in Long Island Sound continued unabated. The campaigns of the main armies in fact seemed to have little effect on this brutal war. In mid-June, for example, a raiding party attacked the guards near Stamford. The militia guards chased the raiders back to their boats, then quickly marched to New Rochelle, New York, in an unsuccessful attempt to intercept the raiders' return. The Connecticut militiamen decided not to waste the day and rounded up some sheep. They in turn were chased all the way back to Connecticut. Stamford was the object of several more raids during the summer. The local militia regiment maintained a guard, but the regiment commander asked Trumbull for a larger permanent guard for the area. A civilian leader of Stamford wrote to Washington while he was still in New York, asking him to send a detachment of Continentals for protection. If he did not, the people of the area would either have to move inland or make their peace with the enemy. They did not receive their detachment. In August, Norwalk was hit, and again the raiders reached their boats before a sufficient number of militia could assemble. On August 31, about 150 Tories and a few British troops landed in West Haven, just west of New Haven. They took some cattle and a few inhabitants, and left the next morning. The civilian leaders of the area asked Trumbull for a stronger guard.[60]

A major event along the coast during the fall was Benedict Arnold's raid of September 6 on New London. He attacked with about 1500 British, Germans, and Tories. After an obstinate defense by about 150 militiamen, Arnold took the local forts and, according to survivors of the Connecticut militia, killed seventy men after they had surrendered. Whether that was true or not, the raid sparked deep fears and resentment along the coast, and Trumbull and the council ordered reinforcements of militia to the ports in anticipation of further such raids. Trumbull and the council also asked Major General Samuel H. Parsons to take command of the militia and state regiments in the southwestern part of the state and along the coast. They gave Parsons the authority to call directly on the local militia brigades for defense. By mid-September, three hundred men in addition to the usual coast guard company garrisoned New Haven against another fleet of British ships sailing east in the Sound. The ships approached New Haven and the militia and men on the ships fired a few shots at each other, but that was all. Another force of about three hundred militia guarded New London. Finally, at the beginning of November, with a detachment of Continentals serving at Fairfield, the governor and council relieved the extra militia-men ordered to the Sound.[61]

In a spirit of retaliation, Connecticut militiamen wanted to raid Long Island and eliminate the Tory post at Lloyd's Neck, which a band of Tory raiders used as a base for their raids. Trumbull asked Heath in late August for the support of a detachment of Heath's troops, but Heath objected to the plan because the British controlled the Sound and had reinforcements that could reach Lloyd's Neck within a day or two. Major Benjamin Tallmadge then took the initia-tive and sent one hundred of his Continental dragoons, who were stationed in Connecticut, to destroy Fort Slongo, another small Tory fort on the island. The party, led by Major Lemuel Trescott, crossed the Sound on October 2 and attacked the fort the next day. They killed four, captured the fort and twenty-one men, and returned to Connecticut with only one man wounded. Since the raid was a suc-cess, Heath did not make an issue of Tallmadge's action. On Octo-ber 23, Parsons again asked Heath for help against Lloyd's Neck, and this time Heath approved. He even sent orders for the dragoons and Waterbury's militia to support the effort. Parsons prepared the men and boats, but the presence of a superior British naval force postponed the attack. Parsons then increased his naval force and planned to cross on November 4, but on the third he received orders from Heath to cancel the plan due to the continuing British naval presence off the Connecticut coast. The Tories thus maintained their base on Lloyd's Neck and continued to raid across the Sound. As in Westchester County, some of the raids by both sides hit people indis-criminately. Inhabitants of Suffolk County, Long Island, who were loyal to the United States complained to Governor Trumbull and Governor Clinton that Connecticut raiders had attacked them while hunting Tories on the island. Their complaints fell on deaf ears.[62]

Far from this partisan war in the middle states, Washington had to decide what to do with the Allied army after Cornwallis had sur-rendered his army on October 19. He decided to split his forces. All of the Continentals from Pennsylvania and the states to the south of Pennsylvania would join Major General Nathanael Greene in South Carolina. The rest would return to New York and New Jersey, and the French would remain in Virginia. Washington asked Heath to prepare winter quarters for the returning soldiers. The New Jersey

Continentals would stay in Morristown, the New York men would enter quarters between there and the Hudson River, and the Continentals from New England would garrison West Point.[63]

While the victorious soldiers marched back toward the Hudson River in November, Heath asked Governor Clinton to hold his militia ready in case the British decided to strike before the main army arrived. At the same time, the New York legislature directed that the militia should seize all livestock between the American and British outposts in Westchester County. Clinton asked Heath for Continental support for this project, and Heath agreed to use regulars to cover the foraging parties. General Waterbury also moved part of his Connecticut militia to Mamaroneck, according to Heath's orders, to help protect the New York militia foragers. They met little resistance.[64]

Despite the skirmishing, no British attack materialized, and the Continental Army returned in late November and moved into its winter quarters. Heath remained in command because Washington stopped first at Mount Vernon and then at Philadelphia, where he stayed until the end of March 1782. While the army settled into its quarters, Governor Trumbull asked for Continentals to be quartered in Connecticut, but Heath responded as Washington presumably would have: the importance of the Highlands precluded the possibility of sending any corps of Continentals too far from the river. Continental and militia parties, however, including Waterbury's militia from Connecticut, resumed their patrols near the British defenses. Heath also stationed a company of 100 Continentals and a company of militia near Bedford through the winter, and another party of 250 Continentals patrolled along the Hudson River in northern Westchester County.[65]

On November 30, Heath dismissed all of the militiamen whose enlistments had ended or were about to end. He thanked them for their efforts and kept the militia soldiers who still had time to serve only until the army was fully settled into its winter quarters.[66] As winter began, the war around New York City returned to the patterns set in the previous years. The contending armies entered winter quarters, and small detachments of militia and Continentals patrolled and skirmished with British parties.

In December, the militia officers and inhabitants of devastated Westchester County asked Clinton for more help. The militiamen

stationed in the area were going home soon, and the one Continental company near Bedford did not provide enough protection. The
people of Westchester said that they could not provide more guards
on their own, and therefore requested Continentals and militia from
other areas to be stationed near Bedford and North Castle. Since no
reinforcements arrived, the raids by Tories continued and the local
militia tried to fight the Tory parties to the best of its ability. One
local militiaman, Captain Daniel Williams, led twenty-five New York
militiamen against the rebuilt Tory base at Morrisania. On the night
of December 23, Williams and twenty-five mounted volunteers raided
Morrisania and captured nine Tories without a loss. A detachment
of Continentals was nearby to cover the militia's retreat if necessary.[67]

In southwest Connecticut, Waterbury maintained about 560 militiamen through the last weeks of 1781. Even with that force, however,
he could not defend everything, and the civilian leaders of Greenwich complained in mid-December that their town again lay between
Waterbury's and the British positions. Some local leaders suggested
a new method of defending the area. Rather than rotations of temporary men who were unacquainted with the territory and people,
they urged the creation of a small corps that would remain in the
area full time. Ironically, these residents had the same idea, in miniature, that Washington had been advocating for the entire region
since 1775. Such new methods would have to wait for the next year.[68]

As for the British, perhaps the best summary to the year's
mistakes and the underestimation of the Americans' strength came
from Frederick Haldimand, governor of Canada. Writing to Secretary of State Germain, he concluded that the British leaders had
been deceived about how hard it was for the rebels to recruit for
their army. Though they had trouble enlisting new Continentals,
there was an abundance of men who would serve for a few months,
"by which means the whole body of the people are become soldiers
and their militia are equipped and as good troops as any they have
and form into amazing bodies on the shortest notice."[69]

As the cold weather set in, Washington, the new Confederation
Congress, and the state governments all had reason to be happy with
the results of the 1781 campaign. Washington had finally combined
with the French for decisive results: the capture of Cornwallis's army
in Virginia. This great victory, however, did not erase the memory of

the frustrations of the campaign in the New York City area. Once again, the projected grand assault on New York had failed to materialize. The contradiction remained between Washington's mistrust of the militia's ability to work with the army in large numbers for an attack against a large British force, and his efforts to mass a large militia force to do exactly that. For once, Washington proved that even he at times tried to force reality to fit his image of the ideal situation. His overwhelming desire to attack New York in conjunction with the French had led him to call for large numbers of militia every summer since 1778. The poor showing of the militia in each of the previous years should have made the failure of 1781 no surprise. Of the thousands of militiamen called, only a few hundred assembled in a timely fashion. The militia again showed itself incapable of large-scale field operations, a fact Washington had understood from the beginning of the war yet kept trying to ignore each time he contemplated an Allied assault on New York.

On the other hand, the militia provided important services once the Allied armies marched for Virginia. Washington left a small force of Continentals and expected the militia of the adjacent states to supplement the corps in order to prevent the British from taking the Highlands or invading New Jersey. The British made no moves toward either of those objectives, yet the state governments and General Heath prepared to meet such attacks. In addition, throughout the year, the militia handled its usual state duties as well as a new duty in January when portions of the Continental Army mutinied. The militia's conduct during these crises increased its value in the eyes of many loyal Whigs. Elsewhere, the war of raids between Tory and Whig militiamen raged on to new heights of brutality.

Thus, with the resumption of active operations by the Continental and French armies, the militia maintained its important place in Washington's plans and continued to serve the states. As the seventh year of the war stretched on, the Americans could not be sure the surrender of Cornwallis would end hostilities. The British still held New York City, and Washington still wanted to take that prize from them. In addition, Tory and Whig irregulars alike remained poised to attack each other's posts. As 1782 began, there seemed to be every prospect that the partisan war would continue around the British posts in New York City.

★ CHAPTER ELEVEN ★

The Final Years, 1782–1783

THE VICTORY at Yorktown in October 1781 left the leaders of the United States in a confusing, though somewhat pleasant, situation. Added to the usual doubts concerning the new year's prospects, they were uncertain whether the British government would continue to prosecute the war in North America. The British might replace the army and renew the fight, they might remain on the defensive against the Americans and concentrate against the French and Spanish, or they might totally withdraw from the war. Not until word arrived in the spring of 1783 that the preliminaries of a peace treaty had been signed did the American leaders know they had won.

The British did not share this uncertainty. Secretary of State George Germain admitted at the beginning of 1782 that Yorktown changed everything. No further reinforcements would be sent to America; Sir Henry Clinton's job was simply to hold what he currently controlled, and perhaps launch raids against ports to stop the rebels' trade and to prevent them from going on the offensive. Germain informed Clinton that the king had decided to authorize no new operations to reduce the colonies. Germain had no fears for New York, especially since Admiral de Grasse's fleet had been decisively defeated by Admiral Sir George Rodney in late 1781 and the surviving French had sailed for Brest, France. Clinton, however, did not wait to see the end. That winter he tendered his resignation, which the king accepted, and Lieutenant General Sir Guy Carleton became commander in chief of the British forces in North America. In April, Germain ordered Carleton to prepare to evacuate New York, Charleston, and Savannah, but Carleton had to delay the execution of this order until the next year because he could not assemble enough transports to remove everything and everyone from New York.[1]

Unaware of the British decision to cease the prosecution of the war with the United States, the state governments prepared for a continuation of the partisan war along the coasts. Not until the summer of 1782 did they notice a slackening of the raids against them. Meanwhile, the usual difficulties of raising men to guard the most threatened areas plagued the governments. In fact, in anticipation of these problems, the Connecticut Assembly in January 1782 asked the Confederation Congress to pay for the raising of one thousand militiamen who would serve for one year. The governments of New York and Massachusetts had had similar requests accepted, and Connecticut's Assembly hoped for the same treatment. Governor Trumbull justified this request by describing how close Connecticut was to the British in New York, and how few Continental detachments guarded Connecticut. He argued that Continental units were stationed in Massachusetts, New York, and New Jersey, states that had no better claim to such support than did Connecticut. In addition, since he planned to station six hundred of the requested men at Stamford and two hundred at New Haven, altogether eight hundred of the men would be readily available to join any operations in New York. Despite Trumbull's careful argument, however, the Congress denied the request. Connecticut's delegates explained to Trumbull that the Congress had decided if it authorized this request, it would get many others.[2]

Therefore, Connecticut was once again mostly on its own, even as the state government's ability to assemble its militiamen was decreasing. Despite the Assembly's decision in January to raise a state regiment of 480 men to defend the southwestern region until April 1783, the militia commanders on the spot were continually short of men. Brigadier General David Waterbury's detachment initially guarded the area, but his men's enlistments were completed in March. The Assembly therefore drafted three hundred men from the local militia brigades, but the commander, Lieutenant Colonel Samuel

Canfield, never received all of them. While Canfield tried to collect the men, General William Heath, who retained command of the army in New York during Washington's prolonged stay in Philadelphia, sent a Continental detachment to help protect the area. Washington approved of this step but ordered Heath to recall the men by May 1. Recruiting for the state regiment went slowly, and Governor Trumbull blamed the weak militia laws. The Assembly revised the laws again in the spring, but Trumbull still could only urge the officers to issue the necessary orders because he had no power to compel men to serve. After seven years of pleading with the Assembly to pass effectual laws, however, he did not expect it to undertake such a revision at this point. As of the end of April, when the detachment of regulars returned to the army, Canfield had only 200 men, and as of May 12, he reported his strength at 160 men.[3]

Along the coast, the war of raids at first seemed unaffected by the changing circumstances of the larger war. Even before 1781 had ended, Trumbull and the Council of Safety had provided several of the coastal towns with guards who would serve during the first few months of 1782, and Trumbull asked Heath for help through the winter months of early 1782. Though Heath would not spare any men, especially since he had orders from Washington not to scatter the army, he ordered Major Benjamin Tallmadge, who was already stationed in Connecticut with two companies of dismounted dragoons, to lend a hand if possible. When the Continentals in Connecticut rejoined the army in New York in the spring, more militia guards were necessary. Often the Assembly would pay the local townsmen to supply their own guards rather than go through the difficulty of mustering a company of militiamen. The townsmen, however, found it increasingly difficult to assemble a guard because the local inhabitants either were unwilling to serve or wanted to be paid more money than was available. The leaders of Fairfield, for example, reported that they could mount a guard only during the night, so the raiders came during the day. Not surprisingly, the plundering raids and illegal trade between Long Island and Connecticut continued.[4]

The New York government began to prepare for 1782 even before 1781 had ended. The Assembly passed an act in November 1781 to authorize Governor George Clinton to assemble a maximum of fifteen hundred militiamen to serve throughout 1782. In the spring, the legislature revised the militia laws, and it empowered the militia officers to assemble their men to serve in or out of the state in case of invasion or insurrection by internal enemies. The Assembly, however, did not resolve the basic problem of compelling men to serve.[5] Compulsory military service, as urged by Washington and the governors for years, was not a politically acceptable option to the legislators of any of the middle states.

Politics notwithstanding, in Westchester County, the brutal war between the two armies continued unabated. On January 10, 1782, a party of volunteer horsemen captured four Tories, and another volunteer band captured six more on February 26. On March 2, a party of one hundred Continental infantry set up an ambush, and eighty volunteer horsemen went forward to try and lure the Tory cavalry into the trap. They attacked on March 4, the Tories pursued but missed the ambush, and the two parties skirmished as the Continentals and militia retreated. The American volunteers captured twenty-one men. On March 14, a militia party surprised a detachment of twelve Tories, killing one and capturing four. On April 10 the Tories raided as far north as Haverstraw, and Heath sent two hundred Continentals to support the militia. In early May, the militia of Westchester complained to Governor Clinton that General Heath had issued orders to the army's advance guards to stop all parties of militia from scouting near the enemy's positions without his direct authorization. The militia officers were upset because the county was basically undefended, and they wanted permission to scout and send out parties whenever the enemy emerged. Clinton could not believe that Heath wanted to "hinder the militia from harassing the Enemy . . . ," but he agreed that it was proper for all militia parties to consult the officers on the front lines in order to avoid unnecessary danger and confusion. He did not believe such precautions would prevent the militia from attacking the enemy or protecting the settlements in the area. He also promised to consult with Washington on this subject so as to avoid future problems.[6]

New Jersey's government experienced similar problems with its militia. At the end of 1781 it passed an act calling for 422 men to be raised by March 1, 1782, and to serve until December 15, 1782. These militiamen were not to leave the state without the permission of the legislature. The law provided for detachments, ranging in size from sixteen to forty-five men, to guard Bergen, Hackensack, New Bridge, Closter, and along the coasts in Middlesex County, and it established a company of forty militia horsemen to protect Monmouth County. Despite these defensive efforts, however, the British and Tories continued to raid into New Jersey throughout the spring of 1782. Monmouth County was the target of constant raids through the first half of the year, and across from Staten Island, parties of British and Tories occasionally attacked, as they did at New Brunswick in early January 1782. About three hundred raiders entered New Brunswick at night, plundered the nearby buildings, took about six inhabitants as prisoners, and fled. The briefness of their stay prevented a large force of local militia from collecting, though the few who assembled harassed the raiding party as best they could. Both sides had four or five casualties.[7]

The growing difficulties that the state governments were experiencing with their own militia defenses did not encourage Washington for the coming summer, but he was unsure of his own plans for the next campaign. Too many circumstances that would determine the year's events were beyond his control. Two groups in particular that he could not control were the French, who might or might not participate in another campaign in North America, and the British, who might withdraw from New York. In order to be ready for any contingency, he wrote to the state governments to prepare for a possible campaign and to authorize the executives to assemble such militia forces as he might deem necessary. He promised to call out the militia only if absolutely necessary, and to wait as long as possible before calling for the men. He emphasized, however, that waiting so long before collecting the militia meant that should an opportunity arise, delays could be fatal. He urged the state leaders to fill their Continental regiments because then he would need less militia. In addition, he requested that any militia sent to the army be engaged by the governments for as long a time of service as possible. In case of a siege of New York, the militia would have to serve for the duration.[8] Washington tried to use everything he had learned from the previous seven years to prepare for the 1782 campaigning season.

Washington remained in Philadelphia until March 22, then headed back to his headquarters in New York, where he arrived at the beginning of April. In mid-April, he met with his generals to consider the situation and how many militia would be necessary to besiege New York, should they get the chance. Washington estimated the number of British soldiers at 12,390, whereas he had 9146 Continentals in the army on April 25. His army would peak at 13,060 men if all the authorized recruits arrived. He believed 37,160 men were necessary to besiege New York, which meant he needed 24,100 militiamen. Since he knew that he could never assemble that many, he decided to settle for about twelve thousand militia. That would give him a total force of about twenty-five thousand men. For the moment, this mathematical exercise was all that he could do, since he was not yet ready to call for the men, and he believed that the state governments tended to muster their militia when they thought it necessary, and not necessarily when he asked. He therefore thought it best to initiate nothing further until he had more definite plans.[9]

Washington spent the months of April, May, and June planning for, yet pessimistic about, a summer campaign. Though he seemed to believe that he could collect a large militia force, he feared that the state governments would wait too long before mustering their men and that the militia would arrive too late to be of help. He therefore warned the governments again in May that any call for the militia would be sudden and leave no time for delays. Connecticut's Assembly took a preliminary step by ordering two regiments totaling 1836 men to be raised and held ready in case Washington needed them for a siege of New York. The regiments would serve until January 1, 1783, or the end of the siege. The New Jersey Assembly also considered Washington's requests, and in June ordered a state militia regiment to be held ready to join the Continental Army when necessary.[10]

Unbeknownst to Washington, General James Robertson, the royal governor of New York, and General Carleton issued orders in May to the soldiers of the British army, and even to the Tory bands, to suspend all offensive operations against the Americans unless they received specific orders to act. News of the declaration by the British leadership spread through the adjoining counties, but Washington did not believe the rumors. Governor Clinton, however, described New York as being in a "State of perfect Tranquility" during the first week of June. Washington was still unconvinced as of August.[11]

Washington was not the only skeptic. In Connecticut, militia officers tried to fill their detachments standing guard along the coast.

In late June, Brigadier General John Mead, commander of the militia brigade in southwest Connecticut, ordered men from his brigade to help guard a nine-mile gap between the areas covered by Lieutenant Colonel Canfield's patrols in southwest Connecticut and the patrols of the New York militia at Bedford. Mead ordered his men to apprehend anyone under arms and not in the service of the United States, and to stop the movement of all livestock, provisions, and people going toward New York City. This temporary measure, however, did not solve the larger problem of how to fill Canfield's regiment on the southwestern frontier. As late as November, Canfield had only 322 men with him.[12]

Despite the problems that the officers and political leaders of Connecticut had trying to muster the militia in the southwest region and along the coast, the local militia showed that it still would respond to an immediate emergency. On June 4, Brigadier General Gold S. Silliman sent a warning along the coast that a fleet of British ships was sailing eastward through Long Island Sound, and New Haven or New London was the expected target. He warned the militia near him to be ready, and asked the officers of the local militia near the coast to pass the warning along to other militia officers to the east. On June 5, Trumbull sent orders to the officers near New London to prepare for an attack. Early on June 6, Silliman's warning arrived in New London, and the militia commander sent calls to the local militia officers. The fleet arrived in sight of the New London defenders on the sixth, and additional militia forces began to collect. Though the fleet sailed past New London and was out of sight by late that afternoon, the militia kept assembling. By the next morning, about six hundred militiamen were on the spot, but since the fleet was gone, they went home.[13]

Even though the raids all but stopped during the summer, the townspeople along the coast continued to send complaints to the governor and Assembly that more money or guards were needed to protect them and stop the illegal trade with the enemy. Finally, the governor and the council decided on July 17 that the Assembly's effort to pay the people to supply their own guards was not working; instead, they ordered the local militia officers near the towns to provide a guard whenever one of the particular towns applied for men. This order helped for the moment.[14]

Meanwhile, in New York, the tranquillity that Governor Clinton noted in June reigned throughout the summer. Occasionally, an American militia party launched a raid against the Tories—as in mid-August, when an independent militia horse company raided southward and captured three Tories. This company, according to the instructions issued the previous spring by General Heath and agreed to by Governor Clinton, stopped first at the Continental outposts before venturing forth against the Tories in Westchester County. Even the garrison inside the defenses around New York City noticed the growing calm. Though British foraging parties still occasionally scoured the county, they met little resistance from American militia patrols or Continentals. This lack of resistance was due partly to Washington's decision to revert to his usual practice during the campaigning season of not detaching from the army for state defense. Therefore few Continental detachments remained near the British outposts. When Governor Clinton asked for help along his frontiers in July, Washington declined and urged Clinton to determine if he needed to call out more militia for that purpose.[15]

As the summer wore on, Washington's hopes for another opportunity to attack New York declined. In late June, he informed the Comte de Rochambeau, who had remained in Virginia, that without French help, he could not try anything against New York. In July, Washington and Rochambeau met in Philadelphia, but neither commander had enough information to form a definite plan of operations. Washington still considered New York as the primary objective, but an impossible one without naval superiority. Charleston, South Carolina, and Canada were other possibilities, but whatever plan they chose, Washington believed the French and American armies should reunite again in New York. At the moment, he was barely able to threaten New York City. Even in mid-August, Washington was unsure of British intentions, but he feared that they might be planning offensive operations. He therefore urged Rochambeau to join him in New York, where they could at least pin down the British in the city and thus prevent them from sending detachments to the West Indies to fight the French in that region.[16]

The garrison inside the city waited in suspense to see if Washington would commence active operations, but ultimately his attempt to combine the French and American armies and to prepare the militia for a campaign led to nothing. The French army did reunite with the Americans in New York in October, but by the end of that month, Washington had moved the Continental Army into winter quarters and the French forces were on their way to Boston, where they embarked in December and sailed to the West Indies, to fight the British there. After they had left the continent, Washington had to know that he would get no further aid from the French.[17] Washington's grand military vision of attacking and capturing New York City with a combined force of French regulars, Continentals, and militiamen never materialized.

In December, Washington contemplated the next year's prospects with even more pessimism. Though he expected the British to send four thousand to five thousand soldiers from New York to the West Indies, he felt certain that the state governments would be unable to furnish him with enough men to expel even such a weakened garrison. To allow the British to maintain their hold of New York City with such a small force, he believed, was a disgrace, but he had become used to this lack of energy in the state governments as well as in the individual Americans themselves. As he explained to General Greene, he believed too many people put their own selfish interests ahead of the country's needs, and therefore the necessary supplies and soldiers could not be collected.[18]

Pessimism notwithstanding, Washington still hoped for an opportunity to launch his pet project. He preferred to make one final effort in 1783 to oust the British rather than allow them to retain New York and prolong the war, but in the opening months of 1783, he understood clearly that events outside of his control would dictate the year's plans. Based on this assumption, he wrote to the Confederation Congress in January 1783 that its members could best determine the possibilities of peace or continued war, and therefore they had to decide whether he should adopt an offensive or defensive policy for the year.[19] Washington did not yet know that he had planned his last campaign.

He believed he had his answer from the Congress by March 1783. In contrast with previous years, the Congress made no requisitions on the state governments for men or provisions, while the Continental Army continued to shrink. He expected to have only nine thousand men in June, too few to do much. He also was convinced that he could not assemble a sizable force of militia. He informed the Marquis de Lafayette in March: "I am impressed with a belief that *no* Militia could be drawn out *previous* to the arrival of a French fleet, and Land force on the Coast. I am not *sanguine* that *many* could be had afterwards . . . ." That sentiment reflected well his experiences in the previous years when trying to coordinate large militia forces with the French. He concluded in his letter to Lafayette that if there were to be any operations that year, "it appears, that little or no dependence is to be placed on any other Troops than the Continentals of this Army."[20]

The good news for the people of the United States during these frustrating months in the fall and winter of 1782–83 was that the partisan war slackened considerably. Most of the aggressive operations were militia raids against Tory posts. In Westchester County, Continental detachments and New York militia units continued to patrol, and occasionally the militia would attack a Tory base. On October 5, a party of militia horse stopped first at the Continental outposts, according to Heath's orders, before moving south to harass the local Tories. The Continental commander of the outpost paralleled the militia with a party of his regulars in boats down the Hudson River. Unfortunately for the Continentals, the militiamen were unaware of the presence of the Continentals, and they fired on the regulars as they rowed back up the river past Tarrytown. Finally the Continentals convinced the militia that they were on the same side. Such activities slowed down even more during the winter months, but in February 1783, Continentals maintained their watch in the county, and as late as mid-March, a party of American militia attacked Morrisania and captured four Tories. The New York Assembly was as unsure as Washington whether the war would continue, and therefore it passed an act in February authorizing the governor to raise a maximum of six hundred militiamen to serve up to eight months for the defense of New York. The legislators applied unsuccessfully for the Confederation Congress to pay for these men.[21]

Next door in New Jersey, the raids also decreased, though the illegal trade between the Tories and the British continued into 1783. Throughout the winter of 1782–83, Washington stationed detachments of Continentals in Bergen, Newark, Elizabethtown, and other points along the Jersey coast used by the traders to carry goods to the British.[22] The effort to isolate the British from the countryside, begun in 1775, continued as the war neared its end.

By late 1782, the Connecticut militia had just about hit the end of its endurance. To illustrate the problems the state government had in mustering its militia, there were 19,041 men enrolled in the state militia as of October 22, 1782, but the legislators could furnish barely several hundred men to guard the coast and the southwest region. Near the New York border certain Tory bands continued to attack despite the British orders to stop, and the government's control over the area diminished. In December 1782, a Continental detachment joined the area's militia and Washington asked Canfield, the local militia officer, to put his men under the command of the Continental officer. Greenwich was still threatened, and in early February 1783, the leaders of Greenwich asked Trumbull and the Council of Safety to order Canfield forward from Stamford to guard their town. Trumbull and the council gave Canfield discretionary orders to return to the western part of Greenwich if he believed it proper. The state Assembly then asked Washington for more regulars to replace Canfield when his regiment went home on April 1, 1783. Washington responded that he could not maintain a detachment in southwest Connecticut once spring came, but he would extend the patrols of his army in Westchester County to the east, in order to cover the ground all the way to the Sound. On March 24, Trumbull and the council ordered two companies of militia to be detached from the local brigades, to serve with Canfield for the defense of the southwest frontier for two months.[23]

Along the coast, the main concern still centered on stopping the trade between the mainland and Long Island, and raiding Tory bases on the island. To help interrupt the trade and support possible raids, Washington stationed Major Tallmadge and a Continental infantry regiment in Fairfield in November 1782, and the Assembly passed an act in January 1783 that again authorized the people along the coast to form guard details in their towns whenever they believed it necessary. Tallmadge, armed with Washington's approval, then planned to raid Long Island in January. He prepared four companies of Continental infantry, a body of dismounted dragoons, and a detachment of Connecticut militia, totaling about seven hundred men, but bad weather delayed and finally forced Tallmadge to cancel his plans. In February, he asked Governor Trumbull to establish a central location where all the boats that were used to cruise the Sound could be stationed. From this central point, Tallmadge could coordinate his Continentals with the various Connecticut raiders should Washington authorize another enterprise against Long Island. Tallmadge was able to use his Continentals on February 20, when he attacked and captured a sloop manned by Tories near Stratford. He killed or captured almost the entire crew while his force sustained no casualties.[24] The Long Island Sound war raged on through its eighth year.

As the partisan war in general abated, the British prepared for the inevitable. In anticipation of the final orders to pull out, the various corps of the British garrison on the islands remained in their quarters as spring returned. Meanwhile, throughout March, news of the signing of a preliminary peace treaty on November 30, 1782, between the United States and Great Britain began to spread throughout the area. Washington received the official news from Philadelphia in mid-March, Governor Trumbull heard the news in late March, and Governor Clinton reported the news to his Assembly on March 28. The treaty, however, would not become effective until a treaty was concluded between Britain and France. On March 26 news arrived at army headquarters that a treaty between France and Britain had been signed on January 20, which made the preliminary treaty between the United States and Britain effective.[25]

On April 5, General Carleton received an official announcement from Britain of the two peace treaties and the king's instructions for withdrawing from the posts in North America. Carleton was not to begin the evacuation yet, but to prepare everything for the withdrawal while attempting to reestablish cordial relations between the two countries. On April 6 he wrote to Washington to inform him of the king's orders to stop all fighting. Washington received this statement from the British commander on April 8, and answered the next day that he had no authority from the Congress to end the fighting, but he did issue orders to his men at the forward outposts "to suspend all Acts of Hostilities until further Orders . . . ." On April 11 the Confederation Congress issued a proclamation asking all citizens of the United States to undertake no further hostile acts against the British on land or sea. Washington received official orders from the Congress on April 16 to terminate hostilities, and he announced them to the army. All fighting was to end immediately.[26]

The state governments had already begun to react to the news of peace. In Connecticut, Colonel Samuel Canfield and Brigadier General John Mead decided on their own to disregard the March 24 orders from Trumbull and the council for two companies to join them. Instead, they engaged only about thirty men to stay at their posts in southwestern Connecticut, to guard the equipment and defensive works in the area until the state government decided what to do with the property. Mead informed Trumbull that even if official word of a peace treaty did not arrive before they implemented this plan, twenty-five men at most should be enough to guard the area. The governor and council agreed, and ordered Canfield to maintain a guard of only ten to twelve men at Stamford to secure the posts and property from plundering until peace became official. Trumbull and the council also suspended the recent orders for the raising of a new detachment to go to the southwest region. In New Jersey, Governor Livingston issued a proclamation to the people of his state on April 14 that the officers of New Jersey's military forces were to stop all hostile actions against the British.[27]

Disengaging the troops in Westchester County was not as easy. On May 6–7, Washington, Carleton, and Governor Clinton met at Dobb's Ferry to discuss the eventual evacuation of the city. Carleton, however, promised only an immediate withdrawal from Westchester County, and not from the city itself. He informed Washington on May 12 that he was unsure when he would have the necessary shipping to withdraw fully from the city. On May 13, he wrote to Governor Clinton that all British troops would be withdrawn from the county except for small parties that were escorting wagons through the area, and he promised to pull even these detachments out when New York's civil officers told him they were not necessary.[28]

The situation in Westchester remained volatile after eight years of civil war and raids between neighbors, and at this point even New York's government could not guarantee the safety of parties moving through the county. Clinton wanted to reestablish civil government in the area as quickly as possible, and he accordingly planned to send militia troops into the county to protect and support the civil authorities. Washington helped Clinton with this effort by ordering the commander of the Continental detachment in the county to aid the returning civil officers. Despite these efforts, Governor Clinton and New York's legislators, as well as Generals Washington and Carleton, all feared that the raiding parties who had infested the county for years would continue their attacks. Some of the people engaged in the predatory war in Westchester County were loyal to no side but worked only for themselves. Neither the civil nor the military authorities had much control over such groups.[29]

These fears proved well founded, because a few renegade bands of armed men still roamed Westchester County. In June, Carleton complained to Governor Clinton that a Captain Isaac Honeywell, Jr., and a band of fifty armed men were committing depredations in the county. Clinton responded that Honeywell and a few others were indeed still causing trouble, but on their own and not with the approval of the state government. He promised to try to stop such hostilities. His main difficulty, however, was that he had not been able to establish any kind of civil control in Westchester until after the British had left. Lawlessness thus reigned throughout the county for several weeks. He promised Carleton that he was trying to improve the situation, and Carleton accepted Clinton's assurances, though he did accuse the local civil magistrates of refusing to intervene to stop the depredations. Such acts, Carleton argued, practically gave Honeywell's raids official sanction.[30]

Ultimately, Clinton established some order after sending in New York militiamen to stop the raiding, and Clinton informed Washington that men such as Honeywell would be punished. Nothing, however, was done to carry out this threat. As late as August, Carleton was complaining that several committees and associations had emerged in America, and not just in New York, that specialized in committing outrages against Loyalists. He informed Elias Boudinot, president of Congress, that the violence against the Loyalists led to more Loyalists applying for permission to leave with the British, and such applications only delayed his eventual withdrawal. Carleton even accused the Americans of having no government to control the people or of secretly allowing such violence to occur. Some Americans were suspicious of these delaying tactics, such as Mercy Otis Warren, one of the earliest historians of the war, who recorded her growing suspicion of Carleton's actions during these summer months.[31]

Throughout that summer and fall, Connecticut militiamen continued to serve, though now they guarded against a new threat. Guards remained on duty in New London to protect the posts from the area's inhabitants, who seemed intent on plundering and vandalizing the public property. By mid-September, there were only three men on duty in New London, and Captain Benjamin Durkee, the officer in charge, wanted to be relieved before something happened. He explained to Trumbull that the people around there "Not only Steall But threaten to Blow up the Magazine and Blow us to hell . . . ." Trumbull sent orders near the end of September for Durkee to enlist men to serve as guards for two months. In December, after the British had evacuated New York City, Durkee engaged thirty-two men to guard the posts for one year.[32] Thus, the militia moved into peacetime without a pause, still protecting the states internally.

Finally the day arrived that Washington had been waiting for since 1776. On November 25, 1783, the British garrison completed its withdrawal from New York City, and in order to prevent violence, Washington immediately sent in a detachment of the army. General Henry Knox, Washington's trusted artillery commander, led the cheering troops into the city. A little later in the day, Washington and Governor Clinton rode into the city side by side, escorted by a troop of the Westchester Light Dragoons, a militia unit. New York City was in bad shape. Almost half of the houses had been burned or destroyed, leaving half of the city's remaining population destitute. The roads had been partially torn up, and the city was filthy. The flag of the United States, however, flew once again over New York City. The British finished their evacuation of Staten Island and Long Island by December 3. Though not exactly in the manner Washington had planned, he had retaken the city from the British.[33]

Many Loyalists feared a bloody rampage against them by the Whig militia now that the British army had left. Though Governor Clinton had to intervene personally to prevent the tarring and feathering of two British officers in town, most people accepted the end of the war calmly and peacefully, and left the Tories alone. A few extremists, however, did exploit the hatred of Tories in December 1783, when running for the state Assembly, by accusing anyone who ran against them of being Tories. They won their election easily. The United States political tradition of mudslinging and name-calling had begun.[34]

In one last effort to secure financial help from the Confederation Congress, Governor Trumbull sent a request in January 1784 for a reimbursement of the expenses for defending the state's frontiers near Horseneck and New London. He argued that the Congress had helped other state governments cover their costs during the war, and therefore Connecticut deserved the same help. The Congress rejected his appeal by explaining that other state governments had similar claims, and it would take such requests under consideration. Nothing was ever done.[35]

The war had finally ended, and with it the duties of the state militia forces against the British and Tories had also ended. The final year and a half, however, had been frustrating as the war slowly ground to a halt. The frustration was strongest for Washington, who wanted to end the war with one final blow to oust the British by force rather than to have the war just crawl to a stop, but his hopes were not realized. The partisan war had not come to an abrupt end after Cornwallis's surrender in 1781; it too had slowly ground to a halt as Whig and Tory militia units continued to fight into 1783. Throughout this gradual cessation of hostilities, the militia retained its place of importance in the war around New York City. By working together, the national and state military forces had confined and finally outlasted the British army, and had achieved the independence of the United States.

★ CHAPTER TWELVE ★

Conclusion

THE COLONIAL rebellion that had started at Lexington and Concord in 1775 finally came to an end eight and a half years later. During these long years of war, the Whig militiamen had showed their mettle on many a battlefield, large and small. Whether in the partisan war that raged from beginning to end, or in the field coordinating with the Continental Army, militia units had fought constantly and had contributed greatly to the ultimate victory of the military forces of the United States.

The militia of Connecticut, New York, and New Jersey, in particular, played a vital role in this victory. Militiamen from these three states not only participated in all of the operations of the regular armies, but they had to stand guard between the two armies after the British captured New York City. For seven years the British retained that city, and throughout that time, the nearby militia forces had to protect their states from raids, internal dangers, and invasions. At the same time, they had to reinforce the understrength Continental Army, act as scouts for Washington, and rally to the army whenever the British emerged from the city. That the militia of these three states could handle all of these duties showed the resiliency and flexibility of the local military institutions. As the British army evacuated New York in 1783, the militia was still on duty, fulfilling to the best of its ability the many functions required of it by the American leadership.

At all times, the militia had the primary responsibility for the defense of the states from internal and external dangers. Along the coasts, rivers, and roads, militiamen stood guard. The militia forces could not always stop invasions or even small raids, but they could converge quickly on a threatened area. Within a couple of days, several hundred or even thousand militiamen would assemble and contest the further progress of the invaders, even while they skirmished with the raiders and inflicted casualties on them. The militia was the first line of defense throughout the states, providing the flexibility to respond wherever the naval superiority of the British allowed them to attack.

One of the key contributions of the Whig militia was its successful suppression of the Tory elements in the states. When the Tories threatened the control of the new Whig governments in the first three years of the war, the state governments turned to their militiamen to locate, apprehend, or kill the Tories. Tories threatened to rise in support of British troops whenever they appeared, and they tried to enlist people to join the British forces. Whig militiamen throughout the war, but particularly during the first half, had to find and stop these recruiters and the men who had enlisted to join the British. In addition, the militia had to fight the brutal war of raids and counterraids between Tories and Whigs. Politicians and generals alike understood the importance of internal control and of retaining the loyalty of the people, and the Whig militia had the responsibility of maintaining the internal security of the state governments and protecting the friendly inhabitants. This was a role for which the militia proved to be well suited. Tories were hunted, apprehended, ousted, or killed throughout the war, and in the end, the militia helped prevent any real threat to Whig control in the governments of the middle states once these governments had been established in 1775–77.

The militiamen's duties in coordination with the Continental Army were equally varied. The militia, however, proved to be an unreliable source of reinforcement for the regular army, despite the initial policy of the Continental Congress to depend on it for that purpose. Militia soldiers did not fare well in large-scale battles against British regulars, and Washington could not plan operations based on militia forces because they often arrived late and left early. Despite its unsuitability for such a role, the militia remained a main source of manpower for the army throughout the war. Neither the Continental nor the Confederation Congress ever created a sufficiently large regular army, and Washington had to turn to the militia every year. This mismatch between militia capabilities and requirements was a source of endless frustration for Washington, and was the basis for the traditionally negative view of the militia in the middle states.

On the other hand, the militia served the army well in other capacities. Whenever British forces maneuvered outside of their defensive works, militiamen would rally to the army in small detachments and hover around the British. They would harass and skirmish, hit and run, and then pull back and find another position from which they could snipe at the enemy. They obstructed British moves, and they joined Continental detachments to create a swirl of activity around the armies. These regular armies did not campaign through an empty countryside, but instead moved through an area swarming with small parties of militia and even Continentals. The British were never able to march from one point to another in these middle states without fighting every mile of the way. In this kind of partisan warfare, the militiamen's constant fluctuation in numbers was not as critical, and their lack of discipline did not matter as much. They proved to be effective partisans in this kind of war, and Washington preferred to use them in this fashion whenever the armies took the field.

An outgrowth of this partisan war was Washington's policy of using the militia as a shield for the army. On their own or in conjunction with small Continental detachments, militia units took positions between the two armies where they could watch for British activity, send intelligence to army headquarters, and then impede British movements while skirmishing with them. These actions enabled Washington to concentrate his army and to decide if he wanted to engage the British or withdraw. Thus, he initiated a strategy of forward defense or defense in depth, where militiamen were the advance guards and the army was free to move forward or back as desired.

Clearly, the activities of the militia and the Continental Army were intricately entwined. Each functioned best when supported by the other. Contrary to the traditional view, these functions did not lead to two separate wars in the middle states, one at the local level and the other between the regular armies. Both wars merged, and the same soldiers, militia and Continental alike, fought at both levels.

Much to the militia's credit, a pattern emerged during this war that demonstrated its willingness to fight when necessary. Many times the state governments or Washington called for militia forces, and they either did not come or came slowly and in small numbers. This unreliability incensed men such as Washington, who needed to plan ahead and know how many men he would have at a certain date. These same forces, however, would respond immediately and in great numbers when the danger was greatest. It was not fear that kept militiamen away, but lack of regulation and enforceable muster laws. Danger and emergencies brought the militia out in droves. Thus, the pattern for militia activity was not seasonal, and often had little to do with how many men the politicians or generals wanted, but was based more on the presence of danger and the likelihood of immediate action. Whenever either of these factors was present, so was the militia.

The impact of this partisan war on the British is more difficult to judge. British and German generals, as well as former royal governors, tended to have nothing but contempt for the American soldiers, whether regular or militia. That the militia affected the British campaigns in the middle states is clear, but did the British leadership recognize the impact of the militia? Sir William Howe and Sir Henry Clinton both blamed many of their problems on the militia, but whether they actually believed that the militia was the problem or were just looking for a scapegoat is less clear. On the other hand, their actions suggest a grudging respect for what the militia could do. Howe backed out of New Jersey in 1777 and sailed south, and Clinton avoided clashing with the New Jersey militia after 1778. Clinton also placed great emphasis on the militia during the critical months leading up to Yorktown. Men such as Johann Ewald and John Simcoe certainly understood what the Whig militia could do, and even Secretary of State George Germain recognized where the militia fit into Washington's plans. Germain's suggestions on the proper employment of the Loyalist militia, his strategy of raids to pin down the militia in other states and thus to weaken Washington, and his realization that the militia would rally to Washington's army after a victory or when French ships or reinforcements arrived, all suggest that he grasped the essential characteristics of the state militia. Without further study, however, it is impossible to say with certainty how much impact the militia's activities had on British planning.

Another important characteristic of the militia was its ability to respond to three different levels of command: local militia officers, state governments, and Washington and the Continental generals. Militia officers often responded to raids or larger invasions before the state government or nearby Continental generals could react. When militia forces were needed for a longer term of service, the state governments took over and authorized the creation of such units. Thus, when Washington tried to plan ahead, or when a particular region was in danger, the state legislatures ordered out the necessary men to serve as long as required. Though such units were rarely filled, even the partially completed formations could serve with the army or guard the exposed area. Once assembled, militia units received commands from the Continental or militia officers. The state governments did not try to command the actual movements of the militia while it served in the field. The only exception to this was George Clinton's activities. After he became governor of New York, he continued to function as a militia general.

The supremacy of the state governments over their state militia went unchallenged during the war. Washington and his generals had some powers over the militia, both for calling it out and for commanding it in the field, and the local governments and their militia officers rarely challenged the Continental generals' authority to command militia units operating near or with the army. On the other hand, Washington carefully worked through the state governments when he needed men. Only when a governor specifically told him to call for militia directly through militia officers did Washington bypass the government. Other Continental commanders were more restricted, but they generally had the authority to apply to the governors for more men without going through the national legislature or Washington.

The state governments thus played an important part in the war, but in the middle states, the governments did not function with equal efficiency. Connecticut's government remained stable during the war, while New York's and New Jersey's underwent dramatic changes early in the war. Connecticut's prewar governor, Jonathan

Trumbull, continued to serve as governor after the rebellion began, retaining that office throughout the entire war. Connecticut's government did not undergo major structural or procedural changes, at least in relation to the command of the militia. The Assembly called out the militia, and Trumbull and the Council of Safety had the authority to act in the recess of the Assembly and in sudden emergencies. This shared responsibility worked well, and neither the governor nor the Assembly challenged the other's powers over the militia.

The Whigs of New York and New Jersey established new governments in both states during the war. New York's governor proved to be more effective than New Jersey's, but that was due more to Clinton's personality than to the structure of the governments. The New York Assembly did not interfere with Clinton's handling of emergencies, and in turn Clinton relied on the Assembly to create longer-term units for the frontiers and border areas. In New Jersey, neither the governor nor the Assembly exerted strong control over the militia. During most invasions of the state, the militia generals, in particular Major General Philemon Dickinson, commanded the militia and called for more men as needed. Governor William Livingston and the Assembly issued orders to establish state regiments and to send militiamen to protect the coast, but did not involve themselves in the field command of the militia. The two governments were similar in structure, but functioned differently under the pressures of the war.

All three state governments shared one problem: the inability to compel militiamen to serve when called. None solved the problem during the war, as all three depended on monetary fines as punishment for delinquent soldiers. The explanation for this failure is complex and still not fully clear, but it has to do with the heritage of the militia forces in the colonies, fear of a regular army that permeated the entire revolutionary period, and basic politics— politicians are loath to pass laws that will be unpopular. The result of this failure could be seen whenever Washington tried to make plans based on the militia, or the state governments attempted to raise units for their own protection.

In spite of these difficulties, and the competing demands placed on the militia by state and national leaders, the state governments did their job, protected their states, and supported the army. In turn,

Washington tried to understand the needs of the states and the problems that the legislators and governors faced. This cooperation between state and national leadership was critical to the American war
effort. Despite some friction between the state governments and
Washington, especially over requests for Continental detachments
to help in local defense, the state governments and Continental commander worked well together. Ultimately, the fear of a standing army,
which was an important feature of the revolutionary period, was not
as important to the state leaders as defending themselves against
raids and invasions. Perhaps the politicians and citizens of the states
would not have wanted to depend solely on a regular army for their
defense, but when the British or Tories were around, they did not
hesitate to ask for the regulars. National and state leaders worked
closely together throughout the war, and this cooperation added
strength to the American military system.

The three governors provided interesting contrasts. Trumbull
functioned solely as the executive of the state, issuing the orders
necessary to assemble and use the militia. He kept in constant communication with Washington, other Continental generals, Congress,
other governors, and militia officers and generals of his state. Throughout a trying war, in which his state's coasts were raided and its cities
burned, Trumbull maintained control of the state and continued to
support the army's efforts in New York and New Jersey. More than the
other two states, his state had to wage the war primarily on its own. It
received the fewest Continentals, yet usually supplied the largest
militia contingents to help its neighbors. Trumbull and Connecticut
proved to be sources of strength for the Americans during the war.

Clinton was not only a governor, but he remained a militia general throughout the war, and Washington and the Congress entrusted
him with important commands. As governor, he had the primary
control over the state's forces, and the Assembly left him in charge
of most of the assembling and positioning of the militia. Clinton did
an excellent job of holding together a state occupied in the north,
west, and south by enemy troops. He helped organize the government through his efforts as governor, and he inspired and led the
militia to support the army's efforts and to defend the state from
further invasion and destruction. Clinton deserved much praise for
his exertions as governor and militia general.

Livingston started the war as a militia general, but after a year relinquished that position to become governor. Unlike Clinton, he never returned to the field to command, leaving that to Dickinson and the other generals. In fact, he left most of the command of the militia to the generals. In terms of direct control of the militia, Livingston was the weakest of the three governors. On the other hand, he was the strongest advocate of revising the militia laws and ending the reliance on fines to compel men to serve, and through-out the war he waged a constant and unsuccessful battle with his state's Assembly to get improved militia regulations and enforceable laws. Perhaps he was wise to put the primary command of the militia in the hands of the generals, because the state government did not function well during emergencies. Overall, he helped direct a state that faced the constant threat of invasion from the British on Staten and Manhattan Islands from 1776 to the end. He made do with what he had available in the state, and after the initial problems of 1776, the New Jersey militia became one of the most effective partisan forces in the middle states.

Unlike the state governments, the Continental Congress had a limited role in the partisan war around New York City. In the begin-ning, its members participated directly, but increasingly they removed themselves from the daily control of the militia, leaving that to Wash-ington, the generals, and the state governments. After 1776, the Congress tended to limit its actions to advising Washington and supporting his calls for more men. Its efforts to coordinate the state governments and Washington's needs, and to establish Washington's relationship with the local governments, was of critical importance in the early years, and in this capacity the Congress helped ensure that the necessary cooperation between the state and national lead-ers would be possible. The transition from the Continental Congress to the Confederation Congress in 1781 had little effect on the role of the Congress in the actual running of the war. The major change in policy came instead after the 1776 disaster in New York and New Jer-sey. The Congress abandoned the official policy of relying on mili-tiamen as a pool of reserves for the army and, in general, supported Washington's call for a larger regular army. Like the state governments, however, the Congress throughout the war failed to devise a policy that could successfully create the kind of army Washington desired.

Washington clearly emerged as the central figure in the partisan war in the middle states. His initial instincts concerning the militia were good, but he had to adapt his views to the experiences gained over the years. His early efforts to assemble large numbers of militia failed, and he quickly learned to employ the militia in small parties in a partisan fashion. He also found that the militia could not muster a large force even with the prospect of French cooperation. That he kept trying to do this suggests how important the capture of New York was to him, and how reluctant he was to give up his cherished project.

Washington learned to recognize both the strengths and the weaknesses of the militia. As regular soldiers, militiamen were deficient, and they even had difficulty handling the needs of local defense. He therefore increasingly detached Continentals to support them when operating against the British army, and he also allowed Continental units to help guard the more exposed regions of the states. In this way, Washington showed that he was capable of adapting his beliefs to his experiences, and he demonstrated his support for the militia's needs as well. In addition, he recognized its strengths. Militiamen were available everywhere and could respond to sudden attacks and invasions often faster than the army could. Washington therefore used the militia to counter these sudden threats, which meant keeping the militia units in the states to provide local defense, to suppress Loyalists, and to rally to the army in case of an invasion. He understood the importance of internal security and encouraged the state governments to control the Tories, and he occasionally made Continental detachments available for such duty.

Washington made full use of the partisan qualities of the militia forces around him. He used them in small parties to harass and raid the British, to gather information and provide forward defense for the army, and to guard all the places he could not send Continentals. He did not try to limit this partisan war, but actually encouraged it and deliberately fought in that fashion when the British emerged from their defenses. Rather than try to turn the militia into a regular fighting force, he used and exploited its irregular qualities in a partisan war against the British and Tories.

One of Washington's earliest opinions of the militiamen did not change during the war. He considered them undependable soldiers whom he would rather keep separate from the regular soldiers in the army. His view of the militiamen attached to the army did not change from the view presented early in the war: "all the General Officers agree that no Dependence can be put on the Militia for a Continuance in Camp, or Regularity and Discipline during the short Time they may stay."[1] This was Washington's major complaint against militiamen. He did not question their bravery, loyalty, or willingness to fight when necessary, but he could never accept their habit of coming and going when they pleased. As commander in chief, he needed a dependable military force in order to formulate his plans, and the militia was definitely not such a force.

On the other hand, militiamen had much to offer, especially when fighting on their own and as partisans, and Washington tried to take advantage of their availability everywhere. As the war came to an end, Washington expressed this attitude clearly: "The Militia of this Country must be considered as the Palladium of our security, and the first effectual resort in case of hostility. . . ."[2] Washington's strength was his flexibility. He used what he had to use, and he tried to employ the resources available in the best manner possible, learning from his experiences. He did not shun militiamen simply because he did not believe that they were dependable, professional soldiers. Instead, he employed them where their talents would be most useful.

Thus, Washington was a successful and victorious leader of a rebellion. The traditional view of him as a general who was obsessed with conventional warfare, and the one-dimensional picture of the persevering general who tried to win the war in European fashion, both miss one of the key features of the man and the general.[3] His military policy was much more complex. Washington crafted a strategy that used the best qualities of the regulars and militia. His careful coordination of conventional (or European) and unconventional (or North American) styles of warfare was the prototype for the strategy so successfully employed later in the South by his protégé, Nathanael Greene. Washington was adept at waging a partisan war in the middle states, and he stands out as the great leader of the war, consistent, yet willing to learn from past events.

Perhaps the early chronicler of the war, Mercy Otis Warren, caught the true character of Washington best. Washington, she wrote, "required at times, the caution of Fabius, the energy of Caesar, and the happy facility of expedient in distress, so remarkable in the military operations of the illustrious Frederick."[4]

Thus, the war around the British stronghold of New York City was as much a partisan war as it was a war between regular armies, and the militia contributed vitally to this American war effort. It provided the states with a ready military force from the beginning of the war, a semiautonomous force when necessary, one that could respond to commands from all levels of authority. Thus, the strengths and weaknesses of the militia, and Washington's use of those militiamen, had a decided impact on the war in the middle states from New Jersey to Connecticut. Without these militia soldiers, and without Washington's exploitation of their capabilities, the leaders of the United States would have found it difficult to wage war for eight years against the military power of the British empire.

★ ★ ★

Notes

ABBREVIATIONS

Manuscript Sources

CGA   Connecticut General Assembly, 1775–82.
CSP   Council of Safety Papers, 1775–82.
GWP   Washington, George. George Washington Papers.
JDP   Douglas, John. Gen. John Douglas Papers, 1775–82.
JTP   Trumbull, Jonathan. Trumbull Papers.
PCNY   Provincial Congress Papers. Military Returns.

Printed Primary Sources

JNY   *Journals of the Provincial Congress, Provincial Convention, Committee of Safety and Council of Safety of the State of New York 1775–1777.*
NJGA   New Jersey. General Assembly Journals, 1776–83.
PGC   Hastings, Hugh, and James Austin Holden, eds. *Public Papers of George Clinton.*

INTRODUCTION

1. Letter to J. Hancock from Washington, July 10[–11], 1775, in W. W. Abbot, ed., *The Papers of George Washington* 1:90; circular to the states, June 8, 1783, in John C. Fitzpatrick, ed., *The Writings of George Washington from the Manuscript Sources 1745–1799* 26:494.

2. For books that emphasize the militia in the Southern campaigns, see in particular Burke Davis, *The Cowpens–Guilford Courthouse Campaign;* John S. Pancake, *This Destructive War: The British Campaign in the Carolinas, 1780–1782;* Hugh F. Rankin, *Francis Marion: The Swamp Fox;* Paul H. Smith, *Loyalists and Redcoats: A Study in British Revolutionary Policy;* Theodore Thayer, *Nathanael Greene: Strategist of the American Revolution;* Russell F. Weigley,

The Partisan War: The South Carolina Campaign of 1780–1782. The campaign in upstate New York against Burgoyne has received attention in Don R. Gerlach, *Proud Patriot: Philip Schuyler and the War of Independence, 1775–1783;* Robert Middlekauff, *The Glorious Cause: The American Revolution, 1763–1789;* Paul David Nelson, *General Horatio Gates: A Biography.* The other Northern campaigns and militia, as well as the militia in general, have received increasing attention in such works as Alfred Hoyt Bill, *The Campaign of Princeton, 1776–1777;* Richard Buel, Jr., *Dear Liberty: Connecticut's Mobilization for the Revolutionary War;* Steven Rosswurm, *Arms, Country, and Class: The Philadelphia Militia and "Lower Sort" during the American Revolution, 1775–1783;* Charles Royster, *A Revolutionary People at War: The Continental Army and American Character, 1775–1783;* Don Higginbotham, *War and Society in Revolutionary America: The Wider Dimensions of Conflict.*

3. For a sample of the works that cover the operations of the main areas in this region, see in particular John R. Alden, *A History of the American Revolution;* Alfred Hoyt Bill, *New Jersey and the Revolutionary War;* Thomas Fleming, *The Forgotten Victory: The Battle for New Jersey—1780;* Don Higginbotham, *The War of American Independence: Military Attitudes, Policies, and Practice, 1763–1789;* Richard M. Ketchum, *The Winter Soldiers;* Robert Leckie, *George Washington's War: The Saga of the American Revolution;* Adrian C. Leiby, *The Revolutionary War in the Hackensack Valley: The Jersey Dutch and the Neutral Ground, 1775–1783;* Leonard Lundin, *Cockpit of the Revolution: The War for Independence in New Jersey;* Lynn Montross, *The Story of the Continental Army;* Russell F. Weigley, *The American Way of War: A History of United States Military Strategy and Policy.*

4. Capitaine De Jeney, *The Partisan: or, the Art of Making War in Detachment,* v, 1–2. A note of interest is that this book was part of Washington's personal library. See Abbot, ed., *Papers of Washington* 2:347.

5. Johann Ewald, *Treatise on Partisan Warfare.*

6. The best modern study of the British war effort, strategy, and policy is Piers Mackesy, *The War for America, 1775–1783.*

7. For studies of Washington's military career during the Revolution, see in particular Burke Davis, *George Washington and the American Revolution;* James Thomas Flexner, *George Washington in the American Revolution, 1775–1783;* Douglas Southall Freeman, *George Washington: A Biography;* Dave Richard Palmer, *The Way of the Fox: American Strategy in the War for America, 1775–1783.*

8. Howard H. Peckham, ed., *The Toll of Independence: Engagements and Battle Casualties of the American Revolution.*

CHAPTER ONE
Initial Plans and Preparation for the Use of the Militia, 1775–1776

1. Mercy Otis Warren, *History of the Rise, Progress and Termination of the American Revolution* 1:103.

2. Mackesy, *War for America,* 19, 30–32; Fred Anderson, *A People's Army: Massachusetts Soldiers and Society in the Seven Years' War,* 167.

3. Anderson, *People's Army,* 61, 167; Eric Robson, ed., *Letters from America, 1773–1780: Being the Letters of a Scots Officer, Sir James Murray, to His Home During the War of American Independence,* 17–18; Alden, *American Revolution,* 180, 251; Frank Moore, comp., *The Diary of the American Revolution, 1775–1781,* 54; Oscar Brand, *Songs of '76: A Folksinger's History of the Revolution,* 59.

4. Stephen Conway, "To Subdue America: British Army Officers and the Conduct of the Revolutionary War," 381; Robson, ed., *Letters from America,* 17.

5. Anderson, *People's Army*, 61; Higginbotham, *War and Society*, 24, 26, 36–37; Fred Anderson, "The Colonial Background to the American Victory," in John Ferling, ed., *The World Turned Upside Down: The American Victory in the War of Independence*, 16–17.

6. Buel, *Dear Liberty*, 39; I. W. Stuart, *Life of Jonathan Trumbull, Sen., Governor of Connecticut*, 233.

7. Glenn Weaver, *Jonathan Trumbull: Connecticut's Merchant Magistrate (1710–1785)*, 117, 141; Stuart, *Trumbull*, 173–74, 179, 180–81, 213, 232; Charles S. Hall, *Life and Letters of Samuel Holden Parsons: Major General in the Continental Army and Chief Judge of the Northwestern Territory, 1737–1789*, 1.

8. Buel, *Dear Liberty*, 30, 39; Hall, *Parsons*, 1; General Assembly, Apr. 26, 1775, in Charles J. Hoadly and J. Hammond Trumbull, eds., *The Public Records of the Colony of Connecticut* 14:417, 422; John C. Dann, ed. *The Revolution Remembered: Eyewitness Accounts of the War for Independence*, 106.

9. Stuart, *Trumbull*, 203–4; General Assembly (May and July 1, 1775), in Hoadly and Trumbull, eds., *Colony of Connecticut* 14:39, 92–93, 99; Resolve, May 1776, in Connecticut General Assembly, 1775–1852, folder 1, 1775–80, Connecticut Historical Society, Hartford (hereafter CGA).

10. [General Assembly, 1775], in CGA, folder 1, 1775–80; letter to Washington from Norwich Committee of Correspondence, Aug. 7, and to Washington from Trumbull, Sept. 5, 1775, in Abbot, ed., *The Papers of Washington* 1:262, 417.

11. Robert V. Hoffman, *The Revolutionary Scene in New Jersey*, 63, 66–67; letters to G. Germain from W. Franklin, Mar. 28, 1776, Nov. 10, 1778, in K. G. Davies, ed., *Documents of the American Revolution, 1770–1783* 12:96–98, 15:241–242, 245.

12. Hoffman, *Revolutionary Scene*, 162; Earl Schenk Miers, *Crossroads of Freedom: The American Revolution and the Rise of a New Nation*, 6; Paul D. Nelson, *William Alexander, Lord Stirling*, 63; Bill, *New Jersey*, 4–8; Lundin, *Cockpit of the Revolution*, 71–72; *Minutes of the Provincial Congress and Council of Safety of the State of New Jersey, 1775–1776*, 187–90, 192.

13. *Rivington's Gazette*, June 1, [1775], in Moore, comp., *Diary*, 39; letter to C. Skinner from D. Coxe, July 4, 1775, in Davies, ed., *Documents* 11:37–38; *Minutes of the Provincial Congress*, 104–6, 111, 151, 179, 187–90, 192.

14. *Minutes of the Provincial Congress*, 241–42.

15. Philip Ranlet, *The New York Loyalists*, 52, 54, 58, 60; Roger J. Champagne, *Alexander McDougall and the American Revolution in New York*, 83–84; Colonel Marinus Willett's narrative, in *New York City During the American Revolution. Being a Collection of Original Papers (Now First Published) from the Manuscripts in the Possession of the Mercantile Library Association, of New York City*, 54–56, 58–59.

16. Edward Countryman, *A People in Revolution: The American Revolution and Political Society in New York, 1760–1790*, 140–41; Bruce Bliven, Jr., *Under the Guns: New York, 1775–1776*, 2; Bernard Mason, *The Road to Independence: The Revolutionary Movement in New York, 1773–1777*, 103–4; May 31, 1775, in *Journals of the Provincial Congress, Provincial Convention, Committee of Safety and Council of Safety of the State of New York 1775–1777* 1:21 (hereafter *JNY*); William L. MacDougall, *American Revolutionary: A Biography of General Alexander Mc Dougall*, xi, 19, 57, 59, 62; Champagne, *McDougall*, 84–85.

17. Ranlet, *Loyalists*, 60; Paul D. Nelson, "William Tryon Confronts the American Revolution, 1771–1780," 267, 270–73; Warren, *History* 1:108; Champagne, *McDougall*, 93; letter to the Earl of Dartmouth from W. Tryon, July 4, 1775, in Davies, ed., *Documents* 11:35; Bliven, *Under the Guns*, 25.

18. Militia bill, Aug. 22, 1775, and letter to the Ulster Committee, Mar. 14, 1776, in *JNY* 1:114–16, 359; resolution of the New York Provincial Congress, Dec. 12, 1775, in Jonathan Trumbull, Trumbull Papers, vol. 4, no. 187, Connecticut Colonial Official

Papers, 1631-1784, Massachusetts Historical Society, Connecticut State Library, Hartford (hereafter JTP).

19. Commission from the Continental Congress, June 19, 1775, in Abbot, ed., *Papers of Washington* 1:6-7.

20. Minutes of the conference [Oct. 18-24, 1775], in ibid. 2:194; Thurs., Dec. 7, 1775, in Worthington C. Ford and Gaillard Hunt, eds., *Journals of the Continental Congress, 1774- 1789* 3:414; letter to certain colonies [Mass., N.H., R.I., and Conn.] from John Hancock, Dec. 8, 1775, in Paul H. Smith, ed., *Letters of Delegates to Congress, 1774-1789* 2:454.

21. E. Wayne Carp, *To Starve the Army at Pleasure: Continental Army Administration and American Political Culture, 1775-1783*, 83.

22. Letter to P. Schuyler from Washington, Aug. 20, 1775, in Abbot, ed., *Papers of Washington* 1:333; letter to Washington from the Massachusetts Council, Oct. 3, to Trumbull from Washington, Dec. 2, and to J. Hancock from Washington, Dec. 18, 1775, ibid. 2:89, 471-72, 574; Massachusetts House of Representatives, Jan. 16, 1776, in George Washington Papers, ser. 4, reel 35, Presidential Papers Microfilm, Library of Congress (hereafter GWP); letter to the Massachusetts legislature from Washington, to Trumbull from Washington, and to the New Hampshire legislature from Washington, Jan. 16, 1776, in Fitzpatrick, ed., *Washington* 4:247, 248, 250.

23. Letter to J. Warren from J. Reed, July 12, and to J. Hancock from Washington, July 14, 1775, in Abbot, ed., *Papers of Washington* 1:105, 116; to the Provincial Congress of Massachusetts from Washington, July 12, 1775, in GWP, ser. 3C, reel 22.

24. Letter to Trumbull from Washington, Nov. 15, 1775, in Abbot, ed., *Papers of Washington* 2:379; to N. Cooke from Washington, Jan. 6, 1776, in Fitzpatrick, ed., *Washington* 4:215-16; Higginbotham, *War and Society*, 113-14.

25. Massachusetts House of Representatives journal, July-Nov. 1775, in editor's note no. 1 and letter to J. Warren from Washington, July [30], 1775, in Abbot, ed., *Papers of Washington* 1:195-96.

26. Letter to the Committee of New London from Washington, Aug. 9, 1775, in GWP, ser. 3C, reel 22; letter to N. Cooke from Washington, Aug. 14, to Trumbull from Washington, Aug. 23, and to D. Wooster from Washington, Sept. 2, 1775, in Abbot, ed., *Papers of Washington* 1:305, 352, 407.

27. Letters to Washington from Trumbull, Aug. 7, 8, Sept. 5, 15, and to Trumbull from Washington, Aug. 14, Sept. 2, 8, 1775, in Abbot, ed., *Papers of Washington* 1:267, 276, 307, 406, 437, 416, 468; meeting of the governor and Council of Safety, Sept. 14, 1775, in Hoadly and Trumbull, eds., *Colony of Connecticut* 15:128.

28. Letter to Trumbull from Washington, Sept. 21, 1775, in Abbot, ed., *Papers of Washington* 2:33-34; Stuart, *Trumbull*, 207-9.

29. Letter to T. Gage from S. Graves, Sept. 1, and to the Earl of Dartmouth from W. Howe, Nov. 27, 1775, in Davies, ed., *Documents* 11:98, 196; letter to the Falmouth Committee of Safety from Washington, Oct. 24, to J. Hancock from Washington, Oct. 24, to Washington from the Inhabitants of North Yarmouth and New Gloucester, Oct. 24, to Washington from J. Sullivan, Oct. 29, to E. Phinney from Washington, Nov. 6, and instructions to J. Sullivan, [Nov. 7], 1775, in Abbot, ed., *Papers of Washington* 2:226, 228, 230-31, 253, 314, 325; letter to J. Sullivan from H. Gates, Oct. 23, 1775, in editor's note no. 2, ibid. 2:254; letter to the Committee of Portsmouth from Washington, Oct. 20, and to S. Freeman from S. Moylan, Nov. 24, 1775, in GWP, ser. 3C, reel 22; letter to J. Sullivan from the Committee of Safety of New Hampshire, Oct. 27, 1775, ibid., ser. 4, reel 34.

30. Ira Gruber, "America's First Battle: Long Island, 27 August 1776," in Charles E. Heller and William A. Stofft, eds., *America's First Battles, 1776-1965*, 12; Mon., Oct. 2, 1775,

in Ford and Hunt, eds., *Journals of Continental Congress* 3:270; Council of War, Oct. 18, and minutes of the conference, [Oct. 18–24] 1775, in Abbot, ed., *Papers of Washington* 2:184, 194.

31. Freeman, *Washington* 2:112–13, 119, 127, 377, 5:483; Rosemarie Zagarri, ed., *David Humphreys' "Life of General Washington" with George Washington's "Remarks,"* 19–20; Don Higginbotham, *George Washington and the American Military Tradition*, 12, 23.

32. Freeman, *Washington* 2:378; Washington's account of the battle in Zagarri, ed., *Humphreys' "Life of Washington,"* 15.

33. Council of War, [July 9] 1775, in Abbot, ed., *Papers of Washington* 1:80; letter to J. Hancock from Washington, Nov. 28, 1775, in ibid. 2:446.

34. Letter to J. Reed from Washington, Nov. 28, Dec. 25, to J. Hancock from Washington, Dec. 4, 11, and circular to the New England states from Washington, Dec. 5, 1775, in Abbot, ed., *Papers of Washington* 2:449, 484, 492, 533, 607; letter to J. Reed from Washington, Jan. 4, 1776, in Fitzpatrick, ed., *Washington* 4:211.

35. Two councils of General Officers, Jan. 16, Feb. 16, 1776, in GWP, ser. 3F, reel 25; letter to C. Lee from Washington, Jan. 23, to J. Reed from Washington, Jan. 23, and to the president of Congress from Washington, Feb. 9, 18, 1776, in Fitzpatrick, ed., *Washington* 4:267, 271, 313, 335–37.

36. Letter to the Massachusetts legislature from Washington, Feb. 26, to the president of Congress from Washington, Mar. 7, and General Orders, Mar. 8, 1776, in Fitzpatrick, ed., *Washington* 4:350–51, 372–74, 384.

37. Letter to John A. Washington from Washington, July 27, 1775, in Abbot, ed., *Papers of Washington* 1:183–84.

CHAPTER TWO
Early Defense of the Middle Colonies, 1775–1776

1. Higginbotham, *War and Society*, 24, 118–19; letter to Washington from Trumbull, Jan. 1, 1776, in GWP, ser. 4, reel 35; letter to G. Clinton from J. McKesson, June 14, 1775, in Hugh Hastings and James Austin Holden, eds., *Public Papers of George Clinton, First Governor of the State of New York. 1777–1797—1801–1804* 1:203 (hereafter *PGC*); resolve of the New York Provincial Congress, Dec. 12, 1775, in JTP, vol. 4, no. 187; Mackesy, *War for America*, 32, 36; Ranlet, *Loyalists*, 158–59.

2. Buel, *Dear Liberty*, 39; Higginbotham, *War of Independence*, 273–74.

3. Letter to E. Dyer from J. Trumbull, June 1, and to the delegates at the Continental Congress from Trumbull, Aug. 4, 1775, in JTP, vol. 28:258, 310; letter to Washington from the Norwich Committee of Correspondence, Aug. 7, 1775, in Abbott, *Papers of Washington* 1:262; meeting of the governor and Council of Safety, Aug. 7, 1775, in Hoadly and Trumbull, eds., *Colony of Connecticut* 15:114–15.

4. Letter to Washington from Trumbull, Sept. 5, 15, 1775, in Abbott, ed., *Papers of Washington* 1:416, 470; letter to Trumbull from the Committee of Inspection of Lyme, Aug. 29, to Trumbull from G. Saltonstall, Aug. 30, 31, and to the Lyme Committee from G. Saltonstall, Aug. 31, 1775, in JTP, vol. 4, nos. 159, 163–65; letter from Trumbull to D. Marvin, J. Huntly, and G. Chadwick, Aug. 31, and to Col. Huntington, Sept. 18, 1775, ibid., vol. 20, nos. 112, 115.

5. At a General Assembly, Oct. 2, Dec. 14, 1775, in JTP, vol. 4, nos. 171, 195; speech by Trumbull to both houses of General Assembly, Dec. 14, 1775, in ibid., 20, no. 119; meeting of the governor and Council of Safety, Aug. 14, Sept. 8, and General Assembly, Oct. 11–25, Dec. 14, 1775, in Hoadly and Trumbull, eds., *Colony of Connecticut* 15:118, 125, 142, 187–89, 201.

6. Letter to Trumbull from S. Nott, Feb. 14, to Trumbull from G. Saltonstall, Apr. 4, 11, and to G. Saltonstall from Trumbull, Apr. 4, 1776, in JTP, vol. 5, nos. 10, 23, 27; meeting of the governor and Council of Safety, Feb. 16, Mar. 14, 1776, in Hoadly and Trumbull, eds., *Colony of Connecticut* 15:241, 247.

7. Warren, *History* 1:107–8; Dann, ed., *Revolution Remembered,* 111–12; letter to W. Tryon from the Earl of Dartmouth, July 1, 1775, in Davies, ed., *Documents* 11:30.

8. Letter to Trumbull from the Committee of New York, May 18, and to Trumbull from D. Wooster, June 16, 1775, in JTP, vol. 4, nos. 91, 116; letter to I. Law from Trumbull, May 22, 1775, ibid., vol. 20, no. 107; letter to the Earl of Dartmouth from W. Tryon, July 4, 1775, in Davies, ed., *Documents* 11:35; Buel, *Dear Liberty,* 43; Thurs., May 25, 1775, in Ford and Hunt, eds., *Journals of Continental Congress* 2:60; May 31, 1775, in *JNY* 1:21.

9. Letter to E. Dyer from the Connecticut General Assembly, May 25, to Trumbull from E. Dyer, June 20, and to [the delegates in the Continental Congress] from Trumbull, June 20, 1775, in JTP, vol. 28:250, 278, 281; letter to D. Wooster from the New York Provincial Congress, June 17, and to P. B. Livingston from Trumbull, June 19, 1775, ibid., vol. 4, nos. 117, 119; Champagne, *McDougall,* 90; to Trumbull from E. Dyer, June 16, and to the New York Provincial Congress from J. Duane, June 17, 1775, in Edmund Burnett, ed., *The Letters of the Members of the Continental Congress* 1:127, 129; resolution, June 16, 1775, in Ford and Hunt, eds., *Journals of Continental Congress* 2:95; letter to D. Wooster from E. Dyer, June 17, 1775, in Smith, ed., *Letters* 1:501; June 13, 1775, in *JNY* 1:40; resolution at a meeting of the Committee of Lebanon, June 19, 1775, in Hoadly and Trumbull, eds., *Colony of Connecticut* 15:89.

10. Letters to Trumbull from D. Wooster, June 16, 1775, in JTP, vol. 4, nos. 115, 116; letter to D. Wooster from Trumbull, June 19, 1775, ibid., vol. 20, no. 110; meeting of the Committee of Lebanon, June 19, 1775, in Hoadly and Trumbull, eds., *Colony of Connecticut* 15:89.

11. Letter to Trumbull from E. Dyer, June 20, and to J. Hancock from Trumbull, June 30, 1775, in JTP, vol. 28:278–79, 289; Stuart, *Trumbull,* 196; Gerlach, *Schuyler,* 13; letter to Washington from P. Schuyler, July 1, 1775, in Abbot, ed., *Papers of Washington* 1:47; letter to the Committee of Safety from the New York delegates, July 29, 1775, in Burnett, ed., *Letters* 1:182.

12. Aug. 7, 1775, in *JNY* 1:102–3; letter to Trumbull from D. Wooster, Aug. 9, to Washington from Trumbull, Aug. 11, and to Washington from D. Wooster, Aug. 29, 1775, in Abbot, ed., *Papers of Washington* 1:294, 377–78; letter to Trumbull from D. Wooster, Aug. 14, 1775, in GWP, ser. 4, reel 33; letter to Trumbull from D. Wooster, Aug. 24, 1775, in JTP, vol. 4, no. 154; Gerlach, *Schuyler,* 1.

13. Sept. 13, 16, 18, and letter to the Continental Congress, Sept. 19, 1775, in *JNY* 1:146, 149, 151–52; Gerlach, *Schuyler,* 17; letter to D. Wooster from Washington, Sept. 2, 1775, in Abbot, ed., *Papers of Washington* 1:407; letter to Washington from D. Wooster, Sept. 28, 1775, in ibid. 2:61.

14. Ranlet, *Loyalists,* 62; Nelson, "Tryon," 274–75; letter to S. Graves from G. Vandeput, Aug. 23, 1775, in Davies, ed., *Documents* 11:82–83; *New York Gazette and Weekly Mercury,* Aug. 28, 1775, in Moore, comp., *Diary,* 64.

15. Nelson, "Tryon," 274; Ranlet, *Loyalists,* 61.

16. Letter to S. Graves from G. Vandeput, Aug. 23–25, and to G. Vandeput from S. Graves, Sept. 10, 1775, in Davies, ed., *Documents* 11:82–83, 104–5.

17. Ranlet, *Loyalists,* 70; Champagne, *McDougall,* 94; Higginbotham, *War of Independence,* 274; Nelson, "Tryon," 275.

18. Letter to T. Gage from the Earl of Dartmouth, Aug. 2, to the Earl of Dartmouth from W. Tryon, Aug. 7, to the Earl of Dartmouth from T. Gage, Aug. 20, and to W. Howe

from the Earl of Dartmouth, Sept. 5, 1775, in Davies, ed., *Documents* 11:63–64, 71–72, 80, 99; Nelson, "Tryon," 275.

19. Letter to D. Wooster from the president of Congress, Oct. 19 [9] 1775, in Burnett, ed., *Letters* 1:224; Oct. 12, 1775, in *JNY* 1:171–72; John Adams's notes of debates, Oct. 7 [1775], in Smith, ed., *Letters* 1:131; resolution, Oct. 7, 1775, in Ford and Hunt, eds., *Journals of Continental Congress* 3:282; letter to J. Hancock from Washington, Oct. 12, and minutes of the conference, [Oct. 18–24] 1775, in Abbot, ed., *Papers of Washington* 2:148, 199.

20. Letter to the Earl of Dartmouth from W. Tryon, Nov. 11, to the Earl of Dartmouth from W. Howe, Nov. 26, to W. Tryon from R. Mansfield, Nov. 29, and to W. Howe from W. Tryon, Dec. 13, 1775, in Davies, ed., *Documents* 11:171, 191, 198–99, 210.

21. Ranlet, *Loyalists,* 62–63; letter to the Earl of Dartmouth from W. Tryon, Dec. 6, and to H. Parker from G. Vandeput, Dec. 18, 1775, in Davies, ed., *Documents* 11:206, 212.

22. Resolution, Nov. 8, 1775, in Ford and Hunt, eds., *Journals of Continental Congress* 3:337–38; E. Wilder Spaulding, *His Excellency George Clinton: Critic of the Constitution,* 9, 37, 40–41, 43–45, 52–53.

23. Nelson, *Stirling,* 65; resolution, Nov. 27, and Fri., Dec. 8, 1775, in Ford and Hunt, eds., *Journals of Continental Congress* 3:376, 416.

24. Wed., Jan. 3, Tues., Jan. 9, Wed., Jan. 10, 1776, in Ford and Hunt, eds., *Journals of Continental Congress* 4:27, 42, 47–48; return of Capt. Samuel Raymond's company, Jan. 3, and return of Capt. Francis Burns's company, [Jan.] 15, 1776, in Provincial Congress Papers, Military Returns, ser. A1815, box 2, folder "Vol. 27, Military Returns etc. 1776," New York State Archives, Albany (hereafter PCNY); Richard Smith diary, [Jan. 3], 6, 1776, in Burnett, ed., *Letters* 1:294, 300; Buel, *Dear Liberty,* 61; Nelson, *Stirling,* 70; Ranlet, *Loyalists,* 70, 154–55; Champagne, *McDougall,* 98; letter to J. Hancock from W. Livingston, Feb. 3, 1776, in Carl E. Prince and Dennis P. Ryan, eds., *The Papers of William Livingston* 1:37.

25. Champagne, *McDougall,* 98; letter to the president of Congress from Washington, Jan. 4, 1776, in Fitzpatrick, ed., *Washington* 4:209; Freeman, *Washington* 3:441; letter to Washington from C. Lee, Jan. 5, 1776, in GWP, ser. 4, reel 35; John R. Alden, *General Charles Lee: Traitor or Patriot?* 75, 89–90, 95–96; [Nicholas Cresswell], *The Journal of Nicholas Cresswell, 1774–1777,* 246; Dann, ed., *Revolution Remembered,* 105; Warren, *History* 1:160.

26. Alden, *Lee,* 96; letter to Washington from J. Adams, Jan. 6, to Washington from Trumbull, Jan. 12, and to Washington from C. Lee, Jan. 16, 1776, in GWP, ser. 4, reel 35; letter to Trumbull from Washington, Jan. 7, letter to the Committee of Safety of New York from Washington, Jan. 8, instructions to C. Lee, Jan. 8, and letter to Stirling from Washington, Jan. 10, 1776, in Fitzpatrick, ed., *Washington* 4:218–19, 220–21, 221–22, 226–27; letter to C. Lee from Trumbull, Jan. 12, 1776, in "Lee Papers," New York Historical Society *Collections* 4:238; letter to P. Schuyler from Trumbull, Jan. 20, 1776, in JTP, vol. 27:41–42.

27. Sir Henry Clinton, *The American Rebellion: Sir Henry Clinton's Narrative of His Campaigns, 1775–1782,* 24; letter to the Earl of Dartmouth from W. Tryon, Jan. 3, and to the Earl of Dartmouth from W. Howe, Jan. 16, 1775, in Davies, ed., *Documents* 12:31–32, 45.

28. Dann, ed., *Revolution Remembered,* 40–41; Champagne, *McDougall,* 99; letter to Trumbull from C. Lee, Jan. 22, 1776, in JTP, vol. 29:253; letter to C. Lee from the chairman of the New York Committee of Safety, Jan. 21, and to the chairman of the New York Committee of Safety from C. Lee, Jan. 23, 1776, in GWP, ser. 4, reel 35; Bliven, *Under the Guns,* 31, 46–47; Jan. 21, Feb. 1, 1776, in *JNY* 1:259, 277; MacDougall, *American Revolutionary,* 79; to the president of Congress from C. Lee, Jan. 22, and to C. Lee from J. Hancock, Jan. 26, 1776, in "Lee Papers" 4:247–49, 251, 262; Buel, *Dear Liberty,* 61; resolution, Jan. 26, 1776, in Ford and Hunt, eds., *Journals of Continental Congress* 4:94.

29. Letter to C. Lee from Washington, Jan. 30, 1776, in Fitzpatrick, ed., *Washington* 4:293; letter to Trumbull from C. Lee, Jan. 31, 1776, in JTP, vol. 29:257; letter to the Committee of Congress from C. Lee, Jan. 31, 1776, in "Lee Papers" 4:268.

30. Champagne, *McDougall*, 99, 101.

31. Clinton, *American Rebellion*, 24; letter to the Earl of Dartmouth from W. Tryon, Jan. 3, 1776, in Davies, ed., *Documents* 12:31–32.

32. Letter to W. Radclift from R. Beck, Feb. 13, 1776, in *New York City during the American Revolution*, 85–86; letter to the New York delegates, Feb. 3, 1776, in *JNY* 1:283; letters to the president of Congress from C. Lee and to R. Morris from C. Lee, Feb. 9, 1776, in "Lee Papers" 4:279, 280; letter to Washington from C. Lee, Feb. 5, 1776, in GWP, ser. 4, reel 35; letter to [Trumbull] from C. Lee, Feb. 7, 1776, in JTP, vol. 29:257–58.

33. Letter to W. Radclift from R. Beck, Feb. 13, 1776, in *New York City during the American Revolution*, 87; "A True State of the 2nd regiment [of] militia in Suffolk County," Feb. 10, 1776, in PCNY; meeting [of the governor and Council of Safety], Feb. 2, 1776, in Hoadly and Trumbull, eds., *Colony of Connecticut* 15:237; letter to C. Lee from J. Hancock, Feb. 12, 1776, in Smith, ed., *Letters* 3:235; letter to C. Lee from the president of Congress, Feb. 12, 1776, in "Lee Papers" 4:293; Mon., Feb. 12, 1776, in Ford and Hunt, eds., *Journals of Continental Congress* 4:127–28; Feb. 15, 1776, in *Minutes of the Provincial Congress*, 369–70; letter to Mrs. Adams from J. Adams, Feb. [13], 1776, in Burnett, ed., *Letters* 1:348–49; letter to Washington from C. Lee, Feb. [14], 1776, in GWP, ser. 4, reel 35; Feb. 19, 1776, in *JNY* 1:310; letter from N. Heard, Feb. 16, 1776, ibid. 2:127.

34. Champagne, *McDougall*, 102–4; Warren, *History* 1:160–62; Alden, *Lee*, 100–101; Ranlet, *Loyalists*, 155.

35. Champagne, *McDougall*, 103–4; Nelson, *Stirling*, 72.

36. Clinton, *American Rebellion*, 24; letter to G. Germain from W. Tryon, Apr. 6, 1776, in Davies, ed., *Documents* 12:106; Nelson, "Tryon," 277.

37. Letter to Washington from C. Lee, Feb. 19, 1776, in GWP ser. 4, reel 35; letter to R. Morris from C. Lee, Feb. 20, and to the president of Congress from C. Lee, Feb. 22, 1776, in "Lee Papers" 4:316–17, 321–22; letter to C. Lee from Washington, Feb. 26, 1776, in Fitzpatrick, ed., *Washington* 4:353.

38. Gerlach, *Schuyler*, 116; Nelson, *Stirling*, 73.

39. Letter to Washington from C. Lee, Feb. 29, Mar. 3, 1776, in GWP, ser. 4, reel 35; Mar. 4, and letter from C. Lee, Mar. 7, 1776, in *JNY* 1:336, 343; letter to the president of Congress from C. Lee, Mar. 5, and report on the defense of New York, Mar. 1776, in "Lee Papers" 4:346–47, 357; letter to J. Reed from Washington, Mar. 3, 1776, in Fitzpatrick, ed., *Washington* 4:366.

CHAPTER THREE
The Armies Arrive at New York, March–August 1776

1. Nelson, *Stirling*, 72–73; Gerlach, *Schuyler*, 127.

2. Letter to the officer commanding the American forces in New York from Washington, Mar. 9, 1776, in GWP, ser. 3B, reel 16; proceedings of a Council of General Officers, Mar. 13, 1776, ibid., ser. 3F, reel 25; letter to the president of Congress from Washington, Mar. 13, to the officer commanding at New York from Washington and to Trumbull from Washington, Mar. 14, 1776, in Fitzpatrick, ed., *Washington* 4:391–92, 395–96, 399; resolution, Mar. 14, 1776, in Ford and Hunt, eds., *Journals of Continental Congress* 4:204; letter to Trumbull from J. Hancock, Mar. 15, 1776, in JTP, vol. 29:43; letter to Stirling from the president of Congress, Mar. 15, 1776, in Burnett, ed., *Letters* 1:393.

3. Two letters to Washington from Stirling, Mar. 15, 1776, in GWP, ser. 4, reel 35.

4. Letter to Washington from Stirling, Mar. 20, 1776, in ibid.; order to raise twenty companies to march to New York, Mar. 18, 1776, in JTP, vol. 20, no. 125; meeting of the governor and Council of Safety, Mar. 18, 1776, in Hoadly and Trumbull, eds., *Colony of Connecticut* 15:249–50; Nelson, *Stirling*, 76; resolution, Mar. 25, 1776, in JNY 1:383.

5. Letter to W. Livingston from Stirling, Mar. 24, 1776, in Prince and Ryan, eds., *Livingston Papers* 1:44–45; Nelson, *Stirling*, 77; letter to the New Jersey Committee of Safety from J. Hancock, Mar. 28, 1776, in Smith, ed., *Letters* 3:458; resolves, Mar. 26, 1776, in *Selections of the Correspondence of the Executive of New Jersey, from 1776 to 1786*, 4–5.

6. Letters to Stirling from Washington, Mar. 17, 19, 24, instructions to Brig. Gen. Heath, Mar. 19, letter to the president of Congress from Washington, Mar. 27, and orders and instructions to Maj. Gen. Israel Putnam, Mar. 29, 1776, in Fitzpatrick, ed., *Washington* 4:402, 408, 410–11, 428, 436–37, 443; letter to Washington from Stirling, Mar. 27, 1776, in GWP, ser. 4, reel 35; letter to G. Germain from W. Tryon, Apr. 6, and to M. Shuldham from H. Parker, Apr. 29, 1776, in Davies, ed., *Documents* 12:106, 117; letter to Putnam from the president of Congress, Apr. 16, 1776, in Burnett, ed., *Letters* 1:422.

7. Letter to J. Hancock from P. Schuyler, Apr. 2, and to Washington from P. Schuyler, Apr. 7, 1776, in GWP, ser. 4, reel 35.

8. Letter to the commanding officer of the four regiments of the Continental troops on their march to New York from N. Cooke and letter to Washington from N. Cooke, Mar. 31, 1776, in GWP, ser. 4, reel 35; letter to N. Cooke from Washington, Mar. 21, 1776, in Fitzpatrick, ed., *Washington* 4:414.

9. Letter to W. Livingston from W. Heath, Apr. 1, 1776, in Prince and Ryan, eds., *Livingston Papers* 1:46; letter to S. Tucker from P. Dickinson, Apr. 9, 1776, no. 938, Emmet Collection, New York Public Library; letter to [Washington] from W. Burnett, May 14, and to Washington from S. Tucker, May 18, 1776, in GWP, ser. 4, reel 36.

10. Letter to Washington from Stirling, Apr. 1, to W. Thompson or officer commanding at New York from P. Schuyler, Apr. 12, return of the garrison at Forts Montgomery and Constitution, Apr. 23, 29, May 29, and letter to Washington from I. Nicoll, Apr. 30, 1776, in GWP, ser. 4, reels 35–36; letter to I. Nicoll from R. H. Harrison, May 4, 1776, ibid., ser. 3B, reel 16.

11. Letter to John Douglas from Trumbull, May 6, 1776, Gen. John Douglas Papers, 1775–82, no. 6, Connecticut Historical Society, Hartford (hereafter JDP); meeting of the governor and Council of Safety, May 6, and of the General Assembly, May, and May 9–June 8, 1776, in Hoadly and Trumbull, eds., *Colony of Connecticut* 15:266–67, 284–86, 291–95, 398–99; letter to Capt. S. Harding from Trumbull, May 18, and General Assembly, May 1776, in JTP, vol. 5, nos. 32, 54, 63, 65; General Assembly, May 1776, in CGA, folder 1.

12. Letter to the president of Congress from Washington, Apr. 15, and to the Committee of Safety of New York from Washington, Apr. 20, 1776, in Fitzpatrick, ed., *Washington* 4:479–80, 498–99; General Orders, May 16, 1776, ibid. 5:50; letter to Washington from P. Van Cortlandt, Apr. 25, 29, and resolution of Provincial Congress, May 30, 1776, in GWP, ser. 4, reels 35–36.

13. Letter to the legislature or Committee of Safety of New Jersey from Washington, Apr. 24, and to Trumbull from Washington, Apr. 26, 1776, in Fitzpatrick, ed., *Washington* 4:509–10, 523.

14. Ranlet, *Loyalists*, 66; letter to the Committee of Safety of New York from Washington, Apr. 17, to John A. Washington from Washington, Apr. 29, 1776, and proclamation, [Apr. or May] 1776, in Fitzpatrick, ed., *Washington* 4:486–88, 531, 533–34; letter to

Washington from the chairman of the Committee of Safety of New York, Apr. 1[8], 1776, in GWP, ser. 4, reel 35.

15. Letter to the Committee of Suffolk, Long Island, from Washington, May 16, and to I. Putnam from Washington, May 21, 1776, in Fitzpatrick, ed., *Washington* 5:48–49, 69–70; Joseph S. Tiedemann, "Patriots by Default: Queens County, New York, and the British Army, 1776–1783," 36–37.

16. Letter to G. Germain from W. Howe, July 7, 1776, in Davies, ed., *Documents* 12:157–58; to the president of Congress from Washington, July 3, 10, 1776, in Fitzpatrick, ed., *Washington* 5:214, 250.

17. Letter to the [Continental Congress] from Trumbull, June 17, and to J. Hancock from Trumbull, July 6, 1776, in JTP, vol. 29:55, 66–67; to [Washington] from Trumbull, July 6, 1776, in GWP, ser. 4, reel 37.

18. Bill, *New Jersey*, 8; letter to the Committee of Essex County, N.J., from Washington, June 30, 1776, in Fitzpatrick, ed., *Washington* 5:203–4; Constitution of the State of New Jersey, 1776, 4–7, 12; July 17, 1776, in *Minutes of the Provincial Congress*, 511; Lundin, *Cockpit of the Revolution*, 110, 120; Countryman, *People in Revolution*, 164; letter to G. Clinton from J. McKesson, Aug. 7, 1776, in *PGC* 1:297.

19. June 20, 30, 1776, in *JNY* 1:500, 512; Ranlet, *Loyalists*, 182; convention of the representatives of the State of New York, July 9, 16, Aug. 10, letter to Washington from R. Benson, July 14, and examination of Balthazar De Hart, [July 16?] 1776, in GWP, ser. 4, reel 37; Spaulding, *George Clinton*, 109–10.

20. In convention of the representatives of the State of New York, Aug. 10, 1776, in GWP, ser. 4, reel 37.

21. Letter to [W. Livingston] from J. Duyckink, July 6, 1776, in GWP, ser. 4, reel 37; letter to John Dickinson from W. Livingston, Aug. 1, 1776, in Prince and Ryan, eds., *Livingston Papers* 1:112; June 26, 29, July 1–3, 27, 1776, in *Minutes of the Provincial Congress*, 476–77, 486–87, 489, 523; Lundin, *Cockpit of the Revolution*, 116.

22. In Congress, June 12, 23, and letter to Washington from J. Hancock, June 25, 1776, in GWP, ser. 4, reel 36; letter to the New Jersey Provincial Congress from J. Witherspoon, July 3, 1776, in Smith, ed., *Letters* 4:377; Wed., July 3, 1776, in Ford and Hunt, eds., *Journals of Continental Congress* 5:508.

23. Letter to the New York Provincial Congress from N. Greene, June 6, and to M. Little from N. Greene, [Aug. 7] 1776, in Richard K. Showman, ed., *The Papers of General Nathanael Greene* 1:229, 278; letter to the president of Congress from Washington, June 10, 28, July 4, to H. Beekman from Washington, June 26, to W. Livingston from Washington, July 5, 6, to the secret committee of the New York legislature from Washington, July 13, 15, to the Committee of the City of New York from Washington, July 19, to G. Clinton from Washington, July 26, to the New Jersey legislature from Washington, Aug. 7, to the New York legislature from Washington, Aug. 11, 12, and to J. Trumbull from Washington, Aug. 16, 1776, in Fitzpatrick, ed., *Washington* 5:121–22, 181, 193–94, 220, 224, 226–27, 267, 284, 311–12, 341, 388, 415, 420, 439; in Provincial Congress of New York, June 24, 30, letter to Washington from N. Greene, July 27, and letter to Washington from [A. Yates], Aug. 13, 1776, in GWP, ser. 4, reels 36–37; determination of brigadier generals, June 27, 1776, ibid., ser. 3F, reel 25.

24. Letter to Washington from Trumbull, Aug. 5, 1776, in GWP, ser. 4, reel 37; meeting of the governor and Council of Safety, July 17, 1776, in Council of Safety Papers, 1775–1782, Connecticut Historical Society, Hartford (hereafter CSP).

25. Letter to [J. Hancock] from Trumbull, July 20, 1776, in JTP, vol. 29:75; letter to Trumbull from J. Wadsworth, July 20, to Trumbull from J. Fitch, Aug. 13, and to Trumbull from O. Wolcott, Aug. 15, 1776, ibid., vol. 5, nos. 122, 144, 147; letter to P. Schuyler from

Trumbull, July 22, and to H. Gates from Trumbull, Aug. 12, 1776, ibid., vol. 26:122, 150; letter to J. Fitch from Trumbull, Aug. 5, 1776, ibid., vol. 20, no. 131; General Assembly, June 14, and meeting of the governor and Council of Safety, July 2, Aug. 12, 1776, in Hoadly and Trumbull, eds., *Colony of Connecticut* 15:422, 460–61, 499; letter to Washington from Trumbull, Aug. 13, and to Washington from J. Mackay, Aug. 20, 1776, in GWP, ser. 4, reel 37.

26. June 7, 1776, in *JNY* 1:483–84; letter to [Trumbull] from J. Huntington, June 6, 1776, in JTP, vol. 5, no. 121; in Provincial Congress of New York, June 9, to Washington from R. Livingston, Aug. 9, to Washington from the convention of the representatives of the State of New York, Aug. 9, and in convention of the representatives of the State of New York, Aug. 10, 1776, in GWP, ser. 4, reels 36–37; Countryman, *People in Revolution*, 166; letter to the president of Congress from Washington, Aug. 12, 1776, in Fitzpatrick, ed., *Washington* 5:417.

27. Dann, ed., *Revolution Remembered*, 155; letter to [G. Clinton] from A. Hawkes Hay, July 13, to the commanding officer of the Continental forces from the Orange County committee, July 13, to Washington from N. Woodhull, July 13, 16, in convention of the representatives of the State of New York, July 16, letter to the representatives of the State of New York from P. Van Cortlandt and Z. Platt, July 18, and to Washington from G. Clinton, July 23, 1776, in GWP, ser. 4, reel 37; letter to Washington from G. Clinton, July 15, to G. Clinton from Capt. Moffat, July 16, to G. Clinton from A. Hawkes Hay, July 20, and to Capt. Moffat from G. Clinton, July 20, 1776, in PGC 1:250–52, 261–63.

28. Henry P. Johnston, *The Campaign of 1776 Around New York and Brooklyn*, 99–100; Andrew Chittenden, *Orderly Book of Lieut. Abraham Chittenden, Adj't. 7th Conn. Regt't.: August 16, 1776 to September 29, 1776*, 10, 12; Peckham, ed., *Toll of Independence*, 22; Freeman, *Washington* 4:151; letter to Lt. Col. Cuyper from G. Clinton, Aug. 18, 1776, in *PGC* 1:311; Aug. 13, 1776, in *JNY* 1:570.

29. Letter to Washington from A. McDougall, July 26, and to Washington from R. Livingston, Aug. 9, 1776, in GWP, ser. 4, reel 37.

30. Letters to Col. J. Hasbrouck from G. Clinton, July 14, Aug. 4, to the Committee of Poughkeepsie from G. Clinton, July 14, to Washington from G. Clinton, July 15, to unknown recipient from G. Clinton, July 17, and to A. Hawkes Hay from G. Clinton, July 17, 1776, in *PGC* 1:249–51, 259–60, 291; letter to Washington from G. Clinton, July 23, 1776, in GWP, ser. 4, reel 37.

31. Letter to Col. J. Hasbrouck from G. Clinton, Aug. 4, to G. Clinton from H. Howell, Aug. 12, and to G. Clinton from W. Smith, Aug. 19, 1776, in *PGC* 1:291, 308–9, 315–16; Johnston, *Campaign of 1776*, 109; Spaulding, *George Clinton*, 48–49, 55.

32. Letter to the New York legislature from Washington, Aug. 8, 1776, in Fitzpatrick, ed., *Washington* 5:398; letter to Washington from the convention of the representatives of the State of New York, Aug. 6, 13, 1776, in GWP, ser. 4, reel 37; in convention of the representatives of the State of New York, Aug. 8, to Brig. Gen. Morris from G. Clinton, Aug. 9, to Capt. Salisbury from G. Clinton, Aug. 9, to Lt. Col. Jansen from G. Clinton, Aug. 9, to Lt. Col. Cuyper from G. Clinton, Aug. 9, to Brig. Gen. Ten Broeck from G. Clinton, Aug. 9, and to Maj. Thompson from G. Clinton, Aug. 12, 1776, in *PGC* 1:298–99, 301–5, 306–7.

33. In convention of the representatives of the State of New York, Aug. 10, and letter to Washington from A. Yates, Aug. 13, 1776, in GWP, ser. 4, reel 37; to Col. Nicoll from G. Clinton, Aug. 9, 1776, in *PGC* 1:301–2.

34. In Provincial Congress of New York, June 29, letter to Washington from N. Woodhull, July 20, and in convention of the representatives of the State of New York, July 20, Aug. 24, 1776, in GWP, ser. 4, reel 37; to unknown recipient from N. Woodhull,

Aug. 8, 1776, no. 6966, Emmet Collection; Aug. 20, 26, 1776, in *JNY* 1:587–91.

35. Letter to S. Howell from B. Tusten, Jr., July 23, to G. Clinton from S. Logan, July 25, to Capt. Dorland from G. Clinton, Aug. 1, to S. Logan from G. Clinton, Aug. 2, to Maj. Cuyper from G. Clinton, Aug. 2, and to Col. Thomas from G. Clinton, Aug. 12, 1776, in *PGC* 1:266, 272–73, 280, 288–90, 309; to Washington from A. Hawkes Hay, July 25, 1776, in GWP, ser. 4, reel 37.

36. An ordinance for raising 3,300 of the militia, June 14, June 29, 1776, in *Minutes of the Provincial Congress,* 484, 550; letter to Washington from J. Covenhoven, July 24, and to Washington from W. Livingston, Aug. 12, 1776, in GWP, ser. 4, reel 37.

37. Lundin, *Cockpit of the Revolution,* 274; letter to Washington from W. Livingston, June 28, to W. Livingston from E. Johnson, June 30, to W. Livingston from J. Deare, July 4, to J. Deare from W. Livingston, July 5, to J. Duyckink from W. Livingston, July 6, to W. Livingston from J. Reed, July 6 [7], to H. Mercer from W. Livingston, July 10, 15, to S. Tucker from W. Livingston, July 13–15, to A. Quick from W. Livingston, July 19, W. Livingston order, Aug. 13, to P. Dickinson from W. Livingston, Aug. 13, and to W. Livingston from H. Mercer, Aug. 22, 1776, in Prince and Ryan, eds., *Livingston Papers* 1:57, 59, 64, 71, 76–77, 89, 97, 99, 104, 117, 118, 122, 177; letter to Washington from W. Livingston, July 5, 6, 1776, in GWP, ser. 4, reel 37.

38. Letters to S. Tucker from W. Livingston, July 6, 16, to J. Reed from W. Livingston, July 7, to W. Livingston from J. Duyckink, July 7, and to H. Mercer from W. Livingston, Aug. 22, 1776, in Prince and Ryan, eds., *Livingston Papers* 1:72–74, 78–79, 100, 121–22; to Washington from P. Bradley, July 22, 1776, in GWP, ser. 4, reel 37; Peckham, ed., *Toll of Independence,* 20.

39. Mon., June 3, 1776, in Ford and Hunt, eds., *Journals of Continental Congress* 4:412–13; letter to Washington from J. Hancock, June 4, 1776, in GWP, ser. 4, reel 36; letter to certain colonies from J. Hancock, June 4, 1776, in Smith, ed., *Letters* 4:136–37; letter to A. Wayne from J. Morton, Aug. 16, and to S. H. Parsons from J. Adams, Aug. 19, 1776, ibid. 5:8, 23; letter to A. Wayne from J. Morton, Aug. 16, 1776, Anthony Wayne Papers, no. 378, Bancroft Collection, New York Public Library, New York City; letter to the Assembly of Connecticut from J. Hancock, July 16, 1776, in JTP, vol. 29:71–72.

40. "June 11," an ordinance for raising 3,300 of the militia of New Jersey, June 14, an ordinance for detaching 2,000 of the militia, July 18, and an ordinance for detaching half the militia, Aug. 11, 1776, in *Minutes of the Provincial Congress,* 447–48, 548–49, 563–64, 568–70; General Assembly, June 14, 1776, in Hoadly and Trumbull, eds., *Colony of Connecticut* 15:417, 419; Tues., July 16, and Sat., July 20, 1776, in Ford and Hunt, eds., *Journals of Continental Congress* 5:565–66, 598; in Congress, [July 24, 1776], in GWP, ser. 4, reel 37.

41. Letter to certain colonies from J. Hancock, June 18, and to H. Mercer from J. Hancock, July 14, 1776, in Smith, ed., *Letters* 4:264–65, 453; to the president of Congress from Washington, June 20, 1776, in Fitzpatrick, ed., *Washington* 5:160; to J. Hancock from Trumbull, July 6, 1776, in JTP, vol. 29:68; in Provincial Congress of New York, June 22, and in Congress, July 16, 1776, in GWP, ser. 4, reels 36–37; to W. Livingston from Washington, June 28, 1776, in Prince and Ryan, eds., *Livingston Papers* 1:56.

42. Letter to J. Clinton from Washington, June 14, General Orders, July 2, and to the president of Congress from Washington, July 10, 1776, in Fitzpatrick, ed., *Washington* 5:138, 211, 247–50; in committee of Queens County, July 1, to Washington from L. Ogden, July 4, to Washington from N. Woodhull, July 13, and to Washington from James Hamman, July 15, 1776, in GWP, ser. 4, reels 36–37.

43. Letter to Trumbull from Washington, June 10, to J. Wadsworth from Washington, June 27, to the Massachusetts legislature or the Committee of Safety from Wash-

ington, June 28, and to the president of Congress from Washington, June 29, 1776, in Fitzpatrick, ed., *Washington* 5:124, 186, 188, 199; letter to Washington from S. Tucker, June 11, 1776, in GWP, ser. 4, reel 36; letter to J. Wadsworth from Washington, June 28, 1776, ibid., ser. 3B, reel 16; letter to the New York Convention from Washington, June 28, 1776, ibid., ser. 3C, reel 22; letter to W. Livingston from Washington, June 28, 1776, in Prince and Ryan, eds., *Livingston Papers* 1:56–57.

44. Letters to the president of Congress from Washington, July 10, 27, to John A. Washington from Washington, July 22, to the New Jersey legislature from Washington, Aug. 7, to J. Root from Washington, Aug. 7, and to Trumbull from Washington, Aug. 18, 1776, in Fitzpatrick, ed., *Washington* 5:249, 325, 344, 389, 391, 453; to Trumbull from J. Wadsworth, July 20, 1776, in JTP, vol. 5, no. 122; William M. Dwyer, *The Day Is Ours! November 1776—January 1777: An Inside View of the Battles of Trenton and Princeton,* 62–63.

45. Letters to Trumbull from Washington, July 11, 19, 1776, in Fitzpatrick, ed., *Washington* 5:260, 308; to [J. Hancock] from Trumbull, Aug. 22, 1776, in JTP, vol. 29:76.

46. June 21, July 24, 1776, in *Minutes of the Provincial Congress,* 468–69, 518; letter to Washington from W. Livingston, June 28, 1776, in Prince and Ryan, eds., *Livingston Papers* 1:57; letter to W. Livingston from Washington, June 29, July 5, 6, to H. Mercer from Washington, July 4, and to the New Jersey legislature from Washington, July 21, 1776, in Fitzpatrick, ed., *Washington* 5:198, 217–18, 225, 227, 317; letter to N. Heard from Washington, June 29, 1776, in GWP, ser. 3B, reel 16; letter to Washington from W. Livingston, July 5, 7, Aug. 12, and to Washington from H. Mercer, July 30, Aug. 11, 1776, ser. 4, reel 37.

47. Letters to the New York legislature from Washington, June 27, Aug. 8, to G. Clinton from Washington, July 12, 17, 26, to Col. J. Woodhull from Washington, July 14, to Washington from G. Clinton, July 15, and to the Committee of Safety from Washington, Aug. 17, 1776, in Fitzpatrick, ed., *Washington* 5:187, 248, 252, 265–66, 288, 340, 398, 450; in convention of the representatives of the State of New York, July 10, Aug. 24, to Washington from the secret committee, July 17, to Washington from G. Clinton, July 23, and to Washington from N. Woodhull, Aug. 6, 1776, in GWP, ser. 4, reel 37.

48. Letter to W. Livingston from Washington, June 28, 1776, in Prince and Ryan, eds., *Livingston Papers* 1:56–57; to the New Jersey convention from Washington, June 28, 1776, in GWP, ser. 3C, reel 22; letter to Washington from Trumbull, July 6, 1776, ibid., ser. 4, reel 37; letter to Col. J. Fitch from Washington, Aug. 7, to Trumbull from Washington, Aug. 7, and to W. Livingston from Washington, [Aug. 8] 1776, in Fitzpatrick, ed., *Washington* 5:396, 387, 390; letter to Trumbull from J. Wadsworth, Aug. 1, to Trumbull from J. Cooke, Aug. 9, to Trumbull from J. Fitch, Aug. 10, to Trumbull from B. Hinman, Aug. 14, to Trumbull from I. Lewis, Aug. 15, and to Trumbull from R. Law, Aug. 16, 1776, in JTP, vol. 5, nos. 130, 139, 141, 145, 148–49.

49. Letter to Washington from Stirling, June 1, and to Washington from N. Greene, Aug. 1, 1776, in GWP, ser. 4, reels 36–37; General Orders, June 25, July 1, 2, Aug. 24, letter to W. Livingston from Washington, July 5, and to I. Putnam from Washington, Aug. 25, 1776, in Fitzpatrick, ed., *Washington* 5:176, 209, 211, 225, 482, 489; letter to Col. J. Smith from N. Greene, Aug. 9, 1776, in Showman, ed., *Greene* 1:279–80.

50. Letter to S. Tucker from W. Livingston, July 6, and to J. Reed from W. Livingston, Aug. 24, 1776, in Prince and Ryan, eds., *Livingston Papers* 1:72, 125; letter to the Massachusetts legislature from Washington, July 9, to the president of Congress from Washington, July 10, 14, 27, to the New York legislature from Washington, July 24, and to A. Hawkes Hay from Washington, Aug. 10, 1776, in Fitzpatrick, ed., *Washington* 5:239, 250, 271, 333, 343, 408; in committee of Queens County, July 1, letter to Washington

from N. Woodhull, July 13, 20, to Washington from J. Hamman, July 15, to Washington from John [Cole], July 16, to Washington from H. Mercer, July 24, Aug. 15, to Washington from G. Clinton, July 23, Aug. 2, to Washington from A. Hawkes Hay, Aug. 2, and to Washington from W. Heath, Aug. 18, 1776, in GWP, ser. 4, reels 36-37; orders for the Fort Montgomery garrison, July 25, 1776, in *PGC* 1:268.

51. Letters to the president of Congress from Washington, July 19, Aug. 26, letter to A. Stephen from Washington, July 20, and to Trumbull from Washington, Aug. 24, 1776, in Fitzpatrick, ed., *Washington* 5:307, 313, 486, 491; letter to Washington from H. Mercer, July 14, 1776, in GWP, ser. 4, reel 37.

52. Letter to J. Reed from W. Livingston, July 3, 1776, in Prince and Ryan, eds., *Livingston Papers* 1:60; letter to Washington from H. Mercer, July 9, 27, and to J. Hancock from H. Mercer, July 20, 1776, in GWP, ser. 4, reel 37; proceedings of a Council of General Officers, July 12, 1776, ibid., ser. 3F, reel 25; letter to the president of Congress from Washington, July 30, 1776, in Fitzpatrick, ed., *Washington* 5:354.

53. Letters to the president of Congress from Washington, Aug. 18, 19, letter to Lund Washington from Washington, Aug. 19, and to W. Heath from Washington, Aug. 23, 1776, in Fitzpatrick, ed., *Washington* 5:451, 457, 463, 475; Weigley, *American Way of War,* 4.

CHAPTER FOUR
New York Lost and New Jersey Saved, August 1776–January 1777

1. Gruber, "First Battle," 4-5, 18; Johnston, *Campaign of 1776,* 102; Thayer, *Greene,* 94.

2. Letter to Mrs. Smyth from J. Murray, Aug. 31, 1776, in Robson, ed., *Letters from America,* 31; Gruber, "First Battle," 20-21; Johnston, *Campaign of 1776,* 103, 144, 148, and letter to his wife from G. Silliman, Aug. 25, 1776, in pt. 2:53; Charles P. Whittemore, *A General of the Revolution: John Sullivan of New Hampshire,* 1, 17, 25, 32-33, 40; letter to J. Sullivan from J. Hancock, Aug. 10, 1776, in Otis G. Hammond, ed., "Letters and Papers of Major-General John Sullivan, Continental Army" 1:293.

3. Letter to Mrs. Smyth from J. Murray, Aug. 31, 1776, in Robson, ed., *Letters from America,* 32-33; Johnston, *Campaign of 1776,* 152, and letter to his wife from G. Silliman, Aug. 25, 1776, in pt. 2:53.

4. Letters to the Committee of Safety from N. Woodhull, Aug. 27, 1776, in *JNY* 1:593.

5. Johnston, *Campaign of 1776,* 151, 155-58; Gruber, "First Battle," 21; Dann, ed., *Revolution Remembered,* 48, 111, 113, 155-56.

6. Gruber, "First Battle," 21-22; letter to Mrs. Smyth, from J. Murray, Aug. 31, 1776, in Robson, ed., *Letters from America,* 32; to G. Germain from W. Howe, Sept. 3, 1776, in Davies, ed., *Documents* 12:216-17.

7. Johnston, *Campaign of 1776,* 190; letter to Mrs. Smyth from J. Murray, Aug. 31, 1776, in Robson, ed., *Letters from America,* 33; Lewis Carroll, Jr., qtd. in Whittemore, *Sullivan,* 39, 43.

8. Letter to Washington from Stirling, Aug. 29, 1776, in GWP, ser. 4, reel 38; Dann, ed., *Revolution Remembered,* 48, 50.

9. Peckham, ed., *Toll of Independence,* 22; letter to G. Germain from W. Howe, Sept. 3, 1776, in Davies, ed., *Documents* 12:217; Lt. Gen. Sir William Howe, *The Narrative of Lt. Gen. Sir William Howe,* 4-5.

10. Letter to G. Germain from W. Howe, Sept. 3, 1776, in Davies, ed., *Documents* 12:217-18; Johnston, *Campaign of 1776,* 208, 211, and letter to his wife from G. Silliman, Aug. 29, 1776, pt. 2: 54; letter to the convention of the State of New York from N. Woodhull, Aug. 27, and to Washington from A. Yates, Aug. 28, 1776, in GWP, ser. 4,

reel 37; Benjamin Tallmadge, *Memoir of Colonel Benjamin Tallmadge*, 10; letter to Trumbull from A. Yates, Aug. 28, and to Trumbull from H. Livingston, Aug. 30, 1776, in JTP, vol. 5, nos. 159, 163; letter to the New York legislature from Washington, Aug. 28, 1776, in Fitzpatrick, ed., *Washington* 5:495–96; Peckham, ed., *Toll of Independence*, 22.

11. Letter to Trumbull from H. Livingston, Aug. 30, 1776, in JTP, vol. 5, no. 163; Dann, ed., *Revolution Remembered*, 42–43; MacDougall, *American Revolutionary*, 83, 85.

12. Council of War, Aug. 29, letter to Trumbull from H. Livingston, Aug. 30, to [Trumbull] from Suffolk County committee, Aug. 31, to Washington from H. Livingston, Aug. 31, and to Washington from Trumbull, Sept. 2, in GWP, ser. 4, reel 38; Ranlet, *Loyalists*, 73; letter to Trumbull from Bridgehampton Committee, Aug. 31, to the Council of War held by Trumbull from H. Livingston, Sept. 4, and to Trumbull from A. Gardiner, Sept. 7, 1776, in JTP, vol. 5, nos. 165, 171, 174; letter to H. Livingston from I. Wood, Sept. 2, 1776, ibid., vol. 7, no. 36; letter to J. Douglas from Trumbull, Sept. 1, 1776, in JDP, no. 7; meeting of the governor and Council of Safety, Sept. 1–3, 1776, in Hoadly and Trumbull, eds., *Colony of Connecticut* 15:511–13; letter to H. Livingston from Washington, Sept. 4, 1776, in Fitzpatrick, ed., *Washington* 6:14.

13. Letter to the Council of War from H. Livingston, Sept. 7, to Trumbull from H. Livingston, Sept. 9, 10, 14, 17, to H. Livingston from Trumbull, Sept. 9, 15, and to Maj. J. Ely from H. Livingston, Sept. 11, 1776, in JTP, vol. 5, nos. 175, 177–78, 181, 183–84, 190, 192; letter to H. Livingston from Trumbull, Sept. 12, 1776, in ibid., vol. 20, no. 134; letter to Washington from H. Livingston, Sept. 11, 1776, in GWP, ser. 4, reel 38; letter to Trumbull from C. Leffingwell, Sept. 16, 1776, no. 5284, Emmet Collection; letter to W. Heath from G. Clinton, Sept. 10, 1776, in PGC 1:343.

14. Aug. 17, 1776, in William Heath, *Memoirs of Major-General William Heath by Himself*, 46; letter to the New York legislature from Washington, Aug. 30, 1776, in Fitzpatrick, ed., *Washington* 5:499; letter to W. Heath from Washington, Aug. 30, and to the president of Congress from Washington, Sept. 2, 8, 16, 1776, ibid., 6:4–5, 32, 58.

15. General Orders, Sept. 1, 1776, in Fitzpatrick, ed., *Washington* 6:4; letter to N. Cooke from W. Ellery, Sept. 7, 1776, in Smith, ed., *Letters* 5:119; in Congress, Sept. 16, 1776, in GWP, ser. 4, reel 38.

16. General Orders, Aug. 30, 1776, in Fitzpatrick, ed., *Washington* 5:500; letters to the New York legislature from Washington, Sept. 1, 8, letter to the president of Congress from Washington, Sept. 2, to H. Mercer from Washington, Sept. 3, and to Trumbull from Washington, Sept. 9, 1776, ibid. 6:3, 6, 9–10, 35, 39–40; in Congress, Sept. 3, letter to Washington from A. Yates, Sept. 9, Massachusetts General Court, Sept. 12, and letter to Washington from J. Powell, Sept. 13, 1776, in GWP, ser. 4, reel 38.

17. Letter to H. Mercer from Washington, Sept. 5, and to W. Heath from Washington, Sept. 5, 1776, in Fitzpatrick, ed., *Washington* 6:18–19.

18. Lundin, *Cockpit of the Revolution*, 96–97, 274–75; Hoffman, *Revolutionary Scene*, 20; Aug. 31, 1776, in New Jersey Legislative Journal, 1776, 3–4; letter to H. Mercer from W. Livingston, Sept. 1, to the legislature from W. Livingston, Sept. 11, and to W. Livingston from M. Williamson, Sept. 15, 1776, in Prince and Ryan, eds., *Livingston Papers* 1:133, 144, 147.

19. Extract of a letter to Gen. Wayne from S. Delany, Sept. 5, 1776, in Wayne Papers; letter to W. Livingston from H. Mercer, Aug. 29, 1776, in Prince and Ryan, eds., *Livingston Papers* 1:130; to Washington from H. Mercer, Sept. 7, 17, 1776, in GWP, ser. 4, reel 38.

20. In Committee of Safety for the State of New York, Aug. 29, and letter to Col. J. Drake from G. Clinton, Aug. 29, to unknown recipient from G. Clinton, Sept. 1, to the president of the Convention of the State of New York from G. Clinton, Sept. 3, and to W. Heath from G. Clinton, Sept. 10, 1776, in PGC 1:328–29, 331, 334, 343–45; letter

356 ★ NOTES TO PAGES 74–78

to Washington from A. Yates, Aug. 30, 31, and in convention, Sept. 7, 1776, in GWP, ser. 4, reel 38; Chittenden, *Orderly Book,* 27.

21. Letter to Washington from Trumbull, Sept. 5, 1776, in GWP, ser. 4, reel 38; meeting of the governor and Council of Safety, Sept. 5–6, 1776, in Hoadly and Trumbull, eds., *Colony of Connecticut* 15:514–15; letter to J. Douglas from Trumbull, Sept. 1, 1776, in JDP, no. 7.

22. Letter to Washington from W. Duer, Aug. 30, and to Washington from Trumbull, Sept. 5, 1776, in GWP, ser. 4, reel 38; in Committee of Safety for the State of New York, Sept. 3, and letter to the president of the convention of the State of New York from G. Clinton, Sept. 8, 1776, in *PGC* 1:332, 338–39.

23. Buel, *Dear Liberty,* 81; in Committee of Safety of the State of New York, Sept. 4, letter to Washington from A. Yates, Sept. 4, and to Washington from Trumbull, Sept. 5, 1776, in GWP, ser. 4, reel 38; letter to the Committee of Safety of New York from Washington, Sept. 6, 1776, in Fitzpatrick, ed., *Washington* 6:20; Sept. 4, 1776, in *JNY* 1:606; meeting of the governor and Council of Safety, Sept. 10, 1776, in Hoadly and Trumbull, eds., *Colony of Connecticut* 15:518–19.

24. Christopher Ward, *The War of the Revolution* 1:240–41; Johnston, *Campaign of 1776,* 232–36; George F. Scheer and Hugh F. Rankin, *Rebels and Redcoats,* 198, 203–5; Peckham, ed., *Toll of Independence,* 23.

25. Scheer and Rankin, *Rebels and Redcoats,* 206; Ward, *War of the Revolution* 1:243; Johnston, *Campaign of 1776,* 237, 239, and letter to his wife from G. Silliman, Sept. 17, 1776, pt. 2:54–55.

26. Letter to the president of Congress from Washington, Sept. 16, 1776, in Fitzpatrick, ed., *Washington* 6:58; Freeman, *Washington* 6:195; Johnston, *Campaign of 1776,* 242.

27. Ward, *War of the Revolution* 1:246, 248, 250; Johnston, *Campaign of 1776,* 256–58; Spaulding, *George Clinton,* 62–63; Peckham, ed., *Toll of Independence,* 23.

28. Chittenden, *Orderly Book,* 40, 42–43, 62, 64; General Orders, Sept. 26, 28, Oct. 14, 1776, in Fitzpatrick, ed., *Washington* 6:119–20, 126, 206; letter to Washington from J. Clinton, Oct. 1, 1776, in GWP, ser. 4, reel 38; letter to the president of Congress from [R. H. Harrison], Oct. 14, 1776, in ibid., ser. 2, reel 5; orders—Heath, Oct. 3, 1776, in JDP, no. 9; letter to Jabez Huntington from Jed Huntington, Oct. 12, 1776, Revolutionary Papers, vol. 1, Bancroft Collection, New York Public Library, New York City; Thayer, *Greene,* 111.

29. Letter to Trumbull from Washington, Sept. 30, to B. Lincoln from Washington, Sept. 30, and to G. Clinton from Washington, Sept. 30, 1776, in Fitzpatrick, ed., *Washington* 6:135–36, 141–42; letter to Washington from N. Cooke, Oct. 5, and to Washington from Trumbull, Oct. 11, 21, 1776, in GWP, ser. 4, reel 38; letter to B. Lincoln from J. Hobart, Oct. 17, 1776, no. 4851, Emmet Collection.

30. Ward, *War of the Revolution* 1:249, 255–57; Johnston, *Campaign of 1776,* 265–66, 271; letter to the president of Congress from Washington, Sept. 18, 1776, in Fitzpatrick, ed., *Washington* 6:67–69; letter to J. Hancock from R. H. Harrison, Oct. 20, 25, 1776, in GWP, ser. 3A, reel 14; Alden, *Lee,* 143–44; Dann, ed., *Revolution Remembered,* 51; letter to G. Germain from W. Howe, Nov. 30, 1776, in Davies, ed., *Documents* 12:258–60.

31. Ward, *War of the Revolution* 1:257; Johnston, *Campaign of 1776,* 271, 273; Dann, ed., *Revolution Remembered,* 51; letter to J. Hancock from R. H. Harrison, Oct. 25, and to J. Hancock from Washington, Oct. 29, 1776, in GWP, ser. 3A, reel 14; letter to G. Germain from W. Howe, Nov. 30, 1776, in Davies, ed., *Documents* 12:258–60.

32. Peckham, ed., *Toll of Independence,* 25; Johnston, *Campaign of 1776,* 273–75, and letter to his wife from G. Silliman, Oct. 29, 1776, in pt. 2:56–57; Dann, ed., *Revolution*

Remembered, 53–54, 113–14; MacDougall, *American Revolutionary*, 88–90; letter to J. Hancock from Washington, Oct. 29, 1776, in GWP, ser. 3A, reel 14; letter to G. Germain from W. Howe, Nov. 30, 1776, in Davies, ed., *Documents* 12:258–60.

33. Letter to Washington from N. Greene, Oct. 31, and to N. Greene from R. H. Harrison, Nov. 5, 1776, in GWP, ser. 4, reel 38; letter to N. Greene from R. H. Harrison, Nov. 3, 1776, ser. 3B, reel 17; letter to G. Germain from W. Howe, Nov. 30, 1776, in Davies, ed., *Documents* 12:260–61; Dann, ed., *Revolution Remembered*, 51.

34. Letters to Washington from Trumbull, Sept. 20, Oct. 31, in Congress, Nov. 4, and to Washington from J. Hancock, Nov. 6, 1776, in GWP, ser. 4, reel 38; letter to Trumbull from R. H. Harrison, Nov. 2, 1776, ser. 3C, reel 22; letter to J. Hancock from Trumbull, Sept. 21, 1776, in JTP, vol. 29:81; letter to the officer commanding the Massachusetts militia from Washington, Sept. 19, to the president of Congress from Washington, Sept. 24, and General Orders, Oct. 7, 1776, in Fitzpatrick, ed., *Washington* 6:74–75, 106, 171; General Assembly, Oct. 10–Nov. 7, 1776, in Charles J. Hoadly, et al., eds., *The Public Records of the State of Connecticut, with the Journal of the Council of Safety, and an Appendix* 1:16–17.

35. Letters to the president of Congress from Washington, Sept. 24, Oct. 4, 1776, in Fitzpatrick, ed., *Washington* 6:110–12, 155; Carp, *Starve the Army*, 67; letter to N. Cooke from N. Greene, Sept. 17, Oct. 11, 1776, in Showman, ed., *Greene* 1:300, 314; letter to the convention of the State of New York from G. Clinton, Sept. 18, 1776, in *PGC* 1:354.

36. Letter to S. Washington from Washington, Oct. 5, 1776, in Fitzpatrick, ed., *Washington* 6:168–69.

37. Letter to L. Carter from F. Lee, Sept. 15, and to the states from J. Hancock, Sept. 24, 1776, in Smith, ed., *Letters* 5:173, 229; letter to Washington from J. Hancock, Sept. 24, 1776, in GWP, ser. 4, reel 38; letter to Trumbull from J. Hancock, Sept. 24, 1776, in JTP, vol. 29:530.

38. Letter to H. Mercer from Washington, Sept. 26, to B. Lincoln from Washington, Oct. 7, to the president of Congress from Washington, Oct. 11, to Col. T. Nash from Washington, Oct. 13, and to Maj. Z. Rogers from Washington, Oct. 21, 1776, in Fitzpatrick, ed., *Washington* 6:120–21, 176, 196–97, 204, 221; Tues., Nov. 5, 1776, in Ford and Hunt, eds., *Journals of Continental Congress* 6:925–26.

39. General Assembly, Oct. 1776, in Hoadly, *State of Connecticut* 1:26–27, 37, 42; letter to Washington from Trumbull, Oct. 13, 1776, in GWP, ser. 4, reel 38; in Committee of Safety of New York, Oct. 10, and to the [convention] from G. Clinton, Oct. 23, 1776, in *PGC* 1:375–76, 390; Oct. 11, 1776, in *JNY* 1:670.

40. Letter to the commanding officers at Mount Washington from W. Miller, Oct. 1, and to Washington from P. Livingston, Oct. 10, 1776, in GWP, ser. 4, reel 38; letter to the president of Congress from [R. H. Harrison], Oct. 14, 1776, ibid., ser. 2, reel 5; letter to G. Clinton from J. McKesson, Sept. 24, and in Committee of Safety of New York, Oct. 10, 1776, in *PGC* 1:361, 376; Oct. 17, 20, 1776, in "Minutes of the Committee and First Commission for Detecting Conspiracies" 57:1–3, 5; General Assembly, Oct. 1776, in Charles J. Hoadly et al., eds., *The Public Records of the State of Connecticut, with the Journal of the Council of Safety, and an Appendix* 1:27–28.

41. Letter to N. Greene from H. Mercer, Nov. 4, 1776, in Showman, ed., *Greene* 1:332; General Assembly, Sept. 14, Oct. 5, 1776, in New Jersey General Assembly Journals, 12, 35–36 (hereafter NJGA); letter to Washington from H. Mercer, Sept. 18, Oct. 16, 1776, in GWP, ser. 4, reel 38; letter to the [General] Assembly from W. Livingston, Sept. 24, Oct. 5, and to N. Greene from W. Livingston, Oct. 24, 1776, in Prince and Ryan, eds., *Livingston Papers* 1:150, 158, 170–71; letter to G. Read from Col. S. Patterson, Oct. 17, 1776, in Revolutionary Papers, vol. 1.

42. Letter to G. Germain from W. Howe, Nov. 30, 1776, in Davies, ed., *Documents* 12:261; General Orders, Nov. 5, letter to the Massachusetts legislature from Washington, Nov. 6, to the president of Congress from Washington, Nov. 6, to N. Greene from Washington, Nov. 7, to C. Lee from Washington, Nov. 10, 12, and to W. Heath from Washington, Nov. 12, 1776, in Fitzpatrick, ed., *Washington* 6:241–42, 247–50, 254, 263–66, 274–75; Council of War, Nov. 6, and letter to Trumbull from [Harrison], Nov. 7, 1776, in GWP, ser. 4, reel 38.

43. Letter to W. Livingston from Washington, Nov. 7, to N. Greene from Washington, Nov. 8, and to the president of Congress from Washington, Nov. 9, 16, 1776, in Fitzpatrick, ed., *Washington* 6:255–58, 261–62, 287; letter to Washington from N. Greene, Nov. 18, 1776, in GWP, ser. 4, reel 38; letter to G. Germain from W. Howe, Nov. 30, 1776, in Davies, ed., *Documents* 12:261.

44. Letter to Washington from W. Livingston, Nov. 9, 1776, in GWP, ser. 4, reel 38; letter to the New Jersey militia colonels from W. Livingston, Nov. 17–23, 1776, in Prince and Ryan, eds., *Livingston Papers* 1:178–79.

45. Letter to G. Germain from W. Howe, Nov. 30, 1776, in Davies, ed., *Documents* 12:262–63; Freeman, *Washington* 4:248–52; Ward, *War of the Revolution* 1:270–71; Dann, ed., *Revolution Remembered,* 117; Peckham, ed., *Toll of Independence,* 26; Thayer, *Greene,* 122–23.

46. Howe, *Narrative,* 7; letter to G. Germain from W. Howe, Nov. 30, 1776, in Davies, ed., *Documents* 12:363; letter to N. Cooke from N. Greene, Dec. 4, 1776, in Showman, ed., *Greene* 1:362; Peckham, ed., *Toll of Independence,* 26.

47. Letter to the president of Congress from Washington, Nov. 14, 19, and to W. Livingston from Washington, Nov. 21, 1776, in Fitzpatrick, ed., *Washington* 6:279, 294, 301–3; letter to C. Lee from W. G., Nov. 20, 1776, in GWP, ser. 4, reel, 38; letter to P. Schuyler from R. H. Harrison, Nov. 20, 1776, in ser. 3B, reel 17; letter to G. Germain from W. Howe, Nov. 30, 1776, in Davies, ed., *Documents* 12:263.

48. Letter to [Jabez Huntington?] from Jed Huntington, Nov. 21, 1776, in JTP, vol. V, no. 267; letter to C. Lee from Washington, Nov. 21, and to the president of Congress from Washington, Nov. 23, 1776, in Fitzpatrick, ed., *Washington* 6:298, 303–4; to P. Dickinson from W. Livingston, Nov. 24, and to M. Williamson from W. Livingston, Nov. 25, 1776, in Prince and Ryan, eds., *Livingston Papers* 1:187–88; letter to Washington from J. Hancock, Nov. 24, in Congress, Nov. 25, to Washington from T. Mifflin, Nov. 26, and to P. Schuyler from [R. H. Harrison?], Nov. 26, 1776, in GWP, ser. 4, reel 38; letter to G. Read from the Committee of Congress, Nov. 25, and to the Maryland Council of Safety from S. Chase, Nov. 26, 1776, in Smith, ed., *Letters* 5:542, 544.

49. Letter to Washington from W. Livingston, Nov. 27, 1776, in GWP, ser. 4, reel 38; "An Act for the raising of four Battalions," Nov. 27, 1776, in New Jersey Session Laws, 1776–83, 9, 11; letter to G. Read from S. Patterson, Nov. 30, 1776, in Revolutionary Papers, vol. 1; letter to W. Livingston from a Committee of Congress, Nov. 25, 1776, in Smith, ed., *Letters* 5:540, 542; *Pennsylvania Journal,* Nov. 27, 1776, in Moore, comp., *Diary,* 183; Dann, ed., *Revolution Remembered,* 51; letter to N. Cooke from N. Greene, Dec. 4, 1776, in Showman, ed., *Greene* 1:362; Thayer, *Greene,* 130; letter to the president of Congress from Washington, Nov. 30, and to W. Livingston from Washington, Nov. 30, 1776, in Fitzpatrick, ed., *Washington* 6:312–15.

50. Letter to D. Forman from Washington, Nov. 24, to the president of Congress from Washington, Nov. 27, 30, and to W. Livingston from Washington, Nov. 30, 1776, in Fitzpatrick, ed., *Washington* 6:307, 310, 312–15.

51. Letter to J. Trumbull from the Provincial Convention, Dec. 8, and Dec. 9, 1776, in *JNY* 1:745–46; letter to Trumbull from P. Van Cortlandt, Dec. [1], 1776, in JTP, vol. 5, no. 276.

52. Letter to W. Livingston from Washington, Dec. 1, to the president of Congress from Washington, Dec. 1, 2, 3, and to C. Lee from Washington, Dec. 3, 1776, in Fitzpatrick, ed., *Washington* 6:320–26.

53. Two letters to Col. J. Reed from C. Lee, Nov. 16, 21, to J. Bowdoin from C. Lee, Nov. 21, and to the president of the Massachusetts Council from C. Lee, Nov. 22, 1776, in "Lee Papers" 5:284, 291–92, 301, 303–4; order from Gen. Lee, Nov. 20, 1776, in JDP, no. 13; in Committee of Safety of New York, Nov. 25, 27, letter to Washington from W. Heath, Nov. 26, and to Washington from C. Lee, Nov. 26, 1776, in GWP, ser. 4, reel 38; letter to C. Lee from Washington, Nov. 21, 24, 1776, in Fitzpatrick, ed., *Washington* 6:299, 306; letter to G. Clinton from J. McKesson, Nov. 26, 1776, in *PGC* 1:434.

54. Letter to W. Heath from Washington, Nov. 29, and to C. Lee from Washington, Nov. 29, 1776, in Fitzpatrick, ed., *Washington* 6:311–12; letter to Washington from C. Lee, Nov. 30, and to Washington from J. Scott, Nov. 30, 1776, in GWP, ser. 4, reel 38; in Committee of Safety of New York, Nov. 30, 1776, in *PGC* 1:437; in Committee of Safety of New York, Dec. 8, 1776, in JTP, vol. 5, no. 277.

55. Letter to C. Lee from D. Wooster, Nov. 12, and to C. Lee from W. Palfrey, Nov. 13, 1776, in "Lee Papers" 5:274–75, 278; letter to D. Wooster from C. Lee, Nov. 13, 1776, no. 5578, Emmet Collection; letter to Trumbull from D. Wooster, Nov. 18, 1776, in JTP, vol. 5, no. 252; letter to [J. Hancock] from Trumbull, Nov. 30, 1776, ibid., vol. 29:84; letter to C. Lee from Washington, Nov. 30, 1776, in GWP, ser. 4, reel 38; Tues., Dec. 10, 1776, in Ford and Hunt, eds., *Journals of Continental Congress* 6:1021.

56. Letter to the president of the Convention of the State of New York from G. Clinton, Dec. 1, 1776, in *PGC* 1:440; letter to Washington from W. Heath, Dec. 2, 1776, in GWP, ser. 4, reel 39; Dec. 2–3, 1776, in Heath, *Memoirs,* 88–89; letter to J. Spencer from C. Lee, Dec. 2, 1776, in "Lee Papers" 5:328; Nov. 30, 1776, in *JNY* 1:725.

57. Letters to the president of Congress from Washington, Dec. 5, 6, 1776, in Fitzpatrick, ed., *Washington* 6:330–34.

58. Two letters to G. Germain from W. Howe, Nov. 30, 1776, in Davies, ed., *Documents* 12:263–64; Johann Ewald, *Diary of the American War: A Hessian Journal,* 18, 22; George Inman, "George Inman's Narrative of the American Revolution," 239.

59. Letter to G. Germain from W. Howe, Dec. 20, 1776, in Davies, ed., *Documents* 12:266; Dann, ed., *Revolution Remembered,* 51; Howe, *Narrative,* 7; Ewald, *Diary,* 24–25, 27, 30.

60. Ewald, *Diary,* 25, 27; letter to G. Germain from W. Howe, Dec. 20, 1776, in Davies, ed., *Documents* 12:266–67; letter to Washington from J. Cadwalader, Dec. 15, 1776, in GWP, ser. 4, reel 39; Howe, *Narrative,* 7; "Observations upon a Pamphlet intitled Letters to a Nobleman," in ibid., 68; Ira Gruber, *The Howe Brothers and the American Revolution,* 339.

61. Letter to G. Germain from W. Howe, Dec. 20, 1776, in Davies, ed., *Documents* 12:266–67; Bill, *Princeton,* 17, 35; Howe, *Narrative,* 8–9.

62. Letter to the Pennsylvania Council of Safety from Washington, Dec. 10, to L. Washington from Washington, Dec. 10, to Trumbull from Washington, Dec. 12, to J. Hancock from Washington, Dec. 16, and to R. Morris from Washington, Dec. 25, 1776, in Fitzpatrick, ed., *Washington* 6:344, 347, 352, 379, 436–37; letter to Washington from M. Williamson, Dec. 8, to Washington from C. Lee, Dec. 11, and to Washington from W. Heath, Dec. 28, 1776, in GWP, ser. 4, reel 39; Dwyer, *Day Is Ours,* 163.

63. Letter to Washington from J. Cadwalader, Dec. 7, 1776, "Revolutionary War Correspondence," no. 54, Revolutionary War, box 27, Department of Defense, Military Records, New Jersey State Archives, Trenton; letter to Col. Cadwalader from W. Grayson, Dec. 15, 1776, ibid., 93–94; letter to W. Maxwell from Washington, Dec. 8, to the Pennsylvania Council of Safety from Washington, Dec. 9, 16, to C. Lee from Washington, Dec. 10, to J. Cadwalader from Washington, Dec. 11, 12, to J. Ewing from Washington,

Dec. 12, to P. Dickinson from Washington, Dec. 12, to the president of Congress from Washington, Dec. 13, to J. Washington from Washington, Dec. 18, to J. Kirkbride from Washington, Dec. 19, to N. Cooke from Washington, Dec. 21, to L. Gordon from Washington, Dec. 22, to the colonels of the militia of Northampton County from Washington, Dec. 22, to J. Spencer from Washington, Dec. 22, and to the commanding officer of the Massachusetts militia on their march to Peekskill from Washington, Dec. 24, 1776, in Fitzpatrick, ed., *Washington* 6:337–38, 341, 347–48, 358, 360–64, 382, 397, 400, 413, 423–24, 426–28, 431; letter to Washington from J. Bowdoin, Dec. 8, to J. Cadwalader from W. G., Dec. 15, in Council of Safety, Dec. 17, and letter to Washington from J. Hancock, Dec. 23, 1776, in GWP, ser. 4, reel 39; letter to the Convention of New York from Trumbull, Dec. 12, 1776, in JTP, vol. 20, no. 137.

64. Memorandum for R. Humpton, Dec. 5, letter to C. Lee from Washington, Dec. 10, to J. Sullivan from Washington, Dec. 15, and to the president of Congress from Washington, Dec. 20, 1776, in Fitzpatrick, ed., *Washington* 6:329, 340–41, 375, 407; Alden, *Lee*, 145, 147–48, 151–55, 161; letter to C. Lee from W. Heath, Dec. 8, to the Committee of Congress from C. Lee, Dec. 8, and to H. Gates from C. Lee, Dec. 12–13, 1776, in "Lee Papers" 5:336, 338–39, 348; letter to Washington from C. Lee, Dec. 4, 8 (two), 11, and to Washington from W. Heath, Dec. 8, 1776, in GWP, ser. 4, reel 39; letter to J. Sullivan from J. Eustace, Nov. 19, to D. Coe from J. Sullivan, Dec. 6, to C. Lee from J. Caldwell, Dec. 12, and to J. Sullivan from Washington, Dec. 15, 1776, in Hammond, ed., "Letters of Sullivan" 13:301, 303, 305; Ewald, *Diary*, 24; Whittemore, *Sullivan*, 44.

65. Dwyer, *Day Is Ours*, 132, 139, 201; letter to the president of Congress from Washington, Dec. 20, 1776, in Fitzpatrick, ed., *Washington* 6:407.

66. Letter to W. Heath from Washington, Dec. 7, 1776, in Fitzpatrick, ed., *Washington* 6:335; in Committee of Safety for the State of New York, Dec. 9, 11, and letter to the colonels in Orange and Ulster counties from G. Clinton, Dec. 9, 1776, in *PGC* 1:454–56, 458, 461–62; letter to Washington from M. Contine, Dec. 11, 1776, in GWP, ser. 4, reel 39.

67. Letter to Washington, from W. Heath, Dec. 11, 15, 1776, in GWP, ser. 4, reel 39; letter to the president of Congress from Washington, Dec. 12, and to W. Heath from Washington, Dec. 16, 1776, in Fitzpatrick, ed., *Washington* 6:356, 385; letter to J. Duane from G. Clinton, Dec. 14, 1776, in *PGC* 1:467; Dec. 13, 14, 1776, in Heath, *Memoirs*, 91.

68. Letter to W. Heath from G. Clinton, Dec. 16, to the president of the Convention of New York from G. Clinton, Dec. 17, and to W. Allison from G. Clinton, Dec. 17, 1776, in *PGC* 1:467–71; Dec. 16, 19–20, 1776, in Heath, *Memoirs*, 93; letter to W. Heath from Washington, Dec. 18, 1776, in Fitzpatrick, ed., *Washington* 6:392–93; Peckham, ed., *Toll of Independence*, 27.

69. Letter to G. Clinton from I. Keith, Dec. 19, to G. Clinton from A. Ten Broeck, Dec. 19, 25, to G. Clinton from W. Allison, Dec. 20, to A. Ten Broeck from G. Clinton, Dec. 21, to the Convention from G. Clinton, Dec. 23, 24, and to Col. Heathorn from G. Clinton, Dec. 23, 1776, in *PGC* 1:472–73, 476–77, 479, 488–92; Dec. 20, 22–23, 1776, in Heath, *Memoirs*, 93, 95.

70. Letter to C. Lee from J. Caldwell, Dec. 12, 1776, in Hammond, ed., "Letters of Sullivan" 13:303–4; letter to Washington from W. Heath, Dec. 11, 21, to A. McDougall from Morristown citizens, Dec. 19, and to Washington from A. McDougall, Dec. 19, 1776, in GWP, ser. 4, reel 39; MacDougall, *American Revolutionary*, 91.

71. Letter to the president of Congress from Washington, Dec. 20, and to W. Maxwell from Washington, Dec. 21, 1776, in Fitzpatrick, ed., *Washington* 6:407, 414–15; letter to Washington from A. McDougall, Dec. 22, 1776, in GWP, ser. 4, reel 39.

72. Ewald, *Diary*, 30–38; Stephen Conway, "'The great mischief Complain'd of': Reflections on the Misconduct of British Soldiers in the Revolutionary War," 370, 377; General Orders, Jan. 1, 1777, in Fitzpatrick, ed., *Washington* 6:466.

73. Letter to Washington from J. Reed, Dec. 22, 1776, in GWP, ser. 4, reel 39; letter to R. Morris from Washington, Dec. 22, and to the president of Congress from Washington, Dec. 24, 1776, in Fitzpatrick, ed., *Washington* 6:421, 432; Peckham, ed., *Toll of Independence*, 27.

74. Letter to G. Germain from W. Howe, Dec. 20, to G. Germain from the Commissioners for Restoring Peace in America, Dec. 22, and to G. Germain from W. Tryon, Dec. 24, 1776, in Davies, ed., *Documents* 12:268, 274, 275; Nelson, "Tryon," 278; Gruber, *Howe Brothers*, 156.

75. Bill, *Princeton*, 12, 15; Higginbotham, *War and Society*, 122; Richard Ketchum, *The Winter Soldiers*, 294–95.

76. Letter to Washington from P. Dickinson, Dec. 24, 1776, in GWP, ser. 4, reel 39; Higginbotham, *War and Society*, 122; Thayer, *Greene*, 140–41.

77. Dwyer, *Day Is Ours*, 211–17; Bill, *Princeton*, 37; Ewald, *Diary*, 38–39, 44.

78. Thayer, *Greene*, 140; letter to J. Cadwalader from Washington, Dec. 25, 1776, in Revolutionary War, box 27, no. 55; letter to J. Cadwalader from Washington, Dec. 25, and to R. Morris from Washington, Dec. 27, 1776, in Fitzpatrick, ed., *Washington* 6:438, 441; Bill, *Princeton*, 45; Higginbotham, *War of Independence*, 166.

79. Scheer and Rankin, *Rebels and Redcoats*, 238; Bill, *Princeton*, 28.

80. Dwyer, *Day Is Ours*, 251; Craig L. Symonds, *A Battlefield Atlas of the American Revolution*, 30; Bill, *Princeton*, 57; Peckham, ed., *Toll of Independence*, 27; letter to R. Morris from Washington, Dec. 27, 1776, in Fitzpatrick, ed., *Washington* 6:441.

81. Letter to I. Putnam from Washington, Dec. 25, and to J. Cadwalader from Washington, Dec. 27, 1776, in Fitzpatrick, ed., *Washington* 6:440, 446–47; letter to Washington from J. Cadwalader, Dec. 25, 26, 27, and to J. Cadwalader from T. Tilghman, Dec. 27, 1776, in GWP, ser. 4, reel 39; letter to I. Putnam from J. Cadwalader, Dec. 27, 1776, in Wayne Papers, vol. 1.

82. Bill, *Princeton*, 72–74; letter to W. Heath from Washington, Dec. 28, 1776, in Fitzpatrick, ed., *Washington* 6:447.

83. Letter to W. Heath from Washington, Dec. 28, to A. McDougall from Washington, Dec. 28, and to W. Maxwell from Washington, Dec. 28, 1776, in Fitzpatrick, ed., *Washington* 6:448–50; MacDougall, *American Revolutionary*, 92; letter to Washington from W. Maxwell, Dec. 29, and to Washington from A. McDougall, Dec. 30, 1776, in GWP, ser. 4, reel 39.

84. Fri., Dec. 27, 1776, in Ford and Hunt, eds., *Journals of Continental Congress* 6:1045; in Congress, Dec. 27, 1776, in GWP, ser. 4, reel 39; letter to J. Trumbull from J. Hancock, Dec. 30, 1776, in JTP, vol. 29:493–94; letter to W. Livingston from the president of the Continental Congress, Dec. 30, 1776, in *Selections from the Correspondence of New Jersey*, 21–22; letter to the Friends of America in New Jersey from Washington, Dec. 31, 1776, and to the president of Congress from Washington, Jan. 1, 1777, in Fitzpatrick, ed., *Washington* 6:460–63.

85. Dwyer, *Day Is Ours*, 293–94, 310; letter to the president of Congress from Washington, Jan. 1, and General Orders, Jan. 1, 1777, in Fitzpatrick, ed., *Washington* 6:460–63, 466; to Washington from J. Cadwalader, Dec. 28, and to Washington from T. Mifflin, Dec. 28, 1776, in GWP, ser. 4, reel 39; Bill, *Princeton*, 82.

86. Letter to G. Germain from W. Howe, Jan. 5, 1777, in Davies, ed., *Documents* 14:27; Inman, "Narrative," 239–40; Dwyer, *Day Is Ours*, 336.

87. Letter to G. Germain from W. Howe, Jan. 5, 1777, in Davies, ed., *Documents* 14:27; Ward, *War of the Revolution* 1:308–9; Dwyer, *Day Is Ours,* 317–18.

88. Letter to the president of Congress from Washington, Jan. 5, 1777, in Fitzpatrick, ed., *Washington* 6:467–68; letter to G. Germain from W. Howe, Jan. 5, 1777, in Davies, ed., *Documents* 14:27.

89. Peckham, ed., *Toll of Independence,* 29; letter to the president of Congress from Washington, Jan. 5, 1777, in Fitzpatrick, ed., *Washington* 6:469; Dwyer, *Day Is Ours,* 337, 341, 344; Ketchum, *Winter Soldiers,* 350, 358–59; letter to G. Germain from W. Howe, Jan. 5, 1777, in Davies, ed., *Documents* 14:27; Bill, *Princeton,* 101–3, 105.

90. Letter to the president of Congress from Washington, Jan. 5, 1777, in Fitzpatrick,ed., *Washington* 6:469; Ketchum, *Winter Soldiers,* 361–62; Freeman, *Washington* 4:355; Dwyer, *Day Is Ours,* 348; Ward, *War of the Revolution* 1:314–15; Sergeant Thomas Sullivan, "Battle of Princeton," 55; Bill, *Princeton,* 108–10; letter to G. Germain from W. Howe, Jan. 5, 1777, in Davies, ed., *Documents* 14:27.

91. Letter to the president of Congress from Washington, Jan. 5, 1777, in Fitzpatrick, ed., *Washington* 6:469; Freeman, *Washington* 4:355; Dwyer, *Day Is Ours,* 354; Sullivan, "Battle of Princeton," 56; Bill, *Princeton,* 112.

92. Letter to the president of Congress from Washington, Jan. 5, 1777, in Fitzpatrick, ed., *Washington* 6:469; Ketchum, *Winter Soldiers,* 373; letter to G. Germain from W. Howe, Jan. 5, 1777, in Davies, ed., *Documents* 14:27; Peckham, ed., *Toll of Independence,* 29; Bill, *Princeton,* 113; "The Old Soldiers of the King," in Brand, *Songs of '76,* 88–89.

93. Sullivan, "Battle of Princeton," 56; letter to G. Germain from W. Howe, Jan. 5, 1777, in Davies, ed., *Documents* 14:28; Ketchum, *Winter Soldiers,* 380; letter to the president of Congress from Washington, Jan. 5, 1777, in Fitzpatrick, ed., *Washington* 6:469–70; Peckham, ed., *Toll of Independence,* 29.

94. Letter to the president of Congress from Washington, Jan. 5, 1777, in Fitzpatrick, ed., *Washington* 6:470; letter to G. Germain from W. Howe, Jan. 5, 1777, in Davies, ed., *Documents* 14:28.

95. Letter to the president of Congress from Washington, Jan. 5, 7, and to I. Putnam from Washington, Jan. 5, 1777, in Fitzpatrick, ed., *Washington* 6:470–72, 477–78; letter to the Council of Safety from J. Cadwalader, Jan. 10, 1777, no. 8781, Emmet Collection.

96. Letter to the president of Congress from Washington, Jan. 7, 9, and to R. Morris, G. Clymer, and G. Walton from Washington, Jan. 12, 1777, in Fitzpatrick, ed., *Washington* 6:477, 487, 504; Peckham, ed., *Toll of Independence,* 29; letter to G. Germain from W. Howe, Jan. 5, 1777, in Davies, ed., *Documents* 14:27; Ketchum, *Winter Soldiers,* 381; letter to the Council of Safety from J. Cadwalader, Jan. 10, 1777, no. 8781, Emmet Collection.

97. Letter to Earl Cornwallis from Washington, Jan. 8, 1777, in Fitzpatrick, ed., *Washington* 6:480.

98. Letter to T. Day from G. Clinton, Dec. 26, to Col. Pawling from G. Clinton, Dec. 27, to Cols. Allison and Heathorn from G. Clinton, Dec. 28, to the president of the Convention of the State of New York from G. Clinton, Dec. 28, 1776, to W. Heath from G. Clinton, Jan. 1, 2, and in Committee of Safety of the State of New York, Jan. 1, 1777, in *PGC* 1:216–17, 494, 498, 502, 504–5, 518, 522.

99. In Committee of Safety of New York, Jan. 4, General Orders, Jan. 6, letter to W. Heath from G. Clinton, Jan. 6, to [the Convention of New York] from G. Clinton, Jan. 6, to W. Allison from G. Clinton, Jan. 13, and to Washington from G. Clinton, Jan. 21, 1777, in *PGC* 1:529, 532–35, 546–47, 564.

100. Letter to Trumbull from Washington, Dec. 12, to B. Lincoln from Washington, Dec. 18, and to W. Heath from Washington, Dec. 27, 1776, in Fitzpatrick, ed., *Washington* 6:353, 394, 445; in convention of the representatives of the State of New York, Dec.

19, 21, 1776, in *PGC* 1:480–81, 485–86; letter to Washington from W. Heath, Dec. 26, 1776, in GWP, ser. 4, reel 39.

101. Letter to Washington from W. Heath, Jan. 4, 9, 19, and [Heath's Summons], Jan. 18, 1777, in GWP, ser. 4, reel 39; Hall, *Parsons,* 81–82; letter to W. Heath from Washington, Jan. 5, 12, and to B. Lincoln from Washington, Jan. 7, 1777, in Fitzpatrick, ed., *Washington* 6:472–73, 476, 497; Jan. 8, 10, 13–15, 17, 1777, in Heath, *Memoirs,* 98–99.

102. Letter to G. Germain from W. Howe, Jan. 20, 1777, in Davies, ed., *Documents* 14:33.

103. Letter to Washington from W. Heath, Jan. 24, 30, Council of War, Jan. 28, and letter to Washington from W. Duer, Jan. 28, 1777, in GWP, ser. 4, reel 39; Jan. 19–20, 22–23, 29, 1777, in Heath, *Memoirs,* 99–102, 104; letter to W. Heath, from Washington, Jan. 27, Feb. 3, 1777, in Fitzpatrick, ed., *Washington* 7:71, 94–95.

104. Dec. 22, 28, 31, 1776, Jan. 3, 6, 1777, in "Minutes of the Committee . . . for Detecting Conspiracies," 30–31, 43, 57, 71, 80, 95–96; General Assembly, Dec., 1776, in Hoadly et al., *State of Connecticut* 1:116–17, 142; letter to Trumbull from A. Ten Broeck, Dec. 24, in JTP, vol. 5, no. 328; letter to Lt. G. Burr from Trumbull, Dec. 26, 1776, ibid., vol. 20, no. 138.

105. Letter to P. Henry from R. H. Lee, Jan. 9, and to J. Hancock from executive committee, Jan. 10, 1777, in Smith, ed., *Letters* 6:74, 79; letter to the Pennsylvania Council of Safety, from Washington, Jan. 12, 1777, in Fitzpatrick, ed., *Washington* 6:504–5; letter to J. Custis from Washington, Jan. 22, 1777, ibid. 7:52–53; extract of Washington's order, [Jan. ?, 1777], in Revolutionary War, box 27, no. 31; letter to Washington from Trumbull, Nov. 30, 1776, in GWP, ser. 4, reel 38.

106. Gruber, "First Battle," 3; idem, *Howe Brothers,* 155–56; letter to G. Germain from W. Howe, Jan. 20, 1777, in Davies, ed., *Documents* 14:33.

107. Mackesy, *War for America,* 17, 47; letter to W. Howe from G. Germain, Mar. 3, 1777, in Davies, ed., *Documents* 14:46–47.

108. Ewald, *Diary,* 44; Ketchum, *Winter Soldiers,* 381–82.

CHAPTER FIVE
Partisan War Erupts, January–May 1777

1. Letter to J. Reed from Washington, Jan. 14, to the president of Congress from Washington, Jan. 17, Feb. 14, to W. Heath from Washington, Feb. 2, 3, to I. Putnam from Washington, Feb. 3, and to S. Parsons from Washington, Feb. 8, 1777, in Fitzpatrick, ed., *Washington* 7:16, 22–23, 90–91, 94–97, 119–20, 146; to J. Cadwalader from Washington, Jan. 23, 1777, in Revolutionary War, box 27, no. 56.

2. Letter to the president of Congress from Washington, Jan. 22, to W. Livingston from Washington, Feb. 4, to the president of Congress from Washington, Feb. 5, 28, to the New York Committee of Safety from Washington, Feb. 8, to P. Schuyler from Washington, Feb. 23, and to J. Washington from Washington, Feb. 24, 1777, in Fitzpatrick, ed., *Washington* 7:48, 99, 105, 118, 196, 198, 205; letter to Washington from P. Dickinson, Feb. 13, 1777, in GWP, ser. 4, reel 40; Harry M. Ward, *Charles Scott and the "Spirit of '76,"* 23, 28–30; Peckham, ed., *Toll of Independence,* 29–30; letter to Mrs. Smyth from J. Murray, Feb. 25, 1777, in Robson, ed., *Letters from America,* 38–39.

3. Ewald, *Treatise,* 117–19.

4. Idem, *Diary,* 53; letter to Mrs. Smyth from J. Murray, Feb. 25, 1777, in Robson, ed., *Letters from America,* 39–41; letter to Washington from I. Putnam, Feb. 18, 1777, in GWP, ser. 4, reel 40.

5. Letter to G. Read from C. Rodney, Jan. 23, 1777, in Revolutionary Papers, vol. 1; letter to I. Putnam from W. McElwy, W. Parker, and S. Davidson, Feb. 7, to Washington

from I. Putnam, Feb. 8, to Washington from P. Dickinson, Feb. 9, 20, to Washington from W. Maxwell, Feb. 18, and to Washington from Stirling, Feb. 26, 1777, in GWP, ser. 4, reel 40; active operations Feb. 8–23, 1777, in *PGC* 1:622–23.

6. Letter to G. Germain from W. Howe, Apr. 24, 1777, in Davies, ed., *Documents* 14:72; Ewald, *Diary*, 56–57; letter to L. Carter from Washington, Apr. 15, and to A. McDougall from Washington, Apr. 17, 1777, in Fitzpatrick, ed., *Washington* 7:413, 427; letter to J. Hancock from I. Putnam, Apr. 9, 1777, in Revolutionary Papers, vol. 1; letter to Trumbull from Joseph Trumbull, Apr. 19, 1777, in JTP, vol. 6, no. 81; Bernhard A. Uhlendorf, trans., *Revolution in America: Confidential Letters and Journals 1776–1784 of Adjutant General Major Baurmeister of the Hessian Forces*, 86–87; Peckham, ed., *Toll of Independence*, 34.

7. Letter to Stirling from Washington, Feb. 4, to G. Clinton from Washington, Mar. 31, and to the president of Congress from Washington, Apr. 18, 1777, in Fitzpatrick, ed., *Washington* 7:101, 340, 434; letter to Washington from P. Dickinson, Feb. 20, 1777, in GWP, ser. 4, reel 40.

8. Letter to L. Carter from Washington, Apr. 15, 1777, in Fitzpatrick, ed., *Washington* 7:413.

9. Champagne, *McDougall*, 120; MacDougall, *American Revolutionary*, 95; letter to Washington from W. Heath, Feb. 7, and to Washington from A. McDougall, Feb. 16, Mar. 7, 1777, in GWP, ser. 4, reel 40; Feb. 6, 1777, in Heath, *Memoirs*, 106.

10. Letter to Washington from A. McDougall, Mar. 7, 12, 1777, in GWP, ser. 4, reel 40; letter to the Convention of the State of New York from G. Clinton, Mar. 16, 23, and to the commanding officer at Ft. Montgomery from A. Hawkes Hay, Mar. 23, 1777, in *PGC* 1:666, 676, 679.

11. Gruber, *Howe Brothers*, 191; letter to P. Stephens from Vice Admiral Howe, Mar. 31, 1777, in Davies, ed., *Documents* 14:58–59; letter to Trumbull from Washington, Mar. 29, and to A. McDougall from Washington, Apr. 2, 1777, in Fitzpatrick, ed., *Washington* 7:333, 347; Mar. 25, 1777, in *JNY* 1:848; letter to Washington from H. Livingston, Mar. 29, and to Washington from A. McDougall, Mar. 29, 1777, in GWP, ser. 4, reel 40; Peckham, ed., *Toll of Independence*, 32.

12. Letter to A. Hawkes Hay from G. Clinton, Mar. 24, to Col. Pawling from G. Clinton, Mar. 24, and to G. Clinton from A. Hawkes Hay, Mar. 24, 1777, in *PGC* 1:679–82.

13. Ranlet, Loyalists, 147, 149; Carl Van Doren, *Secret History of the American Revolution*, 13.

14. Jan. 31, Feb. 1, 1777, in Heath, *Memoirs*, 105; letter to D. Wooster from W. Heath, Feb. 3, 8, 1777, nos. 1203, 8795, Emmet Collection; letter to Washington from W. Heath, Feb. 5, 6, 7, and to W. Heath from W. Duer, Feb. 6, 1777, in GWP, ser. 4, reel 40.

15. Letter to the president of the Convention of New York from W. Duer, Feb. 17, 25, to the Convention of New York from D. Wooster, Feb. 17, and to the president of the Convention of New York from W. Duer, Feb. 25, 1777, in *JNY* 2:366–67, 369, 376; letter to Washington from W. Heath, Feb. 7, to Washington from D. Wooster, Feb. 21, Mar. 2, 28, to Washington from W. Duer, Mar. 2, and to Washington from A. McDougall, Mar. 7, 1777, in GWP, ser. 4, reel 40; letter to W. Duer from Washington, Mar. 6, and to D. Wooster from Washington, Mar. 11, 1777, in Fitzpatrick, ed., *Washington* 7:255, 271.

16. Letter to A. McDougall from N. Sackett, Mar. 12, to Washington from A. McDougall, Mar. 29, Apr. 12, and to Washington from G. Clinton, Apr. 18, 1777, in GWP, ser. 4, reels 40–41; in convention of the representatives of the State of New York, Apr. 7, letter to G. Clinton from Richard Hatfield, Apr. 7, orders from G. Clinton, Apr. 9, and letter to G. Clinton from A. McDougall, Apr. 21, 1777, in *PGC* 1:701, 703–4, 706–7, 724; letter to the president of the Convention of New York from A. McDougall, Apr. 21, 1777, in *JNY* 2:425.

17. Letter to Lt. Daniel [Wail?] from S. Parsons, Feb. 16, and to Washington from S. Parson, Feb. 23, Mar. 6, May 11, 25, 1777, in GWP, ser. 4, reels 40–41; letter to S. Parsons from Washington, Mar. 20, 1777, in Fitzpatrick, ed., *Washington* 7:306–7; Dann, ed., *Revolution Remembered*, 324–25; Ward, *War of the Revolution* 1:323–24; Peckham, ed., *Toll of Independence*, 34.

18. Letter to Trumbull from L. Lay, Jan. 7, to Trumbull from T. Burr, Jan. 20, to Trumbull from T. Burr, Mar. 8, 21, and to T. Burr from Trumbull, Mar. 25, 1777, in JTP, vol. 6, nos. 8, 15, 59, 64, 67; letter to Messrs. Newall and Farmington from Trumbull, Mar. 20, and to G. Silliman from Trumbull, Mar. 24, 1777, ibid., vol. 20, nos. 142–43; letter to P. Schuyler from Trumbull, Mar. 10, 1777, ibid., vol. 26:116–17; meeting of the governor and Council of Safety, Jan. 27, Mar. 8, Apr. 12, 1777, in Hoadly et al., *State of Connecticut* 1:162, 189, 207; letter to Washington from G. Silliman, Mar. 7, 1777, in GWP, ser. 4, reel 40.

19. Letter to Washington from S. Parsons, Apr. 22, 1777, in GWP, ser. 4, reel 41; letter to S. Parsons from Washington, Apr. 23, and to G. Clinton from Washington, Apr. 26, 1777, in Fitzpatrick, ed., *Washington* 7:459–60, 474; letter to W. Howe from G. Germain, Mar. 3, 1777, in Davies, ed., *Documents* 14:48.

20. Letter to G. Germain from W. Howe, Apr. 24, May 22, 1777, in Davies, ed., *Documents* 14:72, 91; letter to A. McDougall from J. Huntington, Apr. 26, 27, to A. McDougall from B. Arnold, Apr. [27], and to Washington from Trumbull, May 4, 1777, in GWP, ser. 4, reel 41; letter to H. Gates from Col. H. Hughes, May 3, 1777, in Revolutionary Papers, vol. 1.

21. Freeman, *Washington* 4:410; Van Doren, *Secret History*, 158–59; Ward, *War of the Revolution* 2:494; letter to A. McDougall from B. Arnold, Apr. [27], to A. McDougall from J. Campbell, Apr. 27, and to A. McDougall from J. Field, Apr. 27, 1777, in GWP, ser. 4, reel 41; letter to G. Germain from W. Howe, May 22, 1777, in Davies, ed., *Documents* 14:91.

22. Letter to H. Gates from H. Hughes, May 3, 1777, in Revolutionary Papers, vol. 1; Ward, *War of the Revolution* 2:494; to G. Germain from W. Howe, May 22, 1777, in Davies, ed., *Documents* 14:91; "A Skirmish in America Between the Kings Troops & Genl. Arnold"; Dann, ed., *Revolution Remembered*, 101; "Mr. [Jesse] Brown's Relation of the Destruction of the Stores, and Burning Buildings in Danbury, 26th Instant," Apr. 30, 1777, in JTP, vol. 6, no. 90; letter to A. McDougall from B. Arnold, Apr. 28, to A. McDougall from [H.] Hughes, Apr. 28, and to Washington from Trumbull, May 4, 1777, in GWP, ser. 4, reel 41.

23. Letter to H. Gates from H. Hughes, May 3, 1777, in Revolutionary Papers, vol. 1; letter to "Gentlemen" from Trumbull, Apr. 29, "Mr. (Jesse) Brown's Relation . . . ," Apr. 30, and letter to Trumbull from J. Wadsworth, May 1, 1777, in JTP, vol. 6, nos. 86, 90, 94; letter to Washington from A. McDougall, Apr. 27, to A. McDougall from B. Arnold, Apr. 28, to A. McDougall from [H.] Hughes, Apr. 28, and to Washington from Trumbull, May 4, 1777, in GWP, ser. 4, reel 41; meeting of the governor and Council of Safety, Apr. 27, 1777, in Hoadly et al., *State of Connecticut* 1:214.

24. Letter to G. Germain from W. Howe, May 22, 1777, in Davies, ed., *Documents* 14:91; Ward, *War of the Revolution* 2:494–95; letter to A. Babcock from G. Silliman, Apr. 29, "Mr. [Jesse] Brown's Relation . . . ," Apr. 30, and letter to Trumbull from J. Wadsworth, May 1, 1777, in JTP, vol. 6, nos. 87, 90, 94; letter to A. McDougall from J. Huntington, Apr. 28, and to A. McDougall from B. Arnold, Apr. 28, 1777, in GWP, ser. 4, reel 41; letter to H. Gates from Col. H. Hughes, May 3, 1777, in Revolutionary Papers, vol. 1.

25. Letter to Washington from A. McDougall, Apr. 29, 1777, in GWP, ser. 4, reel 41; to A. McDougall from Washington, May 1, 1777, in Fitzpatrick, ed., *Washington* 8:1.

26. Letter to W. Ellery from O. Wolcott, Sr., May 13, 1777, no. 2435, Emmet Collection; letter to A. McDougall from J. Huntington, Apr. 28, to A. McDougall from [H.]

Hughes, Apr. 28, to A. McDougall from B. Arnold, Apr. 28, to Washington from J. Hancock, May 3, and to Washington from Trumbull, May 4, 1777, in GWP, ser. 4, reel 41; letter to H. Gates from H. Hughes, May 3, 1777, in Revolutionary Papers, vol. 1; letter to the president of Congress from Washington, May 5, and to Trumbull from Washington, May 11, 1777, in Fitzpatrick, ed., *Washington* 8:17–18, 42; letter to Abigail Adams from J. Adams, Apr. 30, 1777, in Smith, ed., *Letters* 6:687; Peckham, ed., *Toll of Independence,* 33; Van Doren, *Secret History,* 159; letter to G. Germain from W. Howe, May 22, 1777, in Davies, ed., *Documents* 14:91.

27. Letter to G. Germain from W. Howe, May 22, 1777, in Davies, ed., *Documents* 14:91.

28. Warren, *History* 1:201; Ewald, *Diary,* 55; Karl Bauer[?], "Platte Grenadier Battalion Journal," qtd. in Ewald, *Treatise,* 157; letter to Mrs. Smyth from J. Murray, Feb. 25, 1777, in Robson, ed., *Letters from America,* 38, 42; Lundin, *Cockpit of the Revolution,* 319.

29. German journals quoted in Ewald, *Treatise,* 157; Uhlendorf, *Revolution in America,* 86; Inman, "Narrative," 240; Conway, "To Subdue America," 398; idem, "The Great Mischief," 389.

30. Gruber, *Howe Brothers,* 191, 193; letter to W. Howe from G. Germain, Apr. 19, 1777, in Davies, ed., *Documents* 14:69–70.

31. Letter to Trumbull from S. Parsons, Apr. 9, to [Trumbull] from E. Dyer and N. Wale, Jr., Apr. 30, and to Trumbull from J. Shipman, May 1, 1777, in JTP, vol. 6, nos. 74, 92, 96; speech to the Council and House of Representatives by Trumbull, May 8, 1777, ibid., vol. 20, no. 146; letter to J. Douglas from Trumbull, Apr. 30, May 5, 1777, in JDP, nos. 16–17; meeting of the governor and Council of Safety, May 4, and General Assembly, May 2–June 7, 1777, in Hoadly et al., *State of Connecticut* 1:218, 230, 242; Stuart, *Trumbull,* 363.

32. General Assembly, May 2–June 7, 1777, in Hoadly et al., *State of Connecticut* 1:260; letter to Washington from Trumbull, May 4, and to Washington from S. Parsons, May 11, 25, 1777, in GWP, ser. 4, reel 41.

33. Letter to the president of the Convention of the State of New York from G. Clinton, Feb. 13, to Washington from G. Clinton, Feb. 23, to the convention from G. Clinton, Mar. 8, to G. Clinton from A. Ten Broeck, Mar. 18, meeting of the field officers of Brig. Gen. G. Clinton's brigade, Mar. 31, letter to Col. M. Graham from G. Clinton, Apr. 3, and in convention of the representatives of the State of New York, May 13, 1777, in *PGC* 1:593, 619, 655, 671, 687, 695, 836; Spaulding, *George Clinton,* 71.

34. Letter to the Convention of the State of New York from M. Jackson, Apr. 1, 1777, and to the Convention of the State [of New York] from G. Clinton, Apr. 22, 1777, in *PGC* 1:696, 725.

35. Letter to Trumbull from Washington, Mar. 29, 1777, in Fitzpatrick, ed., *Washington* 7:332–33; meeting of the field officers of Brig. Gen. G. Clinton's brigade, Mar. 31, brigade orders, Mar. 31, letter to [Washington] from G. Clinton, Apr. 1, to Col. M. Graham from G. Clinton, Apr. 3, and to the convention of the state from G. Clinton, Apr. 22, 1777, in *PGC* 1:687–88, 692, 695, 726; letter to Washington from A. McDougall, Apr. 12, 17, and to Washington from G. Clinton, Apr. 18, 1777, in GWP, ser. 4, reel 41.

36. Letter to Col. Pawling from G. Clinton, Feb. 10, 24, to the president of the Convention of the State of New York from G. Clinton, Feb 13, 23, to Washington from G. Clinton, Feb. 23, and in the Committee of Safety for the State of New York, Feb. 26, 1777, in *PGC* 1:586, 592, 616–17, 619, 624, 633.

37. Letter to A. St. Clair from G. Clinton, Mar. 22, to the Convention of the State of New York from G. Clinton, Mar. 23, to G. Clinton from Col. Pawling, Mar. 23, brigade orders, Mar. 31, to [Washington] from G. Clinton, Apr. 1, to G. Clinton from J. Blauvalt and J. Bell, Apr. 7, and weekly return of Col. J. Hathorn's regiment, Apr. 18, 1777, in *PGC* 1:673, 676–78, 689, 691, 701–2, 720.

38. Letter to G. Clinton from C. Tappen, Feb. 28, to G. Clinton from Col. Pawling, Mar. 1, to Col. Pawling from G. Clinton, Mar. 7, to [Washington] from G. Clinton, Apr. 1, to S. Mills from G. Clinton, Apr. 5, to G. Clinton from B. Tusten, Apr. 6, to J. Decker from I. Van Campen, P. Van Neste, and S. Westbrook, Apr. 6, to B. Tusten from G. Clinton, Apr. 8, and in convention of the representatives of the State of New York, Apr. 21, 1777, in *PGC* 1:637, 639, 652, 692–93, 696–700, 723–24.

39. Letter to Col. Woodhull from G. Clinton, [Apr. 25], to G. Clinton from J. Blauveldt, Apr. 26, to G. Clinton from G. Cooper, Apr. 26, to G. Clinton from T. Machin, May 2, to the president of the Convention from G. Clinton, May 4, to G. Clinton from J. Hardenburgh, May 5, in convention of the representatives of the State of New York, May 5, return of the troops at Fts. Constitution and Independence, May 13, and return of the troops stationed at Ft. Montgomery, May 29, 1777, in *PGC* 1:733, 734–35, 741, 787, 796, 800, 802; letter to Washington from A. McDougall, May 5, 29, 1777, in GWP, ser. 4, reels 41–42.

40. Letter to Washington from G. Clinton, May 1, 1777, in GWP, ser. 4, reel 41; letter to the convention from G. Clinton, Apr. 26, to Col. Hathorn from G. Clinton, Apr. 26, to G. Clinton from G. Cooper, Apr. 26, General Orders, Apr. 27, and letter to G. Clinton from the Committee of Bedford, May 9, 1777, in *PGC* 1:736–37, 740, 744, 801.

41. Return of the troops at Fts. Constitution and Independence, May 13, and return of the troops stationed at Ft. Montgomery, May 29, 1777, in *PGC* 1:817, 844; letter to Washington from A. McDougall, May 29, and to Washington from I. Putnam, May 31, 1777, in GWP, ser. 4, reel 42.

42. Jan. 24, Feb. 3, 5, 1777, in NJGA, card no. 15466, pp. 52, 56, 58; letter to W. Livingston from Washington, Jan. 24, 1777, in Fitzpatrick, ed., *Washington* 7:56–57; letter to Washington from W. Livingston, Feb. 1, 1777, in GWP, ser. 4, reel 39; letter to J. Jay from W. Livingston, Mar. 3, 1777, in Prince and Ryan, eds., *Livingston Papers* 1:265.

43. Mar. 7, 1777, in NJGA, card no. 15466, p. 94; letter to Washington from W. Livingston, Mar. 3, 1777, in GWP, ser. 4, reel 40; letter to W. Livingston from Washington, Mar. 8, 1777, in Fitzpatrick, ed., *Washington* 7:264; letter to the [General] Assembly from W. Livingston, Mar. 11, 1777, in Prince and Ryan, eds., *Livingston Papers* 1:273–74.

44. "An Act for the better regulating the Militia," Mar. 15, and "An Act for investing the Governor and a Council, consisting of twelve, with certain Powers therein mentioned for a limited Time," Mar. 15, 1777, in New Jersey Session Laws, card no. 15459, pp. 30–31, 40–42; letter to W. Livingston from Washington, Apr. 1, 1777, in Fitzpatrick, ed., *Washington* 7:344; letter to Washington from W. Livingston, Apr. 4, 1777, in GWP, ser. 4, reel 40.

45. Letter to P. Dickinson from W. Livingston, Jan. 14, and to W. Livingston from I. Putnam, Feb. 10, 18, 1777, in Prince and Ryan, eds., *Livingston Papers* 1:197, 220, 241–42; letter to Washington from P. Dickinson, Feb. 13, to I. Putnam from W. Livingston, Feb. 13, to Washington from W. Livingston, Feb. 15, and to Washington from W. Maxwell, Feb. 17, 1777, in GWP, ser. 4, reel 40.

46. Letter to Washington from W. Livingston, Feb. 10, 1777, in GWP, ser. 4, reel 40; letter to P. Dickinson from W. Livingston, Mar. 1, 1777, in Prince and Ryan, eds., *Livingston Papers* 1:260; letter to N. Heard from Washington, Apr. 7, 1777, in Fitzpatrick, ed., *Washington* 7:367; to W. Livingston from P. Dickinson, Feb. 12, 1777, in *Selections from the Correspondence of New Jersey,* 30–31; Feb. 15, 1777, in New Jersey Legislative Journal, 15–16.

47. Letter to Washington from W. Livingston, Apr. 4, 1777, in GWP, ser. 4, reel 40.

48. Letter to Washingtor. from W. Livingston, May 2, to Washington from N. Heard, May 14, and to R. Peters from D. Forman, May 27, 1777, in GWP, ser. 4, reel 41.

49. Letter to G. Clinton from W. Livingston, Jan. 15, and to J. Jay from W. Livingston, Mar. 3, 1777, in Prince and Ryan, eds., *Livingston Papers* 1:198–99, 265.

50. Letters to the president of Congress from Washington, Jan. 19, Feb. 5, 20, to the Pennsylvania Council of Safety from Washington, Jan. 19, circular to the New England states from Washington, Jan. 24, to C. Rodney from Washington, Feb. 18, and to John A. Washington from Washington, Feb. 24, 1777, in Fitzpatrick, ed., *Washington* 7:30, 34–35, 58–59, 104, 160, 168, 198.

51. Letter to the president of Congress from Washington, Feb. 28, Mar. 14, to R. Morris from Washington, Mar. 2, to H. Gates from Washington, Mar. 4, to Trumbull from Washington, Mar. 6, to N. Ramsay from Washington, Mar. 29, and to W. Livingston from Washington, Apr. 1, 1777, in Fitzpatrick, ed., *Washington* 7:205, 223, 245, 253–54, 288, 335, 345.

52. Letter to J. Kirkbride from Washington, Jan. 14, to J. Reed from Washington, Jan. 14, circular to the states from Washington, Jan. 31, to G. Clinton from Washington, Feb. 19, Apr. 23, to W. Livingston from Washington, Apr. 5, to A. Stephen from Washington, Apr. 20, to A. McDougall from Washington, Apr. 23, and to N. Heard from Washington, Apr. 23, 1777, in Fitzpatrick, ed., *Washington* 7:13, 16, 82, 165, 363, 443, 455, 460–61.

53. Letter to J. Reed from Washington, Jan. 15, to Stirling from Washington, Jan. 19, and to I. Putnam from Washington, Feb. 20, 1777, in Fitzpatrick, ed., *Washington* 7:18, 33, 174–75.

54. Letter to P. Dickinson from Washington, Jan. 21, Feb. 18, to W. Maxwell from Washington, Feb. 18, to A. McDougall from Washington, Feb. 20, Apr. 17, to W. Livingston from Washington, Feb. 22, Apr. 1, to Trumbull from Washington, Mar. 6, and to G. Clinton from Washington, Apr. 20, 1777, in Fitzpatrick, ed., *Washington* 7:45–46, 158–59, 179, 186, 254–55, 344–45, 425–26, 444; meeting of the governor and Council of Safety, Mar. 20, 1777, in Hoadly et al., *State of Connecticut* 1:196.

55. Letter to N. Cooke from Washington, Jan. 20, to S. Parsons from Washington, Feb. 18, to G. Silliman from Washington, Mar. 11, to A. McDougall from Washington, Mar. 15, and to the president of Congress from Washington, Mar. 26, 1777, in Fitzpatrick, ed., *Washington* 7:42–44, 156, 269, 293, 317–18.

56. Thomas Burke, abstract of debates, Feb. 24, [1777], in Burnett, ed., *Letters* 2:274; Mon., Feb. 24, 1777, in Ford and Hunt, eds., *Journals of Continental Congress* 7:149–50; letter to W. Livingston from J. Hancock, Feb. 25, and to the New York Convention from J. Hancock, Feb. 25, 1777, in Smith, ed., *Letters* 6:365–67; letter to Washington from J. Hancock, Feb. 25, Apr. 26, May 10, and in Congress, Mar. 18, Apr. 25, 1777, in GWP, ser. 4, reels 40–41.

57. Arrangement and present strength of the army in Jersey, May 20, 1777, in GWP, ser. 4, reel 41; letter to W. Livingston from Washington, Apr. 29, 1777, in Fitzpatrick, ed., *Washington* 7:492; letter to the president of Congress from Washington, May 12, and to P. Henry from Washington, May 17, 1777, ibid. 8:46, 77.

CHAPTER SIX
The Militia Takes Over the Defenses, May–December 1777

1. Council of General Officers, May 2, and letter to Washington from N. Greene, H. Knox, A. Wayne, and G. Clinton, May 17, 1777, in GWP, ser. 4, reel 41; letter to A. McDougall from Washington, May 7, 10, to Trumbull from Washington, May 23, to

I. Putnam from Washington, May 25, 30, and to S. Parsons from Washington, May 25, 1777, in Fitzpatrick, ed., *Washington* 8:26, 39, 104, 121–22, 125, 144; Johann Conrad Dohla, *A Hessian Diary of the American Revolution,* 37.

2. Letter to W. Livingston from P. Dickinson, Feb. 12, 1777, in *Selections of the Correspondence of New Jersey,* 30–31; Feb. 15, 1777, New Jersey Legislative Journal, 15–16; letter to N. Heard from R. Harrison, May 15, and to W. Winds from T. Tilghman, May 16, 1777, in GWP, ser. 3B, reel 17; letter to W. Livingston from Washington, Apr. 29, 1777, in Fitzpatrick, ed., *Washington* 7:493; letter to N. Greene from Washington, May 12, to A. Stephen from Washington, May 19, to N. Heard from Washington, May 24, to J. Olney from Washington, May 28, and to J. Sullivan from Washington, May 29, June 1, 1777, ibid. 8:51, 87, 118–19, 135–36, 163–64.

3. Letter to J. Sullivan from Washington, June 1, and to F. Barber from Washington, June 1, 1777, in Fitzpatrick, ed., *Washington* 8:163, 165–66; letter to Washington from N. Heard, June 5, and to Washington from D. Forman, June 10, 1777, in GWP, ser. 4, reel 42; instructions to Gen. Prudhomme de Borre from J. Sullivan, June 10, 1777, in Hammond, ed., "Letters of Sullivan" 13:378–80.

4. Three letters to S. Parsons from Washington, May 7, 25, 29, to Trumbull from Washington, May 11, 26, to J. Warren from Washington, May 23, and to A. Stephen from Washington, May 24, 1777, in Fitzpatrick, ed., *Washington* 8:27–28, 43–44, 102–3, 119, 124, 126, 140.

5. Letter to N. Greene from J. Sullivan, May 31, to B. Arnold from J. Sullivan, May 31, return of Gen. Sullivan's division, June 1, letter to J. Sullivan from B. Arnold, June 9, and instructions to Brig. Gen. Prudhomme de Borre, June 10, 1777, in Hammond, ed., "Letters of Sullivan" 13:348, 350, 354, 376, 378–79.

6. Ewald, *Diary,* 62; letter to Mrs. Smyth from J. Murray, May 30, [1777], in Robson, ed., *Letters from America,* 45–46; letter to G. Germain from W. Howe, Dec. 20, 1776, in Davies, ed., *Documents* 12:268; letter to G. Germain from W. Howe, Jan. 20, Apr. 2, 1777, ibid. 14:33, 64–65.

7. Letter to G. Germain from W. Howe, Apr. 2, and to G. Carleton from W. Howe, Apr. 5, 1777, in Davies, ed., *Documents* 14:64, 66; Nelson, "Tryon," 279.

8. Gruber, *Howe Brothers,* 325; Howe, *Narrative,* 10, 12–13.

9. Howe, *Narrative,* 18; letter to G. Germain from W. Howe, June 3, 1777, in Davies, ed., *Documents* 14:102.

10. Letter to G. Germain from W. Howe, Jan. 20, Apr. 2, 1777, in Davies, ed., *Documents* 14:33, 65; Howe, *Narrative,* 19.

11. Council of General Officers, June 12, and letter to J. Sullivan from Washington, June 12, 1777, in GWP, ser. 4, reel 42; letter to the president of Congress from Washington, June 2, to Z. Butler from Washington, June 12, and to D. Morgan from Washington, June 13, 1777, in Fitzpatrick, ed., *Washington* 8:168, 236; letter to B. Lincoln from N. Greene, in Showman, ed., *Greene* 2:105.

12. "A Supplemental Act to an Act, entitled, 'An Act for the better regulating the Militia,'" passed June 5, 1777, in New Jersey Session Laws, card no. 15460, pp. 66, 68, 71; June 6, 1777, in New Jersey Legislative Journal, 20–21; letter to J. Sullivan from Washington, June 12, 1777, in Fitzpatrick, ed., *Washington* 8:233.

13. Letter to G. Clinton from J. Hamman, June 4, return of troops at Fort Montgomery, June 12, weekly return of the detachment of militia under Maj. Maurice Pleas, June 12, weekly return of the detachment under Lt. Col. Loring, June 12, and weekly return of Col. Morris Graham's militia at Fort Independence, June 12, 1777, in *PGC* 2:3, 24–27; letter to Washington from I. Putnam, June 9, 13, Council of General Officers, June

12, and letter to Washington from G. Clinton, June 19, 1777, in GWP, ser. 4, reel 42; letter to J. Clinton from Washington, June 8, and to I. Putnam from Washington, June 12, 1777, in Fitzpatrick, ed., *Washington* 8:202, 234.

14. Ewald, *Diary*, 64; letter to G. Germain from W. Howe, July 5, 1777, in Davies, ed., *Documents* 14:127; Dohla, *Hessian Diary*, 37; Peckham, ed., *Toll of Independence*, 35.

15. Letter to the president of Congress from Washington, June 13–15, and to J. Sullivan from Washington, June 14, 1777, in Fitzpatrick, ed., *Washington* 8:241, 244, 246, 248–49; Ewald, *Treatise*, 86.

16. Letter to the president of Congress from Washington, June 13–15, to J. Sullivan from Washington, June 14, 15, and to P. Schuyler from Washington, June 16, 1777, in ibid., 244, 249, 251–53; letter to N. Heard from T. Tilghman, June 14, and to Washington from B. Arnold, June 16, 1777, in GWP, ser. 4, reel 42.

17. Letter to G. Germain from W. Howe, July 5, 1777, in Davies, ed., *Documents* 14:127; letter to P. Schuyler from Washington, June 16, and to B. Arnold from Washington, June 17, 1777, in Fitzpatrick, ed., *Washington* 8:253–54, 259–62; Ewald, *Diary*, 64; Dohla, *Hessian Diary*, 39.

18. Letter to W. Livingston from C. Pettit, June 16, 1777, in Prince and Ryan, eds., *Livingston Papers* 1:355; letter to Washington from P. Dickinson, June 18, 1777, in GWP, ser. 4, reel 42; letter to P. Schuyler from Washington, June 16, and to B. Arnold from Washington, June 17, 1777, in Fitzpatrick, ed., *Washington* 8:253, 261–62; letter to G. Clinton from A. McDougall, June 18, 1777, in *PGC* 2:37.

19. Letter to G. Germain from W. Howe, July 5, 1777, in Davies, ed., *Documents* 14:127; Ewald, *Diary*, 65; letter to Washington from J. Sullivan, June 19, 1777, in GWP, ser. 4, reel 42; letter to [?] Jackson from H. Knox, June 21, 1777, in Revolutionary War, 249–50; letter to the president of Congress from Washington, June 20, 1777, in Fitzpatrick, ed., *Washington* 8:270.

20. Letter to Trumbull from J. Trumbull, June 22, 1777, in JTP, vol. 6, no. 152; letter to the president of Congress from Washington, June 20, and to P. Schuyler from Washington, June 20, 1777, in Fitzpatrick, ed., *Washington* 8:270, 275; letter to the officers and soldiers of the Hunterdon, Burlington, Gloucester, Salem, and Cumberland county militias from Washington, Nov. 20, 1777, ibid. 10:90; letter to [?] Jackson from H. Knox, June 21, 1777, in Revolutionary War, 250–51; letter to his wife from S. Parsons, June 22, 1777, in Hall, *Parsons*, 103; Warren, *History* 1:202.

21. Ewald, *Treatise*, 115; Howe, *Narrative*, 15–16.

22. Hall, *Parsons*, 103; Ewald, *Diary*, 65, 68; *Journal of Cresswell*, 240, 242; letter to G. Germain from W. Howe, July 5, 1777, in Davies, ed., *Documents* 14:127–28; Lt. Col. John G. Simcoe, *Simcoe's Military Journal: A History of the Operations of a Partisan Corps, called the Queen's Rangers, Commanded by Lieut. Col. J. G. Simcoe, During the War of the American Revolution*, 18.

23. Letter to J. Sullivan from Washington, June 21, to the president of Congress from Washington, June 22, 25, and General Orders, June 23, 1777, in Fitzpatrick, ed., *Washington* 8:279–83, 287, 298–99; letter to Trumbull from J. Trumbull, June 22, 1777, in JTP, vol. 6, no. 151.

24. Letter to W. Livingston from P. Dickinson, June 26, 1777, in Prince and Ryan, eds., *Livingston Papers* 1:359; letter to J. Sullivan from Stirling, June 24, 1777, in Hammond, ed., "Letters of Sullivan" 13:401–2; Dohla, *Hessian Diary*, 40.

25. Letter to G. Germain from W. Howe, July 5, 1777, in Davies, ed., *Documents* 14:128; Ewald, *Diary*, 68–69; Dohla, *Hessian Diary*, 40.

26. Letter to G. Germain from W. Howe, July 5, 1777, in Davies, ed., *Documents* 14:128–29; Dohla, *Hessian Diary*, 40; letter to W. Livingston from P. Dickinson, June 26, 1777, in

Prince and Ryan, eds., *Livingston Papers* 1:359; letter to W. Heath from Washington, June 27, and to the president of Congress from Washington, June 28, 1777, in Fitzpatrick, ed., *Washington* 8:305, 307–8; letter to B. Rush from A. Wayne, in Wayne Papers, vol. 1; Ewald, *Diary*, 69; Peckham, ed., *Toll of Independence*, 36.

27. Letter to the president of Congress from Washington, June 28, 29, to I. Putnam from Washington, June 29, 30, and to N. Heard from Washington, July 1, 1777, in Fitzpatrick, ed., *Washington* 8:308–9, 311, 322–23, 325–26; letter to Trumbull from J. Trumbull, June 29, 1777, in JTP, vol. 6, no. 159; letter to B. Rush from A. Wayne, in Wayne Papers, vol. 1.

28. Letter to A. McDougall from Washington, June 20, 1777, in GWP, ser. 3B, reel 17; letter to A. McDougall and J. Glover from Washington, June 20, and to Washington from I. Putnam, June 23, 1777, ser. 4, reel 42; letter to I. Putnam from Washington, June 22, and to G. Clinton from Washington, June 23, 1777, in Fitzpatrick, ed., *Washington* 8:284–85, 292; return of Col. Pawling's regiment, June 25, return of Col. Snyder's regiment, June 25, weekly return of the detachment commanded by Lt. Col. Loring, June 26, weekly return of Col. Morris Graham's regiment, June 26, weekly return of the detachment of militia under Maj. Pleas, June 26, and return of the regiment of foot commanded by Col. Dubois, June 26, 1777, in PGC 2:50, 52, 54–57.

29. Letters to Washington from I. Putnam, June 26, 28, 1777, in GWP, ser. 4, reel 42; letter to I. Putnam from Washington, June 25, 30, July 1, letter to G. Clinton from Washington, July 1, and to the president of Congress from Washington, July 2, 1777, in Fitzpatrick, ed., *Washington* 8:300, 321, 324–27, 329.

30. Letter to the president of the Council of Safety from G. Clinton, July 2, to G. Clinton from the president of the Council of Safety, n.d. [July 2?], and to I. Putnam from G. Clinton, July 3, 1777, in PGC 2:61–62, 74; letter to Washington from I. Putnam, July 4, 1777, in GWP, ser. 4, reel 42.

31. Letter to Trumbull from Washington July 2, to the president of Congress from Washington, July 5, 22, to J. Sullivan from Washington, July 6, 8, 9, 16, General Orders, July 22, and to I. Putnam from Washington, July 22, 1777, in Fitzpatrick, ed., *Washington* 8:336, 353, 358, 371, 373, 414, 446–47, 452–53; letter to J. Washington from Washington, Aug. 5, 1777, ibid. 9:21; letter to Washington from Stirling, July 3, to Washington from I. Putnam, July 21, and to Washington from D. Forman, July 23, 1777, in GWP, ser. 4, reels 42–43; letter to D. Morgan from T. Tilghman, July 11, 1777, no. 1037, Myers Collection, New York Public Library; Sat., July 12, 1777, in Ford and Hunt, eds., *Journals of Continental Congress* 8:549.

32. Letter to W. Winds from W. Livingston, July 3, to W. Livingston from S. Hayes, July 16, and to P. Dickinson from W. Livingston, July 18, 1777, in Prince and Ryan, eds., *Livingston Papers* 2:8, 21–24; July 3, 8, 17, 1777, in *Minutes of the Council of Safety of the State of New Jersey, 1777–1778*, 76–77, 91–92; letter to Washington from D. Forman, July 6, to D. Forman from R. Harrison, July 7, to Washington from W. Livingston, July 8, 11, and to Col. Moylan from D. Forman, July 20, 1777, in GWP, ser. 4, reel 42; letter to J. Armstrong from Washington, July 4, and to W. Livingston from Washington, July 12, 1777, in Fitzpatrick, ed., *Washington* 8:342, 390.

33. Letter to I. Putnam from Washington, July 12, 1777, in Fitzpatrick, ed., *Washington* 8:383; letter to Washington from I. Putnam, July 17, 1777, in GWP, ser. 4, reel 42; return of troops stationed at Forts Montgomery, Constitution, and Independence, July 18, 1777, in PGC 2:119.

34. New York (State) Constitution, 54–55, 92–93, 95.

35. Letter to G. Clinton from C. Tappen, July 7, to the Council of Safety from G. Clinton, July 11, to I. Putnam from G. Clinton, July 14, and to the legislature from

G. Clinton, Aug. 5, 1777, in *PGC* 2:79, 106, 111, 184; in Council of Safety for the State of New York, "A Proclamation," July 30, 1777, New York—State: Governor, 1777–81, Messages and Proclamations of George Clinton, Aug. 1777–Sept. 1781, New York Public Library; letter to the New York Council of Safety from Washington, Aug. 4, 1777, in Fitzpatrick, ed., *Washington* 9:15.

36. Letter to J. Hancock from Trumbull, June 10, 12, 1777, in JTP, vol. 29:109, 119–20; letter to Washington from Trumbull, June 12, 1777, in GWP, ser. 4, reel 42; meeting of the governor and Council of Safety, June 2, 3, July 1, 7, 15, 18, 1777, in Hoadly et al., *State of Connecticut* 1:321, 336, 344, 349, 352.

37. Letter to G. Germain from W. Howe, July 5, 16, 1777, in Davies, ed., *Documents* 14:129, 145; Gruber, *Howe Brothers*, 339.

38. Letter to G. Germain from W. Howe, July 7, 1777, in Davies, ed., *Documents* 14:130; Howe, *Narrative*, 23, 107; Clinton, *American Rebellion*, 63.

39. Letter to Col. Bland from Washington, July 24, 1777, in GWP, ser. 4, reel 43; letter to I. Putnam from Washington, July 24 and 28, General Orders, July 25, to J. Sullivan from Washington, July 29, to H. Gates from Washington, July 30, and to the president of Congress from Washington, July 31, 1777, in Fitzpatrick, ed., *Washington* 8:460, 465, 491–92, 497, 499, 505; letter to I. Putnam from Washington, Aug. 1, to J. Sullivan from Washington, Aug. 3, and to the president of Congress from Washington, Aug. 21, 22, 1777, ibid. 9:1, 6, 111, 118–19.

40. Return of troops at Forts Montgomery, Constitution, and Independence, July 25, letter to I. Putnam from G. Clinton, July 26, and to the Council of Safety from G. Clinton, July 31, 1777, in *PGC* 2:135, 139, 142–43; letter to I. Putnam from Washington, July 25, 31; letter to G. Clinton from Washington, July 25, 1777, in Fitzpatrick, ed., *Washington* 8:466–67, 473–74, 503; letter to Washington from G. Clinton, July 26, to Washington from I. Putnam, July 27, 31, and to I. Putnam from A. Hamilton, July 30, 1777, in GWP, ser. 4, reel 43; letter to Trumbull from Col. J. (Root), July 28, 1777, in JTP, vol. 6, no. 202.

41. Letter to I. Putnam from Washington, July 31, 1777, in Fitzpatrick, ed., *Washington* 8:503; letter to Washington from I. Putnam, July 31, 1777, in GWP, ser. 4, reel 43.

42. Letter to I. Putnam from Washington, Aug. 1, and to G. Clinton from Washington, Aug. 1, 1777, in Fitzpatrick, ed., *Washington* 9:1, 5; letter to P. Schuyler from G. Clinton, Aug. 2, to [various colonels] from G. Clinton, Aug. 5, and to I. Putnam from G. Clinton, Aug. 5, 1777, in *PGC* 2:167, 180, 183–84; letter to Trumbull from I. Putnam, Aug. 3, 1777, in JTP, vol. 7, no. 5; letter to Washington from I. Putnam, Aug. 8, and to Washington from G. Clinton, Aug. 9, 1777, in GWP, ser. 4, reel 43.

43. Letter to I. Putnam from Washington, Aug. 11, and to G. Clinton from Washington, Aug. 13, 1777, in Fitzpatrick, ed., *Washington* 9:55–56, 60–61; letter to Washington from I. Putnam, Aug. 11, 1777, in GWP, ser. 4, reel 43.

44. Letter to I. Putnam from Trumbull, July 30, and to P. Van Cortlandt from Trumbull, Aug. 7, 1777, in JTP, vol. 20, nos. 153–54; letter to [Trumbull] from O. Wolcott, Aug. 5, to O. Wolcott from Trumbull, Aug. 6, and to E. Wolcott from Trumbull, Aug. 6, 1777, ibid., vol. 7, nos. 9, 12, 34; meeting of the governor and Council of Safety, Aug. 6, 1777, in Hoadly et al., *State of Connecticut* 1:362–63; letter to Washington from Trumbull, Aug. 7, 1777, in GWP, ser. 4, reel 43.

45. Buel, *Dear Liberty*, 123; letter to Washington from I. Putnam, Aug. 15, 22, and to Washington from Trumbull, Sept. 1, 1777, in GWP, ser. 4, reel 43; letter to I. Putnam from Washington, Aug. 18, 1777, in Fitzpatrick, ed., *Washington* 9:91–92; letter to Trumbull from I. Putnam, Aug. 21, 1777, in JTP, vol. 7, no. 23; letter to I. Putnam from Trumbull, Aug. 24, 1777, ibid., vol. 20, no. 158.

46. Wed., Aug. 20, 1777, in Ford and Hunt, eds., *Journals of Continental Congress* 8:659; letter to the president of Congress from Washington, Aug. 21, 22, 1777, in Fitzpatrick, ed., *Washington* 9:111, 118–19; letter to W. Winds from W. Livingston, Aug. 28, 1777, in Prince and Ryan, eds., *Livingston Papers* 2:47; letter to Washington from W. Livingston, Aug. 28, 1777, in GWP, ser. 4, reel 43.

47. Letter to Stirling from Washington, July 26, and to E. Dayton from Washington, July 26, 1777, in Fitzpatrick, ed., *Washington* 8:477–78; letter to J. Sullivan from Washington, Aug. 10, and General Orders, Oct. 16, 1777, ibid. 9:44, 380; letter to P. Dickinson from D. Forman, Aug. 17, to Washington from P. Dickinson, Aug. 19, and to Washington from J. Sullivan, Aug. 24, 1777, in GWP, ser. 4, reel 43; Whittemore, *Sullivan*, 55; Clinton, *American Rebellion*, 67–68, 68n.20; Dohla, *Hessian Diary*, 45–46; Frederick Mackenzie, *Diary of Frederick Mackenzie* 1:174–175; letter to J. Hancock from J. Sullivan, Sept. 27, 1777, in Hammond, ed., "Letters of Sullivan" 13:461.

48. Letter to Washington from J. Sullivan, Aug. 24, 1777, in GWP, ser. 4, reel 43; letter to J. Hancock from J. Sullivan, Sept. 27, and to J. Adams from J. Sullivan, Sept. 28, 1777, in Hammond, ed., "Letters of Sullivan" 13:461, 470–71; Peckham, ed., *Toll of Independence*, 39; Whittemore, *Sullivan*, 55; Mackenzie, *Diary* 1:175; Dohla, *Hessian Diary*, 45–46; General Orders, Oct. 16, 1777, in Fitzpatrick, ed., *Washington* 9:380.

49. Letter to S. Parsons from I. Putnam, Aug. 16, 1777, in Hall, *Parsons*, 108; Mackenzie, *Diary* 1:175; Clinton, *American Rebellion*, 67–68, 68n.20; Peckham, ed., *Toll of Independence*, 39.

50. Letter to Col. Webb from S. Parsons, Aug. 29, 1777, in Hall, *Parsons*, 110; Clinton, *American Rebellion*, 69; letter to Washington from I. Putnam, Aug. 30, 1777, in GWP, ser. 4, reel 43.

51. Letter to I. Putnam from Trumbull, July 30, and to P. Van Cortlandt from Trumbull, Aug. 7, 1777, in JTP, vol. 20, nos. 153–54; letter to Washington from I. Putnam, Aug. 11, 1777, in GWP, ser. 4, reel 43.

52. Council, Aug. 14, 1777, in David Bernstein, ed., *Minutes of the Governor's Privy Council, 1777–1789*, 38; letter to Col. Frelinghuysen from Capt. Craig, Aug. 1777, in *Selections of the Correspondence of New Jersey*, 92; letter to W. Livingston from Washington, Aug. 21, 1777, in Fitzpatrick, ed., *Washington* 9:114; letter to Washington from W. Livingston, Aug. 15, 1777, in GWP, ser. 4, reel 43; letter to W. Winds from W. Livingston, Aug. 28, 1777, in Prince and Ryan, eds., *Livingston Papers* 2:47.

53. Lundin, *Cockpit of the Revolution*, 382; letter to W. Livingston from Washington, Sept. 1, and to I. Putnam from R. Harrison, Sept. 10, 1777, in Fitzpatrick, ed., *Washington* 9:159, 201; letter to the Assembly from W. Livingston, Sept. 3, and to J. Hancock from W. Livingston, Sept. 7, 1777, in Prince and Ryan, eds., *Livingston Papers* 2:53–54, 65; Sept. 10, 16, 18, 1777, in NJGA, card no. 16398, pp. 162, 174, 178; letter to I. Putnam from J. Hancock, Sept. 9, 1777, in Smith, ed., *Letters* 7:639.

54. Nelson, "Tryon," 281; Roger Kaplan, "The Hidden War: British Intelligence Operations during the American Revolution," 115, 119, 121.

55. Letter to G. Germain from J. Burgoyne, Aug. 20, and to W. Howe from H. Clinton, Oct. 9, 1777, in Davies, ed., *Documents* 14:166, 198; Clinton, *American Rebellion*, 69–71.

56. Clinton, *American Rebellion*, 71; Dohla, *Hessian Diary*, 47; letter to J. Hancock from P. Dickinson, Sept. 13, and to Washington from W. Malcom, Sept. 13, 1777, in GWP, ser. 4, reel 44; letter to I. Putnam from Washington, Sept. 14, and to A. McDougall or officer commanding the detachment from Peekskill from Washington, Sept. 14, 1777, in Fitzpatrick, ed., *Washington* 9:218, 221; letter to P. Dickinson from W. Livingston, Sept. 14, 1777, in Prince and Ryan, eds., *Livingston Papers* 2:72.

57. Dohla, *Hessian Diary*, 47–50; letter to Washington from W. Malcom, Sept. 14, to Washington from I. Putnam, Sept. 14, to Washington from P. Dickinson, Sept. 15, 17, to

W. Livingston from P. Dickinson, Sept. 16, and to Washington from A. McDougall, Sept. 17, 1777, in GWP, ser. 4, reel 44; letter to J. Hancock from W. Livingston, Sept. 15, 1777, in Prince and Ryan eds., *Livingston Papers* 2:74; letter to Trumbull from I. Putnam, Sept. 17, 1777, in JTP, vol. 7, no. 51.

58. Letter to Washington from P. Dickinson, Sept. 17, to Washington from A. McDougall, Sept. 17, and to J. Hancock from P. Dickinson, Sept. 18, 1777, in GWP, ser. 4, reel 44; Dohla, *Hessian Diary*, 50; Wed., Sept. 17, 1777, in Ford and Hunt, eds., *Journals of Continental Congress* 8:750; letter to Trumbull from S. Parsons, Sept. 19, 1777, in JTP, vol. 7, no. 53; letter to G. Wyllys from J. Wyllys, Sept. 19, 1777, in "Wyllys Papers, 1590–1796," 457.

59. Dohla, *Hessian Diary*, 50; Peckham, ed., *Toll of Independence*, 40.

60. Letter to Washington from P. Dickinson, Sept. 20, Oct. 3, 1777, in GWP, ser. 4, reel 44; letter to P. Dickinson from Washington, Sept. 22, to D. Forman from Washington, Sept. 26, and to W. Livingston from Washington, Oct. 1, 1777, in Fitzpatrick, ed., *Washington* 9:246, 269, 293–94; letter to J. Hancock from W. Livingston, Sept. 17, 1777, in Prince and Ryan, eds., *Livingston Papers* 2:74; Sept. 19, 1777, in NJGA, card no. 16398, p. 178; "An Act for constituting a Council of Safety," Sept. 20, and "An Act to explain and amend an Act, intitled, An act for better regulating the Militia, and the Supplemental Act thereto," Sept. 23, 1777, in New Jersey Session Laws, card no. 15461, pp. 84–86, 98–100.

61. Sept. 10, 13, 17, 1777, Journal of the General Assembly of the State, 1777–92, vol. 1, New York Historical Society, New York City; letter to Brig. Gen. Wolcott from I. Putnam, Sept. 14, and to Trumbull from O. Wolcott, Sept. 16, 1777, in JTP, vol. 7, nos. 48, 50; letter to I. Putnam from Washington, Sept. 14, 1777, in Fitzpatrick, ed., *Washington* 9:219.

62. Two letters to H. Gates from G. Clinton, Sept. 15, 18, and to I. Putnam from G. Clinton, Sept. 15, 1777, in *PGC* 2:322–24, 333; letter to Trumbull from I. Putnam, Sept. 15, 27, and to Trumbull from O. Wolcott, Sept. 16, 25, 1777, in JTP, vol. 7, nos. 49–50, 64, 66; letter to I. Putnam from Washington, Sept. 23, 1777, in Fitzpatrick, ed., *Washington* 9:253.

63. Letter to G. Silliman from S. Parsons, Sept. 27, and to I. Putnam from Trumbull, Sept. 30, 1777, in JTP, vol. 7, nos. 67, 74; letter to I. Putnam from G. Clinton, Sept. [28], 29, to Cols. Field, Ludington, Brinkerhoff, Humphrey, Sutherland, Freer, and Swartwout from G. Clinton, Sept. 29, to Cols. Allison, McClaghry, and Hasbrouck from G. Clinton, Sept. 29, and to G. Clinton from A. Leggett, Sept. 30, 1777, in *PGC* 2:347–51, 353–54; letter to J. Hancock from I. Putnam, Sept. 29, 1777, in GWP, ser. 4, reel 44.

64. Letter to Washington from I. Putnam, Oct. 2, 1777, in GWP, ser. 4, reel 44; letter to Trumbull from S. Parsons, Oct. 3, 1777, in JTP, vol. 7, no. 80; meeting of the governor and Council of Safety, Oct. 3, 1777, in Hoadly et al., *State of Connecticut* 1:407; letter to I. Putnam from Washington, Oct. 7, 1777, in Fitzpatrick, ed., *Washington* 9:325.

65. Letter to H. Clinton from J. Burgoyne, Sept. 27, 28, to J. Burgoyne from H. Clinton, n.d., and to W. Howe from H. Clinton, Oct. 9, 1777, in Davies, ed., *Documents* 14:190–92, 197; Clinton, *American Rebellion*, 72–74, 78.

66. Letter to Trumbull from J. Mead, Oct. 24, 1777, in JTP, vol. 7, no. 150.

67. Letter to W. Howe from H. Clinton, Oct. 9, and to Vice Adm. Howe from Commodore W. Hotham, Oct. 9, 1777, in Davies, ed., *Documents* 14:197–98, 200.

68. Letter to G. Clinton from S. Parsons, Sept. 26, to G. Clinton from J. Clinton, Oct. 4, to J. Clinton from G. Clinton, Oct. 4, to J. Clinton from T. Moffat, Oct. 5, to G. Clinton from I. Putnam, Oct. 6, to G. Clinton from P. Van Cortlandt, Oct. 7, and to G. Clinton from G. Cooper, T. Cuyper, and J. Christie, Oct. 14, 1777, in *PGC* 2:345–46,

360–61, 365, 375–77, 434–35; letter to G. Clinton from I. Putnam, Oct. 4, 1777, no. 8045, Emmet Collection; letter to Washington from A. Hawkes Hay, Oct. 5, and to Washington from I. Putnam, Oct. 8, 1777, in GWP, ser. 4, reel 44.

69. Letter to W. Howe from H. Clinton, Oct. 9, and to Vice Adm. Howe from Commodore W. Hotham, Oct. 9, 1777, in Davies, ed., *Documents* 14:198, 200.

70. Letter to W. Howe from H. Clinton, Oct. 9, and to Vice Adm. Howe from Commodore W. Hotham, Oct. 9, 1777, in ibid., 198, 200; letter to Trumbull from S. Parsons, Oct. 7, 1777, in JTP, vol. 7, no. 93; letter to H. Gates from H. Hughes, Oct. 7, and to the Council of New York from G. Clinton, [Oct. 7, 1777], in Revolutionary Papers, vol. 1; letter to the [legislature] from G. Clinton, Oct. 7, 1777, in *PGC* 2:381–82.

71. Letter to W. Howe from H. Clinton, Oct. 9, and to Vice Adm. Howe from Commodore W. Hotham, Oct. 9, 1777, in Davies, ed., *Documents* 14:198–99, 201; letter to Trumbull from S. Parsons, Oct. 7, 1777, in JTP, vol. 7, no. 93; letter to H. Gates from H. Hughes, Oct. 7, and to the Council of New York from G. Clinton, [Oct. 7, 1777], in Revolutionary Papers, vol. 1; letter to Washington from I. Putnam, Oct. 8, 1777, in GWP, ser. 4, reel 44; letter to the [legislature] from G. Clinton, Oct. 7, 1777, in *PGC* 2:381–82; Warren, *History* 1:243; Peckham, ed., *Toll of Independence*, 42.

72. Letter to W. Howe from H. Clinton, Oct. 9, and to Vice Adm. Howe from Commodore W. Hotham, Oct. 9, 1777, in Davies, ed., *Documents* 14:199, 201.

73. Letter to Washington from I. Putnam, Oct. 8, 1777, in GWP, ser. 4, reel 44; letter to the Council of New York from G. Clinton, [Oct. 7, 1777], in Revolutionary Papers, vol. 1; letter to the [legislature] from G. Clinton, Oct. 7, 1777, in *PGC* 2:382.

74. Letter to Col. Cook and the different colonels of militia on the western border of Connecticut from I. Putnam, Oct. 4, to Col. Canfield and the other commanding officers of militia in Connecticut from I. Putnam, Oct. 5, to Trumbull from S. Parsons, Oct. 7, to J. Wadsworth from S. Parsons, Oct. 8, and to Trumbull from J. Wadsworth, Oct. 11, 1777, in JTP, vol. 7, nos. 81, 84, 93–94, 107.

75. Letter to W. Livingston from Washington, Oct. 8, 1777, in Fitzpatrick, ed., *Washington* 9:339–40; Oct. 10, 1777, in NJGA, card no. 16398, p. 199; letter to Washington from W. Livingston, Oct. 10, 12, 1777, in GWP, ser. 4, reel 44; letter to G. Clinton from P. Dickinson, Oct. 12, 14, to G. Clinton from W. Winds, Oct. 18, and to G. Clinton from J. Clinton, Oct. 20, 23, 1777, in *PGC* 2:420, 432–33, 459–60, 463, 473; letter to H. Gates from G. Clinton, Oct. 21, 1777, in Revolutionary Papers, vol. 1.

76. Letter to W. Howe from H. Clinton, Oct. 9, 1777, in Davies, ed., *Documents* 14:199; letter to Trumbull from J. Wadsworth, Oct. 8, and to G. Clinton from J. Wilkinson, Oct. 9, 1777, in JTP, vol. 7, nos. 96, 101; letter to Washington from I. Putnam, Oct. 8, 1777, in GWP, ser. 4, reel 44; letter to the Council of Safety from G. Clinton, [Oct. 8, 1777], in *PGC* 2:387–89.

77. Letter to the Council of Safety from G. Clinton, Oct. 10, to G. Clinton from W. Floyd, Oct. 10, to Col. Swartwout from G. Clinton, Oct. 10, and to G. Clinton from B. Swartwout, Oct. 11, 1777, in *PGC* 2:402–3, 405, 410, 412.

78. Warren, *History* 1:242–43; letter to G. Wyllys from J. Wyllys, in "Wyllys Papers," 458.

79. Letter to the [Council of Safety] from G. Clinton, Oct. 12, and to I. Putnam from H. Gates, Oct. 15, 1777, in *PGC* 2:423–26, 439–40; return of brigade of militia commanded by G. S. Silliman, Oct. 13, 1777, in JTP, vol. 24, no. 42; letter to Trumbull from I. Putnam, Oct. 15, 1777, ibid., 7, no. 119; letter to G. Wyllys from H. Wyllys, Oct. 14, 1777, in "Wyllys Papers," 459; letter to Washington from I. Putnam, Oct. 16, 1777, in GWP, ser. 4, reel 44.

80. Clinton, *American Rebellion*, 79–80; letter to H. Clinton from J. Vaughan, Oct. 26, 1777, in Davies, ed., *Documents* 14:246–47; letter to H. Gates from G. Clinton, Oct. 16, to

unknown recipient from J. Vaughan, Oct. 17, and to B. Lincoln from G. Clinton, Oct. 22, 1777, in *PGC* 2:444–45, 458, 471; Peckham, ed., *Toll of Independence*, 43.

81. Letter to H. Clinton from J. Vaughan, Oct. 26, 1777, in Davies, ed., *Documents* 14:247; letter to G. Clinton from I. Putnam, Oct. 18, to I. Putnam from G. Clinton, Oct. 18, and to G. Clinton from J. Clinton, Oct. 20, 1777, in *PGC* 2:460–61, 463; letter to Trumbull from R. Flint, Oct. 20, 1777, in JTP, vol. 7, no. 128; Clinton, *American Rebellion*, 80.

82. Letter to H. Gates from G. Clinton, Oct. 21, 1777, in Revolutionary Papers, vol. 1; to G. Clinton from I. Putnam, Oct. 18, and to G. Clinton from J. Clinton, Oct. 23, 1777, in *PGC* 2:460, 473–74.

83. Letter to H. Gates from G. Clinton, Oct. 26, 1777, in *PGC* 2:481; letter to Trumbull from S. Parsons, Oct. 25, 1777, in JTP, vol. 7, no. 144; letter to G. Germain from W. Howe, Oct. 21, and to H. Clinton from J. Vaughan, Oct. 26, 1777, in Davies, ed., *Documents* 14:238, 247; Clinton, *American Rebellion*, 80–81.

84. Letter to unknown recipient from G. Clinton, Oct. 25, to H. Gates from G. Clinton, Oct. 26, to G. Clinton from J. Clinton, Oct. 29, and to the Council of Safety from G. Clinton, Nov. 6, 1777, in *PGC* 2:480–83, 488–89, 500; letter to Trumbull from S. Parsons, Oct. 25, to Trumbull from I. Putnam, Oct. 27, and to H. Gates from I. Putnam, Oct. 31, 1777, in JTP, vol. 7, nos. 144, 146, 155; letter to Washington from I. Putnam, Oct. 25, 27, 31, to H. Gates from G. Clinton, Oct. 30, and to Washington from P. Dickinson, Nov. 6, 1777, in GWP, ser. 4, reels 44–45; Putnam's orders, Oct. 27, 1777, in Numbered Record Books Concerning Military Operations and Service, reel 3, 18:85–86.

85. Letter to G. Clinton from W. Malcom, Oct. 24, 1777, in *PGC* 2:478–79; Council of War convened by I. Putnam, Oct. 31, and to G. Clinton from H. Gates, Nov. 2, 1777, in GWP, ser. 4, reel 45; letter to I. Putnam from Washington, Oct. 26, 1777, in Fitzpatrick, ed., *Washington* 9:440.

86. Letter to I. Putnam from Washington, Oct. 30, 1777, in Fitzpatrick, ed., *Washington* 9:464–65; letter to I. Putnam from Washington, Nov. 4, 9, 11, 1777, ibid. 10:3, 29, 40–41; letter to Washington from I. Putnam, Nov. 3, 1777, in GWP, ser. 4, reel 45; letter to H. Gates from Maj. J. Hughes, Nov. 5, 1777, in Revolutionary Papers, vol. 1; letter to Trumbull from J. Root, Nov. 7, 1777, in JTP, vol. 7, no. 174.

87. Letter to Washington from I. Putnam, Nov. 3, and in Congress, Nov. 5, 1777, in GWP, ser. 4, reel 45; letter to Trumbull from J. Root, Nov. 7, 1777, in JTP, vol. 7, no. 174; letter to I. Putnam from Washington, Nov. 4, to P. Dickinson from Washington, Nov. 4, and to Maj. J. Clark from Washington, Nov. 4, 1777, in Fitzpatrick, ed., *Washington* 10:2–4, 8–9; Wed., Nov. 5, 1777, in Ford and Hunt, eds., *Journals of Continental Congress* 9:865.

88. Letter to Washington from P. Dickinson, Oct. 4, 24, 26, Nov. 1, 2, 28, and to W. Livingston from P. Dickinson, Nov. 7, 1777, in GWP, ser. 4, reels 44–45; letter to P. Dickinson from Washington, Nov. 4, and to J. Varnum from Washington, Nov. 8, 1777, in Fitzpatrick, ed., *Washington* 10:4, 25; Dec. 4, 1777, order book of Maj. Gen. P. Dickinson, in Revolutionary War, box 28, no. 27; Nov. 7, 1777, in NJGA, card no. 16399, p. 13.

89. Letter to [Trumbull] from S. Parsons, Nov. 2, and to Trumbull from J. Ely, Nov. 8, 1777, in JTP, vol. 7, nos. 165, 176; letter to Washington from I. Putnam, Nov. 7, 1777, in GWP, ser. 4, reel 45; letter to G. Clinton from S. Webb, Nov. 10, 1777, in *PGC* 2:512–13.

90. Letter to [Trumbull] from I. Putnam, Nov. 12, and to unknown recipient from Trumbull, Nov. 18, 1777, in JTP, vol. 7, nos. 186, 223; letter to Washington from I. Putnam, Nov. 14, and to Washington from P. Dickinson, Nov. 15, 1777, in GWP, ser. 4, reel 45; meeting of the governor and Council of Safety, Nov. 18, 1777, in Hoadly et al., *State of Connecticut* 1:458.

91. Letter to H. Gates from Col. Hughes, Nov. 27, 1777, in Revolutionary Papers, vol. 3; letter to Washington from P. Dickinson, Nov. 28, to Washington from I. Putnam, Nov. 28, and to Washington from W. Livingston, Dec. 1, 1777, in GWP, ser. 4, reel 45.

92. Letter to Washington from P. Dickinson, Nov. 28, and to Washington from W. Livingston, Dec. 1, 1777, in GWP, ser. 4, reel 45; letter to P. Dickinson from Washington, Dec. 2, 1777, in Fitzpatrick, ed., *Washington* 10:134; letter to Trumbull from I. Putnam, Dec. 16, 1777, in JTP, vol. 7, no. 242.

93. Letter to I. Putnam from Washington, Dec. 2, to H. Gates from Washington, Dec. 2, to P. Dickinson from Washington, Dec. 2, and to G. Clinton from Washington, Dec. 3, 1777, in Fitzpatrick, ed., *Washington* 10:129–31, 134–36; letter to Trumbull from I. Putnam, Dec. 16, 1777, in JTP, vol. 7, no. 242.

94. Letter to G. Clinton from the Committee of Haverstraw, Nov. 22, to the Council of Safety from G. Clinton, Dec. 1, to H. Gates from G. Clinton, Dec. 17, and to G. Clinton from T. Smith, Dec. 25, 1777, in *PGC* 2:537, 558, 587–89, 604; letter to Washington from G. Clinton, Dec. 20, 1777, in GWP, ser. 4, reel 45.

95. Letter to G. Silliman from Trumbull, Dec. 20, and to I. Putnam from Trumbull, Dec. 20, 1777, in JTP, vol. 7, no. 242.

96. Letter to Trumbull from S. Parsons, Dec. 4, prisoners taken by the *Falcon*, Dec. 10, letter to T. Marmford and N. Shaw from J. Ely, Dec. 14, and to Trumbull from Maj. Gen. Huntington, Dec. 14, 1777, in JTP, vol. 7, nos. 214, 228, 237–38; letter to Washington from S. Parsons, Dec. 29, 1777, in GWP, ser. 4, reel 46; letter to I. Putnam from Washington, Dec. 27, 1777, in Fitzpatrick, ed., *Washington* 10:212.

97. Letter to D. Forman from T. Henderson, Oct. 5, to Washington from W. Livingston, Oct. 5, to Washington from D. Forman, Oct. 15, and to Washington from P. Dickinson, Nov. 28, 1777, in GWP, ser. 4, reels 44–45; Dec. 4, 1777, order book of Maj. Gen. P. Dickinson, in Revolutionary War, box 28, no. 27; letter to S. Seely from W. Livingston, Dec. 9, 1777, in Prince and Ryan, eds., *Livingston Papers* 2:133; letter to W. Livingston from Washington, Nov. 24, 1777, in Fitzpatrick, ed., *Washington* 10:103; Dec. 5, 1777, in *Minutes of the Council of Safety,* 169.

98. Letter to G. Germain from W. Howe, Nov. 30, 1777, in Davies, ed., *Documents* 14:264–65; *Journal of Cresswell,* 250, 252; letter to Mrs. Smyth from J. Murray, Sept. 1, 1777, in Robson, ed., *Letters from America,* 48.

99. Letter to Andrew Huntington from Jedediah Huntington, Aug. 5, 1777, in "Huntington Papers," 360.

CHAPTER SEVEN
The Militia in a Changing War, 1778

1. Letter to Washington from La Radiere, Jan. 13, 1778, in GWP, ser. 4, reel 46; letter to Trumbull from I. Putnam, Jan. 14, and to Trumbull from G. Clinton, Mar. 6, 1778, in JTP, vol. 8, nos. 46, 98; letter to H. Gates from G. Clinton, Feb. 5, 1778, in *PGC* 2:711; letter to G. Clinton from S. Parsons, Mar. 10, 1778, ibid. 3:15; proclamation by Gov. Clinton, Feb. 18, and message of Gov. Clinton to the Senate, Mar. 21, 1778, in New York Governor; message from Gov. Clinton, Mar. 10, 1778, in Journal of the General Assembly of New York, vol. 1.

2. Letter to S. Parsons from G. Clinton, [Mar. 11], to Lafayette from G. Clinton, Mar. 13, to G. Clinton from A. McDougall, Apr. 3, to A. McDougall from G. Clinton, Apr. 5, and to G. Clinton from Trumbull, Apr. 10, 1778, in *PGC* 3:26, 37–38, 128, 130, 154; letter to A. McDougall from Washington, Mar. 25, 1778, in Fitzpatrick, ed., *Washington*

11:146; letter to Washington from S. Parsons, Mar. 16, 1778, in GWP, ser. 4, reel 47; message from Gov. Clinton, Mar. 21, 1778, in Journal of the General Assembly of New York, vol. 1.

3. MacDougall, *McDougall*, 107, 116; letter to G. Clinton from A. McDougall, Apr. 5, to A. McDougall from G. Clinton, Apr. 6, and to [Col. Malcom] from G. Clinton, June 9, 1778, in *PGC* 3:131–32, 139, 443; letter to Washington from A. McDougall, Apr. 13, and to Washington from H. Gates, May 23, 1778, in GWP, ser. 4, reels 48–49.

4. Resolution of the Council of Safety, Jan. 4, and message from Gov. Clinton, Feb. 18, 1778, in New York Governor; letter to Trumbull from I. Putnam, Jan. 6, 1778, in JTP, vol. 8, no. 34; letter to Washington from I. Putnam, Feb. 13, to [A. McDougall] from M. Graham, May 17, to Washington from A. McDougall, May 21, and to H. Gates from M. Graham, May 27, 1778, in GWP, ser. 4, reels 47, 49; letter to S. Parsons from H. Hughes, Mar. 11, return of Lt. Col. M. Graham's regiment, Mar. 12, and to G. Clinton from petitioners of Westchester County, Apr. 12, 1778, in *PGC* 3:24, 27, 157.

5. Letter to Washington from A. Hawkes Hay, Feb. 28, 1778, in GWP, ser. 4, reel 47; letter to S. Parsons from Washington, Mar. 5, 1778, in Fitzpatrick, ed., *Washington* 11:25; letter to G. Clinton from A. Hawkes Hay, Apr. 6, and to A. Hawkes Hay from G. Clinton, May 4, 1778, in *PGC* 3:141, 269.

6. General Assembly, Jan. 8, Feb. 12, and meeting of the governor and Council of Safety, Mar. 27, 1778, in Hoadly et al., *State of Connecticut* 1:477–78, 533–34, 576–77; General Assembly, June 13, 1778, ibid. 2:15–16; letter to Trumbull from G. Silliman, May 9, 1778, in JTP, vol. 8, no. 129; letter to H. Gates from Trumbull, May 30, June 3, 1778, vol. 26:212, 214.

7. Letter to Trumbull from I. Putnam, Jan. 26, Feb. 24, to Trumbull from G. Silliman, Feb. 9, Mar. 14, May 1, and to G. Silliman from Trumbull, May 4, 1778, in JTP, vol. 8, nos. 56, 70, 88, 104, 123, 125; letter to G. Silliman from Trumbull, Apr. 1, 1778, ibid., vol. 20, no. 171; letter to H. Gates from Trumbull, May 30, 1778, ibid., vol. 26:212.

8. Letter to Washington from W. Livingston, Jan. 12, 26, to Washington from S. Seely, Mar. 20, to Washington from G. Baylor, Mar. 24, to the Continental Congress from the Legislative Council and General Assembly of New Jersey, Apr. 3, and to Washington from P. Dickinson, June 9, 1778, in GWP, ser. 4, reels 46–49; to the Assembly from W. Livingston, Feb. 16, 1778, in Prince and Ryan, eds., *Livingston Papers* 2:224–25; council, Apr. 2, 1778, in Bernstein, *Privy Council*, 73; Apr. 3, 1778, in New Jersey Legislative Council Journals, 53–54.

9. Letter to Washington from I. Putnam, Jan. 13, 1778, in GWP, ser. 4, reel 46; Jan. 20, Mar. 10, 26, message from Gov. Clinton, Mar. 21, and message from the Council of Revision, Apr. 2, 1778, in Journal of the General Assembly of New York, vol. 1; address to the legislature from G. Clinton, Jan. 16, 1778, in *PGC* 2:677; letter to Lafayette from G. Clinton, Mar. 8, to A. McDougall from G. Clinton, Apr. 6, and to A. Hawkes Hay from G. Clinton, May 4, 1778, ibid. 3:4–5, 139, 269; letter to Trumbull from I. Putnam, Jan. 26, 1778, in JTP, vol. 8, no. 56; "An Act for raising Seven Hundred Men, to be employed in the Defence of this State," Mar. 31, 1778, in New York (State) Laws, Statutes, etc., 23.

10. Letter to G. Morris or J. Duane from G. Clinton, Mar. 4, 1778, in *PGC* 2:838; letter to J. Hunt, P. Leeke, and B. Miller from G. Clinton, May 23, 1778, ibid. 3:346; Mar. 27, 31, 1778, in Journal of the General Assembly of New York, vol.1; "An Act for regulating the Militia of the State of New-York," Apr. 3, 1778, in New York Laws, Statutes, etc., card no. 17630, pp. 30–34.

11. Letter to H. Gates from I. Putnam, June 5, 1778, in JTP, vol. 8, no. 141; letter to H. Gates from Trumbull, June 18, 1778, ibid., vol. 26:217; letter to J. Sullivan from

Trumbull, June 5, 1778, ibid., vol. 27:16; General Assembly, May 14–June 13, 1778, in Hoadly et al., *State of Connecticut* 2:16.

12. Feb. 11, 1778, in NJGA, card no. 16399, pp. 49, 52; "An Act for the Regulating, Training, and Arraying the Militia," Apr. 14, 1778, in New Jersey Session Laws, card no. 15927, pp. 42–43, 47–48, 56.

13. Letter to Washington from W. Livingston, Apr. 14, and to Washington from P. Dickinson, June 10, 1778, in GWP, ser. 4, reels 48–49; "De Lisle," [Apr. 23], and to H. Laurens from W. Livingston, June 8, 1778, in Prince and Ryan, eds., *Livingston Papers* 2:303, 362–63.

14. Letter to Trumbull from I. Putnam, Jan. 6, 1778, in JTP vol. 8, no. 34; letter to Trumbull from H. Gates, May 21, 1778, ibid., vol. 26:208; letter to Washington from I. Putnam, Feb. 13, to Washington from S. Parsons, Mar. 7, to Washington from H. Gates, May 21, 23, and to Washington from A. McDougall, May 21, 1778, in GWP, ser. 4, reels 47, 49; letter to G. Clinton from S. Parsons, Mar. 10, and to G. Clinton from A. McDougall, Apr. 3, 1778, in *PGC* 3:15, 128; letter to the president of Congress from Washington, Mar. 16, and to A. McDougall from Washington, Mar. 16, 1778, in Fitzpatrick, ed., *Washington* 11:90, 96–97.

15. Letter to I. Putnam from Washington, Jan. 25, Feb. 26, to La Radiere from Washington, Jan. 25, 1778, in Fitzpatrick, ed., *Washington* 10:348–49, 516; letter to S. Parsons from Washington, Mar. 5, 18, to G. Clinton from Washington, Mar. 12, to the president of Congress from Washington, Mar. 16, 24, to A. McDougall from Washington, Mar. 25, to W. Livingston from Washington, Mar. 25, and to E. Sheldon from Washington, May 29, 1778, ibid. 11:25, 29–30, 68–69, 90–92, 104, 140, 146, 149, 481.

16. Letter to Trumbull from I. Putnam, Jan. 26, 1778, in JTP, vol. 8, no. 56; Wed., Feb. 18, and Wed., Apr. 15, 1778, in Ford and Hunt, eds., *Journals of Continental Congress* 10:180–81, 354; message from Gov. Clinton, Mar. 10, 1778, in Journal of the General Assembly of New York, vol. 1; letter to G. Clinton from H. Laurens, Mar. 24, Apr. 20, 1778, in Smith, ed., *Letters* 9:328, 455; in Congress, Apr. 20, 1778, in GWP, ser. 4, reel 48.

17. Letter to Washington from B. Lincoln, Mar. 17, and to Washington from A. McDougall, Apr. 13, 1778, in GWP, ser. 4, reel 48; letter to A. McDougall from Washington, Mar. 31, Apr. 22, 1778, in Fitzpatrick, ed., *Washington* 11:178–79, 297; letter to H. Gates from H. Laurens, Apr. 20, 1778, in Revolutionary Papers, vol. 3; letter to G. Clinton from Trumbull, Apr. 10, and to Trumbull from G. Clinton, May 1, 1778, in *PGC* 3:154, 246–47.

18. Letter to W. Livingston from Washington, Apr. 26, May 12, to P. Dickinson from Washington, May 24, and to W. Maxwell from Washington, May 25, 1778, in Fitzpatrick, ed., *Washington* 11:310–11, 378, 445–46, 448; letter to Washington from P. Dickinson, May 27, and to Washington from W. Maxwell, May 28, 1778, in GWP, ser. 4, reel 49.

19. Letter to W. Livingston from Washington, June 1, to P. Dickinson from Washington, June 5, and Council of War, June 17, 1778, in Fitzpatrick, ed., *Washington* 12:1, 19–20, 77–78; letter to Washington from P. Dickinson, June 9, 10, 1778, in GWP, ser. 4, reel 49.

20. Letter to H. Gates from Washington, Apr. 24, May 17, 25, 29, 1778, in Fitzpatrick, ed., *Washington* 11:303–4, 401–2, 447, 476–77; Council of War, June 17, 1778, ibid. 12:77–78; letter to Trumbull from H. Gates, May 30, 1778, in JTP, vol. 26:213; letter to Washington from H. Gates, May 30, 1778, in GWP, ser. 4, reel 49.

21. Letter to G. Morris from G. Clinton, May 14, to H. Gates from J. Mead, May 23, to H. Gates from M. Graham, May 23, to H. Gates from G. Clinton, June 3, and to Brig. Gen. Ten Broeck from G. Clinton, June 8, 1778, in *PGC* 3:308, 347–48, 398–99, 427–28; letter to Trumbull from H. Gates, May 25, 30, June 15, 1778, in JTP, vol. 26:209, 213, 216–17; letter to Washington from H. Gates, May 30, and to H. Gates from M. Graham,

May 27, June 2, 1778, in GWP, ser. 4, reel 49; message from G. Clinton, June 22, 1778, in Journal of the General Assembly of New York, vol. 2.

22. "Thoughts upon a plan of operations for Campaign 1778," n.d., letter to A. Mc-Dougall from Washington, May 5, and Council of War, May 8, 1778, in Fitzpatrick, ed., *Washington* 11:185–93, 352, 364–65; Council of War, June 17, and to H. Gates from Washington, June 12, 1778, ibid. 12:51, 75–76.

23. Letter to T. Wharton from Washington, Feb. 23, 1778, in Fitzpatrick, ed., *Washington* 10:504; letter to the president of Congress from Washington, Apr. 10, to W. Livingston from Washington, Apr. 11, to T. Wharton from Washington, May 11, and to T. Johnson from Washington, May 11, 1778, ibid. 11:235–36, 248, 369–72; letter to Washington from B. Lincoln, Mar. 17, and In Congress, Apr. 4, 1778, in GWP, ser. 4, reel 40.

24. Mackesy, *War for America*, 213; letter to H. Clinton from G. Germain, Mar. 8, and secret instruction for Gen. Sir H. Clinton, Mar. 21, 1778, in Davies, ed., *Documents* 15:57, 74–75; Ira D. Gruber, "The Education of Sir Henry Clinton," 131–53.

25. Mackesy, *War for America*, 219–20; letter to G. Germain from H. Clinton, June 5, 1778, in Davies, ed., *Documents* 15:132.

26. Letter to G. Germain from H. Clinton, June 5, 1778, in Davies, ed., *Documents* 15:132; Clinton, *American Rebellion*, 89.

27. Uhlendorf, *Revolution in America*, 181; letter to Washington from P. Dickinson, June 14, 15, 17, 18, to P. Dickinson from W. Livingston, June 16, and to Washington from B. Arnold, June 20, 1778, in GWP, ser. 4, reels 49–50; letter to G. Germain from H. Clinton, July 5, 1778, in Davies, ed., *Documents* 15:159–60; Ewald, *Diary*, 132; Simcoe, *Journal*, 62–63; letter to the president of Congress from Washington, June 18, and to P. Dickinson from Washington, [June 18], 1778, in Fitzpatrick, ed., *Washington* 12:82–83, 86; council, June 16, 1778, in Bernstein, *Privy Council*, 81.

28. Ewald, *Diary*, p. 132; Uhlendorf, *Revolution in America*, 183.

29. Letter to P. Dickinson from W. Maxwell, June 18, to Washington from P. Dickinson, June 19, 20, 21, 22, and information from Elias Boudinot, June 20, 1778, in GWP, ser. 4, reel 50; letter to B. Arnold from Washington, June 21, and to the president of Congress from Washington, July 1, 1778, in Fitzpatrick, ed., *Washington* 12:103, 140; letter to H. Laurens from W. Livingston, June 20, 1778, in Prince and Ryan, eds., *Livingston Papers* 2:370.

30. Letter to the president of Congress from Washington, June 18, to P. Dickinson from Washington, June 20, 22, to W. Livingston from Washington, June 21, and to H. Gates from Washington, June 21, 1778, in Fitzpatrick, ed., *Washington* 12:83, 95–96, 100, 104, 108; Higginbotham, *War and Society*, 122.

31. Ewald, *Diary*, 132; letter to G. Germain from H. Clinton, July 5, 1778, in Davies, ed., *Documents* 15:160; letter to Washington from P. Dickinson, June 21, 1778, in GWP, ser. 4, reel 50; Peckham, ed., *Toll of Independence*, 52.

32. Letter to Washington from P. Dickinson, June 21, to P. Dickinson from W. Maxwell, [June 21], and to Washington from B. Arnold, June 22, 1778, in GWP, ser. 4, reel 50; General Orders, June 22, and to J. Kirkbride from Washington, June 22, 1778, in Fitzpatrick, ed., *Washington* 12:107–8.

33. Letter to C. Lee from W. Livingston, June 22, 1778, in Prince and Ryan, eds., *Livingston Papers* 2:373–74; Alden, *Lee*, 197–99, 206–7.

34. Letter to Washington from P. Dickinson, June 22, 23, to Washington from C. Stewart, June 23, and to Washington from W. Maxwell, June 24, 1778, in GWP, ser. 4, reel 50; Dann, ed., *Revolution Remembered*, 123; Simcoe, *Journal*, 17, 64; Uhlendorf, *Revolution in America*, 184; Ewald, *Diary*, 134; letter to G. Germain from H. Clinton, July 5, 1778, in Davies, ed., *Documents* 15:160.

35. Letter to Washington from P. Dickinson, June 24, to Washington from J. Morris, June 24, and to Washington from W. Maxwell, June 24, 1778, in GWP, ser. 4, reel 50.

36. Letter to Washington from C. Stewart, June 23, to Washington from J. Kirkbride, June 23, and to Washington from Col. Jackson, June 24, 1778, in GWP, ser. 4, reel 50; letter to P. Dickinson from Washington, June 24, instructions to C. Scott from Washington, June 24, and letter to D. Morgan from Washington, June 24, 1778, in Fitzpatrick, ed., *Washington* 12:113–15.

37. Letter to G. Germain from H. Clinton, July 5, 1778, in Davies, ed., *Documents* 15:160–61; Inman, "Narrative," 243; Clinton, *American Rebellion*, 90; Uhlendorf, *Revolution in America*, 184.

38. Letter to Washington from P. Dickinson, June 23, 1778, in GWP, ser. 4, reel 50; Simcoe, *Journal*, 66; Council of War, June 24, to Lafayette from Washington, June 25, to P. Dickinson from Washington, June 25, 26, to C. Lee from Washington, June 26, and to the president of Congress from Washington, July 1, 1778, in Fitzpatrick, ed., *Washington* 12:115–21, 140–41; Alden, *Lee*, 208–10; Ward, *Charles Scott*, 48–49.

39. Simcoe, *Journal*, 66–67; Ewald, *Diary*, 135; Uhlendorf, *Revolution in America*, 184.

40. Letter to Washington from P. Dickinson, June 25, to Lafayette from A. Hamilton, June 25, and to Washington from D. Morgan, June 25, 1778, in GWP, ser. 4, reel 50; disposition of the New Jersey militia, June 25, 1778, in "Lee Papers" 5:413; letter to J. Neilson from Washington, June 26, 1778, in Fitzpatrick, ed., *Washington* 12:123.

41. Letter to Washington from P. Dickinson, June 26, 1778, in GWP, ser. 4, reel 50; Simcoe, *Journal*, 68; Ewald, *Diary*, 135; Uhlendorf, *Revolution in America*, 185–86.

42. Letter to Washington from P. Dickinson, June 26, 27, to Washington from Capt. J. Morgan, June 26, to [Washington] from J. Neilson, June 26, to Washington from W. Winds, June 26, 27, to P. Dickinson from W. Winds, June 26, and to Washington from D. Morgan, June 27, 1778, in GWP, ser. 4, reel 50; letter to W. Winds from Washington, June 27, 1778, in Fitzpatrick, ed., *Washington* 12:126.

43. Letter to Lafayette from Washington, June 26, to H. Gates from Washington, June 27, and to the president of Congress from Washington, July 1, 1778, in Fitzpatrick, ed., *Washington* 12:122–23, 125, 141–42; account of the Battle of Monmouth, [July 1, 1778], in Prince and Ryan, eds., *Livingston Papers* 2:376.

44. Kaplan, "Hidden War," 122–23; Alden, *Lee*, 213; Thomas Fleming, "George Washington, General," 47.

45. Letter to Washington from P. Dickinson, June 28, 1778, in GWP, ser. 4, reel 50; letter to H. Gates from Washington, June 28, 1778, in Fitzpatrick, ed., *Washington* 12:127; Ewald, *Diary*, 135–36; Simcoe, *Journal*, 68–71; letter to G. Germain from H. Clinton, July 5, 1778, in Davies, ed., *Documents* 15:161; Uhlendorf, *Revolution in America*, 186–87.

46. Court martial, July 23, 25, 1778, in "Lee Papers" 6:140, 162–63; Alden, *Lee*, 216, 221.

47. Letter to G. Germain from H. Clinton, July 5, 1778, in Davies, ed., *Documents* 15:161; Uhlendorf, *Revolution in America*, 186; Alden, *Lee*, 216–21.

48. Letter to the president of Congress from Washington, June 28, 1778, in Fitzpatrick, ed., *Washington* 12:127–28; Alden, *Lee*, 222–25; letter to G. Germain from H. Clinton, July 5, 1778, in Davies, ed., *Documents* 15:161–62.

49. Letter to D. Morgan from Washington, June 28, 1778, in Fitzpatrick, ed., *Washington* 12:126; letter to G. Germain from H. Clinton, July 5, 1778, in Davies, ed., *Documents* 15:162; Clinton, *American Rebellion*, 96–97.

50. Letter to G. Germain from H. Clinton, July 5, 1778, in Davies, ed., *Documents* 15:162; letter to H. Gates from Washington, June 29, to the president of Congress from Washington, July 1, and to J. Washington from Washington, July 4, 1778, in Fitzpatrick, ed., *Washington* 12:129, 142–45, 157; Clinton, *American Rebellion*, 98.

51. Letter to H. Gates from Washington, June 29, and to the president of Congress from Washington, July 1, 1778, in Fitzpatrick, ed., *Washington,* 129, 145; letter to G. Germain from H. Clinton, July 5, 1778, in Davies, ed., *Documents* 15:162; Ewald, *Diary,* 136; Peckham, ed., *Toll of Independence,* 52.

52. Letter to G. Germain from H. Clinton, July 5, and to P. Stephens from Vice Adm. Howe, July 6, 1778, in Davies, ed., *Documents* 15:162–63; Ewald, *Diary,* 136–38; Simcoe, *Journal,* 73; Kaplan, "Hidden War," 123; letter to the president of Congress from Washington, July 1, and to H. Gates from Washington, July 3, 1778, in Fitzpatrick, ed., *Washington* 12:146, 149–50.

53. Letter to P. Dickinson from J. Neilson, June 29, and to Washington from P. Dickinson, June 29, 1778, in GWP, ser. 4, reel 50; letter to P. Dickinson from Washington, June 29, 1778, in Fitzpatrick, ed., *Washington* 12:129–30; letter to Col. Morgan from T. Tilghman, June 29, 30, 1778, in nos. 1044–45, Myers Collection.

54. Letter to Washington from P. Dickinson, June 30, to Washington from W. Winds, June 30, and to Washington from D. Morgan, June 30, 1778, in GWP, ser. 4, reels 49–50.

55. Letter to the president of Congress from Washington, July 1, and to H. Gates from Washington, July 3, 1778, in Fitzpatrick, ed., *Washington* 12:146, 149–50; letter to D. Morgan from R. Meade, July 3, and to Washington from W. Winds, July 8, 1778, in GWP, ser. 4, reel 50.

56. Letter to H. Gates from Washington, June 21, 27, July 3, 1778, in Fitzpatrick, ed., *Washington* 12:104, 125, 149–50; letter to G. Clinton from H. Gates, June 27, and to G. Clinton from W. Malcom, June 29, 1778, in *PGC* 3:496, 501; letter to Trumbull from S. Parsons, June 22, 1778, in JTP, vol. 8, no. 147; letter to Trumbull from H. Gates, June 22, July 5, 1778, ibid. 26:219, 223; letter to Washington from H. Gates, June 25, and to Washington from W. Winds, July 8, 1778, in GWP, ser. 4, reel 50.

57. General Orders, June 29, and letter to J. Washington from Washington, July 4, 1778, in Fitzpatrick, ed., *Washington* 12:130, 157.

58. Ewald, *Diary,* 138–39; Ewald, *Treatise,* 114; Clinton, *American Rebellion,* 90; letter to G. Germain from H. Clinton, July 5, 1778, in Davies, ed., *Documents* 15:159–62; Lundin, *Cockpit of Revolution,* 395.

59. "A Plan of Attack on New York, [June 1778]," letter to H. Gates from Washington, July 14, and to J. Sullivan from Washington, July 17, 1778, in Fitzpatrick, ed., *Washington* 12:136–38, 177, 184; letter to Washington from W. Winds, July 10, 1778, in GWP, ser. 4, reel 50; Sat., July 11, 1778, in Ford and Hunt, eds., *Journals of Continental Congress* 11:684; letter to Trumbull from H. Laurens, July 12, 1778, in JTP, vol. 27:22.

60. Letter to Capt. Hopkins from T. Tilghman, July 16, to Col. Van Schaick from T. Tilghman, July 19, to W. Maxwell from T. Tilghman, July 19, and to [Washington] from R. Hopkins, July 21, 1778, in GWP, ser. 4, reel 50; Freeman, *Washington* 5:47–50; letter to H. Gates from Washington, July 19, to G. Clinton from Washington, July 21, and to the president of Congress from Washington, July 22, 1778, in Fitzpatrick, ed., *Washington* 12:193–94, 211.

61. Letter to J. Sullivan from Washington, July 22, to the president of Congress from Washington, July 22, Council of War, July 25, and to Trumbull from Washington, July 28, 1778, in Fitzpatrick, ed., *Washington* 12:201–2, 230, 245; Freeman, *Washington* 5:51; letter to Washington from Trumbull, July 25, 1778, in GWP, ser. 4, reel 51.

62. Letter to G. Germain from H. Clinton, July 27, and to H. Clinton from G. Germain, Sept. 25, 1778, in Davies, ed., *Documents* 15:173, 207.

63. Council of War, July 25, letter to G. Clinton from Washington, Aug. 28, and to Trumbull from Washington, Sept. 6, 1778, in Fitzpatrick, ed., *Washington* 12:230, 366, 406; letter to Washington from W. Malcom, July 26, to Washington from G. Clinton,

Aug. 29, and to W. Malcom from Washington, Aug. 31, 1778, in GWP, ser. 4, reel 51; letter to R. Benson from S. Ten Broeck, Sept. 15, and to G. Clinton from W. Malcom, Sept. 16, 1778, in *PGC* 4:33–34, 42.

64. Letter to G. Clinton from Washington, July 23, General Orders, July 26, Aug. 8, to C. Scott from Washington, Aug. 14, and to the quartermaster general from Washington, Sept. 15, 1778, in Fitzpatrick, ed., *Washington* 12:220, 231, 300–301, 323–24, 462; Ward, *Charles Scott*, 31, 52–53; letter to Washington from J. Nixon, July [24], S. Parsons's report, July 24, and to Washington from C. Scott, Sept. 8, 9, 10, 12, 13, 14, 1778, in GWP, ser. 4, reels 51–52; Tallmadge, *Memoir*, 43.

65. Simcoe, *Journal*, 74–83, 88; Ewald, *Diary*, 141, 143–51.

66. Letter to W. Maxwell from Washington, Aug. 8, Sept. 19, 1778, in Fitzpatrick, ed., *Washington* 12:295, 468; letter to Washington from W. Maxwell, Sept. 17, 1778, in GWP, ser. 4, reel 52.

67. Letter to Washington from G. Silliman, Sept. 14, and to G. Silliman from Washington, Sept. 22, 1778, in GWP, ser. 4, reel 52; Erna Risch, *Supplying Washington's Army*, 111–12.

68. Council, Aug. 10, 1778, in Bernstein, *Privy Council*, 84; letter to H. Laurens from W. Livingston, Aug. 22, 1778, in Prince and Ryan, eds., *Livingston Papers* 2:423; Aug. 26, 1778, in *Minutes of the Council of Safety*, 278; letter to G. Clinton from P. Van Ness, Aug. 10, to G. Clinton from "Petitioners from . . . Dutchess and . . . the Manor of Livingston," n.d., and to Col. Langdon from G. Clinton, Aug. 23, 1778, in *PGC* 3:619, 674–76, 686; General Orders, Sept. 21, 1778, ibid. 4:56.

69. Letter to G. Clinton from Washington, Aug. 28, to H. Gates from Washington, Sept. 10, to J. Sullivan from Washington, Sept. 13, and to the quartermaster general from Washington, Sept. 15, 1778, in Fitzpatrick, ed., *Washington* 12:367, 419, 444–45, 462; letter to Washington from G. Clinton, Aug. 29, 1778, in GWP, ser. 4, reel 51.

70. Letter to the quartermaster general from Washington, Sept. 15, to Stirling from Washington, Sept. 15, to C. Scott from Washington, Sept. 15, to I. Putnam from Washington, Sept. 19, to J. Sullivan from Washington, Sept. 19, to W. Heath from Washington, Sept. 22, and to N. Greene from Washington, Sept. 22, 1778, in Fitzpatrick, ed., *Washington* 12:452, 463–68, 475–76, 480; letter to G. Germain from H. Clinton, July 27, Aug. 12, Sept. 15, 1778, in Davies, ed., *Documents* 15:173, 186, 201; letter to Washington from C. Scott, Sept. 15, 16, 17, 20, to C. Scott from B. Tallmadge, Sept. 16, and to Washington from H. Gates, Sept. 21, 1778, in GWP, ser. 4, reel 52.

71. James Kirby Martin, "The Continental Army and the American Victory," in Ferling, ed., *World Turned Upside Down*, 28.

CHAPTER EIGHT
Frustration and Partisan Fighting, 1778–1779

1. Two letters to G. Germain from H. Clinton, July 27, Sept. 15, 1778, in Davies, ed., *Documents* 15:173–74, 201; Clinton, *American Rebellion*, 107; Van Doren, *Secret History*, 123; Nelson, "Tryon," 280–82; Gruber, "Education of Henry Clinton," 147.

2. Letter to G. Germain from H. Clinton, Oct. 8, 1778, in Davies, ed., *Documents* 15:210–11; Ewald, *Diary*, 151; Uhlendorf, *Revolution in America*, 216–18; Nelson, *Stirling*, 134.

3. Letter to the president of Congress from Washington, Sept. 23, to Stirling from Washington, Sept. 24, to C. Scott from Washington, Sept. 25, to I. Putnam from Washington, Sept. 27, and to W. Maxwell from Washington, Sept. 27, 1778, in Fitzpatrick,

384 ★ NOTES TO PAGES 227-231

ed., *Washington* 12:492–94, 498–99, 508, 512; letter to [Washington] from G. Baylor, Sept. 23, and to Washington from C. Scott, Sept. 23, 1778, in, GWP, ser. 4, reel 52; letter to T. Smith from J. Haring and G. Cooper, Sept. 25, 1778, in *PGC* 4:86.

4. Council, Sept. 24, 1778, in Bernstein, *Privy Council,* 90; letter to G. Clinton from T. Smith, [Sept. 26], to Col. Woodhull from R. Benson, Sept. 27, to G. Clinton from A. Hay, Oct. 9, and to G. Clinton from the freeholders and inhabitants of Orange County, Oct. 18, 1778, in *PGC* 4:101–2, 159, 170; letter to I. Putnam from G. Cooper, Sept. 26, to W. Winds from W. Maxwell, Sept. 26, to Washington from W. Winds, Sept. 26, and to Washington from W. Maxwell, Sept. 27, 1778, in GWP, ser. 4, reel 52; letter to W. Maxwell from Washington, Sept. 27, 1778, in Fitzpatrick, ed., *Washington* 12:512.

5. Nine letters to Washington from C. Scott, Sept. 25, 26, 27, 28, 30, Oct. 2, 8, and to Maj. Allison from R. Harrison, Oct. 1, 1778, in GWP, ser. 4, reel 52; Uhlendorf, *Revolution in America,* 218; letter to G. Germain from H. Clinton, Oct. 8, 1778, in Davies, ed., *Documents* 15:211.

6. Letter to H. Clinton from C. Cornwallis, Sept. 28, 1778, in Charles Ross, ed., *Correspondence of Charles, First Marquis Cornwallis* 1:35; Simcoe, *Journal,* 90; Uhlendorf, *Revolution in America,* 220; letter to G. Germain from H. Clinton, Oct. 8, 1778, in Davies, ed., *Documents* 15:211; Peckham, ed., *Toll of Independence,* 54–55.

7. Letter to H. Laurens from W. Livingston, Sept. 28, 1778, in Prince and Ryan, eds., *Livingston Papers* 2:448–49; letter to Washington from W. Maxwell, Sept. 28, 29, to Washington from M. Ogden, Sept. 28, to Washington from O. Williams, Sept. 28, to Washington from C. Stewart, Sept. 28, to Washington from W. Winds, Sept. 28, and to W. Winds from Washington, Sept. 28, 1778, in GWP, ser. 4, reel 52; letter to Stirling from Washington, Sept. 28, and to I. Putnam from Washington, Sept. 29, 1778, in Fitzpatrick, ed., *Washington* 12:513–14, 519.

8. Letter to Washington from W. Woodford, Sept. 29, 1778, in GWP, ser. 4, reel 52; Council of War, Sept. 29, 1778, in Fitzpatrick, ed., *Washington* 12:522–23; letter to H. Livingston from W. Livingston, Sept. 29, 1778, in Prince and Ryan, eds., *Livingston Papers* 2:450.

9. Letter to Washington from W. Winds, Sept. 30, to Washington from I. Putnam, Sept. 30, to Washington from Stirling, Oct. 1, 3, 4, 5, 6, 12, and to Washington from W. Woodford, Oct. 4, 1778, in GWP, ser. 4, reels 52–53; letter to W. Woodford from Washington, Sept. 30, and to W. Maxwell from Washington, Oct. 2, 1778, in Fitzpatrick, ed., *Washington* 12:528–29; letter to Stirling from Washington, Oct. 2, 1778, ibid. 13:5; letter to Stirling from W. Livingston, Oct. 5, and to J. Neilson from W. Livingston, Oct. 9, 1778, in Prince and Ryan, eds., *Livingston Papers* 2:455, 460.

10. Letter to G. Germain from H. Clinton, Oct. 8, 1778, in Davies, ed., *Documents* 15:211; Uhlendorf, *Revolution in America,* 222; letter to Washington from Stirling, Oct. 9, 14, 16, and to Stirling from Washington, Oct. 12, 1778, in GWP, ser. 4, reels 52–53.

11. Uhlendorf, *Revolution in America,* 200–201; letter to G. Germain from W. Tryon, Sept. 5, 1778, in Davies, ed., *Documents* 15:198; Simcoe, *Journal,* 93, 95.

12. General Assembly, Oct. 8, 1778, Jan. 7, May, 1779, and meeting of the governor and Council of Safety, Mar. 5, 1779, in Hoadly et al., *State of Connecticut* 2:124–25, 181, 218, 281–82; letter to J. Douglas from Trumbull, Oct. 14, 1778, in JDP, no. 42; letter to Trumbull from G. Silliman, Nov. 2, and to Trumbull from S. Bishop and T. Jones, Nov. 25, 1778, in JTP, vol. 8, nos. 237, 260; letter to Trumbull from the civil authority and selectmen of Stanford and Norwalk, Feb. 16, to Trumbull from the inhabitants of Saybrook, Mar. 3, and to Trumbull from S. Parsons, Apr. 8, 1779, ibid., vol. 9, nos. 45, 73, 170.

13. Letter to Washington from Trumbull, Oct. 28, 1778, to Washington from I. Putnam, Mar. 22, and to Washington from S. Parsons, Apr. 25, 1779, in GWP, ser. 4,

reels 53, 56; letter to I. Putnam from Washington, Nov. 2, 27, to Trumbull from Washington, Nov. 7, Dec. 19, and to the president of Congress from Washington, Nov. 27, 1778, in Fitzpatrick, ed., *Washington* 13:195–96, 212, 340, 350–51, 434–35; letter to Trumbull from I. Putnam, Dec. 20, 1778, in JTP, vol. 27:172; letter to Trumbull from S. Parsons, Apr. 6, 1779, ibid., vol. 9, no. 165; Risch, *Supplying Washington's Army*, 111–12; Simcoe, *Journal*, 99; Uhlendorf, *Revolution in America*, 262.

14. Letter to Washington from S. Parsons, Apr. 25, to Washington from Trumbull, Apr. 27, and to Washington from I. Putnam, May 7, 1779, in GWP, ser. 4, reels 57–58; letter to J. Armstrong from Washington, May 18, and to the president of Congress from Washington, May 25, 1779, in Fitzpatrick, ed., *Washington* 15:97, 143–44.

15. General Assembly, Oct. 8, 1778, in Hoadly et al., *State of Connecticut* 2:124–25; letter to G. Silliman from E. Curtis, Oct. 31, and to Trumbull from R. Enos and J. Mead, Dec. 5, 1778, in JTP, vol. 8, nos. 235, 274; letter to a general from G. Silliman, Feb. 26, to Trumbull from J. Wadsworth, Feb. 27, to Trumbull from J. Huntington, Mar. 3, and to Trumbull from I. Putnam, Mar. 4, 1779, ibid., vol. 9, nos. 57–58, 60, 76, 78; letter to Washington from Trumbull, Oct. 9, to Washington from S. Parsons, Nov. 19, 1778, and to Washington from I. Putnam, Mar. 2, 22, 1779, in GWP, ser. 4, reels 52, 54, 56; letter to Trumbull from Washington, Oct. 11, 1778, in Fitzpatrick, ed., *Washington* 13:63–64; Uhlendorf, *Revolution in America*, 262.

16. General Assembly, Apr. 7, May 1779, in Hoadly et al., *State of Connecticut* 2:233, 292, 328; letter to Trumbull from J. Mead, June 17, 1779, in JTP, vol. 9, no. 244; Ward, *Charles Scott*, 66; letter to Washington from I. Putnam, Mar. 22, 1779, in GWP, ser. 4, reel 56.

17. Speech to the Assembly by Trumbull, Oct. 1778, and Oct. 12, 1780, in JTP, vol. 20, nos. 178, 276; General Assembly, May 13–June 18, 1779, in Hoadly et al., *State of Connecticut* 2:265.

18. Letter to C. Scott from Washington, Oct. 17, to Washington from C. Scott, Nov. 13, 14, and to Washington from I. Putnam, Dec. 17, 1778, in GWP, ser. 4, reels 53–54; letter to Gen. Morris from G. Clinton, Oct. 21, Nov. 18, 1778, in *PGC* 4:181, 297; Uhlendorf, *Revolution in America*, 226.

19. Letter to [G. Clinton] from W. Miller, Dec. 1, and to G. Clinton from S. Lyon, Dec. 10, 1778, in *PGC* 4:320, 361–62; letter to Trumbull from R. Enos and J. Mead, Dec. 5, 1778, in JTP, vol. 8, no. 274; letter to A. Wayne from A. Hay, Dec. 4, 1778, Wayne Papers, vol. 2; letter to G. Clinton from A. McDougall, Dec. 4 and 6, 1778, in *PGC* 4:352, 355–56; letter to N. Greene from R. Harrison, Dec. 6, to T. Clark from Washington, Dec. 6, and to the president of Congress from Washington, Dec. 7, 1778, in Fitzpatrick, ed., *Washington* 13:369–71, 378–79; Ewald, *Diary*, 141, 143–51, 156–57; letter to G. Germain from H. Clinton, Dec. 17, 1778, in Davies, ed., *Documents* 15:287–88; Uhlendorf, *Revolution in America*, 231.

20. Letter to Washington from I. Putnam, Dec. 17, 1778, in GWP, ser. 4, reel 54; letter to G. Clinton from A. McDougall, Dec. 2, 28, 1778, and Mar. 14, 1779, and to A. McDougall from G. Clinton, Dec. 4, 1778, Jan. 14, 1779, in *PGC* 4:347–48, 431–32, 483, 631–32.

21. Ewald, *Diary*, 157; Uhlendorf, *Revolution in America*, 247; Nelson, *Stirling*, 104, 138, 141; letter to G. Clinton from the inhabitants of Orange County, Nov. 14, 1778, Apr. 28, 1779, to G. Clinton from R. Livingston, Nov. 14, 1778, and to A. McDougall from G. Clinton, Apr. 29, 1779, in *PGC* 4:274–75, 633–34, 774–76.

22. Council, Oct. 8, 1778, Jan. 15, Feb. 3, 1779, in Bernstein, *Privy Council*, 93–94, 112–13; letter to W. Livingston from Washington, Nov. 18, Dec. 7, 16, to the president of Congress from Washington, Nov. 27, instructions to W. Maxwell from Washington, Dec. 21, and instructions to T. Clark from Washington, Dec. 21, 1778, in Fitzpatrick, ed.,

Washington 13:276, 350–51, 379–80, 404–5, 443–46; letter to W. Livingston from Washington, Apr. 22, 1779, ibid. 14:427; letter to Washington from Stirling, Oct. 16, to Washington from W. Livingston, Nov. 7, Dec. 21, 1778, and to Washington from J. McHenry, Jan. 23, 1779, in GWP, ser. 4, reels 53–55; letter to Washington from W. Livingston, Dec. 15, 1778, in Prince and Ryan, eds., *Livingston Papers* 2:512; letter to J. Mead from W. Livingston, Feb. 5, 1779, ibid. 3:29; Apr. 26, 1779, in NJGA, card no. 16401, p. 75.

23. Letter to G. Germain from W. Franklin, Dec. 20, 1778, in Davies, ed., *Documents* 15:293–94; E. A. Benians, ed., *A Journal by Thos: Hughes . . . (1778–1789)*, 60; Uhlendorf, *Revolution in America*, 257–58, 262; *New-Jersey Gazette*, Mar. 3, 1779, in Moore, comp., *Diary*, 347, 349; Ewald, *Diary*, 158–59; letter to W. Maxwell from A. Hamilton, Feb. 25, 1779, in GWP, ser. 4, reel 56; letter to the president of Congress from Washington, Feb. 26, 1779, in Fitzpatrick, ed., *Washington* 14:153; Peckham, ed., *Toll of Independence*, 58.

24. Ewald, *Diary*, 159; *New-Hampshire Gazette*, May 25, 1779, in Moore, comp., *Diary*, 356–57; letter to Washington from W. Livingston, Feb. 8, to the militia colonels of Burlington, Hunterdon, and Middlesex counties from W. Livingston, Mar. 1, and to F. Frelinghuysen from W. Livingston, May 26, 1779, in Prince and Ryan, eds., *Livingston Papers* 3:34, 41, 98; letter to Stirling from J. Burrowes, Apr. 26, to Washington from B. Ford, Apr. 26, and to Washington from T. Clark, May 17, 1779, in GWP, ser. 4, reels 56–58.

25. Letter to Washington from W. Livingston, Apr. 24, and to Washington from W. Maxwell, May 12, 14, 1779, in GWP, ser. 4, reel 57; Council, Apr. 9, May 25, June 7, 11, 1779, in Bernstein, *Privy Council*, 112, 116, 118, 120; letter to W. Livingston from Washington, Apr. 22, 1779, in Fitzpatrick, ed., *Washington* 14:427; letter to W. Livingston from Washington, May 14, 1779, ibid. 15:74; Apr. 29, 1779, in New Jersey Legislative Council Journals, card no. 16887, pp. 38–39; letter to J. Neilson from W. Livingston, May 1, 18, to W. Livingston from J. Neilson, May 15, 30, and to N. Heard from W. Livingston, June 7, 1779, in Prince and Ryan, eds., *Livingston Papers* 3:78, 89, 92, 100–101, 107; "An Act to embody, for a limited Time, One Thousand of the Militia of this State, for the defence of the Frontiers thereof," June 2, 1779, in New Jersey Session Laws, card no. 16394, p. 58.

26. "A Supplementary Act to an Act, intitled, An Act for the regulating, training and arraying of the Militia," June 12, 1779, in New Jersey Session Laws, card no. 16394, p. 113; "An Act to provide for the more effectual Defence of the State, in case of Invasions or Incursions of the Enemy," June 16, 1780, ibid., card no. 16885, p. 108; letter to the Assembly from W. Livingston, Mar. 13, 1780 (not sent), in Prince and Ryan, eds., *Livingston Papers* 3:325–27.

27. Letter to Trumbull from Baron von Steuben, Apr. 20, 1779, in JTP, vol. 9, no. 179; Higginbotham, *War of Independence*, 247; Frederick William Baron von Steuben, *Baron von Steuben's Revolutionary War Drill Manual: A Facsimile Reprint of the 1794 Edition*, 3; letter to Baron von Steuben from W. Livingston, May 22, 1779, in Prince and Ryan, eds., *Livingston Papers* 3:95–96; letter to G. Clinton from Baron von Steuben, July 12, and to Baron von Steuben from G. Clinton, July 20, 1779, in *PGC* 5:131.

28. Letter to the president of Congress from Washington, Mar. 15, and to W. Livingston from Washington, Mar. 23, 1779, in Fitzpatrick, ed., *Washington* 14:244, 281–82; letter to G. Clinton from A. McDougall, Mar. 14, to A. McDougall from G. Clinton, Mar. 18, 26, 27, and General Orders, Mar. 18, 1779, in *PGC* 4:630–31, 644–45, 648–49, 668, 671–72; letter to Trumbull from Washington, Mar. 24, to Washington from W. Livingston, Mar. 30, and to Washington from Trumbull, Apr. 27, 1779, in GWP, ser. 4, reels 56–58; speech to the Council and House of Representatives from Trumbull, Apr. 7, 1779, in JTP, vol. 20, no. 191.

29. Letter to H. Clinton from G. Germain, Nov. 4, and to commissioners for quieting disorders from G. Germain, Nov. 4, 1778, in Davies, ed., *Documents* 15:238–41; letter to H. Clinton from G. Germain, Jan. 23, 1779, ibid. 17:44; Mackesy, *War for America*, 256.

30. Letter to G. Germain from H. Clinton, May 5, 21, 1779, in Davies, ed., *Documents* 17:117–18, 126; Clinton, *American Rebellion*, 121–22.

31. Letter to G. Germain from H. Clinton, June 18, 1779, in Davies, ed., *Documents* 17:144–46; letter to Lord Viscount Townshend from J. Pattison, June 9, 1779, in James Pattison, "Official Letters of Major General James Pattison," 73–74; Simcoe, *Journal*, 101.

32. Letter to Trumbull from A. McDougall, May 29, 1779, in JTP, vol. 9, no. 219; letter to Washington from A. McDougall, May 29, 1779, in GWP, ser. 4, reel 59; letter to G. Clinton from A. McDougall, May 30, 31, to A. McDougall from G. Clinton, May 31, to G. Clinton from U. Hay, May 31, and to Col. Hay from G. Clinton, May 31, 1779, in *PGC* 4:860–61, 866, 868–69, 871–72; letter to A. McDougall from Washington, May 31, 1779, in Fitzpatrick, ed., *Washington* 15:194–95; letter to G. Germain from H. Clinton, June 18, 1779, in Davies, ed., *Documents* 17:145; to Lord Viscount Townshend from J. Pattison, June 9, 1779, in "Official Letters of General Pattison," 74–75, 77.

33. Letter to Lord Viscount Townshend from J. Pattison, June 9, 1779, in Pattison, "Official Letters of General Pattison," 76; letter to G. Germain from H. Clinton, June 18, 1779, in Davies, ed., *Documents* 17:145–46; Peckham, ed., *Toll of Independence*, 60.

34. Letter to A. McDougall from Washington, June 1, 2, to Stirling or officer commanding his division from Washington, June 2, to the president of Congress from Washington, June 3, and to W. Livingston from Washington, June 3, 1779, in Fitzpatrick, ed., *Washington* 15:202–3, 210–11, 213, 223–24; letter to G. Clinton from U. Hay, June 1, and to A. McDougall from G. Clinton, June 1, 1779, in *PGC* 5:5–6; letter to Washington from A. St. Clair, June 3, 1779, in GWP, ser. 4, reel 59; letter to Trumbull from J. Huntington, June 4, 1779, in JTP, vol. 9, no. 238.

35. Letter to G. Germain from H. Clinton, June 18, July 25, 1779, in Davies, ed., *Documents* 17:146, 168; letter to Lord Viscount Townshend from J. Pattison, June 9, 1779, in Pattison, "Official Letters of General Pattison," 78; letter to Trumbull from J. Huntington, June 4, 1779, in JTP, vol. 9, no. 238; letter to J. Jay from Trumbull, June 22, 1779, ibid., vol. 20, no. 199; letter to J. Christie from Washington, June 4, to H. Knox from Washington, June 4, and to A. Hay from Washington, June 4, 1779, in Fitzpatrick, ed., *Washington* 15:225, 227–29; letter to G. Clinton from W. Malcom, June 4, to W. Malcom from G. Clinton, June 5, to Col. Ludington from W. Duer, June 5, and to A. McDougall from G. Clinton, June 5, 1779, in *PGC* 5:20, 32–35; letter to Washington from W. Malcom, June 5, 1779, in GWP, ser. 4, reel 59.

36. Letter to F. Frelinghuysen from Washington, June 5, to H. Lee from Washington, June 6, to the president of Congress from Washington, June 6, and to A. St. Clair from Washington, June 6, 1779, in Fitzpatrick, ed., *Washington* 15:231–35, 237–38.

37. Letter to G. Clinton from W. Malcom, June 7, to W. Malcom from J. Woodhull, June 7, and to Col. Beardsly from G. Clinton, June 7, 1779, in *PGC* 5:49–52; letter to P. Schuyler from Washington, June 9, to G. Clinton from Washington, June 9, 10, 27, to W. Malcom from Washington, June 9, to the president of Congress from Washington, June 11, to J. Neilson from Washington, June 13, and instructions to S. Moylan from Washington, June 28, 1779, in Fitzpatrick, ed., *Washington* 15:243–46, 256, 261, 273, 328, 337; letter to Washington from G. Clinton, June 10, 1779, in GWP, ser. 4, reel 59; letter to J. Jay from Trumbull, June 22, 1779, in JTP, vol. 20, no. 199.

38. Letter to Washington from W. Livingston, June 8, 1779, in Prince and Ryan, eds., *Livingston Papers* 3:110; letter to G. Clinton from A. McDougall, June 11, 1779, in *PGC* 5:76–77; letter to the general officers from Washington, June 13, and to the president

of Congress from Washington, July 1, 1779, in Fitzpatrick, ed., *Washington* 15:269–70, 346; letter to G. Germain from H. Clinton, June 18, July 25, 1779, in Davies, ed., *Documents* 17:146, 168; Simcoe, *Journal*, 101–2.

39. Letter to A. Wayne from Washington, July 1, 9, 1779, in Fitzpatrick, ed., *Washington* 15:355, 386.

40. Letter to G. Germain from H. Clinton, June 18, July 25, 1779, in Davies, ed., *Documents* 17:146, 168; Clinton, *American Rebellion*, 130; letter to Trumbull from the Committee of Fairfield, July 2, 1779, in JTP, no. 260.

41. Clinton, *American Rebellion*, 130; letter to H. Clinton from W. Tryon, July 20, 1779, in Davies, ed., *Documents* 17:162–63; Buel, *Dear Liberty*, 190–91; letter to Trumbull from A. Ward, July 5, 6, 7, 1779, in JTP, vol. 9, nos. 265–66, 269; Peckham, ed., *Toll of Independence*, 62.

42. Letter to Trumbull from A. Ward, July 7, to A. Ward from Trumbull, July 7, to Trumbull from H. Wyllys, June [July] 8, and to Trumbull from Col. Whiting, July 9, 1779, in JTP, vol. 9, nos. 240, 269–70, 277; letter to Trumbull from Washington, July 7, to S. Parsons from Washington, July 8, and to J. Glover from Washington, July 8, 1779, in Fitzpatrick, ed., *Washington* 15:379–80, 382–83; letter to H. Clinton from W. Tryon, July 20, 1779, in Davies, ed., *Documents* 17:163; Peckham, ed., *Toll of Independence*, 62.

43. Simcoe, *Journal*, 102; meeting of the governor and Council of Safety, July 8, 10, 11, 1779, in Hoadly et al., *State of Connecticut* 2:357–59; letter to G. Germain from H. Clinton, July 25, 1779, in Davies, ed., *Documents* 17:168; letter to Trumbull from the Men of New Haven, July 9, 1779, in JTP, vol. 9, no. 279; letter to President Ward from Trumbull, July 11, 1779, ibid., vol. 20, no. 202; letter to Washington from the selectmen and justices of Norwalk, July 9, and to Washington from S. Parsons, July 9, 1779, in GWP, ser. 4, reel 59; letter to W. Heath from Washington, July 10, and to Trumbull from Washington, July 12, 1779, in Fitzpatrick, ed., *Washington* 15:394–95, 415.

44. Letter to H. Clinton from W. Tryon, July 20, 1779, in Davies, ed., *Documents* 17:163–64; Buel, *Dear Liberty*, 193–94; letter to Washington from S. Parsons, July 11, 1779, in GWP, ser. 4, reel 60; letter to S. Parsons from Washington, July 11, 1779, in Fitzpatrick, ed., *Washington* 15:407; letter to the men of Middletown from C. Bell, July 12, 1779, in JTP, vol. 10, no. 16.

45. Letter to Washington from S. Moylan, July 12, to Washington from S. Parsons, July 12, 14, to Washington from W. Heath, July 14, and to Washington from J. Glover, July 15, 1779, in GWP, ser. 4, reel 60; to the men of Middletown from C. Bell, July 12, to Trumbull from J. Powell, July 13, and to Trumbull from J. Glover, July 15, 1779, in JTP, vol. 10, nos. 16, 19, 24.

46. Letter to H. Clinton from W. Tryon, July 20, 1779, in Davies, ed., *Documents* 17:164; Clinton, *American Rebellion*, 130–31, 415.

47. Letter to Washington from W. Heath, July 15, to Washington from O. Wolcott, July 17, and to R. Howe from Washington, July 17, 1779, in GWP, ser. 4, reel 60; Buel, *Dear Liberty*, 196; Simcoe, *Journal*, 103–4; letter to G. Germain from H. Clinton, July 25, 1779, in Davies, ed., *Documents* 17:168–69; Clinton, *American Rebellion*, 130–31; letter to Trumbull from S. Parsons, July 17, and to Trumbull from J. Glover, July 18, 1779, in JTP, vol. 10, nos. 27, 35; letter to A. Wayne from Washington, July 1, 9, to W. Heath from Washington, July 16, 17, to G. Clinton from Washington, July 19, to Stirling from Washington, July 24, and Council of War, July 26, 1779, in Fitzpatrick, ed., *Washington* 15:355, 386, 427, 433, 439, 472, 489–90; Peckham, ed., *Toll of Independence*, 62.

48. Mackesy, *War for America*, 270–71; Nelson, "Tryon," 283–84; letter to G. Germain from H. Clinton, Aug. 21, 1779, in Davies, ed., *Documents* 17:189–90.

49. Letter to the president of Congress from Washington, Aug. 11, to W. Livingston from Washington, Aug. 16, to the Board of War from Washington, Aug. 27, and to Stirling from Washington, Aug. 28[–29], 1779, in Fitzpatrick, ed., *Washington* 16:78–79, 155, 184, 198; letter to Trumbull from J. Jay, Aug. 14, 1779, in JTP, vol. 10, no. 91; letter to F. Frelinghuysen from W. Livingston, June 24, 1779, in Prince and Ryan, eds., *Livingston Papers* 3:123.

50. Letter to O. Wolcott from Washington, July 24, and to R. Howe from Washington, July 28, Aug. 24, 1779, in Fitzpatrick, ed., *Washington* 15:473, 496–98; letter to Trumbull from A. Ward, July 29, Aug. 19, and to Trumbull from T. Burr, Aug. 16, 1779, in JTP, vol. 10, nos. 58, 95, 103; letter to A. Ward from Trumbull, Aug. 5, 1779, vol. 20, no. 205; meeting of the governor and Council of Safety, Aug. 2, 3, 1779, in Hoadly et al., *State of Connecticut* 2:379, 393.

51. Simcoe, *Journal*, 104–7; Dann, ed., *Revolution Remembered*, 72–73.

52. General Orders, Aug. 22, 1779, in Fitzpatrick, ed., *Washington* 16:149; Peckham, ed., *Toll of Independence*, 63–64.

53. Uhlendorf, *Revolution in America*, 296; Simcoe, *Journal*, 107–8; letter to Trumbull from A. Ward, Sept. 1, and to Trumbull from J. Avery, Sept. 1, 1779, in JTP, vol. 10, nos. 136–37.

54. Letter to Govs. Trumbull, G. Clinton, and W. Livingston from Washington, Sept. 27, to G. Clinton from Washington, Oct. 4, to the president of Congress from Washington, Oct. 4, and to D'Estaing from Washington, Oct. 4, 1779, in Fitzpatrick, ed., *Washington* 16:344–45, 403–4, 406, 411.

55. Letter to G. Clinton from Washington, Oct. 1, to D'Estaing from Washington, Oct. 7, and to Trumbull from Washington, Oct. 10, 1779, in Fitzpatrick, ed., *Washington* 16:377, 428–29, 451–52; "An Act further to Amend an Act, entitled, An Act for regulating the Militia of the State of New York, and other Purposes therein mentioned," Oct. 9, 1779, and "An Act for regulating the Militia of the State of New York," Mar. 11, 1780, in New York Laws, Statutes, etc., card no. 17630, pp. 78–80, 121–22; message of Gov. Clinton to the [Senate], Jan. 27, 1780, in New York Governor; "An Act to embody, for a limited Time, four Thousand of the Militia of this State . . . ," Oct. 9, 1779, in New Jersey Session Laws, card no. 16395, pp. 135, 137–38; letter to Washington from W. Livingston, Oct. 8 and 9, 1779, in GWP, ser. 4, reel 61; meeting of the governor and Council of Safety, Oct. 9, and General Assembly, Oct. 14, 1779, in Hoadly et al., *State of Connecticut* 2:399–400, 405–8.

56. Letter to R. Caswell from W. Sharpe, Oct. 24, 1779, in Smith, ed., *Letters* 14:108; letter to the president of Congress from Washington, Nov. 14, to Trumbull from Washington, Nov. 16, to G. Clinton from Washington, Nov. 16, and to W. Livingston from Washington, Nov. 22, 1779, in Fitzpatrick, ed., *Washington* 17:105–6, 108–10, 160–61; to the president and Council of Massachusetts from Washington, Nov. 22, and to J. Reed from Washington, Nov. 22, 1779, in GWP, ser. 4, reel 62.

57. Letter to Trumbull from Washington, Oct. 22, 1779, in Fitzpatrick, ed., *Washington* 17:11; letter to G. Germain from H. Clinton, Oct. 26, 1779, in Davies, ed., *Documents* 17:236.

58. Simcoe, *Journal*, 109; Clinton, *American Rebellion*, 147.

59. Simcoe, *Journal*, 109–19; Clinton, *American Rebellion*, 147–48; Peckham, ed., *Toll of Independence*, 65.

60. Letter to W. Heath from Washington, Oct. 27, to J. Sullivan from Washington, Oct. 27, 28, to A. Wayne from Washington, Oct. 27, to W. Heath from R. Harrison, Oct. 28, and to G. Clinton from Washington, Oct. 29, 1779, in Fitzpatrick, ed., *Washington* 17:32–34, 36–38.

61. Buel, *Dear Liberty*, 196–97, 260; letter to Trumbull from O. Wolcott, Oct. 2, Nov. 30, 1779, in JTP, vol. 10, nos. 174, 252.

62. Letter to Trumbull from Washington, Nov. 20, and order of cantonment, [Nov.] 1779, in Fitzpatrick, ed., *Washington* 17:146–47, 209–10; estimate of troops etc. in the Eastern Dept., [Dec. 13], 1779, in JTP, vol. 10, no. 272; letter to Washington from Trumbull, Nov. 5, 1779, in GWP, ser. 4, reel 62.

63. Letter to A. Holmes from W. Livingston, Aug. 25, 1779, Mar. 21, 1780, to N. Scudder from W. Livingston, Dec. 24, 1779, and to Cols. Philips, Beavers, Blauvert, Taylor and Lt. Col. Chamberlain from W. Livingston, Mar. 18, 1780, in Prince and Ryan, eds., *Livingston Papers* 3:165–66, 280, 339–41, 343–44; order of cantonment, [Nov.] 1779, and to W. Livingston from Washington, Dec. 12, 1779, in Fitzpatrick, ed., *Washington* 17:210–11, 247; letter to Washington from W. Livingston, Dec. 7, 1779, in GWP, ser. 4, reel 62; Council, Dec. 23, 1779, and Mar. 19, 1780, in Bernstein, *Privy Council*, 140–41, 149.

64. Oct. 4, 1779, in NJGA, card no. 16402, p. 194; Dec. 26, 1779, ibid., card no. 16891, pp. 111–12; letter to J. Sullivan from W. Livingston, Nov. 2, 1779, in GWP, ser. 4, reel 62; letter to N. Heard from W. Livingston, Nov. 2, 1779, in Prince and Ryan, eds., *Livingston Papers* 3:191; letter to A. Wayne from Washington, Nov. 5, 9, to W. Maxwell from Washington, Nov. 16, order of troop cantonment, [Nov.], to W. Livingston from Washington, Dec. 21, and to W. Heath from Washington, Dec. 21, 1779, in Fitzpatrick, ed., *Washington* 17:77–78, 88, 114, 210, 294–96; letter to W. Heath from G. Clinton, Dec. 2, 30; letter to G. Clinton from W. Heath, Dec. 27, 1779, in PGC 5:392, 433–35; letter to [S.] Parsons from Washington, Dec. 13, 1779, in Revolutionary War, box 27, no. 65.

65. Clinton, *American Rebellion*, 140, 152; letter to G. Germain from H. Clinton, Mar. 9, 1780, in Davies, ed., *Documents* 18:53; Ewald, *Diary*, 173.

66. Letter to B. Harrison from Washington, Oct. 25, 1779, in Fitzpatrick, ed., *Washington* 17:20.

CHAPTER NINE
Lost Opportunities, 1780

1. General Assembly, Jan. 1780, in Hoadly et al., *State of Connecticut* 2:456–58; and General Assembly, May 1780, ibid. 3:29; letter to Trumbull from J. Cilley, Feb. 21, and to Trumbull from G. Silliman, May 2, 1780, in JTP, vol. 11, nos. 69, 170; letter to Trumbull from G. Silliman, July 7, 24, Sept. 5, to G. Silliman from E. Lockwood, June 13, and to G. Silliman from the justices and selectmen of Stamford, Sept. 4, 1780, ibid., vol. 12, nos. 9, 78, 137, 274, 277; letter to Trumbull from G. Silliman, Sept. 14, 1780, ibid., vol. 13, no. 5.

2. Uhlendorf, *Revolution in America*, 339; Peckham, ed., *Toll of Independence*, 67; General Assembly, Jan. 1780, and meeting of the governor and Council of Safety, Apr. 23, 1780, in Hoadly et al., *State of Connecticut* 2:456–58, 541–42; letter General Assembly, May 1780, ibid. 3:88; letter to [W. Heath] from [Col. Mead], Jan. 21, to Washington from W. Heath, Jan. 23, to S. Moylan from Trumbull, Feb. 19, to [R. Howe] from Col. Mead, Mar. 2, and to Washington from R. Howe, Mar. 7, May 25, 1780, in GWP, ser. 4, reels 63–64, 66; MacDougall, *American Revolutionary*, 128; letter to Trumbull from S. Moylan, Feb. 21, to J. Mead from Trumbull, Feb. 26, to Trumbull from E. Mygatt, Apr. 19, to G. Silliman from J. Mead, May 9, to [Trumbull] from [G. Silliman], May 12, to R. Howe from [Trumbull], May 26, to Trumbull from G. Silliman, June 4, 6; letter to Trumbull from R. Howe, June 7, 1780, in JTP, vol. 11, nos. 68, 75,

145, 177, 183, 209, 239, 253, 255; letter to Trumbull from L. Wells, June 18, and to Trumbull from B. Beebe, June 25, 1780, ibid., vol. 12, nos. 23, 46; letter to R. Howe from Washington, Mar. 10[–11], 1780, in Fitzpatrick, ed., *Washington* 18:104; Dann, ed., *Revolution Remembered*, 75.

3. Letter to G. Clinton from T. Thomas, Mar. 13, General Orders, Apr. 11, and to R. Howe from G. Clinton, Apr. 30, 1780, in *PGC* 5:539–40, 602–3, 660–61; Uhlendorf, *Revolution in America*, 340; Spaulding, *George Clinton*, 132; letter to G. Clinton from S. Huntington, Apr. 6, 1780, in Smith, ed., *Letters* 15:17–18; letter to Washington from R. Howe, May 25, 1780, in GWP, ser. 4, reel 66.

4. Letter to Lord Viscount Townshend from J. Pattison, July 26, 1779, and circular, Jan. 19, and to H. Clinton from J. Pattison, Feb. 21, 1780, in Pattison, "Official Letters of General Pattison," 98, 146–47, 346–47; letter to G. Germain from J. Pattison, Feb. 22, 1780, in Davies, ed., *Documents* 18:50–51.

5. Letter to Stirling from Washington, Jan. 12, 14, and to the president of Congress from Washington, Jan. 18, 1780, in Fitzpatrick, ed., *Washington* 7:379–80, 390, 406; Simcoe, *Journal*, 120–28; to W. Knyphausen, to T. Stirling, Jan. 15, 1780, in Davies, ed., *Documents* 18:34–35; letter to Washington from Stirling, Jan. 16, 1780, in GWP, ser. 4, reel 63; letter to A. Nesbitt from W. Stewart, Feb. 1, 1780, Col. Walter Stewart, Stewart Papers, 1776–95, New York Historical Society, New York City.

6. Letter to Lord Amherst from J. Robertson, Mar. 25, 1780, in Milton M. Klein and Ronald W. Howard, eds., *The Twilight of British Rule in Revolutionary America: The New York Letter Book of General James Robertson, 1780–1783*, 77–78; Uhlendorf, *Revolution in America*, 340, 345–46; Simcoe, *Journal*, 130–34; Peckham, ed., *Toll of Independence*, 67–68; letter to Washington from A. St. Clair, Feb. 11, 20, 1780, in GWP, ser. 4, reel 64; letter to the president of Congress from Washington, Jan. 27, 1780, in Fitzpatrick, ed., *Washington* 17:449; letter to [W.] Irvine from unknown sender, Jan. [?], 1780, in Revolutionary War, box 27, no. 77; Council, Feb. 3, 1780, in Bernstein, *Privy Council*, 144–46.

7. Uhlendorf, *Revolution in America*, 340; letter to Washington from A. St. Clair, Feb. 11, 20, to C. Stuart from magistrates, sheriff, and officers of militia, Mar. 22, to Washington from C. Stuart, Mar. 24, to Washington from J. Hallett, Apr. 16, and to Washington from W. Maxwell, May 26, 1780, in GWP, ser. 4, reels 64–66; letter to the president of Congress from Washington, Jan. 27, 1780, in Fitzpatrick, ed., *Washington* 17:449; letter to A. St. Clair from Washington, Feb. 12, 1780, ibid. 18:7; letter to [W.] Irvine from unknown sender, Jan. [?], 1780, in Revolutionary War, box 27, no. 77; Council, Dec. 21, 1779, Jan. 28, Feb. 3, Apr. 3, May 12, 18, June 13, 1780, in Bernstein, *Privy Council*, 141–46, 150, 152–53, 156; "An Act to amend an Act, intitled, An Act for the regulating, training and arraying of the Militia, and the supplementary Act thereto," Mar. 18, 1780, in New Jersey Session Laws, card no. 16884, pp. 67–68; "An Act to raise and embody, for a limited Time, Six Hundred and Twenty-Four Men, for the Defence of the Frontiers of this State," June 7, 1780, ibid., card no. 16885, p. 86; letter to P. Ward from W. Livingston, Apr. 19, and to J. Neilson from W. Livingston, May 12, 1780, in Prince and Ryan, eds., *Livingston Papers* 3:363–64, 378.

8. Letter to R. Howe from Washington, Mar. 11, to Baron de Kalb from Washington, Mar. 11, 1780, in Fitzpatrick, ed., *Washington* 8:106–8; letter to G. Clinton from R. Howe, Mar. 15, 1780, in *PGC* 5:542–43.

9. Letter to Trumbull from J. Huntington, Apr. 2, 1780, in JTP, vol. 11, no. 126; letter to the president of Congress from Washington, Apr. 2, and to G. Clinton from Washington, Apr. 5, 1780, in Fitzpatrick, ed., *Washington* 8:198, 220; General Orders, [May 1780?], in *PGC* 5:710–11.

10. Letter to G. Germain from J. Robertson, May 18, July 1, and to G. Germain from W. Knyphausen, July 3, 1780, in Davies, ed., *Documents* 18:96–97, 107–8, 110; Uhlendorf, *Revolution in America,* 353.

11. Letter to G. Germain from J. Robertson, July 1, and to G. Germain from W. Knyphausen, July 3, 1780, in Davies, ed., *Documents* 18:108, 110; letter to Maj. J. Talbot or officer commanding at Paramus from Washington, June 7, 1780, in Fitzpatrick, ed., *Washington* 18:487–88.

12. Uhlendorf, *Revolution in America,* 353–54; letter to G. Germain from J. Robertson, July 1, and to G. Germain from W. Knyphausen, July 3, 1780, in Davies, ed., *Documents* 18:108, 110; Ewald, *Diary,* 244; letter to Maj. J. Talbot or officer commanding at Paramus from Washington, June 7, to Stirling from Washington, June 7, and to the president of Congress from Washington, June 10, 1780, in Fitzpatrick, ed., *Washington* 18:487–88, 493; letter to W. Livingston from W. Maxwell, June 14, and to R. Ogden from A. Ogden, June 15, 1780, in Revolutionary War, box 27, nos. 33, 40.

13. Letter to Maj. J. Talbot or officer commanding at Paramus from Washington, June 7, to Stirling from Washington, June 7, and to the president of Congress from Washington, June 10, 1780, in Fitzpatrick, ed., *Washington* 18:487–88, 493; letter to G. Germain from J. Robertson, July 1, and to G. Germain from W. Knyphausen, July 3, 1780, in Davies, ed., *Documents* 18:108, 110–11; Uhlendorf, *Revolution in America,* 354.

14. Letter to Stirling from Washington, June 8, to the president of Congress from Washington, June 10, and to the Committee of Cooperation from Washington, June 11, 1780, in Fitzpatrick, ed., *Washington* 18:490, 493, 505–6; letter to W. Livingston from N. Heard, June 10, 1780, in Prince and Ryan, eds., *Livingston Papers* 3:425; letter to Washington from P. Dickinson, June 11, 1780, in GWP, ser. 4, reel 67.

15. Letter to S. Huntington from W. Livingston, June 11, and to J. Reed from W. Livingston, June 11, 1780, in Prince and Ryan, eds., *Livingston Papers* 3:432–33; letter to Washington from S. Huntington, June 12, and to Washington from G. Clinton, June 17, 1780, in GWP, ser. 4, reel 67; letter to P. Dickinson from Washington, June 13, and to R. Howe from Washington, June 15, 1780, in Fitzpatrick, ed., *Washington* 19:6, 14–15; letter to certain states from S. Huntington, June 15, 1780, in Smith, ed., *Letters* 15:321; letter to G. Clinton from R. Howe, June 15, 16, and to R. Howe from G. Clinton, June 17, 1780, in *PGC* 5:826–27, 832, 841.

16. Uhlendorf, *Revolution in America,* 354–55; letter to G. Germain from J. Robertson, July 1, and to G. Germain from H. Clinton, July 4, 1780, in Davies, ed., *Documents* 18:108, 112; Clinton, *American Rebellion,* 190–92.

17. Letter to Trumbull from Washington, June 18, General Orders, June 22, and to the president of Congress from Washington, June 25, 1780, in Fitzpatrick, ed., *Washington* 19:30–31, 54–55, 63–64; Thayer, *Greene,* 274; meeting of the governor and Council of Safety, June 20, 21, 1780, in Hoadly et al., *State of Connecticut* 3:109–10; letter to Brig. Gen. Hart from Trumbull, June 21, and to A. Ward from Trumbull, June 21, 1780, in JTP, vol. 20, nos. 255–56; letter to G. Clinton from R. Howe, June 19, 1780, in *PGC* 5:853.

18. Letter to G. Germain from J. Robertson, July 1, and to G. Germain from H. Clinton, July 4, 1780, in Davies, ed., *Documents* 18:108, 112–13; Clinton, *American Rebellion,* 193; Simcoe, *Journal,* 143; Ewald, *Diary,* 245.

19. Letter to Washington from P. Dickinson, June 20, to Washington from Baron von Steuben, June 20, and to Washington from N. Greene, June 23, 1780, in GWP, ser. 4, reel 67; letter to S. Huntington from W. Livingston, June 20, and to Baron von Steuben from W. Livingston, June 21, 1780, in Prince and Ryan, eds., *Livingston Papers* 3:436, 438; meeting of the governor and Council of Safety, June 23, 1780, in Hoadly et al., *State*

of Connecticut 3:112; General Orders, June 22, and to the president of Congress from Washington, June 25, 1780, in Fitzpatrick, ed., *Washington* 19:54–55, 63–64.

20. Simcoe, *Journal,* 143; letter to G. Germain from J. Robertson, July 1, 1780, in Davies, ed., *Documents* 18:108–9; Greene's orders, June 24, 1780, in Showman, ed., *Greene* 6:41.

21. Letter to Washington from Stirling, June 23, to Washington from R. Meade, June 23, and to Washington from N. Greene, June 24, 1780, in GWP, ser. 4, reel 67; letter to A. Irvine from W. Irvine, June 24, 1780, in Revolutionary War, box 27, no. 17; letter to the president of Congress from Washington, June 25, 1780, in Fitzpatrick, ed., *Washington* 19:64; Greene's orders, June 24, 1780, in Showman, ed., *Greene* 6:41; Dohla, *Hessian Diary,* 131; Simcoe, *Journal,* 144–45.

22. Letter to Washington from R. Meade, June 23, and to Washington from N. Greene, June 24, 1780, in GWP, ser. 4, reel 67; letter to the president of Congress from Washington, June 25, 1780, in Fitzpatrick, ed., *Washington* 19:64; Simcoe, *Journal,* 145–48; Greene's orders, June 24, 1780, in Showman, ed., *Greene* 6:41; Dohla, *Hessian Diary,* 131–32; Ewald, *Diary,* 245–46.

23. Letter to Trumbull from R. Howe, June 24, 28, 1780, in JTP, vol. 12, nos. 43, 55; letter to Lt. Gov. Cortlandt from G. Clinton, June 25, 1780, in *PGC* 5:887; letter to R. Howe from Washington, June 27, to Trumbull from Washington, June 27, and to G. Clinton from Washington, June 27, 1780, in Fitzpatrick, ed., *Washington* 19:77–78, 81–82, 84; letter to P. Dickinson from N. Greene, June 26, 1780, in Showman, ed., *Greene* 6:44.

24. Clinton, *American Rebellion,* 194–95; letter to G. Germain from J. Robertson, July 1, to G. Germain from H. Clinton, July 4, and to H. Clinton from G. Germain, Aug. 3, 1780, in Davies, ed., *Documents* 18:109, 113, 134; letter to Lord Amherst from J. Robertson, July 25, 1780, in Klein and Howard, eds., *Twilight of British Rule,* 138; Benians, *Journal by Hughes,* 89.

25. Letter to the president of Congress from Washington, June 25, 1780, in Fitzpatrick, ed., *Washington* 19:65; poem in Klein and Howard, eds., *Twilight of British Rule,* 129n.19.

26. Kaplan, "Hidden War," 129; letter to G. Germain from H. Clinton, July 4, 1780, in Davies, ed., *Documents* 18:113; letter to G. Clinton from Washington, May 18, 1780, in Fitzpatrick, ed., *Washington* 18:383–84; letter to H. Clinton from J. Robertson, May 31, 1780, in Klein and Howard, eds., *Twilight of British Rule,* 117.

27. Letter to G. Clinton from Washington, May 18, and to the Committee of Cooperation from Washington, May 25, 31, 1780, in Fitzpatrick, ed., *Washington* 18:383–84, 418–19, 456–58.

28. Letter to certain states from the committee at headquarters, June 2, 1780, in Smith, ed., *Letters* 15:231–32; circular to the states from Washington, June 2, 1780, in Fitzpatrick, ed., *Washington* 18:468–69; circular to the states from Washington, June 30, 1780, ibid. 19:104–5; letter to Lord Amherst from J. Robertson, July 25, 1780, in Klein and Howard, eds., *Twilight of British Rule,* 138.

29. Freeman, *Washington* 5:178; letter to G. Germain from H. Clinton, Aug. 25, 1780, in Davies, ed., *Documents* 18:152–53; letter to Lord Amherst from J. Robertson, July 25, 1780, in Klein and Howard, eds., *Twilight of British Rule,* 140–41; letter to the president of Congress from Washington, Aug. 3, 1780, in Fitzpatrick, ed., *Washington* 19:318.

30. Letter to G. Germain from H. Clinton, Aug. 25, 1780, in Davies, ed., *Documents* 18:152–53; letter to the president of Congress from Washington, July 27, to R. Howe from Washington, July 27, to Rochambeau from Washington, July 31, to Trumbull from Washington, Aug. 1, to W. Livingston from Washington, Aug. 1, to P. Dickinson from Washington, Aug. 1, and to the president of Congress from Washington, Aug. 3, 1780, in Fitzpatrick, ed., *Washington* 19:270–73, 281, 291–93, 295–96, 318; letter to Lord

Amherst from J. Robertson, July 25, 1780, in Klein and Howard, eds., *Twilight of British Rule*, 138; Peckham, ed., *Toll of Independence*, 73; letter to Col. Hopkins from G. Clinton, July 13, to G. Clinton from R. Howe, July 29, and to Gen. Swartwout, and Cols. Drake, Thomas, Crane, Hammond, Platt, and Benedict from G. Clinton, Aug. 1, 1780, in *PGC* 6:8, 66, 71-72; letter to the colonels of the New Jersey militia from W. Livingston, July 17, 1780, in Prince and Ryan, eds., *Livingston Papers* 4:12; letter to the officers commanding the Massachusetts and New Hampshire militia from Washington, Aug. 3, 1780, in GWP, ser. 4, reel 68.

31. Letter to Washington from W. Livingston, Aug. 4, to Washington from W. Malcom, Aug. 4, to Washington from B. Arnold, Aug. 6, 12, to Washington from J. Goetchius, Aug. 8, to Washington from S. Seely, Aug. 10, return of the militia in garrison at West Point, Aug. 12, and letter to Washington from J. Reed, Aug. 17, 1780, in GWP, ser. 4, reels 68-69; Council, Aug. 4, 1780, in Bernstein, *Privy Council*, 165-66.

32. Letter to G. Germain from H. Clinton, Aug. 25, 1780, in Davies, ed., *Documents* 18:152-53; letter to Lord Amherst from J. Robertson, July 25, 1780, in Klein and Howard, eds., *Twilight of British Rule*, 140-41; letter to the president of Congress from Washington, Aug. 3, 1780, in Fitzpatrick, ed., *Washington* 19:318; letter to W. Livingston from Washington, Aug. 17 and 26, 1780, in Prince and Ryan, eds., *Livingston Papers* 4:38, 52-53.

33. Freeman, *Washington* 5:180; letter to S. Seely from Washington, Aug. 6, to Trumbull from Washington, Aug. 8, to W. Livingston from Washington, Aug. 17, and to the Committee of Cooperation from Washington, Aug. 17, 1780, in Fitzpatrick, ed., *Washington* 19:331, 339, 386-87, 392-93; letter to the states from the committee at headquarters, Aug. 19, 1780, in Smith, ed., *Letters* 15:601-2.

34. Letter to W. Livingston from Washington, Aug. 20, and to the president of Congress from Washington, Aug. 20, 1780, in Fitzpatrick, ed., *Washington* 19:400, 409-11; letter to J. Reed from N. Greene, Sept. 5, 1780, in Showman, ed., *Greene* 6:260.

35. Letter to W. Livingston from Washington, Aug. 26, to the president of Congress from Washington, Aug. 28, and to Trumbull from Washington, Aug. 28, 1780, in Fitzpatrick, ed., *Washington* 19:439, 456-57, 462; letter to N. Greene from Washington, Sept. 16, 1780, ibid., 20:58-59.

36. Letter to G. Germain from J. Robertson, Sept. 1, 1780, in Klein and Howard, eds., *Twilight of British Rule*, 161; letter to [W. Eden] from H. Clinton, Sept. 1, 1780, in Clinton, *American Rebellion*, 456; to G. Germain from H. Clinton, Aug. 25, 1780, in Davies, ed., *Documents* 18:153.

37. Letter to G. Germain from H. Clinton, Oct. 11, 1780, in Davies, ed., *Documents* 18:183-84.

38. Council of War, Sept. 6, letter to C. Low from Washington, Sept. 25, to W. Betts from Washington, Sept. 25, to the president of Congress from Washington, Sept. 26, to A. St. Clair from Washington, [Oct. 1], and to N. Greene from Washington, Oct. 6, 1780, in Fitzpatrick, ed., *Washington* 20:7, 87-88, 92, 106, 126.

39. Letter to the president of Congress from Washington, Sept. 15, and circular to the states from Washington, Oct. 18, 1780, in Fitzpatrick, ed., *Washington* 20:49-50, 209.

40. Letter to G. Clinton from L. Morris, T. Thomas, S. Drake, and S. Delivan, Sept. 9, to G. Clinton from W. Heath, Nov. 1, General Orders, Dec. 3, to G. Clinton from T. Thomas, Dec. 4, to Col. Thomas from G. Clinton, Dec. 6, and to Col. Benson from P. Pell, Dec. 22, 1780, in *PGC* 6:187-89, 365-66, 461-64, 477-78, 515; letter to Washington from W. Heath, Dec. 23, 1780, in GWP, ser. 4, reel 73; letter to Trumbull from L. Wells, Sept. 21, and to G. Silliman from J. Mead, Sept. 23, 1780, in JTP, vol. 8, nos. 21, 27; "An Act to raise Troops for the further Defence of the Frontiers,

and for other Purposes therein mentioned," Sept. 29, 1780, New York Laws, Statutes, etc., card no. 17630, p. 151.

41. Letter to W. Livingston from Washington, Nov. 19, 1780, in Prince and Ryan, eds., *Livingston Papers* 4:92; Oct. 7, 1780, in NJGA, card no. 16894, p. 298; Nov. 4, 1780, ibid., card no. 16897, p. 17; Council, July 8, 19, Aug. 4, 22, Sept. 14, 24, 29, Nov. 1, 20, 28, Dec. 25, 1780, in Bernstein, *Privy Council*, 159–60, 163, 165, 169, 170–72, 181, 184–86, 190; Nov. 25, 1780, in New Jersey Legislative Council Journals, card no. 17262, p. 21; letter to Washington from J. Goetchius, Oct. 8, 1780, in GWP, ser. 4, reel 71; letter to J. Goetchius from Washington, Oct. 7, and to S. Moylan from Washington, Nov. 21, 1780, in Fitzpatrick, ed., *Washington* 20:130, 381–82; "An Act to raise, by voluntary Enlistment, eight hundred and twenty Men, for the Defence of the Frontiers of this State," Dec. 26, 1780, in New Jersey Session Laws, card no. 17259, pp. 23–25.

42. Letter to G. Silliman from B. Beebe, July 1, to Trumbull from S. Parsons, July 3, to G. Silliman from J. Fitch, July 7, to Trumbull from L. Wells, Aug. 19, to Trumbull from J. Mackay, Aug. 21, to G. Silliman from J. Mead, Sept. 8, and to Trumbull from G. Silliman, Sept. 11, 1780, in JTP, vol. 12, nos. 66, 71, 79, 238, 242, 280, 292; letter to Trumbull from L. Wells, Sept. 21, to G. Silliman from J. Mead, Sept. 23, to Trumbull from G. Silliman, Sept. 23, Oct. 26, Nov. 18, and Dec. 27, to G. Silliman from B. Beebe, Oct. 23, to Trumbull from N. Peters, Dec. 11, and brigade orders by G. Silliman, Dec. 18, 28, ibid., vol. 13, nos. 21, 27–28, 97, 114, 156, 204, 234, 249, 252; letter to G. Silliman from Trumbull, Sept. 16, 1780, ibid., vol. 20, no. 274; meeting of the governor and Council of Safety, Aug. 15, Sept. 6, Dec. 25, and General Assembly, Oct. and Nov., 1780, in Hoadly et al., *State of Connecticut* 3:149, 166, 184, 239, 248, 281–82; letter to B. Arnold from L. Wells, Aug. 29, and to Washington from Trumbull, Sept. 16, 26, 1780, in GWP, ser. 4, reels 70–71; letter to J. Douglas from Trumbull, Dec. 16, 1780, in JDP, no. 67.

43. Dann, ed., *Revolution Remembered*, 76; Ewald, *Diary*, 250.

44. Letter to Adm. Arbuthnot from H. Clinton, Nov. 1, Dec. 13, 1780, in Clinton, *American Rebellion*, 471–72, 481; letter to M. Arbuthnot from H. Clinton, Dec. 9, 1780, in Davies, ed., *Documents* 18:251–52.

45. Letter to G. Ludlow from G. Silliman, Sept. 23, Oct. 12, to G. Silliman from G. Ledyard [Ludlow], Sept. 26, Oct. 12, Dec. 7, and to Trumbull from G. Silliman, Oct. 13, Dec. 13, 1780, in JTP, vol. 13, nos. 26, 34, 67, 69, 197, 217.

46. Letter to Trumbull from G. Silliman, Dec. 8, and to Trumbull from Lauzun, Dec. 24, 1780, in ibid., 199, 243; letter to Washington from Trumbull, Dec. 15, 1780, in GWP, ser. 4, reel 73.

47. Zagarri, ed., *Humphreys' "Life of Washington,"* 20–21.

CHAPTER TEN
The Militia Helps Seize an Opportunity, 1781

1. Letter to Washington from A. Wayne, Jan. 2, 1781, in GWP, ser. 4, reel 73; Council, Jan. 3, 7, 1781, in Bernstein, *Privy Council*, 192, 194.

2. Anderson, *People's Army*, 61; letter to Lord Amherst from J. Robertson, Jan. 24, 1781, in Klein and Howard, eds., *Twilight of British Rule*, 169–70; letter to G. Germain from H. Clinton, Jan. 25, 1781, in Davies, ed., *Documents* 20:43; Mackenzie, *Diary* 2:441.

3. Letter to Washington from P. Dickinson, Jan. 12, 1781, in GWP, ser. 4, reel 74; letter to G. Clinton from Washington, Jan. 4, 16, and to the president of Congress from Washington, Jan. 15, 1781, in Fitzpatrick, ed., *Washington* 21:58–59, 104, 113; Spaulding, *George Clinton*, 136.

396 • ★ NOTES TO PAGES 283–286

4. Mackenzie, *Diary* 2:448, 450; letter to G. Germain from H. Clinton, Jan. 25, 1781, in Davies, ed., *Documents* 20:43; letter to Lord Amherst from J. Robertson, Jan. 24, 1781, in Klein and Howard, eds., *Twilight of British Rule,* 169–70.

5. Letter to Washington from P. Dickinson, Jan. 12, 1781, in GWP, ser. 4, reel 74; Mackenzie, *Diary* 2:451–52; Uhlendorf, *Revolution in America,* 404; Wed., Jan. 24, 1781, in Ford and Hunt, eds., *Journals of Continental Congress* 19:78–79, 81.

6. Wed., Jan. 24, 1781, in Ford and Hunt, eds., *Journals of Continental Congress* 19:78–79, 81; letter to J. Wadsworth from S. Parsons, Jan. 14, 1781, in Hall, *Parsons,* 321; letter to Lord Amherst from J. Robertson, Jan. 24, 1781, in Klein and Howard, eds., *Twilight of British Rule,* 170; Uhlendorf, *Revolution in America,* 404–5; letter to G. Germain from H. Clinton, Jan. 25, 29, 1781, in Davies, ed., *Documents* 20:43, 51; letter to the president of Congress from Washington, Jan. 15, and to P. Dickinson from Washington, Jan. 16, 1781, in Fitzpatrick, ed., *Washington* 21:104, 111.

7. Letter to R. Howe from Washington, Jan. 22, 1781, in Fitzpatrick, ed., *Washington* 21:128–29; letter to W. Livingston from Washington, Jan. 23, 1781, in Prince and Ryan, eds., *Livingston Papers* 4:128.

8. Letter to G. Germain from H. Clinton, Jan. 29, 1781, in Davies, ed., *Documents* 20:52; letter to Lord Amherst from J. Robertson, Jan. 24, 1781, in Klein and Howard, eds., *Twilight of British Rule,* 172; letter to Washington from F. Frelinghuysen, Jan. 23, Feb. 3, and to Washington from E. Dayton, Jan. 24, 1781, in GWP, ser. 4, reel 74; Freeman, *Washington* 5:247; letter to W. Livingston from Washington, Jan. 27, 1781, in Fitzpatrick, ed., *Washington* 21:148.

9. "An Act for the regulating, training, and arraying of the Militia, and for providing more effectually for the Defence and Security of the State," Jan. 8, 1781, New Jersey Session Laws, card no. 17259, pp. 39, 45–47; Council, Mar. 28, 1781, in Bernstein, *Privy Council,* 197; letter to H. Van Dycke from W. Livingston, Apr. 8, 1781, in Prince and Ryan, eds., *Livingston Papers* 4:175–76; May 28, 1781, in NJGA, card no. 17265, p. 18; to Washington from P. Dickinson, Jan. 29, 1781, in GWP, ser. 4, reel 74.

10. Letter to Trumbull from S. Bishop and T. Jones, Jan. 6, to Trumbull from J. Denison, P. Crary, N. Palmers, and N. Minor, Jan. 16, to Trumbull from the civil authority and selectmen of Norwalk, Jan. 19, to Trumbull from G. Silliman, Jan. 20, Feb. 8, to Trumbull from W. Worthington, Jan. 30, Petition to Trumbull and the Council of Safety from E. Russell, Feb. 2, and to G. Faining and S. Bilings from A. Sheffield, May 12, 1781, in JTP, vol. 14, nos. 15, 42, 48, 53, 69, 88, 109, 230; Buel, *Dear Liberty,* 251; meeting of the governor and Council of Safety, Feb. 2, 8, and General Assembly, Feb. 21, May, 1781, in Hoadly et al., *State of Connecticut* 3:299, 303, 318–19, 396; letter to Trumbull from C. Conroy, Feb. 10, 1781, CSP.

11. Letter to G. Silliman from Col. St. John, Jan. 8, to Trumbull from D. Austin and T. Jones, Feb. 4, to G. Silliman from the selectmen and civil authority of Fairfield and J. Dimon, Mar. 6, and to Trumbull from J. Fitch, Apr. 21, 1781, in JTP, vol. 14, nos. 20, 81, 120, 194; letter to J. Fitch from D. Waterbury, May 19, 1781, in David Waterbury, Col. David Waterbury's Orderly Book (1775–81), 144, Connecticut State Library, Hartford; meeting of the governor and Council of Safety, Jan. 25, May 30, and June 3, 1781, in Hoadly et al., *State of Connecticut* 3:297, 448, 453; Mackenzie, *Diary* 2:552–53.

12. Letter to G. Silliman from J. Mead, Jan. 3, and to Trumbull from G. Silliman, Jan. 5, 9, 1781, in JTP, vol. 14, nos. 6, 12, 22; brigade orders—G. Silliman, Jan. 5, 1781, ibid., vol. 13, no. 25.

13. Letter to [Trumbull] from the civil authority and selectmen of Greenwich, Jan. 15, to Trumbull from J. Mead, Jan. 6, Mar. 1, brigade orders—G. Silliman, Jan. 23, 27, and to Trumbull from G. Silliman, Feb. 5, 1781, in JTP, vol. 14, nos. 36–37, 56, 63, 79,

111; meeting of the governor and Council of Safety, Jan. 23, 1781, in Hoadly et al., *State of Connecticut* 3:293–94.

14. Meeting of the governor and Council of Safety, Mar. 24, 1781, in Hoadly et al., *State of Connecticut* 3:351; letter to Trumbull from D. Waterbury, Apr. 1, 1781, in JTP, vol. 15, no. 310; letter to Trumbull from D. Waterbury, Apr. 16, May 7, June 9, 1781, ibid., vol. 14, nos. 187, 216, 278; letter to Washington from D. Waterbury, June 14, 1781, in GWP, ser. 4, reel 78.

15. Letter to W. Heath from W. Hull, Jan. 1, 6, and to S. Parsons from W. Hull, Jan. 25, 1781 in GWP, ser. 4, reels 73–74; Freeman, *Washington* 5:52; letter to W. Heath from Washington, Jan. 7, 1781, in Fitzpatrick, ed., *Washington* 21:68–69.

16. Letter to W. Heath from S. Parsons, Jan. 25, and to Maj. Tallmadge from Maj. Alden, n.d., 1781, in Hall, *Parsons*, 330–34; letter to Trumbull from S. Parsons, Jan. 23, 30, 1781, in JTP, vol. 14, nos. 54, 68; return of killed, wounded, and missing on the expedition to Morrisania, Jan. 21, and to S. Parsons from W. Hull, Jan. 25, 1781, in GWP, ser. 4, reel 74; Peckham, ed., *Toll of Independence*, 79.

17. Feb. 6, 9, 1781, in Journal of the General Assembly of New York, vol. 4; letter to Maj. Morrill from J. Fogg, Apr. 2, 1781, in GWP, ser. 4, reel 76; letter to J. Jay from G. Clinton, Apr. 6, 1781, in *PGC* 6:747.

18. Letter to J. Jay from G. Clinton, Apr. 6, 1781, in *PGC* 6:747; letter to G. Clinton from [N. Delivan], June 18, 1781, ibid. 7:30; Journal of the Comte de Clermont-Crevecoeur, July 1, 2, and Journal of Louis-Alexandre Berthier, July 6, 1781, in Howard C. Rice, Jr., and Anne S. K. Brown, trans. and eds., *The American Campaigns of Rochambeau's Army, 1780, 1781, 1782, 1783* 1:31–32, 249.

19. Letter to Col. Humphries from W. Heath, Mar. 14, 1781, in GWP, ser. 4, reel 75; letter to G. Clinton from R. Van Rensselaer, Apr. 16, to Col. Willett from G. Clinton, Apr. 28, and to Maj. Logan from G. Clinton, May 2, 1781, in *PGC* 6:779–80, 807–9, 826–27; "An Act to raise Troops for the immediate Defence of the State," Mar. 10, 1781, in New York Laws, Statutes, etc., card no. 17630, p. 172.

20. Peckham, ed., *Toll of Independence*, 86; letter to Brig. Gen. Patterson from J. Pray, May 14, to [Washington] from J. Lawrence, May 16, and to Washington from A. Scammel, May 24, 1781, in GWP, ser. 4, reels 77–78; letter to Maj. Logan from G. Clinton, May 2, 1781, in *PGC* 6:826–27; letter to A. Scammel from Washington, May 17, 1781, in Fitzpatrick, ed., *Washington* 22:94–95.

21. Letter to W. Heath from Washington, Feb. 23, circular to the colonels of the Orange and Ulster militia from Washington, Feb. 25, to P. Dickinson from Washington, Mar. 1, to W. Livingston from Washington, Mar. 1, and to Rochambeau from Washington, Apr. 7, 1781, in Fitzpatrick, ed., *Washington* 21:280–81, 290–91, 324, 326, 426–27; letter to Washington from G. Clinton, Jan. 26, and to Washington from P. Dickinson, Mar. 14, 1781, in GWP, ser. 4, reels 74–75.

22. Freeman, *Washington* 5:266; Thur., Mar. 1, 1781, in Ford and Hunt, eds., *Journals of Continental Congress* 19:214, 216, 219; Higginbotham, *War of Independence*, 206; Thomas Rodney, Diary, Apr. 18, 1781, in Burnett, ed., *Letters* 6:62.

23. Letter to R. Howe from Washington, May 7, strength of the army, May 22, circular to the New England states from Washington, May 24, to W. Livingston from Washington, May 27, and to J. Reed from Washington, May 27, 1781, in Fitzpatrick, ed., *Washington* 22:51, 102, 109–11, 116–18; Freeman, *Washington* 5:286–89.

24. General Assembly, May 10–June 16, 1781, in Hoadly et al., *State of Connecticut* 3:377–78; May 31, 1781, in NJGA, card no. 17265, pp. 25–26; letter to G. Clinton from S. Parsons, June 7, 1781, in Hall, *Parsons*, 248.

25. Letter to Rochambeau from Washington, June 13, to W. Heath from Washington, June 15, to Trumbull from Washington, June 15, to W. Livingston from Washington,

June 15, and to J. Reed from Washington, June 15, 1781, in Fitzpatrick, ed., *Washington* 22:207- 8, 217, 222, 224.

26. Meeting of the governor and Council of Safety, June 19, 1781, in Hoadly et al., *State of Connecticut* 3:462; letter to Trumbull from D. Waterbury, June 16, 1781, in JTP, vol. 14, no. 290; letter to Washington from Trumbull, June 20, 1781, in GWP, ser. 4, reel 78; letter to G. Clinton from Washington, June 25, and to J. Hancock from Washington, June 25, 1781, in Fitzpatrick, ed., *Washington* 22:265–66; "An Act for a further Levy of Troops, for the Defence of this State," July 1, 1781, in New York Laws, Statutes, etc., card no. 17630, p. 201; June 27, 1781, in New York Senate Journals, card no. 44424, p. 103.

27. June 27, 1781, in NJGA, card no. 17265, p. 98; "An Act to authorize the Governor or Commander in Chief of this State for the Time being, to call out a Part of the Militia of this State, and to continue them in Service for three Months," June 27, 1781, in New Jersey Session Laws, card no. 17260, pp. 112–13; Council, June 27, 1781, in Bernstein, *Privy Council*, 201–2; letter to W. Livingston from A. Holmes, June 23, and petition of the inhabitants of Bergen County, June 26, 1781, in Prince and Ryan, eds., *Livingston Papers* 4:224–25, 233–34; Mackenzie, *Diary* 2:548, 550, 555; Peckham, ed., *Toll of Independence*, 87.

28. Letter to G. Germain from H. Clinton, Jan. 25, and to H. Clinton from G. Gemain, Mar. 7, 1781, in Davies, ed., *Documents* 20:44, 76.

29. Letter to G. Germain from H. Clinton, Apr. 5–20, and to G. Germain from B. Arnold, June 25, 1781, in Davies, ed., *Documents* 20:104, 163.

30. Letter to G. Germain from H. Clinton, June 9–12, 1781, in Davies, ed., ibid., 154–56; letter to C. Cornwallis from H. Clinton, June 11, 1781, in Clinton, *American Rebellion*, 530.

31. Letter to C. Cornwallis from H. Clinton, June 11, 1781, in Clinton, *American Rebellion*, 530–31.

32. Journal of Clermont-Crevecoeur, June 10, July 1, 1781, in Rice, *American Campaigns* 1:27, 31; Mackenzie, *Diary* 2:556; letter to D. Waterbury from Washington, June 30, July 1, to W. Sackett from Washington, June 30, to Rochambeau from Washington, June 30, to G. Clinton from Washington, June 30, to Lauzun from Washington, July 1, and to H. Knox from Washington, July 2, 1781, in Fitzpatrick, ed., *Washington* 22:290–95, 304, 308–9, 322; to Washington from D. Waterbury, July 1, 1781, in GWP, ser. 4, reel 79.

33. Journal of Clermont-Crevecoeur, July 1, 2, 1781, in Rice and Brown, eds., *American Campaigns* 1:31; letter to the president of Congress from Washington, July 6, 1781, in Fitzpatrick, ed., *Washington* 22:329–31; July 2, 1781, in Waterbury, Col. David Waterbury's Orderly Book (1775–81), 58–59.

34. Mackenzie, *Diary* 2:556–58; letter to Lord Amherst from J. Robertson, July 5, 1781, in Klein and Howard, eds., *Twilight of British Rule*, 206; letter to the president of Congress from Washington, July 6, 1781, in Fitzpatrick, ed., *Washington* 22:329–31.

35. Letter to the president of Congress from Washington, July 6, 1781, in Fitzpatrick, ed., *Washington* 22:329–31; July 2, 1781, in Waterbury, Col. David Waterbury's Orderly Book (1775–81), 58–59; Mackenzie, *Diary* 2:558–59.

36. Letter to the president of Congress from Washington, July 6, 1781, in Fitzpatrick, ed., *Washington* 22:329–31; Mackenzie, *Diary* 2:559; journal of Clermont-Crevecoeur, July 3, 1781, in Rice and Brown, eds., *American Campaigns* 1:32; letter to Lord Amherst from J. Robertson, July 5, 1781, in Klein and Howard, eds., *Twilight of British Rule*, 206.

37. Journal of Clermont-Crevecoeur, July 6, and journal of Berthier, July 6, 1781, in Rice and Brown, eds., *American Campaigns* 1:32, 249; letter to Washington from Rochambeau, July 4, 1781, in GWP, ser. 4, reel 79; General Orders, July 3, and letter to Lafayette from Washington, July 13, 1781, in Fitzpatrick, ed., *Washington* 22:326, 367–

68; Peckham, ed., *Toll of Independence*, 88; Mackenzie, *Diary* 2:570–73; Dann, ed., *Revolution Remembered*, 83–84.

38. Journal of Jean-Baptiste-Antoine de Verger, July 10, 1781, in Rice and Brown, eds., *American Campaigns* 1:130–32.

39. Brigade orders—J. Mead, July 5, letter to Trumbull from R. Enos, July 9, and to Trumbull from J. Mead, July 10, 1781, in JTP, vol. 14, nos. 325, 330, 338; letter to Trumbull from J. Douglas, July 14, and brigade orders—J. Mead, July 20, ibid. 15, nos. 10, 24; letter to J. Douglas from Trumbull, July 11, and to J. Stodder and E. Lewis from Trumbull, July 11, 1781, ibid., vol. 20, nos. 304, 308; letter to W. Livingston from S. Condict, July 20, 1781, in Prince and Ryan, eds., *Livingston Papers* 4:243; conference at Dobb's Ferry, July 19, 1781, in Fitzpatrick, ed., *Washington* 22:395–96.

40. Letter to G. Germain from H. Clinton, July 13, and to C. Cornwallis from H. Clinton, July 15, 1781, in Davies, ed., *Documents* 20:186, 190.

41. Letter to W. Knox from J. Robertson, July 12, 1781, in Klein and Howard, eds., *Twilight of British Rule*, 211; letter to Right Hon. T. Townshend from Hon. H. Brodrick, Sept. 30, 1781, in Ross, ed., *Correspondence of Cornwallis* 1:123.

42. Letter to D. Waterbury from Washington, July 21, to D. Forman from Washington, July 21, and to S. Seely from Washington, July 27, 1781, in Fitzpatrick, ed., *Washington* 22:406–8, 422–23; letter to Washington from E. Dayton, July 23, return of the detachment of militia of New Jersey, July 29, to Washington from S. Seely, July 30, to Washington from A. McDougall, July 30, and to Washington from Trumbull, July 31, 1781, in GWP, ser. 4, reel 79; Council, Aug. 2, 1781, in Bernstein, *Privy Council*, 203; letter to Trumbull from S. Heart, July 30, 1781, in JTP, vol. 15, no. 46; MacDougall, *American Revolutionary*, 129, 137, 141.

43. Letter to the president of Congress from Washington, Aug. 2, circular to New Hampshire, Massachusetts, Connecticut, and New Jersey from Washington, Aug. 2, and to G. Clinton from Washington, Aug. 5, 1781, in Fitzpatrick, ed., *Washington* 22:446–47, 451–52, 468; letter to Washington from A. McDougall, Aug. 3, and to Washington from W. Livingston, Aug. 6, 1781, in GWP, ser. 4, reel 80.

44. Letter to H. Livingston from G. Clinton, Aug. 6, 1781, in *PGC* 7:57; letter to Washington from Trumbull, Aug. 8, and to Washington from S. Seely, Aug. 10, 1781, in GWP, ser. 4, reel 80; Aug., 1781, in Heath, *Memoirs* 273–74.

45. Mackenzie, *Diary* 2:576, 581–82, 595; letter to G. Germain from H. Clinton, Aug. 20, 1781, in Davies, ed., *Documents* 20:217.

46. Letter to H. Clinton from C. Cornwallis, Aug. 20, and to Maj. Gen. Leslie from C. Cornwallis, Aug. 27, 1781, in Ross, ed., *Correspondence of Cornwallis* 1:114–15, 118.

47. Aug. 17, 1781, in Heath, *Memoirs*, 275; letter to de Grasse from Washington, Aug. 17, to W. Heath from Washington, Aug. 19, and circular to the states from Washington, Aug. 21, 1781, in Fitzpatrick, ed., *Washington* 23:7–8, 20–22, 26–27.

48. Letter to E. Dayton from Washington, Aug. 19, 1781, in Fitzpatrick, ed., *Washington* 23:23–24; Aug. 21–23, 1781, in Heath, *Memoirs*, 279–80; letter to Trumbull from D. Waterbury, Aug. 24, 1781, in JTP, vol. 15, no. 73; letter to Col. Weissenfels from G. Clinton, [Aug. 25, 1781], in *PGC* 7:255.

49. Letter to W. Heath from Washington, Aug. 29, 1781, in Fitzpatrick, ed., *Washington* 23:67–68.

50. Letter to C. Cornwallis from H. Clinton, Aug. 27, Sept. 2, 6, 1781, in Clinton, *American Rebellion*, 562–64; letter to G. Germain from H. Clinton, Sept. 7, 12, 1781, in Davies, ed., *Documents* 20:222–23, 230–31.

51. Mackenzie, *Diary* 2:606, 624, 638–39; letter to Hon. T. Townshend from Hon. H. Brodrick, Sept. 30, 1781, in Ross, ed., *Correspondence of Cornwallis* 1:122–23.

52. Freeman, *Washington* 5:300, 310; Sept. 1, 5, 1781, in Orderly Books, Aug. 22, 1781–Aug. 9, 1782, vols. 55–60, in War Department Collection, M853, reel 9, vol. 60:44–45, 66–67, National Archives; letter to Washington from W. Heath, Sept. 1, 1781, in GWP, ser. 4, reel 80; letter to W. Heath from G. Clinton, Sept. 1, 2, and to G. Clinton from W. Heath, Sept. 3, 1781, in *PGC* 7:284, 288, 293–94; letter to Trumbull from W. Heath, Sept. 2, 1781, in JTP, vol. 15, no. 89.

53. Letter to Washington from W. Heath, Sept. 9, 12, 1781, in GWP, ser. 4, reel 80; letter to Trumbull from W. Heath, Sept. 10, 1781, in JTP, vol. 15, no. 109; Sept. 11, 13, 1781, in Heath, *Memoirs*, 284–85.

54. Letter to J. Reed from W. Livingston, Sept. 8, 1781, in Prince and Ryan, eds., *Livingston Papers* 4:288; letter to the states of New Jersey and Pennsylvania from the president of Congress, Sept. 11, 1781, in Burnett, ed., *Letters* 6:216; letter to Washington from W. Heath, Sept. 12, 1781, in GWP, ser. 4, reel 80.

55. Letter to J. Reed from W. Livingston, Sept. 14, to W. Heath from W. Livingston, Sept. 15, Oct. 11, and to W. Livingston from S. Seely, Oct. 16, 1781, in Prince and Ryan, eds., *Livingston Papers* 4:292–94, 313, 315; Sept. 21, 25, 1781, in NJGA, card no. 17266, pp. 5–6, 9–10; letter to Washington from W. Heath, Sept. 30, 1781, in GWP, ser. 4, reel 81; letter to G. Germain from H. Clinton, Oct. 29, 1781, in Davies, ed., *Documents* 20:552.

56. Letter to Trumbull from W. Heath, Sept. 15, 16, Oct. 1, 12, 1781, in JTP, vol. 15, nos. 131, 134, 165, 186; letter to W. Heath from G. Clinton, Sept. 25, 1781, in *PGC* 7:358.

57. Extracts from minutes of a Council of War, Sept. 14, 1781, in Clinton, *American Rebellion*, 570; letter to G. Germain from H. Clinton, Oct. 14, 29, 1781, in Davies, ed., *Documents* 20:240–41, 252.

58. Letter to Washington from T. McKean, Oct. 14, and to Washington from W. Heath, Oct. 30, 1781, in GWP, ser. 4, reel 81; letter to W. Heath from Washington, Oct. 16, 1781, in Fitzpatrick, ed., *Washington* 23:230; letter to Trumbull from W. Heath, Oct. 17, 1781, in JTP, vol. 15, no. 201; letter to G. Clinton from W. Heath, Oct. 17, 21, and to W. Heath from G. Clinton, Oct. 18, 1781, in *PGC* 7:411, 416–17, 431.

59. Letter to Trumbull from S. Weed, Aug. 22, and to Trumbull from D. Waterbury, Sept. 7, 1781, in JTP, vol. 15, nos. 68, 101; return of a brigade of Connecticut state troops commanded by Brig. Gen. Waterbury, Oct. 29, 1781, ibid., vol. 24, no. 166; in Council of Safety, Aug. 30, 1781, in CSP; meeting of the governor and Council of Safety, Aug. 31, 1781, in Hoadly et al., *State of Connecticut* 3:499.

60. Return of a brigade of Connecticut state troops commanded by Brig. Gen. Waterbury, June 19, 1781, in JTP, vol. 24, no. 153; letter to Trumbull from T. Fitch, June 29, and to W. Ledyard from A. Shapley, July 4, 1781, ibid., vol. 14, nos. 298, 323; letter to Trumbull from J. Mead, July 23, to J. Mead from A. Davenport, T. Fitch, T. Betts, E. Lockwood, July 23, to Trumbull from T. Betts, E. Lockwood, C. Raymond, A. Betts, Aug. 22, to Trumbull from T. Jones and C. Chauncey, Sept. 1, and to Trumbull from T. Jones and H. Sabin, Jr., Sept. 6, 1781, ibid., vol. 15, nos. 31–32, 66, 87, 340; meeting of the governor and Council of Safety, July 25, 1781, in Hoadly et al., *State of Connecticut* 3:477; letter to Washington from A. Davenport, Aug. 10, 1781, in GWP, ser. 4, reel 80.

61. Letter to Trumbull from T. Ledyard, Sept. 9, brigade orders—J. Mead, Sept. 9, to Trumbull from J. Tyler, Sept. 10, to Trumbull from S. Parsons, Sept. 13, 17, to Trumbull from Lt. Col. Austin, Sept. 17, to Trumbull from C. Leffingwell, Sept. 19, and to Trumbull from S. McClellan, Sept. 28, 1781, in JTP, vol. 15, nos. 99, 105, 110, 119, 136, 142, 159, 321; Peckham, ed., *Toll of Independence*, 90; meeting of the governor and Council of Safety, Sept. 10, 11, Nov. 7, 1781, in Hoadly et al., *State of Connecticut* 3:504, 506, 547.

62. Letter to Trumbull from J. Fitch, July 24, to W. Heath from [Trumbull], Aug. 23, to Trumbull from W. Heath, Aug. 27, to Trumbull from B. Tallmadge, Oct. 5, to W. Heath from S. Parsons, Oct. 23, to S. Parsons from W. Heath, Oct. 23, 31, and to Trumbull from S. Parsons, Nov. 8, 1781, in JTP, vol. 15, nos. 33, 70, 78, 174, 207, 225, 243; Dann, ed., *Revolution Remembered*, 77; Peckham, ed., *Toll of Independence*, 91; Tallmadge, *Memoir*, 68–69; letter to G. Clinton from W. Heath, Oct. 6, 1781, in *PGC* 7:375; Ranlet, *Loyalists*, 80.

63. Instructions to T. Pickering from Washington, Oct. 27, and letter to W. Heath from Washington, Oct. 29, 1781, in Fitzpatrick, ed., *Washington* 23:280, 290–91.

64. Letter to W. Heath from G. Clinton, Nov. 6, and to G. Clinton from W. Heath, Nov. 7, 8, 1781, in *PGC* 7:435, 488–89, 491; after orders, Nov. 13, and brigade orders, Nov. 14, 1781, David Waterbury, Brig.-Gen. David Waterbury's Orderly Book (1781–82), 38–40; Nov. 18, 1781, in Orderly Books, War Department Collection, reel 9, 61:105–6.

65. Letter to G. Clinton from W. Heath, Nov. 26, Dec. 7, 1781, in *PGC* 7:525, 564–65; Nov. 11, 1781, in Orderly Books, War Department Collection, reel 9, 61:84; letter to the president of Congress from Washington, [Nov. 28, 1781], in Fitzpatrick, ed., *Washington* 23:361; Freeman, *Washington* 5:401–3, 410–11; letter to Trumbull from W. Heath, Nov. 25, and to Trumbull from D. Waterbury, Nov. 26, 1781, in JTP, vol. 15, nos. 266–67.

66. Nov. 30, 1781, in Orderly Books, War Department Collection, reel 9, 61:137–39.

67. Letter to G. Clinton from W. Heath, Dec. 7, 25, to G. Clinton from T. Thomas, Dec. 20, and to G. Clinton from the field officers and other inhabitants of Westchester County, n.d. [Dec.] 1781, in *PGC* 7:565, 605, 625–26, 630–31; letter to Washington from W. Heath, Dec. 26, 1781, in GWP, ser. 4, reel 82; Peckham, ed., *Toll of Independence*, 93.

68. Monthly return of the brigade of Connecticut state troops, commanded by Brig. Gen. Waterbury, Nov. 30, Dec. 31, 1781, in JTP, vol. 24, nos. 169–70; letter to Trumbull from the selectmen of Greenwich, Dec. 17, and "a Representation of the past and present Situation of the western frontiers of the State," [Dec.] 1781, ibid., vol. 15, nos. 290, 304.

69. Letter to G. Germain from F. Haldimand, Nov. 18, 1781, in Davies, ed., *Documents* 20:261.

CHAPTER ELEVEN
The Final Years, 1782–1783

1. Three letters to H. Clinton from G. Germain, Jan. 2, Feb. 6, to G. Carleton from [the Earl of Shelburne], Apr. 4, and to the Earl of Shelburne from G. Carleton, May 14, 1782, in Davies, ed., *Documents* 21:27–28, 38–39, 52–53, 75–76.

2. General Assembly, Jan. 1782, in Hoadly et al., *State of Connecticut* 4:17–18; letter to J. Hanson from Trumbull, Feb. 21, 1782, in JTP, vol. 20, no. 322; letter to Trumbull from the Connecticut delegates, Apr. 29, 1782, in Burnett, ed., *Letters* 6:337–38.

3. Letter to Trumbull from W. Heath, Feb. 4, 24, to Trumbull from R. Newbury, Feb. 24, to Trumbull from S. Canfield, Mar. 13, and to Trumbull from O. Wolcott, Apr. 29, 1782, in JTP, vol. 16, nos. 32, 47–48, 64, 105; letter to W. Heath from Trumbull, Jan. 21, and to R. Newbury from Trumbull, Feb. 25, 1782, ibid., vol. 20, nos. 319, 324; resolve, Jan. 10, and General Assembly, Jan., May 9–June 15, 1782, in Hoadly et al., *State of Connecticut* 4:9–10, 16–17, 24, 138–41, 150, 152–53; (town meeting), Mar. 8, 1782, in CGA, folder 2, "General Assembly, 1781–1783"; letter to Washington from W. Heath, Feb. 23, Apr. 29, to Washington from Trumbull, Feb. 24, to W. Heath from Maj. Maxwell, Apr. 9, to Washington from A. Davenport, Apr. 12, to Maj. Maxwell from D. Humphreys, Apr. 14, and return of a Connecticut battalion under Col. S. Canfield,

[May 12], 1782, in GWP, ser. 4, reels 83–84; brigade orders, in Waterbury, Brig.-Gen. David Waterbury's Orderly Book (1781–82), 55; letter to Trumbull from the Connecticut delegates, Apr. 29, 1782, in Burnett, ed., *Letters* 6:337–38; letter to W. Heath from Washington, Mar. 12, and to W. Heath from D. Humphreys, Apr. 10, 1782, in Fitzpatrick, ed., *Washington* 14:59, 105–6.

4. Meeting of the governor and Council of Safety, Dec. 27, 1781, in Hoadly et al., *State of Connecticut* 3:558; brigade orders, Jan. 1, 1782, in Waterbury, Brig.-Gen. David Waterbury's Orderly Book (1781–82), 72–73; letter to W. Heath from Trumbull, Jan. 21, 1782, in JTP, vol. 20, no. 319; letter to Trumbull from W. Heath, Feb. 4, to Trumbull from S. McClellan, Feb. 7, to Trumbull from G. Silliman, Mar. 1, to Trumbull from T. Burr, Mar. 30, to Trumbull from R. Newbury, Apr. 18, to Trumbull from the civil authority and selectmen of New Haven, Apr. 23, to Trumbull and the Council of Safety from the Committee of Saybrook, Apr. 26, to Trumbull from T. Shaw, May 22, and to Trumbull from J. Dimon, May 23, 1782, ibid., vol. 16, nos. 32–33, 54, 76, 98, 103–4, 140, 144; letter to J. Douglas from Trumbull, Mar. 7, 1782, in JDP, no. 70.

5. "An Act for the further Defence of the frontiers of this State," Nov. 17, 1781, and "An Act to regulate the Militia," Apr. 4, 1782, in New York Laws, Statutes, etc., card no. 17630, pp. 209, 225, 227–29; Mar. 22, 1782, in New York Senate Journals, card no. 44238, n.p.

6. Letter to G. Clinton from Col. Thomas, Jan. 7, 1782, in George Clinton Papers, box 30, no. 4273, New York State Archives, Albany; letter to G. Clinton from I. Honeywell, Apr. [?], 1782, ibid., box 32, no. 4412; letter to Col. Thomas from G. Clinton, [May 3], and to G. Clinton from Col. [Thomas], May 4, 1782, ibid., box 33, nos. 4491–92; letter to Washington from W. Heath, Jan. 14, Feb. 28, Mar. 20, Apr. 10, to W. Heath from J. Woodbridge, Mar. 5, and to W. Heath from J. Pray, Apr. 10, 1782, in GWP, ser. 4, reels 81, 83–84.

7. "An Act to provide for the Defence of the Frontiers, and for defraying the Expenses of the Government of this State," Dec. 29, 1781, in New Jersey Session Laws, card no. 17620, pp. 48–50; letter to Washington from W. Livingston, Jan. 1, 1782, in GWP, ser. 4, reel 82; letter to Stirling from W. Livingston, Jan. 11, and to W. Livingston from D. Forman, Feb. 17, 1782, in Prince and Ryan, eds., *Livingston Papers* 4:359–60, 380; address to the citizens of Monmouth, Apr. 14, 1782, and resolution of Congress supporting retaliation against cruelty of the enemy, Apr. 20, 1782, in Revolutionary War, box 28, nos. 79–80; Peckham, ed., *Toll of Independence,* 94.

8. Circular to the eastern and middle states from Washington, Mar. 5, 1782, in Fitzpatrick, ed., *Washington* 24:44–46.

9. Editor's note 38, Council of General Officers, Apr. 15, and letter to the secretary at war from Washington, Apr. 25, 1782, in Fitzpatrick, ed., *Washington* 24:88, 121–24, 165, 168–71; extract from General Orders, Apr. 4, 1782, in Heath, *Memoirs,* 307.

10. Letter to the Chevalier de la Luzerne from Washington, Apr. 28, and circular to the states from Washington, May 4[–8]. 1782, in Fitzpatrick, ed., *Washington* 24:180, 237; Assembly, May, 1782, in Hoadly et al., *State of Connecticut* 4:166–67; May 17, June 4, 1782, in NJGA, card no. 17626, pp. 4, 23; letter to Washington from W. Livingston, June 24, 1782, in GWP, ser. 4, reel 85.

11. Letter to Lord Amherst from J. Robertson, May 12, 1782, in Klein and Howard, eds., *Twilight of British Rule,* 251; letter to Washington from E. Dayton, May 6, to W. Heath from J. Woodbridge, May 6, and to E. Dayton from Washington, May 7, 1782, in GWP, ser. 4, reel 84; letter to J. Scott from G. Clinton, June 6, 1782, in *PGC* 8:12; letter to Rochambeau from Washington, Aug. 16, 1782, in Fitzpatrick, ed., *Washington* 25:26.

12. Letter to J. Hayt from J. Mead, June 26, 1782, in JTP, vol. 26, no. 185; monthly return of a Connecticut state regiment commanded by Samuel Canfield, Nov. 1, 1782, ibid., vol. 24, no. 192.

13. Letter to Ccl. H. Sabin or other commanding officer at New Haven from G. Silliman, June 4, and to Trumbull from S. McClellan, June 6, 7, 1782, in JTP, vol. 16, nos. 156, 162, 164; letter to J. Douglas from Trumbull, June 5, 1782, in JDP, no. 73.

14. Letter to J. Douglas from Trumbull, June 20, 1782, in JDP, no. 74; letter to Trumbull from the selectmen and civil authority of Branford, June 25, and to Trumbull from the civil authority and selectmen of Killingsworth, June 27, 1782, in JTP, vol. 16, nos. 182, 187; letter to Trumbull from T. Shaw, July 1, to Trumbull from T. Burr, July 2, and to Trumbull from R. Sherman, T. Jones, H. Daggett, and P. Seward, July 10, 1782, ibid., vol. 17, nos. 2, 4, 13; proclamation by Trumbull, July 1, 1782, ibid., vol. 20, no. 325; meeting of the governor and Council of Safety, July 17, 1782, in Hoadly et al., *State of Connecticut* 4:268, 270.

15. Letter to W. Heath from M. Ashley, Aug. 19, 1782, in GWP, ser. 4, reel 87; Uhlendorf, *Revolution in America*, 512; letter to G. Clinton from Washington, July 30, 1782, in Fitzpatrick, ed., *Washington* 24:443.

16. Letter to Rochambeau from Washington, June 24, and substance of a conference between the Comte de Rochambeau and General Washington, July 19, 1782, in Fitzpatrick, ed., *Washington* 24:382, 433–34; letter to Rochambeau from Washington, Aug. 16, 1782, ibid. 25:26–27; Freeman, *Washington* 5:417.

17. Letter to Rochambeau from Washington, Aug. 16, to the president of Congress from Washington, Oct. 30, and to N. Greene from Washington, Dec. 18, 1782, in Fitzpatrick, ed., *Washington* 25:27, 307, 446; Uhlendorf, *Revolution in America*, 523; Freeman, *Washington* 5:425–26.

18. Letter to N. Greene from Washington, Dec. 18, 1782, in Fitzpatrick, ed., *Washington* 25:448–49.

19. Letter to the president of Congress from Washington, Jan. 30, and to S. Adams and T. Dalton from Washington, Feb. 22, 1783, in Fitzpatrick, ed., *Washington* 26:83, 85, 155.

20. Letter to N. Greene from Washington, Dec. 18, 1782, in Fitzpatrick, ed., *Washington* 25:449; letter to the president of Congress from Washington, Jan. 30, and to Lafayette from Washington, Mar. 23, 1783, ibid. 26:83, 253–54.

21. Letter to [S. Webb] from Capt. Webb, Oct. 7, 1782, and to Washington from J. Pope, Mar. 18, 1783, in GWP, ser. 4, reels 88, 90; letter to the president of Congress from Washington, Feb. 26, 1783, in Fitzpatrick, ed., *Washington* 26:165–66; "An Act to authorize his Excellency the Governor, to raise Troops for the Defence of the Frontiers," Feb. 21, 1783, in New York Laws, Statutes, etc., card no. 18060, p. 272.

22. Letter to the president of Congress from Washington, Feb. 26, 1783, in Fitzpatrick, ed., *Washington* 26:165–66.

23. Return of the cavalry and infantry in the state of Connecticut commanded by Trumbull, Oct. 22, 1782, in JTP, vol. 24, no. 191; letter to Trumbull and the Council of Safety from J. Mead and T. Fitch, Feb. 5, 1783, ibid., vol. 18, no. 19; letter to S. Canfield from Washington, Dec. 3, 1782, and to Washington from Trumbull, Feb. 24, 1783, in GWP, ser. 4, reels 89–90; letter to Trumbull from Washington, Mar. 5, 1783, in Fitzpatrick, ed., *Washington* 26:192–93; meeting of the governor and Council of Safety, Mar. 24, 1783, in Hoadly et al., *State of Connecticut* 5:102.

24. Letter to Trumbull from E. Ledyard, Nov. 29, 1782, in JTP, vol. 17, no. 183; letter to Trumbull from B. Tallmadge, Jan. 4, Feb. 8, 1783, ibid., vol. 18, nos. 2, 22; General Assembly, Jan. 8, 1783, in Hoadly et al., *State of Connecticut* 5:30; letter to Washington from T. Burr, Nov. 23, 1782, in GWP, ser. 4, reel 88; heads of bills passed, Jan. 17, 1783, in CGA, folder 2; Tallmadge, *Memoir,* 71–74, 77–79; Peckham, ed., *Toll of Independence,* 99.

25. Uhlendorf, *Revolution in America,* 545; Freeman, *Washington* 5:438–39; Mar. 28, 1783, in New York General Assembly Journals, n.p.; Mar. 28, 1783, in New York Senate Journals, card no. 44425, p. 165; letter to Trumbull from R. Livingston, Mar. 24, 1783, in JTP, vol. 18, no. 70.

26. Letter to G. Carleton from [T. Townshend], Feb. 16, and to Washington from G. Carleton, Apr. 6, 1783, in Davies, ed., *Documents* 21:156, 161; letter to Trumbull from J. Trumbull, Jr., Apr. 9, 1783, in JTP, vol. 18, no. 87; letter to G. Carleton from Washington, Apr. 9, and to the general officers of the army from Washington, Apr. 17, 1783, in Fitzpatrick, ed., *Washington* 26:307, 328; Fri., Apr. 11, 1783, in Ford and Hunt, eds., *Journals of Continental Congress* 24:238, 240.

27. Letter to Trumbull from S. Canfield, Mar. 30, and to Trumbull from J. Mead, Mar. 30, 1783, in JTP, vol. 18, nos. 78–79; Stuart, *Trumbull,* 587; meeting of the governor and Council of Safety, Apr. 4, 1783, in Hoadly et al., *State of Connecticut* 5:104–5; proclamation by W. Livingston, Apr. 14, 1783, in Prince and Ryan, eds., *Livingston Papers* 4:516–18.

28. Spaulding, *George Clinton,* 139; Uhlendorf, *Revolution in America,* 559–60; letter to Washington from G. Carleton, May 12, 1783, in Davies, ed., *Documents* 21:165; letter to G. Clinton from G. Carleton, May 13, 1783, in *PGC* 8:176.

29. Letter to Chief Justice Morris from G. Clinton, May 15, 1783, in *PGC* 8:183; letter to the commanding officer of troops in Westchester County from Washington, May 21, 1783, in Fitzpatrick, ed., *Washington* 26:447.

30. Letter to G. Clinton from G. Carleton, June 18, and to G. Carleton from G. Clinton, July 1, 1783, in *PGC* 8:209, 213–14; Ranlet, *Loyalists,* 165; letter to G. Clinton from G. Carleton, July 25, 1783, in Davies, ed., *Documents* 21:197.

31. Ranlet, *Loyalists,* 166; letter to Pres. E. Boudinot from G. Carleton, Aug. 17, and to Lord North from G. Carleton, Aug. 29, 1783, in Davies, ed., *Documents* 21:208–9, 214; Warren, *History* 2:603–4.

32. Letter to Trumbull from B. Durkee, Sept. 11, 20, Dec. 17, 1783, in JTP, vol. 18, nos. 203, 206, 238.

33. Ranlet, *Loyalists,* 169; Spaulding, *George Clinton,* 139; Freeman, *Washington* 5:460–61; Nov., 1783, in Heath, *Memoirs,* 355; letter to the president of Congress from Washington, Dec. 3, 1783, in Fitzpatrick, ed., *Washington* 27:255; Champagne, *McDougall,* 201; MacDougall, *American Revolutionary,* 153.

34. Spaulding, *George Clinton,* 111; Ranlet, *Loyalists,* 169–70.

35. Stuart, *Trumbull,* 630–31.

CHAPTER TWELVE
Conclusion

1. Letter to J. Hancock from Washington, July 10[–11], 1775, in Abbot, ed., *Papers of Washington* 1:90.

2. Circular to the states, June 8, 1783, in Fitzpatrick, ed., *Washington* 26:494.

3. For example, see Weigley, *American Way of War,* 13–17, 20, 29; Russell F. Weigley, "Generals Building an Army; American Military Command in the War of Independence," in Russell F. Weigley, John R. Galvin, and Allen R. Millett, *Three George Rogers Clark Lectures,* 10–12; Higginbotham, *War and Society,* 156–58, 169.

4. Warren, *History* 1:128.

★ ★ ★

Bibliography

MANUSCRIPTS

Clinton, George. Boxes 30–33, vol. 15, Jan.–June 1782. George Clinton Papers. New York State Archives, Albany.

Connecticut General Assembly, 1775–1852. Folder 1, 1775–80; folder 2, 1781–83. Connecticut Historical Society, Hartford.

Council of Safety Papers, 1775–82. Connecticut Historical Society, Hartford.

Douglas, John. Gen. John Douglas Papers, 1775–82. Connecticut Historical Society, Hartford.

Emmet Collection. Nos. 938, 1203, 2435, 4851, 5284, 5578, 6950, 6966, 8045, 8263, 8781, 8795, 10915. New York Public Library, New York City.

Journal of the General Assembly of the State [of New York], 1777–92. 20 vols. New-York Historical Society, New York City.

Myers Collection. Nos. 572, 1026, 1027, 1029, 1037, 1044, 1045, 1046, 1203, 1232, 1237, 1349. New York Public Library, New York City.

New York. Governor. Messages and Proclamations of George Clinton, First governor of the State of New York, with Some Responses or Addresses from the Senate or the Assembly to Him, from August 1777 to September 1781. New York Public Library, New York City.

Numbered Record Books Concerning Military Operations and Service, Pay and Settlement Accounts, and Supplies in the War Department Collection of Revolutionary War Records. M853, 41 reels. RG 93. War Department Collection of Revolutionary War Records. National Archives, Washington, D.C.

Provincial Congress Papers. Military Returns. Folder "vol. 27, Military Returns etc. 1776," box 2. Ser. A1815. New York State Archives, Albany.

Revolutionary Papers. 3 vols. Nos. 79–81. Bancroft Collection. New York Public Library, New York City.

Revolutionary War. Boxes 1, 27–29. Book 43C, Military Records. Typescript. Department of Defense. New Jersey State Archives, Trenton.

Stewart, Col. Walter. Stewart Papers, 1776–95. New-York Historical Society, New York City.

Trumbull, Jonathan. Trumbull Papers. 31 vols. Connecticut Colonial Official Papers, 1631–1784. Massachusetts Historical Society, Connecticut State Library, Hartford.

Washington, George. George Washington Papers. Presidential Papers Microfilm. 7 ser., 124 reels. 3rd ser., Varick Transcripts, 1755–83 (ser. 3A, Continental Congress; ser. 3B, Continental and State Military Personnel; ser. 3C, Civil Officials and Citizens). 4th ser., General Correspondence, 1697–1799. Library of Congress, Washington, D.C.

Waterbury, David. Brig.-Gen. David Waterbury's Orderly Book, October 1, 1781–February 27, 1782. Connecticut State Library, Hartford.

————. Colonel David Waterbury's Orderly Book, June 3, 1775–September 16, 1781. Connecticut State Library, Hartford.

Wayne, Anthony. Anthony Wayne Papers. 2 vols. Nos. 378–79. Bancroft Collection, New York Public Library, New York City.

PRINTED PRIMARY SOURCES

Abbot, W. W., ed. *The Papers of George Washington.* 2 vols. Revolutionary War Series. Ed. Philander D. Chase. Charlottesville: University Press of Virginia, 1985–87.

Benians, E. A., ed. *A Journal by Thos: Hughes . . . (1778–1789).* Cambridge, Mass.: Harvard University Press, 1947.

Bernstein, David, ed. *Minutes of the Governor's Privy Council, 1777–1789.* New Jersey Archives, 3rd ser., vol. 1. Trenton: New Jersey State Archives Library Archives and History Bureau, 1974.

Burnett, Edmund, ed. *The Letters of the Members of the Continental Congress.* 8 vols. Washington, D.C.: Carnegie Institution of Washington, 1921–38.

Chittenden, Abraham. *Orderly Book of Lieut. Abraham Chittenden, Adj't. 7th Conn. Reg't: August 16, 1776 to September 29, 1776.* Hartford, Conn.: The Case, Lockwood & Brainard, 1922.

Clinton, Sir Henry. *The American Rebellion: Sir Henry Clinton's Narrative of His Campaigns, 1775–1782.* Ed. William B. Willcox. New Haven: Yale University Press, 1954.

Cresswell, Nicholas. *The Journal of Nicholas Cresswell, 1774–1777.* 1924. Port Washington, N.Y.: Kennikat Press, 1968.

Dann, John C., ed. *The Revolution Remembered: Eyewitness Accounts of the War for Independence.* Chicago: University of Chicago Press, 1980.

Davies, K. G., ed. *Documents of the American Revolution, 1770–1783.* Colonial Office Series, 21 vols. Dublin: Irish University Press, 1972–81.

De Jeney, Capitaine. *The Partisan: or, The Art of Making War in Detachment.* Trans. by an officer in the army [J. Berkenhout]. London: Printed for R. Griffiths, 1760.

Dohla, Johann Conrad. *A Hessian Diary of the American Revolution.* Trans. and ed. Bruce E. Burgoyne. Norman: University of Oklahoma Press, 1990.

Ewald, Johann. *Diary of the America War: A Hessian Journal.* Trans. and ed. Joseph P. Tustin. New Haven: Yale University Press, 1979.

———. *Treatise on Partisan Warfare.* Trans. Robert A. Selig and David Curtis Skaggs. New York: Greenwood Press, 1991.

Fitzpatrick, John C., ed. *The Writings of George Washington from the Original Manuscript Sources, 1745–1799.* 39 vols. Washington, D.C.: Government Printing Office, 1931–44.

Ford, Worthington C., and Gaillard Hunt, eds. *Journals of the Continental Congress, 1774–1789.* 34 vols. Washington, D.C.: Government Printing Office, 1904–37.

Hammond, Otis G. "Letters and Papers of Major-General John Sullivan, Continental Army." *Collections* of the New Hampshire Historical Society 13–15 (1930, 1931, 1939).

Hastings, Hugh, and James Austin Holden, eds. *Public Papers of George Clinton, First Governor of the State of New York. 1777–1797—1801–1804.* 10 vols. New York and Albany: State Printers, 1899–1914.

Heath, William. *Memoirs of Major-General William Heath by Himself.* 1798. Ed. William Abbatt. New York: William Abbatt, 1901.

Hoadly, Charles J., and J. Hammond Trumbull, eds. *The Public Records of the Colony of Connecticut.* 15 vols. 1850–90. New York: AMS, 1968.

Hoadly, Charles J., et al., eds. *The Public Records of the State of Connecticut, with the Journal of the Council of Safety, and an Appendix.* 11 vols. Hartford, Conn.: Various printers, 1894–1967.

Howe, Lt. Gen. Sir William. *The Narrative of Lt. Gen. Sir William Howe.* London: H. Baldwin, 1780.

"Huntington Papers." *Collections* of the Connecticut Historical Society 20 (1923).

Inman, George. "George Inman's Narrative of the American Revolution." *The Pennsylvania Magazine of History and Biography* 7 (1883): 237–48.

Journals of the Provincial Congress, Provincial Convention, Committee of Safety and Council of Safety of the State of New York 1775–1777. 2 vols. Albany: Thurlow Weed, 1842.

Klein, Milton M., and Ronald W. Howard, eds. *The Twilight of British Rule in Revolutionary America: The New York Letter Book of General James Robertson, 1780–1783.* Cooperstown: New York State Historical Association, 1983.

Lee, Charles. "Lee Papers." New York Historical Society *Collections* 4–7 (1871–74).

Mackenzie, Frederick. *Diary of Frederick Mackenzie.* 2 vols. Cambridge, Mass.: Harvard University Press, 1930.

"Minutes of the Committee and First Commission for Detecting Conspiracies." New York Historical Society *Collections* 57–58 (1924–25).

Minutes of the Council of Safety of the State of New Jersey, 1777–1778. Jersey City, N.J.: John H. Lyon, 1872.

Minutes of the Provincial Congress and Council of Safety of the State of New Jersey, 1775–1776. Trenton, N.J.: Naar, Day and Naar, 1879.

Moore, Frank, comp. *The Diary of the American Revolution, 1775–1781.* 1860. Ed. John Anthony Scott. New York: Washington Square Press, 1967.

New Jersey. Constitution of the State of New Jersey, 1776 (Burlington, 1776). Card no. 14912. In Shipton, ed., *Early American Imprints.*

———. General Assembly Journals, 1776–83. Votes and Proceedings of the General Assembly (Burlington and Trenton, 1777–83). Card nos. 15466, 16398–16399, 16401–16402, 16891, 16894, 16897, 17265–17266, 17626. In Shipton, ed., *Early American Imprints.*

———. Legislative Council Journals, 1777–83. Journals of the Proceedings of the Legislative Council (Burlington and Trenton, 1777–83). Card nos. 16397, 16887, 16889, 17262. In Shipton, ed., *Early American Imprints.*

———. Legislative Journal, 1776. Minutes and Proceedings of the Council and General Assembly in Joint Meeting [August 30, 1776–May 1780] (Trenton, 1780). Card no. 16890. In Shipton, ed., *Early American Imprints.*

———. Session Laws, 1776–83. Acts of Council and General Assembly, 1776–83 (Burlington and Trenton, 1777–84). Card nos. 15459–61, 15927, 16394–95, 16884–85, 17259–60, 17620. In Shipton, ed., *Early American Imprints.*

New York [State]. The Constitution of the State of New York. (Fishkill, 1777). Card no. 15472. In Shipton, ed., *Early American Imprints.*

———. General Assembly Journals, 1783. Votes and Proceedings of the Assembly, Jan. 27[–Mar. 28, 1783]. (Poughkeepsie, 1783). Card no. 44421. In Shipton, ed., *Early American Imprints.*

———. Laws, Statutes, etc., 1782. Laws of the State of New York, Commencing with the First Session . . . after the Declaration of Independency. (Poughkeepsie, 1782). Card nos. 17630, 18060. In Shipton, ed., *Early American Imprints.*

———. Senate Journals, 1777–83. Votes and Proceedings of the Senate. (Fishkill, Poughkeepsie, 1777–83). Card nos. 44424–25, 44238. In Shipton, ed., *Early American Imprints.*

New York City During the American Revolution. Being a Collection of Original Papers (Now First Published) from the Manuscripts in the Possession of the Mercantile Library Association, of New York City. New York, 1861.

Pattison, James. "Official Letters of Major General James Pattison." *Collections of the New-York Historical Society* 8 (1875).

Prince, Carl E., and Dennis P. Ryan, eds. *The Papers of William Livingston.* 4 vols., 1774–83. Trenton and New Brunswick: New Jersey Commission and Rutgers University Press, 1979–87.

Rice, Howard C., Jr., and Anne S. K. Brown, trans. and eds. *The American Campaigns of Rochambeau's Army, 1780, 1781, 1782, 1783.* 2 vols. Princeton: Princeton University Press, 1972.

Robson, Eric, ed. *Letters from America, 1773–1780: Being the Letters of a Scots Officer, Sir James Murray, to His Home During the War of American Independence.* Manchester: Manchester University Press, 1951.

Ross, Charles, ed. *Correspondence of Charles, First Marquis Cornwallis.* 3 vols. London: John Murray, 1859.

Selections from the Correspondence of the Executive of New Jersey, from 1776 to 1786. Newark, N.J.: Newark Daily Advertisers, 1848.

Shipton, Dr. Clifford K., ed. *Early American Imprints, 1639–1800.* Worcester, Mass.: American Antiquarian Society, 1955–64; supp. 1966–68.

Showman, Richard K., ed. *The Papers of General Nathanael Greene.* 7 vols., 1766–81. Chapel Hill: University of North Carolina, 1976–94.

Simcoe, Lt. Col. John Graves. *Simcoe's Military Journal: A History of the Operations of a Partisan Corps, Called the Queen's Rangers, Commanded by Lieut. Col. J. G. Simcoe, During the War of the American Revolution.* New York: Bartlett & Welford, 1844.

"A Skirmish in America Between the Kings Troops & Genl. Arnold." London: Jas. Sharpe, 1780. Print.

Smith, Paul H., ed. *Letters of Delegates to Congress, 1774–1789.* 22 vols., 1774–85. Washington, D.C.: Library of Congress, 1976–95.

Steuben, Frederick William. *Baron von Steuben's Revolutionary War Drill Manual: A Facsimile Reprint of the 1794 Edition.* New York: Dover Publications, Inc., 1985.

Sullivan, Sergeant Thomas. "Battle of Princeton." *The Pennsylvania Magazine of History and Biography* 32 (1908): 54–57.

Tallmadge, Benjamin. *Memoir of Colonel Benjamin Tallmadge.* 1858. Ed. H. P. Johnston. New York: The Gillis Press, 1904.

Uhlendorf, Bernhard A., trans. *Revolution in America: Confidential Letters and Journals 1776–1784 of Adjutant General Major Baurmeister of the Hessian Forces.* New Brunswick, N.J.: Rutgers University Press, 1957.

"Wyllys Papers, 1590–1796." Connecticut Historical Society *Collections* 21 (1924).

Zagarri, Rosemarie, ed. *David Humphreys' "Life of General Washington" with George Washington's "Remarks."* Athens: University of Georgia Press, 1991.

SECONDARY SOURCES CITED

Alden, John Richard. *General Charles Lee: Traitor or Patriot?* Baton Rouge: Louisiana State University Press, 1951.

———. *A History of the American Revolution.* New York: Da Capo Press, 1969.

Anderson, Fred. *A People's Army: Massachusetts Soldiers and Society in the Seven Years' War.* Chapel Hill: University of North Carolina Press, 1984.

Bill, Alfred Hoyt. *The Campaign of Princeton, 1776–1777.* Princeton: Princeton University Press, 1948.

———. *New Jersey and the Revolutionary War.* Princeton: Van Nostrand Company, 1964.

Bliven, Bruce, Jr. *Under the Guns: New York, 1775–1776.* New York: Harper & Row, 1972.

Brand, Oscar. *Songs of '76: A Folksinger's History of the Revolution.* New York: M. Evans and Company, 1972.

Buel, Richard, Jr. *Dear Liberty: Connecticut's Mobilization for the Revolutionary War.* Middletown, Conn.: Wesleyan University Press, 1980.

Carp, E. Wayne. *To Starve the Army at Pleasure: Continental Army Administration and American Political Culture, 1775–1783.* Chapel Hill: University of North Carolina Press, 1984.

Champagne, Roger J. *Alexander McDougall and the American Revolution in New York.* Schenectady, N.Y.: Union College Press, 1975.

Conway, Stephen. " 'The great mischief Complain'd of': Reflections on the Misconduct of British Soldiers in the Revolutionary War." *The William and Mary Quarterly* 3rd ser., 47 (July 1990): 370–90.

———. "To Subdue America: British Army Officers and the Conduct of the Revolutionary War." *The William and Mary Quarterly* 3rd ser., 43 (July 1986): 381–407.

Countryman, Edward. *A People in Revolution: The American Revolution and Political Society in New York, 1760–1790.* Baltimore: Johns Hopkins University Press, 1981.

Davis, Burke. *The Cowpens-Guilford Courthouse Campaign.* Philadelphia: J. B. Lippincott Company, 1962.

———. *George Washington and the American Revolution.* New York: Random House, 1975.

Dwyer, William M. *The Day is Ours! November 1776—January 1777: An Inside View of the Battles of Trenton and Princeton.* New York: Viking, 1983.

Ferling, John, ed. *The World Turned Upside Down: The American Victory in the War of Independence.* New York: Greenwood Press, 1988.

Fleming, Thomas. *The Forgotten Victory: The Battle for New Jersey—1780.* New York: Reader's Digest Press, 1973.

———. "George Washington, General." *MHQ: The Quarterly Journal of Military History* 2 (Winter 1990): 38–47.

Flexner, James Thomas. *George Washington in the American Revolution, 1775–1783.* Boston: Little, Brown, 1968.

Freeman, Douglas Southall. *George Washington: A Biography.* 7 vols. New York: Charles Scribner's Sons, 1948–57.

Gerlach, Don R. *Proud Patriot: Philip Schuyler and the War of Independence, 1775–1783.* Syracuse, N.Y.: Syracuse University Press, 1987.

Gruber, Ira D. "The Education of Sir Henry Clinton." *Bulletin of the John Rylands University Library of Manchester* 72 (Spring 1990): 131–53.

———. *The Howe Brothers and the American Revolution.* Chapel Hill: University of North Carolina Press, 1974.

Hall, Charles S. *Life and Letters of Samuel Holden Parsons: Major General in the Continental Army and Chief Judge of the Northwestern Territory, 1737–1789.* Binghamton, N.Y.: Otseningo, 1905.

Heller, Charles E., and William A. Stofft, eds. *America's First Battles, 1776–1965.* Lawrence: University Press of Kansas, 1986.

Higginbotham, Don. *George Washington and the American Military Tradition.* Athens: University of Georgia Press, 1985.

————. *The War of American Independence: Military Attitudes, Policies, and Practice, 1763–1789.* New York: Macmillan, 1971.

————. *War and Society in Revolutionary America: The Wider Dimensions of Conflict.* Columbia: University of South Carolina Press, 1988.

Hoffman, Robert V. *The Revolutionary Scene in New Jersey.* New York: American Historical Company, 1942.

Johnston, Henry P. *The Campaign of 1776 Around New York and Brooklyn.* 1878. New York: Da Capo, 1971.

Kaplan, Roger. "The Hidden War: British Intelligence Operations During the American Revolution." *The William and Mary Quarterly* 3rd ser., 47 (Jan. 1990): 115–38.

Ketchum, Richard M. *The Winter Soldiers.* Garden City, N.Y.: Doubleday, 1973.

Leiby, Adrian C. *The Revolutionary War in the Hackensack Valley: The Jersey Dutch and the Neutral Ground, 1775–1783.* New Brunswick, N.J.: Rutgers University Press, 1962.

Lundin, Leonard. *Cockpit of the Revolution: The War for Independence in New Jersey.* Princeton: Princeton University Press, 1940.

MacDougall, William L. *American Revolutionary: A Biography of General Alexander McDougall.* Westport, Conn.: Greenwood Press, 1977.

Mackesy, Piers. *The War for America, 1775–1783.* 1964. Lincoln: University of Nebraska Press, 1993.

Mason, Bernard. *The Road to Independence: The Revolutionary Movement in New York, 1773–1777.* Lexington: University Press of Kentucky, 1966.

Middlekauff, Robert. *The Glorious Cause: The American Revolution, 1763–1789.* New York: Oxford University Press, 1982.

Miers, Earl Schenk. *Crossroads of Freedom: The American Revolution and the Rise of a New Nation.* New Brunswick, N.J.: Rutgers University Press, 1971.

Montross, Lynn. *The Story of the Continental Army.* [*Rag, Tag and Bobtail,* 1952] New York: Barnes and Noble, 1967.

Nelson, Paul David. *General Horatio Gates: A Biography.* Baton Rouge: Louisiana State University Press, 1976.

————. *William Alexander, Lord Stirling.* Tuscaloosa: University of Alabama Press, 1987.

————. "William Tryon Confronts the American Revolution, 1771–1780." *Historian: A Journal of History* 53 (Winter 1991): 267–84.

Palmer, Dave Richard. *The Way of the Fox: American Strategy in the War for America, 1775–1783.* Westport, Conn.: Greenwood Press, 1975.

Pancake, John S. *This Destructive War: The British Campaign in the Carolinas, 1780–1782.* Tuscaloosa: University of Alabama Press, 1985.

Peckham, Howard H., ed. *The Toll of Independence: Engagements and Battle Casualties of the American Revolution.* Chicago: University of Chicago Press, 1974.

Rankin, Hugh F. *Francis Marion: The Swamp Fox.* New York: Thomas Y. Crowell, 1973.

Ranlet, Philip. *The New York Loyalists.* Knoxville: University of Tennessee Press, 1986.

Risch, Erna. *Supplying Washington's Army.* Washington, D.C.: Center of Military History, 1981.

Rosswurm, Steven. *Arms, Country, and Class: The Philadelphia Militia and "Lower Sort" During the American Revolution, 1775–1783.* New Brunswick, N.J.: Rutgers University Press, 1987.

Royster, Charles. *A Revolutionary People at War: The Continental Army and American Character, 1775–1783.* Chapel Hill: University of North Carolina Press, 1979.

Scheer, George F., and Hugh F. Rankin. *Rebels and Redcoats.* New York: New American Library, 1957.

Smith, Paul H. *Loyalists and Redcoats: A Study in British Revolutionary Policy.* Chapel Hill: University of North Carolina Press, 1964.

Spaulding, E. Wilder. *His Excellency George Clinton: Critic of the Constitution.* New York: Macmillan, 1938.

Stuart, I. W. *Life of Jonathan Trumbull, Sen., Governor of Connecticut.* Hartford: Belknap & Warfield, 1859.

Symonds, Craig L. *A Battlefield Atlas of the America Revolution.* Cart. William J. Clipson. N.p.: Nautical & Aviation Publishing Company of America, 1986.

Thayer, Theodore. *Nathanael Greene: Strategist of the American Revolution.* New York: Twayne, 1960.

Tiedemann, Joseph S. "Patriots by Default: Queens County, New York, and the British Army, 1776–1783." *The William and Mary Quarterly* 3rd ser., 48 (Jan. 1986): 35–63.

Van Doren, Carl. *Secret History of the American Revolution.* New York: Viking, 1941.

Ward, Christopher. *The War of the Revolution.* 2 vols. Ed. John R. Alden. New York: Macmillan, 1952.

Ward, Harry. *Charles Scott and the "Spirit of '76."* Charlottesville: University of Virginia Press, 1988.

Warren, Mercy Otis. *History of the Rise, Progress and Termination of the American Revolution.* 2 vols. 1805. Ed. Lester H. Cohen. Indianapolis: Liberty Classics, 1988.

Weaver, Glenn. *Jonathan Trumbull: Connecticut's Merchant Magistrate (1710–1785).* Hartford: Connecticut Historical Society, 1956.

Weigley, Russell F. *The American Way of War: A History of United States Military Strategy and Policy.* Bloomington: Indiana University Press, 1973.

———. *The Partisan War: The South Carolina Campaign of 1780–1782.* Columbia: University of South Carolina Press, 1970.

Weigley, Russell F., John R. Galvin, and Allen R. Millett. *Three George Rogers Clark Lectures.* Washington, D.C.: University Press of America, 1991.

Whittemore, Charles P. *A General of the Revolution: John Sullivan of New Hampshire.* New York: Columbia University Press, 1961.

★ ★ ★

Index

Canada, 42, 44, 142, 220, 320
Canfield, Samuel, 314–15, 319, 323, 325
Carleton, Sir Guy, 142, 314, 318, 324, 325, 326, 327
Caribbean Sea, 199
Carlisle Commission, 199
Cavalry: British army, 169, 208, 246, 263, 292; Connecticut militia, 45, 52, 74, 79, 169; Continental Army, 195, 204, 250, 264, 295, 297; Continental detachments of, in Connecticut, 247, 252, 255–56, 309, 315; Continental detachments of, in New Jersey, 153, 228, 229; Continental detachments of, in New York, 217, 232, 242, 302; French, 298; New Jersey militia, 105, 259, 317; New York militia, 55, 67, 327; Tory, 119, 180
Charleston, S.C., 314, 320
Chatham, N.J., 96, 281, 282, 284, 303
Chatterton's Hill, N.Y., 78
Chesapeake Bay, 156, 161, 238, 260, 302, 304, 306–7
Clermont-Crevecoeur, Jean-François-Louis, Comte de, 288
Clinton, George, 9, 32, 54, 76, 237, 249, 266, 327; analysis of, 222, 334, 335; as brigadier general, 128; coordinates command with Washington, 54, 60, 61, 81; elected governor, 154–55, 257; at forts in the Highlands, commanded by, 144, 152–53, 157, 158, 167–68; Highland forts lost, 170, 171, 172, 173–74, 175, 176; Highlands in 1777 commanded by, 118, 119, 128, 129, 130–31, 177; initial commands of, 53, 54, 55, 61; and militia responsibility, 195–96, 198, 219, 233, 257, 263, 275, 303; and New York City attack, 270, 307; opinion of militia, 79, 192, 217, 287–88; and Pennsylvania mutiny, 282; reputation of, 32, 54–55, 128, 136, 191–92; supports Washington's reconquest of New Jersey, 88–89, 94, 95, 106–7; Tory control by, 49, 54–55, 56, 73, 74, 130, 191–92, 219; urges revised militia laws, 128, 192; and Verplank's and Stony Points attack, 239, 241, 242; and war's end, 316, 325–26; and West Point, 181, 188–89

Clinton, James, 32; appointed brigadier general, 227, 228; Highlands command of, 118, 130, 145, 152, 177; Highland forts lost while defended by, 171, 172, 175, 176
Clinton, Sir Henry, 195, 293; and Arnold defection, 272–73; and British army command, 196, 199; and Burgoyne, 163, 164; and Continental mutinies, 282–83, 284; and French alliance, 199–200, 225; French fleet targeted by, 220; and French in Rhode Island, 269, 271; Highland forts captured by, 169, 170, 171, 172, 173, 175, 176; intelligence activities of, 163, 208, 211–12; and Long Island, 67, 276–77, 298; militia influences, xiii, 200, 214–15, 332; and Monmouth campaign, 200, 202–3, 205, 209–10, 211; and nature of war, 3, 163, 199, 247; New Jersey operations in 1780 by, 264, 265, 266, 267; and New York City defense, 216, 250, 268, 272, 293–94, 299, 303–4; New York City garrison commanded by, 156, 161, 163; pessimistic views of, 110, 246–47; resignation of, 313–14; South Carolina campaign of, 253, 261, 263, 264; Southern expedition by, 33, 35, 37, 67; strategy of raids by, 226–27, 229, 233, 235, 236; and Tryon's raid, 242, 243, 244, 245–46; and Verplank's and Stony Points, 239–40, 241, 246; during the Yorktown campaign, 294, 295, 299, 301, 303–4, 306–7
Clinton, Fort, 170, 171
Closter, N.J., 129, 317
Committee for Detecting Conspiracies, 81, 130
Compo Hill, Conn., 122, 124, 231
Concord: battle of, xi, 1, 5, 7, 39, 329
Confederation Congress. See Articles of Confederation
Connecticut, 4, 5–6, 22, 23–25, 46; analysis of, 333–34; and attack on Highland forts, 172, 174; and attacks on ships on Hudson River, 53; British raids resisted in, 121, 141, 243, 247, 248; Continental Army reinforced by, 58, 78–79, 158, 159, 160, 290–91, 299, 300; Continental detachments (1777)

Washington's Partisan War, 1775–1783
was composed in 10.3/13 New Baskerville
in PageMaker 6.0 on a Micro 133MHz Pentium system
by Cornerstone Compositon Services;
imaged to film from PostScript files,
printed by sheet-fed offset on
50-pound Glatfelter Supple Opaque natural stock
(an acid-free, recycled paper)
with halftones printed on 70-pound Richgloss enamel,
notch casebound over 88-point binder's boards
in ICG Kennett cloth,
and wrapped with dustjackets printed in three colors
on 100-pound enamel stock
finished with matte film lamination
by Thomson-Shore, Inc.;
designed by Will Underwood;
and published by
The Kent State University Press
KENT, OHIO 44242